ANALYTICAL ROBOTICS AND MECHATRONICS

McGraw-Hill Series in Electrical and Computer Engineering

Senior Consulting Editor

***Stephen W. Director**, Carnegie Mellon University*

Circuits and Systems
Communications and Signal Processing
Computer Engineering
Control Theory
Electromagnetics
Electronics and VLSI Circuits
Introductory
Power and Energy
Radar and Antennas

Previous Consulting Editors

Ronald N. Bracewell, Colin Cherry, James F. Gibbons, Willis W. Harman, Hubert Heffner, Edward W. Herold, John G. Linvill, Simon Ramo, Ronald A. Rohrer, Anthony E. Siegman, Charles Susskind, Frederick E. Terman, John G. Truxal, Ernst Weber, and John R. Whinnery

Computer Engineering

Senior Consulting Editors
Stephen W. Director, *Carnegie Mellon University*
C. L. Liu, *University of Illinois at Urbana-Champaign*

Bartee: *Computer Architecture and Logic Design*
Bell and Newell: *Computer Structures: Readings and Examples*
Feldman and Retter: *Computer Architecture: A Designer's Text Based on a Generic RISC*
Gardland: *Introduction to Microprocessor System Design*
Hamacher, Vranesic, and Zaky: *Computer Organization*
Hayes: *Computer Architecture and Organization*
Horvath: *Introduction to Microprocessors using the MC 6809 or the MC 68000*
Hwang: *Advanced Computer Architecture: Parallelism, Scalability, Programmability*
Kohavi: *Switching and Finite Automata Theory*
Lawrence-Mauch: *Real-Time Microcomputer System Design: An Introduction*
Levine: *Vision in Man and Machine*
Navabi: *VHDL: Analysis and Modeling of Digital Systems*
Peatman: *Design of Digital Systems*
Peatman: *Design with Microcontrollers*
Peatmen: *Digital Hardware Design*
Ritterman: *Computer Circuit Concepts*
Rosen: *Discrete Mathematics and Its Applications*
Sandige: *Modern Digital Design*
Stadler: *Analytical Robotics and Mechatronics*
Sze: *VLSI Technology*
Taub: *Digital Circuits and Microprocessors*
Wear, Pinkert, Wear, and Lane: *Computers: An Introduction to Hardware and Software Design*
Wiatrowski and House: *Logic Circuits and Microcomputer Systems*

Control Theory

Senior Consulting Editor
Stephen W. Director, *Carnegie Mellon University*

D'Azzo and Houpis: *Linear Control System Analysis and Design: Conventional and Modern*
Emanuel and Leff: *Introduction to Feedback Control Systems*
Friedland: *Control System Design: An Introduction to State Space Methods*
Houpis and Lamont: *Digital Control Systems: Theory, Hardware, Software*
Raven: *Automatic Control Engineering*
Rohrs, Melsa, and Schultz: *Linear Control Systems*
Saadat: *Computational Aids in Control Systems Using MATLAB™*
Schultz and Melsa: *State Functions and Linear Control Systems*
Stadler: *Analytical Robotics and Mechatronics*
Vaccaro: *Digital Control: A State-Space Approach*

Also Available from McGraw-Hill

Schaum's Outline Series in Electronics & Electrical Engineering

Most outlines include basic theory, definitions and hundreds of example problems solved in step-by-step detail, and supplementary problems with answers.

Related titles on the current list include:

Analog & Digital Communications
Basic Circuit Analysis
Basic Electrical Engineering
Basic Electricity
Basic Mathematics for Electricity & Electronics
Digital Principles
Electric Circuits
Electric Machines & Electromechanics
Electronic Power Systems
Electromagnetics
Electronic Circuits
Electronic Communication
Electronic Devices & Circuits
Electronics Technology
Feedback & Control Systems
Introduction to Digital Systems
Microprocessor Fundamentals
Signals & Systems

Schaum's Solved Problems Books

Each title in this series is a complete and expert source of solved problems with solutions worked out in step-by-step detail.

Related titles on the current list include:

3000 Solved Problems in Calculus
2500 Solved Problems in Differential Equations
3000 Solved Problems in Electric Circuits
2000 Solved Problems in Electromagnetics
2000 Solved Problems in Electronics
3000 Solved Problems in Linear Algebra
2000 Solved Problems in Numerical Analysis
3000 Solved Problems in Physics

Available at most college bookstores, or for a complete list of titles and prices, write to: Schaum Division
McGraw-Hill, Inc.
1221 Avenue of the Americas
New York, NY 10020

ANALYTICAL ROBOTICS AND MECHATRONICS

Wolfram Stadler

San Francisco State University

McGraw-Hill, Inc.

New York St. Louis San Francisco Auckland Bogotá Caracas Lisbon
London Madrid Mexico City Milan Montreal New Delhi
San Juan Singapore Sydney Tokyo Toronto

This book was set in Times Roman by Science Typographers, Inc.
The editors were George T. Hoffman and John M. Morriss;
the production supervisor was Richard A. Ausburn.
The cover was designed by Merrill Haber.
Project supervision was done by Science Typographers, Inc.
R. R. Donnelley & Sons Company was printer and binder.

ANALYTICAL ROBOTICS AND MECHATRONICS

This book is printed on acid-free paper.

2 3 4 5 6 7 8 9 0 DOC DOC 9 0 9 8 7 6 5

ISBN 0-07-060608-0

Library of Congress Cataloging-in-Publication Data

Stadler, Wolfram.
Analytical robotics and mechatronics / Wolfram Stadler.
p. cm.—(McGraw-Hill series in electrical and computer engineering)
Includes index.
ISBN 0-07-060608-0
1. Robotics. 2. Mechatronics. I. Title. II. Series.
TJ211.S728 1995
629.8′92—dc20 94-44838

ABOUT THE AUTHOR

Wolfram Stadler was born in Germany, where he received all of his basic education. He emigrated to the United States at the age of 17. After a variety of jobs, including four years of service in the U.S. Air Force, he began his university studies at Georgia Institute of Technology, in Aerospace Engineering. There he earned a B.S. and an M.S. in Aerospace Engineering, as well as an M.S. and a Ph.D. in Engineering Science and Mechanics.

He was an Assistant Professor at Georgia Institute of Technology, with a joint appointment in Mathematics and Mechanics. Subsequently he went to the University of California at Berkeley as a post-doctoral fellow. There he began studies in optimal control and multicriteria optimization, which are still his main research areas. He has been at San Francisco State University since 1978.

Professor Stadler has been a visiting professor at the University of Munich, at the University of Bonn, and at Osaka University. (At the latter, he was the recipient of a senior research fellowship from the Japan Society for the Promotion of Science.) He has presented invited lectures all over the world.

He has more than 50 publications, on topics such as Newtonian dynamics, shell theory, control theory, and optimal structural design, as well as numerous contributions to multicriteria optimization, including surveys and historical articles. He has published four books and has contributed chapters to several others. He is an associate editor on three international journals dealing with control and optimization.

Professor Stadler has taught 23 different courses in Engineering and Mathematics, ranging from basic calculus to Laplace transforms and a graduate course in linear algebra, and from gas dynamics to courses in robotics, controls and optimization. He is bilingual (English and German), is conversant in Spanish and French, and has a nodding acquaintance with Russian.

CONTENTS

PREFACE

In 1983 I received an offer I could not refuse: Teach robotics or be out of a job. At that time, junior/senior courses in robotics were not in evidence and neither were any texts dedicated to this level; so I began to write this textbook. Since similar offers are quite likely still being made, I hope to ease the task for others who cannot refuse.

My approach to the subject was a didactic one, with the goal of presenting the student with the background needed for any endeavor connected with robotics. Rather than emphasizing current and rapidly changing technology, the emphasis here is on established fundamental concepts. This ultimately leads to an understanding of any related evolving technology. The student should thus feel comfortable with *any* robot.

The basic concepts are no different for robotics than they are for the description of other physical phenomena. Robotics differs in the extensive integration of concepts from a variety of individual disciplines. Thus, concepts from solid-state physics, computer science, fluids, dynamics, controls, circuits, and machine design, to name a few, all play a role in robotics. This collection of separate parts is frequently termed *mechatronics*, with robotics as its central application.

The material of the book builds on a presumed background course each in circuits, in dynamics, and in systems analysis—a background common to all of our students at the end of their fifth semester (ideally speaking). An effort has been made throughout the textbook to tie in new topics to previous experience and expertise for both the students and the instructor. To ease this transition, many topics from mathematics and physics are reviewed and presented where they are needed. A "just in time" approach is taken, rather than relegating the transitions and background material to an appendix.

With the exception of this just-in-time approach, the book is written in a rather traditional textbook style, with discussion, examples, exercises, and numerous figures to aid in the visualization of topics. The book also lends itself to course structures tailored to an individual instructor's tastes and aims. The course offered at San Francisco State University is a one-semester course which serves as an elective for both electrical and mechanical engineering majors; this book could easily be used for a two-semester sequence. With some variations, the course here is usually comprised of the following chapters and sections: most of Chapters 1, 2, and 3, which deal with a synopsis of fundamental ideas and problems in robotics, and with motion fundamentals embodied in three-dimensional rigid body dynamics; selections from Chapter 4, including a discussion of semiconductors and the depletion region; a selection of several sensors, which usually includes accelerometers and force and tactile sensors, from Chapter 5; and most of Chapter 6, since I believe that an understanding of the limitations and promise of vision systems is essential. The remainder of the course deals with actuators, power transmission devices, and the planning and implementation of robot trajectories. The course also includes weekly homework, two exams, a final examination, a term project, and an essay on the social implications of automation and robotics. The course is not an easy course since it draws on virtually all of the student's background. However, when asked if he or she would feel comfortable in dealing with any robot, even the average student answers with a confident "yes."

Ideally, a robotics laboratory course should be taken concurrently with this course, to provide the needed hands-on experience. In fact, it should be made an integral part of the course. When this is not done, students tend to avoid the lab with the usual aversion to any laboratory experience.

Robotics has changed dramatically since my first foray into the subject in 1983, when a certain amount of science fiction still imbued the subject with an almost other-worldly atmosphere. There were industry projections of billions of dollars in sales, and the market contained more than 40 companies involved in robotics. Experts were making statements such as, "In 20 years we will have robots with intelligence and emotions equivalent to those of human beings." My projection in 1983 was that robots would begin to catch on in about 15 years after the general public—as well as engineers—had learned to routinely accept them in their work environment, and that no robot would act or feel like a human being in the foreseeable future. I believe that these projections are still true.

The primary purpose of the robot as a machine is controlled motion: If it does not move, it is not a robot. All of the robotic design endeavor has controlled, sensitive, and intelligent motion as its collective goal. The variety of uses for robots is increasing, although their main use still seems to reside in automobile manufacturing. The number of producers of robots has decreased considerably, so that now there are only between five to ten manufacturers left, the biggest market share being occupied by ABB (ASAE, Brown, Boveri) and by GMF (General Motors, Fanuc).

Now there is a consolidation of robotics, as well as a broadening to the mix of applied mechanics and electronics termed mechatronics. This is a collective viewpoint to which mechanics should have evolved long ago. Robotics and mechatronics have become part of most modern curricula in mechanical and electrical engineering. Although the technology will continue to evolve, the background needed to understand it will remain the same. I believe that this book provides that background.

Wolfram Stadler

ACKNOWLEDGMENTS

Robotics and mechatronics are a high-tech joining of a number of classical fields and engineering theories. Thus we stand not so much on the shoulders of a few giants as on a multitude of competent individuals who have managed to see classical results in a new light. The basic concepts have not changed; the way we view and combine them has.

This textbook could not have come to be without the numerous texts on robotics that preceded it. Their viewpoints influenced mine, and their emphases created a standard. There were two which proved particularly helpful, not so much because of their detailed treatment of individual topics, but more so because of the timeliness of their appearance and because of what they treated. One was Engelberger's book *Robotics in Practice*; the other was *Freiprogrammierbare Manipulatoren* by C. Blume and R. Dillmann.

As one reviewer remarked, a better treatment of diodes can be found in a basic electrical engineering text, and similar comments may well apply to much of what I have presented. To some extent, the electrical material was written for the mechanical engineer, and the mechanics for the electrical engineer; both of them may find the math and physics useful. Part of my contribution consists of putting it all together and presenting it in a unified form.

I have avoided citing large numbers of often irrelevant references. Instead, I have cited desk references, treating the specific topic and related ones in greater detail. Whenever feasible, I then adhered to the notation used in the cited reference. The viewpoints, treatments, and interpretations are my own (as are any errors). When I saw myself unable to improve upon a particularly lucid explanation, I quoted it.

By and large, I have treated homework problems and problems in general as part of the public domain; and I would like to offer those who find some of my problems particularly interesting or useful the freedom to use them in their own writings. In addition, I would encourage those who have some favorite problems they would like to see included in some future edition to send them to me with their solutions. If I find myself in agreement, I should like to include them, together with a proper citation of their authors.

Mechatronics is such an interdisciplinary subject that, even with a relatively broad background, I found myself constantly studying and learning new concepts and methods. Absorbing this information, assuring myself of its correctness, and then recording it in an acceptable form would not have been possible without my colleagues' willingness to share their expertise, listen to my questions, and study various segments of the manuscript. I am grateful to S. Franco, S. Hu, S. S. Liou, and R. Zimmerman for their critical reading of the material on electronics, computer logic, and electric motors; to J. Lockhart from the Physics Department for his help and patience with the Hall effect; to A. Wheeler and A. Ganji for their perusal of the segments on hydraulic and pneumatic actuators; and to V. Krishnan for his comments on the material concerning statistics and control theory. I am also grateful to my European colleagues W. Schiehlen and E. Kreuzer for sharing their robotics notes with me.

I owe a great deal to B. Zellner, of Loral-Fairchild-Schlumberger's imaging division, for his help in reading the exposition on CCD vision systems and for his patience in supplying me with information and figures. In this connection, I also found the comments of T. Coogan of Adept, Inc., extremely helpful.

My obligation to my students provided stimulation to continue writing, and their comments, criticisms, and corrections were essential contributions. My particular thanks go to Jon Moore, who read and commented upon much of the manuscript.

The active support and patience of the editors and staff of McGraw-Hill were an extremely positive influence. I appreciated the editors' work in searching out suitable and knowledgeable reviewers, whose remarks provided essential expert guidance with respect to content and completeness: Harvey Lipkin, Georgia Institute of Technology; Mahmood Nahvi, California Polytechnic State University; and Ronald A. Perez, University of Wisconsin, Milwaukee, as well as others who commented on incomplete versions of the book.

I am deeply grateful to my wife for her well nigh infinite patience and skill in typing and editing the many variants of this book as it evolved.

Finally, there is One without whom none of this would have been written. He prepared the beginning, provided the direction, sustained me when the task seemed onerous, and gave me the understanding to complete it: God.

Wolfram Stadler

AUTOMATION WITH A SOCIAL CONSCIENCE

We are discovering that the more triumphant our technology, the less does society function automatically.

—Eric Hoffer

For approximately 10 years I have used the last class of all my courses for a discussion of ethics—not engineering ethics, not business ethics, but simply ethics. I offered my first course in robotics in 1983, and since 1984 I have required that each student taking the course write an essay on the social impact of robotics and automation in society. No great literary pieces emerged; but the students did present me with a plethora of ideas and they were forced to take such issues under consideration. Every manager who implements automation should have to write an essay about the impact of his decision to automate a particular routine in the work cycles under his purview. Similarly, all who work on or promote concepts of automation should be made to consider the possible social impact of their work. Since I require it of others, I feel compelled to provide such an assessment of my own views on this topic.

Our physical existence demands that we have food and a place to lay our heads, and our social well being demands that we perform some useful function for society. If we do not produce our own food and dwelling, then we must acquire them indirectly by providing a product or service in exchange for food and lodging. If we consider these essential for all of humanity, then a modicum of mass production and automation is needed in an industrial society to achieve some uniform standard or level of existence for a given population segment. If this had been the sole aim, the needed modicum could have been achieved long ago.

In modern society, the capability to provide these basic needs has existed some time and could provide a reasonable living standard. The intent of this capability, however, is frequently usurped by greed and the obsession with the acquisition of wealth and individual power. Excessive advertising and manipulation of the society have continued to increase individual need far beyond the basic requirements in order to meet the economic dictum of growth. Not only has modern western society accepted this view, but it has also managed to infect the aspirations of the remaining nations of the world to make it their primary goal to acquire these same material comforts. We shall first look at the benefits or detriments of automation the way it is presently imposed upon society in this presumed state of the world.

If we deem it desirable to continue to raise the material living standard of ever-increasing segments of the human population, then mass production and the associated technology are essential. The "we" referred to is crucial here, presumably composed of those who benefit from automation. Potential beneficiaries are the producer and the stockholder, the salesperson and the worker, and society as a whole.

Suppose we begin the analysis by looking at producer and stockholder. Generally, efficiency, when applied to automation, may be taken to be equivalent to more, quicker, cheaper, and sometimes better quality, ultimately again meaning cheaper. The immediate savings (and increased profits) primarily derive from the elimination of a category of jobs. The decision is usually carried out with the assurance (lamely given) that more highly skilled and, presumably, better paying jobs will, of course, eventually be created in the not too distant future. But these jobs are *never* provided at the time when automation is introduced. Thus the corporation no longer pays salaries or provides insurance, retirement, or other benefits, and in some cases is even granted a tax write-off for work force reduction. More often than not, the initial cost of automation is amortized in less than two years. The short-term monetary benefits to corporation and stockholder thus are obvious.

This wholesale and indiscriminate elimination of segments of a corporate work force, frequently consisting of the elimination of whole departments whose expertise is deemed outdated, brings about a reduction of the technical capabilities, and eliminates the seeds of innovation, since the collective experience of the worker, his or her interaction and exchange of ideas with other workers, is also eliminated. This can be destructive in much the same way the now recognized arbitrary elimination of a segment of the ecological chain can have devastating effects. Machines simply do not discuss innovation or improvements, or anything else, for that matter.

Finally, excessive automation tends to stagnate an industry, since replacement and upgrading of an automated system will now involve real cost without the immediate savings derived from employees who were laid off. This should be evident from the almost biennial required upgrading of computational tools, which may cost companies far more now than upgrading the employees. A major effect of this stagnation and implied resistance to real change is that the public must now be manipulated with fads and fashions that imitate change and thus allow the company to continue making the same product. This can only be accomplished with ever-increasing marketing and advertising expenditures. Thus the net result is a shifting of expenditures from production to sales. The best examples are the relics of automobile industries and the clothing industry.

This brings us to the laid-off employee. The immediate benefits are zero, or negative. Those with a strong constitution adjust, possibly improve their skills, and move on to another job, which *always* requires a reduction in income. The employee's personal involvement in the next job will quite likely be reduced to loyalty to oneself. Those with weaker constitutions will tend to remain on state support for some time, and any subsequent job will be at considerably reduced pay. In summary, I can see few benefits to the laid-off employee (in spite of the occasional, somewhat random exception).

The benefits to society of this approach are also dubious. The laid-off individuals often become an immediate financial burden to society, not only in terms of actual employment benefits, for example, but they also no longer pay taxes, they may not be able to pay off their debts, and they are less likely to purchase anything even if they do have sufficient savings. More indirect effects are those on their children, who will lack proper care, and the strain that the situation puts on families. None of us is isolated from these effects.

The approach we are talking about also produces an enormously self-centered moral climate, where individuals are looked at as commodities or percentages in a battle-like scenario, and where we accept a percentage of people without jobs as normal as long as we can maintain our own relatively affluent (generally speaking) standard of living.

Based on the preceding analysis, only marketing, sales, and advertising reap direct benefits from this approach to automation. Regardless of whether this societal state is desirable or not, it cannot continue to exist without the continuous introduction of new technology and automation. In particular, competing members and proponents of this society will find it essential to continue to automate, with the attendant reduction in work force, in order to remain competitive—to create a pool of jobless in order to maintain the eventually excessive lifestyles of a few. The final result would seem to be an expert marketing and sales force, selling foreign products to those few still capable of buying them.

I think there is another approach to the introduction and use of automation in society. The effect on society as a whole must be of primary importance.

Automation and technology are inextricably linked; we cannot have one without the other. At present, new technology is often viewed like an old mountain: we use it and, in the case of technology produce it, because it is there. Nary a thought is given to the desirability of new technology and its effect on society. Our lives are expected to continuously adjust to new technology foisted upon us by impressionable management and by an ever-increasing sales force. Faced with this continuous adjustment, there is little time to consider the quality of life, the kind of life we should like to lead as enlightened and educated individuals.

Automation and technology can benefit all of us, but we need to maintain control rather than be pulled hither and yon by more and more things that we neither need nor want. Only few would wish to return to an agrarian society where virtually all have to till the soil in order to eat. Our food is abundant because of the mechanization of every aspect of food production.

We should learn to plan the evolution of society over several centuries and learn to plan in such a grand framework rather than the minute plans whose failures are constantly in evidence. We should visualize and plan this ideal society and then evolve the technology and introduce automation which harmonizes with this goal. This would require the will to say no to some technology and to accept new technology only after it has passed a societal impact statement of sorts. It is relatively easy to deduce some of the basic edicts of such a society, although their refinement and implementation may be difficult and arduous.

Clearly, every member of such a society would have to be considered essential and indispensable, and each individual would have to be given the opportunity to realize his or her implied potential. Automation would thus need to be an evolutionary process, not the warlike and revolutionary process it now tends to be. Rather than being used to increase competitiveness and profit, it should be used in the service of society; it should free society from a great many onerous or dangerous jobs. The greatest challenge then would be how to use the freedom gained in a productive, constructive, and sensitive manner.

Once a desire for a more peaceful and less disruptive introduction of automation has been established within a society, acceptable rules for its implementation can be established. It is clear what these rules must accomplish. At present, the brunt of the introduction of automation is borne by the displaced employee, with benefits mostly accruing to company and stockholder. A more equitable distribution of the burden as well as benefits must be achieved by these rules. It then falls upon both employees and management to adjust (which might include retraining) and to create a new and productive niche for those who are displaced by automation.

The introduction of automation must occur without the loss of jobs. Its purpose must be service rather than competition. As long as automation threatens the jobs of those whose work it is designed to perform, the efforts of management and employee should go into the smooth transition to an automated environment, with benefits to all of society and not just a select few.

CHAPTER

ONE

INTRODUCTION TO ROBOTICS CONCEPTS AND PROBLEMS

1-1 WHENCE THE ROBOT?

This brief introduction will bring out the relative youth of the subject area and put it within the proper present technological framework.

In 1954 George C. Devol filed a U.S. patent for a programmable method for transferring articles between different parts of a factory. He wrote, in part:

> The present invention makes available for the first time a more or less general purpose machine that has universal application to a vast diversity of applications where cyclic control is desired.

In 1956 Devol met Joseph F. Engelberger, a young engineer in the aerospace industry. With others, they set up the world's first robot company, Unimation, Inc., and built their first machine in 1958. Their initiative was a great deal ahead of its time; according to Engelberger, Unimation did not show a profit until 1975.

The first industrial robot saw service in 1961 in a car factory run by General Motors in Trenton, New Jersey. The robot lifted hot pieces of metal from a die-casting machine and stacked them.

Japan, by comparison, imported its first industrial robot from AMF in 1967, at which time the United States was a good 10 years ahead in robotics technology. The enormous effort put forth by Japanese industry is best evidenced by the fact that Unimation was eventually reduced to handing over its pioneering robot technology to Kawasaki Heavy Industries in a licensing deal in 1968. A former Unimation executive states:

> I doubt if the royalty payments have been more than a tenth of the money it would have cost Kawasaki to work out the same technology itself.

By 1990 there were more than 40 Japanese companies, including giants like Hitachi and Mitsubishi, that were producing commercial robots. By comparison, there were approximately one dozen U.S. firms, led by Cincinnati Milacron and Westinghouse's Unimation. In 1979 the U.S. leader, Unimation, was the only company in the world actively marketing an advanced assembly robot. In 1982 GM, the largest single user of robots in the world, signed a pact with Fanuc Ltd. for a joint robotics venture to make and market robots in the United States. In the first six months of operation, more than half of the 100 robots sold by the joint venture went to GM, locking out other U.S. companies from the largest single buyer in the market.

There were other joint operations: Bendix signed to market Yaskawa robots, while Yaskawa was already selling through Hobart Industries and Nordson Corporation; IBM signed with Seiki to market the SCARA assembly robot, which sells for one-half the price of the Unimation advanced PUMA model but does 85% of what the PUMA does. As of 1987 the U.S. market was valued at more than $170 billion.

No introductory discussion of robotics would be complete without delving briefly into the origin of the word *robot*. The first mention of the word occurs in Karel Capek's play, *Rossum's Universal Robot*, written in 1922. In Czech, the word *robot* means *worker*. In the play, Rossum and his son discover the chemical formula for artificial protoplasm, the very basis of life, and they set out to make a robot. After 20 years they look at their construction, and the young Rossum decides to trim off any organs which he considers unnecessary for the ideal worker. He says:

> A man is something that feels happy, plays piano, likes going for a walk and, in fact, wants to do a whole lot of things that are unnecessary... but a working machine must not play piano, must not feel happy, must not do a whole lot of other things. Everything that doesn't contribute directly to the progress of work should be eliminated.

Based on this sample dialogue, the play does not seem to have been one which everybody rushed to see. It does, however, suggest the introduction of a

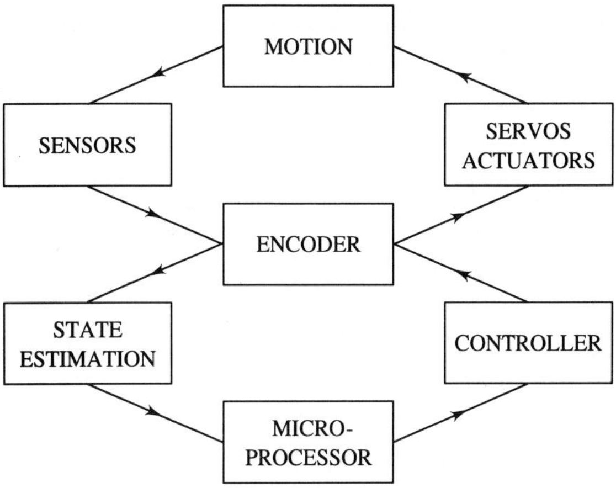

FIGURE 1-1
Robot operating diagram.

new verb into the English language:

> **robot** (ro'bət) *v.* [< Czech *robotnik*, serf, or *robota*, compulsory service]. 1. To perform boring or repetitive work; 2. to perform subhuman or dangerous work; 3. to perform work which is void of dignity or promise of improvement.

The reader may addend his own definitions. As for myself, I could do with a lot less "roboting."

Numerical comparisons of robots available in various countries make little sense unless there is agreement on what constitutes a robot. Such an agreement was reached recently when the International Standards Organization (ISO) settled on the following definition.

> **Definition 1-1 Industrial robot.** An industrial robot is an automatic, servo-controlled, freely programmable, multipurpose manipulator, with several axes, for the handling of work pieces, tools or special devices. Variably programmed operations make possible the execution of a multiplicity of tasks.

This definition was previously the German definition. It provides a clear distinction between pick-and-place robots which race from point to point at full speed and those robots where path control between points is provided.

In this context, *free programmability* implies that robots are capable of performing more than one task; and *manipulation* (and transport) indicates that a robot is not a tool but instead uses tools to carry out prescribed tasks—generally, manufacturing tasks within a production environment. A rough operating diagram for a robot is shown in Fig. 1-1. Since controlled motion is the prime purpose of robots, it is motion that is sensed, processed, and controlled.

Essential components of a robot are further illustrated in Fig. 1-2, depicting what might be termed a "roboach." The items depicted are present in every robot, although immobile robots may have no independent power supply or communications units. The components may be described briefly in the following manner:

Actuator—serves as the muscle of the system, produces the motion, with power supplied either electrically, pneumatically, or by hydraulics.

Communicator—a unit transmitting information and receiving instructions from a remote operator.

Control computer—a central computer that integrates the activity of several microprocessors.

End effector—a gripping device at the end of the manipulator arm; used to make intentional contact with an object or to produce the robot's final effect on its surroundings.

Manipulator—a mechanism consisting of several segments or arms.

Power supply—generally, some energy storage device, such as a battery, for a mobile unit; otherwise, the hook-up to the power grid.

Sensor—usually, a transducer of some kind whose inputs are physical phenomena and whose outputs consist of electronic signals.

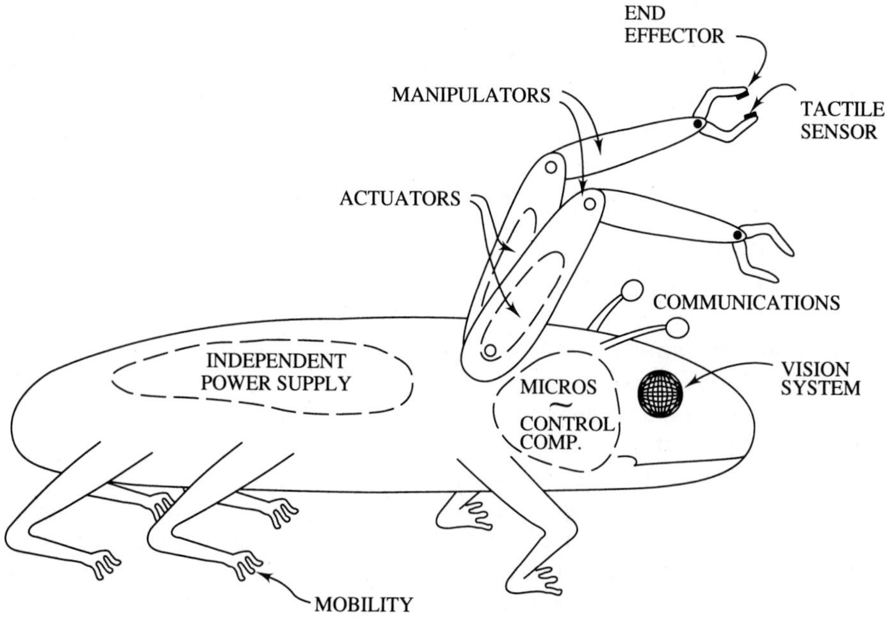

FIGURE 1-2
Robot components.

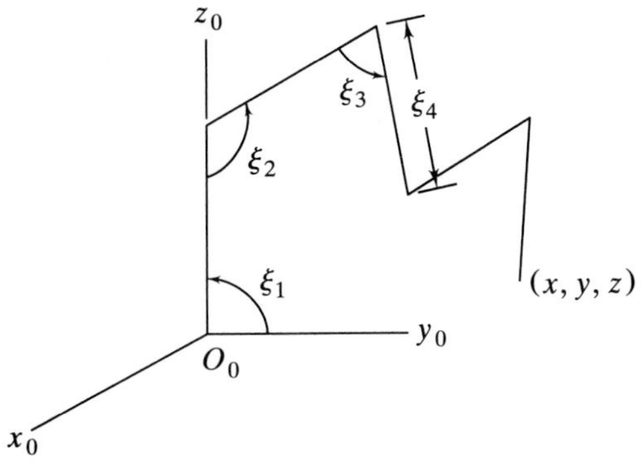

FIGURE 1-3
Robot variables and world variables.

The further classification of robots involves their physical configuration. There are two sets of variables for a robot which are of primary importance: the *external variables* or *world coordinates*, which will be denoted throughout simply by (x, y, z); and the corresponding *internal variables* or *robot coordinates* $(\xi_1, \ldots, \xi_N)$ whose values must generally be determined in such a way that some point of the robot structure coincides with the world coordinates (x, y, z). The general situation is depicted in Fig. 1-3.

Suppose now that the ξ_i have been chosen in such a way that only those are kept which may be actively changed by means of some internal actuator. For example, in Fig. 1-3, ξ_1 would not be included if it is fixed at 90°; and the inclusion of ξ_4 would require that the length ξ_4 can be changed. These requirements form the basis of the following definition.

Definition 1-2 Number of axes. The number of axes of a robot is equal to the number of robot variables that are actively controlled.

The use of the word *axes* here is deliberate, since it is clearly identifiable with robotics. The terms *degrees of mobility* and *degrees of freedom* are also in use in this context. Every joint, whether controllable or not, adds a degree of mobility to the robot. The term *degrees of freedom* has a very specific meaning in mechanics. A rigid body freely moving in $\mathbb{R}^3$ has six degrees of freedom: three translational and three rotational. Suppose a robot were to grip a rigid body; then the different motions that the robot could impart to the rigid body would constitute the degrees of freedom of the robot. Thus, if it were to mimic the free motion of the rigid body, it would need to have six degrees of freedom. A rigid body in planar motion has three degrees of freedom: two translational and one rotational. For example, the simple polar manipulator in Fig. 1-4a has two actively controlled variables (a two-axes robot) and two degrees of freedom; a joint at the gripper end provides it with three degrees of freedom (Fig. 1-4b). At this point it should be evident that in order to have n degrees of freedom, a robot must have at least n axes. When there are more axes than degrees of freedom, then these axes are redundant, although they may serve to improve

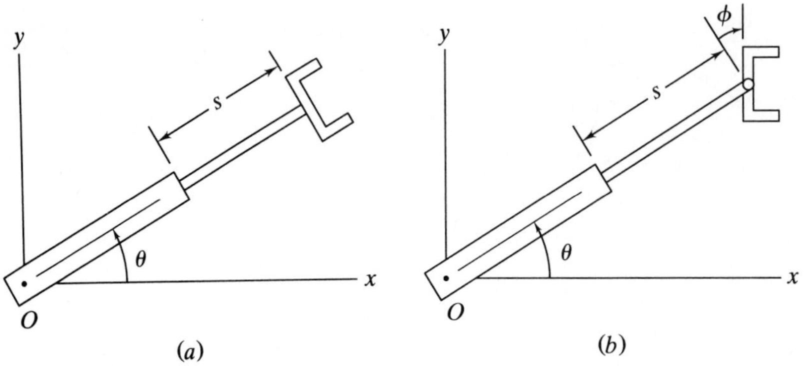

FIGURE 1-4
Degrees of freedom of the simple polar manipulator.

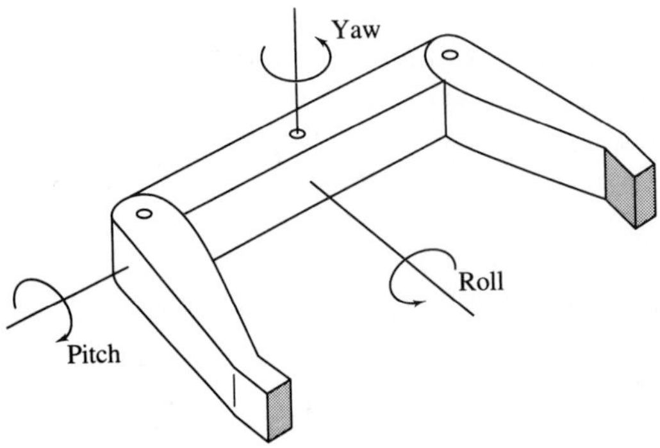

FIGURE 1-5
Motion terminology for gripper.

the motion characteristics. Additional axes also cause problems when a specific motion in space is to be described in terms of the robot variables.

The type of internal variables implied by the robot construction may be used as further means of classification. For example, the internal variables—all or some of them—may correspond to cylindrical or spherical coordinates. Another common subdivision of the internal variables singles out the number of axes of the end effector. A six-axes robot might have three manipulator axes and three axes for the end effector.† Somewhere along the line there was a nautical engineer among the roboticists who imagined the end effector as "plying" under the support of the manipulator, and he most probably introduced the terms *roll*, *pitch*, and *yaw* for the possible motions of the end effector, as shown in Fig. 1-5.

†By comparison, the human arm may move about more than 20 axes.

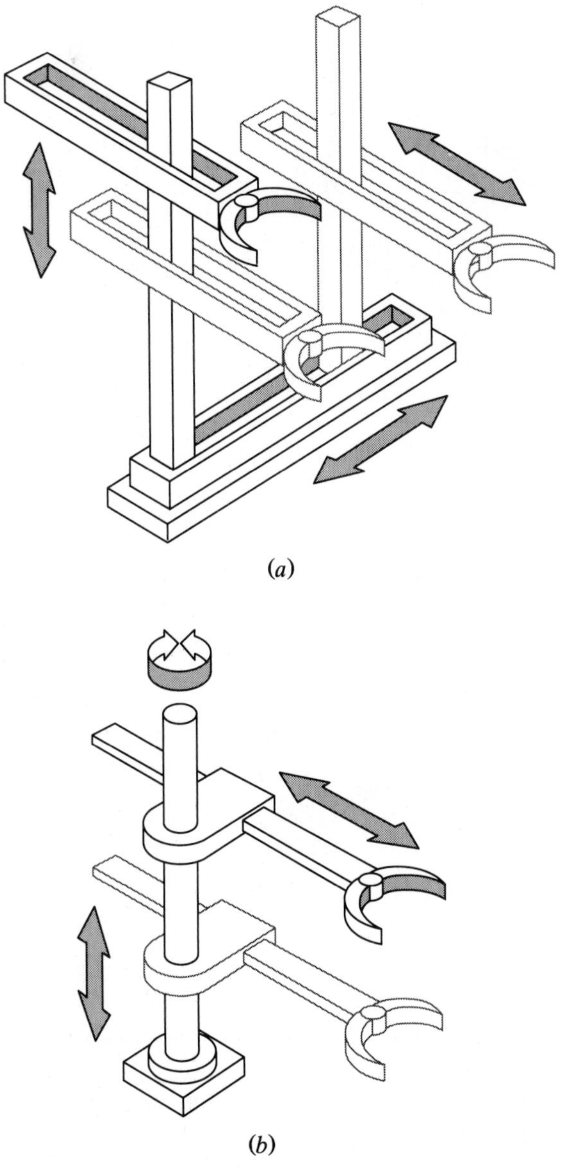

FIGURE 1-6
Standard robot configurations: (*a*) Cartesian robot; (*b*) cylindrical robot; (*c*) spherical robot; (*d*) revolute robot; (*e*) SCARA robot.

The manipulator axes are involved in the following five major robot classifications in terms of their physical configurations.

Definition 1-3 Robot classifications. (The five major robot types and their primary motion capabilities—standard robot configurations—are illustrated in Figs. 1-6*a*–*e*.)

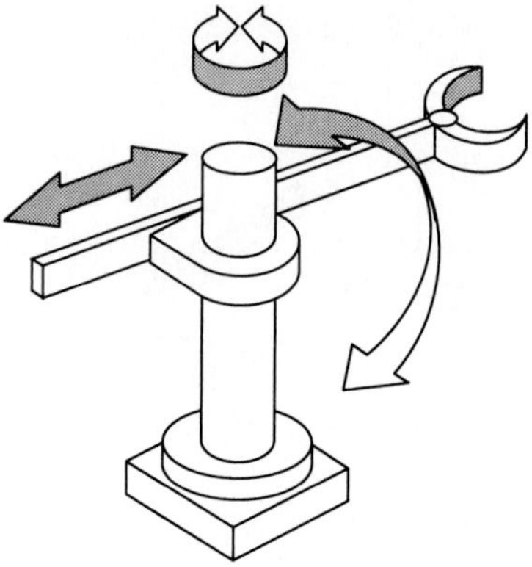

(*c*)

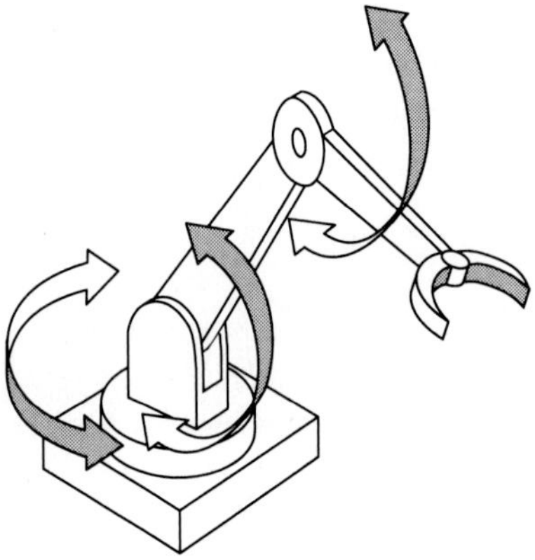

(*d*)

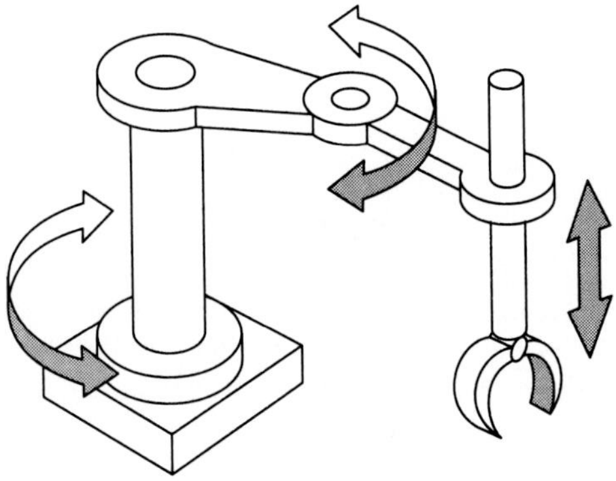

(*e*)

FIGURE 1-6 (*Continued*)

The Cartesian robot. Here the robot moves along the three basic translational axes x_0, y_0, and z_0 (Fig. 1-6*a*).

The cylindrical robot. The manipulator motion possibilities are defined by cylindrical coordinates (r, θ, z) (Fig. 1-6*b*).

The spherical robot. The manipulator motion possibilities are defined by spherical coordinates (r, θ, ϕ) (Fig. 1-6*c*).

The revolute robot. The manipulator motion possibilities are such that they mimic human arm motion. Such a robot is also known as an *articulated* or *anthropomorphic* robot. (Fig. 1-6*d*).

The SCARA robot. The manipulator motion possibilities are revolute motions confined to the horizontal plane, together with translation of this plane. The acronym stands for selective compliance assembly robot arm (Fig. 1-6*e*).

Each configuration has its advantages and disadvantages—in particular, as they concern the points within reach of the robot.

Definition 1-4 Work space and work envelope. Let A be a suitably defined point on the end effector of the robot. Then all of the world points (x, y, z) that A *can* occupy constitute the *work space* of the robot; the boundary of the work space is called the *work envelope*.

Clearly, obstacles consist of points that A cannot occupy; thus the given definition of work space also excludes any possible intrinsic obstacles such as the robot's supporting substructure.

The previous discussion provided an overall picture of robots and some specific robotics concepts. The remainder of the chapter is devoted to the introduction of some of the technical topics that need to be treated before we can hope to provide a partial or integrated mathematical model of a robot. The following introductory comments are by no means exhaustive; they merely introduce some of the fundamental problems that need to be considered.

1-2 COORDINATES AND THE COORDINATE INVERSION PROBLEM

There are a number of ways in which a robot may be made to move along a given trajectory. Such a motion always provides a relationship between the robot's surroundings, described in terms of the world coordinates (x, y, z), and the robot's perception of these surroundings, described in terms of $(\xi_1, \ldots, \xi_n)$. If the robot variables are specified first in some fashion, then one usually has the single-valued mapping

$$x = x(\xi_1, \ldots, \xi_n)$$
$$y = y(\xi_1, \ldots, \xi_n)$$
$$z = z(\xi_1, \ldots, \xi_n)$$

relating them to the corresponding world points to be occupied by the robot. However, it is often desirable, indeed imperative, that the world points be specified and the corresponding robot variables be calculated from an *inverse* mapping

$$\begin{aligned} \xi_1 &= \xi_1(x, y, z) \\ \xi_2 &= \xi_2(x, y, z) \\ &\vdots \\ \xi_n &= \xi_n(x, y, z) \end{aligned}$$

It is this inverse problem that causes most of the geometric difficulties involved in robot control. Since these relations are always dealt with in connection with the robot's motion, the former is also referred to as the *forward kinematics problem*, and the latter as the *inverse kinematics problem*. Collectively, one is dealing with coordinate transformations although not in the strict mathematical sense of the term.

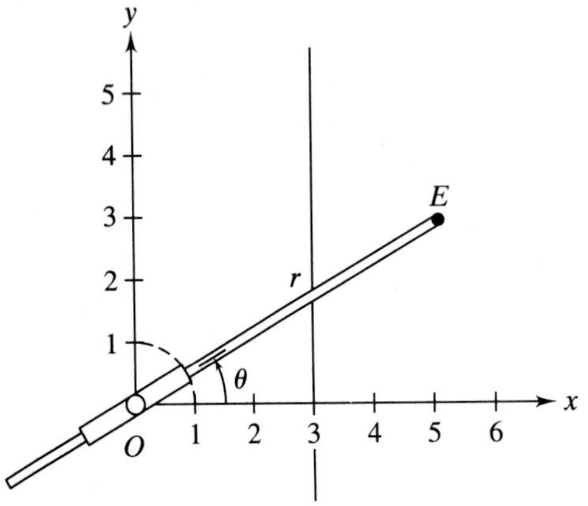

FIGURE 1-7
A polar manipulator.

Example 1-1. Suppose the "polar manipulator" in Fig. 1-7 is mounted in a rotating sleeve at the origin of the fixed world reference frame $(0xy)$. The robot arm with end effector E may slide radially within the sleeve. The values of r and θ are constrained to lie in the ranges

$$1 \le r \le 4.5 \qquad \text{and} \qquad 0 \le \theta \le 50^\circ$$

(*a*) Sketch the work space and the work envelope of this manipulator—that is, the set of all points reached by the end effector E.

(*b*) Let the world variables (x, y) be known as functions of the robot variables (r, θ):

$$x = r\cos\theta = x(r,\theta) \qquad \text{and} \qquad y = r\sin\theta = y(r,\theta)$$

Determine the robot variables (coordinates) (r, θ) as functions of the world variables and discuss the limitations of your solution.

(*c*) Suppose the end effector E is to move in the direction of increasing y along the straight line $x = 3$, beginning at $(3, 0)$. How far can it move along this line? State your limitations in terms of both the world variables and the robot variables.

Solution

(*a*) The boundary of the work space is specified by the rays $\theta = 0^\circ$ and $\theta = 50^\circ$ along with the circular arcs at $r = 1$ and $r = 4.5$. (See Fig. 1-8.)

(*b*) The objective is to obtain the robot variables as a function of the world variables, or

$$r = r(x, y)$$
$$\theta = \theta(x, y)$$

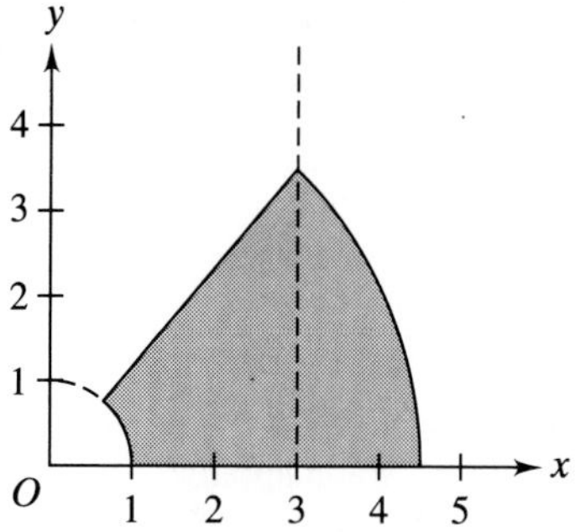

FIGURE 1-8
Work space of the polar manipulator.

The given equations are a set of simultaneous transcendental equations. The first one may be solved for r,

$$r = \frac{x}{\cos\theta}$$

which may be substituted into the second to yield

$$\tan\theta = \frac{y}{x}$$

With

$$\cos\theta = \frac{x}{\sqrt{x^2 + y^2}}$$

one then obtains

$$r = \sqrt{x^2 + y^2}$$

This completes the formal solution of the problem. It remains to check the limitations of this result.

A brief review of coordinate systems (as found in Fleming,[1] for example) may be helpful. Let S (open) $\subset \mathbb{R}^n$. A mapping $\mathbf{g}(\cdot)$ is *regular* on S if:

(*a*) $\mathbf{g}(\cdot)$ is of class $C^{(1)}$,

(*b*) $\mathbf{g}(\cdot)$ is univalent, and

(*c*) the Jacobian of $\mathbf{g}(\cdot)$, $J(\mathbf{g}(t)) \neq 0$ for every t in S.

Now, let S (open) $\subset \mathbb{R}^2$. Then any regular mapping $\mathbf{f}(x, y) = (f_1(x, y), f_2(x, y))$ from S to $\mathbb{R}^2$ is a coordinate system on S. Since the mapping is univalent, $\mathbf{f}(x_1, y_1) = \mathbf{f}(x_2, y_2)$ implies $(x_1, y_1) = (x_2, y_2)$. The so-called identity map on S thus yields the usual Cartesian coordinate system.

Suppose we now consider the *principal* range of the arctangent function with

$$-\frac{\pi}{2} \leq \text{Arctan}\, a \leq \frac{\pi}{2}$$

the use of the capital A indicating this restriction, and let

$$S = \mathbb{R}^2 - \{(x, y)\colon x \leq 0,\ y = 0\}$$

that is, the plane minus the nonpositive segment of the x-axis. Then the mapping

$$f_1(x, y) = r(x, y) = \sqrt{x^2 + y^2}$$

$$f_2(x, y) = \theta(x, y) = \begin{cases} \text{Arctan}\,\dfrac{y}{x} & x > 0 \\ \pi + \text{Arctan}\,\dfrac{y}{x} & x < 0 \end{cases}$$

is a *polar coordinate system* for S with implied θ-range, $-\pi < 0 < \pi$. With a priori restrictions given in the original problem statement, the mapping

$$r(x, y) = \sqrt{x^2 + y^2}$$

$$\theta(x, y) = \text{Arctan}\,\frac{y}{x}$$

is a coordinate system without further restriction.

The previous discussion has dealt only with the mathematical difficulties encountered in establishing a one-to-one correspondence between the two sets of coordinates; nothing has been said concerning possible computational difficulties based on the ranges of the Arctangent function.

(c) The maximum length vertical line segment attainable by the robot is to be determined. There are two possibilities to consider—either the vertical line intersects the ray $\theta = 50°$ or it intersects the circular arc with radius $r = 4.5$. Since $4.5 \cos 50° = 2.89 < 3$, the vertical line intersects the curved portion. Consequently,

$$\theta = \text{Arccos}\,\frac{3}{4.5} = 48.19°$$

is the critical angle. The maximum length line segment is thus specified with $(\bar{x}, \bar{y}) = (3, 3.35)$ corresponding to $(\bar{r}, \bar{\theta}) = (4.5, 48.19°)$.

In this example the proper restrictions established the univalence of the mapping and hence a one-to-one correspondence between the coordinate descriptions. For cylindrical robots these restrictions are met by design. Most robots, however, generally have a number of configurations, with the end effector occupying the same world point; that is, the equations

$$x = x(\xi_1, \ldots, \xi_n)$$
$$y = y(\xi_1, \ldots, \xi_n)$$
$$z = z(\xi_1, \ldots, \xi_n)$$

when attempting to solve for the ξ_i in terms of (x, y, z), will have a multiplicity of solutions which may range from two to infinity, as illustrated by the manipulator configurations shown in Fig. 1-9.

For the manipulator depicted in Fig. 1-9a, there are again two robot variables to describe a point in $\mathbb{R}^2$. Ambiguity may again be eliminated by an appropriate restriction of the robot variables, as in Example 1-1. For example,

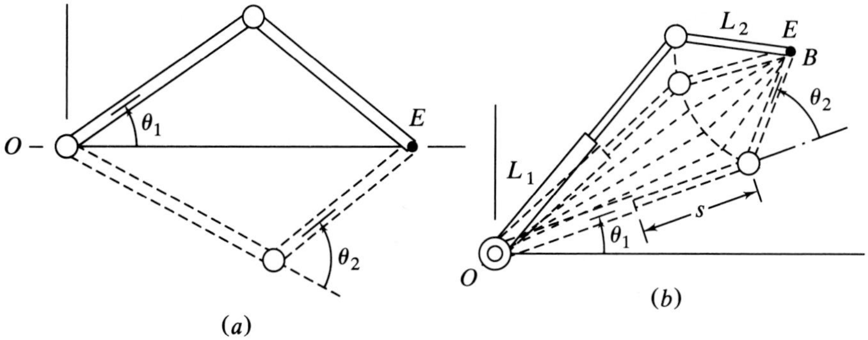

FIGURE 1-9
Manipulators with multiple configurations for a given world point.

one may insist on $\theta_2 \geq 0$ to resolve the difficulty, resulting in a so-called "below arm" positioning of the robot. The difficulty is considerably exacerbated when there are more robot coordinates than the dimension in which the robot is to move. For the manipulator shown in Fig. 1-9*b*, the first link is allowed to rotate an amount θ_1, the second link to translate an amount s, and the third—again a fixed-length link—to rotate an amount θ_2. Note that there are now an infinite number of configurations for the prescribed position of E. Can you deduce a constraint on only one of the variables which will allow only one configuration to reach a given point E? The inverse kinematics problem deals with these questions, in general, as well as in a tailored form, adjusted to a particular robot type.

1-3 TRAJECTORY PLANNING

Trajectory planning refers to the planning of a sequence of world points $(x(t), y(t), z(t))$ to be occupied by, say, the end effector of the robot and the planning of a sequence of values to be taken on by a specific joint variable ξ_i. The former is often referred to as *path planning*, and the latter as *trajectory planning*. Suppose we now take a brief look at desirable aspects of such trajectories from a purely physical point of view.

Once we have dealt with the coordinate inversion problem, we have the essential tool for the planning of robot motion, since we are now able to describe its motion either in terms of the world coordinates or the robot coordinates. The use of world variables in describing the motion allows easy visualization of the motion in terms of some characteristic point on the robot. However, since actual control is usually carried out in terms of the robot variables, a coordinate inversion is required in effecting control. This delay can cause difficulties, for example, when the robot is to be guided in interaction with an external sensor—that is, a sensor perceiving the robot's surroundings rather than measuring some internal robot variable. These difficulties are avoided when the robot motion is planned in terms of the robot variables. That, however, would be at the expense of having any intuitive awareness of the robot's interaction with its surroundings, since it is generally difficult to visualize the resultant motion when only the joint motions are known.

The study of curves or trajectories is essential to an understanding of robot kinematics, since all points of a robot move on curves. A student's first encounter with kinematics occurs in the analytic geometry part of his or her analytic geometry and calculus course sequence. We shall now expand upon the basics acquired there as well as in a first course on dynamics.

The ultimate purpose of every aspect of robotics is to produce controlled motion. Without motion a robot is no more than a computer. Generally, there are three ways in which a robot can be made to move: (1) it may be taught its motion by "taking it by the hand" or by means of a *teach pendant*; (2) it may be programmed "off line" to perform a particular motion; and (3) it may "create" its own motion as a response to sensory data. In order to provide a relevant context, suppose we consider the first possibility.

In essence, world variables (x, y, z), along with a total velocity v, are being specified. This, in turn, implies the specification of corresponding discrete values for each of the robot (or link) variables ξ_i, along with corresponding velocity components η_i. Note that at this point the velocity components η_i need not be derivatives of the ξ_i since they are specified as separate discrete parameters. They are, however, ultimately taken to be related in this fashion.

When replaying such a recorded motion, it is, of course, expected that the robot will traverse its path (including nonrecorded points) in a smooth fashion. The assurance of such smoothness is provided by trajectory planning. Suppose we plan the trajectory in terms of the world variables. This requires the prescription of intermediate positions and velocities for the world variables, with the robot variables taking on the values implied by the coordinate inversion. There are three steps for the proper specification of such a trajectory:

1. We first specify a space curve which passes through all of the recorded points and satisfies all constraints imposed by the robot's surroundings [a collection of points (x, y, z)].
2. We then specify a parametrization of the space curve, which will assure that the robot will traverse the curve in the desired fashion, that is, with the desired velocity. Thus we specify *when* the previous sequence of values is to be taken on.
3. We calculate the corresponding robot variables $\xi_i(t)$.

Again, the three concepts from differential geometry that enter the problem are space curves, parametrization of space curves, and coordinate transformations. To fix these ideas in our minds, we follow their application through a planar problem.

Example 1-2. Suppose that the world points $P_1(2,0)$, $P_2(1,2)$, and $P_3(0,2)$, together with the velocities $v_1 = 0$, $v_2 = \sqrt{2}\pi$ (admittedly contrived), and $v_3 = 0$, have been recorded for the end effector E of a polar manipulator. Prescribe a suitable interpolated path C for the two-dimensional "robot" in the sketch. Assume that the required transfer time from P_1 to P_3 is $t_1 = 1$ s (see Fig. 1-10).

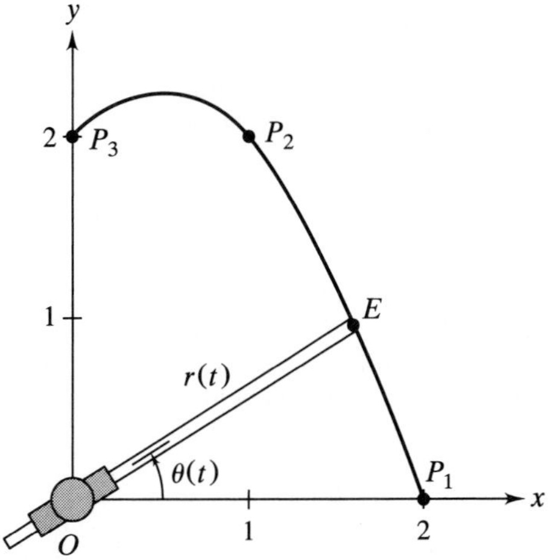

FIGURE 1-10
Parametrization of end-effector path.

Solution. First, suppose we prescribe a parabola through the three points. Then

$$y = ax^2 + bx + c$$

and we obtain the simultaneous equations

$$0 = 4a + 2b + c$$
$$2 = a + b + c$$
$$2 = c$$

which are to be solved for the parameters a, b, and c. The result is

$$y = -x^2 + x + 2 = f(x) \qquad 0 \le x \le 2$$

We now write

$$\boldsymbol{r}(t) = x(t)\hat{\imath} + y(t)\hat{\jmath}$$
$$\boldsymbol{v}(t) = \dot{x}(t)\hat{\imath} + \dot{y}(t)\hat{\jmath}$$

for the motion and the velocity of E, respectively. In these terms, the following requirements need to be imposed:

$$\boldsymbol{r}(0) = x(0)\hat{\imath} + y(0)\hat{\jmath} = 2\hat{\imath} \qquad x(0) = 2 \qquad y(0) = 0$$

$$\boldsymbol{r}(1) = x(1)\hat{\imath} + y(1)\hat{\jmath} = 2\hat{\jmath} \qquad x(1) = 0 \qquad y(1) = 2$$

$$\boldsymbol{v}(0) = \dot{x}(0)\hat{\imath} + \dot{y}(0)\hat{\jmath} = \mathbf{0}$$

$$\boldsymbol{v}(1) = \dot{x}(1)\hat{\imath} + \dot{y}(1)\hat{\jmath} = \mathbf{0}$$

Note that with $y = f(x)$, we now have

$$\dot{y}(t) = \frac{df}{dx}(x(t))\dot{x}(t)$$

so that $\boldsymbol{v}$ is 0 whenever $\dot{x}$ is 0. Furthermore, if we satisfy the endpoint conditions on x, then those on y will follow automatically from $y = f(x)$. Hence it suffices to construct $x(t)$, subject to

$$x(0) = 2 \qquad \dot{x}(0) = 0$$

$$x(1) = 0 \qquad \dot{x}(1) = 0$$

and $v = \sqrt{2}\pi$ when E passes through P_2.

The most obvious choice is a polynomial of sufficient degree to provide the needed number of adjustable constraints. To reduce the amount of algebra, we choose a sinusoid here. For a transfer from rest to rest,

$$x(t) = a\sin^2 b(c - t) = \tfrac{1}{2}a(1 - \cos 2b(c - t))$$

is a well-behaved choice. The use of the previous conditions yields $a = 2$, $b = \pi/2$, and $c = 1$, with

$$x(t) = 1 - \cos\pi(1 - t) = 2\sin^2\frac{\pi}{2}(1 - t)$$

as a consequence. The corresponding expression for y is

$$y(t) = -4\sin^4\frac{\pi}{2}(1 - t) + 2\sin^2\frac{\pi}{2}(1 - t) + 2$$

The final condition to be satisfied is $v = \sqrt{2}\pi$. When x passes through 1, we have

$$x(t^*) = 1 - \cos\pi(1 - t^*) = 1$$

or $t^* = \frac{1}{2}$ as the corresponding instant. At that time, the x-component of the velocity is

$$\dot{x}\left(\tfrac{1}{2}\right) = -\pi\sin\pi(1 - t)|_{t=1/2} = -\pi$$

For the y-component of the velocity, we use

$$\begin{aligned}\dot{y}\left(\frac{1}{2}\right) &= \frac{df}{dx}\left(x\left(\frac{1}{2}\right)\right)\frac{dx}{dt}\left(\frac{1}{2}\right)\\ &= [-2(1 - \cos\pi(1 - t)) + 1]\dot{x}(t)|_{t=1/2}\\ &= \pi\end{aligned}$$

Hence we have

$$v\left(\tfrac{1}{2}\right) = \sqrt{\dot{x}^2\left(\tfrac{1}{2}\right) + \dot{y}^2\left(\tfrac{1}{2}\right)} = \sqrt{2}\,\pi$$

as required. Thus the desired space curve is completely determined at this point.

It remains to describe the robot variables (r, θ) as a function of time. The coordinate transformation between Cartesian and polar coordinates yields

$$\begin{aligned} r(t) &= \sqrt{x^2(t) + y^2(t)} \\ &= \Bigg[16 \sin^8 \frac{\pi}{2}(1-t) - 16 \sin^6 \frac{\pi}{2}(1-t) \\ &\quad -8 \sin^4 \frac{\pi}{2}(1-t) + 8 \sin^2 \frac{\pi}{2}(1-t) + 4\Bigg]^{1/2} \end{aligned}$$

$$\theta(t) = \operatorname{Arctan} \frac{y(t)}{x(t)} = \operatorname{Arctan}\left[-2 \sin^2 \frac{\pi}{2}(1-t) + 1 + \operatorname{cosec}^2 \frac{\pi}{2}(1-t)\right]$$

Although not a pretty sight, it fulfills all of the requirements.

Collectively, we may envision the choice of curve and parametrization as a way of ensuring that nothing drastic will happen to the acceleration. In essence, we want a "smooth" (continuous derivative) velocity. If $\hat{e}_t$ is a unit tangent vector to the curve C at a point P and $\hat{e}_n$ is a unit normal vector (pointing toward the center of curvature), recall that for planar motion the acceleration in intrinsic coordinates is

$$\boldsymbol{a}(t) = \ddot{s}(t)\hat{e}_t(t) + \frac{\dot{s}^2(t)}{\rho(t)}\hat{e}_n(t)$$

Clearly, then, the parametrization basically takes care of the tangential component, and the shape of the curve itself takes care of the normal component.

The following two examples illustrate phenomena to be avoided in planning the accelerated motion of a robot end effector.

Example 1-3. Consider the unit circle in the first quadrant along with the parametrization

$$x(t) = \left(-\tfrac{1}{2}t^2 + t\right)u(t) + (t-1)^2 u(t-1) \qquad 0 \le t \le 2$$

$$y(t) = \sqrt{1 - x^2(t)}$$

where $u(t)$ is the unit step function. Sketch $x(t)$, $\dot{x}(t)$, and $\ddot{x}(t)$ versus t on $[0, 2]$.

Solution. The sketches and the corresponding needed derivatives are shown in Fig. 1-11. Note carefully that the seemingly innocuous parametrization of the curve

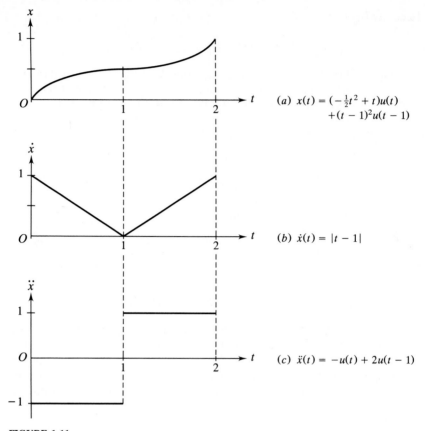

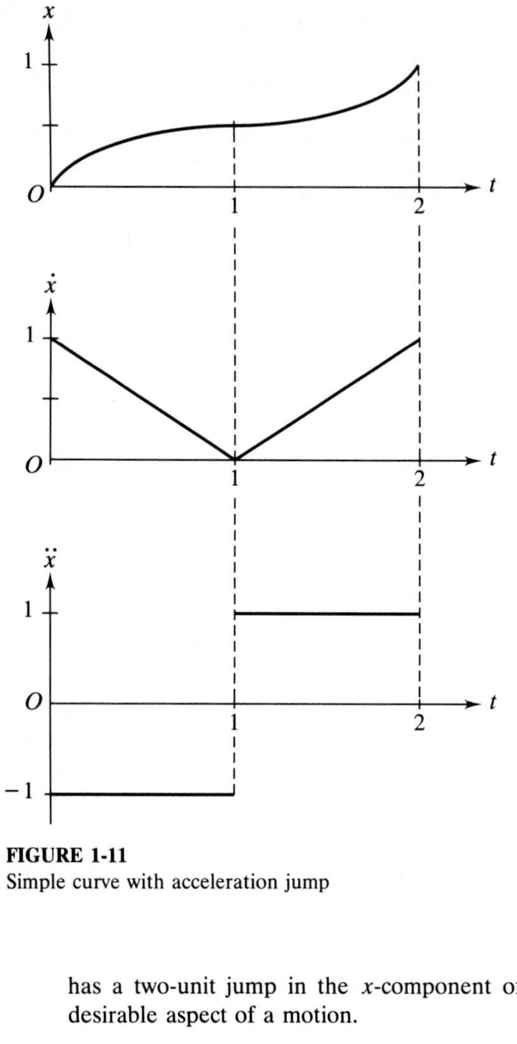

$$(a)\ x(t) = (-\tfrac{1}{2}t^2 + t)u(t) + (t-1)^2u(t-1)$$

$$(b)\ \dot{x}(t) = |t-1|$$

$$(c)\ \ddot{x}(t) = -u(t) + 2u(t-1)$$

FIGURE 1-11
Simple curve with acceleration jump

has a two-unit jump in the x-component of the acceleration, not a particularly desirable aspect of a motion.

Example 1-4. Consider the curve C in Fig. 1-12, consisting of two connected quarter circles with radii b_1 and b_2. Suppose a point P moves along the curve with constant speed v. Discuss the acceleration of P over the curve segment indicated.

Solution. Note that in spite of the smooth appearance of the curve, there is a jump of magnitude

$$^-a_n^+ = v^2\left(\frac{1}{b_2} - \frac{1}{b_1}\right)$$

in the normal acceleration component.

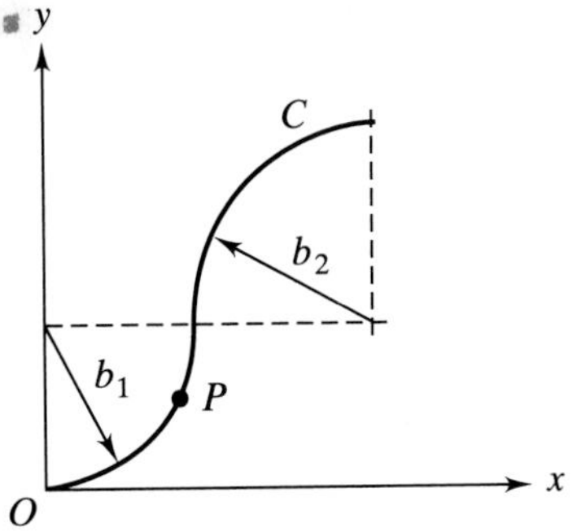

FIGURE 1-12
A jump in curvature.

It is clear from these examples and comments that both the curve and its parametrization must be carefully chosen to assure a smooth operation of the robot. That is, they must avoid jumps in the acceleration.

The next example deals with an organized approach to the construction of curves that specifically avoid jumps in slope as well as curvature. The approach is called *cubic splining*. Each interval is bridged by a new cubic equation which ties into the preceding one by requiring that the slope and curvature be continuous.

Example 1-5. Draw the cubic splines between the four points $P_1, \ldots, P_4$ in Fig. 1-13. Specify the equations and indicate the intervals of validity.

Solution. The first interval is from P_1 to P_2 with $1 \le x \le 2$. We specify the cubic

$$y_1(x) = a_1x^3 + b_1x^2 + c_1x + d_1$$

Two equations are obtained from the points P_1 and P_2 through which the cubic is to pass. Since there are no continuity conditions from the left, we arbitrarily

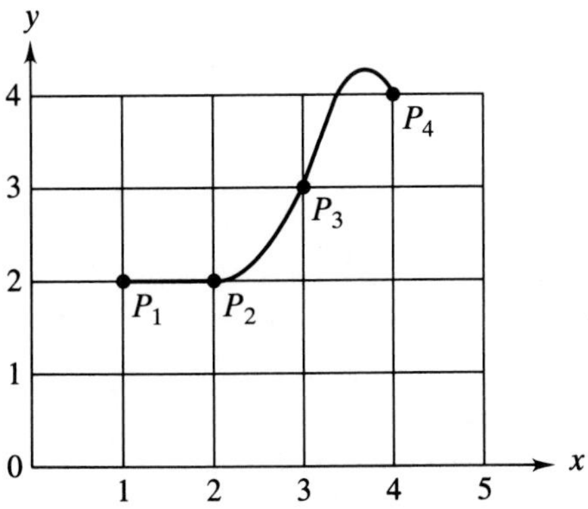

FIGURE 1-13
A cubic spline.

specify $y_1'(0) = 0$ and $y_1''(0) = 0$. Even in the general case, such conditions must be provided. However, this is usually done by specifying the second derivative at each end of the curve. The resultant simultaneous equations are

$$2 = a_1 + b_1 + c_1 + d_1$$

$$2 = 8a_1 + 4b_1 + 2c_1 + d_1$$

$$0 = 3a_1 + 2b_1 + c_1$$

$$0 = 6a_1 + 2b_1$$

The solution yields

$$y_1(x) = 2 \qquad 1 \le x \le 2$$

We next turn to the interval from P_2 to P_3. The cubic is taken to be

$$y_2(x) = a_2 x^3 + b_2 x^2 + c_2 x + d_2 \qquad 2 \le x \le 3$$

This cubic must pass through P_2 and P_3, and the slope as well as the second derivative must match at P_2 or at $x = 2$. The simultaneous equations are

$$2 = 8a_2 + 4b_2 + 2c_2 + d_2$$

$$3 = 27a_2 + 9b_2 + 3c_2 + d_2$$

$$0 = 12a_2 + 4b_2 + c_2$$

$$0 = 12a_2 + 2b_2$$

yielding the cubic

$$y_2(x) = x^3 - 6x^2 + 12x - 6 \qquad 2 \le x \le 3$$

For the final interval between P_3 and P_4, we have

$$y_3(x) = a_3 x^3 + b_3 x^2 + c_3 x + d_3 \qquad 3 \le x \le 4$$

The curve must pass through P_3 and P_4 with first and second derivatives matching at P_3. The set of equations is

$$3 = 27a_3 + 9b_3 + 3c_3 + d_3$$

$$4 = 64a_3 + 16b_3 + 4c_3 + d_3$$

$$3 = 27a_3 + 6b_3 + c_3$$

$$6 = 18a_3 + 2b_3$$

with corresponding cubic

$$y_3(x) = -5x^3 + 48x^2 - 150x + 156$$

The result of connecting these cubics end to end is depicted in Fig. 1-13. With different specified values of y' and y'' at P_1, a different total curve would, of course, be obtained.

Note, finally, that the continuity of the first and second derivative as imposed previously implies the continuity of the curvature

$$\kappa(x) = \frac{y''(x)}{\left[1 + y'(x)^2\right]^{3/2}}$$

The preceding discussion and examples dealt with some rudimentary aspects of trajectory planning. Trajectory planning in terms of world coordinates has been emphasized since they are more easily visualized. The cubic splining example, however, is equally applicable to the planning of the two-dimensional motion of the robot as well as to the planning of the position of a particular link as a function of time. All of these aspects are discussed in greater detail in Chap. 8.

1-4 SOME SYSTEMS CONCEPTS

By this time, the electrical engineering student may be tempted to inquire: "When do we get to the electrical stuff? This is supposed to be a course for electrical as well as mechanical engineers!" We are about to delve into some "electrical stuff."

Some readers may feel that general systems concepts should be presented in an appendix. However, this short review (or introduction) should considerably ease the study of the remaining part of the first chapter, and it reflects my own preference for having a review where I need it, rather than having it tucked away in an appendix.

Systems concepts should be—and sometimes are—a part of the fundamental education of every engineer. More often than not, they are used by electrical engineers and mechanical engineers working in control. For an integrated linear viewpoint of the robot as an electromechanical system, the concepts of system functions and block diagrams become indispensable. System functions are usually defined for systems governed by linear equations or linear differential equations. Suppose then that we take our general system here to be governed by an equation of the form

$$a_0(t)\frac{d^n y}{dt^n} + a_1(t)\frac{d^{n-1}y}{dt^{n-1}} + \cdots + a_n(t)y$$

$$= b_0(t)\frac{d^m f}{dt^m} + \cdots + b_m(t)f \qquad \text{(S)}$$

where we define $f(\cdot)$: $[0, \infty) \to \mathbb{R}$ as the *input* and the response $y(\cdot)$: $[0, \infty) \to \mathbb{R}$ as the *output*, unless otherwise stated. Furthermore, we shall denote the Laplace transform of a function $g(\cdot)$: $[0, \infty) \to \mathbb{R}$ by

$$\mathscr{L}\{g(t)\} = G(s) = \int_0^\infty e^{-st} g(t)\, dt$$

(With few exceptions, the use of a lowercase letter to denote a function in t-space and the corresponding uppercase letter to denote the transform function in s-space will be maintained throughout.)

Definition 1-5 System function. Let (S) be a linear time-invariant system and let $Y(s)$ and $F(s)$ be the Laplace transforms of $y(t)$ and $f(t)$, respectively. Let them be related by the Laplace transform of the system equation (S) taken with all initial conditions set equal to 0. Then the ratio

$$G(s) = \frac{Y(s)}{F(s)}$$

as computed from the transformed equation (S) is the system function for the system (S).

Example 1-6. Obtain the system function for the system (S) when all of the coefficients are constant.

Solution. The Laplace transform of both sides of (S) with all initial conditions set equal to 0 is

$$\left[a_0 s^n + a_1 s^{n-1} + \cdots + a_n\right] Y(s) = \left[b_0 s^m + b_1 s^{m-1} + \cdots + b_m\right] F(s)$$

and the system function thus is

$$G(s) = \frac{Y(s)}{F(s)} = \frac{b_0 s^m + \cdots + b_m}{a_0 s^n + \cdots + a_n}$$

In complex variable theory, such functions, represented by the ratio of two polynomials, are called *rational functions*, and they enjoy a number of nice properties germane to the class of entire, or meromorphic, functions.

Example 1-7. Determine the system function for the inverting op-amp differentiating circuit shown in Fig. 1-14. Unless noted otherwise, all voltages are stated with ground as the reference voltage.

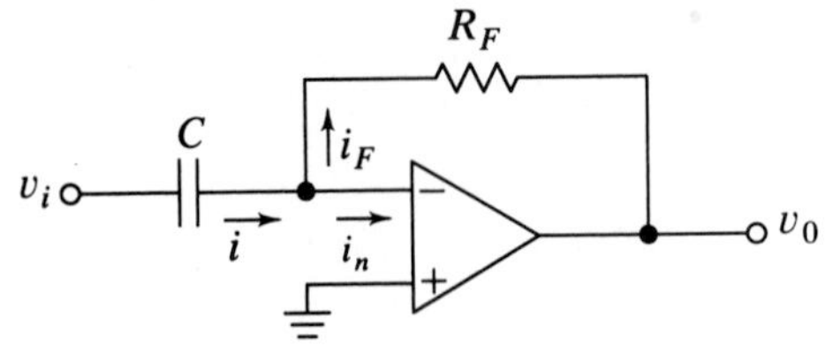

FIGURE 1-14
A differentiator.

Solution. We first determine the governing differential equation for the circuit. At the so-called summing junction, we have

$$i = i_n + i_F$$

Substitution of the corresponding current-voltage laws yields

$$C\frac{d}{dt}(v_i - v_n) = i_n + \frac{1}{R_F}(v_n - v_0)$$

and the usual operating assumptions for the op amp, $i_n \approx 0$ and $v_n \approx 0$, then result in

$$v_0 = -R_F C\frac{dv_i}{dt}$$

Thus the system function with input v_i and output v_0 is given by

$$G(s) = \frac{V_0(s)}{V_i(s)} = -ks \qquad k = R_F C$$

We now turn to a brief summary of block diagrams and their manipulation as used in systems analysis. By definition, the algebraic meaning of the symbols in Fig. 1-15 is

$$Y(s) = G(s)F(s)$$

with the arrows denoting the direction of signal flow. Furthermore, the symbols in Fig. 1-16 denote a *summing point* with

$$F(s) + (-A(s)) - B(s) = 0$$

and a *pick-off point*, respectively. At a summing point, the signals are summed as at a current node, with the exception that the signals carry with them the sign indicated in the quadrant of the circle, with a "blank" denoting a plus (+) sign. All branches leaving a pick-off point have the signal value indicated at the pick-off point. Although generally drawn for four directions, both of these symbols obviously extend to the possible meeting of n-branches. These are the basic rules. They are used in reducing extensive combinations of subsystems to a single equivalent system function.

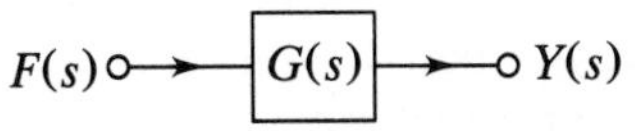

FIGURE 1-15
Fundamental block diagram segment.

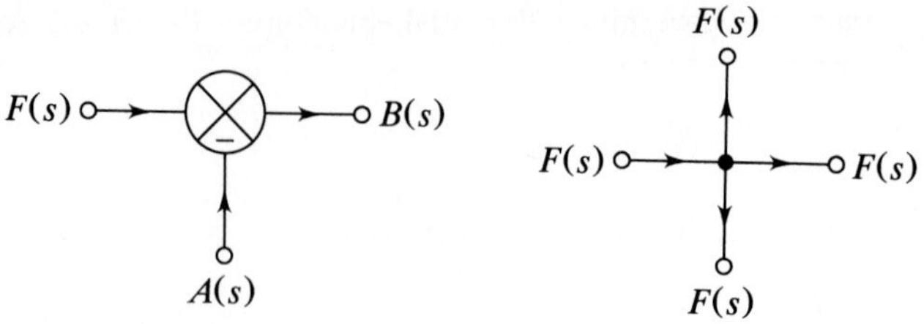

FIGURE 1-16
Graph conventions.

Example 1-8. Deduce a single equivalent system function for the sequence of subsystems shown in Fig. 1-17.

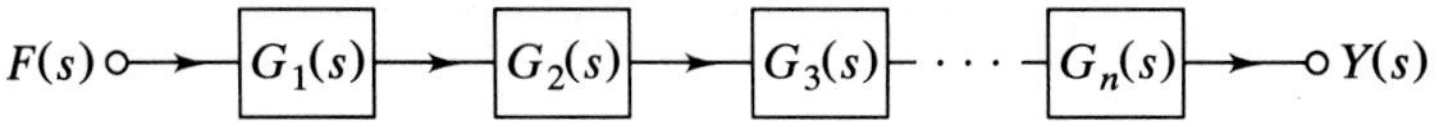

FIGURE 1-17
n subsystems in tandem.

Solution. With $A_1(s)$ denoting the output at $G_1(s)$, $A_2(s)$ the output at $G_2(s)$, and so on, we obtain

$$A_1(s) = F(s)G_1(s)$$

$$A_2(s) = A_1(s)G_2(s) = F(s)G_1(s)G_2(s)$$

$$\vdots$$

$$Y(s) = A_n(s)G_n(s) = F(s)G_1(s)G_2(s)\dots G_n(s)$$

so that

$$G(s) = \frac{Y(s)}{F(s)} = G_1(s)G_2(s)\dots G_n(s) = \prod_{k=1}^{n} G_k(s)$$

where the symbol $\prod_{k=1}^{n}$ denotes the product of n terms in a manner similar to the summation symbol (Σ) denoting a sum of the terms.

Example 1-9. Deduce a single equivalent system function for the combination of subsystems depicted in Fig. 1-18.

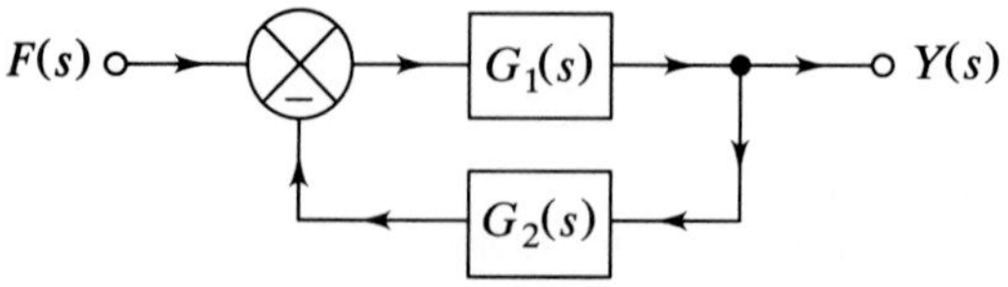

FIGURE 1-18
Simple negative feedback.

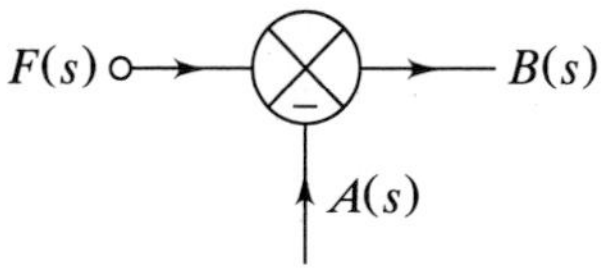

FIGURE 1-19
Summing point.

Solution. Again, we introduce symbols for the unknown outputs and solve the resultant set of simultaneous equations. Based on Fig. 1-19,

$$F(s) - A(s) - B(s) = 0$$

and

$$Y(s) = G_1(s)B(s)$$

$$A(s) = G_2(s)Y(s)$$

the result, in terms of the given system function, input, and output, is

$$F(s) = Y(s)\left(G_2(s) + \frac{1}{G_1(s)}\right)$$

or

$$G(s) = \frac{Y(s)}{F(s)} = \frac{G_1(s)}{1 + G_1(s)G_2(s)}$$

frequently occurring result of considerable importance.

This sketchy collection of basic system manipulations suffices for the treatment of a number of systems and system control topics.

1-5 CLOCKS

For ease in signal processing, a robot should run on a clock that is common to all of its signal components. The same clock that drives the stepper motor should drive the Charge Coupled Device (CCD) vision sensor; the same clock that samples the data should process them through the system. Clocks serve as impetus and conveyance for all digital signals. Clocks are as ubiquitous as time, and they are treated as a primitive concept, just as time is a primitive in physics; that is, a student is expected to have absorbed the notion as a part of his or her everyday experience. Just as other system components, clocks may simply be used without knowing how they function. This section is included to satisfy the curiosity of those who wish to know.

Running on a master clock also has its disadvantages, since this may require delays and queuing of events that happen faster than a clock cycle. What about such delays?

"Real time" appears to be another robotics primitive. It is often used and rarely defined. In essence, there are two concepts of real time—one in connection with the feedback of sensory information. Suppose a real event is being computer simulated. Then, if the real event occurs during a time Δt, the simulation may be said to be real time if the simulated event also has duration Δt. Otherwise, the simulation is "time scaled," analogous to the concept of time scaling in analog computation. In a feedback context, the concept deals with the robot's reaction to external stimuli. Real-time response of the robot then, for example, may be taken to mean its reaction to a visual input. If the robot continues its motion without interruption (i.e., as perceived by a human observer), then the numerical evaluation of the input is said to have been done in real time. Thus motion on a television is generally perceived to be smooth, although, in fact, the image is changed every 1/30th of a second. (Sixteen frames per second seem to suffice to make movies appear natural.) The fastest human reaction time to an external impulse lies between 10 and 20 ms and so on. Collectively, it is clear that an operation qualifies as real time if it is carried out in an amount of time less than some critical time. All of these considerations prompt the following formal definition.

Definition 1-6 Real time. Let t_1 be some critical human response time. Then any robot response to its surroundings, occurring in a time $t < t_1$, will be termed a real-time response, and the calculations required to produce this response will be termed real-time calculations.

I had a little trouble finding out about clocks, at least the kind that are of interest here. One logical place seemed to be a basic book in computer architecture, but there the discussion ranged from a single paragraph to "we assume we have a clock." It turns out that clocks are variously known as "timers," "multivibrators," "oscillators," "waveform generators," and a litany of other terms.

Basically, a clock is a signal generator producing a square wave signal, as shown in Fig. 1-20. Such a signal has a period T, in seconds, and a frequency

$$f = \frac{1}{T}$$

with units of cycles/second. It is usual to use 1 cycle/s = 1 Hz (hertz). Thus a

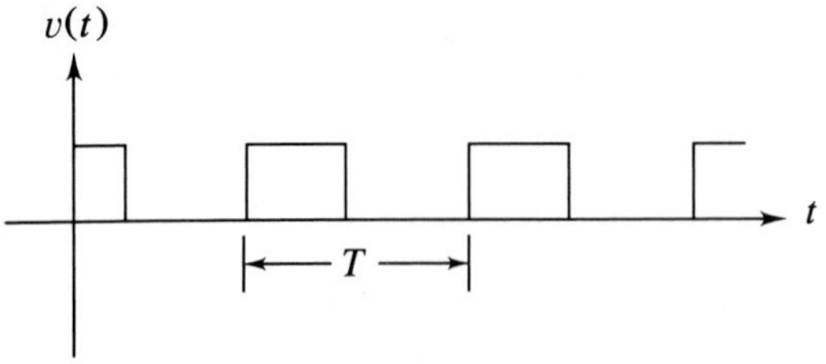

FIGURE 1-20
Basic clock signal.

computer operating at 20 MHz (megahertz) is based on a clock for which

$$f = 20 \times 10^6 \text{ Hz}$$

or $T = [20 \times 10^6]^{-1}$ s.

We now turn to some simple circuits that can serve as signal generators in this context. One point of interest is that in such circuits instability as well as positive feedback play a useful role—situations that the student is usually exhorted to avoid. In particular, they are told that it is generally desirable that the poles of the system function be in the left half of the complex plane. The first example deals with a situation where the poles (a conjugate pair for real systems) lie on the imaginary axis of the complex plane, constituting an unstable pole location.

Example 1-10 *The Wien bridge oscillator.* Its main use is as a generator of sinusoidal signals in the 0.001 Hz to 1 MHz frequency range. The corresponding circuit is shown in Fig. 1-21.

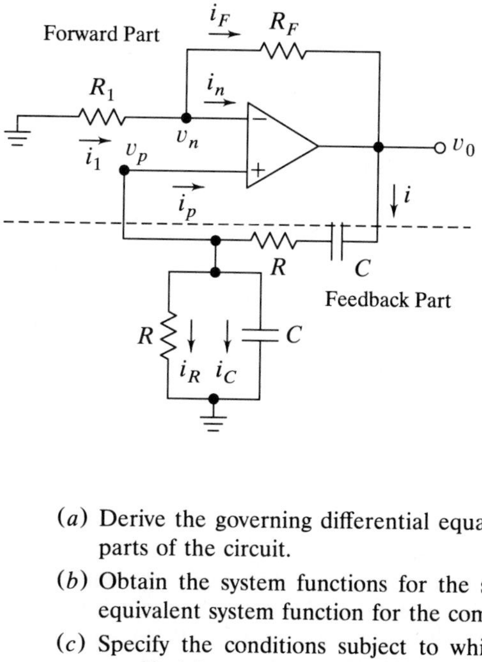

FIGURE 1-21
Wien bridge oscillator.

(a) Derive the governing differential equations for the forward and the feedback parts of the circuit.

(b) Obtain the system functions for the subsystems treated in part (a) and the equivalent system function for the combined system.

(c) Specify the conditions subject to which the output will be a sinusoid at a specified frequency and amplitude.

Solution

(a) At the summing junction of the op amp, we have

$$i_1 = i_n + i_F$$

or

$$-\frac{v_n}{R_1} = \frac{v_n - v_0}{R_F} + i_n$$

With the standard op amp operating assumptions $v_p - v_n \approx 0$, $i_n \approx 0$, and $i_p \approx 0$, this equation may also be written in terms of v_p as

$$-\frac{v_p}{R_1} = \frac{v_p - v_0}{R_F} \quad \Rightarrow \quad v_0 = \frac{R_1 + R_F}{R_1} v_p$$

For the feedback segment below the dashed line, we have the current equation

$$i = i_p + i_C + i_R = C\frac{dv_p}{dt} + \frac{v_p}{R} \qquad i_p \approx 0$$

and the voltage equation

$$v_0 = v_p + v_C + v_R = v_p + \frac{1}{C}\int i\,d\tau + iR$$

Differentiation of the voltage equation and substitution of the current equation yield

$$\frac{dv_0}{dt} = \frac{dv_p}{dt} + \frac{1}{C}i + R\frac{di}{dt}$$

$$= \frac{dv_p}{dt} + \frac{1}{C}\left[C\frac{dv_p}{dt} + \frac{v_p}{R}\right] + R\left[C\frac{d^2v_p}{dt^2} + \frac{1}{R}\frac{dv_p}{dt}\right]$$

(*b*) The system function for the forward subsystem is

$$G_1(s) = \frac{V_0(s)}{V_p(s)} = \frac{R_1 + R_F}{R_1}$$

For the feedback function, we first take the Laplace transform of the differential equation with all initial conditions equal to 0:

$$sV_0(s) = \left[3s + \frac{1}{CR} + RCs^2\right]V_p(s)$$

The system function with input $v_0(t)$ and output $v_p(t)$ then is

$$G_2(s) = \frac{V_p(s)}{V_0(s)} = \frac{RCs}{(RC)^2s^2 + 3RCs + 1}$$

To obtain the system function for the combined system, we consider the positive feedback loop (Fig. 1-22). The input $F(s)$ may be viewed as an artifice to start up the system; we eventually simply take it equal to 0. (In real systems, the ever-present internal noise provides the impetus.) The equivalent single

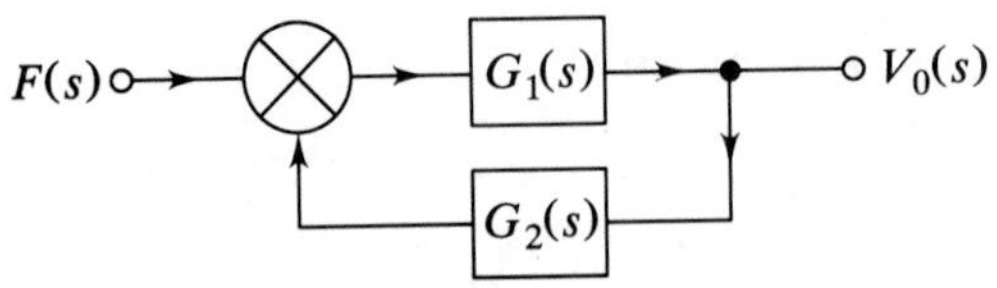

FIGURE 1-22
Positive feedback.

system function thus is

$$G(s) = \frac{G_1(s)}{1 - G_1(s)G_2(s)}$$

(*c*) The so-called Barkhausen criterion for sustained oscillation of this system at frequency ω_0 is

$$M(\omega_0) = |G_1(j\omega_0)G_2(j\omega_0)| = 1$$

$$\phi(\omega_0) = \operatorname{Arg} G_1(j\omega_0)G_2(j\omega_0) = 0$$

Exact fulfillment of the criterion assures that the system response will have the form $v_0(t) = A\sin(\omega_0 t + \theta)$, A and θ being a function of the initial conditions. (See also Problem 1-15.)

We now turn to one of the simplest circuits producing a square wave output, as used in clocks. Whereas the op amp was used in its stable configuration for the Wien bridge oscillator, it will now be used in its saturated mode.

Example 1-11 The free-running multivibrator as a square wave generator. In essence, the feedback arrangement here is such that the capacitor alternately charges and discharges, resulting in either a high or a low op amp saturation output. The circuit is shown in Fig. 1-23.

(*a*) Derive the governing equations for the circuit and discuss its input and output configurations.

(*b*) Sketch $v_n(t)$ and $v_0(t)$ versus time.

(*c*) Determine the period and the frequency of the resultant square wave.

Solution

(*a*) Due to the capacitance and the positive feedback, the op amp output will always be at the saturation levels

$$v_0 = \begin{cases} v_H & v_p > v_n \\ v_L & v_p < v_n \end{cases}$$

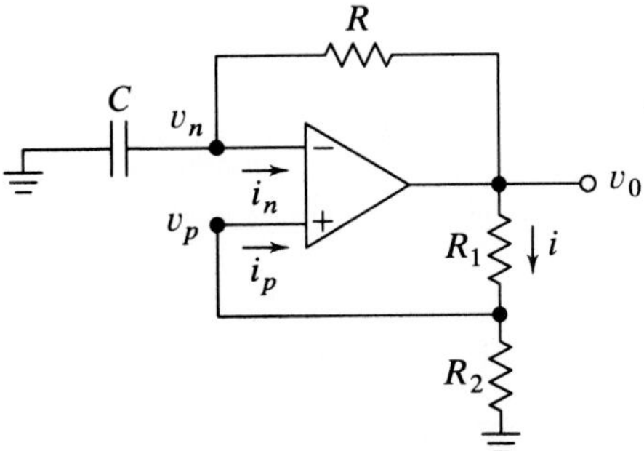

FIGURE 1-23
Free-running multivibrator.

The governing equation for the positive feedback branch (recall a voltage divider) is given by

$$v_0 = i(R_1 + R_2)$$

$$v_p = iR_2 \qquad i_p \approx 0$$

$$\Rightarrow \quad v_p = \frac{R_2}{R_1 + R_2} v_0 = kv_0 \qquad k = \frac{R_2}{R_1 + R_2}$$

The differential equation governing the negative feedback branch is

$$-C\frac{dv_n}{dt} = \frac{v_n - v_0}{R} \quad \Rightarrow \quad RC\frac{dv_n}{dt} + v_n = v_0$$

Strictly speaking, v_0 could now be 0, v_H, or v_L. Since 0 is unstable, the input into the last equation will always be v_H or v_L.

(*b*) Since the response $v_n(t)$ will be periodic, it is somewhat irrelevant what we take to be our initial conditions. Suppose we begin with

$$v_p > v_n \quad \Rightarrow \quad v_0 = v_H \qquad \text{and with} \quad v_n(0) = 0$$

the latter indicating a capacitor with zero charge. (Note that the initial charge on the capacitor, together with whether v_0 is high or low initially, determines the phase shift of the square wave.) No matter which constant value v_0 assumes, the general integral for $v_n(t)$ will always be

$$v_n(t) = v_0 + Ae^{-t/RC}$$

This equation is the central equation which now is evaluated for $v_0 = v_L$ or v_H and for the relevant initial and continuity conditions. We shall carry out the process for three consecutive time segments, enough to establish the procedure.

$\mathbf{0 \le t \le t_1}$. $v_p > v_n$, $v_0 = v_H$, and $v_n(0) = 0$. The result of the application of these conditions is

$$A = -v_H \quad \Rightarrow \quad v_n(t) = v_H(1 - e^{-t/RC})$$

This response will continue until a time t_1 for which v_p becomes equal to v_n, to be followed by $v_p < v_n$, resulting in a switch from v_H to v_L. This switching time t_1 is given by

$$v_n(t_1) = v_p = kv_0 = kv_H = v_H(1 - e^{-t_1/RC})$$

$$\Rightarrow \quad t_1 = RC \ln \frac{1}{1 - k}$$

$\mathbf{t_1 \le t \le t_2}$. $v_p < v_n$ and $v_0 = v_L$. Instead of an initial condition, we now have the continuity condition $v_n(t) = kv_H$, at $t = t_1$. The response $v_n(t)$ on this interval is

$$A = \frac{kv_H - v_L}{1 - k} \quad \Rightarrow \quad v_n(t) = v_L + \frac{kv_H - v_L}{1 - k} e^{-t/RC}$$

This response will continue until a time t_2 for which v_p again becomes greater than v_n and for which v_0 will again switch to v_L. This time is given by

$$v_n(t_2) = kv_L = v_L + \frac{kv_H - v_L}{1-k} e^{-t_2/RC}$$

$$\Rightarrow \quad t_2 = RC \ln \frac{v_L - kv_H}{v_L(1-k)^2}$$

Note that, to assure the existence of such a t_2 at this point, there are some magnitude requirements imposed on v_L, k, and v_H.

$t_2 \le t \le t_3$. $v_p > v_n$, $v_0 = v_H$, and the continuity condition $v_n(t_2) = kv_L$. The response on this interval is

$$A = \frac{(kv_L - v_H)(v_L - kv_H)}{v_L(1-k)^2}$$

$$\Rightarrow \quad v_n(t) = v_H + \frac{(kv_L - v_H)(v_L - kv_H)}{v_L(1-k)^2} e^{-t/RC}$$

Based on the previous reasoning, the time t_3 is obtained as

$$v(t_3) = kv_H$$

$$\Rightarrow \quad t_3 = RC \ln \frac{(v_H - kv_L)(v_L - kv_H)}{v_H v_L (1-k)^3}$$

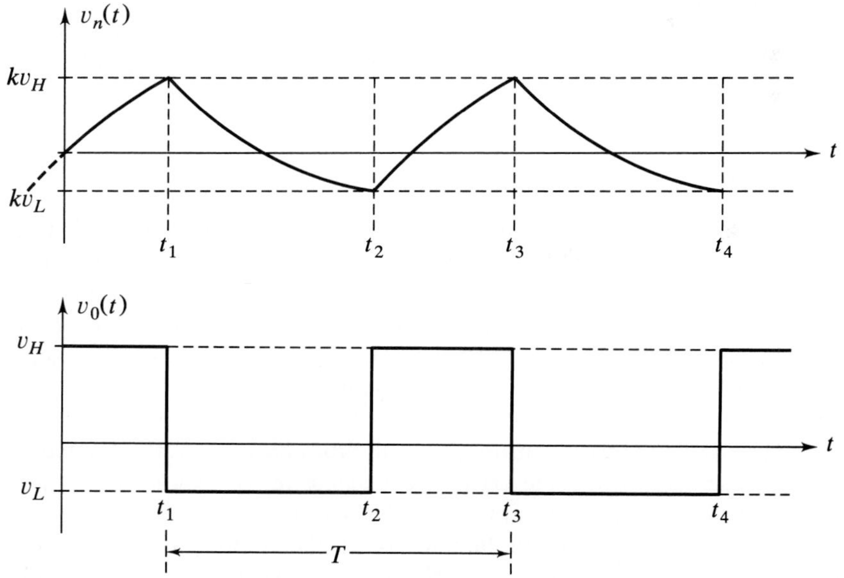

FIGURE 1-24
Square wave with $|v_L| < |v_H|$, $v_L < 0$.

A graph of v_n and v_0 versus t over several periods of the motion is shown in Fig. 1-24.

(*c*) From the sketch of the response, it is clear that the period of the square wave is given by

$$T = t_3 - t_1$$

$$= RC \ln \frac{(v_H - kv_L)(v_L - kv_H)}{v_H v_L (1-k)^2}$$

with corresponding frequency $f = 1/T$.

As pointed out in Franco,[2] the maximum operating frequency of the oscillator is limited by the response speed (slew rate) of the comparator. For example, if a 301 comparator is used, the circuit is adequate up to the 10-kHz range; the use of a 311 comparator extends the range to several hundred kilohertz.

The previous oscillator is sensitive to temperature changes, and the precision of the shape of the square wave decreases at the higher frequencies. The wave form may be improved by clamping v_0. Complementary metal oxide silicon (CMOS) quartz crystal oscillators, whose equivalent circuit characteristics are also less sensitive to temperature changes, are used for the higher megahertz frequency ranges.

Such square wave generators or timers may be used with additional circuitry to generate derived signals having a multiple of the original period or a phase shifted with respect to the original one. Such integrated circuit timing devices became popular with the introduction of the 555 timer, the granddaddy of such devices.

1-6 SENSORS

All control hinges on being able to measure the quantity we wish to control. Quite generally, this measurement consists of the construction of a sensor, a device that is in some manner affected by the quantity we wish to measure and hence displaying and interpreting this reaction. In robotics, there are two main classes of sensors: those that allow the robot to interact with its surroundings, and those that let the robot know its own present state.

Within the former category, force sensors and tactile sensors seem to arouse the greatest interest. Transducers of all types have been constructed to accomplish these tasks with some extremely imaginative contributions.

Here we shall give an example of a classical approach to force sensing without any great regard to the limitations of the approach or its actual implementation. We shall make use of changes in capacitance because of the variety of its uses in measurement and sensing and because of the student's relative familiarity with the concept.

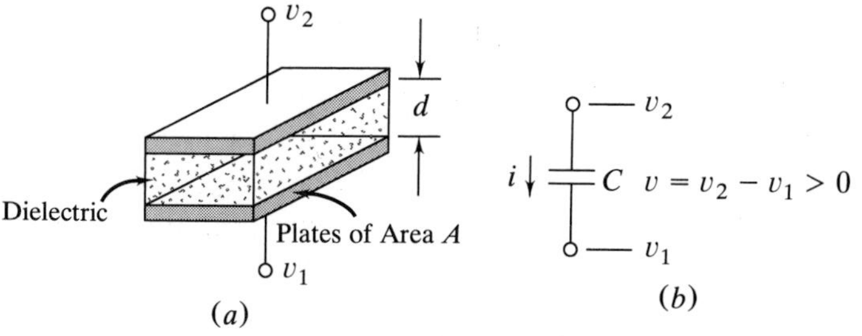

FIGURE 1-25
The capacitor: (*a*) physical aspects; (*b*) circuit symbol.

Recall that an ideal capacitor consists of two conducting plates, say of area A, separated by a dielectric insulator. Within the present context, we assume that these plates are essentially rigid (see Fig. 1-25). Energy may be stored in the electric field between the plates. When the applied voltage is constant, no current flows through the device. When the voltage is time varying, current flows through the device in accordance with the linear relationship

$$i(t) = C\frac{dv}{dt}(t)$$

with capacitance C is given by

$$C = \frac{\beta A}{d}$$

where β is the permittivity of the dielectric, A is the plate area, and d is the distance between the plates. Clearly, then, varying either the distance or the plate area changes the capacitance. A great variety of sensors is based on changes in these two variables.

Using capacitance as a measure is useless in itself, unless we are able to measure capacitance quickly and efficiently. Traditionally, this has been accomplished by a variety of bridge circuits. More recent and dynamic approaches make use of oscillators, such as the 555 timer.[3] Here the variation of capacitance with distance is of interest, and it will be assumed that the circuitry ultimately has been devised so as to produce a linear relationship between displacement and output voltage (Fig. 1-26)

$$v_s = K_s d$$

As the basic vehicle for our force measurement, consider a loaded, linearly elastic bar with cross-sectional area A and unstressed length L. Let $u(x)$ denote the displacement of a cross section a distance x from the left end

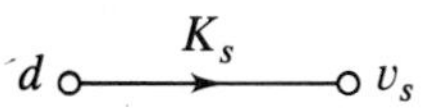

FIGURE 1-26
Linear voltage-displacement relation.

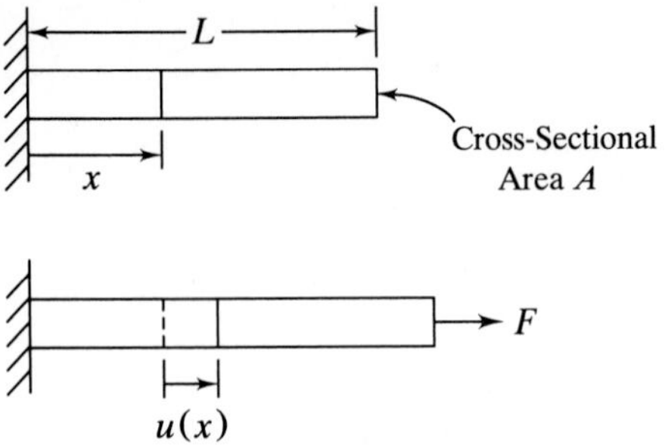

FIGURE 1-27
Stretching of an elastic bar.

(Fig. 1-27), and let E be the elastic modulus of the bar. We have the kinematic relationship

$$\epsilon(x) = \frac{du}{dx}(x)$$

relating the strain at x to the rate of change of the displacement. The constant stress in the bar is given by

$$\sigma(x) = \frac{F}{A}$$

and we ultimately relate force and displacement with the constitutive expression

$$\epsilon(x) = \frac{1}{E}\sigma(x)$$

Collectively,

$$\frac{du}{dx}(x) = \frac{F}{EA}$$

which may be integrated to yield

$$u_L = u(L) = \frac{FL}{EA}$$

for the total change in length of the bar. In this context, tension has been taken as positive.

Example 1-12 A force sensor. Consider the gripper schematic in Fig. 1-28. The gripper is to be equipped with force sensors at its tips, as shown. Assume that as the gripper closes on an object, rigid or elastic, the dielectric between the end plates of the capacitors compresses and the relative displacement of the end plates is Δ; the elastic modulus of the dielectric again is E. In the zero-force reading, the capacitor plates are separated by a distance d. Determine the bound on the output voltage v_s of the sensor if the allowable compressive force is F_0. Take compression as producing a positive voltage.

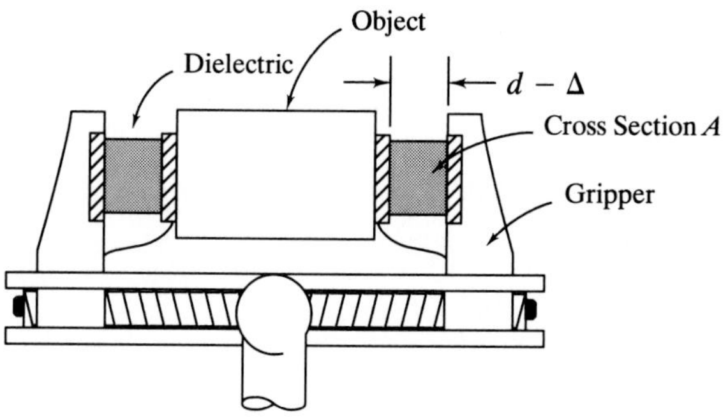

FIGURE 1-28
Gripper with force sensor.

Solution. Let Δ be the amount of compression. Then the new gap width is $d - \Delta$, resulting in the output voltage

$$v_s = K_s(d - \Delta) = K_s\left(d - \frac{FL}{EA}\right)$$

$$\Rightarrow F = \frac{EA}{L}\left(d - \frac{v_s}{K_s}\right) \le F_0$$

$$\Rightarrow v_s \ge K_s\left(d - \frac{F_0 L}{EA}\right)$$

There are some caveats in the actual implementation of such a sensor. If the capacitor plates are small, then the alignment of the top and bottom plates must be maintained during compression to assure that changes in area do not affect the reading. Furthermore, the permittivity of the dielectric must not be a function of its stress state.

1-7 ACTUATORS AND CONTROL

The parts become the whole when we exercise control. All of the previous topics and more need to be combined in controlling the robot. What then is *control*?

The simplest viewpoint considers a system with input and output. Common educational lore takes the input as given, with the output to be calculated. In some ways, control is the inverse of this process—we have a pretty good idea of what we should like the output to be, and we need to choose the input that will provide us with the desired output.

Thus we may clearly determine a force that will move an object of mass m along a straight line (rectilinear motion) in such a way that $x(0) = 0$ and $x(t_1) = 1$. Then the motion $x(\cdot)$ from $x = 0$ to $x = 1$ in time $[0, t_1]$ is the output, and the force that produces it is the input. One such motion might be specified by

$$x(t) = \frac{1}{t_1^2}t^2$$

As a consequence of Newton's second law, the force that produces this motion is

$$f(t) = ma = m\frac{2}{t_1^2}$$

That is, the choice of an input (control)

$$f(t) = \frac{2m}{t_1^2}$$

into the system

$$\frac{d^2x}{dt^2} = \frac{1}{m}f(t)$$

upon integration will yield

$$x(t) = \frac{1}{t_1^2}t^2$$

a response with the desired properties (obviously, since we just fixed things to work out this way).

For the beginner who is used to integrating a given differential equation for a specified right-hand side, the crucial idea here is that *the right-hand side of the equation may*, in fact, *be used to obtain a desired response*. More often than not, there will be more than one function producing a specified response [e.g., a function $f(\cdot)$ such that $x(0) = 0$ and $x(t_1) = 1$]. Generally, the set of, say, continuous functions that work would be termed a set of *admissible* controls for the problem. The type of control that we have just discussed, one depending on t only, is called *open loop control*. In essence, we simply specify the function $f(\cdot)$ as we begin the process and stand by as it evolves the desired response.

Open loop control works fine as long as everything functions perfectly. There are no errors in the physical generation of $f(\cdot)$, nor are there any disturbances in the system; that is, $x(t)$ is the exact state at the instant t. If either of these is inaccurate, then we generally do not end up where and when we had expected we would. It then becomes advisable to check on the state $x(\cdot)$ during the process and, depending on whether we are where we should be or not, to make adjustments in the control. The control itself becomes a function of the state $x(t)$. Suppose, then, instead of simply $f(t)$, we now attempt to use a forcing function defined by

$$g(x(t)) = -kx(t)$$

a linear negative *feedback control* with adjustable constant k to achieve our results. With this feedback control, the state equation now has the form

$$m\frac{d^2x}{dt^2} = -kx$$

again, as obtained from an application of Newton's second law. The resultant state $x(\cdot)$ is given by

$$x(t) = A\sin(\omega t + \phi) \qquad \omega^2 = \frac{k}{m}$$

Note that a response

$$x(t) = \frac{\sin \omega t}{\sin \omega t_1}$$

again satisfies $x(0) = 0$ and $x(t_1) = 1$ for any k or t_1.

Remark 1-1. Note carefully that the system equation in the open loop case was

$$\frac{d^2x}{dt^2} = \frac{1}{m}f(t)$$

whereas for the closed loop case, we eventually had

$$\frac{d^2x}{dt^2} + \frac{k}{m}x = 0$$

The use of feedback *changes* the original system. This requires additional care. For example, the original system may have been stable; the system with feedback may turn out to be unstable.

As before, there usually is a whole set of admissible feedback controllers. With so many possible controls available, often an infinite number of possibilities, the question of which of them to actually use naturally arises. Ease of use, availability, technical feasibility—all might be considered in the selection process. A more formal analytical approach might be to select the control $f(\cdot)$ that minimizes the integral

$$J[f(\cdot)] = \int_0^{t_1} f^2(t)\,dt$$

The use of such a selection criterion also allows us to compare two different controls, since we may order the set of controls by requiring

$$f_1(t) \prec f_2(t) \qquad \text{iff} \qquad J[f_1(\cdot)] < J[f_2(\cdot)]$$

where the symbol $\prec$ is to be read as "is smaller than."

Example 1-13 Better control. Recall that

$$f_1(t) = \frac{2m}{t_1^2}$$

was a force (control) that provided for $x(0) = 0$ and $x(t_1) = 1$. Another control that moves the particle in the required manner is given by

$$f_2(t) = m\left(\frac{1}{t_1}\ln 2\right)^2 e^{(\ln 2)t/t_1}$$

Determine which of these is the better control in accordance with the criterion

$$J[f(\cdot)] = \int_0^{t_1} f^2(t)\,dt$$

That is, our ultimate aim is to select a control $f(\cdot)$ for which $J[f(\cdot)]$ is a minimum.

Solution. We need only evaluate the criterion for $f_1(\cdot)$ and $f_2(\cdot)$. We have

$$J[f_1(\cdot)] = \int_0^{t_1}\left(\frac{2m}{t_1^2}\right)^2 dt = \frac{4m^2}{t_1^3}$$

and

$$J[f_2(\cdot)] = \int_0^{t_1} m^2\left(\frac{1}{t_1}\ln 2\right)^4 e^{2(\ln 2)t/t_1}\,dt$$

$$= \frac{3}{2}m^2\frac{1}{t_1^3}(\ln 2)^3$$

We now claim that $f_2(t) \prec f_1(t)$; that is, that $f_2(t)$ is the better open loop control. Clearly,

$$\frac{3}{2}(\ln 2)^3 < 4$$

$$\Rightarrow \quad \frac{3}{2}m^2\frac{1}{t_1^3}(\ln 2)^3 < 4\frac{m^2}{t_1^3}$$

Of course, the best control in this context would be one that minimizes the criterion $J[f(\cdot)]$. Such a control is also called an *optimal control.*

A common feedback approach in automatic control theory is one where the instantaneously measured state is fed back and compared to a desired state; the difference between the two of them is then used to guide further adjustments in the motion. When the difference is 0, that is, when the actual state is the same as the desired state, no further adjustments are made. As a particular example (preempting some of the material that follows later), we consider a velocity servo control problem.

Example 1-14 Design of a velocity control system. Suppose a DC servo motor is to rotate the simple robot arm shown in Fig. 1-29. It is required that the angular velocity of the arm as a function of time be maintained at $\omega_0(t)$. Use velocity feedback of the motor-load output angular velocity $\omega(t)$ and the velocity error

$$e(t) = \omega_0(t) - \omega(t)$$

to provide the needed corrections in maintaining the required angular velocity.

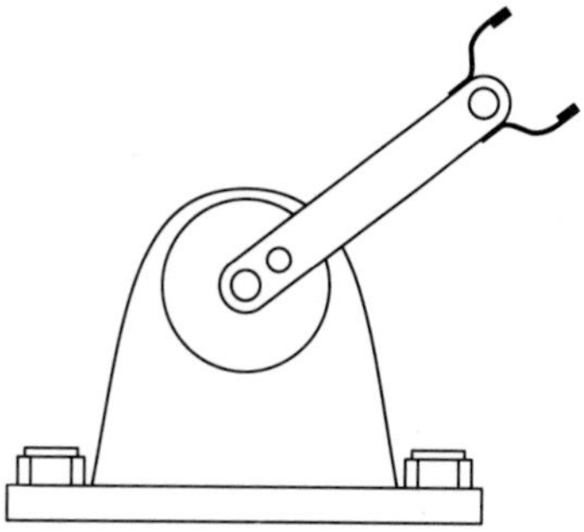

FIGURE 1-29
Servo-controlled simple robot arm.

Solution. In general terms, we shall use the overall control configuration shown in Fig. 1-30. The system components indicated are taken to have the following governing equations and corresponding system functions:

for motor and load

$$k_T i = J\frac{d\omega}{dt} + b\omega \qquad G_m(s) = \frac{\Omega(s)}{I(s)} = \frac{k_T}{Js + b}$$

for the current amplifier

$$Av = \tau\frac{di}{dt} + i \qquad G_a(s) = \frac{I(s)}{V(s)} = \frac{A}{\tau s + 1}$$

for the tachometer and input transducer

$$v = k\omega \qquad G_t(s) = \frac{V(s)}{\Omega(s)} = k$$

where k_T = torque constant for the motor
J = mass moment of inertia of tachometer load and armature
b = viscous damping coefficient
A = DC gain of the amplifier
τ = amplifier time constant
k = tachometer constant

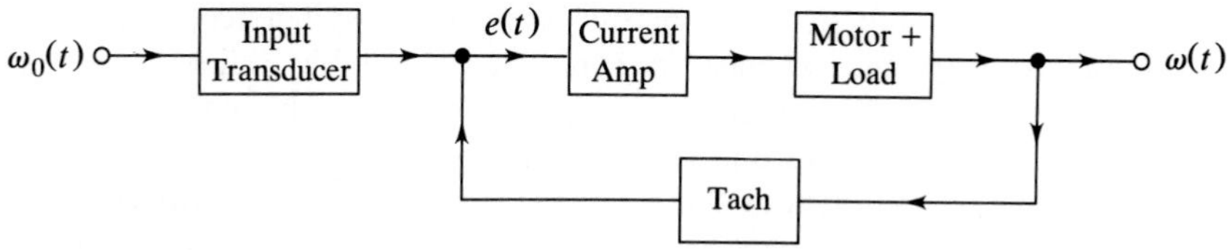

FIGURE 1-30
Component configuration.

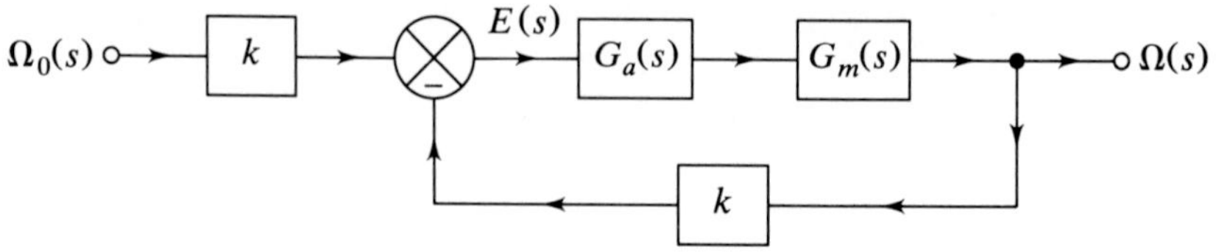

FIGURE 1-31
Block diagram for velocity feedback control system.

The input transducer here simply indicates some way in which the velocity signal is transformed to an appropriate voltage signal for comparison with the tachometer voltage.

The block diagram for the feedback control system, which follows from the preceding subsystem representations, is shown in Fig. 1-31. Note, particularly, that the output at the summing point is

$$E(s) = V_0(s) - V(s) = k(\Omega_0(s) - \Omega(s))$$

the difference between the desired value and the current value, essentially serving as the input signal to the motor-load combination.

1-8 SIGNAL PROCESSING

The ingredients and major problems in robotics have now been touched upon; we have a rough robot with an outline of what its behavior should be. Nothing yet has been said about the brains needed to run such an operation. We now discuss in a rudimentary form the manner in which a robot may take "intelligent" action.

Intelligence is defined, in part, as

> the ability to learn or understand from experience; ability to acquire and retain knowledge; the use of the faculty of reason in solving problems, directing conduct, etc.

"Reason" I take to be out of reach for robots. In essence, robots are intelligent to the extent one has managed to construct computer intelligence, since they may be made to respond, at least in concept, to suitably refined sensors, hardware, and software. The manner in which robots may be endowed with artificial intelligence is a separate area of investigation.

At this point, let us consider the relatively standard manner with which a sensor signal is processed in order to produce a corresponding response. A schematic of such a signal processing loop is shown in Fig. 1-32. We now discuss the signal as it proceeds around the loop in terms of its transition from one

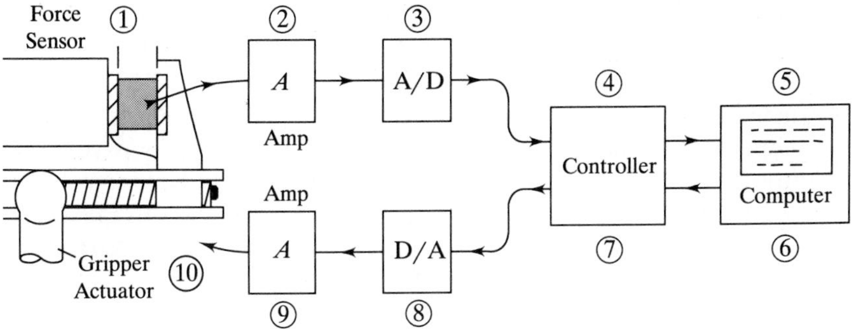

FIGURE 1-32
Sensor-to-actuator signal processing.

numbered station to the next:

1 → 2 We suppose that the force sensor has been calibrated so that a force F_0 corresponds to an output voltage v_0. Since this signal is generally rather weak, it needs to be amplified.

2 → 3 The amplified signal voltage is then fed into an analog-to-digital (A/D) converter, replacing the analog (continuous) signal with discrete signal levels. Generally, such analog-to-digital converters may include an encoder which assigns a binary code corresponding to each signal level.

3 → 4 This binary signal now continues to a controller, a piece of hardware that basically keeps track of where a signal comes from and where it is going. Here the controller will note that it received a signal of a certain level, say from force sensor 1 on the gripper.

4 → 5 The controller will then pass this binary signal to the computer, with an identifying code indicating that the signal comes from force sensor 1. The computer, in turn, through its software, may now display a statement of the form "force sensor 1 indicates a force F_0." That is, it recognizes where the signaled force level exists and displays this to an operator or operating program.

5 → 6 The computer now processes this information by comparing F_0 to some required force F_1, for example, with $F_0 < F_1$ implying an order to continue closing the gripper.

6 → 7 Hence the computer now sends a signal to the controller, indicating a certain coded binary voltage level for the gripper motor and an identifying code for the motor.

7 → 8 The controller again identifies where the signal is to go and sends out a binary signal to the motor. If the motor runs on an analog signal, then there is a decoder and a digital-to-analog (D/A) converter, which eventually provides the specified analog voltage level.

8 → 9 Since computer and controller voltages may run between 0 and 5 V, this may not be enough to drive the motor, so that amplification is again necessary.

9 → 10 The motor now turns the amount indicated by the voltage level. If it is a stepper motor, the signal voltage may simply be enough to have it step through a specified number of segments, or we might have some other device indicating the amount of rotation of the motor. Finally, of course, in the absence of these, the preceding cycle may be repeated as often as needed to reach the required force level $F_0 = F_1$, at which time the motor is provided with just enough voltage (torque) to maintain this level.

This type of cycle is repeated for every sensor that the robot has, all of the information being sent in time with the pulses of some universal clock. In each case, the incoming signal must be interpreted, a response prescribed, and a signal fed back, indicating that the desired response has been carried out. Computational power clearly is of the essence in this context, from microprocessor to mainframe. The level of artificial intelligence in connection with the resolution of the sensors determines the sophistication of the robotic response.

Not much more can be said at this point, since the student is expected to have little background in either computer architecture or in programming. Generally, the student has had no more than a single course in FORTRAN or some other computer language. We thus turn now to some closing remarks concerning the outline presented in this chapter.

1-9 GENERATIONS OF ROBOTS

Hopefully, the student now has some idea of what a robot is and of the more prevalent problems encountered in robotics. All of the topics will be discussed in more detail in later sections.

A robot can be made quite accurate, both in terms of being able to attain a given point in space and in being able to attain the same point repetitively. However, the sophistication of a robot depends on its sensory perception and the software that provides the interpretation and corresponding action. There is general agreement that any advanced robot requires real-time vision, which to date can be achieved in a limited fashion for binary vision, but causes considerable difficulties for gray level vision. Compared to human vision, gray level vision is extremely slow, the speed being determined by the image identification algorithm rather than the electronics of the image acquisition process. In the area of sensors and the corresponding interpretative software, the robot's artificial intelligence, there is still a long way to go until we obtain the anthropomorphic robot depicted in science fiction.

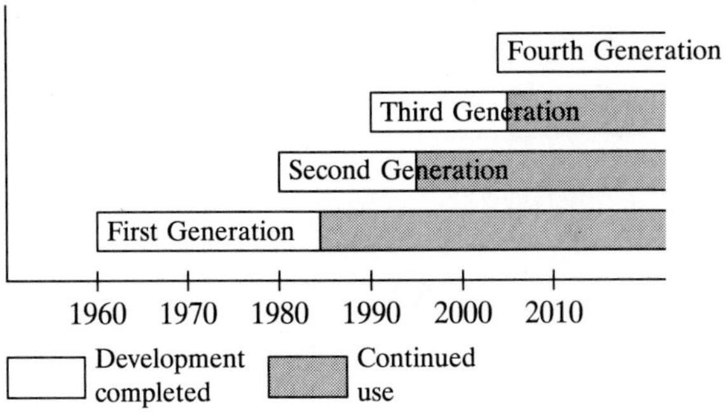

FIGURE 1-33
Generations of robots.

We close this chapter with a brief look at robot generations as projected by Dr. Eiji Nakano, head of the Planning Department of Japan's Mechanical Engineering Laboratory[4]:

First generation. Repeating robots. These are generally pneumatically powered pick-and-place robots or non-servo point-to-point robots. It is estimated that more than 90% of the robots in use belong to this category.

Second generation. These robots exhibit path control and they are equipped with sensing devices, enabling the robot to alter its movements in response to feedback from its surroundings. The United States is estimated to be leading in the development of this category.

Third generation. The central brain of this kind of robot would not be an ordinary computer, but one based on artificial intelligence. Such a learning capability would allow robots to draw conclusions from past experience and alter their operation correspondingly.

Fourth generation. This and further classifications are best given in retrospect. For example, the production of a true android—or an artificial biological robot—might provide the impetus for fifth- and higher-generation robots.

A visualization of these overlapping generations of robots is provided in Fig. 1-33.

EXERCISES

1-1. Determine the segment of the ray OA which can be traversed by the end effector E of the revolute manipulator in Fig. E1-1. Assume that θ, measured counterclockwise from OB to BE, is restricted to $10° \leq \theta \leq 170°$. State the Cartesian coordinates of the two points bounding the line segment on OA.

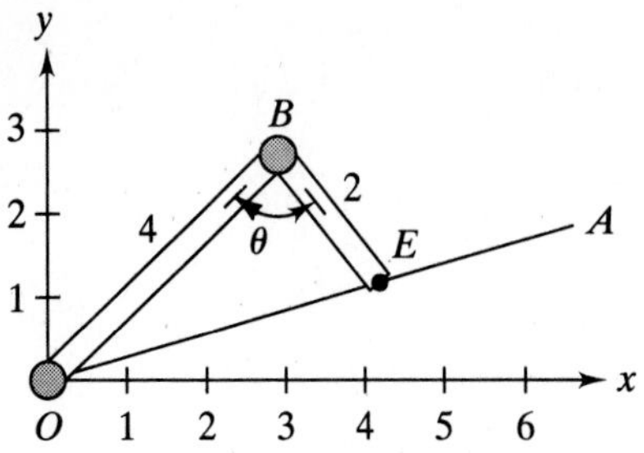

FIGURE E1-1

1-2. The simple robots in Fig. E1-2 have restrictions on the robot variables as indicated. In each case, determine the work space and the work envelope traced out by E. The point O is fixed throughout. All angles are positive in the counterclockwise direction.

(*a*)

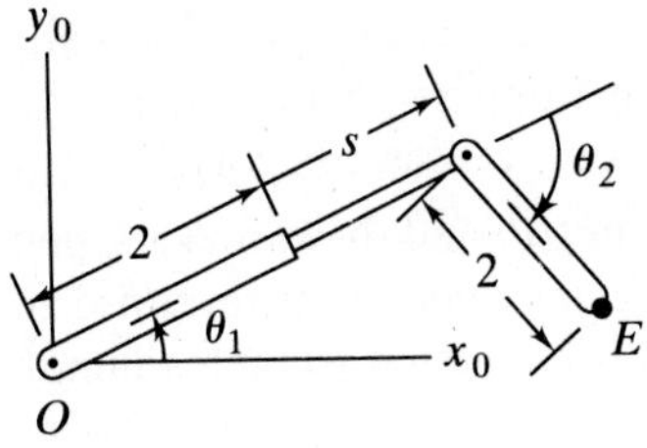

(*a*)

FIGURE E1-2*a*

$$0° \leq \theta_1 \leq 90° \qquad -30° \leq \theta_2 \leq 60° \qquad 0 \leq s \leq 2$$

(*b*)

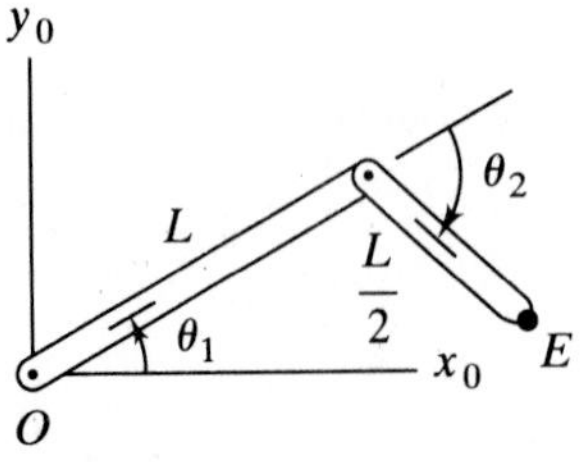

(*b*)

FIGURE E1-2*b*

$$-30° \leq \theta_1 \leq 60° \qquad -30° \leq \theta_2 \leq 60°$$

(c)

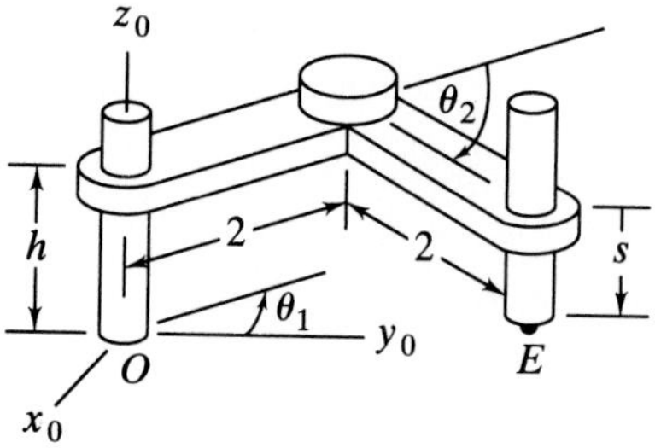

(c) FIGURE E1-2c

$$-50° \leq \theta_1 \leq 150° \qquad -90° \leq \theta_2 \leq 90°$$

$$1 \leq h \leq 2 \qquad 1 \leq s \leq 1.5$$

1-3. The anthropomorphic robot in the sketch (Fig. E1-3) is holding a book in its rigid gripper (no wrist action). The robot is free to rotate about the z_0-axis and about axes through its joints A and B. Determine the number of axes of the robot, the number of degrees of mobility, and the number of degrees of freedom. Explain your results in light of the fact that the book may be both displaced and rotated.

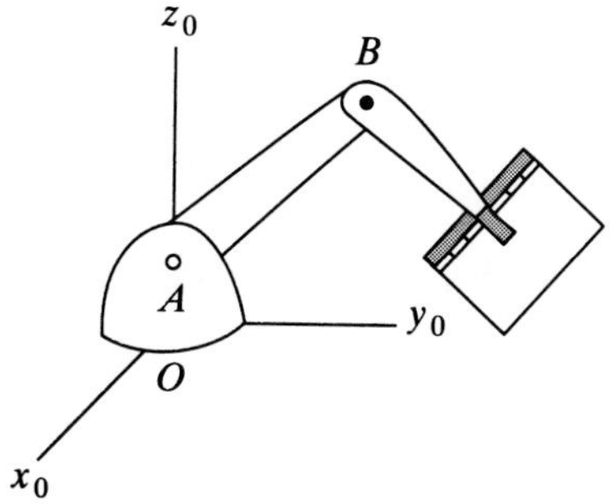

FIGURE E1-3

1-4. One of the aspects of the coordinate inversion problem concerns the maximum region on which a mapping relating two coordinate systems is one to one. That is, locating a point P uniquely in one coordinate system also locates it uniquely in terms of the other. Consider the coordinate systems illustrated in Figs. E1-4a and b.

(a) The standard mapping between cylindrical coordinates and Cartesian coordinates is defined by

$$x = x(r, \theta, h) = r \cos \theta$$

$$y = y(r, \theta, h) = r \sin \theta$$

$$z = z(r, \theta, h) = h$$

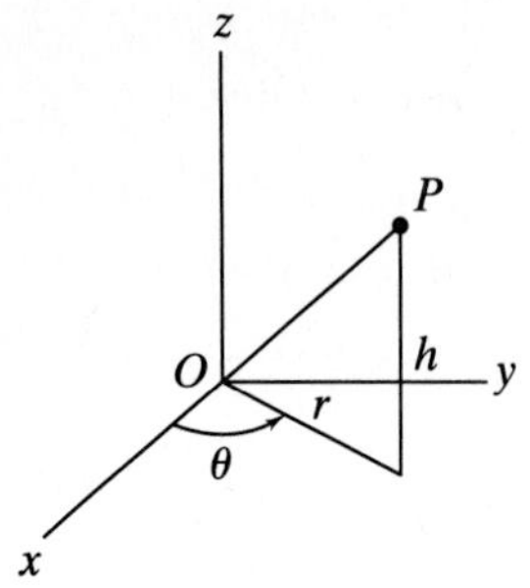

FIGURE E1-4*a*

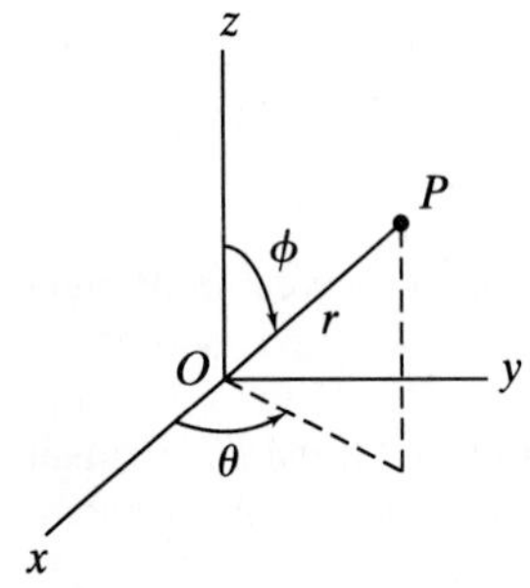

FIGURE E1-4*b*

Determine the inverse mapping $\theta(x, y, z)$, $r(x, y, z)$, and $h(x, y, z)$ and indicate a maximum subset of $\mathbb{R}^3$ on which the relationship between (x, y, z) and (r, θ, h) is one to one.

(*b*) The standard mapping between spherical coordinates and Cartesian coordinates is defined by

$$x = r \sin \phi \cos \theta = x(r, \theta, \phi)$$

$$y = r \sin \phi \sin \theta = y(r, \theta, \phi)$$

$$z = r \cos \phi = z(r, \theta, \phi)$$

Determine the inverse mapping $r(x, y, z)$, $\theta(x, y, z)$, and $\phi(x, y, z)$ and indicate a maximum subset of $\mathbb{R}^3$ on which the relationship between (x, y, z) and (r, θ, ϕ) is one to one.

1-5. Consider again the manipulator in Fig. 1-9*b*. Assume that O is a fixed point and B is a specified point which the end effector E is to occupy. Determine a constraint of the form $a \leq \omega \leq b$, where ω stands for either θ_1, θ_2, or s, which will yield only one possible configuration to reach this particular point. The interval $[a, b]$ must be nonzero.

1-6. Consider the rectilinear motion of a point P between points A and B, as shown in Fig. E1-6. The point is to move from A to B in time t_f in such a way that the following conditions are satisfied:

1. $x(0) = \dot{x}(0) = 0,\ x(t_f) = 10,\ \dot{x}(t_f) = 0.$
2. The acceleration of the point P is bounded by $|\ddot{x}(t)| \leq 10$.
3. The speed is to be $v(t) = 10$ ft/sec for as long as possible on $[0, t_f]$ and $|v(t)| \leq 10$ is always required.

(*a*) Parametrize the motion from A to B in at least two different ways and select the one that takes the lesser amount of total time for P to travel from A to B.
(*b*) Suppose that a further requirement is that the jerk be 0 at both ends of the motion; that is, $\dddot{x}(0) = \dddot{x}(t_f) = 0$. Provide a suitable parametrization for this case.

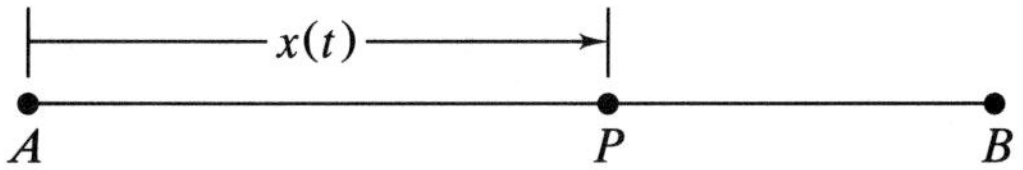

FIGURE E1-6

1-7. Consider again the rectilinear motion specified in Exercise 1-6 and assume the following conditions:

$$x(0) = 0 \qquad v(0) = 0 \qquad a(0) = 0 \qquad |v(t)| \leq 5$$

$$x(t_f) = 10 \text{ ft} \qquad v(t_f) = 0 \qquad a(t_f) = 0 \qquad |a(t)| \leq 10$$

Show that

$$v(t) = \begin{cases} 2.5(1 - \cos 4t) & 0 \leq t < \dfrac{\pi}{4} \\ 5 & \dfrac{\pi}{4} \leq t < t_1 \\ 2.5\left[1 - \cos 4\left(t - t_1 + \dfrac{\pi}{4}\right)\right] & t_1 < t \leq t_1 + \dfrac{\pi}{4} \end{cases}$$

is a motion that satisfies all of the requirements for an appropriate choice of t_1. Proceed as follows:

(*a*) Integrate $v(t)$ to determine t_1 and t_f with $x(t_f) = 10$ ft and $x(0) = 0$.
(*b*) Show that all of the boundary conditions and inequality constraints are satisfied.
(*c*) Sketch x, v, and a versus t.

1-8. In each of the linkages of Fig. E1-8, the two rods are connected by a slider block P. The indicated constant velocity v is the velocity of the slider P relative to the rod on which it slides. In each case, determine the angular velocities of the rods for the positions shown.

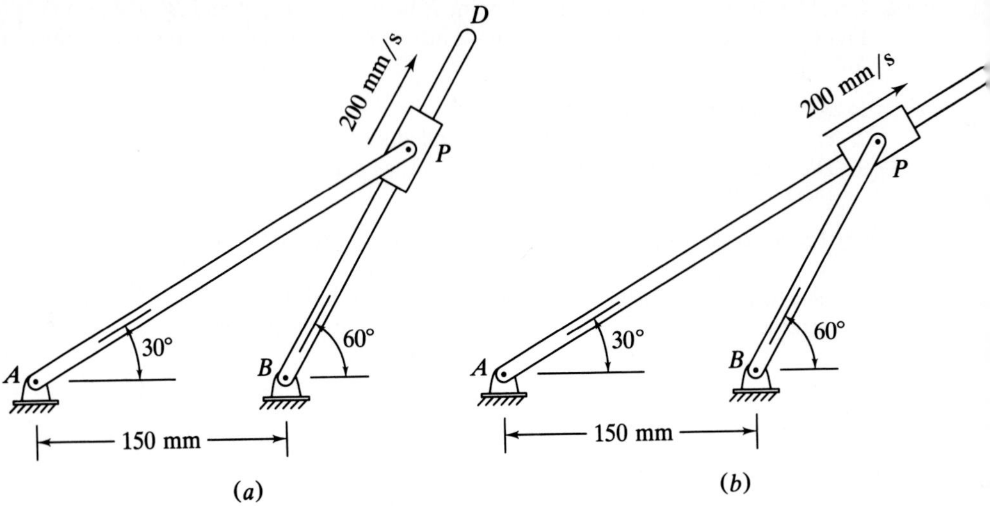

FIGURE E1-8

1-9. The rod BC in Fig. E1-9 is hinged to a slider which is free to move horizontally in the groove. The hydraulic actuator is fixed to the incline and its piston rod is hinged to the rod BC at A. The piston starts from rest at $\theta = 0°$ and it has an acceleration of 0.4 m/s^2 in the direction shown. Compute the initial angular acceleration of the rod BC.

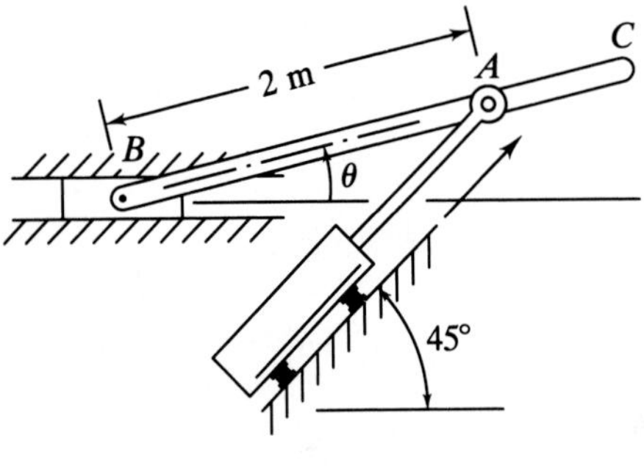

FIGURE E1-9

1-10. Consider again the linkage in Fig. E1-9. Assume that at the instant when $\theta = 0$, the velocity and acceleration of A are $v = 0.2$ m/s and $a = 0.3$ m/s^2 in the indicated direction, respectively. Determine the corresponding angular acceleration of the rod BC at this instant.

1-11. The piston rod of the hydraulic actuator is hinged to the linkage at B. At the instant shown in Fig. E1-11, the piston rod has a constant velocity of 0.2 m/s in the direction shown. Compute the acceleration of A for this instant and the angular velocities and accelerations of the rods.

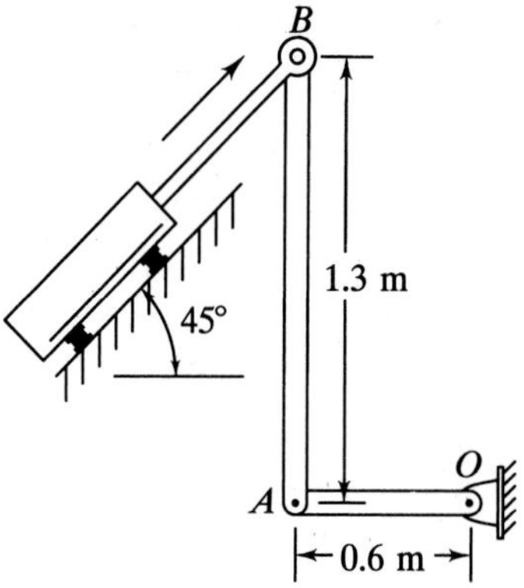

FIGURE E1-11

1-12. Deduce the system function for each of the following systems with $f(\cdot)$ considered as the input and $y(\cdot)$ as the output.

(*a*)

$$\frac{d^2y}{dt^2} + 3\frac{dy}{dt} + 2y = \frac{df}{dt} + 2f$$

(*b*) In the following system, deduce system functions for both $y(\cdot)$ and $z(\cdot)$ as outputs with input $f(\cdot)$:

$$\frac{d^2y}{dt^2} + 2\frac{dy}{dt} + z = f(t)$$

$$\frac{d^2z}{dt^2} + \frac{dy}{dt} + 2y = 3f(t)$$

(*c*)

$$\frac{d^2y}{dt^2} - 2a\frac{dy}{dt} + a^2y = f(t)$$

1-13. A system is represented by the block diagram in Fig. E1-13. Draw the corresponding signal flow graph and use Mason's rule to deduce a single equivalent system function for this system.

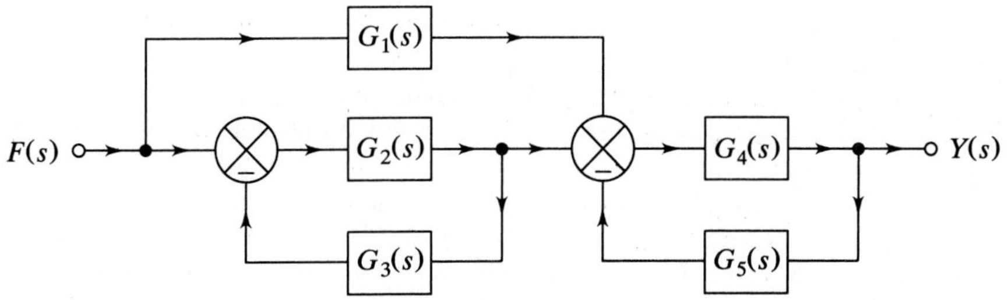

FIGURE E1-13

1-14. (*Sallen-Key filter*) Filters are an essential electronic design tool. The filter designed by R. P Sallen and E. L. Key in 1955 is a classical low-pass filter. Its standard circuit representation is shown in Fig. E1-14.

(*a*) Derive the system function for this filter with v_1 as input and v_0 as output. (*Hint:* Determine the system function for the boxed circuit, then sum currents at a and b.)

(*b*) The system function for a standard low-pass filter has the form

$$G_{\mathrm{LP}}(s) = \frac{K\omega_0^2}{s^2 + \left(\dfrac{\omega_0}{Q}\right)s + \omega_0^2}$$

Determine K, Q, and ω_0 for the Sallen-Key filter.

(*c*) Suppose we choose $R_A = R_B = R$ and set $\omega_0 = 1$ and $R_1 = C_1 = 1$. Sketch the circuit and indicate the appropriate parameter values for all circuit elements in terms of R and Q.

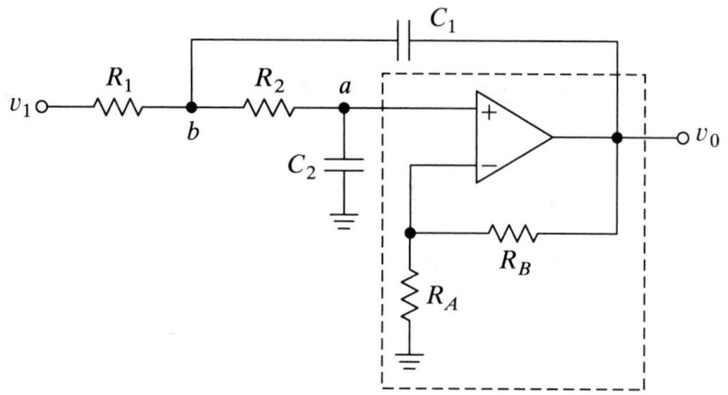

FIGURE E1-14

1-15. Complete the calculations implied by the Barkhausen criterion.

(*a*) Obtain the corresponding values of ω_0 and K in terms of R and C.

(*b*) Show that the Wien bridge oscillator does indeed have a sinusoidal response in the time domain.

(*c*) Note that the output of the oscillator in Fig. 1-21 is $v_0(t)$, a continuous sinusoidal signal, without an apparent voltage input. What supplies the power to this signal generator? Discuss the supply and any possible limitations on the signal being generated.

1-16. (*a*) Derive the expression for the period T of the free-running multivibrator of Example 1-11 with $v_H = v$, $v_L = -v$.

(*b*) Take $v = 5$ V, $R_2/R_1 = 0.86$ and determine R and C so as to obtain a 10-kHz clock. Draw reasonably accurate sketches of $v_n(t)$ and $v_0(t)$ versus t, indicating the amplitudes and zeros of $v_n(t)$.

1-17. Consider the astable multivibrator[5] shown in Fig. E1-17. In order to obtain more precise amplitude control, the output limiting Zener diodes are included in the basic circuit of Example 1-11. Take the combined voltage of the Zener diodes to be given by $V_Z = V_{D1} + V_{Z2}$ and $-V_Z = -V_{Z1} - V_{D2}$ and assume that all voltages remain within the operating limits of the op amp.

(*a*) Set up the governing equations for the circuit by summing currents at the op amp input nodes.

(*b*) Discuss the circuit behavior in broad terms with regard to v_1 across the capacitor, the output v_0 clamped at $\pm V_Z$, and the condition for the triggering of the op amp. Sketch your results to indicate the square wave output.

(*c*) Determine the period T of the oscillation.

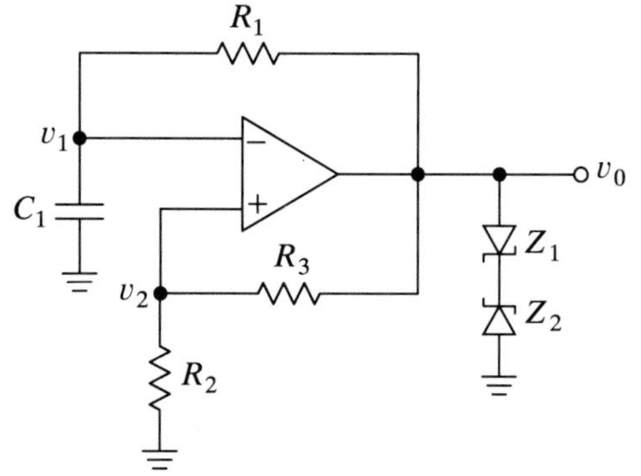

FIGURE E1-17

1-18. You are to use a capacitor as the basic transducer for the measurement of a number of physical quantities. In each case, you are given the basic configuration and you are to solve for the "measured" variable in terms of the total capacitance C and any remaining fixed dimensions or parameters. You may assume that the capacitance C can be measured in some fashion.

(*a*) *Angular displacement*. The capacitor has a movable plate, as shown in Fig. E1-18*a*. Solve for $\theta \geq 0$.

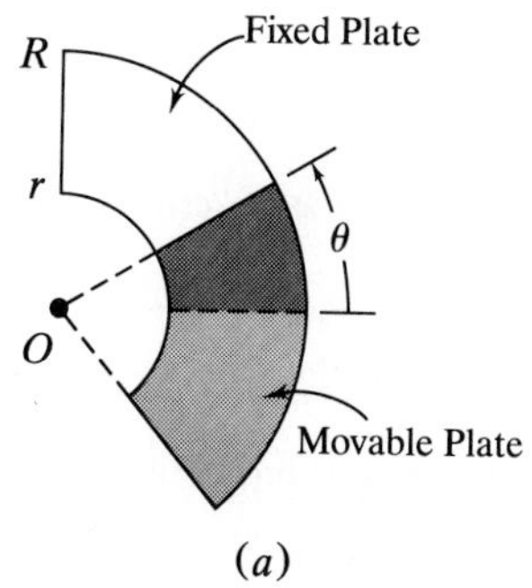

FIGURE E1-18*a*

(*b*) *Linear displacement*. The capacitor again has a movable plate, as shown in Fig. E1-18*b*. Solve for $x \geq 0$.

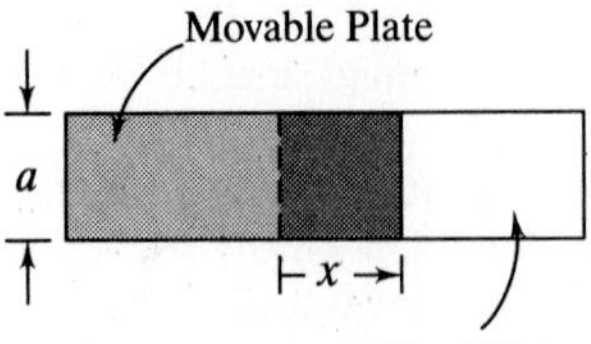

(*b*) **FIGURE E1-18*b***

(*c*) *Liquid level*. A cylindrical "capacitor" of radius r and total height L has permeable walls so that liquid may freely flow in and out. (See Fig. E1-18*c*.) There is air above the liquid. If the cylinder is all air, the total permittivity is β_1; if the cylinder is all liquid, it is β_2. Assume that permittivity is linearly distributed. Obtain an expression for the liquid level t.

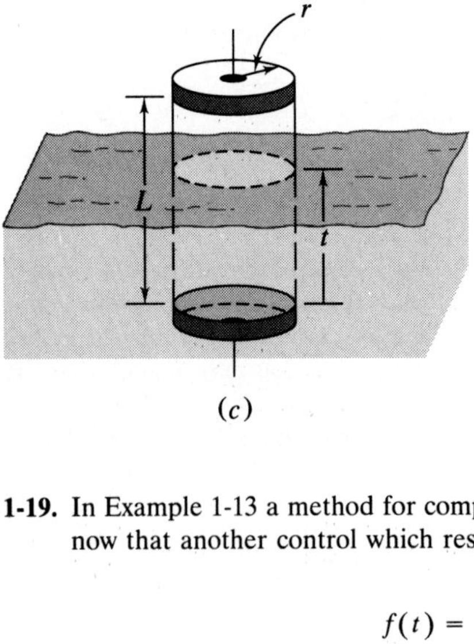

(*c*) **FIGURE E1-18*c***

1-19. In Example 1-13 a method for comparing different controls was introduced. Recall now that another control which resulted in $x(0) = 0$ and $x(t_1) = 1$ was given by

$$f(t) = -m\left(\frac{\pi}{2t_1}\right)^2 \sin\frac{\pi}{2t_1}t$$

How does this control compare to the other two controls if the same criterion is used for the comparison?

1-20. Consider the feedback system represented by the block diagram in Fig. E1-20.

(*a*) Determine the overall system function for this system and the corresponding governing equation.

(*b*) Assume $\zeta < 1$ and determine the homogeneous system response subject to $x(0) = 0$ and $x(t_1) = 1$.

(*c*) Note that both the system velocity and the position have been fed back. Determine the system feedback function $g(x, \dot{x})$.

(*d*) Assume $\zeta < 1$. Determine the poles for this feedback system and compare them to those when only position feedback was used. Sketch the location of the poles in the complex plane with $s = \alpha + j\beta$ and discuss the stability implications.

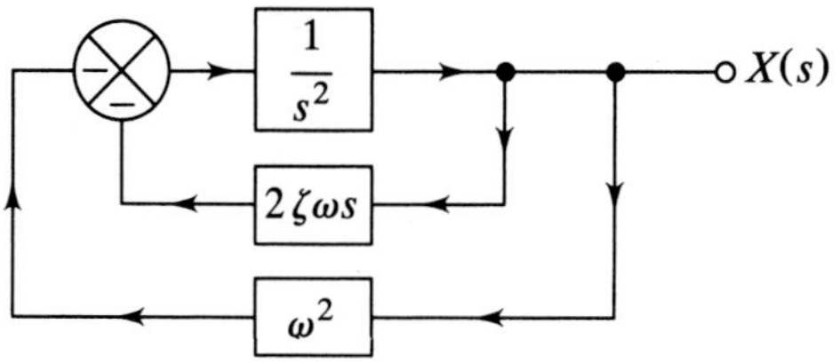

FIGURE E1-20

REFERENCES

1. Fleming, W. H.: *Functions of Several Variables*, Addison-Wesley, Reading, Mass., 1965.
2. Franco, S.: *Design with Operational Amplifiers and Analog Integrated Circuits*, McGraw-Hill, New York, 1988.
3. Horton, R.: "555 Timer Makes Simple Capacitance Meter," *EDN Magazine*, p. 81, November 5, 1973.
4. Nakano, E.: *An Introduction to Robot Engineering* (in Japanese), Omusha, Tokyo, 1983.
5. Kennedy, E. J.: *Operational Amplifier Circuits (Theory and Applications)*, Holt, Rinehart and Winston, New York, 1988.

CHAPTER

TWO

BASIC KINEMATICS

2-1 INTRODUCTION

As mentioned earlier, it is assumed that the student has had no more than a first course in dynamics, meaning that he or she has some idea of particle dynamics and some notion of energy methods, and that he or she moves, if somewhat precariously, in two dimensions. Rarely does such a course include three-dimensional rigid body-dynamics—concepts essential to the treatment of the dynamics of robots.

Dynamics, as a subject, may be separated into three distinct areas of endeavor: kinematics, kinetics, and constitutive relations or laws. The first deals exclusively with the descriptive geometry of the motion of points, without regard to how the motion may have come about. Thus one talks about points in space and the manner in which they may be located, about collections of points (curves), and about the motion of points along such mathematically smooth curves, introducing concepts such as position, velocity, and acceleration. The primitives are length and time, used in the presentation of units such as meters per second or meters per second squared. Kinetics deals with the discussion of forces, which need not involve a corresponding discussion of motion (e.g., the concept of force as used in statics). Indeed, there were those who did not wish to go beyond this static concept of force, who felt that force, now used in a dynamic context as equivalent to mass times acceleration, was a vague and misleading concept. Finally, there are the constitutive relations which provide the connection between forces and motion. Some relations are provided as general laws, such as Newton's laws, and other relations provide a quantitative description of internal forces, such as gravitation. It is common to give a unified treatment of kinetics and constitutive relations and to present only the geometric aspects as a separate topic. This has been done here.

We begin with a discussion of kinematics as it pertains to robotics. Although such a discussion is sometimes given in the context of kinematic chains and multibody systems, most practical robots may be treated as sequences of moving reference frames. This approach provides an easy extension of the discussion of moving reference frames found in textbooks on fundamental dynamics. Additional kinematic concepts are presented in later sections dealing with trajectory planning and control.

To provide the connection with the student's presumed background, the chapter begins with a discussion of two-dimensional translation and rotation. From these, it evolves to the central topics in the description of motion, the rotation matrix, the concept of angular velocity, and eventually, the compact description of rigid body motion, including the framework of homogeneous coordinates. The chapter closes with a section of kinematic examples relevant to robotics.

2-2 REFERENCE FRAMES

Clearly, a moving rigid body may be identified with a moving reference frame by embedding the reference within the body. We shall have need of a number of such embedded reference frames, and we shall thus denote a particular frame by $(0xyz)_i$, $i = 0, 1, \ldots, n$; $i = 0$ will always be used to denote a fixed reference frame (sometimes termed the *base reference frame*). Generally, $\boldsymbol{r}_0$ will denote the position vector of the point P with respect to the origin O_0 of the fixed reference, that is, the absolute position of P, and $\boldsymbol{r}_i$ will denote the position vector of P with respect to an origin O_i which may be moving or nonmoving.

We shall use a right-handed orthogonal unit basis $(\hat{\boldsymbol{\imath}}\hat{\boldsymbol{\jmath}}\hat{\boldsymbol{k}})_i$ in the directions (x_i, y_i, z_i), respectively, corresponding to a reference frame $(0xyz)_i$ (see Fig. 2-1).

We shall also develop vector and matrix representations side by side. Note that vectors are entities that are independent of the choice of basis; matrices are

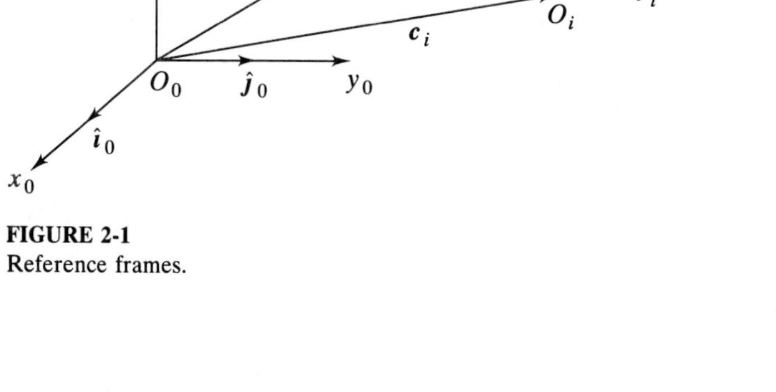

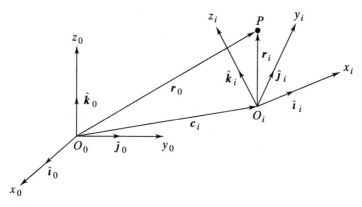

FIGURE 2-1
Reference frames.

not. Here matrices will always be written with respect to the basis of the corresponding reference frame. That is, we write

$$\boldsymbol{r}_i = x_i\hat{\boldsymbol{\imath}}_i + y_i\hat{\boldsymbol{\jmath}}_i + z_i\hat{\boldsymbol{k}}_i \qquad \text{and} \qquad \mathbf{r}_i = \begin{pmatrix} x_i \\ y_i \\ z_i \end{pmatrix} = (x_i y_i z_i)^{\mathrm{T}}$$

where T denotes the transpose, to denote the vector and matrix representation with respect to a particular basis, respectively. Whenever possible, lowercase letters will be used to denote vectors and column or row matrices, and uppercase letters to denote rectangular or square matrices. Throughout, we shall also maintain the distinction by using one font for vectors and another for matrices. Thus $\boldsymbol{r}_i$ will be used to denote the position vector, and $\mathbf{r}_i$ the corresponding column matrix; similarly, $\mathbf{A}$ denotes an $m \times n$ matrix, for example.

The development of the dynamics will be based on the assumption that the student's first course in dynamics included a rudimentary study of plane rigid body motion, with some mention of three-dimensional dynamics.

2-3 TRANSLATION

In describing the motion of a given point P in a rigid body $\mathscr{B}$, there are two aspects that need to be considered: the motion itself and the coordinate system within which to express the motion. This leads to the introduction of two types of transformations: point transformation and coordinate transformation. The former generally deals with the change of position of a point P, described with respect to the same coordinate system; the latter, with the same point described with respect to two different coordinate systems. As we shall see, these two types of transformations are closely related. We shall treat translation in some detail, since it will form the model for the treatment of rotation.

THE COORDINATE TRANSFORMATION. As indicated, we here view the position of a given point P from two different reference frames. Generally, the aim is to express the coordinates of the reference frame $(0xyz)_1$ in terms of those of the fixed frame $(0xyz)_0$ (see Fig. 2-2).

The position vectors are related by

$$\boldsymbol{r}_1 = \boldsymbol{r}_0 - \boldsymbol{c}_1 \tag{2-1}$$

In this form, the expression is still independent of any choice of coordinates. We now write each vector with respect to its corresponding basis. Since $\boldsymbol{r}_0$ and $\boldsymbol{c}_1$

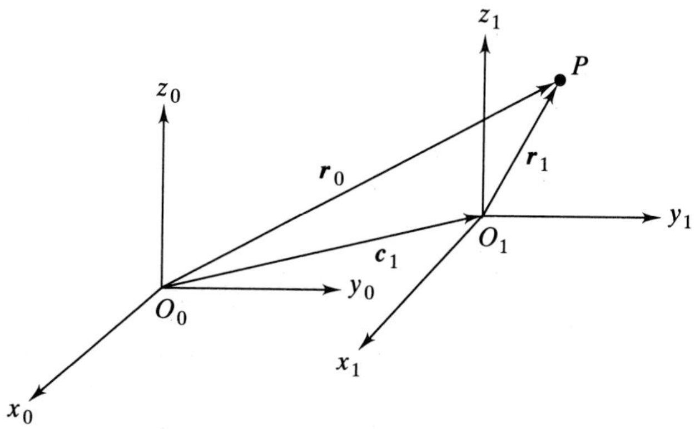

FIGURE 2-2
Translation-coordinate transformation.

are position vectors in $(0xyz)_0$ we use $(\hat{\imath}\hat{\jmath}\hat{k})_0$, and for r_1 we use $(\hat{\imath}\hat{\jmath}\hat{k})_1$ to obtain

$$x_1\hat{\imath}_1 + y_1\hat{\jmath}_1 + z_1\hat{k}_1 = x_0\hat{\imath}_0 + y_0\hat{\jmath}_0 + z_0\hat{k}_0 - \left(a_1\hat{\imath}_0 + b_1\hat{\jmath}_0 + c_1\hat{k}_0\right) \tag{2-2}$$

Recall that the aim is to express (x_1, y_1, z_1) in terms of the coordinates of $(0xyz)_0$. In order to be able to compare the components on both sides of the vector equation (the coordinates of P as determined by the choice of basis), both sides need to be expressed in terms of the same basis; that is, we need the relationship between the basis vectors. For reference frames that are *translated* with respect to each other, this relationship is given by

$$\hat{\imath}_1 = \hat{\imath}_0 \qquad \hat{\jmath}_1 = \hat{\jmath}_0 \qquad \hat{k}_1 = \hat{k}_0$$

With this in mind, we obtain the equations

$$\begin{aligned} x_1 &= x_0 - a_1 \\ y_1 &= y_0 - b_1 \\ z_1 &= z_0 - c_1 \end{aligned} \quad \Rightarrow \quad \begin{pmatrix} x_1 \\ y_1 \\ z_1 \end{pmatrix} = \begin{pmatrix} x_0 \\ y_0 \\ z_0 \end{pmatrix} - \begin{pmatrix} a_1 \\ b_1 \\ c_1 \end{pmatrix} \tag{2-3}$$

defining the relationship between the coordinates (x_1, y_1, z_1) and (x_0, y_0, z_0). In accordance with our previously introduced conventions, this may be written in matrix form as

$$\mathbf{r}_1 = \mathbf{r}_0 - \mathbf{c}_1 \tag{2-4}$$

In order to gain some understanding concerning the potential time dependence of these coordinates, consider the following possibility. Take $(0xyz)_0$ as the fixed frame and let the $(0xyz)_1$ frame be moving (translating). Then, if P is taken to be a fixed point within the $(0xyz)_0$ frame, we have

$$\begin{pmatrix} x_1(t) \\ y_1(t) \\ z_1(t) \end{pmatrix} = \begin{pmatrix} x_0 \\ y_0 \\ z_0 \end{pmatrix} - \begin{pmatrix} a_1(t) \\ b_1(t) \\ c_1(t) \end{pmatrix}$$

$$\mathbf{r}_1(t) = \mathbf{r}_0 - \mathbf{c}_1(t)$$

as the time-dependent relationship between the coordinates. Differentiation yields

$$\begin{pmatrix} \dot{x}_1(t) \\ \dot{y}_1(t) \\ \dot{z}_1(t) \end{pmatrix} = -\begin{pmatrix} \dot{a}_1(t) \\ \dot{b}_1(t) \\ \dot{c}_1(t) \end{pmatrix}$$

or

$$\mathbf{v}_1(t) = \dot{\mathbf{r}}_1(t) = -\dot{\mathbf{c}}_1(t)$$

and the velocity $\mathbf{v}_1(t)$ is that of the point P as seen by an observer moving with the translating reference frame.

THE POINT TRANSFORMATION. Recall that we now consider the translation of a point P from a position P' to a position P described with respect to a single fixed reference frame $(0xyz)_0$. Suppose we denote the position P' with respect to O_0 by $\boldsymbol{r}_1$. That is, we briefly abandon the previously introduced notation (see Fig. 2-3). Then these position vectors are related by

$$\boldsymbol{r}_1 = \boldsymbol{r}_0 - \boldsymbol{c}_1$$

Since all of these are now expressed within the same basis vectors, we immediately have

$$\begin{pmatrix} x_1 \\ y_1 \\ z_1 \end{pmatrix} = \begin{pmatrix} x_0 \\ y_0 \\ z_0 \end{pmatrix} - \begin{pmatrix} a_1 \\ b_1 \\ c_1 \end{pmatrix}$$

$$\mathbf{r}_1 = \mathbf{r}_0 - \mathbf{c}_1$$

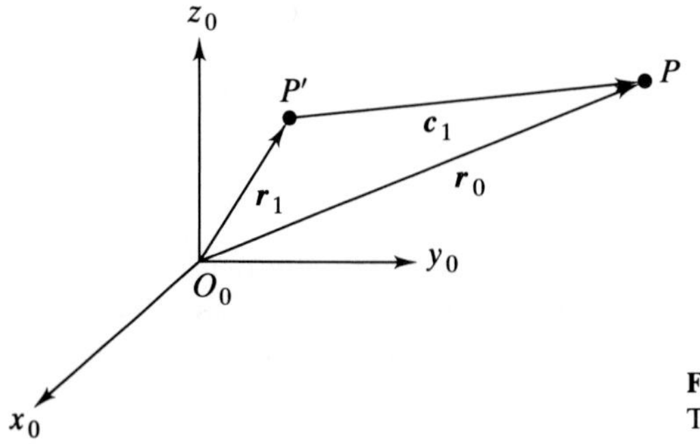

FIGURE 2-3
Translation-point transformation.

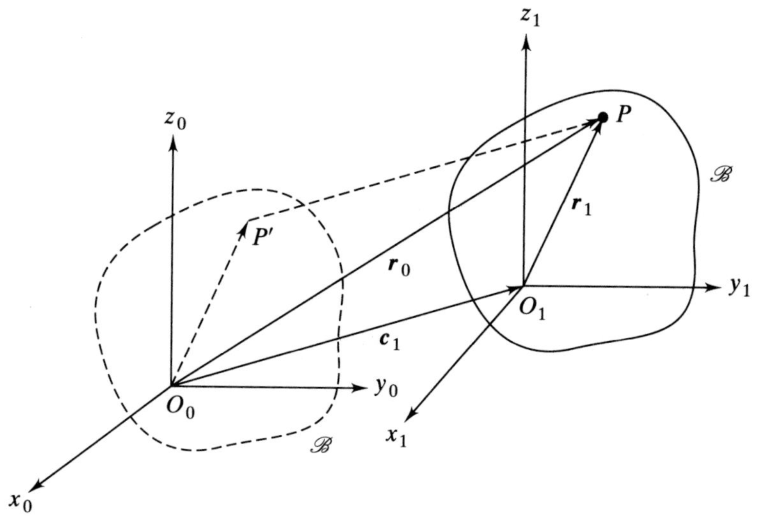

FIGURE 2-4
A mixture of coordinate transformation and point transformation.

Note that this equation is numerically indistinguishable from (2-3); however, the meanings of $\mathbf{r}_0$ and $\mathbf{r}_1$ are completely different.

We shall now look at the point transformation in a somewhat altered form, where we return to the specified terminology of Sec. 2-2. Consider a fixed reference frame $(0xyz)_0$ and a translating reference frame $(0xyz)_1$ (see Fig. 2-4). Then we may view $\mathscr{B}'$ (or P') as some reference configuration, and $\mathscr{B}$ (or P) as the translated configuration of the body. Consequently, $\boldsymbol{r}_0$ retains its meaning as the position vector of P relative to the fixed frame; however, $\boldsymbol{r}_1$ is now the position vector of P relative to O_1 as before. The relationship between the vectors is

$$\boldsymbol{r}_0 = \boldsymbol{c}_1 + \boldsymbol{r}_1 \qquad \text{or} \qquad \boldsymbol{r}_1 = \boldsymbol{r}_0 - \boldsymbol{c}_1$$

which yields

$$\begin{pmatrix} x_1 \\ y_1 \\ z_1 \end{pmatrix} = \begin{pmatrix} x_0 \\ y_0 \\ z_0 \end{pmatrix} - \begin{pmatrix} a_1 \\ b_1 \\ c_1 \end{pmatrix} \tag{2-5}$$

$$\mathbf{r}_1 = \mathbf{r}_0 - \mathbf{c}_1$$

when combined with the results of the coordinate transformation.

Again, it is instructive to consider some time dependence. Suppose P is now a point which is fixed in the body $\mathscr{B}$ which is translating through space. We then have

$$\begin{pmatrix} x_1 \\ y_1 \\ z_1 \end{pmatrix} = \begin{pmatrix} x_0(t) \\ y_0(t) \\ z_0(t) \end{pmatrix} - \begin{pmatrix} a_1(t) \\ b_1(t) \\ c_1(t) \end{pmatrix}$$

$$\mathbf{r}_1 = \mathbf{r}_0(t) - \mathbf{c}_1(t)$$

with time derivative

$$\begin{pmatrix} 0 \\ 0 \\ 0 \end{pmatrix} = \begin{pmatrix} \dot{x}_0(t) \\ \dot{y}_0(t) \\ \dot{z}_0(t) \end{pmatrix} - \begin{pmatrix} \dot{a}_1(t) \\ \dot{b}_1(t) \\ \dot{c}_1(t) \end{pmatrix}$$

$$\mathbf{0} = \dot{\mathbf{r}}_0(t) - \dot{\mathbf{c}}_1(t)$$

or

$$\mathbf{v}_0(t) = \dot{\mathbf{r}}_0(t) = \dot{\mathbf{c}}_1(t)$$

where the entries in $\mathbf{v}_0(t)$ are now the absolute velocity components of the velocity $\boldsymbol{v}_0(t)$ of P; that is,

$$\boldsymbol{v}_0(t) = \dot{\boldsymbol{c}}_1(t) \tag{2-6}$$

is the velocity of P as seen by an observer in the fixed reference frame $(0xyz)_0$.

It is this combined viewpoint of point transformation and coordinate transformation that is the most useful within the present context.

2-4 TWO-DIMENSIONAL ROTATION

General rigid body motion (or motion of reference frames) consists of a combination of translation and rotation. It is advantageous to take a close look at a two-dimensional treatment of rotation before proceeding to the general three-dimensional case. We shall again look at the coordinate transformation and the point transformation.

THE COORDINATE TRANSFORMATION. Accordingly, we consider a fixed point P referred to two different reference frames. For pure rotation (i.e., no translation), we assume that the origins O_0 and O_1 coincide and that the reference frame $(0xyz)_1$ has been rotated by an angle θ, counterclockwise, with respect to $(0xyz)_0$ (see Fig. 2-5). Again, we would like to obtain the new coordinates (x_1, y_1) in terms of the old (fixed) coordinates (x_0, y_0).

Evidently, we have

$$\begin{aligned} \boldsymbol{r}_1 &= \boldsymbol{r}_0 \\ x_1\hat{\imath}_1 + y_1\hat{\jmath}_1 &= x_0\hat{\imath}_0 + y_0\hat{\jmath}_0 \end{aligned} \tag{2-7}$$

To be able to compare the two sides, we need the transformation equations of the unit vectors for rotation. Since we want to solve for (x_1, y_1) in terms of

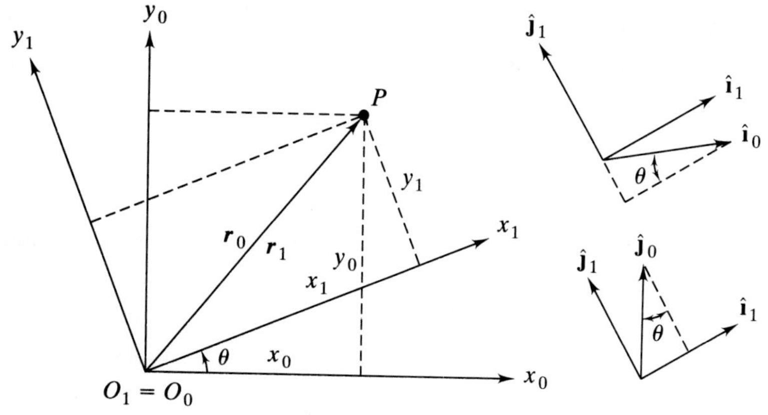

FIGURE 2-5
Rotated coordinate system and its unit vectors.

(x_0, y_0), we shall replace $(\hat{\imath}\hat{\jmath})_0$ in terms of $(\hat{\imath}\hat{\jmath})_1$. From Fig. 2-5 we deduce

$$\begin{aligned} \hat{\imath}_0 &= \cos\theta\, \hat{\imath}_1 - \sin\theta\, \hat{\jmath}_1 \\ \hat{\jmath}_0 &= \sin\theta\, \hat{\imath}_1 + \cos\theta\, \hat{\jmath}_1 \end{aligned} \tag{2-8}$$

Substitution in (2-7) results in

$$x_1\hat{\imath}_1 + y_1\hat{\jmath}_1 = (x_0\cos\theta + y_0\sin\theta)\hat{\imath}_1 + (-x_0\sin\theta + y_0\cos\theta)\hat{\jmath}_1$$

and hence

$$\begin{aligned} x_1 &= x_0\cos\theta + y_0\sin\theta \\ y_1 &= -x_0\sin\theta + y_0\cos\theta \end{aligned}$$

or

$$\begin{pmatrix} x_1 \\ y_1 \end{pmatrix} = \begin{bmatrix} \cos\theta & \sin\theta \\ -\sin\theta & \cos\theta \end{bmatrix} \begin{pmatrix} x_0 \\ y_0 \end{pmatrix} \tag{2-9}$$

$$\mathbf{r}_1 = \mathbf{K}\mathbf{r}_0$$

As before, consider now some time dependence. With fixed point P and rotating reference frame $(0xy)_1$, we have

$$\begin{pmatrix} x_1(t) \\ y_1(t) \end{pmatrix} = \begin{bmatrix} \cos\theta(t) & \sin\theta(t) \\ -\sin\theta(t) & \cos\theta(t) \end{bmatrix} \begin{pmatrix} x_0 \\ y_0 \end{pmatrix}$$

$$\mathbf{r}_1(t) = \mathbf{K}(t)\mathbf{r}_0$$

Differentiation with respect to t yields

$$\dot{\mathbf{r}}_1(t) = \dot{\mathbf{K}}(t)\mathbf{r}_0$$

$$\begin{pmatrix} \dot{x}_1(t) \\ \dot{y}_1(t) \end{pmatrix} = \dot{\theta}(t)\begin{bmatrix} -\sin\theta(t) & \cos\theta(t) \\ -\cos\theta(t) & -\sin\theta(t) \end{bmatrix}\begin{pmatrix} x_0 \\ y_0 \end{pmatrix} \tag{2-10}$$

since x_0 and y_0 are constant.

To interpret this result, it is instructive to consider the vector equation (2-7) with

$$\boldsymbol{r}_1(t) = \boldsymbol{r}_0$$

since the point P is fixed in the base reference frame $(0xy)_0$. Consequently, the absolute velocity of P is $\mathbf{0}$ and we have

$$\boldsymbol{v}_1(t) = \frac{d\boldsymbol{r}_1}{dt}(t) = \frac{d\boldsymbol{r}_0}{dt} = \boldsymbol{v}_0(t) = \mathbf{0}$$

and it follows that

$$\begin{aligned} \frac{d\boldsymbol{r}_1}{dt}(t) &= \frac{d}{dt}(x_1(t)\hat{\imath}_1(t) + y_1(t)\hat{\jmath}_1(t)) \\ &= \dot{x}_1(t)\hat{\imath}_1(t) + \dot{y}_1(t)\hat{\jmath}_1(t) + x_1(t)\dot{\hat{\imath}}_1(t) + y_1(t)\dot{\hat{\jmath}}_1(t) \\ &= \mathbf{0} \end{aligned} \tag{2-11}$$

To evaluate this expression, we need the time derivatives of the rotating unit vectors. We first express $(\hat{\imath}(t)\hat{\jmath}(t))_1$ in terms of $(\hat{\imath}\hat{\jmath})_0$,

$$\dot{\hat{\imath}}_1(t) = \cos\theta(t)\hat{\imath}_0 + \sin\theta(t)\hat{\jmath}_0$$

$$\dot{\hat{\jmath}}_1(t) = -\sin\theta(t)\hat{\imath}_0 + \cos\theta(t)\hat{\jmath}_0$$

with derivatives

$$\begin{aligned} \dot{\hat{\imath}}_1(t) &= \dot{\theta}(t)(-\sin\theta(t)\hat{\imath}_0 + \cos\theta(t)\hat{\jmath}_0) \\ &= \dot{\theta}(t)\hat{\jmath}_1(t) \\ \dot{\hat{\jmath}}_1(t) &= \dot{\theta}(t)(-\cos\theta(t)\hat{\imath}_0 - \sin\theta(t)\hat{\jmath}_0) \\ &= -\dot{\theta}(t)\hat{\imath}_1(t) \end{aligned} \tag{2-12}$$

As a preview, we take this result one step further. Suppose we introduce a vector $\boldsymbol{\omega}(t) = \dot{\theta}(t)\hat{\boldsymbol{k}}_1$ where $(\hat{\imath}\hat{\jmath}\hat{k})_1$ form an orthonormal triad; then the previous derivatives can also be written in the form

$$\begin{aligned} \frac{d\hat{\imath}_1}{dt}(t) &= \boldsymbol{\omega}(t) \times \hat{\imath}_1(t) = \dot{\theta}(t)\hat{\jmath}_1(t) \\ \frac{d\hat{\jmath}_1}{dt}(t) &= \boldsymbol{\omega}(t) \times \hat{\jmath}_1(t) = -\dot{\theta}(t)\hat{\imath}_1(t) \end{aligned} \tag{2-13}$$

a completely general result, as we shall see in a subsequent section.

The substitution of (2-12) into (2-11) yields

$$\begin{aligned}\dot{x}_1(t)\hat{\imath}_1(t) &+ \dot{y}_1(t)\hat{\jmath}_1(t) \\ &+ x_1(t)\boldsymbol{\omega}(t)\times\hat{\imath}_1(t) + y_1(t)\boldsymbol{\omega}(t)\times\hat{\jmath}_1(t) \\ &= \dot{x}_1(t)\hat{\imath}_1(t) + \dot{y}_1(t)\hat{\jmath}_1(t) + \boldsymbol{\omega}(t)\times\boldsymbol{r}_1(t) \\ &= \mathbf{0}\end{aligned} \tag{2-14}$$

or

$$\begin{aligned}\dot{x}_1(t)\hat{\imath}_1(t) + \dot{y}_1(t)\hat{\jmath}_1(t) &= -\boldsymbol{\omega}(t)\times\boldsymbol{r}_1(t) \\ &= \dot{\theta}(t)y_1(t)\hat{\imath}_1(t) - \dot{\theta}(t)x_1(t)\hat{\jmath}_1(t)\end{aligned} \tag{2-15}$$

The physical interpretation is clearest at this stage. The left-hand side of (2-15) is the time rate of change of the position of P, which would be seen by an observer in the moving reference frame. To such an observer, $\hat{\imath}_1(t)$ and $\hat{\jmath}_1(t)$ would appear constant and only their components would change with time. As we shall see, the right-hand side represents the rotational motion of a point about O_1 in the counterclockwise direction. That is, the point P will appear to have moved from P' to P (see Fig. 2-6 in conjunction with Fig. 2-5).

To continue, a comparison of both sides of (2-15) yields

$$\begin{aligned}\dot{x}_1(t) &= \dot{\theta}(t)y_1(t) \\ \dot{y}_1(t) &= -\dot{\theta}(t)x_1(t)\end{aligned} \quad\Rightarrow\quad \begin{pmatrix}\dot{x}_1(t)\\ \dot{y}_1(t)\end{pmatrix} = \dot{\theta}(t)\begin{bmatrix}0 & 1\\ -1 & 0\end{bmatrix}\begin{pmatrix}x_1(t)\\ y_1(t)\end{pmatrix}$$

The use of (2-9) yields

$$\begin{aligned}\begin{pmatrix}\dot{x}_1(t)\\ \dot{y}_1(t)\end{pmatrix} &= \dot{\theta}(t)\begin{bmatrix}0 & 1\\ -1 & 0\end{bmatrix}\begin{bmatrix}\cos\theta(t) & \sin\theta(t)\\ -\sin\theta(t) & \cos\theta(t)\end{bmatrix}\begin{pmatrix}x_0\\ y_0\end{pmatrix} \\ &= \dot{\theta}(t)\begin{bmatrix}-\sin\theta(t) & \cos\theta(t)\\ -\cos\theta(t) & -\sin\theta(t)\end{bmatrix}\begin{pmatrix}x_0\\ y_0\end{pmatrix}\end{aligned}$$

which is the same as (2-10).

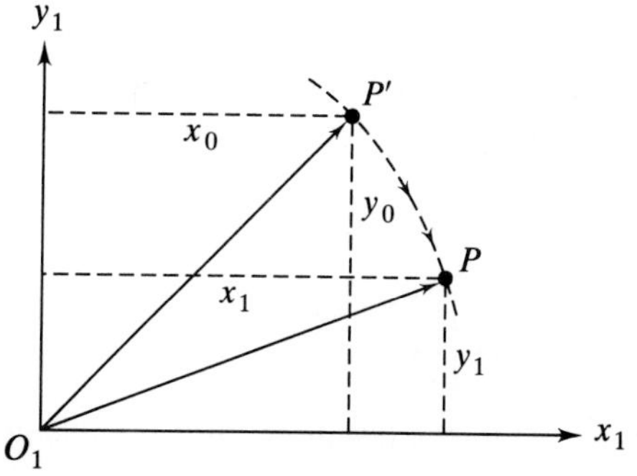

FIGURE 2-6
Apparent motion of P in the moving reference frame.

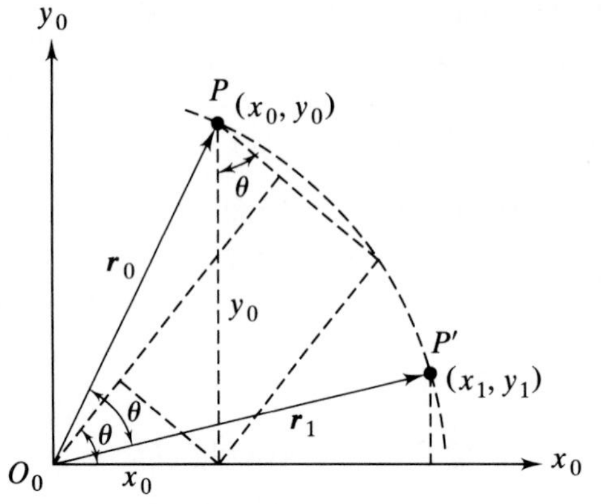

FIGURE 2-7
Point rotation.

THE POINT TRANSFORMATION. We consider a clockwise rotational displacement of a point P from P to P' with respect to the same reference frame—say, the base frame. A point P is *rotated* from P to P' by first passing a line O_0P through the point P with coordinates (x_0, y_0) and then rotating the line by an angle θ to the line O_0P' passing through P' with coordinates (x_1, y_1). Based on the geometry, as illustrated in Fig. 2-7, we deduce the following relationship between the coordinates (x_1, y_1) and (x_0, y_0):

$$x_1 = x_0 \cos\theta + y_0 \sin\theta$$

$$y_1 = y_0 \cos\theta - x_0 \sin\theta$$

$$\begin{pmatrix} x_1 \\ y_1 \end{pmatrix} = \begin{bmatrix} \cos\theta & \sin\theta \\ -\sin\theta & \cos\theta \end{bmatrix} \begin{pmatrix} x_0 \\ y_0 \end{pmatrix}$$

$$\mathbf{r}_1 = \mathbf{K}\mathbf{r}_0$$

which is the same as (2-9). Again, the meaning of the entries is completely different.

We now combine the concepts by considering a point P fixed in a rotating reference frame $(0xy)_1$ whose position initially coincided with $(0xy)_0$, and which is then rotated by an amount θ (see Fig. 2-8). Clearly, this is now the same situation as that depicted in Fig. 2-5, and we conclude that

$$\begin{pmatrix} x_1 \\ y_1 \end{pmatrix} = \begin{bmatrix} \cos\theta & \sin\theta \\ -\sin\theta & \cos\theta \end{bmatrix} \begin{pmatrix} x_0 \\ y_0 \end{pmatrix}$$

The obvious time dependence to consider here consists of

$$\begin{pmatrix} x_1 \\ y_1 \end{pmatrix} = \begin{bmatrix} \cos\theta(t) & \sin\theta(t) \\ -\sin\theta(t) & \cos\theta(t) \end{bmatrix} \begin{pmatrix} x_0(t) \\ y_0(t) \end{pmatrix}$$

since (x_1, y_1) is a point P fixed in $(0xy)_1$. Differentiation of the expression

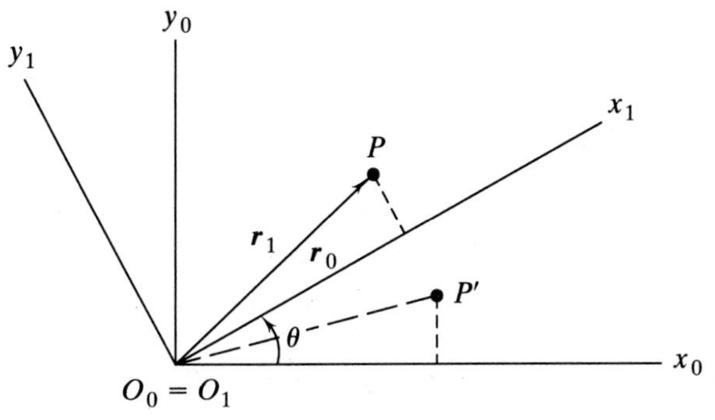

FIGURE 2-8
Combined transformation.

results in

$$\begin{pmatrix} 0 \\ 0 \end{pmatrix} = \begin{bmatrix} \cos\theta & \sin\theta \\ -\sin\theta & \cos\theta \end{bmatrix} \begin{pmatrix} \dot{x}_0 \\ \dot{y}_0 \end{pmatrix} + \dot{\theta} \begin{bmatrix} -\sin\theta & \cos\theta \\ -\cos\theta & -\sin\theta \end{bmatrix} \begin{pmatrix} x_0 \\ y_0 \end{pmatrix}$$

where, for convenience, t has been suppressed. Solving for $(\dot{x}_0 \quad \dot{y}_0)^{\mathrm{T}}$ yields

$$\begin{pmatrix} \dot{x}_0 \\ \dot{y}_0 \end{pmatrix} = -\dot{\theta} \begin{bmatrix} \cos\theta & -\sin\theta \\ \sin\theta & \cos\theta \end{bmatrix} \begin{bmatrix} -\sin\theta & \cos\theta \\ -\cos\theta & -\sin\theta \end{bmatrix} \begin{bmatrix} \cos\theta & -\sin\theta \\ \sin\theta & \cos\theta \end{bmatrix} \begin{pmatrix} x_1 \\ y_1 \end{pmatrix}$$

$$= -\dot{\theta} \begin{bmatrix} 0 & 1 \\ -1 & 0 \end{bmatrix} \begin{bmatrix} \cos\theta & -\sin\theta \\ \sin\theta & \cos\theta \end{bmatrix} \begin{pmatrix} x_1 \\ y_1 \end{pmatrix}$$

$$= -\dot{\theta} \begin{bmatrix} \sin\theta & \cos\theta \\ -\cos\theta & \sin\theta \end{bmatrix} \begin{pmatrix} x_1 \\ y_1 \end{pmatrix}$$

In terms of the basis $(\hat{\imath}\hat{\jmath})_0$, we may now write the vector expression

$$\begin{aligned} \dot{\boldsymbol{r}}_0 &= \dot{x}_0 \hat{\boldsymbol{\imath}}_0 + \dot{y}_0 \hat{\boldsymbol{\jmath}}_0 \\ &= -\dot{\theta}(x_1 \sin\theta + y_1 \cos\theta)\hat{\boldsymbol{\imath}}_0 + \dot{\theta}(x_1 \cos\theta - y_1 \sin\theta)\hat{\boldsymbol{\jmath}}_0 \\ &= x_1\left(-\dot{\theta}\sin\theta\,\hat{\imath}_0 + \dot{\theta}\cos\theta\,\hat{\jmath}_0\right) + y_1\left(-\dot{\theta}\cos\theta\,\hat{\imath}_0 - \dot{\theta}\sin\theta\,\hat{\jmath}_0\right) \\ &= \dot{\theta} x_1 \hat{\boldsymbol{\jmath}}_1 - y_1 \dot{\theta} \hat{\boldsymbol{\imath}}_1 \\ &= \boldsymbol{\omega} \times x_1 \hat{\boldsymbol{\imath}}_1 + \boldsymbol{\omega} \times y_1 \hat{\boldsymbol{\jmath}}_1 \\ &= \boldsymbol{\omega} \times \boldsymbol{r}_1 \end{aligned}$$

where we have again made use of the vector $\boldsymbol{\omega} = \dot{\theta}\hat{\boldsymbol{k}}_1 = \dot{\theta}\hat{\boldsymbol{k}}_0$, with $\hat{k}_1 = \hat{k}_0$ normal to the plane of motion.

In a similar fashion, one may begin with the vector identity

$$\boldsymbol{r}_0(t) = x_0(t)\hat{\boldsymbol{\imath}}_0 + y_0(t)\hat{\boldsymbol{\jmath}}_0 = x_1\hat{\boldsymbol{\imath}}_1(t) + y_1\hat{\boldsymbol{\jmath}}_1(t) = \boldsymbol{r}_1(t)$$

and differentiate to obtain

$$\begin{aligned}\dot{\boldsymbol{r}}_0(t) &= \dot{x}_0(t)\hat{\boldsymbol{\imath}}_0 + \dot{y}_0(t)\hat{\boldsymbol{\jmath}}_0 \\ &= x_1\boldsymbol{\omega}\times\hat{\boldsymbol{\imath}}_1 + y_1\boldsymbol{\omega}\times\hat{\boldsymbol{\jmath}}_1 \\ &= \boldsymbol{\omega}\times\boldsymbol{r}_1\end{aligned}$$

It should be evident at this point that vector notation is somewhat more general than matrix notation. General vector expressions are valid, independent of the basis used to write the vectors. Thus $\boldsymbol{r}_1 = \boldsymbol{r}_0$ is a vector identity independent of any basis used to express it; we have introduced the convention that the basis and the subscript are to agree. By contrast, matrix equations are always bound by a particular basis.

In either case, once a basis has been chosen, both approaches contain the same information. For example, either expression may be used to derive the absolute velocity or acceleration.

2-5 THE ROTATION MATRIX

We shall now take a closer look at the description of rotating coordinate systems. In particular, we shall consider the mixture of point transformation and coordinate transformation. As indicated before, this would be the most useful description in representing the motion of rigid body systems.

In the previous section (see Fig. 2-8), we arrived at the transformation equation

$$\begin{pmatrix} x_1 \\ y_1 \end{pmatrix} = \begin{bmatrix} \cos\theta & \sin\theta \\ -\sin\theta & \cos\theta \end{bmatrix}\begin{pmatrix} x_0 \\ y_0 \end{pmatrix} \tag{2-16}$$

where (x_1, y_1) were the coordinates of a point fixed in $(0xy)_1$, a reference frame that had been rotated through a counterclockwise angle θ with respect to the base frame $(0xy)_0$; thus (x_0, y_0) were the coordinates of the same point with respect to the base frame. The crucial step in the derivation was the transformation equation relating the unit bases of the two systems. Here we shall begin in the same fashion by equating the position vectors with respect to the two reference frames. However, we shall obtain the transformation equation in a somewhat more direct manner.

Consider the situation depicted in Fig. 2-9. In Fig. 2-9a the two reference frames coincide, and the point, fixed with respect to $(0xyz)_i$, occupies the position P'; in Fig. 2-9b the point has been rotated to the position P along with the reference frame $(0xyz)_i$. In this position we now have

$$\begin{aligned}\boldsymbol{r}_0 &= \boldsymbol{r}_i \\ x_0\hat{\boldsymbol{\imath}}_0 + y_0\hat{\boldsymbol{\jmath}}_0 + z_0\hat{\boldsymbol{k}}_0 &= x_i\hat{\boldsymbol{\imath}}_i + y_i\hat{\boldsymbol{\jmath}}_i + z_i\hat{\boldsymbol{k}}_i\end{aligned} \tag{2-17}$$

Previously, we solved for the coordinates (x_i, y_i, z_i) in terms of the coordinates (x_0, y_0, z_0) of the base frame. Within the present context, however,

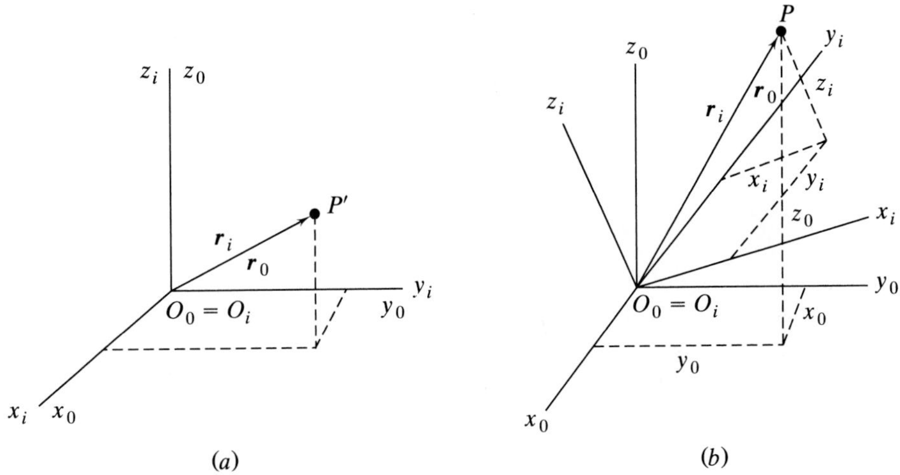

FIGURE 2-9
General rotation of a point.

the $(0xyz)_i$, $i \neq 0$, reference frames serve as "robot variables," and it is of interest to know "where the robot is" in terms of the world or base coordinates. In addition, one traditionally defines the rotation matrix as the transformation matrix, expressing the coordinates (x_0, y_0, z_0) in terms of (x_i, y_i, z_i) of the rotated reference frame. This is what we shall do.

Take the dot product of both sides of (2-17) successively with $\hat{\imath}_0$, $\hat{\jmath}_0$, and $\hat{k}_0$, to obtain

$$x_0 = \hat{\imath}_0 \cdot \hat{\imath}_i x_i + \hat{\imath}_0 \cdot \hat{\jmath}_i y_i + \hat{\imath}_0 \cdot \hat{k}_i z_i$$

$$y_0 = \hat{\jmath}_0 \cdot \hat{\imath}_i x_i + \hat{\jmath}_0 \cdot \hat{\jmath}_i y_i + \hat{\jmath}_0 \cdot \hat{k}_i z_i$$

$$z_0 = \hat{k}_0 \cdot \hat{\imath}_i x_i + \hat{k}_0 \cdot \hat{\jmath}_i y_i + \hat{k}_0 \cdot \hat{k}_i z_i$$

which we can write in the form

$$\begin{pmatrix} x_0 \\ y_0 \\ z_0 \end{pmatrix} = \begin{bmatrix} \hat{\imath}_0 \cdot \hat{\imath}_i & \hat{\imath}_0 \cdot \hat{\jmath}_i & \hat{\imath}_0 \cdot \hat{k}_i \\ \hat{\jmath}_0 \cdot \hat{\imath}_i & \hat{\jmath}_0 \cdot \hat{\jmath}_i & \hat{\jmath}_0 \cdot \hat{k}_i \\ \hat{k}_0 \cdot \hat{\imath}_i & \hat{k}_0 \cdot \hat{\jmath}_i & \hat{k}_0 \cdot \hat{k}_i \end{bmatrix} \begin{pmatrix} x_i \\ y_i \\ z_i \end{pmatrix} \tag{2-18}$$

$$\mathbf{r}_0 = \mathbf{A}_i \mathbf{r}_i$$

Suppose we now take a closer look at the matrix $\mathbf{A}_i$. From the definition of the dot product, it follows that

$$\hat{\imath}_0 \cdot \hat{\imath}_i = \cos \theta_{x_0 x_i} = a_{x_0 x_i}$$

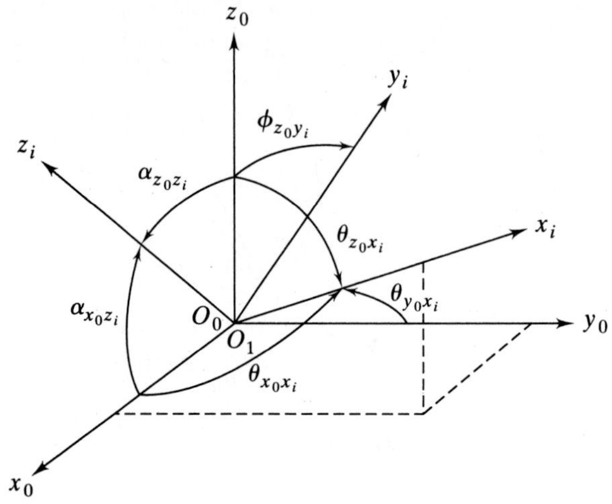

FIGURE 2-10
Direction cosines.

for example (see Fig. 2-10). In a similar fashion, we obtain

$$\hat{\imath}_0 \cdot \hat{\jmath}_i = \cos \phi_{x_0y_i} = b_{x_0y_i}$$

$$\hat{\imath}_0 \cdot \hat{k}_i = \cos \alpha_{x_0z_i} = c_{x_0z_i}$$

Here we have made use of the following notational convention:

$\theta_{x_0x_i}$,	$\theta_{y_0x_i}$,	$\theta_{z_0x_i}$	locate the x_i-axis
$\phi_{x_0y_i}$,	$\phi_{y_0y_i}$,	$\phi_{z_0y_i}$	locate the y_i-axis
$\alpha_{x_0z_i}$,	$\alpha_{y_0z_i}$,	$\alpha_{z_0z_i}$	locate the z_i-axis

all with respect to the x_0-, y_0-, and z_0-axes, respectively. The corresponding matrix of direction cosines

$$\mathbf{A}_i = \begin{bmatrix} a_{x_0x_i} & b_{x_0y_i} & c_{x_0z_i} \\ a_{y_0x_i} & b_{y_0y_i} & c_{y_0z_i} \\ a_{z_0x_i} & b_{z_0y_i} & c_{z_0z_i} \end{bmatrix} \tag{2-19}$$

is called the *rotation matrix*.

Convention 2-1. All angles are measured between the positive segments of the axes. Angles are measured *from* the positive axis segments of the $(0xyz)_0$ frame to the positive axis segments of the $(0xyz)_i$ frame. Thus $\theta_{y_0x_i}$ is the positive angle measured from the positive segment of the y_0-axis to the positive segment of the x_i-axis.

Remark 2-1. Some care must be exercised when dealing with the rotation matrix in other texts. A rotation matrix $\mathbf{Q}$ is often defined in the context of the transformation

$$\mathbf{r}_1 = \mathbf{Q}\mathbf{r}_0$$

that is, their $\mathbf{Q}$ is the transpose of our $\mathbf{A}_i$, $\mathbf{Q} = \mathbf{A}_i^{\mathrm{T}}$.

Definition 2-1 The rotation matrix. The following special rotation matrices shall be used:

(*a*) *The absolute rotation matrix*. Let the frame $(0xyz)_0$ be a fixed reference frame and let $(0xyz)_i$ be rotated with respect to $(0xyz)_0$ in such a way that $O_0 = O_i$. Let P be a point fixed in the rotated frame $(0xyz)_i$ and let $\mathbf{r}_i = (x_i \quad y_i \quad z_i)^{\mathrm{T}}$ be the components of P relative to this frame; let $\mathbf{r}_0 = (x_0 \quad y_0 \quad z_0)^{\mathrm{T}}$ denote the components of the same point relative to the fixed frame $(0xyz)_0$. Then the absolute rotation matrix $\mathbf{A}_i$ is the matrix of direction cosines for which

$$\mathbf{r}_0 = \mathbf{A}_i\mathbf{r}_i$$

(see Fig. 2-9).

(*b*) *Relative rotation matrix*. Let the reference frames be numbered successively and assume $i < j$. Then $\mathbf{A}_{ij}$ is the rotation of $(0xyz)_j$ relative to $(0xyz)_i$; that is,

$$\mathbf{r}_i = \mathbf{A}_{ij}\mathbf{r}_j$$

(*c*) *Basic rotation matrices*. Again, let the reference frames be numbered successively and assume $i < j$. In the following, the angles α, ϕ, and θ are measured from the coincident position of $(0xyz)_i$ and $(0xyz)_j$. Then, as illustrated in Fig. 2-11,

$$\mathbf{A}_{ij}(x,\alpha) = \begin{bmatrix} 1 & 0 & 0 \\ 0 & C\alpha & -S\alpha \\ 0 & S\alpha & C\alpha \end{bmatrix}$$

is the rotation of $(0xyz)_j$ about the x_i-axis by an angle α;

$$\mathbf{A}_{ij}(y,\phi) = \begin{bmatrix} C\phi & 0 & S\phi \\ 0 & 1 & 0 \\ -S\phi & 0 & C\phi \end{bmatrix}$$

is the rotation of $(0xyz)_j$ about the y_i-axis by an angle ϕ;

$$\mathbf{A}_{ij}(z,\theta) = \begin{bmatrix} C\theta & -S\theta & 0 \\ S\theta & C\theta & 0 \\ 0 & 0 & 1 \end{bmatrix}$$

is the rotation of $(0xyz)_j$ about the z_i-axis by an angle θ.

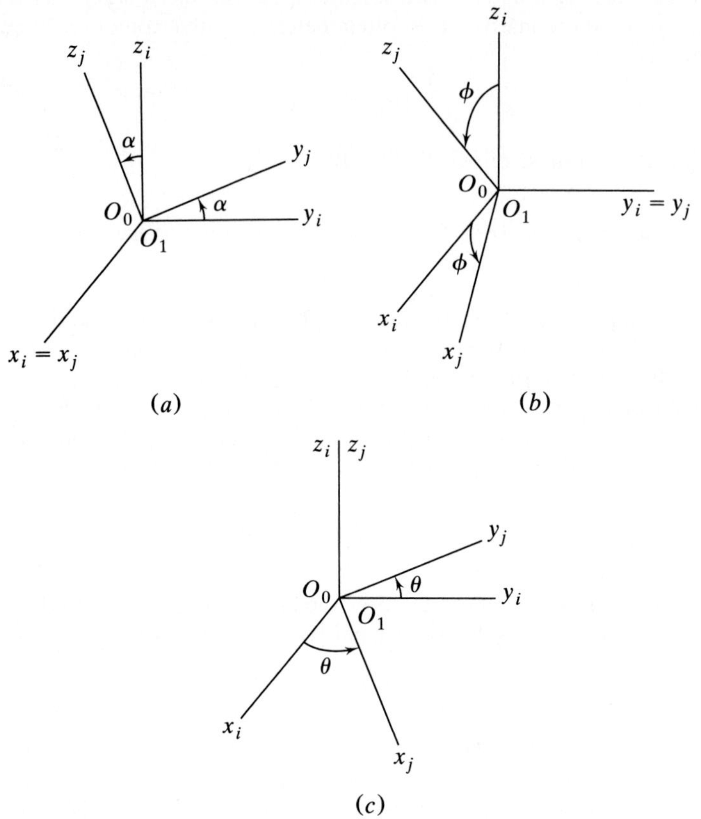

FIGURE 2-11
(*a*) Basic rotation about the *x*-axis. (*b*) basic rotation about the *y*-axis. (*c*) basic rotation about the *z*-axis.

The notational convenience $C\alpha = \cos\alpha$ and $S\alpha = \sin\alpha$, etc., has established itself in robotics; generally, we shall make use of it mainly in this context. For the basic rotation matrices, we introduce the following conventions (see Fig. 2-12):

(*a*) The rotations α, ϕ, and θ are taken as positive in the counterclockwise direction, based on looking along the positive segment of the axis toward the origin.

(*b*) The remaining direction angles are used as before; that is, they are the angles measured *from* the positive *i*-segment to the positive *j*-segment.

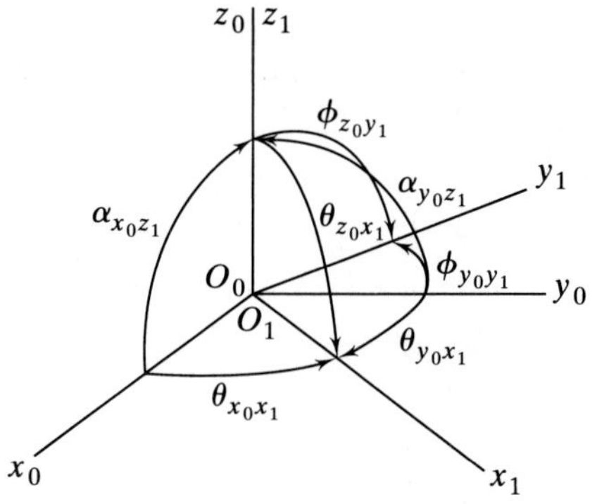

FIGURE 2-12
Convention for the direction angles.

Example 2-1. Suppose the $(0xyz)_1$ frame is rotated through an angle θ (counterclockwise) about the z_0-axis in such a way that $O_1 = O_0$ and z_1 remains coincident with z_0. Determine the corresponding rotation matrix.

Solution. In accordance with Fig. 2-13, we have the following direction cosines:

$$a_{x_0x_1} = \hat{\imath}_0 \cdot \hat{\imath}_1 = \cos\theta$$

$$a_{y_0x_1} = \hat{\jmath}_0 \cdot \hat{\imath}_1 = \cos(90 - \theta)$$

$$a_{z_0x_1} = \hat{k}_0 \cdot \hat{\imath}_1 = 0$$

$$b_{x_0y_1} = \hat{\imath}_0 \cdot \hat{\jmath}_1 = -\cos(90 - \theta)$$

$$b_{y_0y_1} = \hat{\jmath}_0 \cdot \hat{\jmath}_1 = \cos\theta$$

$$b_{z_0y_1} = \hat{k}_0 \cdot \hat{\jmath}_1 = 0$$

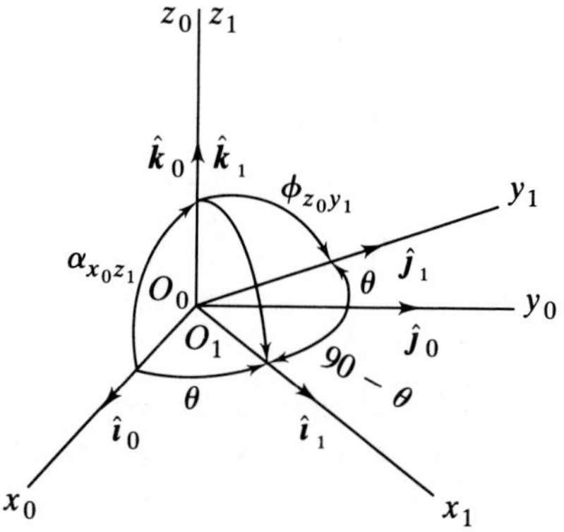

FIGURE 2-13
A rotation about the z_0-axis.

and

$$c_{x_0 z_1} = \hat{\imath}_0 \cdot \hat{k}_1 = 0$$

$$c_{y_0 z_1} = \hat{\jmath}_0 \cdot \hat{k}_1 = 0$$

$$c_{z_0 z_1} = \hat{k}_0 \cdot \hat{k}_1 = 1$$

The rotation matrix is thus given by

$$\mathbf{A}_1 = \begin{bmatrix} \cos\theta & -\sin\theta & 0 \\ \sin\theta & \cos\theta & 0 \\ 0 & 0 & 1 \end{bmatrix}$$

We shall now note some of the properties of the rotation matrix:

(*a*) Suppose we carry out the dot product in (2-17), successively with the unit vectors $\hat{\imath}_i$, $\hat{\jmath}_i$, and $\hat{k}_i$. The result then is

$$\begin{pmatrix} x_i \\ y_i \\ z_i \end{pmatrix} = \begin{bmatrix} \hat{\imath}_i \cdot \hat{\imath}_0 & \hat{\imath}_i \cdot \hat{\jmath}_0 & \hat{\imath}_i \cdot \hat{k}_0 \\ \hat{\jmath}_i \cdot \hat{\imath}_0 & \hat{\jmath}_i \cdot \hat{\jmath}_0 & \hat{\jmath}_i \cdot \hat{k}_0 \\ \hat{k}_i \cdot \hat{\imath}_0 & \hat{k}_i \cdot \hat{\jmath}_0 & \hat{k}_i \cdot \hat{k}_0 \end{bmatrix} \begin{pmatrix} x_0 \\ y_0 \\ z_0 \end{pmatrix}$$

Since the dot product is commutative, it follows that the transformation matrix here is simply $\mathbf{A}_i^{\mathrm{T}}$ or

$$\mathbf{r}_i = \mathbf{A}_i^{\mathrm{T}} \mathbf{r}_0$$

However, from (2-18) we deduce that

$$\mathbf{r}_i = \mathbf{A}_i^{-1} \mathbf{r}_0$$

and, consequently, that $\mathbf{A}_i^{-1} = \mathbf{A}^{\mathrm{T}}$. Matrices that have this property are called *orthogonal* matrices. Note that orthogonality also implies

$$\mathbf{A}_i \mathbf{A}_i^{\mathrm{T}} = \mathbf{A}_i^{\mathrm{T}} \mathbf{A}_i = \mathbf{E}$$

where $\mathbf{E}$ is the identity matrix in $\mathbb{R}^3$.

(*b*) Next, we show that if $\mathbf{A}$ is an orthogonal matrix, then $\det \mathbf{A} = \pm 1$. This follows directly from

$$\mathbf{A}^{\mathrm{T}}\mathbf{A} = \mathbf{E} \qquad \det \mathbf{A}^{\mathrm{T}} \cdot \det \mathbf{A} = 1 \qquad (\det \mathbf{A})^2 = 1$$

since an interchange of all rows and columns does not affect the value of a determinant.

2-6 RIGID BODY MOTION

We now turn to the description of the general motion of rigid bodies consisting of a combined rotation and translation. As before, we may take several different viewpoints in deriving our results.

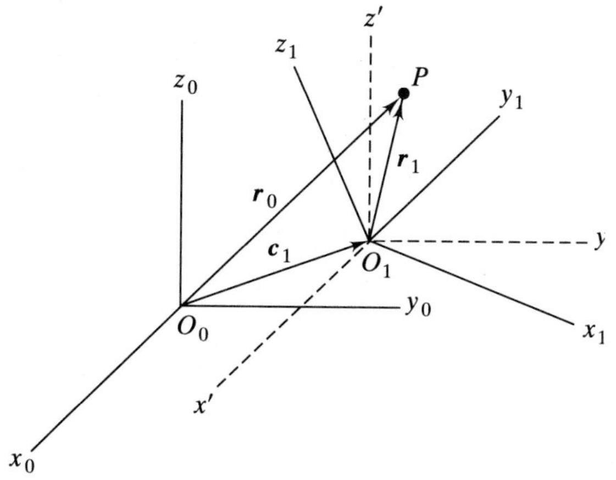

FIGURE 2-14
Coordinate transformation for combined translation and rotation.

THE COORDINATE TRANSFORMATION. These words have a familiar ring by now. That is, we know that we are to represent the position of a fixed point P with respect to two different reference frames. The situation is illustrated in Fig. 2-14.

We shall use only the matrix representation in our description. The first step in obtaining $\mathbf{r}_0$ in terms of $\mathbf{r}_1$ consists of a rotation that aligns the rotated frame with the base frame, as indicated by the dashed lines in Fig. 2-14. This results in

$$\mathbf{r}' = \mathbf{A}_1\mathbf{r}_1$$

This is followed by a translation, to yield

$$\mathbf{r}_0 = \mathbf{c}_1 + \mathbf{A}_1\mathbf{r}_1 \tag{2-20}$$

which constitutes the desired coordinate transformation.

Example 2-2. In order to visualize the geometry of this result, let us consider a two-dimensional example in accordance with Fig. 2-15. We read off directly

$$x_0 = a_1 + x_1 \cos\theta - y_1 \sin\theta$$

$$y_0 = b_1 + x_1 \sin\theta + y_1 \cos\theta$$

$$\begin{pmatrix} x_0 \\ y_0 \end{pmatrix} = \begin{pmatrix} a_1 \\ b_1 \end{pmatrix} + \begin{bmatrix} \cos\theta & -\sin\theta \\ \sin\theta & \cos\theta \end{bmatrix} \begin{pmatrix} x_1 \\ y_1 \end{pmatrix} \tag{2-21}$$

THE POINT TRANSFORMATION. We remind the reader that the meaning of $\mathbf{r}_1$ and $\mathbf{r}_0$ in the point transformation differs from our standard definitions; here $\mathbf{r}_1$ simply denotes the initial position P' of the point, and $\mathbf{r}_0$ denotes the final position P, both with respect to one and the same reference frame which we take to be $(0xyz)_0$.

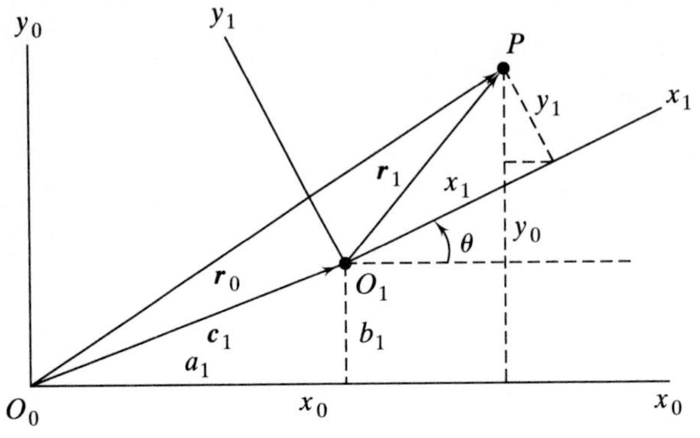

FIGURE 2-15
Geometry of the two-dimensional coordinate transformation.

In accordance with Fig. 2-16, we first take a rotation from P' to Q,

$$\mathbf{r}' = \mathbf{A}_1\mathbf{r}_1$$

followed by a translation

$$\mathbf{r}_0 = \mathbf{c}_1 + \mathbf{r}'$$

with the result

$$\mathbf{r}_0 = \mathbf{c}_1 + \mathbf{A}_1\mathbf{r}_1 \tag{2-22}$$

Example 2-3. Again, we look at a two-dimensional case for geometric insight (see Fig. 2-17). Based on Fig. 2-17, we evidently have

$$\begin{pmatrix} x_0 \\ y_0 \end{pmatrix} = \begin{pmatrix} a_1 \\ b_1 \end{pmatrix} + \begin{bmatrix} \cos\theta & -\sin\theta \\ \sin\theta & \cos\theta \end{bmatrix} \begin{pmatrix} x_1 \\ y_1 \end{pmatrix} \tag{2-23}$$

THE MOTION OF A RIGID BODY. We have now finished with the building material needed for the description of rigid body motion. We turn to the combined description which we used previously. The objective is the description of the motion of a rigid body.

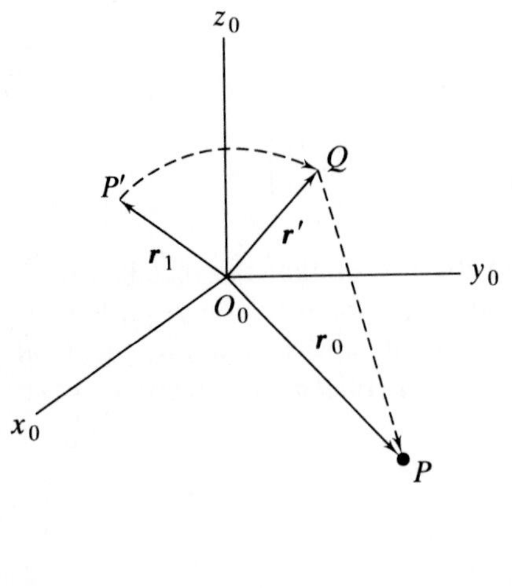

FIGURE 2-16
A rotation followed by a translation.

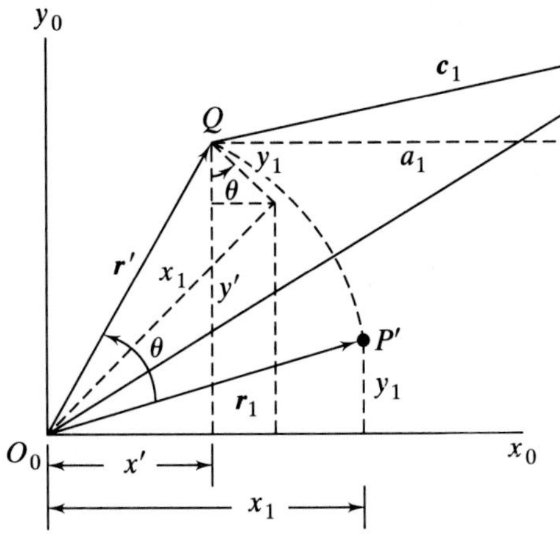

FIGURE 2-17
Two-dimensional rotation plus translation.

Definition 2-2 Rigid body. Let P_1 and P_2 be any two points in a body $\mathscr{B}$ and let $\boldsymbol{r}_1(t)$ and $\boldsymbol{r}_2(t)$ be their position vectors relative to some fixed frame $(0xyz)_0$. Then $\mathscr{B}$ is a rigid body if and only if (iff), for all times t,

$$|\boldsymbol{r}_1(t) - \boldsymbol{r}_2(t)| = \text{const.}$$

As always, $(0xyz)_0$ denotes the fixed or base reference frame, and $(0xyz)_1$ denotes a reference frame that is embedded in a rigid body $\mathscr{B}_1$. Let P be a point in $\mathscr{B}_1$ and let

$$\boldsymbol{r}_1(t) = x_1\hat{\boldsymbol{\imath}}_1(t) + y_1\hat{\boldsymbol{\jmath}}_1(t) + z_1\hat{\boldsymbol{k}}_1(t)$$

be the position vector of P relative to O_1; let

$$\boldsymbol{r}_0(t) = x_0(t)\hat{\boldsymbol{\imath}}_0 + y_0(t)\hat{\boldsymbol{\jmath}}_0 + z_0(t)\hat{\boldsymbol{k}}_0$$

be the position vector of P relative to O_0. The vector $\boldsymbol{r}_0(t)$ will also be termed the *motion* of the point P of $\mathscr{B}_1$, since it describes the path along which P moves for all time t (see Fig. 2-18). The vector $\boldsymbol{c}_1(t)$ is the motion of O_1.

Independent of the choice of basis, we have

$$\boldsymbol{r}_0(t) = \boldsymbol{c}_1(t) + \boldsymbol{r}_1(t)$$

or

$$\mathbf{r}_0(t) = \mathbf{c}_1(t) + \mathbf{A}_1(t)\mathbf{r}_1$$

when we refer to a particular basis.

Definition 2-3 Rigid body motion. The transformation

$$\mathbf{r}_0(t) = \mathbf{c}_1(t) + \mathbf{A}_1(t)\mathbf{r}_1$$

with all terms as defined previously, is called a *rigid body motion*.

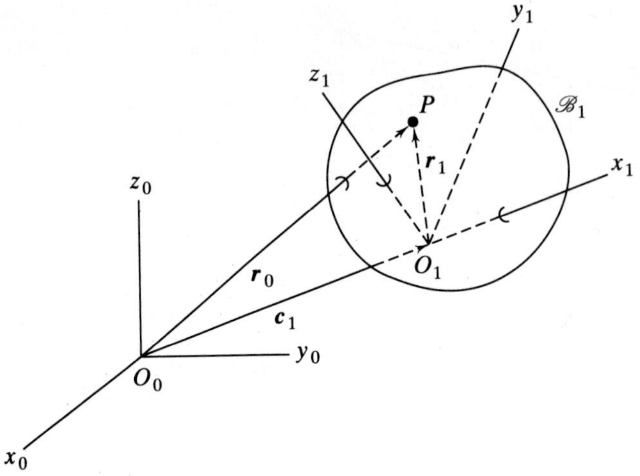

FIGURE 2-18
Rigid body motion.

2-7 ANGULAR VELOCITY OF A RIGID BODY

Suppose we consider the plane rotation of a rigid body $\mathscr{B}$ about a fixed point which we identify with O_0 and O_1. Then

$$\boldsymbol{r}_0(t) = \boldsymbol{r}_1(t)$$

and with $(\hat{\imath}\hat{\jmath}\boldsymbol{k})_0$ as the comparison basis,

$$\begin{pmatrix} x_0(t) \\ y_0(t) \end{pmatrix} = \begin{bmatrix} \cos\theta(t) & -\sin\theta(t) \\ \sin\theta(t) & \cos\theta(t) \end{bmatrix} \begin{pmatrix} x_1 \\ y_1 \end{pmatrix}$$

Differentiating both sides yields

$$\begin{pmatrix} \dot{x}_0 \\ \dot{y}_0 \end{pmatrix} = \dot{\theta} \begin{bmatrix} -\sin\theta & -\cos\theta \\ \cos\theta & -\sin\theta \end{bmatrix} \begin{pmatrix} x_1 \\ y_1 \end{pmatrix}$$

corresponding to the vector equation

$$\begin{aligned} \boldsymbol{v}_0 &= (-x_1 \sin\theta - y_1 \cos\theta)\dot{\theta}\hat{\imath}_0 + (x_1 \cos\theta - y_1 \sin\theta)\dot{\theta}\hat{\jmath}_0 \\ &= x_1\dot{\theta}\hat{\jmath}_1 - y_1\dot{\theta}\hat{\imath}_1 \\ &= (\dot{\theta}\hat{\boldsymbol{k}}_1) \times (x_1\hat{\imath}_1) + (\dot{\theta}\hat{\boldsymbol{k}}_1) \times (y_1\hat{\jmath}_1) \\ &= (\dot{\theta}\hat{\boldsymbol{k}}_1) \times (x_1\hat{\imath}_1 + y_1\hat{\jmath}_1) \\ &= \boldsymbol{\omega}_1 \times \boldsymbol{r}_1 \end{aligned}$$

For obvious reasons, we call $\boldsymbol{\omega}_1(t) = \dot{\theta}(t)\hat{\boldsymbol{k}}_1$ the angular velocity of the rigid body $\mathscr{B}$.

Remark 2-2. Note that the result is independent of the choice of the point of rotation. That is, no matter which fixed point we chose to rotate about, the same $\boldsymbol{\omega}(t)$ would be obtained. Thus we generally say the rigid body $\mathscr{B}$ has an angular velocity $\boldsymbol{\omega}(t)$ without referring to some particular axis of rotation.

We now generalize the preceding deviation to three-dimensional motion. Again, we begin with

$$\boldsymbol{r}_0(t) = \boldsymbol{r}_1(t) \tag{2-24}$$

and

$$\mathbf{r}_0(t) = \mathbf{A}_1(t)\mathbf{r}_1$$

Differentiation yields

$$\mathbf{v}_0 = \dot{\mathbf{A}}_1\mathbf{r}_1$$
$$= \dot{\mathbf{A}}_1\mathbf{A}_1^{\mathrm{T}}\mathbf{r}_0$$

where we omit the argument t, since it should be clear by now which quantities depend on time. Next, we note that $\mathbf{W} = \dot{\mathbf{A}}_1\mathbf{A}_1^{\mathrm{T}}$ is a skew-symmetric matrix; that is, $\mathbf{W} = -\mathbf{W}^{\mathrm{T}}$. This follows immediately from

$$\mathbf{A}_1\mathbf{A}_1^{\mathrm{T}} = \mathbf{E} \quad \Rightarrow \quad \dot{\mathbf{A}}_1\mathbf{A}_1^{\mathrm{T}} + \mathbf{A}_1\dot{\mathbf{A}}_1^{\mathrm{T}} = \mathbf{0}$$

$$\dot{\mathbf{A}}_1\mathbf{A}_1^{\mathrm{T}} = -\mathbf{A}_1\dot{\mathbf{A}}_1^{\mathrm{T}} = -\left(\dot{\mathbf{A}}_1\mathbf{A}_1^{\mathrm{T}}\right)^{\mathrm{T}}$$

With the skew-symmetric matrix $\mathbf{W}$ we now associate its so-called *axial* vector

$$\boldsymbol{\omega}_1 = \omega_{x_0}\hat{\boldsymbol{\imath}}_0 + \omega_{y_0}\hat{\boldsymbol{\jmath}}_0 + \omega_{z_0}\hat{\boldsymbol{k}}_0 \tag{2-25}$$

identified with

$$\mathbf{W} = \begin{bmatrix} 0 & -\omega_{z_0} & \omega_{y_0} \\ \omega_{z_0} & 0 & -\omega_{x_0} \\ -\omega_{y_0} & \omega_{x_0} & 0 \end{bmatrix}$$

It follows that

$$\mathbf{v}_0 = \mathbf{W}\mathbf{r}_0$$

$$= \begin{bmatrix} 0 & -\omega_{z_0} & \omega_{y_0} \\ \omega_{z_0} & 0 & -\omega_{x_0} \\ -\omega_{y_0} & \omega_{x_0} & 0 \end{bmatrix} \begin{pmatrix} x_0 \\ y_0 \\ z_0 \end{pmatrix} = \begin{pmatrix} \omega_{y_0}z_0 - \omega_{z_0}y_0 \\ \omega_{z_0}x_0 - \omega_{x_0}z_0 \\ \omega_{x_0}y_0 - \omega_{y_0}x_0 \end{pmatrix}$$

These latter components are the components of the vector product

$$\boldsymbol{v}_0 = \boldsymbol{\omega}_1 \times \boldsymbol{r}_0$$

and from (2-24) it then follows that

$$\boldsymbol{v}_0(t) = \boldsymbol{\omega}_1(t) \times \boldsymbol{r}_1(t) \tag{2-26}$$

where $\boldsymbol{\omega}_1(t)$ must, of course, be expressed in terms of $\hat{\boldsymbol{\imath}}_1$, $\hat{\boldsymbol{\jmath}}_1$, and $\hat{\boldsymbol{k}}_1$, if the cross product is to be carried out with $\boldsymbol{r}_1(t)$ in its usual form.

Example 2-4. Consider again the rotation treated in Example 2-1. Let $\theta = \theta(t)$ and use the preceding procedure to determine the vector $\boldsymbol{\omega}_1(t)$.

Solution. We have

$$\dot{\mathbf{A}}_1(t) = \dot{\theta}(t)\begin{bmatrix} -\sin\theta(t) & -\cos\theta(t) & 0 \\ \cos\theta(t) & -\sin\theta(t) & 0 \\ 0 & 0 & 0 \end{bmatrix}$$

so that

$$\dot{\mathbf{A}}_1(t)\mathbf{A}_1^{\mathrm{T}}(t) = \dot{\theta}(t)\begin{bmatrix} -\sin\theta(t) & -\cos\theta(t) & 0 \\ \cos\theta(t) & -\sin\theta(t) & 0 \\ 0 & 0 & 0 \end{bmatrix}\begin{bmatrix} \cos\theta(t) & \sin\theta(t) & 0 \\ -\sin\theta(t) & \cos\theta(t) & 0 \\ 0 & 0 & 1 \end{bmatrix}$$

$$= \dot{\theta}(t)\begin{bmatrix} 0 & -1 & 0 \\ 1 & 0 & 0 \\ 0 & 0 & 0 \end{bmatrix}$$

and it follows that

$$\boldsymbol{\omega}_1(t) = \dot{\theta}(t)\hat{\boldsymbol{k}}_0$$

This result is a clear justification for the use of the label "angular velocity" in connection with $\boldsymbol{\omega}_1(t)$; $\dot{\theta}(t)$ is the time rate of change of an angle (angular speed) and a direction is specified by defining a counterclockwise rotation to correspond with the positive z_0-direction ($\hat{\boldsymbol{k}}_0$).

Example 2-5 Successive rotations of a rigid body. Assume that the $(0xyz)_1$ frame is embedded in a rigid body $\mathscr{B}_1$ and that the initial position of the frame coincides with that of the $(0xyz)_0$ frame. Assume that the final position of the body $\mathscr{B}_1$ [the frame $(0xyz)_1$] is reached by applying two successive rotations: (1) a 90° (ccw) rotation about the z_0-axis so that the $(0xyz)_1$ system occupies the position $(0xyz)_{11}$; (2) a 90° (ccw) rotation of the $(0xyz)_1$ frame about the x_{11}-axis.

(*a*) Determine the separate rotation matrices for cases 1 and 2.

(*b*) Determine the single rotation matrix that locates the final position of $(0xyz)_1$ with respect to $(0xyz)_0$.

(*c*) Check your result by locating the point $\mathbf{r}_1 = (0 \quad 0 \quad 1)^{\mathrm{T}}$ with respect to $(0xyz)_0$.

Solution. Cases 1 and 2 are depicted in Fig. 2-19. At each step, the dashed lines show the initial position of the $(0xyz)_1$ frame, and the drawn-out lines, the final position of the frame.

The first rotation essentially relates $\mathbf{r}_{11}$ to $\mathbf{r}_0$ with

$$\mathbf{r}_0 = \mathbf{A}\mathbf{r}_{11} \qquad \text{where} \qquad \mathbf{A} = \begin{bmatrix} 0 & -1 & 0 \\ 1 & 0 & 0 \\ 0 & 0 & 1 \end{bmatrix}$$

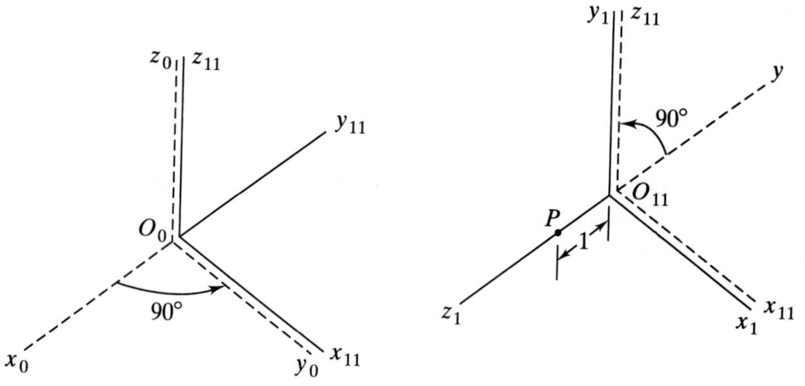

FIGURE 2-19
Two successive rotations.

and the second rotation about the x_{11}-axis is given by

$$\mathbf{r}_{11} = \mathbf{B}\mathbf{r}_1 \qquad \text{where} \quad \mathbf{B} = \begin{bmatrix} 1 & 0 & 0 \\ 0 & 0 & -1 \\ 0 & 1 & 0 \end{bmatrix}$$

The single rotation matrix relating $\mathbf{r}_1$ to $\mathbf{r}_0$ follows from

$$\mathbf{r}_0 = \mathbf{A}\mathbf{r}_{11} = \mathbf{A}\mathbf{B}\mathbf{r}_1$$

as

$$\mathbf{A}_1 = \mathbf{A}\mathbf{B} = \begin{bmatrix} 0 & -1 & 0 \\ 1 & 0 & 0 \\ 0 & 0 & 1 \end{bmatrix} \begin{bmatrix} 1 & 0 & 0 \\ 0 & 0 & -1 \\ 0 & 1 & 0 \end{bmatrix} = \begin{bmatrix} 0 & 0 & 1 \\ 1 & 0 & 0 \\ 0 & 1 & 0 \end{bmatrix}$$

We check this result with

$$\mathbf{r}_0 = \begin{bmatrix} 0 & 0 & 1 \\ 1 & 0 & 0 \\ 0 & 1 & 0 \end{bmatrix} \begin{pmatrix} 0 \\ 0 \\ 1 \end{pmatrix} = \begin{pmatrix} 1 \\ 0 \\ 0 \end{pmatrix}$$

as expected.

Remark 2-3. It is sometimes of interest to trace the successive rotations of a given reference frame (or rigid body). We shall use a second subscript on x, y, and z to denote these positions. For example, x_{12} is the second position of the x_1-axis, x_{13} is its third position, and so on.

2-8 TIME RATE OF CHANGE OF VECTORS IN TERMS OF ROTATING BASIS VECTORS

We shall now derive the expression for the absolute time rate of change of *any* vector that is expressed in terms of the rotating basis $\hat{\imath}_1(t)$, $\hat{\jmath}_1(t)$, $\hat{k}_1(t)$. Suppose $(0xyz)_0$ is fixed and $\boldsymbol{\omega}_1(t)$ is the angular velocity of the rotating reference frame $(0xyz)_1$.

Consider a vector

$$\mathbf{s}_1(t) = u(t)\hat{\imath}_1(t) + v(t)\hat{\jmath}_1(t) + w(t)\hat{\mathbf{k}}_1(t) \tag{2-27}$$

In order to differentiate such an expression, we clearly need the derivatives of the unit vectors.

These may be obtained in a straightforward manner by considering $\mathbf{r}_1(t)$ in the preceding section to be successively replaced by $\hat{\imath}_1(t)$, $\hat{\jmath}_1(t)$, $\hat{\mathbf{k}}_1(t)$. For example, we may begin with

$$\mathbf{r}_0(t) = \hat{\imath}_1(t)$$

It then follows that

$$\frac{d\mathbf{r}_0}{dt}(t) = \mathbf{v}_0(t) = \frac{d\hat{\imath}_1}{dt}(t) = \boldsymbol{\omega}_1(t) \times \hat{\imath}_1(t) \tag{2-28}$$

In a similar manner, we have

$$\frac{d\hat{\jmath}_1}{dt}(t) = \boldsymbol{\omega}_1(t) \times \hat{\jmath}_1(t) \qquad \text{and} \qquad \frac{d\hat{\mathbf{k}}_1}{dt}(t) = \boldsymbol{\omega}_1(t) \times \hat{\mathbf{k}}_1(t) \tag{2-29}$$

Equations (2-28) and (2-29) represent the single most important result in rigid body kinematics. Once the derivatives of moving unit vectors are available, the derivative of any vector, such as (2-27), may be obtained in a straightforward manner. The result is

$$\begin{aligned}\frac{d\mathbf{s}_1}{dt}(t) &= \frac{du}{dt}(t)\hat{\imath}_1(t) + \frac{dv}{dt}(t)\hat{\jmath}_1(t) + \frac{dw}{dt}(t)\hat{\mathbf{k}}_1(t)\\ &\quad + u(t)\frac{d\hat{\imath}_1}{dt}(t) + v(t)\frac{d\hat{\jmath}_1}{dt}(t) + w(t)\frac{d\hat{\mathbf{k}}_1}{dt}(t)\\ &= \left(\frac{d\mathbf{s}_1}{dt}(t)\right)_1 + \boldsymbol{\omega}_1(t) \times \mathbf{s}_1(t)\end{aligned} \tag{2-30}$$

where the notation $(d\mathbf{s}_1(t)/dt)_1$ is used to denote the derivative of $\mathbf{s}_1(t)$ as seen by an observer stationed within the moving reference frame, to whom the unit basis $\hat{\imath}_1(t)$, $\hat{\jmath}_1(t)$, $\hat{\mathbf{k}}_1(t)$ would appear fixed.

Consequently, we define the derivative operator for differentiation in a rotating reference frame by

$$\frac{d}{dt}(\cdot) = \left(\frac{d}{dt}(\cdot)\right)_1 + \boldsymbol{\omega}_1(t) \times (\cdot) \tag{2-31}$$

where $(\cdot)$ may be replaced by any vector that has been expressed in terms of the moving basis vectors.

We note that this represents the absolute time rate of change of a vector as long as $\boldsymbol{\omega}_1(t)$ is measured with respect to a fixed reference frame.

Example 2-6. Calculate the angular acceleration $\boldsymbol{\alpha}_1(t)$ of a rotating reference frame whose angular velocity is given by

$$\boldsymbol{\omega}_1(t) = \omega_{x_1}(t)\hat{\imath}_1(t) + \omega_{y_1}(t)\hat{\jmath}_1(t) + \omega_{z_1}(t)\hat{\boldsymbol{k}}_1(t)$$

Solution. The use of the operator [Eq. (2-31)] yields

$$\begin{aligned}\boldsymbol{\alpha}_1(t) &= \frac{d\boldsymbol{\omega}_1}{dt}(t) = \left(\frac{d\boldsymbol{\omega}_1}{dt}(t)\right)_1 + \boldsymbol{\omega}_1(t) \times \boldsymbol{\omega}_1(t) \\ &= \left(\frac{d\boldsymbol{\omega}_1}{dt}(t)\right)_1 \\ &= \dot{\omega}_{x_1}(t)\hat{\imath}_1(t) + \dot{\omega}_{y_1}(t)\hat{\jmath}_1(t) + \dot{\omega}_{z_1}(t)\hat{\boldsymbol{k}}_1(t) \end{aligned} \tag{2-32}$$

a result well worth remembering.

2-9 VELOCITY AND ACCELERATION FOR GENERAL RIGID BODY MOTION

As always, let $(0xyz)_0$ be fixed and let $(0xyz)_1$ be a moving reference frame. A rigid body motion in vector form is given by

$$\boldsymbol{r}_0(t) = \boldsymbol{c}_1(t) + \boldsymbol{r}_1(t)$$

where the subscripts indicate the respective bases in terms of which these vectors have been expressed (with the exception of $\boldsymbol{c}_i$ which is usually expressed in terms of the reference frame $(0xyz)_{i-1}$). With the result embodied in (2-26), it is now a simple matter to derive the vector expression for the absolute velocity and acceleration of the point P in the rigid body $\mathscr{B}_1$. Suppose $\boldsymbol{\omega}_1(t)$ is the absolute angular velocity of the moving reference frame and $\boldsymbol{\alpha}_1(t)$ is the absolute angular acceleration. Then we immediately obtain

$$\begin{aligned}\boldsymbol{v}_0(t) &= \dot{\boldsymbol{c}}(t) + \dot{\boldsymbol{r}}_1(t) \\ &= \dot{\boldsymbol{c}}_1(t) + \boldsymbol{\omega}_1(t) \times \boldsymbol{r}_1(t)\end{aligned}$$

for the absolute velocity of the point P, and

$$\begin{aligned}\boldsymbol{a}_0(t) &= \ddot{\boldsymbol{c}}_1(t) + \boldsymbol{\omega}_1(t) \times \dot{\boldsymbol{r}}_1(t) + \dot{\boldsymbol{\omega}}_1(t) \times \boldsymbol{r}_1(t) \\ &= \ddot{\boldsymbol{c}}_1(t) + \boldsymbol{\alpha}_1(t) \times \boldsymbol{r}_1(t) + \boldsymbol{\omega}_1(t) \times (\boldsymbol{\omega}_1(t) \times \boldsymbol{r}_1(t))\end{aligned}$$

for the absolute acceleration.

If we retain the matrix notation, then the component form of these equations is given by

$$\mathbf{r}_0(t) = \mathbf{c}_1(t) + \mathbf{A}_1(t)\mathbf{r}_1$$

along with

$$\mathbf{v}_0(t) = \dot{\mathbf{c}}_1(t) + \dot{\mathbf{A}}_1(t)\mathbf{r}_1$$

for the velocity and

$$\mathbf{a}_0(t) = \ddot{\mathbf{c}}_1(t) + \ddot{\mathbf{A}}_1(t)\mathbf{r}_1$$

for the absolute acceleration.

Example 2-7. Suppose P is a given point in a rotating rigid body. Let $(0xyz)_1$ be a body-fixed reference frame which rotates with constant absolute angular velocity $\boldsymbol{\omega}_1$ in such a way that $\hat{\boldsymbol{k}}_1(t) = \hat{\boldsymbol{k}}_0$ for all time, $(0xyz)_0$ being the fixed base frame. Let

$$\boldsymbol{r}_1(t) = x_1\hat{\boldsymbol{\imath}}_1(t) + y_1\hat{\boldsymbol{\jmath}}_1(t) + z_1\hat{\boldsymbol{k}}_1(t)$$

be the position vector of P relative to $(0xyz)_1$ and let

$$\boldsymbol{r}_0(t) = x_0(t)\hat{\boldsymbol{\imath}}_0 + y_0(t)\hat{\boldsymbol{\jmath}}_0 + z_0(t)\hat{\boldsymbol{k}}_0$$

be its position vector with respect to $(0xyz)_0$. Show that the vector expression for the acceleration has the same components as the matrix expression.

Solution. The situation is depicted in Fig. 2-20. The vector expression for the acceleration is given by

$$\boldsymbol{a}_0 = \boldsymbol{\omega}_1 \times (\boldsymbol{\omega}_1 \times \boldsymbol{r}_1) + \boldsymbol{\alpha}_1 \times \boldsymbol{r}_1$$

With $\boldsymbol{\omega}_1 = \dot{\theta}\hat{\boldsymbol{k}}_1$ and $\boldsymbol{\alpha}_1 = \mathbf{0}$, the acceleration is given by

$$\begin{aligned}\boldsymbol{a}_0 &= \left(\dot{\theta}\hat{\boldsymbol{k}}_1\right) \times \left(\left(\dot{\theta}\hat{\boldsymbol{k}}_1\right) \times \boldsymbol{r}_1\right) = \left(\dot{\theta}\hat{\boldsymbol{k}}_1\right) \times \left(-\dot{\theta}y_1\hat{\boldsymbol{\imath}}_1 + \dot{\theta}x_1\hat{\boldsymbol{\jmath}}_1\right) \\ &= -\dot{\theta}^2x_1\hat{\boldsymbol{\imath}}_1 - \dot{\theta}^2y_1\hat{\boldsymbol{\jmath}}_1 \\ &= -\dot{\theta}^2x_1\left(\cos\theta\,\hat{\boldsymbol{\imath}}_0 + \sin\theta\,\hat{\boldsymbol{\jmath}}_0\right) - \dot{\theta}^2y_1\left(-\sin\theta\,\hat{\boldsymbol{\imath}}_0 + \cos\theta\,\hat{\boldsymbol{\jmath}}_0\right) \\ &= \dot{\theta}^2\left[(-x_1\cos\theta + y_1\sin\theta)\hat{\boldsymbol{\imath}}_0 + (-x_1\sin\theta - y_1\cos\theta)\hat{\boldsymbol{\jmath}}_0\right]\end{aligned}$$

We now show that the matrix components are the same.

The rotation matrix is given by

$$\mathbf{A}_1 = \begin{bmatrix} \cos\theta & -\sin\theta & 0 \\ \sin\theta & \cos\theta & 0 \\ 0 & 0 & 1 \end{bmatrix}$$

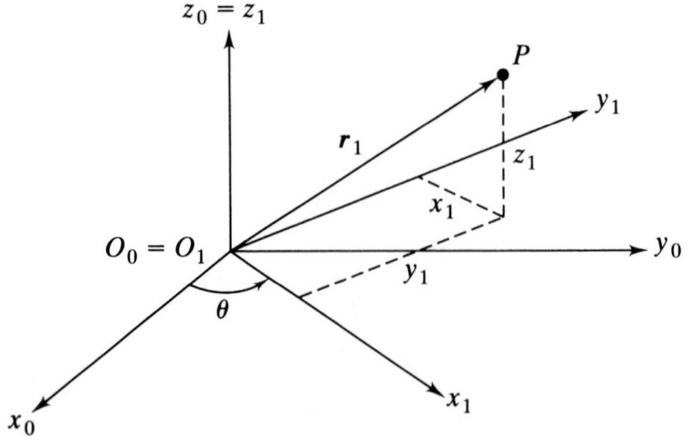

FIGURE 2-20
Rotation about the z_0-axis.

and the absolute acceleration has the components

$$\mathbf{a}_0 = \frac{d^2}{dt^2}\mathbf{A}_1\mathbf{r}_1 = \ddot{\mathbf{A}}_1\mathbf{r}_1$$

We have

$$\dot{\mathbf{A}}_1 = \dot{\theta}\begin{bmatrix} -\sin\theta & -\cos\theta & 0 \\ \cos\theta & -\sin\theta & 0 \\ 0 & 0 & 0 \end{bmatrix}$$

$$\ddot{\mathbf{A}}_1 = \dot{\theta}^2\begin{bmatrix} -\cos\theta & \sin\theta & 0 \\ -\sin\theta & -\cos\theta & 0 \\ 0 & 0 & 0 \end{bmatrix} + \ddot{\theta}\begin{bmatrix} -\sin\theta & -\cos\theta & 0 \\ \cos\theta & -\sin\theta & 0 \\ 0 & 0 & 0 \end{bmatrix}$$

or

$$\mathbf{a}_0 = \dot{\theta}^2\begin{bmatrix} -\cos\theta & \sin\theta & 0 \\ -\sin\theta & -\cos\theta & 0 \\ 0 & 0 & 0 \end{bmatrix}\begin{pmatrix} x_1 \\ y_1 \\ z_1 \end{pmatrix}$$

$$= \dot{\theta}^2\begin{pmatrix} -x_1\cos\theta + y_1\sin\theta \\ -x_1\sin\theta - y_1\cos\theta \\ 0 \end{pmatrix}$$

which has the same components as $\boldsymbol{a}_0$ above.

Remark 2-4. It must be emphasized that the components of the angular velocity generally are not the time derivatives of simple angles unless a suitable succession of rotations is chosen—for example, the Euler angles (see also Exercise 2-17). It is known, however, that $\boldsymbol{\omega}$ is a vector, and from this it follows that angular velocities about different axes may be added vectorially. This latter fact, as well as the numbering scheme for successive reference frames, is illustrated in the next example.

Example 2-8. Shown in Fig. 2-21 is a wheel with radius $b = 20$ cm rotating with constant angular speed $\omega_w = 20$ rad/s (clockwise) relative to the platform, which, in turn, is rotating with constant angular speed $\omega_p = 8$ rad/s (counterclockwise) relative to the ground.

(*a*) Obtain the general expression for the velocity of a point P on the rim of the wheel by using both the rotation matrix and the vector approach.

(*b*) Obtain the general expression for the acceleration by using the vector approach.

(*c*) Obtain numerical values for $\boldsymbol{v}_0$ and $\boldsymbol{a}_0$ when P is vertically above O_0 and the axis of the wheel is aligned with the x_0-axis.

Solution. Suppose we first look at the matrix approach. Note that we now have to deal with separate successive embedded frames rather than the successive rotations of a single coordinate frame.

As always, we take $(0xyz)_0$ to be the base frame; we take $(0xyz)_1$ to be fixed in the platform and $(0xyz)_2$ to be fixed in the wheel. The components of $\boldsymbol{r}_2$ in the

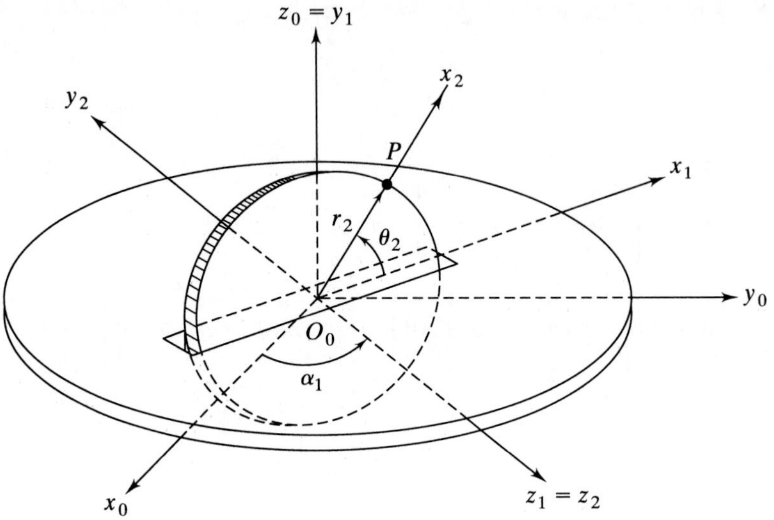

FIGURE 2-21
Wheel within a platform.

$(0xyz)_1$ frame are given by

$$\mathbf{r}_1 = \mathbf{A}_{12}\mathbf{r}_2$$

$$\begin{pmatrix} x_1 \\ y_1 \\ z_1 \end{pmatrix} = \begin{bmatrix} \cos\theta_2 & -\sin\theta_2 & 0 \\ \sin\theta_2 & \cos\theta_2 & 0 \\ 0 & 0 & 1 \end{bmatrix} \begin{pmatrix} b \\ 0 \\ 0 \end{pmatrix}$$

and those of $\boldsymbol{r}_1$ relative to the fixed frame $(0xyz)_0$ by

$$\mathbf{r}_0 = \mathbf{A}_1\mathbf{r}_1$$

$$\begin{pmatrix} x_0 \\ y_0 \\ z_0 \end{pmatrix} = \begin{bmatrix} -\sin\alpha_1 & 0 & \cos\alpha_1 \\ \cos\alpha_1 & 0 & \sin\alpha_1 \\ 0 & 1 & 0 \end{bmatrix} \begin{pmatrix} x_1 \\ y_1 \\ z_1 \end{pmatrix}$$

These may be combined to relate $\mathbf{r}_2$ to $\mathbf{r}_0$ with

$$\mathbf{r}_0 = \mathbf{A}_1\mathbf{r}_1 = \mathbf{A}_1\mathbf{A}_{12}\mathbf{r}_2 = \mathbf{A}_2\mathbf{r}_2$$

or

$$\begin{pmatrix} x_0 \\ y_0 \\ z_0 \end{pmatrix} = \begin{bmatrix} -\sin\alpha_1 & 0 & \cos\alpha_1 \\ \cos\alpha_1 & 0 & \sin\alpha_1 \\ 0 & 1 & 0 \end{bmatrix} \begin{bmatrix} \cos\theta_2 & -\sin\theta_2 & 0 \\ \sin\theta_2 & \cos\theta_2 & 0 \\ 0 & 0 & 1 \end{bmatrix} \begin{pmatrix} b \\ 0 \\ 0 \end{pmatrix}$$

$$= \begin{bmatrix} -\sin\alpha_1\cos\theta_2 & \sin\alpha_1\sin\theta_2 & \cos\alpha_1 \\ \cos\alpha_1\cos\theta_2 & -\cos\alpha_1\sin\theta_2 & \sin\alpha_1 \\ \sin\theta_2 & \cos\theta_2 & 0 \end{bmatrix} \begin{pmatrix} b \\ 0 \\ 0 \end{pmatrix}$$

with the result

$$x_0 = -b \sin \alpha_1 \cos \theta_2$$

$$y_0 = b \cos \alpha_1 \cos \theta_2$$

$$z_0 = b \sin \theta_2$$

Rather than calculating the derivative directly at this point to obtain the velocity, it is instructive to differentiate the matrix $\mathbf{A}_2$ to obtain the result. We have

$$\dot{\mathbf{A}}_2 = \mathbf{A}_1\dot{\mathbf{A}}_{12} + \dot{\mathbf{A}}_1\mathbf{A}_{12}$$

$$= \begin{bmatrix} -\sin \alpha_1 & 0 & \cos \alpha_1 \\ \cos \alpha_1 & 0 & \sin \alpha_1 \\ 0 & 1 & 0 \end{bmatrix} \dot{\theta}_2 \begin{bmatrix} -\sin \theta_2 & -\cos \theta_2 & 0 \\ \cos \theta_2 & -\sin \theta_2 & 0 \\ 0 & 0 & 0 \end{bmatrix}$$

$$+ \dot{\alpha}_1 \begin{bmatrix} -\cos \alpha_1 & 0 & -\sin \alpha_1 \\ -\sin \alpha_1 & 0 & \cos \alpha_1 \\ 0 & 0 & 0 \end{bmatrix} \begin{bmatrix} \cos \theta_2 & -\sin \theta_2 & 0 \\ \sin \theta_2 & \cos \theta_2 & 0 \\ 0 & 0 & 1 \end{bmatrix}$$

$$= \dot{\theta}_2 \begin{bmatrix} \sin \alpha_1 \sin \theta_2 & \sin \alpha_1 \cos \theta_2 & 0 \\ -\cos \alpha_1 \sin \theta_2 & -\cos \alpha_1 \cos \theta_2 & 0 \\ \cos \theta_2 & -\sin \theta_2 & 0 \end{bmatrix}$$

$$+ \dot{\alpha}_1 \begin{bmatrix} -\cos \alpha_1 \cos \theta_2 & \cos \alpha_1 \sin \theta_2 & -\sin \alpha_1 \\ -\sin \alpha_1 \cos \theta_2 & \sin \alpha_1 \sin \theta_2 & \cos \alpha_1 \\ 0 & 0 & 0 \end{bmatrix}$$

As a result, we obtain

$$\mathbf{v}_0 = \dot{\mathbf{r}}_0 = \dot{\mathbf{A}}_2 \mathbf{r}_2$$

$$\begin{pmatrix} \dot{x}_0 \\ \dot{y}_0 \\ \dot{z}_0 \end{pmatrix} = \begin{bmatrix} (\dot{\theta}_2 \sin \alpha_1 \sin \theta_2 - \dot{\alpha}_1 \cos \alpha_1 \cos \theta_2) & (\dot{\theta}_2 \sin \alpha_1 \cos \theta_2 + \dot{\alpha}_1 \cos \alpha_1 \sin \theta_2) & -\dot{\alpha}_1 \sin \alpha_1 \\ (-\dot{\theta}_2 \cos \alpha_1 \sin \theta_2 - \dot{\alpha}_1 \sin \alpha_1 \cos \theta_2) & (-\dot{\theta}_2 \cos \alpha_1 \cos \theta_2 + \dot{\alpha}_1 \sin \alpha_1 \sin \theta_2) & \dot{\alpha}_1 \cos \alpha_1 \\ \dot{\theta}_2 \cos \theta_2 & -\dot{\theta}_2 \sin \theta_2 & 0 \end{bmatrix} \begin{pmatrix} b \\ 0 \\ 0 \end{pmatrix}$$

so that the components are given by

$$\dot{x}_0 = b\left(\dot{\theta}_2 \sin \alpha_1 \sin \theta_2 - \dot{\alpha}_1 \cos \alpha_1 \cos \theta_2\right)$$

$$\dot{y}_0 = -b\left(\dot{\theta}_2 \cos \alpha_1 \sin \theta_2 + \dot{\alpha}_1 \sin \alpha_1 \cos \theta_2\right)$$

$$\dot{z}_0 = b\dot{\theta}_2 \cos \theta_2$$

Again, we now work out the same result using vectors. We know that

$$\boldsymbol{v}_0 = \dot{\boldsymbol{r}}_0 = \boldsymbol{\omega}_2 \times \boldsymbol{r}_2 \tag{2-33}$$

is the absolute velocity as long as $\boldsymbol{\omega}_2$ is the absolute angular velocity of the rotating reference frame. In line with Remark 2-4, all we need to do is to add the angular velocities vectorially. We have one rotation about the z_0-axis,

$$\boldsymbol{\omega}_1 = \dot{\alpha}_1 \hat{\boldsymbol{k}}_0$$

clearly the absolute angular velocity of $(0xyz)_1$, expressed in terms of the $(0xyz)_0$ basis, and

$$\boldsymbol{\omega}_{12} = \dot{\theta}_2 \hat{\boldsymbol{k}}_2$$

the angular velocity of $(0xyz)_2$ relative to $(0xyz)_1$, expressed in terms of the $(0xyz)_2$ basis. The absolute angular velocity of $(0xyz)_2$ is

$$\begin{aligned} \boldsymbol{\omega}_2 &= \boldsymbol{\omega}_1 + \boldsymbol{\omega}_{12} \\ &= \dot{\alpha}_1 \hat{\boldsymbol{k}}_0 + \dot{\theta}_2 \hat{\boldsymbol{k}}_2 \end{aligned}$$

In order to calculate the cross product [see Eq. (2-33)], we need $\boldsymbol{\omega}_2$ in terms of $\hat{\boldsymbol{\imath}}_2$, $\hat{\boldsymbol{\jmath}}_2$, and $\hat{\boldsymbol{k}}_2$. We have

$$\hat{\boldsymbol{k}}_0 = \sin\theta_2\, \hat{\boldsymbol{\imath}}_2 + \cos\theta_2\, \hat{\boldsymbol{\jmath}}_2$$

so that

$$\boldsymbol{\omega}_2 = \dot{\alpha}_1 \sin\theta_2\, \hat{\boldsymbol{\imath}}_2 + \dot{\alpha}_1 \cos\theta_2\, \hat{\boldsymbol{\jmath}}_2 + \dot{\theta}_2 \hat{\boldsymbol{k}}_2$$

The velocity [see Eq. (2-33)] now becomes

$$\begin{aligned} \boldsymbol{v}_0 &= \left(\dot{\alpha}_1 \sin\theta_2\, \hat{\boldsymbol{\imath}}_2 + \dot{\alpha}_1 \cos\theta_2\, \hat{\boldsymbol{\jmath}}_2 + \dot{\theta}_2 \hat{\boldsymbol{k}}_2\right) \times \left(b\hat{\boldsymbol{\imath}}_2\right) \\ &= -\dot{\alpha}_1 b \cos\theta_2\, \hat{\boldsymbol{k}}_2 + b\dot{\theta}\hat{\boldsymbol{\jmath}}_2 \end{aligned}$$

This is a perfectly good end result. However, in order to compare this with the earlier matrix result, we need to express $\boldsymbol{v}_0$ in terms of the basis $(\hat{\boldsymbol{\imath}}\hat{\boldsymbol{\jmath}}\hat{\boldsymbol{k}})_0$. With

$$\begin{aligned} \hat{\boldsymbol{\jmath}}_2 &= -\sin\theta_2\, \hat{\boldsymbol{\imath}}_1 + \cos\theta_2 \hat{\boldsymbol{\jmath}}_1 \\ &= -\sin\theta_2\left(-\sin\alpha_1\, \hat{\boldsymbol{\imath}}_0 + \cos\alpha_1\, \hat{\boldsymbol{\jmath}}_0\right) + \cos\theta_2\, \hat{\boldsymbol{k}}_0 \\ &= \sin\alpha_1 \sin\theta_2\, \hat{\boldsymbol{\imath}}_0 - \cos\alpha_1 \sin\theta_2\, \hat{\boldsymbol{\jmath}}_0 + \cos\theta_2\, \hat{\boldsymbol{k}}_0 \\ \hat{\boldsymbol{k}}_2 &= \cos\alpha_1\, \hat{\boldsymbol{\imath}}_0 + \sin\alpha_1\, \hat{\boldsymbol{\jmath}}_0 \end{aligned}$$

we obtain the final result

$$\begin{aligned} \boldsymbol{v}_0 = &-b\dot{\alpha}_1 \cos\theta_2\left(\cos\alpha_1\, \hat{\boldsymbol{\imath}}_0 + \sin\alpha_1\, \hat{\boldsymbol{\jmath}}_0\right) \\ &+ b\dot{\theta}_2\left(\sin\alpha_1 \sin\theta_2\, \hat{\boldsymbol{\imath}}_0 - \cos\alpha_1 \sin\theta_2\, \hat{\boldsymbol{\jmath}}_0 + \cos\theta_2\, \hat{\boldsymbol{k}}_0\right) \\ = &\left(b\dot{\theta}_2 \sin\alpha_1 \sin\theta_2 - b\dot{\alpha}_1 \cos\alpha_1 \cos\theta_2\right)\hat{\boldsymbol{\imath}}_0 \\ &+\left(-b\dot{\alpha}_1 \sin\alpha_1 \cos\theta_2 - b\dot{\theta}_2 \cos\alpha_1 \sin\theta_2\right)\hat{\boldsymbol{\jmath}}_0 \\ &+ b\dot{\theta}_2 \cos\theta_2\, \hat{\boldsymbol{k}}_0 \end{aligned}$$

We shall calculate the acceleration only in vector form. The standard expression is given by

$$\boldsymbol{a}_0 = \boldsymbol{\omega}_2 \times (\boldsymbol{\omega}_2 \times \boldsymbol{r}_2) + \boldsymbol{\alpha}_2 \times \boldsymbol{r}_2$$

Here we have

$$\begin{aligned}\boldsymbol{\alpha}_2 = \dot{\boldsymbol{\omega}}_2 &= \dot{\alpha}_1\dot{\theta}_2 \cos\theta_2\, \hat{\boldsymbol{\imath}}_2 - \dot{\alpha}_1\dot{\theta}_2 \sin\theta_2\, \hat{\boldsymbol{\jmath}}_2 + 0\hat{\boldsymbol{k}}_2 \\ &= \dot{\alpha}_1\dot{\theta}_2(\cos\theta_2\, \hat{\boldsymbol{\imath}}_2 - \sin\theta_2\, \hat{\boldsymbol{\jmath}}_2)\end{aligned}$$

since $\dot{\theta}_2$ is a constant. Note, specifically, that the components of $\boldsymbol{\omega}_2$ were not simply the derivatives of angles. We now have

$$\begin{aligned}\boldsymbol{a}_0 &= \left(\dot{\alpha}_1 \sin\theta_2\, \hat{\boldsymbol{\imath}}_2 + \dot{\alpha}_1 \cos\theta_2 \hat{\boldsymbol{\jmath}}_2 + \dot{\theta}_2\, \hat{\boldsymbol{k}}_2\right) \times \left(-b\dot{\alpha}_1 \cos\theta_2\, \hat{\boldsymbol{k}}_2 + b\dot{\theta}_2\, \hat{\boldsymbol{\jmath}}_2\right) \\ &\quad + \dot{\alpha}_1\dot{\theta}_2(\cos\theta_2 \hat{\boldsymbol{\imath}}_2 - \sin\theta_2\, \hat{\boldsymbol{\jmath}}_2) \times (b\hat{\boldsymbol{\imath}}_2) \\ &= -\hat{\boldsymbol{\jmath}}_2(-\dot{\alpha}_1^2 b \sin\theta_2 \cos\theta_2) + \hat{\boldsymbol{k}}_2(\dot{\alpha}_1\dot{\theta}_2 b \sin\theta_2) \\ &\quad - \hat{\boldsymbol{\imath}}_2(\dot{\alpha}_1^2 b \cos^2\theta_2) - \hat{\boldsymbol{\imath}}_2\dot{\theta}_2^2 b + \dot{\alpha}_1\dot{\theta}_2 b \sin\theta_2\, \hat{\boldsymbol{k}}_2 \\ &= -(\dot{\alpha}_1^2 b \cos^2\theta_2 + \dot{\theta}_2^2 b)\hat{\boldsymbol{\imath}}_2 + \dot{\alpha}_1^2 b \sin\theta_2 \cos\theta_2\, \hat{\boldsymbol{\jmath}}_2 + 2\dot{\alpha}_1\dot{\theta}_2 b \sin\theta_2\, \hat{\boldsymbol{k}}_2\end{aligned}$$

With

$$\begin{aligned}\hat{\boldsymbol{\imath}}_2 &= \cos\theta_2\, \hat{\boldsymbol{\imath}}_1 + \sin\theta_2\, \hat{\boldsymbol{k}}_1 \\ &= \cos\theta_2(-\sin\alpha_1\, \hat{\boldsymbol{\imath}}_0 + \cos\alpha_1\, \hat{\boldsymbol{\jmath}}_0) + \sin\theta_2\, \hat{\boldsymbol{k}}_0 \\ &= -\sin\alpha_1 \cos\theta_2\, \hat{\boldsymbol{\imath}}_0 + \cos\alpha_1 \cos\theta_2\, \hat{\boldsymbol{\jmath}}_0 + \sin\theta_2\, \hat{\boldsymbol{k}}_0\end{aligned}$$

and with $\hat{\boldsymbol{\jmath}}_2$ and $\hat{\boldsymbol{k}}_2$ as given previously, we obtain

$$\begin{aligned}\boldsymbol{a}_0 &= -(\dot{\alpha}_1^2 b \cos^2\theta_2 + \dot{\theta}_2^2 b)(-\sin\alpha_1 \cos\theta_2\, \hat{\boldsymbol{\imath}}_0 + \cos\alpha_1 \cos\theta_2\, \hat{\boldsymbol{\jmath}}_0 + \sin\theta_2\, \hat{\boldsymbol{k}}_0) \\ &\quad + \dot{\alpha}_1^2 b \sin\theta_2 \cos\theta_2(\sin\alpha_1 \sin\theta_2\, \hat{\boldsymbol{\imath}}_0 - \cos\alpha_1 \sin\theta_2\, \hat{\boldsymbol{\jmath}}_0 + \cos\theta_2\, \hat{\boldsymbol{k}}_0) \\ &\quad + 2\dot{\alpha}_1\dot{\theta}_2 b \sin\theta_2(\cos\alpha_1\, \hat{\boldsymbol{\imath}}_0 + \sin\alpha_1\, \hat{\boldsymbol{\jmath}}_0) \\ &= \left[(\dot{\alpha}_1^2 b \cos^2\theta_2 + \dot{\theta}_2^2 b + \dot{\alpha}_1^2 b \sin^2\theta_2) \sin\alpha_1 \cos\theta_2 + 2\dot{\alpha}_1\dot{\theta}_2 b \sin\theta_2 \cos\alpha_1\right]\hat{\boldsymbol{\imath}}_0 \\ &\quad + \left[(-\dot{\alpha}_1^2 b \cos^2\theta_2 - \dot{\theta}_2^2 b - \dot{\alpha}_1^2 b \sin^2\theta_2) \cos\alpha_1 \cos\theta_2 + 2\dot{\alpha}_1\dot{\theta}_2 b \sin\alpha_1 \sin\theta_2\right]\hat{\boldsymbol{\jmath}}_0 \\ &\quad + \left[(-\dot{\alpha}_1^2 b \cos^2\theta_2 - \dot{\theta}_2^2 b + \dot{\alpha}_1^2 b \cos^2\theta_2) \sin\theta_2\right]\hat{\boldsymbol{k}}_0 \\ &= \left[(\dot{\alpha}_1^2 b + \dot{\theta}_2^2 b) \sin\alpha_1 \cos\theta_2 + 2\dot{\alpha}_1\dot{\theta}_2 b \sin\theta_2 \cos\alpha_1\right]\hat{\boldsymbol{\imath}}_0 \\ &\qquad + \left[-(b)(\dot{\alpha}_1^2 + \dot{\theta}_2^2) \cos\alpha_1 \cos\theta_2 + 2\dot{\alpha}_1\dot{\theta}_2 b \sin\alpha_1 \sin\theta_2\right]\hat{\boldsymbol{\jmath}}_0 \\ &\qquad + \left[-\dot{\theta}_2^2 b \sin\theta_2\right]\hat{\boldsymbol{k}}_0 \\ &= b\left[(\dot{\alpha}_1^2 + \dot{\theta}_2^2) \sin\alpha_1 \cos\theta_2 + 2\dot{\alpha}_1\dot{\theta}_2 \cos\alpha_1 \sin\theta_2\right]\hat{\boldsymbol{\imath}}_0 \\ &\qquad + b\left[-(\dot{\alpha}_1^2 + \dot{\theta}_2^2) \cos\alpha_1 \cos\theta_2 + 2\dot{\alpha}_1\dot{\theta}_2 \sin\alpha_1 \sin\theta_2\right]\hat{\boldsymbol{\jmath}}_0 \\ &\qquad + b\left[-\dot{\theta}_2^2 \sin\theta_2\right]\hat{\boldsymbol{k}}_0\end{aligned}$$

For the numerical results, we now use the following values of the variables:

$$\alpha_1 = 0 \qquad \theta_2 = \frac{\pi}{2} \qquad b = 20 \text{ cm}$$

$$\dot{\alpha}_1 = 8 \text{ rad/s} \qquad \dot{\theta}_2 = -20 \text{ rad/s}$$

The velocity then is

$$v_0 = -20(-20)\hat{j}_0 = 400\hat{j}_0 \text{ cm/s}$$

For the acceleration we have

$$\boldsymbol{a}_0 = (20)(2)(8)(-20)\hat{\imath}_0 + (20)\left[-(-20)^2\right]\hat{\boldsymbol{k}}_0$$

$$= -6400\hat{\imath}_0 - 8000\hat{\boldsymbol{k}}_0 \text{ cm/s}^2$$

2-10 MOTION RELATIVE TO ROTATING REFERENCE FRAMES

Previously, we described the absolute motion of points P which were fixed relative to the body-fixed frame. We now include the possibility of motion of the point P relative to the body-fixed coordinates (e.g., a fly crawling on a moving rigid body).

The basic relationships between the position vectors are the same as those we depicted previously (see Fig. 2-18). The major exception is that we now allow x_1, y_1, and z_1 to vary with the time t; that is, the coordinates of P with respect to $(0xyz)_1$ may now be time dependent.

The matrix equations for the velocity and for the acceleration may be derived in a straightforward manner. We have

$$\mathbf{r}_0(t) = \mathbf{c}_1(t) + \mathbf{A}_1(t)\mathbf{r}_1(t)$$

resulting in the absolute velocity

$$\mathbf{v}_0(t) = \dot{\mathbf{c}}_1(t) + \mathbf{A}_1(t)\dot{\mathbf{r}}_1(t) + \dot{\mathbf{A}}_1(t)\mathbf{r}_1(t) \tag{2-34}$$

and in the absolute acceleration

$$\mathbf{a}_0(t) = \ddot{\mathbf{c}}_1 + \mathbf{A}_1(t)\ddot{\mathbf{r}}_1(t) + 2\dot{\mathbf{A}}_1(t)\dot{\mathbf{r}}_1(t) + \ddot{\mathbf{A}}_1(t)\mathbf{r}_1(t) \tag{2-35}$$

Note that one has the following correspondence for $\dot{\mathbf{r}}_1(t)$ and $\ddot{\mathbf{r}}_1(t)$—namely, the components of these column vectors are the same as those of

$$\left(\frac{d\boldsymbol{r}_1}{dt}(t)\right)_1 \qquad \text{and} \qquad \left(\frac{d^2\boldsymbol{r}_1}{dt^2}(t)\right)_1$$

respectively.

The vectorial approach again is more geometrically descriptive. The position vector is

$$\boldsymbol{r}_0(t) = \boldsymbol{c}_1(t) + \boldsymbol{r}_1(t)$$

$$= \boldsymbol{c}_1(t) + x_1(t)\hat{\imath}_1(t) + y_1(t)\hat{j}_1(t) + z_1(t)\hat{\boldsymbol{k}}_1(t)$$

Before proceeding with the differentiation, we note that $\boldsymbol{r}_1(t)$ now qualifies as one of the vectors mentioned in Sec. 2-8. Thus, with $\boldsymbol{\omega}_1(t)$ as the absolute angular velocity of the rotating reference frame (or, equivalently, of the rigid body $\mathscr{B}$), we calculate the velocity as

$$\boldsymbol{v}_0 = \dot{\boldsymbol{c}}_1 + (\dot{\boldsymbol{r}}_1)_1 + \boldsymbol{\omega}_1 \times \boldsymbol{r}_1 \tag{2-36}$$

Note now that the vector $(\dot{\boldsymbol{r}}_1)_1$ again qualifies, so that the acceleration becomes

$$\begin{aligned} \boldsymbol{a}_0 &= \ddot{\boldsymbol{c}}_1 + (\ddot{\boldsymbol{r}}_1)_1 + \boldsymbol{\omega}_1 \times (\dot{\boldsymbol{r}}_1)_1 + \boldsymbol{\alpha}_1 \times \boldsymbol{r}_1 + \boldsymbol{\omega}_1 \times ((\dot{\boldsymbol{r}}_1)_1 + \boldsymbol{\omega}_1 \times \boldsymbol{r}_1) \\ &= \ddot{\boldsymbol{c}}_1 + (\ddot{\boldsymbol{r}}_1)_1 + 2\boldsymbol{\omega}_1 \times (\dot{\boldsymbol{r}}_1)_1 + \boldsymbol{\omega}_1 \times (\boldsymbol{\omega}_1 \times \boldsymbol{r}_1) + \boldsymbol{\alpha}_1 \times \boldsymbol{r}_1 \end{aligned} \tag{2-37}$$

where $\boldsymbol{\alpha}_1 = \dot{\boldsymbol{\omega}}_1$ is the absolute angular acceleration of $(0xyz)_1$. We illustrate the meaning of these terms by the following relative motion example.

Example 2-9. At the instant depicted in Fig. 2-22, the armature of the motor is rotating at a constant rate of 30 rpm in the ccw direction as shown. The motor itself is mounted on a platform which is rotating about the z-axis with angular speed $\Omega = 10$ rad/sec ccw and angular acceleration $\dot{\Omega} = 2$ rad/sec^2 ccw. The center of the motor is 3 ft from the axis of rotation of the platform, and the armature has a $\frac{1}{2}$-ft radius. Determine the acceleration of a point P on the rim of the armature at the instant when $\theta = 0°$. Assume that the $(0xyz)_1$ frame is embedded in the platform.

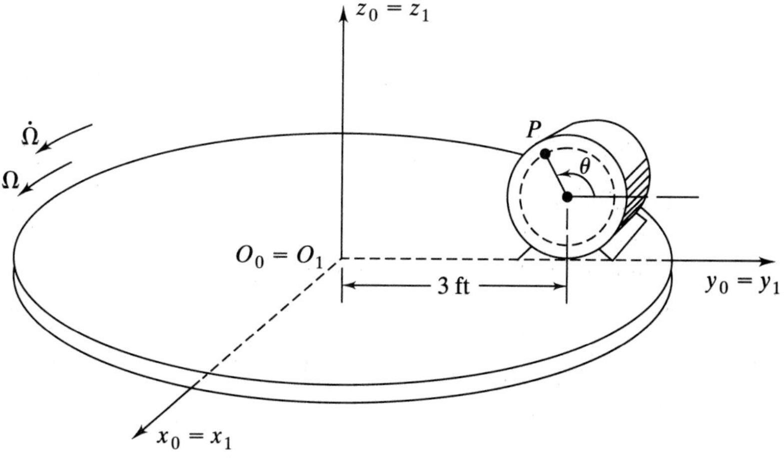

FIGURE 2-22
Motor mounted on a rotating platform.

Solution. We shall have need of the relative velocity and acceleration of the $(0xyz)_1$ frame, rotating with the platform. With

$$\boldsymbol{r}_1 = \left(3 + \frac{1}{2}\cos\theta\right)\hat{\jmath}_1 + \left(\frac{1}{2} + \frac{1}{2}\sin\theta\right)\hat{\boldsymbol{k}}_1$$

these derivatives are given by

$$(\dot{\boldsymbol{r}}_1)_1 = -\frac{1}{2}\dot{\theta}\sin\theta\,\hat{\jmath}_1 + \frac{1}{2}\dot{\theta}\cos\theta\,\hat{\boldsymbol{k}}_1$$

and

$$(\ddot{\boldsymbol{r}}_1)_1 = +\frac{1}{2}\dot{\theta}^2\left(-\cos\theta\,\hat{\jmath}_1 - \sin\theta\,\hat{\boldsymbol{k}}_1\right) + \frac{1}{2}\ddot{\theta}\left(-\sin\theta\,\hat{\jmath}_1 + \cos\theta\,\hat{\boldsymbol{k}}_1\right)$$

The given data are

$$\dot{\theta} = \frac{30 \times 2\pi}{60}\frac{\text{rad}}{\text{sec}} = \pi\frac{\text{rad}}{\text{sec}}$$

$$\omega_1 = \Omega\hat{\boldsymbol{k}}_1 = 10\hat{\boldsymbol{k}}_1 \text{ rad/sec}$$

$$\alpha_1 = \dot{\Omega}\hat{\boldsymbol{k}}_1 = 2\hat{\boldsymbol{k}}_1 \text{ rad/sec}^2$$

We now calculate all the quantities needed in the acceleration for the instant in question:

$$\boldsymbol{r}_1 = \left(3 + \frac{1}{2}\right)\hat{\jmath}_1 + \frac{1}{2}\hat{\boldsymbol{k}}_1 = 3.5\hat{\jmath}_1 + 0.5\hat{\boldsymbol{k}}_1$$

$$(\dot{\boldsymbol{r}}_1)_1 = \frac{1}{2}\pi\hat{\boldsymbol{k}}_1 \qquad \boldsymbol{\omega}_1 \times \boldsymbol{r}_1 = \left(10\hat{\boldsymbol{k}}_1\right) \times \left(3.5\hat{\jmath}_1 + 0.5\hat{\boldsymbol{k}}_1\right) = -35\hat{\imath}_1$$

$$(\ddot{\boldsymbol{r}}_1)_1 = -\frac{1}{2}\pi^2\hat{\jmath}_1 \qquad \boldsymbol{\omega}_1 \times (\boldsymbol{\omega}_1 \times \boldsymbol{r}_1) = \left(10\hat{\boldsymbol{k}}_1\right) \times (-35\hat{\imath}_1) = -350\hat{\jmath}_1$$

$$\boldsymbol{\alpha}_1 \times \boldsymbol{r}_1 = \left(2\hat{\boldsymbol{k}}_1\right) \times \left(3.5\hat{\jmath}_1 + 0.5\hat{\boldsymbol{k}}_1\right) = -7\hat{\imath}_1$$

$$2\boldsymbol{\omega}_1 \times (\dot{\boldsymbol{r}}_1)_1 = 2\left(10\hat{\boldsymbol{k}}_1\right) \times \left(\frac{1}{2}\pi\hat{\boldsymbol{k}}_1\right) = \boldsymbol{0}$$

The instantaneous absolute acceleration of the point P thus is given by

$$\begin{aligned}\boldsymbol{a}_0 &= \ddot{\boldsymbol{c}}_0 + (\ddot{\boldsymbol{r}}_1)_1 + 2\boldsymbol{\omega}_1 \times (\dot{\boldsymbol{r}}_1)_1 + \boldsymbol{\omega}_1 \times (\boldsymbol{\omega}_1 \times \boldsymbol{r}_1) + \boldsymbol{\alpha}_1 \times \boldsymbol{r}_1 \\ &= \boldsymbol{0} + \left(-\frac{\pi^2}{2}\hat{\jmath}_1\right) + \boldsymbol{0} + (-350\hat{\jmath}_1) + (-7\hat{\imath}_1) \\ &= -7\hat{\imath}_1 - 354.93\hat{\jmath}_1 \text{ ft/sec}^2\end{aligned}$$

2-11 HOMOGENEOUS COORDINATES

Homogeneous coordinates in themselves are nothing new. They were first used within the present context in the treatment of mechanisms. They are now used extensively in the manipulation of image matrices for computer vision and in the theoretical treatment of rigid body motion; but they are somewhat less useful in computational applications. This description of motion is an embedding of three-dimensional rigid body motion in $\mathbb{R}^4$, where the homogeneous coordinates make possible the representation of both translation and rotation as a matrix multiplication.

For an understanding of the origin of the concept, it is useful to precede the main discussion with some motivation for the term *homogeneous coordinates*. The basic definition is that of a homogeneous function, another concept introduced by Leonhard Euler.

Definition 2-4 Homogeneous function. A function $f(\cdot)$: $(\mathscr{D} \subset \mathbb{R}^n) \to \mathbb{R}$ of n variables x_i is homogeneous of degree r on $\mathscr{D}$ iff for every $\lambda > 0$,

$$f(\lambda x_1, \lambda x_2, \ldots, \lambda x_n) = \lambda^r f(x_1, x_2, \ldots, x_n)$$

Example 2-10. Show that the function $f(x, y) = x^2 + y^2$ is homogeneous of degree 2.

Solution. We need to show that

$$f(\lambda x, \lambda y) = \lambda^2 f(x, y)$$

We have

$$f(\lambda x, \lambda y) = \lambda^2 x^2 + \lambda^2 y^2 = \lambda^2(x^2 + y^2) = \lambda^2 f(x, y)$$

Definition 2-5 Homogeneous equation. Let $f(\cdot)$: $(\mathscr{D} \subset \mathbb{R}^n) \to \mathbb{R}$ be a function of n variables defined on the domain $\mathscr{D}$. Then the equation

$$f(x_1, x_2, \ldots, x_n) = 0$$

is homogeneous of degree r on $\mathscr{D}$ iff $f(x_1, x_2, \ldots, x_n)$ is homogeneous of degree r on $\mathscr{D}$.

Example 2-11. Is the equation

$$x^2 + y^2 = a^2$$

homogeneous of degree 2? Explain.

Solution. Let

$$f(x, y) = x^2 + y^2 - a^2 = 0$$

Then

$$f(\lambda x, \lambda y) = (\lambda x)^2 + (\lambda y)^2 - a^2 = \lambda^2(x^2 + y^2) - a^2 \neq \lambda^2 f(x, y)$$

and we conclude that the equation is not homogeneous of degree 2.

Definition 2-6 Homogeneous coordinates. Let $\boldsymbol{x} = (x_1, \ldots, x_n)$ be the Cartesian coordinates of a point in $\mathbb{R}^n$. Then any set of $(n + 1)$ numbers $(y_1, y_2, \ldots, y_n, y_{n+1})$, $y_{n+1} \neq 0$, for which

$$\frac{y_1}{y_{n+1}} = x_1, \frac{y_2}{y_{n+1}} = x_2, \ldots, \frac{y_n}{y_{n+1}} = x_n$$

is called a set of homogeneous coordinates for the point $\boldsymbol{x}$.

The connection with the preceding discussion of homogeneity is established by noting that *any* algebraic equation in $x_1, \ldots, x_n$, when transformed to a set of homogeneous coordinates, becomes a homogeneous equation in the homogeneous coordinates.

Example 2-12. Transform the equation

$$f(x, y) = x^3 + y = 0$$

to homogeneous coordinates and determine the degree of homogeneity of the transformed equation.

Solution. Introduce

$$x = \frac{y_1}{y_3} \qquad y = \frac{y_2}{y_3} \qquad y_3 \neq 0$$

with the result that

$$\frac{y_1^3}{y_3^3} + \frac{y_2}{y_3} = 0 \quad \Rightarrow \quad y_1^3 + y_2 y_3^2 = 0$$

Define the new function in the homogeneous variables by

$$\bar{f}(y_1, y_2, y_3) = f\left(\frac{y_1}{y_3}, \frac{y_2}{y_3}\right)$$

Then this new function satisfies

$$\begin{aligned} \bar{f}(\lambda y_1, \lambda y_2, \lambda y_3) &= (\lambda y_1)^3 + (\lambda y_2)(\lambda y_3)^2 \\ &= \lambda^3\left[y_1^3 + y_2 y_3^2 \right] \\ &= \lambda^3 \bar{f}(y_1, y_2, y_3) \end{aligned}$$

so that the new function is homogeneous of degree 3.

Generally, Denavit and Hartenberg[1] are credited with the introduction of homogeneous coordinates in the analysis of mechanisms. They, in turn, built on the incomplete results obtained by Reuleaux[2]. For another synopsis of the subject, the student is directed to Lee[3], and a continuation of the subject at a more advanced level may be found in Paul.[4]

We now take a closer look at the use of homogeneous coordinates in the description of rigid body motion. In particular, we shall always set the scale factor $y_{n+1} = 1$ so that a point P in $\mathbb{R}^3$ and its homogeneous coordinates are related by

$$\begin{pmatrix} x \\ y \\ z \end{pmatrix} \Leftrightarrow \begin{pmatrix} x \\ y \\ z \\ 1 \end{pmatrix}$$

physical $\mathbb{R}^3$ homogeneous $\mathbb{R}^4$

Remark 2-5. Note that, in general, any constant multiple of the homogeneous coordinates is another set of homogeneous coordinates for the physical point. We have forced a unique relationship by insisting on a 1 as the fourth entry. In view of this unique relationship, the use of $\mathbf{r}_1$ for both representations should cause no confusion, since the dimension will be apparent from the context.

Example 2-13. Given the homogeneous vector $\mathbf{p}_1 = (2 \quad 0 \quad -1 \quad 5)^T$, deduce the corresponding physical vector.

Solution. Multiplication by $1/\sigma = 1/5$ and dropping the fourth coordinate yields

$$\mathbf{r}_1 = \left(\frac{2}{5} \quad 0 \quad -\frac{1}{5}\right)^T$$

Our aim is to describe previous physical motions in homogeneous space. As it turns out, scaling, perspective, rotation, and translation can all be combined within a single homogeneous transformation matrix $\mathbf{H}$ partitioned as follows:

$$\mathbf{H} = \left[\begin{array}{c:c} \mathbf{A}_{3\times3} & \mathbf{c}_{3\times1} \\ \hdashline \mathbf{p}_{1\times3} & \sigma_{1\times1} \end{array}\right] = \left[\begin{array}{l:l} \text{Rotation} & \text{Translation} \\ \text{matrix} & \text{vector} \\ \hdashline \text{Perspective} & \text{Scaling} \\ \text{transformation} & \text{factor} \end{array}\right] \tag{2-38}$$

Within the present context, the perspective transformation is taken to be $\mathbf{p} = (0 \quad 0 \quad 0)$ and the scaling factor $\sigma = 1$. The matrix $\mathbf{H}_1$ is used to carry out coordinate transformations in $\mathbb{R}^4$ in the form

$$\mathbf{r}_0 = \mathbf{H}_1 \mathbf{r}_1$$

where $\mathbf{r}_0$ and $\mathbf{r}_1$ now clearly are our standard (fourth coordinate equal to 1) homogeneous representations of the corresponding three-dimensional vectors.

Example 2-14. Express rigid body translation

$$\mathbf{r}_0 = \mathbf{c}_1 + \mathbf{r}_1$$

by a suitable homogeneous transformation matrix $\mathbf{H}_1$ on $\mathbb{R}^4$.

Solution. In view of the general form of $\mathbf{H}$, we first note that "no rotation" is equivalent to

$$\mathbf{A} = \begin{bmatrix} 1 & 0 & 0 \\ 0 & 1 & 0 \\ 0 & 0 & 1 \end{bmatrix} = \mathbf{E}$$

and "no translation" to $\mathbf{c}_1 = (0 \quad 0 \quad 0)^T$. Here, however, the "translation quadrant" of the homogeneous matrix is

$$\mathbf{c}_1 = (a_1 \quad b_1 \quad c_1)^T$$

where we note again that the components of $\mathbf{c}_1$ have been taken in $(0xyz)_0$.

Consequently, the appropriate translation matrix is given by

$$\mathbf{H}_1 = \left[\begin{array}{ccc:c} 1 & 0 & 0 & a_1 \\ 0 & 1 & 0 & b_1 \\ 0 & 0 & 1 & c_1 \\ \hdashline 0 & 0 & 0 & 1 \end{array}\right]$$

A simple check yields

$$\begin{pmatrix} x_0 \\ y_0 \\ z_0 \\ 1 \end{pmatrix} = \begin{bmatrix} 1 & 0 & 0 & a_1 \\ 0 & 1 & 0 & b_1 \\ 0 & 0 & 1 & c_1 \\ 0 & 0 & 0 & 1 \end{bmatrix} \begin{pmatrix} x_1 \\ y_1 \\ z_1 \\ 1 \end{pmatrix} = \begin{pmatrix} x_1 + a_1 \\ y_1 + b_1 \\ z_1 + c_1 \\ 1 \end{pmatrix}$$

the homogeneous representations of the corresponding physical vectors.

Example 2-15. Express the rigid body rotation

$$\mathbf{r}_0 = \mathbf{A}_1 \mathbf{r}_1$$

by means of a suitable homogeneous transformation matrix $\mathbf{H}_1$ on $\mathbb{R}^4$.

Solution. With zero translation the homogeneous rotation matrix is given by

$$\mathbf{H}_1 = \left[\begin{array}{ccc:c} a_{x_1} & b_{x_1} & c_{x_1} & 0 \\ a_{y_1} & b_{y_1} & c_{y_1} & 0 \\ a_{z_1} & b_{z_1} & c_{z_1} & 0 \\ \hdashline 0 & 0 & 0 & 1 \end{array}\right]$$

with the result

$$\mathbf{r}_0 = \mathbf{H}_1 \mathbf{r}_1$$

$$\begin{pmatrix} x_0 \\ y_0 \\ z_0 \\ 1 \end{pmatrix} = \begin{bmatrix} a_{x_1} & b_{x_1} & c_{x_1} & 0 \\ a_{y_1} & b_{y_1} & c_{y_1} & 0 \\ a_{z_1} & b_{z_1} & c_{z_1} & 0 \\ 0 & 0 & 0 & 1 \end{bmatrix} \begin{pmatrix} x_1 \\ y_1 \\ z_1 \\ 1 \end{pmatrix} = \begin{pmatrix} x_1 a_{x_1} + y_1 b_{x_1} + z_1 c_{x_1} \\ x_1 a_{y_1} + y_1 b_{y_1} + z_1 c_{y_1} \\ x_1 a_{z_1} + y_1 b_{z_1} + z_1 c_{z_1} \\ 1 \end{pmatrix}$$

The following definition for homogeneous rigid body motion is now apparent.

Definition 2-7 Homogeneous rigid motion. A physical rigid body motion

$$\mathbf{r}_0(t) = \mathbf{c}_1(t) + \mathbf{A}_1(t)\mathbf{r}_1$$

has the homogeneous representation

$$\mathbf{r}_0(t) = \mathbf{H}_1(t)\mathbf{r}_1 \tag{2-39}$$

where
$$\mathbf{H}_1(t) = \begin{bmatrix} a_{x_1}(t) & b_{x_1}(t) & c_{x_1}(t) & a_1(t) \\ a_{y_1}(t) & b_{y_1}(t) & c_{y_1}(t) & b_1(t) \\ a_{z_1}(t) & b_{z_1}(t) & c_{z_1}(t) & c_1(t) \\ 0 & 0 & 0 & 1 \end{bmatrix}$$

Equation (2-39) is referred to as *homogeneous rigid motion.*

Remark 2-6. Note that, as before, rotation and translation do not commute, and it must therefore be kept in mind that the standard homogeneous rigid motion is composed of a translation followed by a rotation. We have

$$\mathbf{r}_0 = \mathbf{H}_{\text{trans}}\mathbf{r}_{01} \qquad \mathbf{H}_{\text{trans}} = \left[\begin{array}{c:c} \mathbf{E} & \mathbf{c}_1 \\ \hdashline \mathbf{0} & 1 \end{array}\right]$$

and
$$\mathbf{r}_{01} = \mathbf{H}_{\text{rot}}\mathbf{r}_1 \qquad \mathbf{H}_{\text{rot}} = \left[\begin{array}{c:c} \mathbf{A}_1 & \mathbf{0} \\ \hdashline \mathbf{0} & 1 \end{array}\right]$$

resulting in

$$\mathbf{H} = \mathbf{H}_{\text{trans}}\mathbf{H}_{\text{rot}} = \begin{bmatrix} 1 & 0 & 0 & a_1 \\ 0 & 1 & 0 & b_1 \\ 0 & 0 & 1 & c_1 \\ 0 & 0 & 0 & 1 \end{bmatrix} \begin{bmatrix} a_{x_1} & b_{x_1} & c_{x_1} & 0 \\ a_{y_1} & b_{y_1} & c_{y_1} & 0 \\ a_{z_1} & b_{z_1} & c_{z_1} & 0 \\ 0 & 0 & 0 & 1 \end{bmatrix} = \begin{bmatrix} a_{x_1} & b_{x_1} & c_{x_1} & a_1 \\ a_{y_1} & b_{y_1} & c_{y_1} & b_1 \\ a_{z_1} & b_{z_1} & c_{z_1} & c_1 \\ 0 & 0 & 0 & 1 \end{bmatrix}$$

Example 2-16. Consider again the simple two-dimensional rigid body displacement given in Example 2-2. Construct the corresponding homogeneous rigid displacement.

Solution. The corresponding homogeneous rigid displacement matrix is given by

$$\mathbf{H}_1 = \begin{bmatrix} C\theta & -S\theta & 0 & a_1 \\ S\theta & C\theta & 0 & b_1 \\ 0 & 0 & 1 & 0 \\ 0 & 0 & 0 & 1 \end{bmatrix}$$

resulting in

$$\mathbf{r}_0 = \mathbf{H}_1\mathbf{r}_1$$

$$\begin{pmatrix} x_0 \\ y_0 \\ z_0 \\ 1 \end{pmatrix} = \begin{bmatrix} C\theta & -S\theta & 0 & a_1 \\ S\theta & C\theta & 0 & b_1 \\ 0 & 0 & 1 & 0 \\ 0 & 0 & 0 & 1 \end{bmatrix} \begin{pmatrix} x_1 \\ y_1 \\ z_1 \\ 1 \end{pmatrix} = \begin{pmatrix} a_1 + x_1C\theta - y_1S\theta \\ b_1 + x_1S\theta + y_1C\theta \\ z_1 \\ 1 \end{pmatrix}$$

as expected.

We are now in a position to introduce the *basic homogeneous rotation matrices*

$$\mathbf{A}_{ij}(x,\alpha) = \begin{bmatrix} 1 & 0 & 0 & 0 \\ 0 & C\alpha & -S\alpha & 0 \\ 0 & S\alpha & C\alpha & 0 \\ 0 & 0 & 0 & 1 \end{bmatrix} \qquad \mathbf{A}_{ij}(y,\phi) = \begin{bmatrix} C\phi & 0 & S\phi & 0 \\ 0 & 1 & 0 & 0 \\ -S\phi & 0 & C\phi & 0 \\ 0 & 0 & 0 & 1 \end{bmatrix}$$

$$\mathbf{A}_{ij}(z,\theta) = \begin{bmatrix} C\theta & -S\theta & 0 & 0 \\ S\theta & C\theta & 0 & 0 \\ 0 & 0 & 1 & 0 \\ 0 & 0 & 0 & 1 \end{bmatrix}$$

The use of the same notation should cause no confusion, since the dimension of the matrix will be apparent from the context.

The *basic homogeneous translation matrix* is

$$\mathbf{T}_{ij}(a_{ij}, b_{ij}, c_{ij}) = \begin{bmatrix} 1 & 0 & 0 & a_{ij} \\ 0 & 1 & 0 & b_{ij} \\ 0 & 0 & 1 & c_{ij} \\ 0 & 0 & 0 & 1 \end{bmatrix}$$

locating O_j with respect to O_i.

With these rudiments of homogeneous matrix manipulation, the student should find the literature on robot kinematics accessible.

Remark 2-7. In practice, it may not be useful to replace matrix addition by matrix multiplication. In fact, in the estimation of operational steps, it is usual to omit addition and subtraction in the count. From a theoretical point of view, the homogeneous coordinates do unify the approach, since a single mathematical operation allows the treatment of several different effects.

2-12 RUDIMENTARY EXAMPLES IN A ROBOTICS CONTEXT

Prior to treating actual robotics applications, it is useful to consider some rudimentary examples that illustrate these applications for two-degree-of freedom manipulators where exact solutions may still be obtained.

Since much of what robots are designed to do is tracking—that is, motion along a prescribed path with a particular speed and acceleration—we shall deal with several such problems and related ones, such as interception and path interpolation problems. The first example deals with a two-dimensional polar manipulator whose end effector is to move along a prescribed path; the next, with a simple spray-painting arrangement. Further examples include conditions for path interception, illustrated by the need of timing in taking objects from a conveyor, and the exact solution for the two-dimensional anthropomorphic manipulator.

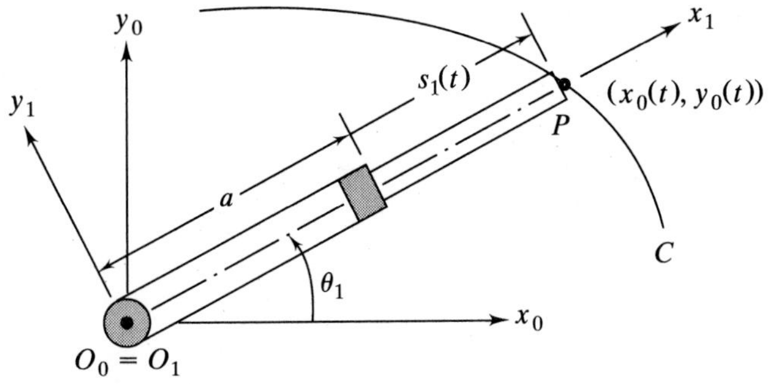

FIGURE 2-23
Polar manipulator

Example 2-17. Consider the two-dimensional manipulator shown in Fig. 2-23. Suppose that the end effector P is to move along a curve C whose parametric equations are $x_0(t)$ and $y_0(t)$.

(*a*) Obtain closed form expressions for the robot variables $\theta_1(t)$ and $s_1(t)$.

(*b*) Assume that the end effector P is to move along the straight line $y_0(t) = h$ with constant speed v to the right. Determine the robot variables for this particular case. Assume $x_0(t) = 0$ at $t = 0$.

Solution

(*a*) The position vector of P in $(0xyz)_1$ is

$$\begin{aligned} \boldsymbol{r}_1(t) &= (a + s_1(t))\hat{\imath}_1(t) \\ &= (a + s_1(t))(\cos\theta_1(t)\hat{\imath}_0 + \sin\theta_1(t)\hat{\jmath}_0) \end{aligned}$$

resulting in

$$x_0(t) = (a + s_1(t))\cos\theta_1(t)$$

$$y_0(t) = (a + s_1(t))\sin\theta_1(t)$$

These must now be solved for the robot variables $s_1(t)$ and $\theta_1(t)$ in terms of the world variables $x_0(t)$ and $y_0(t)$. This is nothing more than the inverse transformation for polar coordinates. Thus

$$s_1(t) = \sqrt{x_0^2(t) + y_0^2(t)} - a$$

$$\theta_1(t) = \text{Arctan}\frac{y_0(t)}{x_0(t)}$$

where $x_0(t)$ and $y_0(t)$ are the parametric equations of C.

(*b*) The world position vector is

$$\boldsymbol{r}_0(t) = vt\hat{\imath}_0 + h\hat{\jmath}_0$$

Consequently, the robot variables are given by

$$s_1(t) = \sqrt{(vt)^2 + h^2} - a$$

$$\theta_1(t) = \text{Arctan}\frac{h}{vt}$$

Remark 2-8. Note that the robot in the preceding example is a two-axis robot with two degrees of freedom (one rotational, one translational).

Example 2-18. Suppose that the end effector of the robot in Example 2-17 is a spray gun whose spray nozzle must move with constant speed v parallel to the x_0-axis as illustrated in Fig. 2-24. Determine the corresponding robot variables θ_1, θ_2, and s_1.

Solution. We simply note that $(0xyz)_2$ is a translating reference frame, so that the absolute angular velocity of the frame is $\boldsymbol{\omega}_2(t) = (\dot{\theta}_1(t) + \dot{\theta}_2(t))\hat{\boldsymbol{k}}_2 = \mathbf{0}$, resulting in the kinematic constraint

$$\dot{\theta}_2(t) = -\dot{\theta}_1(t)$$

or

$$\theta_2(t) = -\theta_1(t)$$

between the robot variables. Consequently, the velocity of P is the same as that

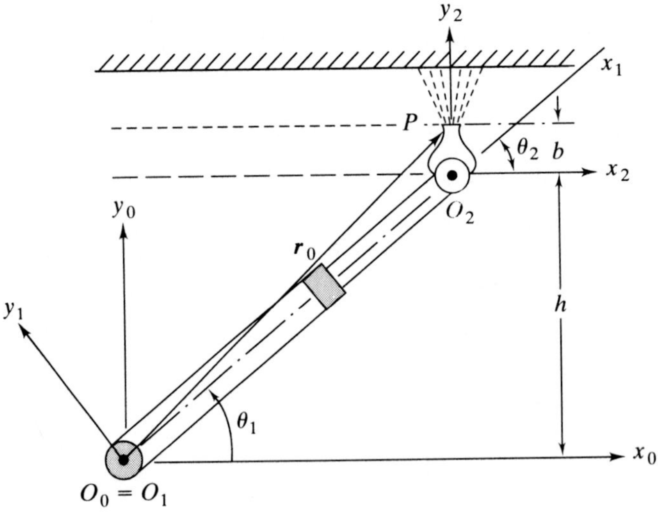

FIGURE 2-24
Spraying operation

of the point O_2, and it thus follows that the robot variables for this motion are given by

$$s_1(t) = \sqrt{(vt)^2 + h^2} - a$$

$$\theta_1(t) = \text{Arctan}\frac{h}{vt}$$

$$\theta_2(t) = -\text{Arctan}\frac{h}{vt}$$

with $s_1(t)$ and $\theta_1(t)$ the same as in the preceding example.

Remark 2-9. The robot in this example is a three-axis, three-degree-of-freedom robot. The three axes (and degrees of freedom) are described by the variables θ_1, θ_2 and s_1.

Another frequently occurring problem concerns the kinematics that must e programmed into the robot if it is to grasp a moving object. This situation ccurs, for example, when an object is to be grasped off a conveyor belt.

The general situation is depicted in Fig. 2-25. As before, $\boldsymbol{r}_0(t)$ denotes the osition vector of the end effector relative to the fixed $(0xyz)_0$ frame. We shall se $\boldsymbol{s}_0(t)$ as the corresponding position vector of the moving object.

The condition for interception—that is, the coincidence of end effector E .nd object P—requires that we have

$$\boldsymbol{r}_0(t_1) = \boldsymbol{s}_0(t_1)$$

Hence there must exist a common time t_1 for which both effector and object occupy the same point. Consider the following specific example.

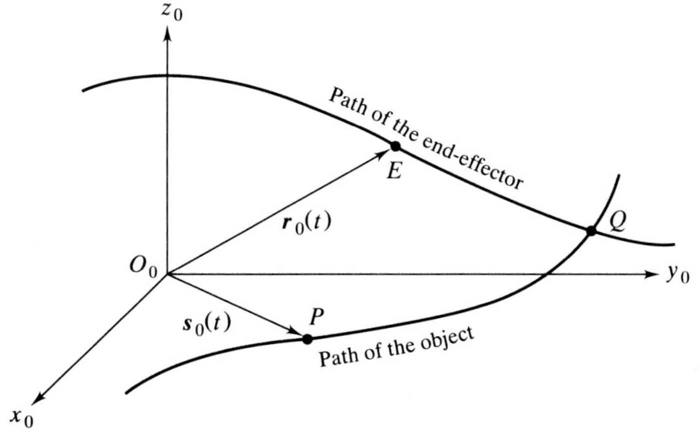

FIGURE 2-25
Interception problem

Example 2-19. Suppose the object P is to be picked off the conveyor belt at the point Q by the end effector E of the two-dimensional manipulator shown in Fig. 2-26. Assume that E is in the position E_0 when P is at P_0 and that the conveyor belt is moving with constant velocity $\boldsymbol{v} = v\hat{\boldsymbol{j}}_0$. The effector is to be guided from rest along a straight line EQ in such a way that P and E arrive at Q at the same instant, and the effector is again at rest at Q. Determine suitable robot variables $s_1(t)$ and $\theta_1(t)$ to accomplish this task.

Solution. The position of the end effector E is given by

$$\boldsymbol{r}_0(t) = x_0(t)\hat{\boldsymbol{i}}_0 + h\hat{\boldsymbol{j}}_0$$

The position of the point P is specified by

$$\boldsymbol{s}_0(t) = k\hat{\boldsymbol{i}}_0 + vt\hat{\boldsymbol{j}}_0$$

Our task is to obtain an $x_0(t)$ in such a way that

$$\boldsymbol{r}_0(t_1) = x(t_1)\hat{\boldsymbol{i}}_0 + h\hat{\boldsymbol{j}}_0 = k\hat{\boldsymbol{i}}_0 + vt_1\hat{\boldsymbol{j}}_0$$

implying

$$h = vt_1 \qquad \text{or} \qquad t_1 = \frac{h}{v}$$

and

$$x_0(t_1) = x\left(\frac{h}{v}\right) = k$$

Clearly, there exist an infinite number of possibilities for accomplishing this task. There are four conditions to be satisfied by $x_0(t)$—namely:

$$x_0(0) = 0 \qquad v_0(0) = 0$$

$$x_0\left(\frac{h}{v}\right) = k \qquad v_0\left(\frac{h}{v}\right) = 0$$

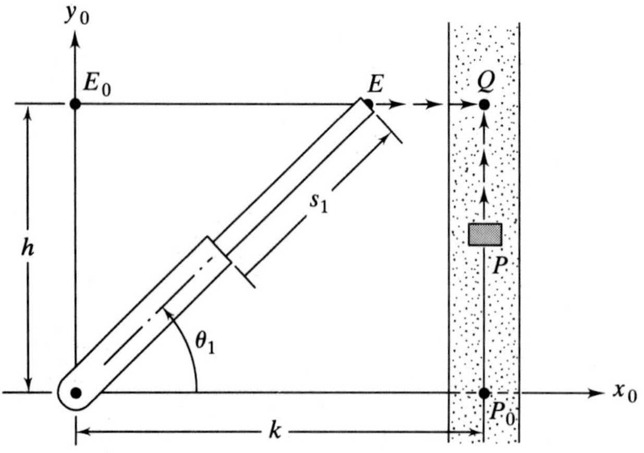

FIGURE 2-26
Interception of objects on a conveyor

We shall take the most obvious approach—namely, we set up $x_0(t)$ in the form

$$x_0(t) = at^3 + bt^2 + ct + d$$

and determine the constants. We have

$$v_0(0) = c = 0$$

$$v_0\left(\frac{h}{v}\right) = 3a\left(\frac{h}{v}\right)^2 + 2b\left(\frac{h}{v}\right) = 0 \quad \Rightarrow \quad 3a\left(\frac{h}{v}\right) + 2b = 0$$

along with

$$x_0(0) = d = 0$$

$$x_0\left(\frac{h}{v}\right) = a\left(\frac{h}{v}\right)^3 + b\left(\frac{h}{v}\right)^2 = k \quad \Rightarrow \quad a + b\left(\frac{v}{h}\right) = k\left(\frac{v}{h}\right)^3$$

The simultaneous solution for a and b yields

$$a = -2k\left(\frac{v}{h}\right)^3 \qquad \text{and} \qquad b = 3k\left(\frac{v}{h}\right)^2$$

Hence

$$x_0(t) = -2k\left(\frac{v}{h}\right)^3 t^3 + 3k\left(\frac{v}{h}\right)^2 t^2$$

$$= k\left(\frac{v}{h}\right)^2 t^2\left(3 - 2\left(\frac{v}{h}\right)t\right)$$

From the general results of Example 2-17, it then follows that the robot variables are given by

$$s_1(t) = \sqrt{\left[k\left(\frac{v}{h}\right)^2 t^2\left(3 - 2\left(\frac{v}{h}\right)t\right)\right]^2 + h^2} - a$$

$$\theta_1(t) = \operatorname{Arctan}\frac{h}{k\left(\frac{v}{h}\right)^2 t^2\left(3 - 2\left(\frac{v}{h}\right)t\right)}$$

Example 2-20 The two-arm revolute manipulator. This is another simple example, where the robot variables can be obtained in terms of the world variables explicitly. Consider the two-bar linkage in the sketch (Fig. 2-27) with robot variables θ_1 and θ_2 and suppose that the endpoint P is to trace a curve C whose parametric equations are $(x_0(t), y_0(t))$.

(*a*) Obtain the robot variables θ_1 and θ_2 in terms of $(x_0(t), y_0(t))$ and the manipulator dimensions if the curve is located in the first quadrant.

(*b*) Determine the work envelope of the robot if $0 \le \theta_1 \le \pi/2$ and $0 \le \theta_2 \le \pi$. That is, determine the set of points that may be reached by the point P. Assume $L_2 < L_1$.

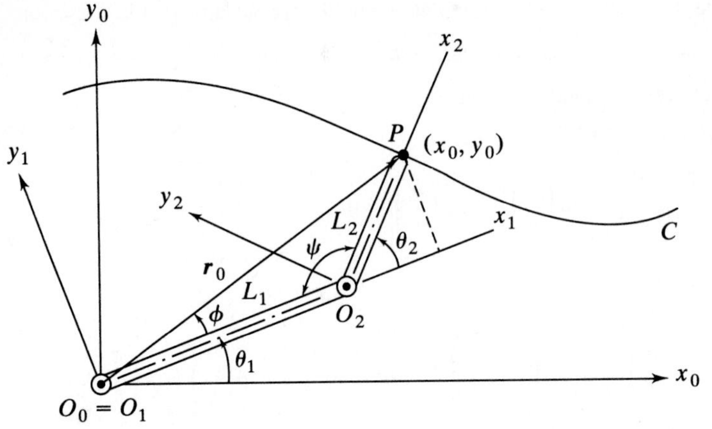

FIGURE 2-27
Two-arm revolute manipulator

Solution

(a) The law of cosines applied to O_1O_2P yields

$$r_0^2 = L_1^2 + L_2^2 - 2L_1L_2\cos\psi$$
$$= L_1^2 + L_2^2 + 2L_1L_2\cos\theta_2$$

and hence

$$\cos\theta_2 = \frac{r_0^2 - L_1^2 - L_2^2}{2L_1L_2}$$

where $r_0^2 = x_0^2 + y_0^2$. Furthermore, we clearly have

$$\sin\phi = \frac{L_2}{r_0}\sin\theta_2$$

$$= \frac{L_2}{r_0}\sqrt{1 - \left(\frac{r_0^2 - L_1^2 - L_2^2}{2L_1L_2}\right)^2}$$

Finally,

$$\tan(\phi + \theta_1) = \frac{y_0}{x_0}$$

from which we deduce

$$\theta_1 = \tan^{-1}\frac{y_0}{x_0} - \sin^{-1}\frac{L_2}{r_0}\sqrt{1 - \left(\frac{r_0^2 - L_1^2 - L_2^2}{2L_1L_2}\right)^2}$$

(b) With the assumption $L_2 < L_1$ we have the work envelope indicated in Fig. 2-28.

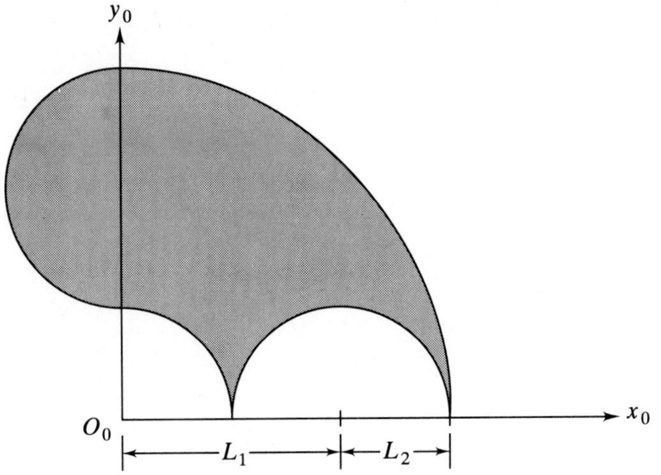

FIGURE 2-28
Work envelope of the two-arm manipulator

Remark 2-10. The robot is a two-axis, two-degree-of-freedom manipulator. The two axes are $(0xy)_1$ and $(0xy)_2$, and the degrees of freedom are expressed by the two robot variables θ_1 and θ_2.

Example 2-21. Consider the two-dimensional manipulator in Fig. 2-29. The base frame is $(0xyz)_0$. The frame $(0xyz)_1$ is embedded in the manipulator, and the arrows in the sketch indicate the possible motions for the manipulator and gripper. The length of the manipulator arm is $L = 17$ in. At some instant $a = 5$ in, $\dot{a} = 4$ in/sec (the arm is *retracting* at a constant rate), $d = 2$ in, $\dot{d} = 3$ in/sec (the gripper is *opening* at a constant rate), $\theta = 90°$ and the manipulator is rotating with constant angular speed $\dot{\theta} = 3$ rad/sec. For this instant, calculate the following quantities:

(*a*) Write the unit vectors $\hat{\imath}_0$, $\hat{\jmath}_0$, and $\hat{k}_0$ in terms of $\hat{\imath}_1$, $\hat{\jmath}_1$, and $\hat{k}_1$.
(*b*) Obtain the homogeneous transformation matrix $\mathbf{H}_1$ for which $\mathbf{r}_0 = \mathbf{H}_1\mathbf{r}_1$.
(*c*) Determine the absolute velocity of the point P in terms of $\hat{\imath}_0$, $\hat{\jmath}_0$, and $\hat{k}_0$.
(*d*) Determine the absolute acceleration of the point P in terms of $\hat{\imath}_0$, $\hat{\jmath}_0$, and $\hat{k}_0$.

Solution. In this example virtually all of the kinematics learned to date come into play.

(*a*) For the indicated position the unit vectors are obviously related by

$$\hat{\imath}_0 = -\hat{\jmath}_1 \qquad \hat{\jmath}_0 = \hat{\imath}_1 \qquad \hat{k}_0 = \hat{k}_1$$

(*b*) Recall that the physical rigid body motion

$$\mathbf{r}_0(t) = \mathbf{c}_1(t) + \mathbf{A}_1(t)\mathbf{r}_1$$

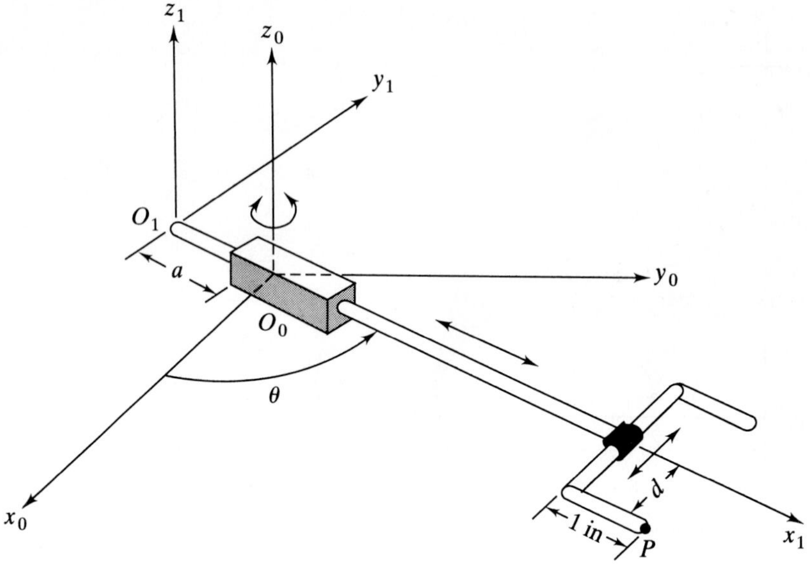

FIGURE 2-29
A two-dimensional manipulator

has the homogeneous representation

$$\mathbf{r}_0(t) = \mathbf{H}_1(t)\mathbf{r}_1(t)$$

where
$$\mathbf{H}_1(t) = \begin{bmatrix} \mathbf{A}_1(t) & \vdots & \mathbf{c}_1 \\ \cdots & \cdots & \cdots \\ \mathbf{0} & \vdots & 1 \end{bmatrix}$$

For the present situation

$$\boldsymbol{c}_1 = b_0\hat{\boldsymbol{j}}_0 = -5\hat{\boldsymbol{j}}_0$$

and the rotation is a rotation about the z-axis, a basic rotation with rotation matrix

$$\mathbf{A}_1(t) = \mathbf{A}_{01}(z,\theta) = \begin{bmatrix} C\theta & -S\theta & 0 \\ S\theta & C\theta & 0 \\ 0 & 0 & 1 \end{bmatrix}_{\theta=90^\circ} = \begin{bmatrix} 0 & -1 & 0 \\ 1 & 0 & 0 \\ 0 & 0 & 1 \end{bmatrix}$$

Consequently, the homogeneous transformation matrix is

$$\mathbf{H}_1 = \begin{bmatrix} 0 & -1 & 0 & 0 \\ 1 & 0 & 0 & -5 \\ 0 & 0 & 1 & 0 \\ 0 & 0 & 0 & 1 \end{bmatrix}$$

(*c*) The general expression for the velocity (including motion relative to a rotating reference frame) is

$$\boldsymbol{v}_0 = \dot{\boldsymbol{c}}_1 + \left(\frac{d\boldsymbol{r}_1}{dt}\right)_1 + \boldsymbol{\omega}_1 \times \boldsymbol{r}_1$$

At a specified instant we may use any convenient basis. We shall use the 0-basis for the remainder. The velocity of O_1 (radial plus θ-component) is given by

$$\dot{\boldsymbol{c}}_1 = \left[\dot{r}\hat{\boldsymbol{e}}_r + r\dot{\theta}\hat{\boldsymbol{e}}_\theta\right] = -4\hat{\boldsymbol{j}}_0 + 15\hat{\boldsymbol{\imath}}_0$$

The motion relative to the moving reference frame is

$$\left(\frac{d\boldsymbol{r}_1}{dt}\right)_1 = 3\hat{\boldsymbol{\imath}}_0$$

The angular velocity of the moving reference frame is

$$\boldsymbol{\omega}_1 = \dot{\theta}\hat{\boldsymbol{k}}_1 = 3\hat{\boldsymbol{k}}_0$$

so that the rigid body motion component is given by

$$\boldsymbol{\omega}_1 \times \boldsymbol{r}_1 = \left(3\hat{\boldsymbol{k}}_0\right) \times \left(2\hat{\boldsymbol{\imath}}_0 + 18\hat{\boldsymbol{j}}_0\right) = 6\hat{\boldsymbol{j}}_0 - 54\hat{\boldsymbol{\imath}}_0$$

(Note carefully that $\boldsymbol{r}_1$ is the position vector of P with respect to O_1.) The final result is

$$\begin{aligned}\boldsymbol{v}_0 &= (15 + 3 - 54)\hat{\boldsymbol{\imath}}_0 + (-4 + 6)\hat{\boldsymbol{j}}_0 \\ &= -36\hat{\boldsymbol{\imath}}_0 + 2\hat{\boldsymbol{j}}_0 \text{ in/sec}\end{aligned}$$

(*d*) The general expression for the acceleration is

$$\begin{aligned}\boldsymbol{a}_0 &= \ddot{\boldsymbol{c}}_1 + \left(\frac{d^2\boldsymbol{r}_1}{dt^2}\right)_1 + 2\boldsymbol{\omega}_1 \times \left(\frac{d\boldsymbol{r}_1}{dt}\right)_1 + \boldsymbol{\omega}_1 \times (\boldsymbol{\omega}_1 \times \boldsymbol{r}_1) + \boldsymbol{\alpha}_1 \times \boldsymbol{r}_1 \\ &= \ddot{\boldsymbol{c}}_1 + 2\boldsymbol{\omega}_1 \times \left(\frac{d\boldsymbol{r}_1}{dt}\right)_1 + \boldsymbol{\omega}_1 \times (\boldsymbol{\omega}_1 \times \boldsymbol{r}_1)\end{aligned}$$

For the acceleration of the point O_1, we have a centripetal component as well as the Coreolis component

$$\begin{aligned}\ddot{\boldsymbol{c}}_1 &= \left[(\ddot{r} - r\dot{\theta}^2)\hat{\boldsymbol{e}}_r + (2\dot{r}\dot{\theta} + r\ddot{\theta})\hat{\boldsymbol{e}}_\theta\right] \\ &= 5(3)^2\hat{\boldsymbol{j}}_0 + 2(4)(3)\hat{\boldsymbol{\imath}}_0 = 24\hat{\boldsymbol{\imath}}_0 + 45\hat{\boldsymbol{j}}_0\end{aligned}$$

(Note that $\dot{r}$ is positive here since $\hat{\boldsymbol{e}}_r$ points away from O_0 in the direction of $\dot{a}$.) The Coreolis part of the total acceleration is

$$2\boldsymbol{\omega}_1 \times \left(\frac{d\boldsymbol{r}_1}{dt}\right)_1 = 2\left(3\hat{\boldsymbol{k}}_0\right) \times (3\hat{\boldsymbol{\imath}}_0) = 18\hat{\boldsymbol{j}}_0$$

The rigid body motion component is

$$\boldsymbol{\omega}_1 \times (\boldsymbol{\omega}_1 \times \boldsymbol{r}_1) = \left(3\hat{\boldsymbol{k}}_0\right) \times \left(-54\hat{\boldsymbol{\imath}}_0 + 6\hat{\boldsymbol{j}}_0\right) = -18\hat{\boldsymbol{\imath}}_0 - 162\hat{\boldsymbol{j}}_0$$

The final expression for the acceleration is

$$\begin{aligned}\boldsymbol{a}_0 &= (24 - 18)\hat{\boldsymbol{\imath}}_0 + (45 + 18 - 162)\hat{\boldsymbol{j}}_0 \\ &= 6\hat{\boldsymbol{\imath}}_0 - 99\hat{\boldsymbol{j}}_0 \text{ in/sec}^2\end{aligned}$$

2-13 NOTATION AND TERMINOLOGY

$(0xyz)$	world reference frame with coordinates (x, y, z)
$(0xyz)_0$	base reference frame with coordinates (x_0, y_0, z_0)
$(0xyz)_i$	ith moving reference frame, $i \geq 1$, with coordinates (x_i, y_i, z_i)
$(\hat{\imath}\hat{\jmath}\hat{k})_i$	orthonormal right-handed basis of the ith reference frame, $i \geq 0$
$\boldsymbol{r}_0, \boldsymbol{v}_0, \boldsymbol{a}_0$	position, velocity, and acceleration vectors for a point P with respect to the fixed frame $(0xyz)_0$; absolute position, velocity, and acceleration
$\boldsymbol{c}_{ij}$	position of O_j relative to O_i
$\boldsymbol{c}_i$	position of O_i relative to O_0
$\boldsymbol{r}_i, (\frac{d\boldsymbol{r}_i}{dt})_i, (\frac{d^2\boldsymbol{r}_i}{dt^2})_i$	position, velocity, and acceleration vectors for a point P relative to $(0xyz)_i$; relative position, velocity, and acceleration
$\boldsymbol{\omega}_i$	angular velocity of the $(0xyz)_i$ frame with respect to the fixed base frame $(0xyz)_0$; absolute angular velocity
$\boldsymbol{\omega}_{ij}$	angular velocity of the jth reference frame relative to the jth, $i < j$
$\mathbf{A}_i$	rotation matrix for $(0xyz)_i$ relative to $(0xyz)_0$; the absolute rotation matrix
$\mathbf{A}_{ij}$	rotation matrix for $(0xyz)_j$ relative to $(0xyz)_i$, $i < j$
$\mathbf{A}_{ij}(x, \alpha)$	rotation matrix for a positive (counterclockwise in accordance with the right-hand rule) rotation of the frame $(0xyz)_j$ about the x-axis of the frame $(0xyz)_i$ by an amount α
$\mathbf{A}_{ij}(y, \phi)$	same for the frame $(0xyz)_j$ about the y-axis of the frame $(0xyz)_i$ by an amount ϕ
$\mathbf{A}_{ij}(z, \theta)$	same for the frame $(0xyz)_j$ about the z-axis of the frame $(0xyz)_i$ by an amount θ

EXERCISES

2-1. A container for waste materials is dumped by the hydraulically actuated linkage shown in Fig. E2-1. If the piston rod starts from rest in the position indicated and has an acceleration of 0.5 m/s^2 in the direction shown, compute the initial angular acceleration of the container.

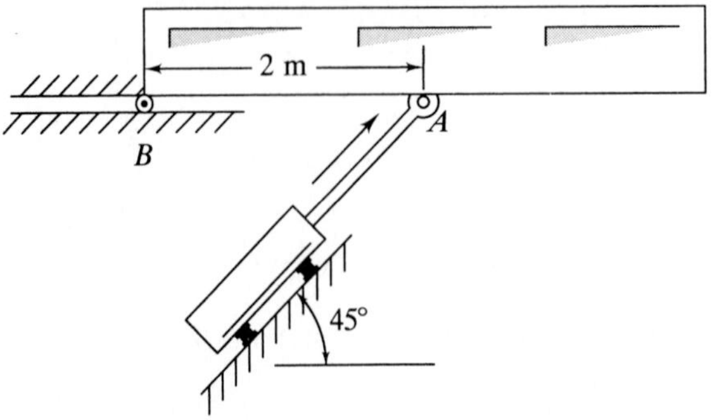

FIGURE E2-1

2-2. Assume that the piston rod of the dumping device of Exercise 2-1 has a velocity of 300 mm/s in the direction of the arrow as point A passes through the horizontal through B. If A has an acceleration of 40 mm/s^2 in the same direction, determine the corresponding angular acceleration of the container and the magnitude of the acceleration of B.

2-3. The piston is inclined at a 45° angle and it has a velocity of 80 mm/s in the direction shown in Fig. E2-3. The bar OA is horizontal. Calculate the angular velocities and angular accelerations of both bars and the acceleration of the point A for this instant.

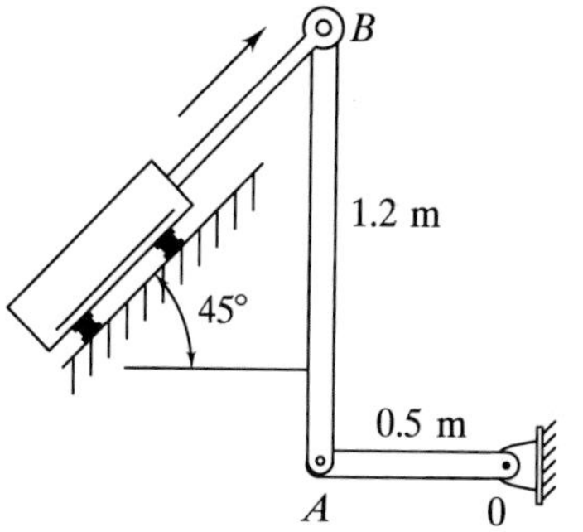

FIGURE E2-3

2-4. Each of the 4-kg balls is mounted on the frame of negligible mass and is rotating freely at a speed of 90 rpm about the vertical with $\theta = 60°$. If the force F on the vertical control rod is increased so that the frame rotates with $\theta = 30°$, determine the new rotational speed Ω and the work W done by F. Point O on the rotating collar remains fixed (see Fig. E2-4).

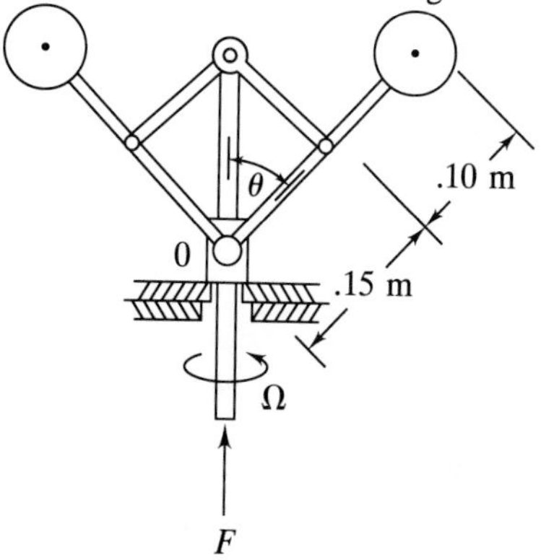

FIGURE E2-4

2-5. The polar manipulator in Fig. E2-5 has an offset moveable arm DE which can translate with respect to the cylinder C. At the instant shown the manipulator is rotating about O with angular velocity $\omega = 2$ rad/sec and an angular acceleration

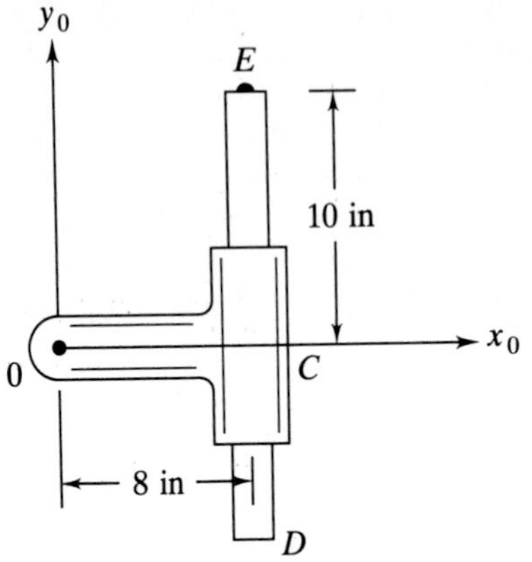

FIGURE E2-5

of $\alpha = 1$ rad/sec^2. The end effector E is moving upward with a constant speed of 15 in/sec relative to the cylinder C. Calculate the absolute velocity and acceleration of the point E at this instant.

2-6. Assume a clockwise rotation to be positive. Determine the points $\mathbf{q}_1$, $\mathbf{r}_1$, and $\mathbf{s}_1$ into which the points

$$\mathbf{q}_0 = (3 \quad 1)^T \qquad \mathbf{r}_0 = (-1 \quad 5)^T \qquad \mathbf{s}_0 = (-3 \quad -1)^T$$

are transformed by a *point transformation* about the origin equal to rotations: (a) 45°, (b) $-60°$, and (c) 180°. Sketch your results for $\mathbf{r}_0$ in each case. Assume plane transformations.

2-7. Let the coordinate axes (x_1, y_1) be rotated through an angle of 60° in the counterclockwise direction and let $\mathbf{q}_1$, $\mathbf{r}_1$, and $\mathbf{s}_1$ be the points $(2\sqrt{3} \quad -4)^T$, $(\sqrt{3} \quad 0)^T$, and $(0 \quad -2\sqrt{3})^T$, respectively, as located with respect to $(0xy)_1$. Determine the corresponding coordinates of $\mathbf{q}_0$, $\mathbf{r}_0$, and $\mathbf{s}_0$ with respect to the base frame $(0xy)_0$. Assume plane transformations.

2-8. This exercise serves as a brief review of the solution of simultaneous equations in connection with coordinate transformations.

(a) Suppose we have the linear transformation

$$\begin{pmatrix} x \\ y \end{pmatrix} = \begin{bmatrix} a_{11} & a_{12} \\ a_{21} & a_{22} \end{bmatrix} \begin{pmatrix} u \\ v \end{pmatrix}$$

Solve for u and v in terms of x and y and state necessary and sufficient conditions for the validity of your solution. Is your solution one to one? Are there any excluded values of the variables?

(b) Suppose now that you have the nonlinear transformation

$$\begin{pmatrix} x \\ y \end{pmatrix} = \begin{bmatrix} a_{11} & a_{12} \\ a_{21} & a_{22} \end{bmatrix} \begin{pmatrix} u^2 \\ v^2 \end{pmatrix}$$

Solve for u and v in terms of x and y. Can you provide similar guarantees to those in part (a)? Consider the specific solution for $u(x, y)$ for $\mathbf{A} = \begin{bmatrix} 2 & -1 \\ -2 & 3 \end{bmatrix}$.

Determine the region in the x, y-plane for which your solution exists and calculate the values of u corresponding to $(1, 1)$.

2-9. This exercise provides a review of partial differentiation.

(*a*) Consider the transformation equations

$$u^2 + v^2 = x$$

$$u^3 + v^3 = 3x + 2$$

Suppose that x is the independent variable, with u and v as dependent variables. Calculate du/dx and dv/dx without solving explicitly for u and v in terms of x.

(*b*) Suppose a transformation has the form

$$2u + v^2 = 3x^2 + y$$

$$u^3 - 2v = 2y - x$$

Take x and y to be independent variables and calculate $\partial u/\partial x$ by using implicit differentiation as before.

2-10. In matrix form, the inner product of two $n \times 1$ column matrices $\mathbf{a}$ and $\mathbf{b}$ is defined by $\mathbf{a}^T\mathbf{b}$. Show that premultiplication by an orthogonal $n \times n$ matrix $\mathbf{Q}$ preserves inner products; that is, show that

$$(\mathbf{Qa})^T(\mathbf{Qb}) = \mathbf{a}^T\mathbf{b}$$

2-11. Suppose we define the length of a column matrix $\mathbf{r} = (x \quad y \quad z)^T$ by $\|\mathbf{r}\| = \sqrt{x^2 + y^2 + z^2}$. Show that the premultiplication of $\mathbf{r}$ by an orthogonal 3×3 matrix $\mathbf{Q}$ preserves this length; that is, show that

$$\|\mathbf{Qr}\| = \|\mathbf{r}\|$$

2-12. In Example 2-9 calculate the velocity and the acceleration of the point P for $\theta = 30°$ and $\theta = 90°$.

2-13. Consider the general point transformation consisting of rotation and translation. Show by example that these operations generally do not commute. That is, a given rotation $\mathbf{A}$ followed by a translation $\mathbf{c}_0$ and a translation $\mathbf{c}_0$ followed by a rotation $\mathbf{A}$ do not yield the same final point.

2-14. (*a*) Show by example that successive rotations do not commute.

(*b*) Do translations commute? Explain.

2-15. Consider again Example 2-8. Calculate the general expression for the velocity and acceleration of the point P using only one moving reference frame, $(0xyz)_1$, embedded in the platform. Check your answer by using the specific point and values in the example. Use only the vector approach.

2-16. Pose and solve two problems on any of the preceding material. Your grade will be based on originality, clarity of the problem statement, correctness, and completeness, in that order.

2-17. (*The Euler angles*) See Fig. E2-17. Let the $(0xyz)_1$ frame be embedded in a rigid body $\mathscr{B}$. Here its final position with respect to $(0xyz)_0$ is attained by the three successive rotations indicated. The corresponding angles ϕ, θ, and ψ are called the *Euler angles*. As shown the first rotation is an amount ϕ about the z_0-axis, the second an amount θ about the x_{11}-axis, and the third an amount ψ about the

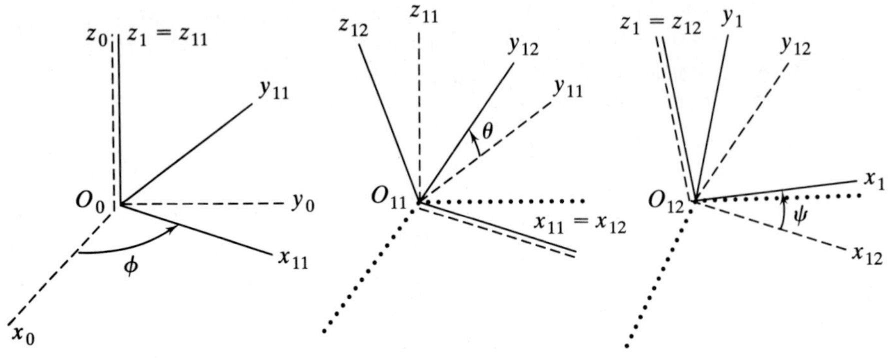

FIGURE E2-17

z_{12}-axis. The solid lines represent successive positions of the $(0xyz)_1$ frame denoted by $(0xyz)_{1i}$. The preceding position in each case is indicated by dashed lines.

(*a*) Determine the individual rotation matrices for the three relative rotations.

(*b*) Determine the resultant rotation matrix which relates the final position of $(0xyz)_1$ to its coordinates with respect to the base frame.

(*c*) Prove that this resultant rotation matrix is orthogonal. Note that there is an algebraically less cumbersome way to prove this.

(*d*) Note that the angular velocity of the $(0xyz)$ frame is

$$\boldsymbol{\omega}_1 = \dot{\phi}\hat{\boldsymbol{k}}_0 + \dot{\theta}\hat{\boldsymbol{\imath}}_{11} + \dot{\psi}\hat{\boldsymbol{k}}_1$$

Write $\boldsymbol{\omega}_1$ in terms of the bases $(\hat{\boldsymbol{\imath}}\hat{\boldsymbol{\jmath}}\hat{\boldsymbol{k}})_0$ and $(\hat{\boldsymbol{\imath}}\hat{\boldsymbol{\jmath}}\hat{\boldsymbol{k}})_1$.

2-18. Show that for two matrices $\mathbf{A}(t)$ and $\mathbf{B}(t)$ one has

$$\frac{d}{dt}(\mathbf{A}(t)\mathbf{B}(t)) = \mathbf{A}(t)\frac{d\mathbf{B}}{dt}(t) + \frac{d\mathbf{A}}{dt}(t)\mathbf{B}(t)$$

where the derivative of a matrix is obtained by differentiating the components of the matrix.

2-19. Four successive positions of a rigid body are shown in Fig. E2-19. Suppose a reference frame $(0yz)_1$ is embedded in the body as shown by the dashed lines. Write the rotation matrices that will take the body from position (1) to (2) to (3) to (4). Show that the successive applications correspond to a single rotation matrix and calculate the matrix. Check your result by calculating the coordinates of the point (2, 1, 0) in $(0xyz)_1$ with respect to $(0xyz)_0$.

2-20. Consider again Example 2-17. Suppose the point P is to move on the parabola (Fig. E2-20)

$$y = 4 - x^2$$

in such a way that it begins from rest at P_0 and comes to rest again at P_1 after 2 s. All of the dimensions are given in meters. The acceleration is not to exceed 12 m/s^2. Obtain analytical expressions for the robot variables $\theta_1(t)$ and $s_1(t)$. Be sure to check your restrictions.

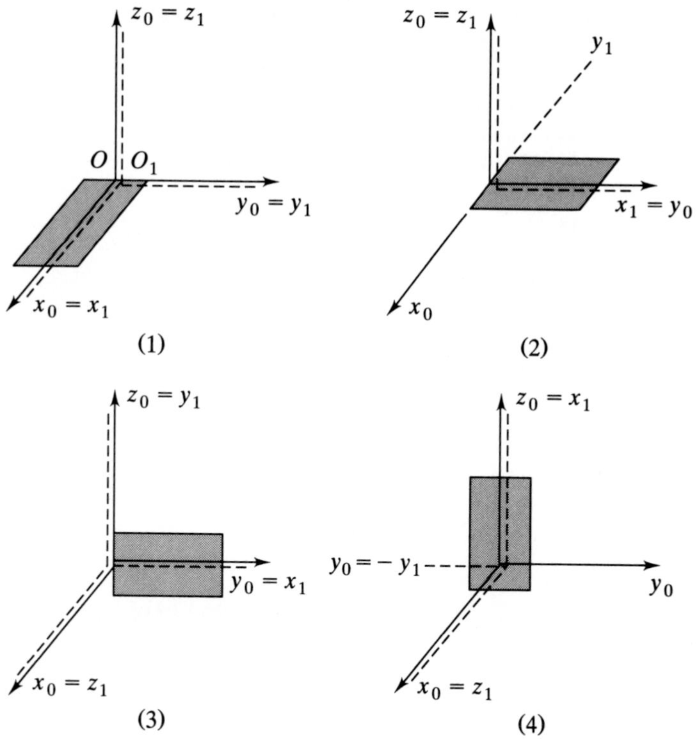

FIGURE E2-19

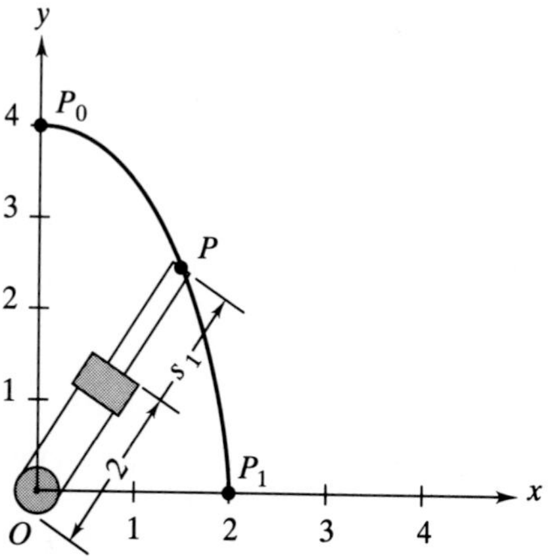

FIGURE E2-20

2-21. Suppose the two-dimensional Cartesian manipulator in Fig. E2-21 is to be programmed in such a way that the end effector E will move along the indicated line with constant tangential velocity $\dot{s}(t) = v_0$. Assume that the motion is to begin at $(x_0, y_0) = (3, 0)$ for $t = 0$ and terminate at $(x_0, y_0) = (0, 2)$ for $t = t_1$.
(*a*) Determine the $x_0(t)$ and $y_0(t)$ that will yield this kind of motion.
(*b*) Determine the time $t = t_1$ at which the manipulator should be shut off.

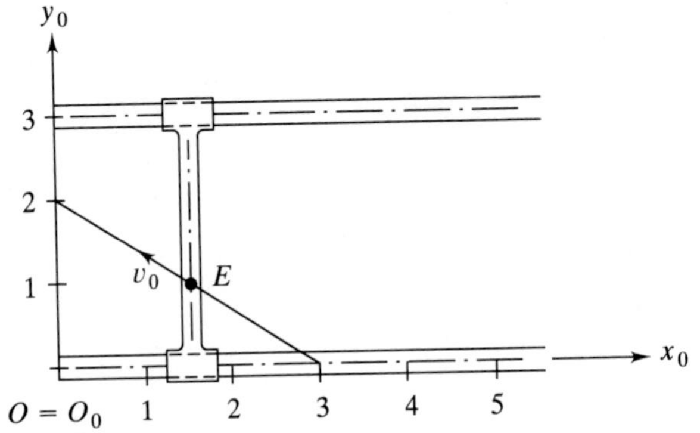

FIGURE E2-21

2-22. Show that if $\mathbf{A}$ is a 3×3 orthogonal matrix, then the homogeneous transformation matrix

$$\mathbf{H} = \left[\begin{array}{ccc:c} & \mathbf{A} & & 0 \\ & & & 0 \\ & & & 0 \\ \hdashline 0 & 0 & 0 & 1 \end{array}\right]$$

is also orthogonal.

2-23. Obtain the inverse matrix for the homogeneous translation matrix $\mathbf{T}(a_0, b_0, c_0)$ and for the homogeneous combined translation and rotation matrix $\mathbf{H}$ with zero perspective terms and scalar factor $\sigma = 1$.

2-24. Consider the two-axis, two-dimensional manipulator in Fig. E2-24. The world path the arm is to follow is a straight line described by

$$y = mx + b$$

where m and b are constants. Suppose the point P is to move along this path with speed $v(t)$. Derive expressions for the angular speeds $\dot{\theta}_1$ and $\dot{\theta}_2$ in terms of $v(t)$, L, m, and the angles θ_1 and θ_2. Use both the vector and the matrix approaches to derive these results. [Observe that this is a set of simultaneous nonlinear differential equations which would have to be solved for $\theta_1(t)$ and $\theta_2(t)$ in order to properly guide the robot along the given path.]

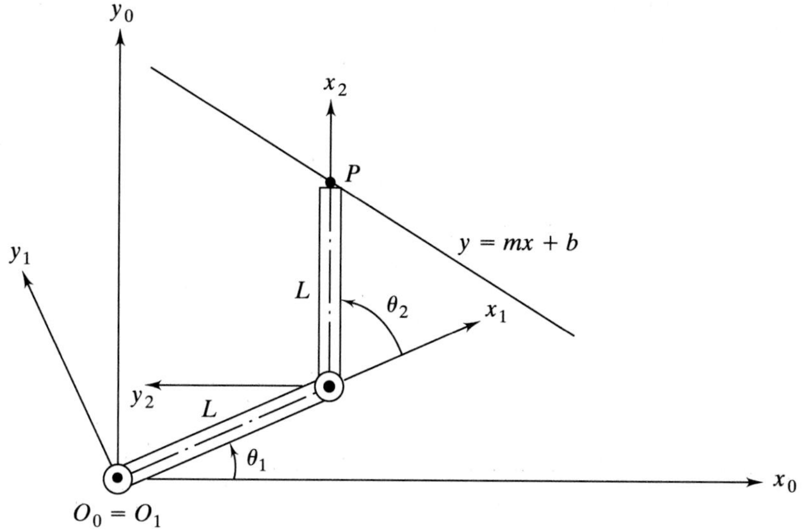

FIGURE E2-24

2-25. As usual, let $(0xyz)_0$ be an inertial reference frame embedded in the base A. Let $(0xyz)_1$ rotate about the z_0-axis in such a way that $z_0 = z_1$. The lower arm of length L_2 makes an angle $\theta_2(t)$ with respect to x_1 and has embedded in it a coordinate system $(0xyz)_2$. The outer member has a length L_3 and makes an angle $\theta_3(t)$ with respect to the x_2-axis; $(0xyz)_3$ is the corresponding embedded coordi-

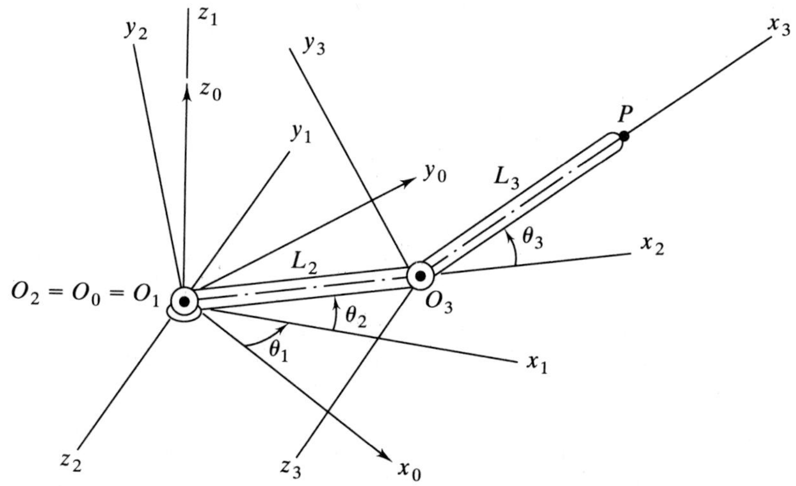

FIGURE E2-25

nate system (see Fig. E2-25).

(*a*) Express the unit vectors of $(0xyz)_3$ in terms of those of $(0xyz)_2$, those of $(0xyz)_2$ in terms of those of $(0xyz)_1$, and finally those of $(0xyz)_1$ in terms of those of $(0xyz)_0$.

(*b*) Write the absolute angular velocity of $(0xyz)_3$ in terms of the unit vectors of $(0xyz)_3$.

(*c*) Write the position vector $\mathbf{r}_0$ in terms of the unit vectors of $(0xyz)_3$ and differentiate it to obtain the velocity of *P*.

(*d*) Write the expression for the velocity in terms of the unit vectors of $(0xyz)_0$.

2-26. The manipulator in Fig. E2-26 has two rotational links and one translational link; rotations around the z_0- and z_2-axes and a translation along the x_1-axis. Suppose that at the given instant the velocities $\dot{\theta}_1$, $\dot{\theta}_2$, and $\dot{a}_1$ and the accelerations $\ddot{\theta}_1$, $\ddot{\theta}_2$, and $\ddot{a}_1$ are prescribed, all of them in the respective positive directions (counterclockwise rotations in accordance with the right-hand rule are considered positive). For the depicted *instant*:

(*a*) Obtain the individual homogeneous transformation matrices between reference frames and the collective homogeneous transformation matrix for the point *P* with respect to the base point O_0.

(*b*) Calculate the absolute angular velocity $\boldsymbol{\omega}_2$ and angular acceleration $\boldsymbol{\alpha}_2$ of $(0xyz)_2$.

(*c*) Calculate the absolute velocity $\mathbf{v}_0$ and the absolute acceleration $\mathbf{a}_0$ of the point *P* and write them in terms of $(\hat{\imath}\hat{\jmath}\hat{k})_2$.

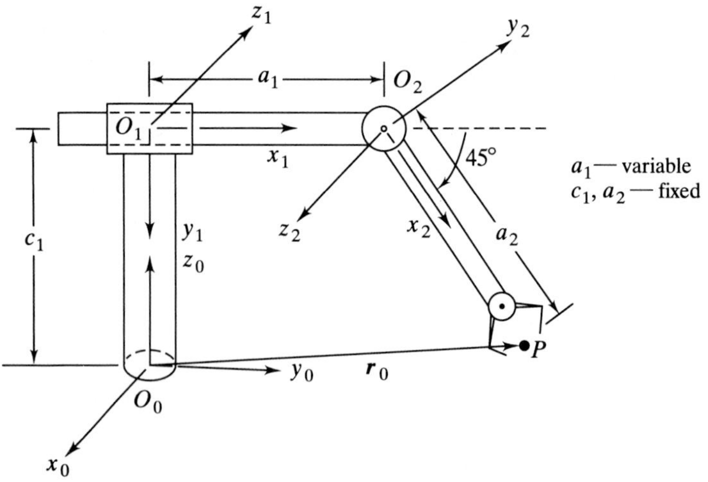

FIGURE E2-26

2-27. At the instant depicted in Fig. E2-27, the bar *AB* is rotating about the vertical axis with angular speed $\Omega = 20$ rad/s (ccw) and angular acceleration $\dot{\Omega} = 5$ rad/s (ccw). The point *P* is moving at a constant speed of 4 m/s relative to the point *B*. Determine the acceleration of the point *P* at the instants when $\theta = 0°$, 60°, and 90°. Take $a = 2$ m.

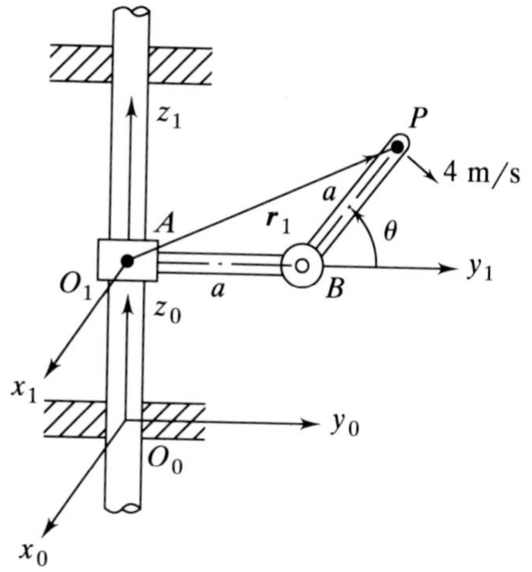

FIGURE E2-27

2-28. Consider the kinematics necessary for two points to arrive at the same instant t_0 at a given intersection P. As shown in Fig. E2-28, P_1 is moving on a circle of radius a with constant tangential speed v and P_2 is moving on the indicated horizontal line with constant speed V. Suppose that at $t = 0$, P_1 is at $(a, 0)$ and P_2 is at $(0, h)$. Solve for the ratio V/v which will assure that the two points will meet at P. [*Hint:* Begin with the velocities $\boldsymbol{v}_1(t)$ and $\boldsymbol{v}_2(t)$ and integrate to obtain $\boldsymbol{r}_1(t)$ and $\boldsymbol{r}_2(t)$.]

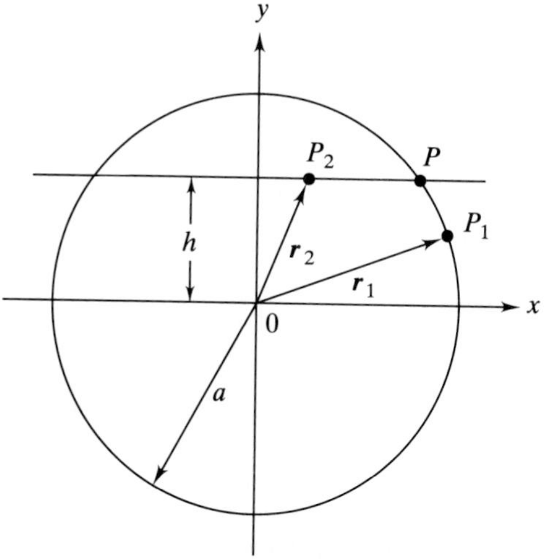

FIGURE E2-28

2-29. The vertical shaft in Fig. E2-29 is rotating with angular velocity $\boldsymbol{\Omega}$ and simultaneously rising with constant rate $\dot{s} = v$. The rod of length L is attached to the rotating shaft and rotates at an angular speed $\dot{\theta} = \omega$ with respect to the shaft.

(*a*) Write the position vector $\boldsymbol{r}_0(t)$ of the point P in terms of the $(0xyz)_1$ basis.
(*b*) Determine the absolute angular velocity of $(0xyz)_1$.
(*c*) Differentiate $\boldsymbol{r}_0(t)$ to obtain the velocity of P.
(*d*) Write the basis $(\hat{\boldsymbol{\imath}}\hat{\boldsymbol{\jmath}}\hat{\boldsymbol{k}})_1$ in terms of the basis $(\hat{\boldsymbol{\imath}}\hat{\boldsymbol{\jmath}}\hat{\boldsymbol{k}})_0$ and use your results to write $\dot{\boldsymbol{r}}_0(t)$ in terms of $(\hat{\boldsymbol{\imath}}\hat{\boldsymbol{\jmath}}\hat{\boldsymbol{k}})_0$.
(*e*) If the total length of the vertical shaft is also L, draw a sketch of the work envelope of the manipulator. Assume that $s(t)$ may extend to a distance L and that $0 \le \theta(t) \le \pi/2$ and $0 \le \psi(t) \le \pi/2$.

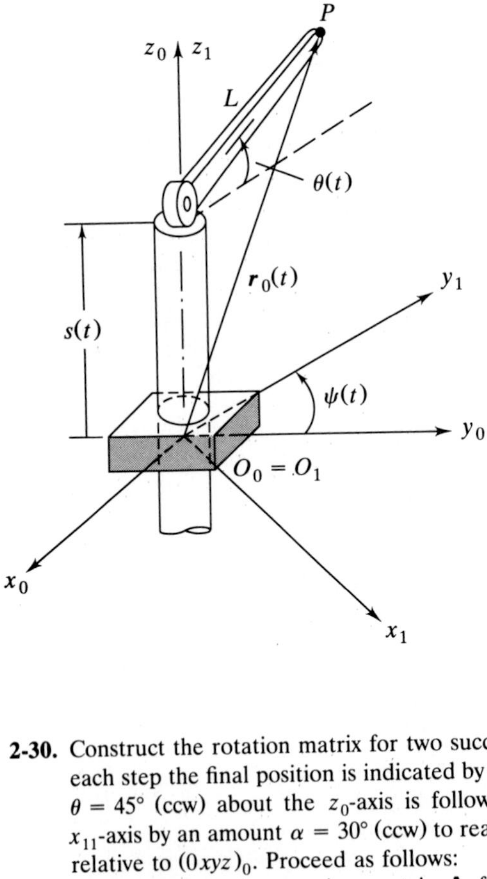

FIGURE E2-29

2-30. Construct the rotation matrix for two successive rotations shown in Fig. E2-30. At each step the final position is indicated by the solid line. In particular, a rotation of $\theta = 45°$ (ccw) about the z_0-axis is followed by a rotation of $(0xyz)_{11}$ about the x_{11}-axis by an amount $\alpha = 30°$ (ccw) to reach the final position of the frame $(0xyz)_1$ relative to $(0xyz)_0$. Proceed as follows:
(*a*) Determine the rotation matrix $\mathbf{A}$ for the rotation of $(0xyz)_{11}$ relative to $(0xyz)_0$.
(*b*) Determine the rotation matrix $\mathbf{B}$ for the rotation of $(0xyz)_1$ relative to $(0xyz)_{11}$.
(*c*) Use your results from parts (*a*) and (*b*) to write the rotation matrix $\mathbf{A}_1$ for $(0xyz)_1$ relative to $(0xyz)_0$.
(*d*) Check your results in part (*c*) by using $\mathbf{A}_1$ to calculate the coordinates of P relative to $(0xyz)_0$.

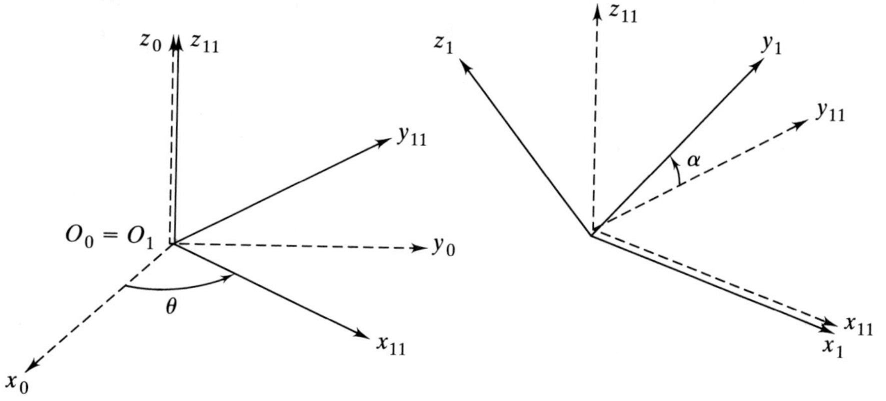

FIGURE E2-30

2-31. Write the basic homogeneous representation of the physical vector $\mathbf{r} = (-1 \quad 2 \quad 3)^T$ and state another homogeneous representation of the same vector.

2-32. Obtain the homogeneous transformation matrix relating the homogeneous representations of $\mathbf{r}_1$ and $\mathbf{r}_0$; that is, obtain $\mathbf{H}$ in $\mathbf{r}_0 = \mathbf{H}\mathbf{r}_1$ for the physical situation depicted in Fig. E2-32. The markings are unit markings.

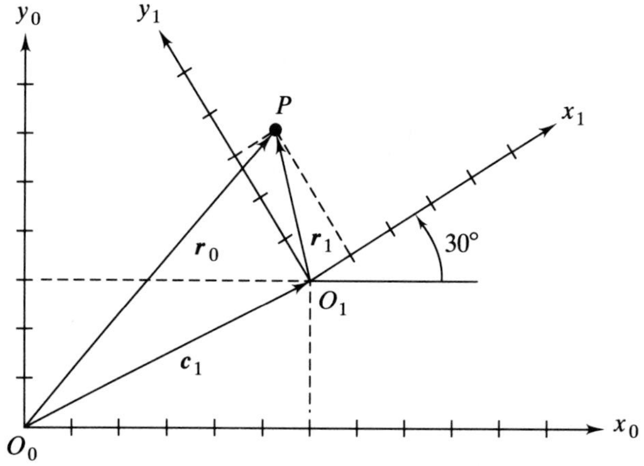

FIGURE E2-32

2-33. Consider a rigid body rotation about a fixed point O_0. We may begin with $\mathbf{r}_0(t) = \mathbf{A}_1(t)\mathbf{r}_1$ and differentiate twice to obtain the acceleration $\mathbf{a}_0(t) = \ddot{\mathbf{r}}_0(t) = \ddot{\mathbf{A}}_1(t)\mathbf{r}_1$. Show that this same result may be obtained by beginning with $\mathbf{r}_1 = \mathbf{A}_1^T(t)\mathbf{r}_0(t)$, differentiating twice, and solving for $\ddot{\mathbf{r}}_0(t)$. [*Hint:* You will need to use $\mathbf{r}_0 = \mathbf{A}(t)\mathbf{r}_1$ and the fact that $\mathbf{A}^T(t)\mathbf{A}(t) = \mathbf{E}$, the unit matrix.]

2-34. Consider the instantaneous position of the manipulator in Fig. E2-34 where $\theta_1 = 90°$, $\theta_2 = 30°$, and the z_2-axis is parallel to the x_0-axis.
(a) Obtain the homogeneous transformation matrix $\mathbf{H}_{12}$ for which $\mathbf{r}_1 = \mathbf{H}_{12}\mathbf{r}_2$.
(b) Obtain the homogeneous transformation matrix $\mathbf{H}_1$ for which $\mathbf{r}_0 = \mathbf{H}_1\mathbf{r}_1$.
(c) Finally, obtain the homogeneous transformation matrix $\mathbf{H}_2$ for which $\mathbf{r}_0 = \mathbf{H}_2\mathbf{r}_2$ and check your result by calculating the coordinates (x_0, y_0, z_0) of P.

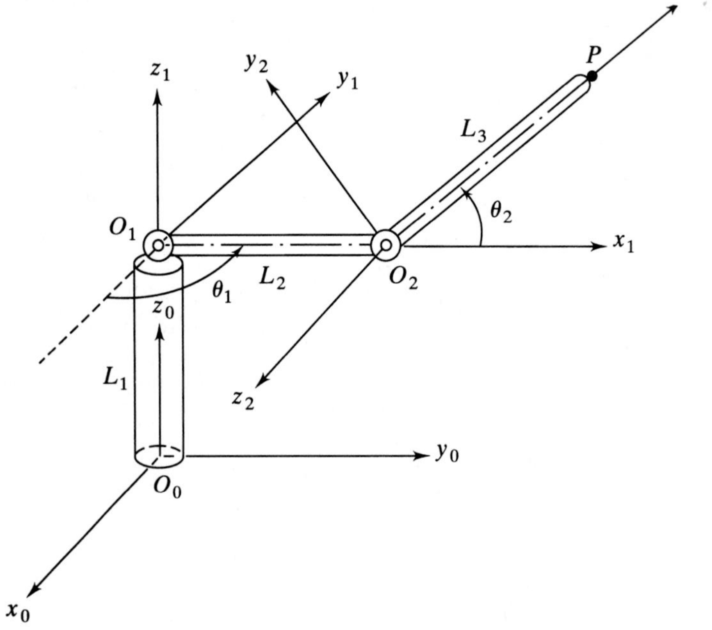

FIGURE E2-34

2-35. Consider the rectilinear motion of a point P between points A and B as shown in Fig. E2-35. The point is to move from A to B in time t_f in such a way that the following conditions are satisfied:

1. $x(0) = \dot{x}(0) = 0$, $x(t_f) = 10$ ft, $\dot{x}(t_f) = 0$.
2. The acceleration of the point P is bounded by $|\ddot{x}(t)| \leq 10$ ft/sec^2.
3. The velocity is to be $v(t) = 10$ ft/sec for as long as possible on $[0, t_f]$ and $|v(t)| \leq 10$ ft/sec is always required.

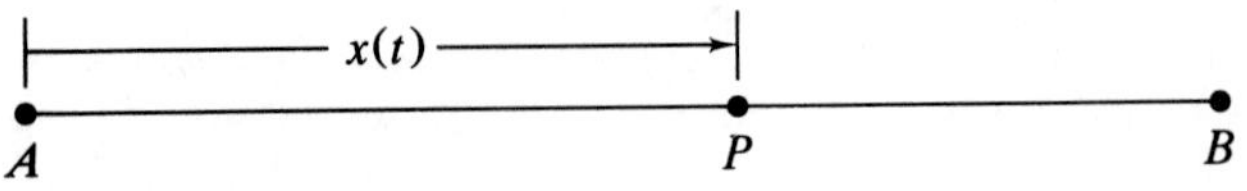

FIGURE E2-35

(*a*) Parametrize the motion from A to B in at least two different ways and select the one that takes the least amount of total time for P to travel from A to B.

(*b*) Suppose that a further requirement is that the jerk be 0 at both ends of the motion; that is, $\dddot{x}(0) = \dddot{x}(t_f) = 0$. Provide a suitable parametrization for this case.

2-36. Obtain the rotation matrix needed for $(0xyz)_1$ to attain the final position shown in Fig. E2-36; the z_1-axis is perpendicular to the plane. Check your results by calculating the $(0xyz)_0$ coordinates of the $(0xyz)_1$ points $\mathbf{r}_1 = (2 \quad 0 \quad 0)^T$ and $\mathbf{s}_1 = (0 \quad 0 \quad 2)^T$.

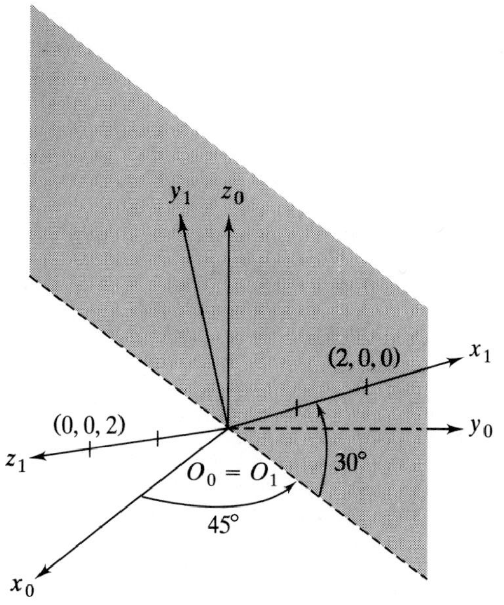

FIGURE E2-36

2-37. Some basic concepts of trajectory planning were discussed in Sec. 1-3. We note, in particular, that a given curve C has an infinite number of parametrizations, each representing a different mode of motion upon the curve. Suppose the curve C is given by $y = \sqrt{1 - x^2}$.

(*a*) Determine the parametrization $x(t)$ and $y(t)$ of C in terms of the time t, such that the speed of the point P moving along C is given by

$$v(t) = \frac{ds}{dt}(t) = t(1 - t)$$

Take $x(0) = 0$ and deal only with the case $dx/dt > 0$.

(*b*) Based on your parametrization, determine any required limitations on t and the location of P at $t = 1$.

2-38. Some trajectory planning was discussed in Sec. 1-3. We note that corresponding to each curve, there exists an infinite number of parametrizations, one corresponding to each mode of motion upon the curve. Suppose that the curve has already been parametrized in terms of a parameter θ (not the time), with

$$x(\theta) = \theta$$

$$y(\theta) = \theta^2$$

(*a*) Deduce the curve C as described by this parametrization.

(*b*) Determine a change of parametrization, $\theta(t)$ to the time t, in such a way that the speed of the point P moving on the curve C is

$$v(t) = \frac{ds}{dt}(t) = t$$

You need only determine the transcendental equation to be solved for θ in terms of t. For definiteness, take $\theta(0) = 0$.

2-39. Consider again the rectilinear motion specified in Exercise 2-35 and assume the following conditions:

$$x(0) = 0 \qquad v(0) = 0 \qquad a(0) = 0 \qquad |v(t)| \le 5\text{ ft/sec}$$

$$x(t_f) = 10\text{ ft} \qquad v(t_f) = 0 \qquad a(t_f) = 0 \qquad |a(t)| \le 10\text{ ft/sec}^2$$

Show that

$$v(t) = \begin{cases} \sin^4 4t & 0 \le t < \dfrac{\pi}{8} \\ 1 & \dfrac{\pi}{8} \le t < t_1 \\ \sin^4 4\left(t - t_1 + \dfrac{\pi}{8}\right) & t_1 \le t \le t_1 + \dfrac{\pi}{8} \end{cases}$$

is a motion that satisfies all of the requirements for an appropriate choice of t_1. Proceed as follows:

(*a*) Integrate $v(t)$ to determine t_1 and t_f with $x(t_f) = 10$ ft and $x(0) = 0$.

(*b*) Show that all of the boundary conditions and inequality constraints are satisfied.

(*c*) Sketch x, v, and a versus t.

2-40. Suppose a rigid body motion is described by $\mathbf{r}_0(t) = \mathbf{A}_1(t)\mathbf{r}_1$, where

$$\mathbf{A}_1(t) = \begin{bmatrix} C\theta(t) & -S\theta(t)C\alpha(t) & S\theta(t)S\alpha(t) \\ S\theta(t) & C\theta(t)C\alpha(t) & -C\theta(t)S\alpha(t) \\ 0 & S\alpha(t) & C\alpha(t) \end{bmatrix}$$

(*a*) Calculate the angular velocity $\boldsymbol{\omega}_1$ of the rigid body in terms of $(\hat{\imath}\hat{\jmath}\hat{k})_0$. Assume that the reference frame $(0xyz)_1$ is embedded in the rigid body.

(*b*) Discuss the meaning of $\boldsymbol{\omega}_1$ in terms of successive rotations of the rotating reference frame.

2-41. The degree of homogeneity of a function may be any real number. With this in mind, determine the degrees of homogeneity of the following functions:

(*a*) $f(x, y) = 4 + \cos\left(\dfrac{y}{x}\right)$.

(*b*) $f(x, y) = x^{2/3}y^{-5/3}\tan^{-1}\dfrac{y}{x}$.

2-42. Prove Euler's theorem. Suppose $f(\cdot)$: $(\mathscr{D} \subset \mathbb{R}^2) \to \mathbb{R}$ is differentiable on $\mathscr{D}$. [This implies that the partial derivatives of $f(x, y)$ with respect to x and y exist.] Suppose, furthermore, that $f(\cdot)$ is homogeneous of degree r on $\mathscr{D}$. Show that

$$x\frac{\partial f}{\partial x}(x, y) + y\frac{\partial f}{\partial y}(x, y) = rf(x, y)$$

[*Hint:* Differentiate the equation that expresses the homogeneity of $f(\cdot)$ and set $\lambda = 1$.]

2-43. (Contributed by Jon Moore) The polar manipulator shown in Fig. E2-43 is positioned in front of two conveyor belts. The bottom one is moving with 1 ft/sec to the right; the top one, with 2 ft/sec to the left. The manipulator is to pick objects off the bottom conveyor, carry them along the semicircular path shown, and place them on the top belt. The total time allotted to the transfer of the object is 2 sec. If the velocity of the manipulator's end effector E is to match that of the object when picking up or placing the object, determine a corresponding parametrization of the path in terms of the robot variables $(s_1(t), \theta_1(t))$ illustrated in Fig. 2-23.

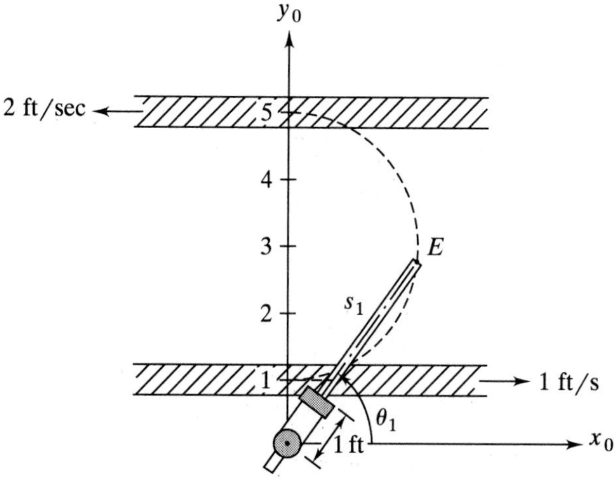

FIGURE E2-43

REFERENCES

1. Denavit, J., and R. S. Hartenberg: "A Kinematic Notation for Lower Pair Mechanisms Based on Matrices," *J. Appl. Mech.*, vol. 22, pp. 215–221, June 1955.
2. Reuleaux, F.: *Kinematics of Machinery*, English translation by A. B. W. Kennedy, Macmillan, London, 1876.
3. Lee, C. S. G.: "Robot Arm Kinematics, Dynamics and Control," *Computer*, vol. 15, no. 12, pp. 62–80, 1982.
4. Paul, R. P.: *Robot Manipulators (Mathematics, Programming and Control)*, MIT Press, Cambridge, Mass. 1981.

CHAPTER

THREE

FORCES, MOMENTS, AND EULER'S LAWS

3-1 INTRODUCTION

This chapter provides the fundamentals needed for the derivation of equations of motion, the essence of modeling system dynamics. Much of robot motion is based on the sensing and control of velocity and displacements, a prevalent approach in automatic feedback control systems. It does not suffice, however, to monitor only the kinematics. The forces and moments generated by actuators must also be monitored to assure that they are ample to sustain the prescribed motions. Laws of motion furnish the essential link—for a given motion, they provide the forces and moments required to sustain the motion; for given forces and moments, they allow the deduction of the resultant system motion or response. Knowledge of forces and moments is required for force-controlled motion as well as the estimation of power and energy requirements. High speed, together with tight turns and extreme accuracy, generally require both force and kinematic control, particularly in direct drive robots.

There are two basic approaches to the derivation of system equations of motion: the Lagrangian approach and the Eulerian approach. The former has established itself as the primary approach in robotics. Part of its appeal is that it lends itself to routine and computerization and that it is a scalar rather than vector approach. Lagrange prided himself for not having used any figures in his text *Mecanique Analytique* (1788); however, it is precisely this emphasis on analysis that is a weakness of the approach. Based on our education and experience, we tend to visualize and conceptualize in terms of forces rather than energy. Euler's equations are a background acquired in a first course in dynamics, while the Lagrangian approach is a topic of courses in advanced dynamics. These are some of the reasons for choosing the Eulerian approach in this text.

Contrary to popular exposition, the Eulerian axioms are not derivable from Newton's laws by some kind of limiting process. They must be separately postulated, just as Euler did in 1776, when he stated them as applicable to both the motion of rigid as well as of deformable bodies. Mass moments of inertia play a crucial role. It is worth noting that they were first used by Jakob Bernoulli in the investigation of the center of oscillation for physical pendula. In the same paper, published in the *Acta Eruditorum* of 1686, Bernoulli also introduced the axiom of moment of momentum, thus preceding Newton's *Principia* (1687) by a whole year.

We take Fox[1] and Greenwood[2] as our desk references for this material. Prior to the presentation of Euler's law of motion, we need to introduce some additional definitions and notation.

3-2 DEFINITIONS AND NOTATION

There are three central concepts that need to be defined for a rigid body: its linear momentum, its moment of momentum, and its inertia matrix. As before, we shall develop the matrix expressions along with the vector expressions whenever suitable.

Definition 3-1 Linear momentum. The linear momentum of a rigid body is given by

$$\boldsymbol{P}(t) = \int_{m(t)} \dot{\boldsymbol{r}}\, dm = \int_{V(t)} \rho \dot{\boldsymbol{r}}\, dV \tag{3-1}$$

where ρ is the mass density per unit volume, $V(t)$ is the volume occupied by $\mathscr{B}$ at the instant t, and $\dot{\boldsymbol{r}}$ is a velocity considered as a function of the points occupied by the body $\mathscr{B}$.

Remark 3-1. Note that the linear momentum is absolute or relative depending on whether $\dot{\boldsymbol{r}}$ is an absolute or relative velocity. Usually, the absolute velocities of the points are used.

Remark 3-2. Note also that the limits of integration in the definition are time dependent if the integration is carried out with respect to the absolute variables (x_0, y_0, z_0) since the body $\mathscr{B}$ occupies a different region in space at each instant t. Avoiding this time dependence of the limits of integration is one of the reasons one generally introduces a body-fixed reference frame.

Example 3-1. Assume that a uniform homogeneous bar of length L is rotating about the fixed point O with angular velocity $\boldsymbol{\omega} = \dot{\theta}(t)\hat{\boldsymbol{k}}_0$ as shown in Fig. 3-1. The

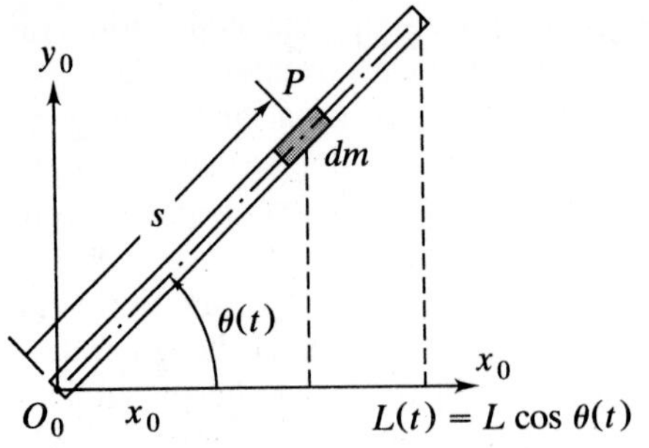

FIGURE 3-1
Integration with respect to a space-fixed frame.

mass density per unit length is ρ. Calculate the linear momentum of the bar at an instant t.

Solution. We shall work the problem from both viewpoints: an integration with respect to a fixed-space frame, and one with respect to a body-fixed frame. In either case, the actual integration is to be carried out over the arc length s along the bar.

In the first case we shall integrate over x_0 from O to $L(t)$. We have

$$s = \frac{x_0}{\cos\theta(t)} \quad \Rightarrow \quad ds = \frac{dx_0}{\cos\theta(t)}$$

The velocity of a point P a distance s from O is given by

$$\boldsymbol{v}_0(t) = s\dot{\theta}(t)(-\sin\theta(t)\hat{\imath}_0 + \cos\theta(t)\hat{\jmath}_0)$$

The linear momentum of the body $\mathscr{B}$ (the rod of length L) is given by

$$\begin{aligned}
\boldsymbol{P}(t) &= \int_0^{L\cos\theta(t)} \rho\frac{x_0}{\cos\theta(t)}\dot{\theta}(t)(-\sin\theta(t)\hat{\imath}_0 + \cos\theta(t)\hat{\jmath}_0)\frac{dx_0}{\cos\theta(t)} \\
&= \frac{\rho\dot{\theta}(t)}{\cos^2\theta(t)}(-\sin\theta(t)\hat{\imath}_0 + \cos\theta(t)\hat{\jmath}_0)\int_0^{L\cos\theta(t)} x_0\,dx_0 \\
&= (\rho L)\frac{1}{2}L\dot{\theta}(t)(-\sin\theta(t)\hat{\imath}_0 + \cos\theta(t)\hat{\jmath}_0) \\
&= m\boldsymbol{v}_G(t)
\end{aligned} \tag{3-2}$$

where m is the total mass of the rod and $\boldsymbol{v}_G$ is the velocity of its center of mass.

Suppose we now consider a reference frame embedded in the rod (see Fig. 3-2). The absolute velocity of an arbitrary point in the rod is given by

$$\boldsymbol{v}_0(t) = x_1\dot{\theta}(t)\hat{\jmath}_1(t)$$

and the linear momentum follows as

$$\begin{aligned}
\boldsymbol{P}(t) &= \int_0^L \rho x_1\dot{\theta}(t)\hat{\jmath}_1(t)\,dx_1 \\
&= (\rho L)\frac{L}{2}\dot{\theta}(t)\hat{\jmath}_1(t) \\
&= m\boldsymbol{v}_G(t)
\end{aligned} \tag{3-3}$$

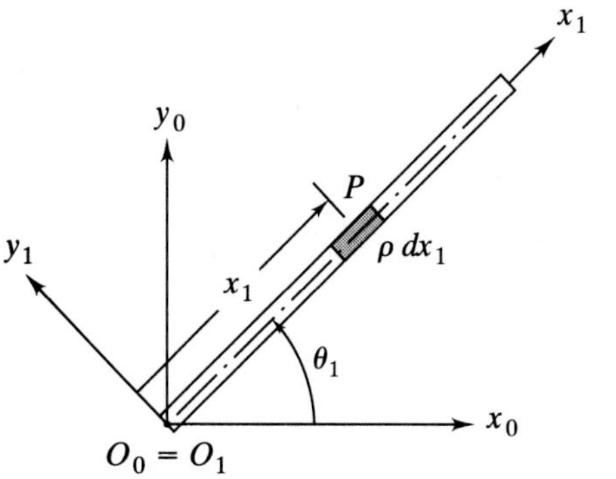

FIGURE 3-2
Integration with respect to a body-fixed frame.

as before. The advantages of the second approach are obvious. Furthermore, the end result is general, as will be seen in the next section.

Definition 3-2 Moment of momentum. The moment of momentum of a body $\mathscr{B}$ with respect to an arbitrary point A (moving or nonmoving) is given by

$$\boldsymbol{H}_A(t) = \int_{V(t)} \rho(\boldsymbol{r}_0 - \boldsymbol{r}_A) \times (\dot{\boldsymbol{r}}_0 - \dot{\boldsymbol{r}}_A)\, dV \tag{3-4}$$

where $V(t)$ is the region in space occupied by the body $\mathscr{B}$ at the instant t; $\boldsymbol{r}_0$ and $\dot{\boldsymbol{r}}_0$ are the absolute position and velocity, respectively, of an arbitrary point P of the body $\mathscr{B}$, and $\boldsymbol{r}_A$ and $\dot{\boldsymbol{r}}_A$ are the absolute position and velocity, respectively, of the point A (see Fig. 3-3).

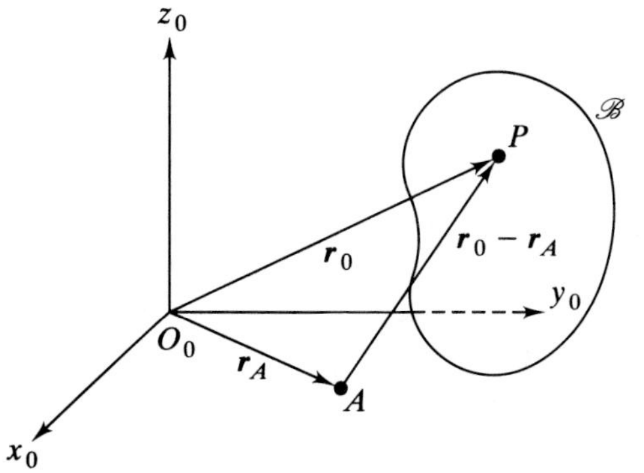

FIGURE 3-3
Definition of moment of momentum.

Example 3-2. The previous example again serves to illustrate the concept. We shall calculate the moment of momentum of the rod with respect to the fixed point O.

Solution. The element of mass is given by

$$dm = \rho\, dx_1$$

The position and velocity of an arbitrary point P in $\mathscr{B}$ are

$$\boldsymbol{r}_0 = x_1\hat{\imath}_1(t) \qquad \text{and} \qquad \dot{\boldsymbol{r}}_0 = x_1\dot{\theta}(t)\hat{\jmath}_1(t)$$

The moment of momentum thus is

$$\begin{aligned}
\boldsymbol{H}_O(t) &= \int_0^L \boldsymbol{r}_0 \times \rho\dot{\boldsymbol{r}}_0\,dx_1 = \int_0^L (x_1\hat{\imath}_1(t)) \times \left(\rho x_1\dot{\theta}_1(t)\hat{\jmath}_1(t)\right) dx_1 \\
&= \dot{\theta}_1(t)\hat{\boldsymbol{k}}_1(t)\int_0^L \rho x_1^2\,dx_1 \\
&= \frac{1}{3}\rho L^3\dot{\theta}_1(t)\hat{\boldsymbol{k}}_1(t) = \frac{1}{3}mL^2\dot{\theta}_1(t)\hat{\boldsymbol{k}}_1(t) \\
&= I_O\dot{\theta}_1(t)\hat{\boldsymbol{k}}_1(t) \qquad\qquad (3\text{-}5)
\end{aligned}$$

where I_O is the mass moment of inertia of the rod with respect to an axis through O perpendicular to the plane of the paper.

With every rigid body we may associate an inertia matrix, a formal array of the mass moments of inertia of the body.

Definition 3-3 Inertia matrix. Consider a rigid body $\mathscr{B}$ with mass density ρ per unit volume. Introduce a rectangular Cartesian reference frame $(0xyz)$. Then the quantities

$$I_{xx} = \int_V (y^2 + z^2)\rho\,dV$$

$$I_{yy} = \int_V (x^2 + z^2)\rho\,dV$$

$$I_{zz} = \int_V (x^2 + y^2)\rho\,dV$$

are called the mass moments of inertia of the body $\mathscr{B}$, and

$$I_{xy} = -\int_V xy\rho\,dV = I_{yx}$$

$$I_{xz} = -\int_V xz\rho\,dV = I_{zx}$$

$$I_{yz} = -\int_V yz\rho\,dV = I_{zy}$$

are the products of inertia of $\mathscr{B}$, all with respect to the specific choice of axes $(0xyz)$. The array

$$\mathbf{I}_O = \begin{bmatrix} I_{xx} & I_{xy} & I_{xz} \\ I_{yx} & I_{yy} & I_{yz} \\ I_{zx} & I_{zy} & I_{zz} \end{bmatrix} \qquad (3\text{-}6)$$

is called the inertia matrix of the body $\mathscr{B}$ with respect to $(0xyz)$. The subscript denotes the location of the origin of coordinates.

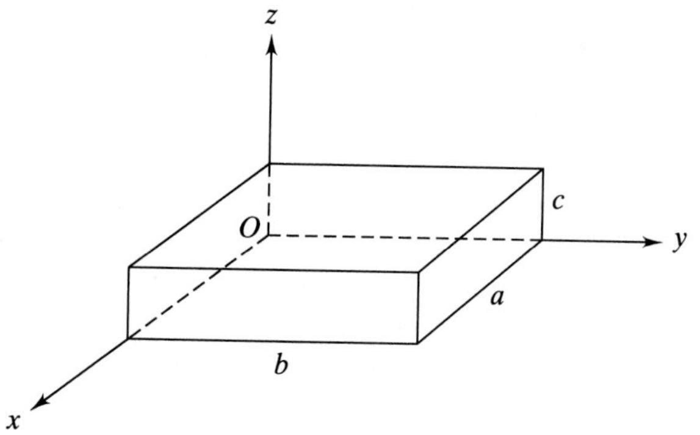

FIGURE 3-4
Calculation of the mass moment of inertia.

Example 3-3. Calculate the inertia matrix of the homogeneous parallelopipedon with respect to the axes system shown in Fig. 3-4.

Solution. Corresponding to the side lengths a, b, and c, we have

$$
\begin{aligned}
I_{xx} &= \int_0^c \int_0^b \int_0^a (y^2 + z^2)\rho \, dV \\
&= a\rho \int_0^c \int_0^b (y^2 + z^2) \, dy \, dz \\
&= a\rho \int_0^c \left(\frac{1}{3} b^3 + z^2 b \right) dz \\
&= a\rho \left[\frac{1}{3} b^3 c + \frac{1}{3} c^3 b \right] \\
&= abc\rho \frac{1}{3} [b^2 + c^2] \\
&= \frac{1}{3} m(b^2 + c^2)
\end{aligned}
\tag{3-7}
$$

In a similar manner, we obtain

$$I_{yy} = \tfrac{1}{3} m(a^2 + c^2) \qquad \text{and} \qquad I_{zz} = \tfrac{1}{3} m(a^2 + b^2)$$

The products of inertia are given by

$$
\begin{aligned}
I_{xy} &= -\int_0^a \int_0^b \int_0^c xy\rho \, dx \, dy \, dz \\
&= -\int_0^c \int_0^b \frac{1}{2} a^2 y \rho \, dy \, dz \\
&= -\int_0^c \frac{1}{2} a^2 \frac{1}{2} b^2 \rho \, dz \\
&= -\tfrac{1}{4}(abc\rho)ab = -\tfrac{1}{4} mab
\end{aligned}
\tag{3-8}
$$

along with

$$I_{xz} = -\tfrac{1}{4}mac \qquad \text{and} \qquad I_{yz} = -\tfrac{1}{4}mbc$$

The corresponding inertia matrix is thus given by

$$\mathbf{I}_0 = \begin{bmatrix} \frac{1}{3}m(b^2+c^2) & -\frac{1}{4}mab & -\frac{1}{4}mac \\ -\frac{1}{4}mba & \frac{1}{3}m(a^2+c^2) & -\frac{1}{4}mbc \\ -\frac{1}{4}mca & -\frac{1}{4}mcb & \frac{1}{3}m(a^2+b^2) \end{bmatrix} \tag{3-9}$$

Remark 3-3. Observe that the entries of the inertia matrix depend on the orientation and location of the coordinate axes $(0xyz)$ with respect to the body $\mathscr{B}$. The matrix is obviously symmetric. The moments of inertia are always positive, whereas the products of inertia may be both positive and negative.

In the next section we shall show that the orientation of the axes may always be chosen in such a way that the products of inertia are 0.

3-3 SOME NEEDED THEOREMS AND FACTS ABOUT THE MOMENTA

In the previous section we introduced some rather general integral definitions of linear momentum and moment of momentum. They apply to both rigid and deformable bodies. Within a rigid body context, some other representations are more useful. In the following discussion we shall drop the distinction between the body $\mathscr{B}$ and the volume $V(t)$ occupied by $\mathscr{B}$ at the instant t.

Theorem 3-1. Let $\dot{\boldsymbol{r}}_0$ describe the absolute velocity field over the body $\mathscr{B}$ at the instant t. Then

$$\boldsymbol{P}(t) = m\boldsymbol{v}_{G/0}(t) \tag{3-10}$$

where $\boldsymbol{v}_{G/0}(t)$ is the absolute velocity of the center of mass of the body $\mathscr{B}$.

Proof. Let $(0xyz)_1$ be a reference frame embedded in the body $\mathscr{B}$. The velocity of an arbitrary point P in $\mathscr{B}$ may be written in the form

$$\dot{\boldsymbol{r}}_0(t) = \dot{\boldsymbol{r}}_{0_1/0}(t) + \boldsymbol{\omega}_1(t) \times \boldsymbol{r}_1$$

The integral then becomes

$$\boldsymbol{P}(t) = \int_{V(t)} \rho \dot{\boldsymbol{r}}\, dV = \int_V \left(\dot{\boldsymbol{r}}_{0_1/0_1}(t) + \boldsymbol{\omega}_1(t) \times \boldsymbol{r}_1\right)\rho\, dV$$

$$= \dot{\boldsymbol{r}}_{0_1/0_1}(t)\int_V \rho\, dV + \boldsymbol{\omega}_1(t) \times \int_V \boldsymbol{r}_1 \rho\, dV$$

$$= \dot{\boldsymbol{r}}_{0_1/0}(t)m + \boldsymbol{\omega}_1(t) \times m\boldsymbol{r}_{G/0_1}$$

$$= m\left(\dot{\boldsymbol{r}}_{0_1/0}(t) + \boldsymbol{\omega}_1(t) \times \boldsymbol{r}_{G/0_1}\right)$$

$$= m\boldsymbol{v}_{G/0}$$ ■

Generally, we shall drop the subscript 0 when it is clear that the absolute position, velocity, or acceleration is intended.

Next, we carry out a similar reduction with respect to the definition of moment of momentum.

Theorem 3-2. Let A be an arbitrary point, let G be the center of mass of the body $\mathscr{B}$, and let $\boldsymbol{r}_A$ and $\boldsymbol{r}_G$ be the corresponding absolute motions. Then

$$\boldsymbol{H}_A(t) = (\boldsymbol{r}_G(t) - \boldsymbol{r}_A(t)) \times m(\boldsymbol{v}_G(t) - \boldsymbol{v}_A(t)) + \boldsymbol{H}_G(t) \qquad (3\text{-}11)$$

Proof. Consider a body-fixed reference frame $(0xyz)_1$ and let O_1 be located at the center of mass G of the body $\mathscr{B}$. Then the motion of an arbitrary point in $\mathscr{B}$ may be written in the form

$$\boldsymbol{r}_p(t) = \boldsymbol{r}_G(t) + \boldsymbol{r}_1$$

with

$$\boldsymbol{v}_p(t) = \boldsymbol{v}_G(t) + \boldsymbol{\omega}_1(t) \times \boldsymbol{r}_1$$

so that

$$\begin{aligned}
\boldsymbol{H}_A(t) &= \int_{V(t)} (\boldsymbol{r}_p - \boldsymbol{r}_A) \times (\boldsymbol{v}_p - \boldsymbol{v}_A)\rho\, dV \\
&= \int_V (\boldsymbol{r}_G + \boldsymbol{r}_1 - \boldsymbol{r}_A) \times (\boldsymbol{v}_G + \boldsymbol{\omega}_1 \times \boldsymbol{r}_1 - \boldsymbol{v}_A)\rho\, dV \\
&= \boldsymbol{r}_G \times \boldsymbol{v}_G \int_V \rho\, dV + \boldsymbol{r}_G \times \left(\boldsymbol{\omega}_1 \times \int_V \boldsymbol{r}_1 \rho\, dV\right) \\
&\quad - \boldsymbol{r}_G \times \boldsymbol{v}_A \int_V \rho\, dV - \boldsymbol{v}_G \times \int_V \boldsymbol{r}_1 \rho\, dV \\
&\quad + \int_V \boldsymbol{r}_1 \times (\boldsymbol{\omega}_1 \times \boldsymbol{r}_1)\rho\, dV + \boldsymbol{v}_A \times \int_V \boldsymbol{r}_1 \rho\, dV \\
&\quad - \boldsymbol{r}_A \times \boldsymbol{v}_G \int_V \rho\, dV - \boldsymbol{r}_A \times \left(\boldsymbol{\omega}_1 \times \int_V \boldsymbol{r}_1 \rho\, dV\right) \\
&\quad + \boldsymbol{r}_A \times \boldsymbol{v}_A \int_V \rho\, dV \\
&= \boldsymbol{r}_G \times m\boldsymbol{v}_G - \boldsymbol{r}_G \times m\boldsymbol{v}_A + \boldsymbol{H}_G - \boldsymbol{r}_A \times m\boldsymbol{v}_G + \boldsymbol{r}_A \times m\boldsymbol{v}_A \\
&= (\boldsymbol{r}_G - \boldsymbol{r}_A) \times m(\boldsymbol{v}_G - \boldsymbol{v}_A) + \boldsymbol{H}_G
\end{aligned}$$

■

Some immediate special cases are given by:

(*a*) A is a fixed point. Then $\boldsymbol{v}_A = \boldsymbol{0}$ and

$$\boldsymbol{H}_A(t) = (\boldsymbol{r}_G(t) - \boldsymbol{r}_A) \times m\boldsymbol{v}_G(t) + \boldsymbol{H}_G(t) \qquad (3\text{-}12)$$

(*b*) A is a fixed point coinciding with O. Then $\boldsymbol{r}_A = \boldsymbol{v}_A = \boldsymbol{0}$ and

$$\boldsymbol{H}_O(t) = \boldsymbol{r}_G(t) \times m\boldsymbol{v}_G(t) + \boldsymbol{H}_G(t) \qquad (3\text{-}13)$$

Suppose we now take a closer look at $\boldsymbol{H}_G(t)$. (Recall that G coincides with O_1.) With

$$\boldsymbol{r}_1 = x_1\hat{\boldsymbol{\imath}}_1(t) + y_1\hat{\boldsymbol{\jmath}}_1(t) + z_1\hat{\boldsymbol{k}}_1(t)$$

and
$$\boldsymbol{\omega}_1(t) = \omega_{x_1}(t)\hat{\boldsymbol{\imath}}_1(t) + \omega_{y_1}(t)\hat{\boldsymbol{\jmath}}_1(t) + \omega_{z_1}(t)\hat{\boldsymbol{k}}_1(t)$$

we have
$$\boldsymbol{H}_G(t) = \int_V \boldsymbol{r}_1 \times (\boldsymbol{\omega}_1 \times \boldsymbol{r}_1)\rho\, dV$$

The triple product is most easily evaluated by using the vector identity

$$\boldsymbol{a} \times (\boldsymbol{b} \times \boldsymbol{c}) = (\boldsymbol{a} \cdot \boldsymbol{c})\boldsymbol{b} - (\boldsymbol{a} \cdot \boldsymbol{b})\boldsymbol{c}$$

resulting in

$$\begin{aligned}
\boldsymbol{H}_G(t) &= \int_V [(\boldsymbol{r}_1 \cdot \boldsymbol{r}_1)\boldsymbol{\omega}_1 - (\boldsymbol{r}_1 \cdot \boldsymbol{\omega}_1)\boldsymbol{r}_1]\rho\, dV \\
&= \int_V \left[\left(x_1^2 + y_1^2 + z_1^2\right)\boldsymbol{\omega}_1 - \left(x_1\omega_{x_1} + y_1\omega_{y_1} + z_1\omega_{z_1}\right)\boldsymbol{r}_1\right]\rho\, dV \\
&= \hat{\boldsymbol{\imath}}_1\int_V \left[\left(y_1^2 + z_1^2\right)\omega_{x_1} - x_1y_1\omega_{y_1} - x_1z_1\omega_{z_1}\right]\rho\, dV \\
&\quad + \hat{\boldsymbol{\jmath}}_1\int_V \left[-y_1x_1\omega_{x_1} + \left(x_1^2 + z_1^2\right)\omega_{y_1} - y_1z_1\omega_{z_1}\right]\rho\, dV \\
&\quad + \hat{\boldsymbol{k}}_1\int_V \left[-z_1x_1\omega_{x_1} - z_1y_1\omega_{y_1} + \left(x_1^2 + y_1^2\right)\omega_{z_1}\right]\rho\, dV \\
&= H_{x_1}(t)\hat{\boldsymbol{\imath}}_1(t) + H_{y_1}(t)\hat{\boldsymbol{\jmath}}_1(t) + H_{z_1}(t)\hat{\boldsymbol{k}}_1(t)
\end{aligned} \tag{3-14}$$

where we have set

$$\begin{aligned}
H_{x_1}(t) &= I_{x_1x_1}\omega_{x_1}(t) + I_{x_1y_1}\omega_{y_1}(t) + I_{x_1z_1}\omega_{z_1}(t) \\
H_{y_1}(t) &= I_{y_1x_1}\omega_{x_1}(t) + I_{y_1y_1}\omega_{y_1}(t) + I_{y_1z_1}\omega_{z_1}(t) \\
H_{z_1}(t) &= I_{z_1x_1}\omega_{x_1}(t) + I_{z_1y_1}\omega_{y_1}(t) + I_{z_1z_1}\omega_{z_1}(t)
\end{aligned} \tag{3-15}$$

The advantages of using a body-fixed reference frame are clear. Collectively, (3-15) may also be summarized in the matrix form

$$\mathbf{H}_G(t) = \mathbf{I}_G\boldsymbol{\omega}_1(t) \tag{3-16}$$

In this expression it must be kept in mind that $\mathbf{I}_G$ is calculated with respect to a reference frame with origin at the center of mass of the body $\mathscr{B}$ and that the basis used for $\boldsymbol{\omega}_1$ must conform with this choice of reference frame.

The preceding development also makes apparent the reason for defining the products of inertia with a minus sign included. We are now able to write the general equations with plus signs, an advantage in the further theoretical development.

As another special case, we note that for two-dimensional motion with $\boldsymbol{\omega}_1(t) = \omega_{z_1}(t)\hat{\boldsymbol{k}}_1$, the moment of momentum simplifies to

$$\boldsymbol{H}_G(t) = H_{z_1}(t)\hat{\boldsymbol{k}}_1 = I_{z_1z_1}\omega_{z_1}(t)\hat{\boldsymbol{k}}_1 \tag{3-17}$$

a form that is familiar from the usual treatment of a planar motion.

Clearly, the general expression for the moment of momentum would be greatly simplified if all of the products of inertia were 0—that is, if the inertia matrix were diagonal. We now indicate how one may obtain a matrix $\mathbf{S}$ such that

$$\mathbf{S}^{\mathrm{T}}\mathbf{I}\mathbf{S} = \boldsymbol{\Lambda}$$

where $\boldsymbol{\Lambda}$ is a diagonal matrix whose entries are the eigenvalues of the inertia matrix $\mathbf{I}$. That is, we may obtain an orientation of the embedded frame $(0xyz)_1$ for which all of the products of inertia vanish.

The modal matrix $\mathbf{S}$ of $\mathbf{I}$ may be obtained in the following manner:

1. The eigenvalues of $\mathbf{I}$ are the roots of the characteristic (or secular) equation

   $$|\mathbf{I} - \lambda\mathbf{E}| = 0$$

   where $\mathbf{E}$ is again the identity matrix in $\mathbb{R}^3$.

   Since $\mathbf{I}$ is a real and symmetric matrix, the eigenvalues are always real. Multiple eigenvalues, however, may occur.

2. Within the present context there are three eigenvalues: λ_1, λ_2, and λ_3. Corresponding to each *eigenvalue* λ_i, we may construct a unit vector $\mathbf{e}_i$ such that

   $$\mathbf{I}\mathbf{e}_i = \lambda_i\mathbf{e}_i$$

   The vector $\mathbf{e}_i$ which is a solution of this equation is an eigenvector corresponding to the eigenvalue λ_i.

   The eigenvectors corresponding to distinct eigenvalues are orthogonal. Even if the roots are not distinct—say an eigenvalue is of multiplicity 3—then there still exist three linearly independent eigenvectors which may be orthogonalized by means of a Gram-Schmidt orthogonalization process.

   We note that every scalar multiple of an eigenvector is also an eigenvector, so that eigenvectors are not unique.

3. Let $\mathbf{e}_1$, $\mathbf{e}_2$, and $\mathbf{e}_3$ be an orthonormal (orthogonal and unit magnitude) set of eigenvectors. Construct the matrix $\mathbf{S}$ given by

   $$\mathbf{S} = [\mathbf{e}_1 \quad \mathbf{e}_2 \quad \mathbf{e}_3]$$

   that is, the eigenvectors form the columns of $\mathbf{S}$. It follows that

   $$\mathbf{S}\mathbf{S}^{\mathrm{T}} = \mathbf{E}$$

or that $\mathbf{S}$ is orthogonal. Furthermore,

$$\mathbf{S}^T \mathbf{I} \mathbf{S} = \mathbf{\Lambda}$$

where

$$\mathbf{\Lambda} = \begin{bmatrix} \lambda_1 & 0 & 0 \\ 0 & \lambda_2 & 0 \\ 0 & 0 & \lambda_3 \end{bmatrix}$$

The three mutually orthogonal directions $\mathbf{e}_i$ are called the *principal directions* for the rigid body $\mathscr{B}$, and the corresponding eigenvalues λ_i, the *principal moments of inertia* of the body $\mathscr{B}$.

The final ingredient needed for a prescription of Euler's laws of motion is the total time rate of change of the moment of momentum. Note that $\boldsymbol{H}_G(t)$ is a vector expressed in terms of a moving basis. Its derivative is thus given by

$$\frac{d\boldsymbol{H}_G}{dt}(t) = \left(\frac{d\boldsymbol{H}_G}{dt}(t)\right)_1 + \boldsymbol{\omega}_1(t) \times \boldsymbol{H}_G(t) \tag{3-18}$$

resulting in

$$\begin{aligned} \dot{\boldsymbol{H}}_G(t) = & \left[\dot{H}_{x_1} + (H_{z_1}\omega_{y_1} - H_{y_1}\omega_{z_1})\right]\hat{\boldsymbol{\imath}}_1 \\ & + \left[\dot{H}_{y_1} + (H_{x_1}\omega_{z_1} - H_{z_1}\omega_{x_1})\right]\hat{\boldsymbol{\jmath}}_1 \\ & + \left[\dot{H}_{z_1} + (H_{y_1}\omega_{x_1} - H_{x_1}\omega_{y_1})\right]\hat{\boldsymbol{k}}_1 \end{aligned} \tag{3-19}$$

This expression will be written in terms of the moments of inertia in the next section, in connection with Euler's laws of motion.

3-4 EULER'S LAWS OF MOTION

With these preliminaries we are now able to give a concise statement of Euler's laws of motion. These laws were stated by Euler in 1776 as applicable to both rigid and deformable bodies.

Axiom 3-1. Euler's first law, the law of linear momentum:

$$\boldsymbol{F}(t) = \frac{d\boldsymbol{P}}{dt}(t) \tag{3-20}$$

where $\boldsymbol{F}(t)$ is the resultant external force acting on the rigid body and where $\boldsymbol{P}(t)$ is the absolute linear momentum of the body $\mathscr{B}$.

In light of Theorem 3-1, this may also be written in the form

$$\boldsymbol{F}(t) = m\boldsymbol{a}_G(t) \tag{3-21}$$

where $\boldsymbol{a}_G(t)$ is the absolute acceleration of the center of mass of the rigid body $\mathscr{B}$. Generally, the law is used in this form.

Axiom 3-2. Euler's second law, the law of moment of momentum:

$$\boldsymbol{M}_O(t) = \frac{d\boldsymbol{H}_0}{dt}(t) \tag{3-22}$$

where O is a fixed point, $\boldsymbol{M}_O(t)$ is the resultant external moment with respect to O, including the moments of the forces and any couples that might be present, and $\boldsymbol{H}_O(t)$ is the moment of momentum of the body with respect to O.

Theorem 3-3. Suppose the motion of a body satisfies Euler's first law and Euler's second law with respect to a fixed point O. Then the law of moment of momentum also holds with respect to the center of mass of the body $\mathscr{B}$. That is,

$$\boldsymbol{M}_G(t) = \frac{d\boldsymbol{H}_G}{dt}(t) \tag{3-23}$$

Proof. Let $\boldsymbol{M}_i$ denote the ith couple and let $\boldsymbol{r}_{0i}$ be the position vector from O to the line of action of the ith force, $\boldsymbol{F}_i$. Furthermore, note that $\boldsymbol{r}_{0i}$ may be written as the sum

$$\boldsymbol{r}_{0i} = \boldsymbol{r}_G + \boldsymbol{r}_{i/G}$$

where $\boldsymbol{r}_G$ is the position vector of G with respect to O and $\boldsymbol{r}_{i/G}$ is the vector from G to the point on the line of action of $\boldsymbol{F}_i$. Then

$$\begin{aligned}
\boldsymbol{M}_O &= \sum_{i=1}^{n} \boldsymbol{M}_i + \sum_{i=1}^{m} (\boldsymbol{r}_G + \boldsymbol{r}_{i/G}) \times \boldsymbol{F}_i \\
&= \sum_{i=1}^{n} \boldsymbol{M}_i + \sum_{i=1}^{m} \boldsymbol{r}_{i/G} \times \boldsymbol{F}_i + \boldsymbol{r}_G \times \sum_{i=1}^{m} \boldsymbol{F}_i \\
&= \boldsymbol{M}_G + \boldsymbol{r}_G \times \boldsymbol{F} \\
&= \boldsymbol{M}_G + \boldsymbol{r}_G \times m\boldsymbol{a}_G
\end{aligned}$$

In view of Theorem 3-2, however, we also have

$$\boldsymbol{H}_O = \boldsymbol{r}_G \times m\boldsymbol{v}_G + \boldsymbol{H}_G$$

and $$\dot{\boldsymbol{H}}_O = \boldsymbol{r}_G \times m\boldsymbol{a}_G + \dot{\boldsymbol{H}}_G$$

Collectively, we thus have

$$\boldsymbol{M}_O = \boldsymbol{M}_G + \boldsymbol{r}_G \times m\boldsymbol{a}_G = \dot{\boldsymbol{H}}_O = \boldsymbol{r}_G \times m\boldsymbol{a}_G + \dot{\boldsymbol{H}}_G$$

and hence $$\boldsymbol{M}_G = \dot{\boldsymbol{H}}_G$$ ■

It is instructive to state the law of moment of momentum with respect to the center of mass in its expanded form. With

$$\boldsymbol{M}_G = M_{x_1}\hat{\boldsymbol{\imath}}_1 + M_{y_1}\hat{\boldsymbol{\jmath}}_1 + M_{z_1}\hat{\boldsymbol{k}}_1$$

the resultant component equations are

$$\begin{aligned}
M_{x_1} &= I_{x_1x_1}\dot{\omega}_{x_1} + I_{x_1y_1}\left(\dot{\omega}_{y_1} - \omega_{x_1}\omega_{z_1}\right) + I_{x_1z_1}\left(\dot{\omega}_{z_1} + \omega_{x_1}\omega_{y_1}\right) \\
&\quad + \left(I_{z_1z_1} - I_{y_1y_1}\right)\omega_{y_1}\omega_{z_1} + I_{y_1z_1}\left(\omega_{y_1}^2 - \omega_{z_1}^2\right) \\
M_{y_1} &= I_{x_1y_1}\left(\dot{\omega}_{x_1} + \omega_{y_1}\omega_{z_1}\right) + I_{y_1y_1}\dot{\omega}_{y_1} + I_{y_1z_1}\left(\dot{\omega}_{z_1} - \omega_{x_1}\omega_{y_1}\right) \\
&\quad + \left(I_{x_1x_1} - I_{z_1z_1}\right)\omega_{x_1}\omega_{z_1} + I_{x_1z_1}\left(\omega_{z_1}^2 - \omega_{x_1}^2\right) \\
M_{z_1} &= I_{x_1z_1}\left(\dot{\omega}_{x_1} - \omega_{y_1}\omega_{z_1}\right) + I_{y_1z_1}\left(\dot{\omega}_{y_1} + \omega_{x_1}\omega_{z_1}\right) \\
&\quad + I_{z_1z_1}\dot{\omega}_{z_1} + \left(I_{y_1y_1} - I_{x_1x_1}\right)\omega_{x_1}\omega_{y_1} + I_{x_1y_1}\left(\omega_{x_1}^2 - \omega_{y_1}^2\right)
\end{aligned} \tag{3-24}$$

Remark 3-4. Naturally, we include Newton's third law as one of the "axioms." It may be shown, however, by means of a straightforward argument that Newton's third law is a consequence of Euler's first law of motion, a proof of which was first given by Noll in 1957. The argument is reproduced in Fox.[1]

3-5 EXAMPLES

As before, we shall now work some comparatively simple examples which deal with applications in robotics. The examples have been simplified to allow exact solutions within a reasonable amount of time. Their main aim is to present relevant topics and to produce a way of thinking in dynamics which is tailored to robotics.

Throughout, it is of interest to distinguish between actuator and nonactuator forces and moments rather than making the usual distinction between internal and external forces and moments. Particular emphasis is placed on the calculation of the forces and moments needed to produce given motions along with any limitations that might be imposed by allowable stresses and actuator capabilities.

The laws of motion provide the connection between the motion and the forces and moments needed to sustain a given motion. This is not a cause-and-effect relationship since both are taken to occur simultaneously. Rather, we have a natural phenomenon which is described by the simultaneous occurrence of forces and motions. Satisfaction of the laws determines the possibility or impossibility of the phenomenon. We begin with some simple examples from particle dynamics.

Example 3-4. Let the absolute motion of a particle P with mass $m = 2$ kg be prescribed as $\boldsymbol{r}_0(t) = 2t^2\hat{\imath}_0 + \frac{1}{6}t^3\hat{\jmath}_0$ meters. Suppose it is known that an external force $\boldsymbol{R}(t) = 4\hat{\imath}_0 + 2t\hat{\jmath}_0$ N is acting on P. Is this a possible combination of force and motion? If not, what additional force must be provided to make this motion possible?

Solution. Since the motion of the system is completely specified, the resultant force required to sustain the motion is determined from an application of Newton's second law. Let $\boldsymbol{F}^a(t)$ denote any additional (or external actuator) force that might be required. Then we must have

$$\boldsymbol{F}^a(t) + \boldsymbol{R}(t) = m\ddot{\boldsymbol{r}}_0(t)$$

$$\boldsymbol{F}^a(t) + (4\hat{\imath}_0 + 2t\hat{\jmath}_0) = 2(4\hat{\imath}_0 + t\hat{\jmath}_0)$$

We conclude that the motion would not be possible without an actuator force (i.e., $4\hat{\imath}_0 \neq 8\hat{\imath}_0$). An actuator force of $\boldsymbol{F}^a(t) = 4\hat{\imath}_0$ N is needed to sustain the prescribed motion.

Example 3-5. Consider again the motion of a 2-kg particle P. Suppose we prescribe a velocity $\boldsymbol{v}_0(t) = t^2\hat{\imath}_0 + v\hat{\jmath}_0$ m/s, a constant $\hat{\jmath}_0$-component of the velocity. Let the known external force be $\boldsymbol{R}(t) = 4t\hat{\imath}_0 + 2t\hat{\jmath}_0$ N. Suppose that only an actuator force in the $\hat{\jmath}_0$-direction is available. Can this actuator be used to sustain the prescribed motion?

Solution. The available additional force has the form

$$\boldsymbol{F}^a(t) = F^a(t)\hat{\jmath}_0$$

The use of Newton's second law yields

$$\boldsymbol{F}^a(t) + \boldsymbol{R}(t) = m\dot{\boldsymbol{v}}_0$$

as a condition that must be satisfied. We have

$$F^a(t)\hat{\jmath}_0 + (4t\hat{\imath}_0 + 2t\hat{\jmath}_0) = 2(2t\hat{\imath}_0)$$

Thus the presence of the actuator force is again required. Without the presence of the actuator, the $\hat{\jmath}_0$-component of the velocity could not remain constant. An actuator force of $\boldsymbol{F}^a(t) = -2t\hat{\jmath}_0$ is needed to assure a constant $\hat{\jmath}_0$-component.

Thus the force cannot be used directly to keep a velocity constant (which might be expected), but it can be used to cancel disturbances.

We now proceed to a slightly more complicated example.

Example 3-6 A physical pendulum. Consider the one-armed manipulator in Fig. 3-5. Suppose that the motion begins ($t = 0$) at $\theta_1 = \pi/2$, where P has a downward vertical velocity component v. The component is to be maintained at this constant value until $\theta_1 = \pi/4$. The manipulator may be considered as a slender rod of length L, mass m, and hinged at the point O.

(*a*) Determine $\theta_1(t)$ if the vertical component of the velocity of P is v.
(*b*) Determine the motion of the system in a gravitational field $\boldsymbol{g}$.
(*c*) Show that the motion as obtained in part (*b*) has a nonconstant vertical component of velocity for P.
(*d*) Introduce additional external forces or moments, or both, which may serve to maintain the vertical component of the velocity of P at v.

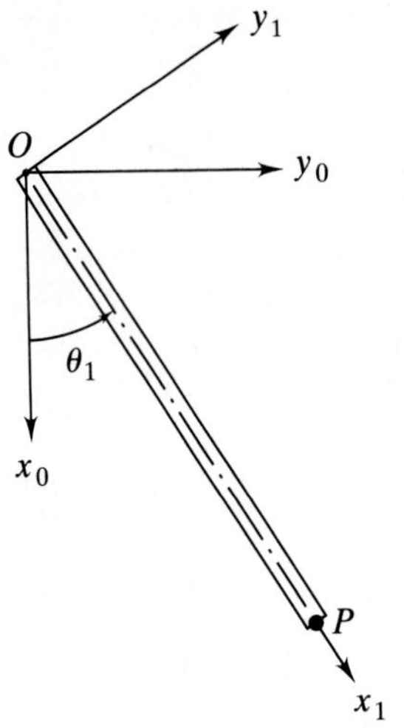

FIGURE 3-5
One-armed manipulator.

Solution

(*a*) The velocity of the point P is given by

$$\boldsymbol{v}_p(t) = L\dot{\theta}_1(t)\,\hat{\boldsymbol{j}}_1(t) = L\dot{\theta}_1(t)(-\sin\theta_1(t)\hat{\boldsymbol{\imath}}_0 + \cos\theta_1(t)\,\hat{\boldsymbol{j}}_0)$$

$$= v\hat{\boldsymbol{\imath}}_0 + v_y(t)\,\hat{\boldsymbol{j}}_0$$

Consequently,

$$-L\dot{\theta}_1(t)\sin\theta_1(t) = v$$

This may be integrated to yield

$$L\cos\theta_1(t) = vt + C$$

The initial conditions $\theta_1(t) = \pi/2$ at $t = 0$ imply $C = 0$, so that

$$\theta_1(t) = \text{Arccos}\frac{v}{L}t \tag{3-25}$$

(*b*) Based on the free body in Fig. 3-6, the forces and moments are given by

$$\boldsymbol{R} = R_x\hat{\boldsymbol{\imath}}_0 + R_y\hat{\boldsymbol{j}}_0$$

$$\boldsymbol{W} = mg\boldsymbol{i}_0$$

$$\boldsymbol{M}_O = \boldsymbol{r}_G \times \boldsymbol{W}$$

$$= \frac{L}{2}(\cos\theta_1(t)\hat{\boldsymbol{\imath}}_0 + \sin\theta_1(t)\,\hat{\boldsymbol{j}}_0) \times (mg\hat{\boldsymbol{\imath}}_0)$$

$$= -mg\frac{L}{2}\sin\theta_1\,\hat{\boldsymbol{k}}_0$$

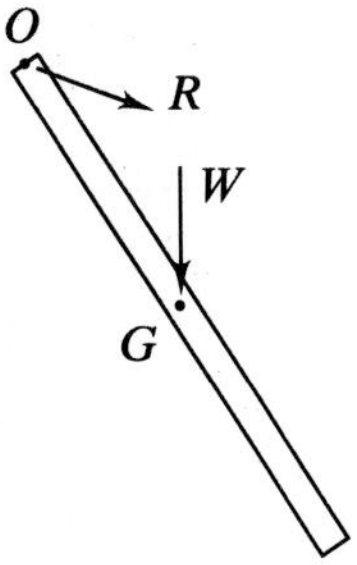

FIGURE 3-6
Force free body.

For the kinematics of the motion, we have

$$\boldsymbol{\alpha}(t) = \ddot{\theta}_1(t)\hat{\boldsymbol{k}}_0$$

and

$$\begin{aligned}\boldsymbol{a}_G(t) &= \frac{L}{2}\left(-\dot{\theta}_1^2(t)\hat{\imath}_1(t) + \ddot{\theta}_1(t)\hat{\jmath}_1(t)\right)\\ &= -\frac{L}{2}\left[\dot{\theta}_1^2\cos\theta_1 + \ddot{\theta}_1\sin\theta_1\right]\boldsymbol{i}_0 + \frac{L}{2}\left[-\dot{\theta}_1^2\sin\theta_1 + \ddot{\theta}_1\cos\theta_1\right]\hat{\jmath}_0\end{aligned}$$

The rate of change of the moment of momentum with respect to O is

$$\dot{\boldsymbol{H}}_O(t) = I_O\boldsymbol{\alpha}(t) = \tfrac{1}{3}mL^2\ddot{\theta}_1(t)\hat{\boldsymbol{k}}_0$$

Euler's laws of motion for the problem have the form

$$\boldsymbol{R} + \boldsymbol{W} = m\boldsymbol{a}_G$$

$$\boldsymbol{M}_O = \dot{\boldsymbol{H}}_O$$

resulting in the component equations

$$R_x = -mg - m\frac{L}{2}\left(\dot{\theta}_1^2(t)\cos\theta_1(t) + \ddot{\theta}_1(t)\sin\theta_1(t)\right)$$

$$R_y = m\frac{L}{2}\left[-\dot{\theta}_1^2(t)\sin\theta_1(t) + \ddot{\theta}_1(t)\cos\theta_1(t)\right]$$

$$-mg\frac{L}{2}\sin\theta_1(t) = \frac{1}{3}mL^2\ddot{\theta}_1(t)$$

The last of these may be written in the form

$$\ddot{\theta}_1 + \frac{3g}{2L}\sin\theta_1 = 0$$

This is the pendulum equation with the initial conditions $\theta_1(0) = \pi/2$ and $\dot{\theta}_1(0) = -v/L$. A first integration yields

$$\dot{\theta}_1^2(t) = \left(\frac{v}{L}\right)^2 + \frac{3g}{L}\cos\theta_1(t)$$

After a considerable amount of algebra, the integral of this equation may eventually be written in the form

$$t = \sqrt{\frac{2L}{3g}} \int_{\sqrt{2}/2k}^{u} \frac{du}{\sqrt{(1-u^2)(1-k^2u^2)}}$$

with $\qquad ku = \sin\frac{1}{2}\theta_1 \qquad$ and $\qquad k^2 = \frac{1}{2} + \frac{v^2}{6gL}$

The expression for t is an elliptic integral in the Legendre canonical form.

The expressions for $\ddot{\theta}_1$ and $\dot{\theta}_1^2$ in terms of θ_1 may be used to write the reaction components in the form

$$R_x = -mg - m\frac{L}{2}\left[\left(\frac{v}{L}\right)^2 \cos\theta_1 + \frac{3g}{L}\left(\cos^2\theta_1 - \frac{1}{2}\sin^2\theta_1\right)\right]$$

$$R_y = -m\frac{L}{2}\sin\theta_1\left[\left(\frac{v}{L}\right)^2 + \frac{9g}{2L}\cos\theta_1\right]$$

(*c*) It suffices to show that the $\hat{\imath}_0$-component of the acceleration is nonzero. The use of $\dot{\theta}_1$ and $\ddot{\theta}_1$ in terms of θ_1 in the expression for the acceleration of the center of mass yields

$$\cos^2\theta_1 + \frac{2v^2}{9Lg}\cos\theta_1 - \frac{1}{3} \neq 0$$

(*d*) Part (*c*) consisted of what is called a mixed problem in dynamics. Some of the forces and the path of motion of the center of mass were prescribed.

Here the motion is completely prescribed with

$$\theta_1(t) = \mathrm{Cos}^{-1}\left(\frac{v}{L}t\right)$$

and we are to determine any additional forces that might be required to maintain this motion. These additional needed forces or moments are to be supplied by actuators.

As the first such possibility, consider a linear actuator, attached at P in such a way that it remains aligned with the $\hat{\imath}_0$-direction. Thus the applied *external* force has the form

$$\boldsymbol{F}^a = F^a(t)\hat{\imath}_0$$

(see Fig. 3-7*a*.) An application of Euler's second law yields

$$F^a(t)L\sin\theta_1(t) - W\frac{L}{2}\sin\theta_1(t) = \frac{1}{3}mL^2\ddot{\theta}_1(t)$$

The calculation of the second derivative of the specified $\theta_1(t)$ yields

$$\ddot{\theta}_1(t) = -\dot{\theta}_1^2(t)\cot\theta_1(t) = -\left(\frac{v}{L}\right)^2\frac{1}{\sin^2\theta_1(t)}\cot\theta_1(t)$$

$$= -\left(\frac{v}{L}\right)^2\frac{\cos\theta_1(t)}{\sin^3\theta_1(t)}$$

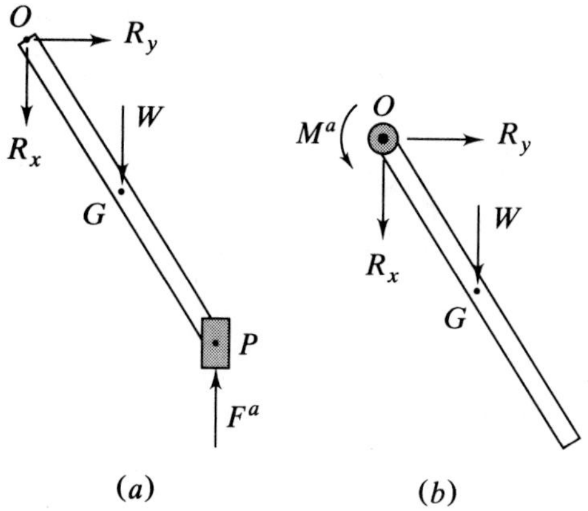

FIGURE 3-7
(*a*) A linear actuator, (*b*) a rotary actuator.

The required actuator force may thus be written in terms of θ_1 as

$$F^a(t) = \frac{1}{L\sin\theta_1}\left[\frac{1}{2}mgL\sin\theta_1 + \frac{1}{3}mL^2\left(-\left(\frac{v}{L}\right)^2\frac{\cos\theta_1}{\sin^3\theta_1}\right)\right]$$

$$= \frac{1}{2}mg - \frac{1}{3}\frac{mv^2}{L}\frac{\cos\theta_1}{\sin^4\theta_1}$$

Note that the force may be positive or negative, with ranges depending on the problem parameters and on the prescribed speed v. That is, the force may have to speed up or retard the natural action of the system.

A final possibility consists of the introduction of a rotary actuator at O —a device that supplies a moment suitable for sustaining the motion. Thus we simply introduce a moment, as yet unknown:

$$\boldsymbol{M}^a(t) = M^a(t)\hat{\boldsymbol{k}}_0$$

The use of Euler's second law yields

$$M^a(t) - mg\frac{L}{2}\sin\theta_1(t) = \frac{1}{3}mL^2\ddot{\theta}_1(t)$$

(see Fig. 3-7*b*). The use of $\ddot{\theta}_1$ in terms of θ_1 as before yields

$$M^a(t) = \frac{1}{2}mgL\sin\theta_1 - \frac{1}{3}mv^2\frac{\cos\theta_1}{\sin^3\theta_1}$$

Example 3-7. Consider again the two-dimensional manipulator of Example 2-17 (see Fig. 3-8). Assume that the motion is to occur in the x_0y_0-plane and that it is to be sustained by a linear actuator at the joint and a rotary actuator at the base O. The manipulator components have moments of inertia I_{G_1} and I_{G_2} with respect to

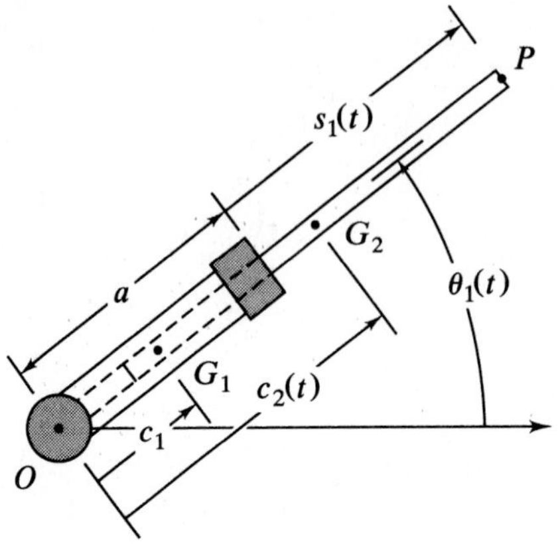

FIGURE 3-8
Polar manipulator (again). Shaded areas indicate actuator locations: (○) rotary actuator; (□) linear actuator.

their centers of mass located at distances c_1 and $c_2(t)$ from point O, respectively. Neglect the actuator masses.

(*a*) Determine the actuator force and moment in terms of $\theta_1(t)$ and $c_2(t)$ and their derivatives.

(*b*) Write the required moments and forces if the required motion of P is one with constant speed v along a ray from O and along a circle of radius $R > a$.

Solution

(*a*) We shall first determine the actuator moment needed at the base O of the manipulator. It suffices to use Euler's second law with respect to the base point O.

The moment of momentum of the system with respect to O is

$$\boldsymbol{H}_O = \boldsymbol{r}_{G_1} \times m_1 \dot{\boldsymbol{r}}_{G_1} + I_{G_1}\dot{\theta}_1 \hat{\boldsymbol{k}}_1 + \boldsymbol{r}_{G_2} \times m_2 \dot{\boldsymbol{r}}_{G_2} + I_{G_2}\dot{\theta}_1 \hat{\boldsymbol{k}}_1$$

The corresponding rate of change is given by

$$\begin{aligned}
\dot{\boldsymbol{H}}_O &= \boldsymbol{r}_{G_1} \times m_1 \ddot{\boldsymbol{r}}_{G_1} + I_{G_1}\ddot{\theta}_1 \hat{\boldsymbol{k}}_1 + \boldsymbol{r}_{G_2} \times m_2 \ddot{\boldsymbol{r}}_{G_2} + I_{G_2}\ddot{\theta}_1 \hat{\boldsymbol{k}}_1 \\
&= (c_1 \hat{\boldsymbol{\imath}}_1) \times m_1\left(-c_1\dot{\theta}_1^2 \hat{\boldsymbol{\imath}}_1 + c_1\ddot{\theta}_1 \hat{\boldsymbol{\jmath}}_1\right) + I_{G_1}\ddot{\theta}_1 \hat{\boldsymbol{k}}_1 \\
&\quad + (c_2 \hat{\boldsymbol{\imath}}_1) \times m_2\left[\left(\ddot{c}_2 - c_2\dot{\theta}_1^2\right)\hat{\boldsymbol{\imath}}_1 + \left(2\dot{c}_2\dot{\theta}_1 + c_2\ddot{\theta}_1\right)\hat{\boldsymbol{\jmath}}_1\right] + I_{G_2}\ddot{\theta}_1 \hat{\boldsymbol{k}}_1 \\
&= m_1 c_1^2 \ddot{\theta}_1 \hat{\boldsymbol{k}}_1 + I_{G_1}\ddot{\theta}_1 \hat{\boldsymbol{k}}_1 + m_2 c_2\left(2\dot{c}_2\dot{\theta}_1 + c_2\ddot{\theta}_1\right)\hat{\boldsymbol{k}}_1 + I_{G_2}\ddot{\theta}_1 \hat{\boldsymbol{k}}_1
\end{aligned}$$

The moment about O is given by

$$\boldsymbol{M}_O = M^a \hat{\boldsymbol{k}}_1 - m_1 g c_1 \cos\theta_1 \,\hat{\boldsymbol{k}}_1 - m_2 g c_2 \cos\theta_1 \,\hat{\boldsymbol{k}}_1$$

(see Fig. 3-9). The use of the law of moment of momentum then yields

$$\boldsymbol{M}_O = \dot{\boldsymbol{H}}_O$$

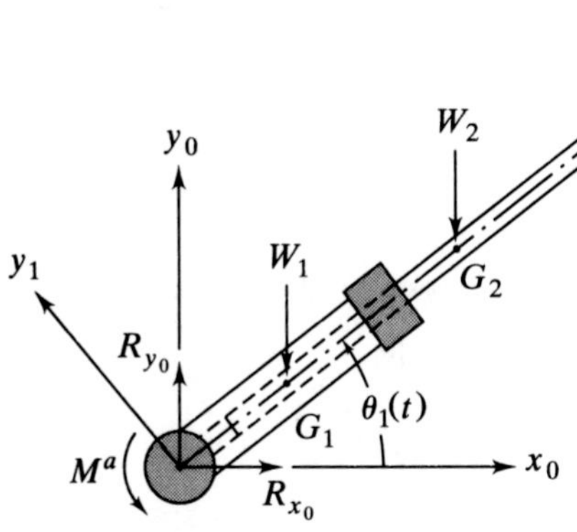

FIGURE 3-9
Polar manipulator (again), with forces.

with

$$M^a(t) = m_1 g c_1 \cos\theta_1 + m_2 g c_2 \cos\theta_1 + \left[c_1^2 m_1 + c_2^2 m_2 + I_{G_1} + I_{G_2}\right]\ddot{\theta}_1 + 2m_2 c_2 \dot{c}_2 \dot{\theta}_1$$

as the required actuator moment.

For the calculation of the linear actuator force at the joint, it suffices to use Euler's first law. The component equation in the $\hat{\imath}_1$-direction yields

$$-F^a - m_2 g \sin\theta_1 = m_2\left(\ddot{c}_2 - c_2\dot{\theta}_1^2\right)$$

or

$$F^a(t) = -m_2\left[g\sin\theta_1 + \ddot{c}_2 - c_2\dot{\theta}_1^2\right]$$

as the required actuator force (see Fig. 3-10).

(*b*) Along a ray we have $\theta_1(t) = \phi = \text{const}$. The result is

$$M^a(t) = m_1 g c_1 \cos\phi + m_2 g(vt + c_{20})\cos\phi$$

that is, the actuator moment needs to be simply enough to maintain "static" equilibrium; c_{20} is simply the initial value of c_2. Note that the actuator moment still is a function of time.

For the actuator force we have

$$F^a(t) = -m_2 g \sin\phi$$

since $\ddot{c}_2(t) = 0$ as a consequence of the required constant speed.

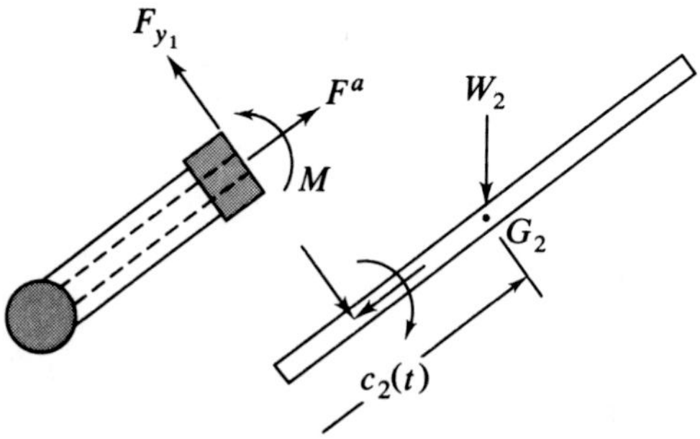

FIGURE 3-10
Polar manipulator (again), in pieces

Some comments may be helpful. As mentioned before, force cannot be used to maintain a constant velocity; the actuator forces and moments are used to maintain the summation of forces and moments at 0. The result here indicates that once we have the center of mass G_2 moving with constant speed v, the only actuator force required is one that is sufficient to maintain static equilibrium with the weight of the arm.

Along a circular path, we have $c_2(t) = c_2 = \text{const}$. With $\dot{c}_2 = \ddot{c}_2 = 0$ and $\theta_1(t) = (v/R)t$, the actuator moment is

$$M^a(t) = (c_1 m_1 + c_2 m_2) g \cos\frac{v}{R}t$$

again indicating that once we have the system moving with constant speed v, all we need to do is maintain static equilibrium at each instant.

The actuator force is

$$F^a(t) = -m_2\left[g \sin\frac{v}{R}t - c_2\left(\frac{v}{R}\right)^2\right]$$

In the manipulator of Example 3-7 we determined both internal and external actuator forces and moments necessary to sustain a prescribed motion. In the next example we shall see that the internal force and moment resultants of a bar are the "actuator" forces and moments needed to sustain the motion of the system in a gravitational field.

Example 3-8. Consider again the physical pendulum of Example 3-6. Assume that the slender bar is moving as a pendulum under the action of gravity. Determine the internal force and moment resultants as functions of the distance r from the point O and as a function of the angle θ_1. For convenience, assume that the arm is released from rest at $\theta_1 = \pi/2$ (see Fig. 3-11).

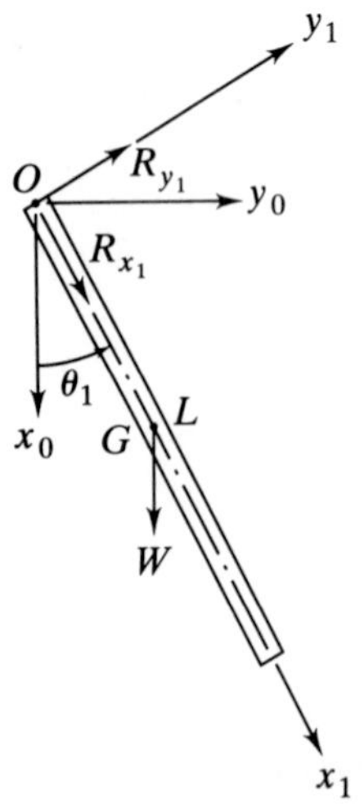

FIGURE 3-11
Physical pendulum.

Solution. In this case, it is more convenient to work with the reaction components in the directions $\hat{\imath}_1$ and $\hat{\jmath}_1$, in view of the intended determination of the internal force and moment distribution. The use of Euler's first law yields

$$\boldsymbol{R} + \boldsymbol{W} = m\boldsymbol{a}_G$$

$$(R_{x_1} + mg\cos\theta_1)\hat{\imath}_1 + (R_{y_1} - mg\sin\theta_1)\hat{\jmath}_1 = m\frac{L}{2}\left(-\dot{\theta}_1^2\hat{\imath}_1 + \ddot{\theta}_1\hat{\jmath}_1\right)$$

and the law of moment of momentum results in

$$\boldsymbol{M}_O = \dot{\boldsymbol{H}}_O$$

$$-mg\frac{L}{2}\sin\theta_1 = \frac{1}{3}mL^2\ddot{\theta}_1$$

An integration of this equation subject to $\dot{\theta}_1(0) = 0$ and $\theta_1(0) = \pi/2$ provides

$$\dot{\theta}_1^2 = \frac{3g}{L}\cos\theta_1 \tag{3-26}$$

The two previous equations together may be used to write the reaction components in the form

$$R_{x_1} = -mg\cos\theta_1 - m\frac{L}{2}\left(\frac{3g}{L}\cos\theta_1\right) = -\frac{5}{2}mg\cos\theta_1$$

$$R_{y_1} = mg\sin\theta_1 - m\frac{L}{2}\left(\frac{3g}{2L}\sin\theta_1\right) = \frac{1}{4}mg\sin\theta_1$$

The integration of the equation for $\dot{\theta}_1$, of course, again yields an elliptic integral.

For the determination of the internal force and moment distribution, we consider the free body in Fig. 3-12 with the positive sign convention indicated on the upper segment of the bar.

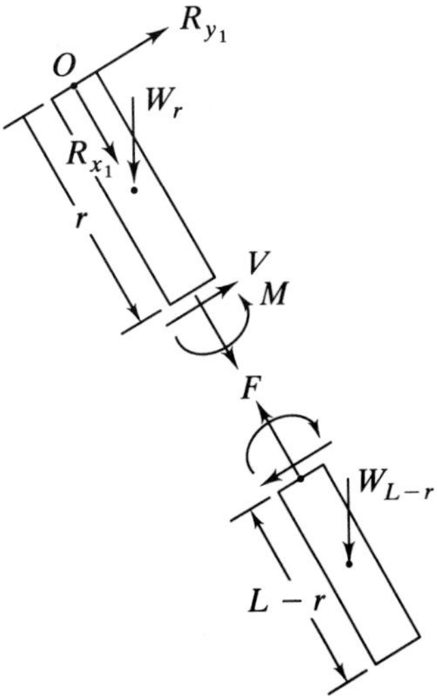

FIGURE 3-12
Internal forces and moments.

It is essential to note that the segments of this pendulum now have the prescribed angular motion $\theta_1(t)$ as determined previously (see Example 3-6). This is not the natural motion of, say, the upper segment in a gravitational field. Rather, it requires the internal "actuator" forces F and V and the moment M to sustain it.

The application of Euler's laws to the upper segment of the bar yields the following shear, axial force, and moment distributions:

Euler's first law provides

$$\boldsymbol{R} + \boldsymbol{W}_r + F\hat{\imath}_1 + V\hat{\jmath}_1 = \left(\frac{m}{L}r\right)\boldsymbol{a}_{G_r}$$

and

$$V(r,\theta_1) = -R_{y_1} + mg\frac{r}{L}\sin\theta_1 + \frac{mr^2}{2L}\ddot{\theta}_1$$

$$= -\frac{1}{4}mg\sin\theta_1\left(1 - \frac{r}{L}\right)\left(1 - 3\frac{r}{L}\right)$$

$$F(r,\theta_1) = -R_{x_1} - mg\frac{r}{L}\cos\theta_1 - \frac{mr^2}{2L}\dot{\theta}_1^2$$

$$= mg\cos\theta_1\left[\frac{5}{2} - \frac{r}{L} - \frac{3}{2}\left(\frac{r}{L}\right)^2\right]$$

Euler's second law provides

$$-\left(\frac{mg}{L}\right)r\left(\frac{r}{2}\sin\theta_1\right) + Vr + M = \frac{1}{3}\left(\frac{mr}{L}\right)r^2\ddot{\theta}_1$$

and

$$M(r,\theta_1) = \left(\frac{mg}{L}\right)\frac{r^2}{2}\sin\theta_1 + \frac{1}{3}\frac{m}{L}r^3\ddot{\theta}_1 - Vr$$

$$= \frac{1}{4}mgr\sin\theta_1\left(1 - \frac{r}{L}\right)^2$$

The resultant internal forces and moments may be considered to be the stress resultants on a cross section a distance r from O when the pendulum is taken to be a flexible beam. They may thus be used to calculate the maximum stresses during the motion of the beam, and, more generally, we may use such dynamic stress calculations to design the members of dynamic machinery to withstand operating loads.

In such a context, the corresponding force and moment diagrams are of interest. Here these may be plotted for a given θ_1. The shear and moment diagrams clearly have their maximum with respect to θ_1 at $\theta_1 = \pi/2$; they are sketched in Fig. 3-13a and b. The axial force has its maximum at $\theta_1 = 0$ (see Fig. 3-13c).

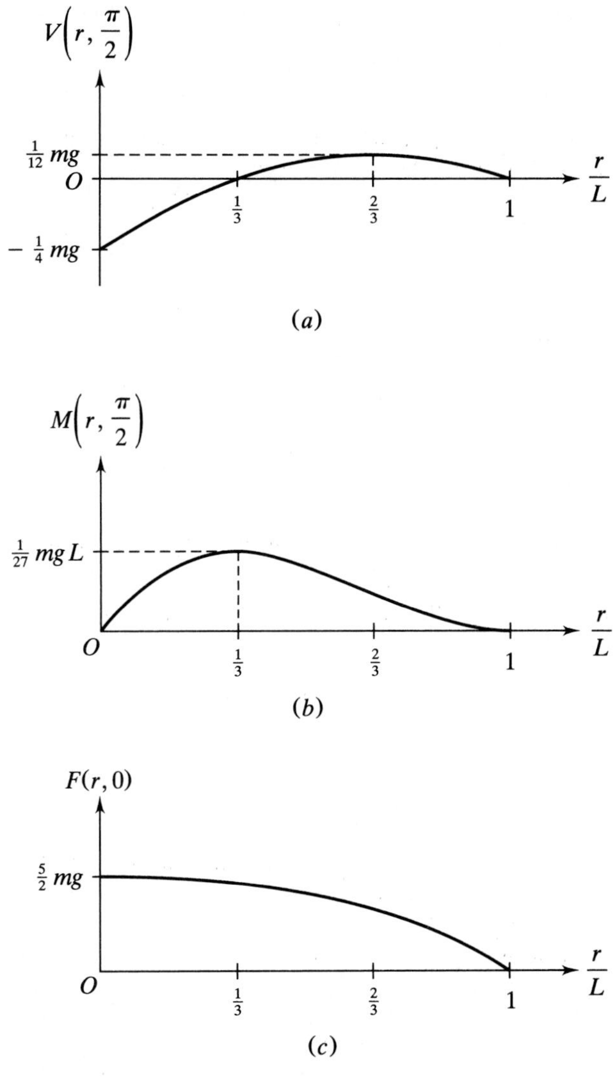

FIGURE 3-13
(*a*) Shear diagram. (*b*) moment diagram. (*c*) axial force diagram.

Example 3-9. Consider the system in Fig. 3-14. The thin disk A at the end of the slender rod B is rotating with constant angular velocity $\dot{\alpha}_2\hat{\imath}_1$ relative to $(0xyz)_1$. The rod B is rigidly connected to the cylinder C which is made to rotate with constant angular velocity $\dot{\theta}_1\hat{k}_0$ relative to $(0xyz)_0$. Calculate the actuator moment $M^a\hat{k}_0$, applied at O_0, which is needed to sustain this motion. Assume homogeneous mass distribution throughout.

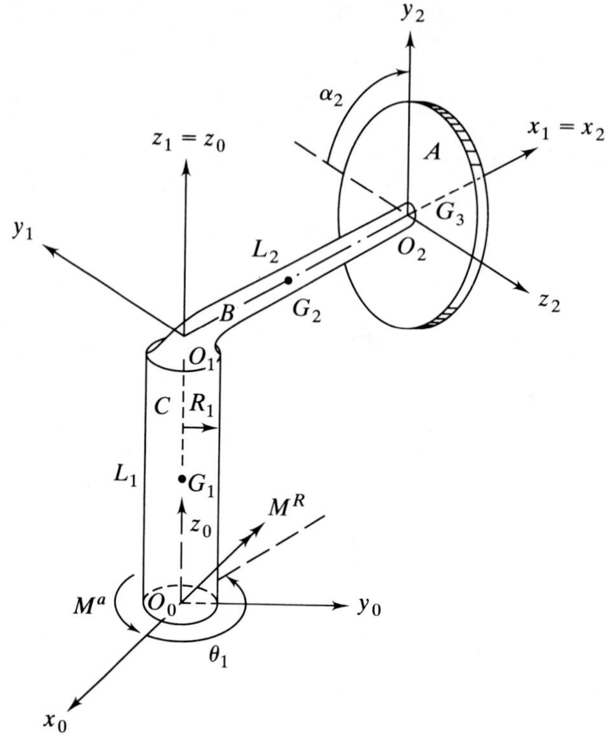

FIGURE 3-14
A manipulator with rotating end effector.

Solution. Ultimately, we shall use Euler's second law, $\dot{\boldsymbol{H}}_{Q_0} = \boldsymbol{M}_{O_0}$, applied with respect to O_0, to determine the actuator moment M^a. The first task is the calculation of the absolute moment of momentum with respect to O_0. We shall obtain the total by first calculating the moment of momentum of each component with respect to O_0. Thus, in each case, we shall use

$$\mathbf{H}_G = \begin{bmatrix} I_{xx} & 0 & 0 \\ 0 & I_{yy} & 0 \\ 0 & 0 & I_{zz} \end{bmatrix} \begin{pmatrix} \omega_x \\ \omega_y \\ \omega_z \end{pmatrix}$$

in view of the geometric and mass symmetry and hence deduce $\boldsymbol{H}_G$ which may then be used in the calculation of

$$\boldsymbol{H}_O = \boldsymbol{r}_G \times m\boldsymbol{v}_G + \boldsymbol{H}_G$$

The disk A. Note that in the matrix expression for $\boldsymbol{H}_G$ the moments of inertia and the angular velocity must be written with respect to the same basis. Furthermore, the absolute angular velocity must be used if the absolute moment of momentum is desired. The absolute angular velocity of the disk is

$$\boldsymbol{\omega}_2 = \dot{\alpha}_2 \hat{\boldsymbol{\imath}}_1 + \dot{\theta}_1 \hat{\boldsymbol{k}}_0$$

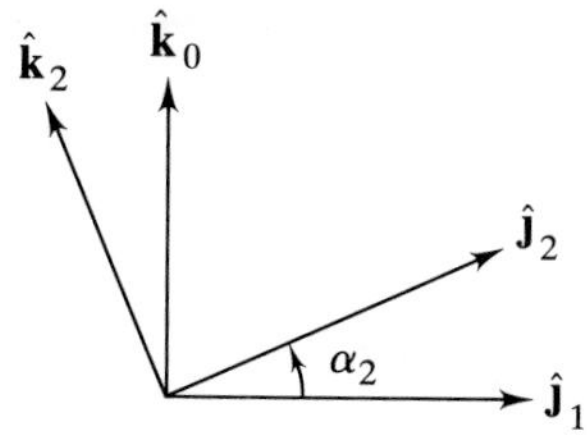

FIGURE 3-15
Relation between unit vectors.

We now write $\boldsymbol{\omega}_2$ in terms of $(\hat{\imath}\hat{\jmath}\hat{k})_2$. Based on Fig. 3-15, we have

$$\hat{\boldsymbol{k}}_0 = \sin\alpha_2\,\hat{\boldsymbol{\jmath}}_2 + \cos\alpha_2\,\hat{\boldsymbol{k}}_2$$

$$\hat{\boldsymbol{\imath}}_1 = \hat{\boldsymbol{\imath}}_2$$

$$\hat{\boldsymbol{\jmath}}_1 = \cos\alpha_2\,\hat{\boldsymbol{\jmath}}_2 - \sin\alpha_2\,\hat{\boldsymbol{k}}_2$$

with

$$\boldsymbol{\omega}_2 = \dot{\alpha}_2\hat{\boldsymbol{\imath}}_2 + \dot{\theta}_1\sin\alpha_2\,\hat{\boldsymbol{\jmath}}_2 + \dot{\theta}_1\cos\alpha_2\,\hat{\boldsymbol{k}}_2$$

The moment of momentum about the center of mass G_3 is

$$\mathbf{H}_G = \begin{bmatrix} \frac{1}{2}m_AR_2^2 & 0 & 0 \\ 0 & \frac{1}{4}m_AR_2^2 & 0 \\ 0 & 0 & \frac{1}{4}m_AR_2^2 \end{bmatrix} \begin{pmatrix} \dot{\alpha}_2 \\ \dot{\theta}_1\sin\alpha_2 \\ \dot{\theta}_1\cos\alpha_2 \end{pmatrix}$$

For the cross-product term we have

$$\boldsymbol{r}_G = L_1\hat{\boldsymbol{k}}_0 + L_2\hat{\boldsymbol{\imath}}_1 = L_2\hat{\boldsymbol{\imath}}_2 + L_1\sin\alpha_2\,\hat{\boldsymbol{\jmath}}_2 + L_1\cos\alpha_2\,\hat{\boldsymbol{k}}_2$$

$$\boldsymbol{v}_G = L_2\dot{\theta}_1\hat{\boldsymbol{\jmath}}_1 = L_2\dot{\theta}_1\cos\alpha_2\,\hat{\boldsymbol{\jmath}}_2 - L_2\dot{\theta}_1\sin\alpha_2\,\hat{\boldsymbol{k}}_2$$

$$\begin{aligned} \boldsymbol{r}_G \times m_A\boldsymbol{v}_G &= \Big(L_2^2\dot{\theta}_1\cos\alpha_2\,\hat{\boldsymbol{k}}_2 + L_2^2\dot{\theta}_1\sin\alpha_2\,\hat{\boldsymbol{\jmath}}_2 \\ &\qquad -L_1L_2\dot{\theta}_1\sin^2\alpha_2\,\hat{\boldsymbol{\imath}}_2 - L_1L_2\dot{\theta}_1\cos^2\alpha_2\,\hat{\boldsymbol{\imath}}_2\Big)m_A \\ &= \Big(-L_1L_2\dot{\theta}_1\hat{\boldsymbol{\imath}}_2 + L_2^2\dot{\theta}_1\sin\alpha_2\hat{\boldsymbol{\jmath}}_2 + L_2^2\dot{\theta}_1\cos\alpha_2\,\hat{\boldsymbol{k}}_2\Big)m_A \end{aligned}$$

The total moment of momentum of the disk A about O thus is

$$\begin{aligned} \boldsymbol{H}_{O_0}^A &= \left(\tfrac{1}{2}m_AR_2^2\dot{\alpha}_2 - L_1L_2\dot{\theta}_1m_A\right)\boldsymbol{i}_2 \\ &\quad + \left(\tfrac{1}{4}m_AR_2^2\dot{\theta}_1\sin\alpha_2 + L_2^2\dot{\theta}_1m_A\sin^2\alpha_2\right)\hat{\boldsymbol{\jmath}}_2 \\ &\quad + \left(\tfrac{1}{4}m_AR_2^2\dot{\theta}_1\cos\alpha_2 + L_2^2\dot{\theta}_1m_A\cos\alpha_2\right)\hat{\boldsymbol{k}}_2 \\ &= m_A\left(\tfrac{1}{2}R_2^2\dot{\alpha}_2 - L_1L_2\dot{\theta}_1\right)\hat{\boldsymbol{\imath}}_2 + m_A\dot{\theta}_1\sin\alpha_2\left(\tfrac{1}{4}R_2^2 + L_2^2\right)\hat{\boldsymbol{\jmath}}_2 \\ &\quad + m_A\dot{\theta}_1\cos\theta_2\left(\tfrac{1}{4}R_2^2 + L_2^2\right)\hat{\boldsymbol{k}}_2 \end{aligned}$$

The slender rod *B*. Everything will be expressed in terms of $(0xyz)_1$ and the corresponding basis. The angular velocity of the rod is

$$\boldsymbol{\omega}_1 = \dot{\theta}_1 \hat{\boldsymbol{k}}_0 = \dot{\theta}_1 \hat{\boldsymbol{k}}_1$$

The moment of momentum about the center of mass is

$$\mathbf{H}_G = \begin{bmatrix} 0 & 0 & 0 \\ 0 & \frac{1}{12} m_B L_2^2 & 0 \\ 0 & 0 & \frac{1}{12} m_B L_2^2 \end{bmatrix} \begin{pmatrix} 0 \\ 0 \\ \dot{\theta}_1 \end{pmatrix}$$

For the cross-product term we have

$$\boldsymbol{r}_G = L_1 \hat{\boldsymbol{k}}_1 + \tfrac{1}{2} L_2 \hat{\boldsymbol{\imath}}_1$$

$$\boldsymbol{v}_G = \tfrac{1}{2} L_2 \dot{\theta}_1 \hat{\boldsymbol{\jmath}}_1$$

$$\Rightarrow \quad \boldsymbol{r}_G \times m_B \boldsymbol{v}_G = -\tfrac{1}{2} L_1 L_2 \dot{\theta}_1 m_B \hat{\boldsymbol{\imath}}_1 + \tfrac{1}{4} L_2^2 \dot{\theta}_1 m_B \hat{\boldsymbol{k}}_1$$

and hence

$$\begin{aligned} \boldsymbol{H}_{O_0}^B &= \tfrac{1}{2} m_B L_1 L_2 \dot{\theta}_1 \hat{\boldsymbol{\imath}}_1 + \left(\tfrac{1}{12} m_B L_2^2 \dot{\theta}_1 + \tfrac{1}{4} L_2^2 m_B \dot{\theta}_1 \right) \hat{\boldsymbol{k}}_1 \\ &= \tfrac{1}{2} m_B L_1 L_2 \dot{\theta}_1 \hat{\boldsymbol{\imath}}_1 + \tfrac{1}{3} m_B L_2^2 \dot{\theta}_1 \hat{\boldsymbol{k}}_1 \end{aligned}$$

The circular cylinder *C*. The angular velocity is

$$\boldsymbol{\omega}_1 = \dot{\theta}_1 \hat{\boldsymbol{k}}_0 = \dot{\theta}_1 \hat{\boldsymbol{k}}_1$$

The moment of momentum about the center of mass is

$$\mathbf{H}_G = \begin{bmatrix} \frac{1}{12} m_C (3R_1^2 + L_1^2) & 0 & 0 \\ 0 & \frac{1}{12} m_C (3R_1^2 + L_1^2) & 0 \\ 0 & 0 & \frac{1}{2} m_C R_1^2 \end{bmatrix} \begin{pmatrix} 0 \\ 0 \\ \dot{\theta}_1 \end{pmatrix}$$

so that

$$\boldsymbol{H}_{O_0}^C = \tfrac{1}{2} m_C R_1^2 \dot{\theta}_1 \hat{\boldsymbol{k}}_1$$

The total moment of momentum. In terms of $(\hat{\imath}\hat{\jmath}\hat{k})_1$ we have

$$\hat{\boldsymbol{\imath}}_2 = \hat{\boldsymbol{\imath}}_1$$

$$\hat{\boldsymbol{\jmath}}_2 = \cos \alpha_2 \hat{\boldsymbol{\jmath}}_1 + \sin \alpha_2 \hat{\boldsymbol{k}}_1$$

$$\hat{\boldsymbol{k}}_2 = -\sin \alpha_2 \hat{\boldsymbol{\jmath}}_1 + \cos \alpha_2 \hat{\boldsymbol{k}}_1$$

resulting in a total moment of momentum given by

$$\begin{aligned} \boldsymbol{H}_{O_0} &= H_{O_0}^A + \boldsymbol{H}_{O_0}^B + \boldsymbol{H}_{O_0}^C \\ &= \left[\tfrac{1}{2} m_A R_2^2 \dot{\alpha}_2 + L_1 L_2 \left(\tfrac{1}{2} m_B - m_A \right) \dot{\theta}_1 \right] \hat{\boldsymbol{\imath}}_1 \\ &\quad + \left[m_A \left(\tfrac{1}{4} R_2^2 + L_2^2 \right) + \tfrac{1}{3} m_B L_2^2 + \tfrac{1}{2} m_C R_1^2 \right] \dot{\theta}_1 \hat{\boldsymbol{k}}_1 \end{aligned}$$

Thus the absolute time rate of change of the moment of momentum is given by

$$\dot{\boldsymbol{H}}_{O_0} = \left[\tfrac{1}{2}m_A R_2^2 \dot{\alpha}_2 \dot{\theta}_1 + L_1 L_2\left(\tfrac{1}{2}m_B - m_A\right)\dot{\theta}_1^2\right]\hat{\boldsymbol{j}}_1$$

(Recall that $\dot{\alpha}_2$ and $\dot{\theta}_1$ are constant.) The total moment at the base consists of an external "reaction" moment

$$\boldsymbol{M}^R = M_{x_1}\hat{\boldsymbol{\imath}}_1 + M_{y_1}\hat{\boldsymbol{j}}_1 + M_{z_1}^a \hat{\boldsymbol{k}}_1$$

and the moments due to the weights. Collectively, we have

$$\boldsymbol{M}_{O_0} = M_{x_1}\hat{\boldsymbol{\imath}}_1 + \left[M_{y_1} + \left(\tfrac{1}{2}m_B + m_A\right)L_2 g\right]\hat{\boldsymbol{j}}_1 + M_{z_1}^a \hat{\boldsymbol{k}}_1.$$

For the case $\dot{\alpha}_2$ and $\dot{\theta}_1$ equal to constants, an application of Euler's second law then yields

$$M_{y_1} = -\left(\tfrac{1}{2}m_B + m_A\right)L_2 g + \tfrac{1}{2}m_A R_2^2 \dot{\alpha}_2 \dot{\theta}_1 + L_1 L_2\left(\tfrac{1}{2}m_B - m_A\right)\dot{\theta}_1^2$$

with $M_{x_1} = M_{z_1}^a = 0$. That is, in the absence of friction, no actuator moment is required to maintain the constant rotations.

Note that M_{x_1} and M_{y_1} are reactions in the usual sense of supports providing the necessary forces and moments to keep a system where it is; the moment $M_{z_1}^a$ is a reactive moment that we choose to produce a desired motion. That is, actuators in this context provide external "reactions" meant to produce a desired motion.

In general, subject to the postulation of a unique relation between motion and forces and moments, the provision of the "correct" reactive forces or moments will produce the according motion in harmony with Euler's laws. (See also Problem 3-13 in this connection.)

Example 3-10. Suppose that the manipulator in Fig. 3-16 is to rotate about the z_0-axis with constant angular velocity Ω and that the arm is to have an angular

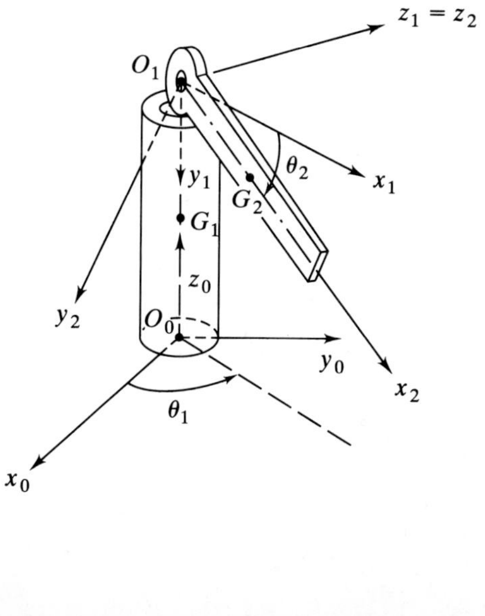

FIGURE 3-16
A simple manipulator.

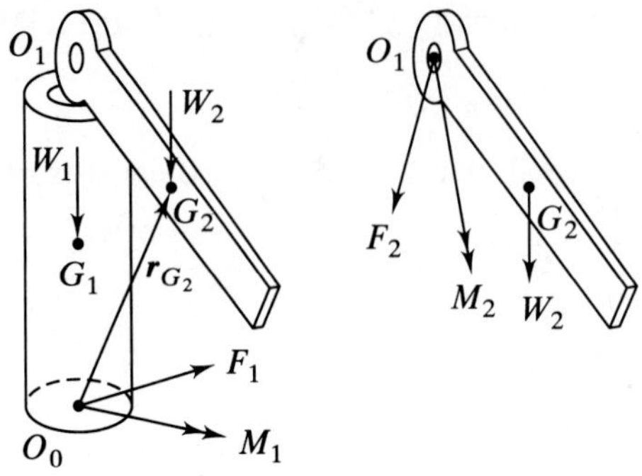

FIGURE 3-17
Some relevant free bodies.

velocity $\dot{\theta}_2 = \omega$ and an angular acceleration $\ddot{\theta}_2 = \alpha$. The base and the arm have masses and lengths m_1, L_1 and m_2, L_2, respetively, and they may be considered to be slender rods. This motion is to be attained by actuators at the base O and at the junction O_1. Calculate the actuator moments necessary at O and at O_1 if the rotary actuators can produce moments about the z_0- and z_1-axes.

Solution. The procedure for the solution of this type of problem remains the same. We first collect the ingredients for a use of Euler's laws so that their application ultimately is almost trivial (in concept, although perhaps not in detail). Again, we separate the solution into a number of more or less well-defined steps.

(*a*) Reference frames. This is nearly always the first step. We introduce suitable moving reference frames for the description of both the kinematics and the kinetics of the problem. Here we shall use essentially the first three reference frames of the PUMA manipulator.

(*b*) Free bodies. Here we introduce the free bodies for the calculations that are to be performed. We are to calculate the required actuator moments at both O_1 and O. The relevant free bodies are illustrated in Fig. 3-17. We shall also give the relations between the unit vectors, since these will be used frequently in the following calculations:

$$\hat{\boldsymbol{\imath}}_i = \cos\theta_2\,\hat{\boldsymbol{\imath}}_2 - \sin\theta_2\,\hat{\boldsymbol{\jmath}}_2 \qquad \hat{\boldsymbol{\imath}}_2 = \cos\theta_2\,\hat{\boldsymbol{\imath}}_1 + \sin\theta_2\,\hat{\boldsymbol{\jmath}}_1$$

$$\hat{\boldsymbol{\jmath}}_1 = \sin\theta_2\,\hat{\boldsymbol{\imath}}_2 + \cos\theta_2\,\hat{\boldsymbol{\jmath}}_2 \qquad \hat{\boldsymbol{\jmath}}_2 = -\sin\theta_2\,\hat{\boldsymbol{\imath}}_1 + \cos\theta_2\,\hat{\boldsymbol{\jmath}}_1$$

$$\hat{\boldsymbol{k}}_1 = \hat{\boldsymbol{k}}_2 \qquad \hat{\boldsymbol{k}}_2 = \hat{\boldsymbol{k}}_1$$

Note that both O and O_1 are fixed points in the problem so that the standard form of the law of moment of momentum may be used.

(*c*) Calculation of the moments $\boldsymbol{M}_O$ and $\boldsymbol{M}_{O_1}$. We begin with the calculation of $\boldsymbol{M}_O$:

$$\boldsymbol{W}_2 = m_2 g\hat{\boldsymbol{\jmath}}_1 \qquad \boldsymbol{M}_1 = M_{x_1}\hat{\boldsymbol{\imath}}_1 + M^a_{y_1}\hat{\boldsymbol{\jmath}}_1 + M_{z_1}\hat{\boldsymbol{k}}_1$$

$$\boldsymbol{r}_{G_2} = -L_1\hat{\boldsymbol{\jmath}}_1 + \tfrac{1}{2}L_2\hat{\boldsymbol{\imath}}_2$$

$$= \tfrac{1}{2}L_2\cos\theta_2\hat{\boldsymbol{\imath}}_1 + \left(\tfrac{1}{2}L_2\sin\theta_2 - L_1\right)\hat{\boldsymbol{\jmath}}_1$$

$$\boldsymbol{r}_{G_2} \times \boldsymbol{W}_2 = \tfrac{1}{2}L_2 m_2 g\cos\theta_2\,\hat{\boldsymbol{k}}_1$$

The total moment at O is

$$\boldsymbol{M}_O = M_{x_1}\hat{\boldsymbol{\imath}}_1 + M^a_{y_1}\hat{\boldsymbol{\jmath}}_1 + \left(M_{z_1} + \tfrac{1}{2}L_2 m_2 g \cos\theta_2\right)\hat{\boldsymbol{k}}_1$$

In a similar fashion, we now calculate $\boldsymbol{M}_{O_1}$. We have

$$\boldsymbol{W}_2 = m_2 g \hat{\boldsymbol{\jmath}}_1 \qquad \boldsymbol{M}_2 = M_{x_2}\hat{\boldsymbol{\imath}}_2 + M_{y_2}\hat{\boldsymbol{\jmath}}_2 + M^a_{z_2}\hat{\boldsymbol{k}}_2$$

$$= m_2 g\left(\sin\theta_2\,\hat{\boldsymbol{\imath}}_2 + \cos\theta_2\,\hat{\boldsymbol{\jmath}}_2\right)$$

$$\boldsymbol{r}_{G_2/O_1} = \frac{1}{2}L_2\hat{\boldsymbol{\imath}}_2$$

so that

$$\boldsymbol{r}_{G_2/O_1} \times \boldsymbol{W}_2 = \tfrac{1}{2}L_2 m_2 g \cos\theta_2\,\hat{\boldsymbol{k}}_2$$

resulting in the total moment

$$\boldsymbol{M}_{O_1} = M_{x_2}\hat{\boldsymbol{\imath}}_2 + M_{y_2}\hat{\boldsymbol{\jmath}}_2 + \left(M^a_{z_2} + \tfrac{1}{2}L_2 m_2 g \cos\theta_2\right)\hat{\boldsymbol{k}}_2$$

Note that we have used the superscript a to denote actuator quantities.

(*d*) Calculation of the time rates of change of the moments of momentum $\dot{\boldsymbol{H}}_O$ and $\dot{\boldsymbol{H}}_{O_1}$. We first note that

$$\dot{\boldsymbol{H}}_O = \dot{H}^1_O + \dot{\boldsymbol{H}}^2_O = \boldsymbol{r}_{G_1} \times m_1\ddot{\boldsymbol{r}}_{G_1} + \dot{\boldsymbol{H}}_{G_1} + \boldsymbol{r}_{G_2} \times m_2\ddot{\boldsymbol{r}}_{G_2} + \dot{\boldsymbol{H}}_{G_2}$$

and

$$\dot{\boldsymbol{H}}_{O_1} = \boldsymbol{r}_{G_2/O_1} \times m_2\ddot{\boldsymbol{r}}_{G_2/O_1} + \dot{\boldsymbol{H}}_{G_2}$$

Furthermore, all of the quantities with respect to O will be expressed in terms of the $(0xyz)_1$ basis, whereas those with respect to O_1 will be expressed in terms of the $(0xyz)_2$ basis.

The angular velocity of the $(0xyz)_2$ frame is

$$\begin{aligned}\boldsymbol{\omega}_2 &= \Omega\hat{\boldsymbol{k}}_0 + \dot{\theta}_2\hat{\boldsymbol{k}}_1\\ &= \Omega(-\hat{\boldsymbol{\jmath}}_1) + \omega\hat{\boldsymbol{k}}_1\\ &= -\Omega\sin\theta_2\,\hat{\boldsymbol{\imath}}_2 - \Omega\cos\theta_2\,\hat{\boldsymbol{\jmath}}_2 + \omega\hat{\boldsymbol{k}}_2\end{aligned}$$

The inertia matrix of body 2 with respect to $(0xyz)_2$ located at G_2 is given by

$$\mathbf{I}_{G_2} = \begin{bmatrix} 0 & 0 & 0 \\ 0 & \frac{1}{12}m_2L_2^2 & 0 \\ 0 & 0 & \frac{1}{12}m_2L_2^2 \end{bmatrix}$$

The moment of momentum thus is

$$\mathbf{H}_{G_2} = \mathbf{I}_{G_2}\boldsymbol{\omega}_2 = \tfrac{1}{12}m_2L_2^2\begin{bmatrix} 0 & 0 & 0 \\ 0 & 1 & 0 \\ 0 & 0 & 1 \end{bmatrix}\begin{pmatrix} -\Omega\sin\theta_2 \\ -\Omega\cos\theta_2 \\ \omega \end{pmatrix}$$

$$= \tfrac{1}{12}m_2L_2^2\begin{pmatrix} 0 \\ -\Omega\cos\theta_2 \\ \omega \end{pmatrix}$$

which has the vector form

$$\boldsymbol{H}_{G_2} = \tfrac{1}{12}m_2L_2^2\left(-\Omega\cos\theta_2\,\hat{\boldsymbol{j}}_2 + \omega\hat{\boldsymbol{k}}_2\right)$$

The time rate of change of this vector is calculated in the usual manner as

$$\dot{\boldsymbol{H}}_{G_2} = \tfrac{1}{12}m_2L_2^2\left[+\Omega\omega\sin\theta_2\,\hat{\boldsymbol{j}}_2 + \alpha\hat{\boldsymbol{k}}_2 + (-\Omega\cos\theta_2)\boldsymbol{\omega}_2\times\hat{\boldsymbol{j}}_2 + \omega\boldsymbol{\omega}_2\times\hat{\boldsymbol{k}}_2\right]$$

$$\boldsymbol{\omega}_2\times\hat{\boldsymbol{j}}_2 = -\Omega\sin\theta_2\,\hat{\boldsymbol{k}}_2 - \omega\hat{\boldsymbol{i}}_2$$

$$\boldsymbol{\omega}_2\times\hat{\boldsymbol{k}}_2 = +\Omega\sin\theta_2\,\hat{\boldsymbol{j}}_2 - \Omega\cos\theta_2\,\hat{\boldsymbol{i}}_2$$

$$\begin{aligned}= \tfrac{1}{12}m_2L_2^2\big[&(\Omega\omega\cos\theta_2 - \omega\Omega\cos\theta_2)\hat{\boldsymbol{i}}_2\\ &+(\Omega\omega\sin\theta_2 + \omega\Omega\sin\theta_2)\hat{\boldsymbol{i}}_2\\ &+\left(\alpha + \Omega^2\sin\theta_2\cos\theta_2\right)\hat{\boldsymbol{k}}_2\big]\end{aligned}$$

$$\begin{aligned}\dot{\boldsymbol{H}}_{G_2} &= \tfrac{1}{12}m_2L_2^2\left[(2\Omega\omega\sin\theta_2)\,\hat{\boldsymbol{j}}_2 + \left(\alpha + \Omega^2\sin\theta_2\cos\theta_2\right)\hat{\boldsymbol{k}}_2\right]\\ &= \tfrac{1}{12}m_2L_2^2\Big[-2\Omega\omega\sin^2\theta_2\,\hat{\boldsymbol{i}}_1 + 2\Omega\omega\sin\theta_2\cos\theta_2\,\hat{\boldsymbol{j}}_1\\ &\qquad +\left(\alpha + \Omega^2\sin\theta_2\cos\theta_2\right)\hat{\boldsymbol{k}}_1\Big]\end{aligned}$$

The angular velocity of the $(0xyz)_1$ frame is

$$\boldsymbol{\omega}_1 = -\Omega\,\hat{\boldsymbol{j}}_1$$

The inertia matrix of body 1 is

$$\mathbf{I}_{G_1} = \tfrac{1}{12}m_1L_1^2\begin{bmatrix}1 & 0 & 0\\ 0 & 0 & 0\\ 0 & 0 & 1\end{bmatrix}$$

with respect to $(0xyz)_1$ located at the mass center. The moment of momentum thus is

$$\mathbf{H}_{G_1} = \mathbf{I}_{G_1}\boldsymbol{\omega}_1 = \tfrac{1}{12}m_1L_1^2\begin{bmatrix}1 & 0 & 0\\ 0 & 0 & 0\\ 0 & 0 & 1\end{bmatrix}\begin{pmatrix}0\\ -\Omega\\ 0\end{pmatrix} = \begin{pmatrix}0\\ 0\\ 0\end{pmatrix}$$

and we conclude that $\boldsymbol{H}_{G_1} = \boldsymbol{0}$, implying $\dot{\boldsymbol{H}}_{G_1} = \boldsymbol{0}$ also.

(*e*) Cross-product terms. We already have

$$\boldsymbol{r}_{G_2} = \tfrac{1}{2}L_2\cos\theta_2\,\hat{\boldsymbol{i}}_1 + \left(\tfrac{1}{2}L_2\sin\theta_2 - L_1\right)\hat{\boldsymbol{j}}_1$$

$$\begin{aligned}\dot{\boldsymbol{r}}_{G_2} &= -\tfrac{1}{2}L_2\omega\sin\theta_2\,\hat{\boldsymbol{i}}_1 + \tfrac{1}{2}L_2\omega\cos\theta_2\,\hat{\boldsymbol{j}}_1\\ &\qquad +\left(\tfrac{1}{2}L_2\cos\theta_2\right)\boldsymbol{\omega}_1\times\hat{\boldsymbol{i}}_1 + \left(\tfrac{1}{2}L_2\sin\theta_2 - L_1\right)\boldsymbol{\omega}_1\times\hat{\boldsymbol{j}}_1\\ &= -\tfrac{1}{2}L_2\omega\sin\theta_2\,\hat{\boldsymbol{i}}_1 + \tfrac{1}{2}L_2\omega\cos\theta_2\,\hat{\boldsymbol{j}}_1 + \tfrac{1}{2}L_2\Omega\cos\theta_2\,\hat{\boldsymbol{k}}_1\end{aligned}$$

and another differentiation then yields

$$\begin{aligned}\ddot{\boldsymbol{r}}_{G_2} = &-\tfrac{1}{2}L_2\left(\omega^2\cos\theta_2 + \Omega^2\cos\theta_2 + \alpha\sin\theta_2\right)\hat{\boldsymbol{i}}_1\\ &+\tfrac{1}{2}L_2\left(-\omega^2\sin\theta_2 + \alpha\cos\theta_2\right)\hat{\boldsymbol{j}}_1\\ &-\tfrac{1}{2}L_2(2\omega\Omega\sin\theta_2)\hat{\boldsymbol{k}}_1\end{aligned}$$

Hence

$$\begin{aligned}\boldsymbol{r}_{G_2} \times m_2 \ddot{\boldsymbol{r}}_{G_2} &= \frac{1}{2} L_2^2 m_2 \Omega \omega \sin\theta_2 \left(\frac{2L_1}{L_2} - \sin\theta_2 \right) \hat{\boldsymbol{\imath}}_1 \\ &\quad + \frac{1}{2} L_2^2 m_2 \Omega \omega \sin\theta_2 \cos\theta_2 \, \hat{\boldsymbol{\jmath}}_1 \\ &\quad + \frac{1}{2} L_2^2 m_2 \left[\frac{1}{2} \Omega^2 \sin\theta_2 \cos\theta_2 + \frac{1}{2}\alpha \right. \\ &\qquad \left. - \frac{L_1}{L_2}(\omega^2 + \Omega^2)\cos\theta_2 - \frac{L_1}{L_2}\alpha \sin\theta_2 \right] \hat{\boldsymbol{k}}_1\end{aligned}$$

For the second cross-product term we begin with

$$\begin{aligned}\boldsymbol{r}_{G_2/O_1} &= \tfrac{1}{2} L_2 \hat{\boldsymbol{\imath}}_2 \\ \dot{\boldsymbol{r}}_{G_2/O_1} &= \tfrac{1}{2} L_2 \boldsymbol{\omega}_2 \times \hat{\boldsymbol{\imath}}_2 \\ &= \tfrac{1}{2} L_2 \left[\omega \hat{\boldsymbol{\jmath}}_2 + \Omega \cos\theta_2 \, \hat{\boldsymbol{k}}_2 \right] \\ \ddot{\boldsymbol{r}}_{G_2/O_1} &= \tfrac{1}{2} L_2 \alpha \hat{\boldsymbol{\jmath}}_2 - \Omega\omega \sin\theta_2 \, \hat{\boldsymbol{k}}_2 \\ &\quad + \tfrac{1}{2} L_2 \omega \boldsymbol{\omega}_2 \times \hat{\boldsymbol{\jmath}}_2 + \tfrac{1}{2} L_2 \Omega \cos\theta_2 \boldsymbol{\omega}_2 \times \hat{\boldsymbol{k}}_2 \\ &= \tfrac{1}{2} L_2 \left(-\omega^2 - \Omega^2 \cos^2\theta_2 \right) \hat{\boldsymbol{\imath}}_2 \\ &\quad + \tfrac{1}{2} L_2 \left(\alpha + \Omega^2 \sin\theta_2 \cos\theta_2 \right) \hat{\boldsymbol{\jmath}}_2 \\ &\quad + \tfrac{1}{2} L_2 \left(-\Omega\omega \sin\theta_2 - \Omega\omega \sin\theta_2 \right) \hat{\boldsymbol{k}}_2\end{aligned}$$

The cross product is then given by

$$\begin{aligned}\boldsymbol{r}_{G_2/O_1} \times m_2 \ddot{\boldsymbol{r}}_{G_2/O_1} &= \tfrac{1}{2} L_2^2 m_2 \Omega\omega \sin\theta_2 \hat{\boldsymbol{\jmath}}_2 \\ &\quad + \tfrac{1}{4} L_2^2 m_2 \left(\alpha + \Omega^2 \sin\theta_2 \cos\theta_2 \right) \hat{\boldsymbol{k}}_2\end{aligned}$$

(*f*) Application of Euler's law of moment of momentum in the form $\dot{\boldsymbol{H}}_O = \boldsymbol{M}_O$ and $\dot{\boldsymbol{H}}_{O_1} = \boldsymbol{M}_{O_1}$. We have the following result:

$$\begin{aligned}\dot{\boldsymbol{H}}_O &= \boldsymbol{r}_{G_2} \times m_2 \ddot{\boldsymbol{r}}_{G_2} + \dot{\boldsymbol{H}}_{G_2} \\ &= m_2 L_2^2 \left[\Omega\omega \sin\theta_2 \left(\frac{L_1}{L_2} - \frac{2}{3} \sin\theta_2 \right) \hat{\boldsymbol{\imath}}_1 + \frac{2}{3} \Omega\omega \sin\theta_2 \cos\theta_2 \, \hat{\boldsymbol{\jmath}}_1 \right. \\ &\quad + \left(\frac{1}{3}\alpha + \frac{1}{3}\Omega^2 \sin\theta_2 \cos\theta_2 - \frac{1}{2}\frac{L_1}{L_2}(\omega^2 + \Omega^2)\cos\theta_2 \right. \\ &\qquad \left. \left. - \frac{1}{2}\frac{L_1}{L_2}\alpha \sin\theta_2 \right) \hat{\boldsymbol{k}}_1 \right] \\ &= \boldsymbol{M}_O = M_{x_1} \hat{\boldsymbol{\imath}}_1 + M_{y_1}^a \hat{\boldsymbol{\jmath}}_1 + \left(M_{z_1} + \frac{1}{2} L_2 m_2 g \cos\theta_2 \right) \hat{\boldsymbol{k}}_1\end{aligned}$$

We thus obtain the reactions

$$M_{x_1} = m_2 L_2^2 \Omega \omega \sin\theta_2 \left(\frac{L_1}{L_2} - \frac{2}{3} \sin\theta_2 \right)$$

$$M_{z_1} = -\frac{1}{2} L_2 m_2 g \cos\theta_2 + m_2 L_2^2 \left[\frac{1}{3}\alpha + \frac{1}{3}\Omega^2 \sin\theta_2 \cos\theta_2 - \frac{1}{2}\frac{L_1}{L_2}(\omega^2 + \Omega^2)\cos\theta_2 - \frac{1}{2}\frac{L_1}{L_2}\alpha \sin\theta_2 \right]$$

and the actuator moment

$$M_{y_1}^a = \tfrac{2}{3} m_2 L_2^2 \Omega \omega \sin\theta_2 \cos\theta_2$$

From the second equation we obtain

$$\begin{aligned}
\dot{\boldsymbol{H}}_{O_1} &= \boldsymbol{r}_{G_2/O_1} \times m_2 \ddot{\boldsymbol{r}}_{G_2/O_1} + \dot{\boldsymbol{H}}_{G_2} \\
&= m_2 L_2^2 \Big[\left(\tfrac{1}{2}\Omega\omega \sin\theta_2 + \tfrac{1}{6}\Omega\omega \sin\theta_2 \right) \hat{\boldsymbol{j}}_2 \\
&\qquad + \left(\tfrac{1}{4}\alpha + \tfrac{1}{4}\Omega^2 \sin\theta_2 \cos\theta_2 + \tfrac{1}{12}\alpha + \tfrac{1}{12}\Omega^2 \sin\theta_2 \cos\theta_2 \right) \hat{\boldsymbol{k}}_2 \Big] \\
&= m_2 L_2^2 \left[\tfrac{2}{3}\Omega\omega \sin\theta_2 \hat{\boldsymbol{j}}_2 + \left(\tfrac{1}{3}\alpha + \tfrac{1}{3}\Omega^2 \sin\theta_2 \cos\theta_2 \right) \hat{\boldsymbol{k}}_2 \right] \\
&= \boldsymbol{M}_{O_1} = M_{x_2} \hat{\boldsymbol{\imath}}_2 + M_{y_2} \hat{\boldsymbol{j}}_2 + \left(M_{z_2}^a + \tfrac{1}{2} L_2 m_2 g \cos\theta_2 \right) \hat{\boldsymbol{k}}_2
\end{aligned}$$

yielding the reaction moments

$$M_{x_2} = 0$$

$$M_{y_2} = \tfrac{2}{3} M_2 L_2^2 \Omega \omega \sin\theta_2$$

and the actuator moment

$$M_{z_2}^a = -\tfrac{1}{2} L_2 m_2 g \cos\theta_2 + \tfrac{1}{3} m_2 L_2^2 \left(\alpha + \Omega^2 \sin\theta_2 \cos\theta_2 \right)$$

There are some questions that arise in connection with these examples. One of the foremost is: Suppose a certain actuator force or moment is supplied; does this necessarily result in the specified motion? Theoretically, the answer is yes, as long as there exists a unique integral of the equations of motion (Euler's laws), that is, a one-to-one correspondence between forces and moments and the motion. Without this uniqueness, it may, in fact, be possible to have a motion other than the one desired. Clearly, the introduction of an actuator into the system changes the system, and different choices of actuators produce different systems. Although we have neglected the actuator mass in our examples, this may not be a reasonable assumption in many cases. To be on the safe side, we should always analyze the changed system. In particular, although it is obvious that we have different states of stress of the system for different prescribed motions, it must also be observed that this state of stress changes with the manner in which the motion is produced. That is, there usually is an infinite number of choices for the production of a given motion. Thus this whole area is ripe for the use of optimal design.

EXERCISES

3-1. Suppose that the waste material container of Exercise 2-1 has a 4 m length, 2 m depth, and 1.5 m height and that the container mass and waste material are homogeneously distributed over the volume. You may also assume that only a normal force is present at B and that the hinge A is located at the edge of the container (Fig. E3-1). Assume that the problem is essentially two dimensional, with all forces applied in the plane of symmetry of the container. Calculate the needed actuator force in terms of θ_1 if the container is to be tipped downward at constant angular velocity $\boldsymbol{\omega}_1$. The total mass of the container is m.

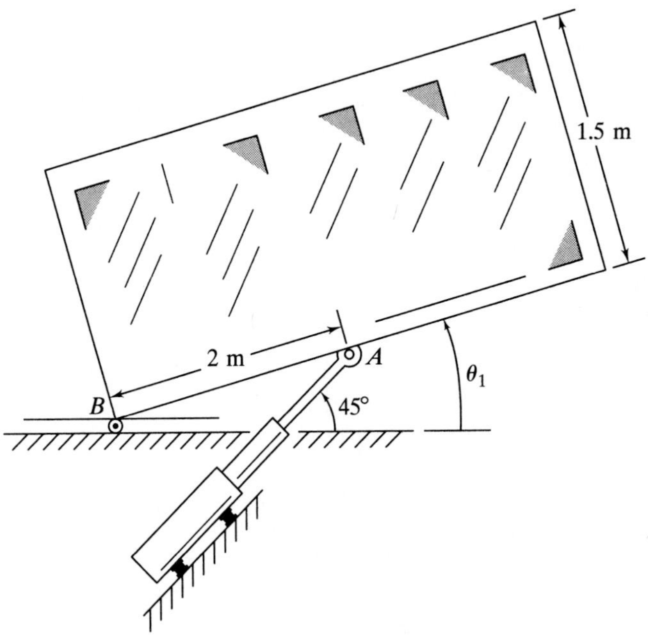

FIGURE E3-1

3-2. Consider the one-arm manipulator of Example 3-6, including the restriction that the vertical component of the velocity be constant with magnitude v. With all other data as before, determine the actuator force needed:

(*a*) if the actuator is kept tangent to the path throughout the range of motion;

(*b*) if the actuator is the one depicted in Fig. E3-2. The actuator is hinged at point B. The distance OB is $\frac{3}{2}L$. In all cases, the actuators themselves may be considered to be massless.

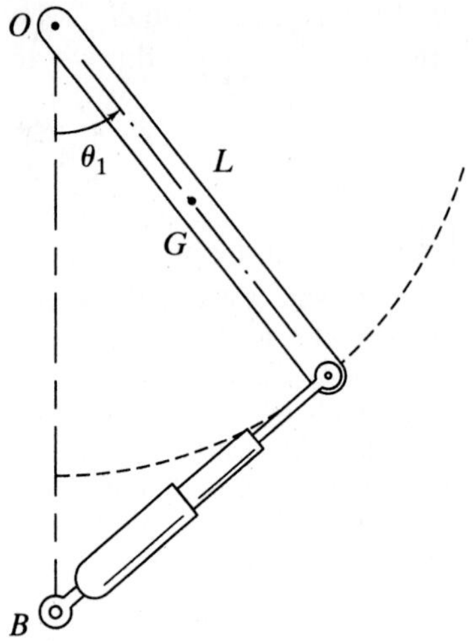

FIGURE E3-2

3-3. Complete the integration for $\theta_1(t)$ in Example 3-8 [Eq. (3-26)]. That is, obtain the elliptic integral corresponding to the initial coditions $\theta_1(0) = \pi/2$ and $\dot{\theta}_1(0) = 0$.

3-4. Consider again the one-arm manipulator of Examples 3-6 and 3-8, including the requirement of a constant downward velocity component v for the end effector P. Suppose the rotary actuator at the base O is used to sustain the motion.

(*a*) Obtain the internal force and moment resultants F, V, and M, respectively, as functions of θ_1 and r.

(*b*) Plot the nondimensional quantities

$$F^* = \frac{F}{mg}, V^* = \frac{V}{mg}, \text{ and } M^* = \frac{2M}{mgL} \qquad \text{versus} \qquad x = \frac{r}{L}$$

for $\theta_1 = \pi/4$ and $v^2/gL = 1$.

3-5. Consider the one-arm manipulator of Example 3-6, including the required constant downward velocity component v of P. Suppose that a vertical actuator at P is used to maintain the motion. Calculate the required actuator force F.

3-6. Consider the two-dimensional manipulator shown in Fig. E3-6. Its motion is governed by angular actuators at O and at O_2. If the motion of the manipulator is such that $\dot{\theta}_1$ and $\dot{\theta}_2$ are *constant* angular velocities, determine the actuator moments necessary to drive the system in such a fashion. Assume that the two slender bars have masses m_1 and m_2, that their lengths are L_1 and L_2, and take $\theta_1(0) = \theta_2(0) = 0$.

3-7. A slender rod with mass density per unit length rotates about the point O under the action of gravity alone. Obtain the resultant internal force and moment distribution as a function of θ_1 and of the distance r from the fixed point O. Obtain the reaction at O and the internal stress resultants as functions of θ_1 if the bar is released from rest at an angle $\theta_1 = \theta_{10}$. That is, work Example 3-8 with this new initial condition. Use the sign convention illustrated in Fig. E3-7.

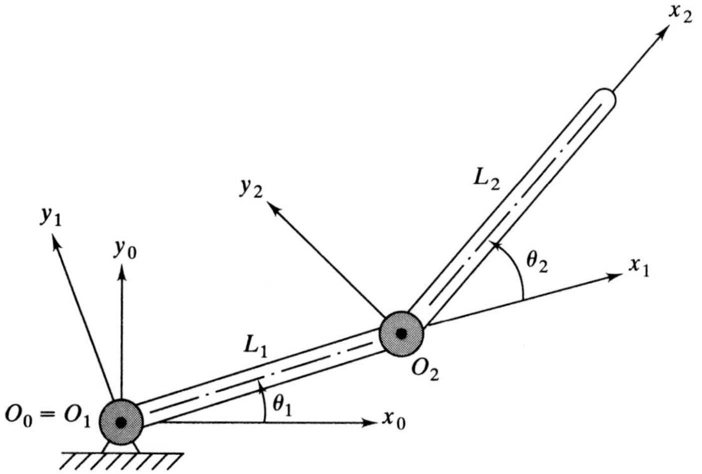

FIGURE E3-6

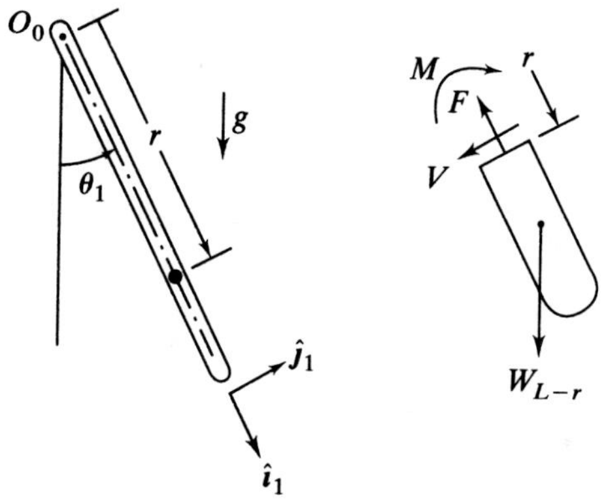

FIGURE E3-7

3-8. Consider again Example 2-8. Assume that the wheel rotating within the platform is homogeneous and "thin," with total mass m. Let $(0xyz)_2$ be embedded in the wheel and let $\boldsymbol{\omega}_2$ be the absolute angular velocity of the wheel. Then

$$\mathbf{H}_O = \mathbf{I}_O \boldsymbol{\omega}_2$$

is the moment of momentum for the wheel with respect to O. Here $\mathbf{I}_O$ is the inertia matrix with respect to the $(0xyz)_2$ axes whose origin coincides with O. Note that $\boldsymbol{\omega}_2$ also has to be expressed with respect to the $(0xyz)_2$ basis. Calculate $\mathbf{H}_O$ for the spinning wheel, first by using general terms (e.g., wheel radius b) and, second, with the particular values used at the end of the example. Use $m = 2$ kg.

3-9. Calculate the inertia matrix with respect to the principal axes for the rigid homogeneous bodies shown in Fig. E3-9 (assume mass density ρ throughout).

3-10. Consider the manipulator in Fig. E3-10 along with the indicated rotations $\dot{\theta}_1 = \Omega$ and $\dot{\theta}_2 = \omega$. The arm is a slender rod of length L and mass m. Calculate the moment of momentum of the rod with respect to the hinge point O_1.

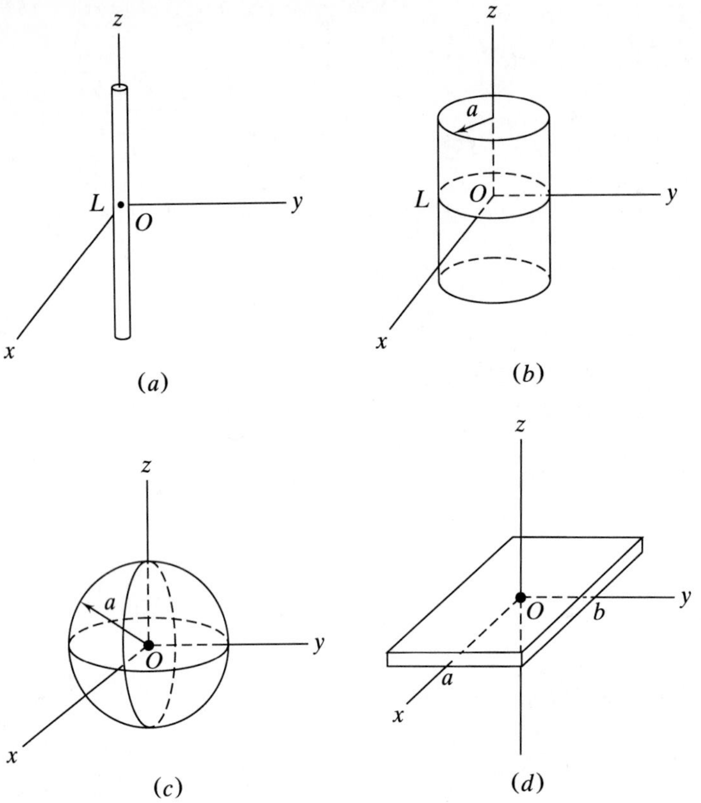

FIGURE E3-9
(*a*) A slender rigid rod of length L; (*b*) a circular cylinder of length L and radius a; (*c*) a sphere with radius a; (*d*) a flat thin plate with side lengths a and b.

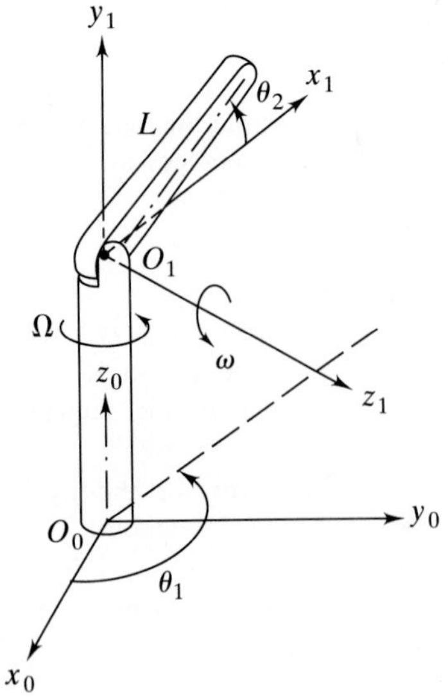

FIGURE E3-10

3-11. A thin uniform bar of length L and mass m is displaced slightly from its vertical equilibrium position at $\theta = 0$ (dashed line position in Fig. E3-11). It slides along a frictionless wall and floor due to gravity. Assuming that the bar remains in a plane perpendicular to both the wall and the floor, solve for the angle at which the bar leaves the wall. Proceed as follows:

(*a*) Draw the free body and derive the equation of motion in terms of θ and $\ddot{\theta}$.

(*b*) Integrate the equation once to obtain an expression for $\dot{\theta}^2$.

(*c*) Obtain the unknown reaction forces in terms of θ only.

(*d*) Use a suitable condition indicating that the bar left the wall and solve for the θ at which the condition is satisfied.

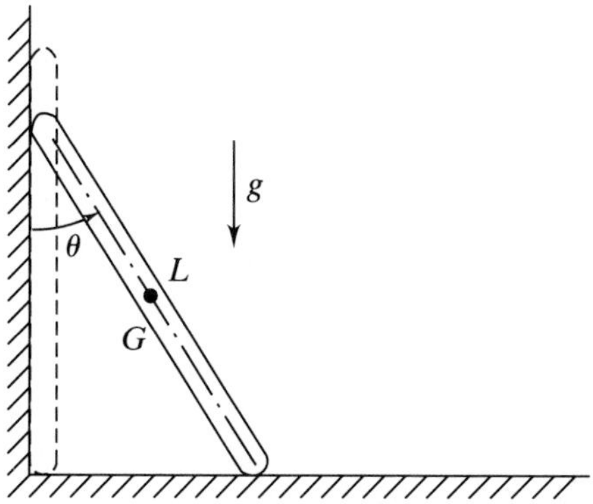

FIGURE E3-11

3-12. Consider the following *plane* motion problem. The thin homogeneous cylinder B with radius R shown in Fig. E3-12 is rotating with constant angular velocity $\dot{\theta}_2\hat{k}_2$ about an axis through O_2, while the slender rod A is made to rotate about O_0

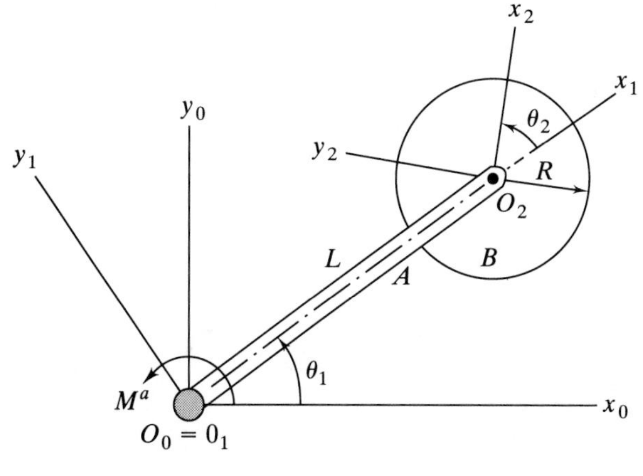

FIGURE E3-12

with constant angular velocity $\dot{\theta}_1 \hat{\boldsymbol{k}}_0$ by means of an actuator moment $M^a \hat{\boldsymbol{k}}_0$. Assume that the bar and the disk have masses m_A and m_B, respectively.

(*a*) Calculate the moment of momentum of the cylinder about O_0.

(*b*) Calculate the moment of momentum of the rod about O_0.

(*c*) Deduce the total moment of momentum $\boldsymbol{H}_{O_0}(t)$ for the system about O_0 and calculate $\dot{\boldsymbol{H}}_{O_0}(t)$.

(*d*) Obtain the actuator moment $\boldsymbol{M}^a(t)$ needed to sustain this motion.

3-13. Obtain the actuator moment $M^a \hat{\boldsymbol{k}}_0$ needed in Example 3-9 if:

(*a*) $\dot{\alpha}_2 \neq$ const. and $\dot{\theta}_1 =$ const.;

(*b*) $\dot{\alpha}_2 =$ const. and $\dot{\theta}_1 \neq$ const.

3-14. Recall that the entries of the inertia matrix depend on both the choice of origin and the orientation of $(0xyz)$ with respect to the body $\mathscr{B}$. For any such point one can find a set of orthogonal Cartesian axes for which the inertia matrix will be diagonal. Given the inertia matrix

$$\mathbf{I} = \begin{bmatrix} 20 & -5 & 2 \\ -5 & 12 & -1 \\ 2 & -1 & 10 \end{bmatrix}$$

determine the principal moments of inertia and the corresponding principal axes. Proceed as follows:

(*a*) Obtain the principal moments of inertia I_i, $i = 1, 2, 3$, for the matrix $\mathbf{I}$.

(*b*) Use the equation $\mathbf{I}\mathbf{e}_i = \lambda_i \mathbf{e}_i$, $i = 1, 2, 3$, to determine the unit vectors $\mathbf{e}_i$ corresponding to λ_i and sketch their orientation with respect to the original axis system.

(*c*) Combine the eigenvectors $\mathbf{e}_i$ in a transformation matrix $\mathbf{S} = [\mathbf{e}_1 \;\; \mathbf{e}_2 \;\; \mathbf{e}_3]$, show that $\mathbf{S}\mathbf{S}^{\mathrm{T}} = \mathbf{E}$, and show that the similarity transformation

$$\mathbf{S}^T \mathbf{I} \mathbf{S} = \boldsymbol{\Lambda} = \begin{bmatrix} I_1 & 0 & 0 \\ 0 & I_2 & 0 \\ 0 & 0 & I_3 \end{bmatrix}$$

is a diagonal matrix whose entries are the principal moments of inertia.

REFERENCES

1. Fox, E. A.: *Mechanics*, Harper and Row, New York, 1967.
2. Greenwood, D. T.: *Principles of Dynamics*, Prentice-Hall, Englewood Cliffs, N.J., 1965.

CHAPTER

FOUR

SOME FUNDAMENTALS IN ELECTRONICS AND COMPUTATION

4-1 INTRODUCTION

One might almost term this chapter, "Some Fundamental Concepts You Always Wanted to Know but Were Afraid to Ask." Computer science students will have had most of the material on logic; electrical engineering students, the material on op amps and solid-state devices. Usually, it is assumed that students know A/D and D/A converters; often, however, there is no formal coverage of those subjects until a senior course on op-amp design.

The attempt here is to provide fundamental concepts and equations that may not have been covered in the students' preceding university training and that will be used in the chapters that follow as well. For example, the operational amplifier is a basic ingredient in all sensory circuitry, yet most mechanical engineering students have little or no background in their function. The discussion of binary concepts and logic gates is essential to an understanding of encoders and decoders, which pervade the whole robotic electronic system. The discussion of solid-state devices (such as the diode and the MOSFET) serves as an essential introduction to the solid-state sensors occurring in vision systems.

This chapter is a reference chapter, with items that can be covered at any time, even when they appear in some other context. Many of the topics were selected because they fill in gaps in the author's own education or simply because they are interesting, even if somewhat peripheral to applied robotics.

Knowing how devices function promotes confidence in and understanding of the large-scale systems into which they are integrated.

4-2 THE OPERATIONAL AMPLIFIER

For the mechanical engineer in particular, the operational amplifier (op amp) would seem to be a fascinating device. In circuitry, it totally eliminates the need for an inductance; that is, capacitors and resistors, in conjunction with op amps, suffice to model all circuits which might previously have been termed *RLC* circuits. In analogous mechanical systems consisting of interconnected damped spring mass oscillators, this would correspond to modeling such systems without springs or mass, depending on the analogy used. It is interesting to think of what such a "mechanical op amp" might be.

The discussion here will be limited to the ideal op amp and its operation as a circuit element. None of the internal workings of the op amp as an integrated circuit is included. The symbol to be used for the op amp is shown in Fig. 4-1. All of the indicated voltages are taken with 0 as the reference voltage. The op amp has an inverting (−) input, a noninverting (+) input, and an output with correspondingly denoted voltages: v_n, v_p, and v_0. The constant a is called the *open loop gain* of the op amp. In normal operation it is desirable to have a be as large as possible; usually, $a \approx 10^5$, but gains $a > 10^5$ are available.

In addition to the input and output terminals, the op amp has terminals that are used to power it. These separate power sources are rarely indicated, so that students often get the impression that op amps are passive elements in a circuit and then have difficulty explaining the source of power—in a positive feedback oscillator, for example—where no power source is apparent in the usual circuit diagram. High and low terminals with ±15 V generally serve as the power sources.

THE VOLTAGE COMPARATOR. When operated in an open loop configuration, the op amp serves as a voltage comparator, or as the simplest analog-to-digital converter, a one-bit ADC. The corresponding symbol is shown in Fig. 4-2a, the additional symbol ⎍ indicating its use as a comparator. Because of the high open loop gain, the op amp saturates in accordance with the ideal operating

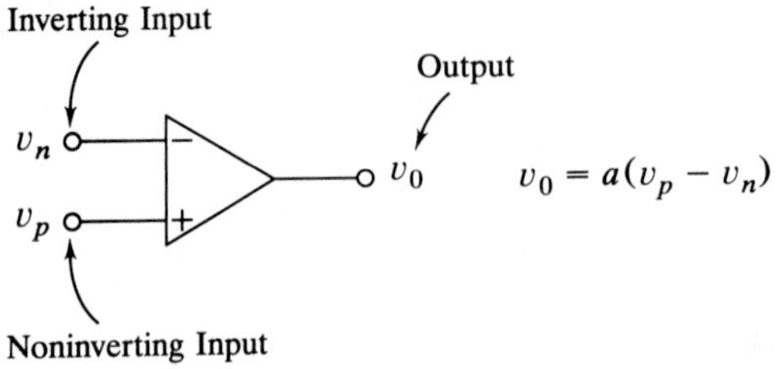

FIGURE 4-1
Op-amp circuit symbol.

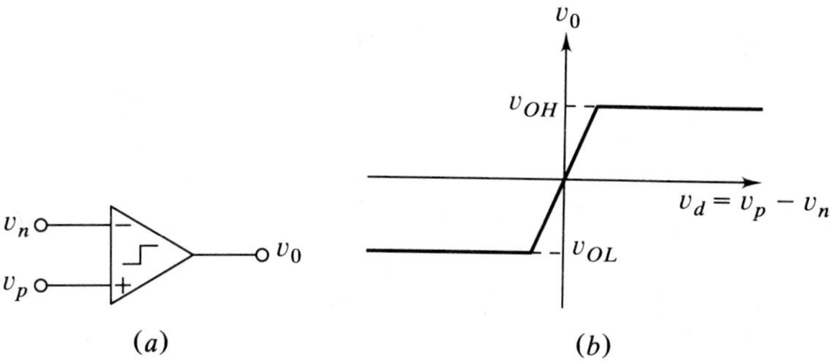

FIGURE 4-2
The comparator.

curve shown in Fig. 4-2*b*, with

$$v_0 = v_{0H} \qquad \text{for} \quad v_p > v_n$$

$$v_0 = v_{0L} \qquad \text{for} \quad v_p < v_n$$

where v_{0H} and v_{0L} are termed the *output saturation voltages*. The inclined linear relation is in the microvolt range so that it is vertical, for all practical purposes, when the comparator is used in a volt range.

When used in logic circuits, it is common to use $v_{0L} = 0$ V and $v_{0H} = 5$ V, the former denoting logic "0," the latter, logic "1."

THE INVERTING SUMMER. In this case the op amp is used in a feedback configuration as shown in Fig. 4-3. The assumptions made for the ideal op amp will be introduced within the analysis of this circuit. Clearly, the objective here is to obtain the output voltage in terms of the input voltages v_1 and v_2.

The use of Kirchhoff's current law (KCL) at the summing junction yields

$$i_1 + i_2 = i_n + i$$

With the use of Ohm's law, this equation may be written in terms of the voltage

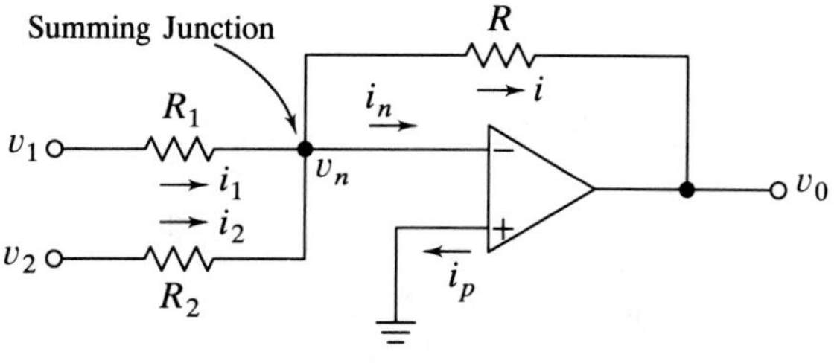

FIGURE 4-3
The inverting summer.

drops as

$$\frac{v_1 - v_n}{R_1} + \frac{v_2 - v_n}{R_2} = i_n + \frac{v_n - v_0}{R}$$

Thus far no assumptions reflecting ideal operation have been made.

At ideal operation, $a \to \infty$. It follows that

$$\lim_{a\to\infty} (v_p - v_n) = \lim_{a\to\infty} \frac{v_0}{a} = 0$$

or, equivalently, $v_p = v_n$; the input ports appear to be shorted. Furthermore, the internal input resistance of the op amp is taken to approach ∞, so that no current flows in or out of either input terminals, implying $i_n \approx 0$ and $i_p \approx 0$. These assumptions of idealness are termed the *virtual short concept* in Franco.[1]

With these assumptions in mind, the previous equation becomes

$$\frac{v_1}{R_1} + \frac{v_2}{R_2} = -\frac{v_0}{R} \quad \Rightarrow \quad v_0 = -\frac{R}{R_1}v_1 - \frac{R}{R_2}v_2$$

It is clear that this approach can be extended to an arbitrary number of input ports. In addition, for a fixed feedback resistance R, the gains of the individual inputs may be adjusted to any value whatsoever simply by making an appropriate choice of R_1 and R_2.

When considered simply as an inverting amplifier, the system function for the circuit is

$$V_0(s) = -kV_1(s)$$

k being the ratio of resistances. The gain may again be made adjustable if the resistance R_1 is taken from a potentiometer.

Example 4-1 The noninverting amplifier. Derive the input-output relationship for the circuit shown in Fig. 4-4. Assume ideal conditions.

Solution. The summation of currents at the summing junction yields

$$\frac{0 - v_n}{R_1} = i_n + \frac{v_n - v_0}{R}$$

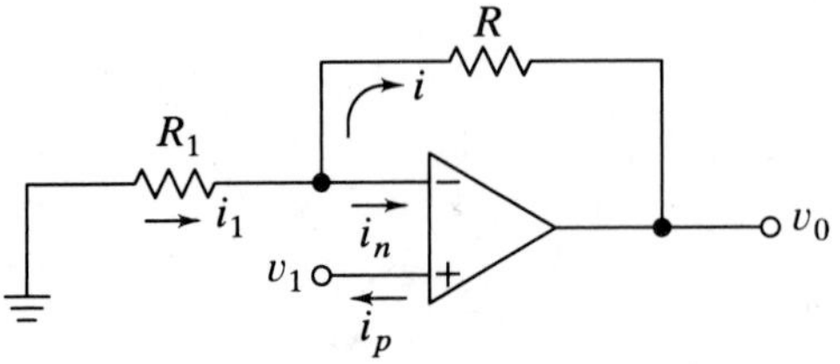

FIGURE 4-4
The noninverting amplifier.

Based on the idealness assumptions given previously, v_n must approach v_1, i_n approaches 0, and we thus have

$$-\frac{v_1}{R_1} = \frac{v_1 - v_0}{R} \quad \Rightarrow \quad v_0 = \left(1 + \frac{R}{R_1}\right) v_1$$

We close this discussion with a few remarks about the limitations of the ideal operating assumptions. For proper operation it must be ascertained that v_0 satisfies $v_{0L} < v_0 < v_{0H}$, since saturation will otherwise end up chopping the response. The saturation voltages usually lie ≈ 2 V below and above the high and the low supply voltages to the op amp, respectively. For example, if the op-amp supply voltages are ± 15 V, then $v_{0L} = -13$ V and $v_{0H} = 13$ V, with similar results for other supply voltages. Further limitations are a decrease in the open loop gain with frequency and a response lag to sudden changes in input, the slew rate of the op amp. Again, we refer the reader to Franco[1] for detailed discussions of these limitations.

4-3 SEMICONDUCTOR DEVICES

4-3-1 Semiconductors

Semiconductors are so prevalent that most engineers are likely to have had at least one course that involved a discussion thereof. However, only the electrical engineer is likely to have followed up on that course. Be that as it may, the discussion here is meant to prepare the student for an understanding of the solid-state vision process.

Semiconductors are crystalline solids whose electrical properties lie somewhere between those of insulators and conductors. Kittel[2] writes:

> The difference between a good conductor and a good insulator is striking. The electrical resistivity of a pure metal may be as low as 10^{-10} ohm · cm at a temperature of 1°K, apart from the possibility of superconductivity. The resistivity of a good insulator may be as high as 10^{22} ohm · cm. This range of 10^{32} may be the widest of any common physical property of solids.

In a conductor valence electrons are free to wander throughout a given crystal segment, forming what is often called an *electron gas*, a model that later gives rise to the involvement of Boltzmann's constant. Insulators, in their purest form, are crystals that have no free electrons at 0 K. Such insulators form the basis for the construction of semiconductors. Some such crystals are germanium and silicon, the latter being the most commonly used by far.

In order to get current to flow in such crystals, it becomes necessary to reintroduce impurities into pure crystals. Current in semiconductors under the action of an applied external field is due to the presence of either *holes* or *electrons*. In terms of their behavior in electric or magnetic fields, holes may best be described as electrons with a charge $q = +e$. More specifically, electrons in

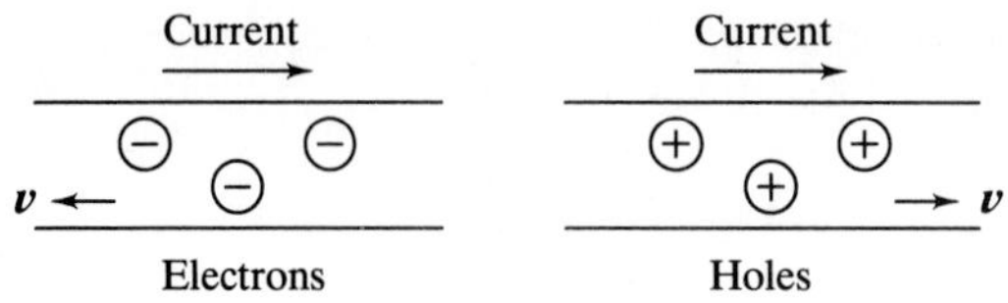

FIGURE 4-5
Electron and hole currents due to an applied field oriented toward the right.

crystals are arranged in energy bands, and a *hole* is a missing electron in one of these bands. A more technically detailed discussion of this topic may be found in Kittel.[2]

Semiconductors are classified into two types: those where holes serve to provide the current, and those where current is due to electrons. This is achieved by introducing appropriate impurities into pure silicon, by "doping" the silicon:

p-type semiconductors—an excess of holes. The corresponding impurities, such as boron, aluminum, and gallium, are called *p-dopants* or *acceptors.* Conduction is due primarily to the presence of holes. These are then termed the *majority carriers*; whatever electrons are present are termed the *minority carriers.*

n-type semiconductors—an excess of electrons. The corresponding impurities, such as phosphorus, arsenic, and antimony, are called *n-dopants* or *donors.* Conduction is due primarily to the presence of electrons. These are thus termed the *majority carriers*, and the holes are termed the *minority carriers.*

Semiconductor devices are constructed by arranging segments of semiconductors in different configurations.

Finally, we note that although the drift velocities of electrons and holes, v (average velocity of a group of electrons or holes), are in opposite directions, the current resulting from an externally applied electric field flows in the same direction as the applied field itself (see Fig. 4-5).

4-3-2 Diodes

It is instructive to begin with a discussion of the simplest semiconductor device obtained by placing a p-type conductor and an n-type conductor in contact with one another. The resulting device is called a *pn-junction*. The device is used here to introduce the student to the analysis of nonlinear circuits, forming a connection to the earlier load line analysis that might have been used in a previous course.

When an external voltage is applied across such a junction, it is called a *bias*, with sign convention as shown in Fig. 4-6. The diode symbol is generally oriented so that the arrowhead points in the direction in which the current flows most easily—the direction of forward bias. In that state the holes move to the

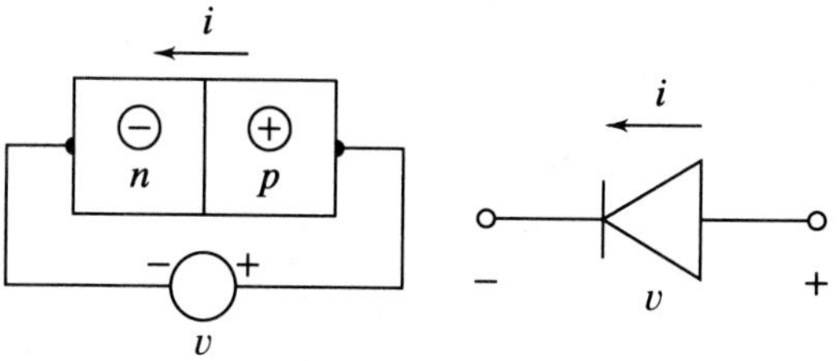

The Physical Diode The Symbol

FIGURE 4-6
The *pn*-junction diode.

left and the electrons move to the right, their cumulative effect being the current i.

The diode is a nonlinear device in the sense that its iv-characteristic is given by $i = f(v)$, where $f(\cdot)$ is a nonlinear function of v. For a *pn*-junction with forward bias, we have the *ideal diode equation*

$$i = I_s(e^{v/V_T} - 1)$$

where $V_T = kT/q$ is the thermal voltage,
$k = 1.38 \times 10^{-23}$ J/K is Boltzmann's constant,
$q = 1.602 \times 10^{-19}$ C is the electron charge,
T is the absolute temperature in kelvins.

In this context the constant I_s is termed the *saturation current*. However, with a reverse bias $|v| \gg V_T$ (e.g., $v \leq -4V_T$), the diode current i also approaches $-I_s$; thus the term *reverse saturation current* is also in use. This limiting value is ideal, and it may differ for forward and reverse bias in practice because of the thermal generation of carriers in reverse bias.

Theoretically, I_s may be written in the form

$$I_s = qA\left(\frac{D_p p_{n_0}}{L_p} + \frac{D_n n_{p_0}}{L_n}\right)$$

where A is the cross-sectional area of the junction, $D_p = L_p^2/\tau_p$ is the diffusion coefficient in the n-region, and $D_n = L_n^2/\tau_n$ is the diffusion coefficient in the p-region.

As we move away from the junction, the concentration of minority carriers decreases exponentially, and we term L_n and L_p the *diffusion lengths*, the distances from the junction at which the excess concentration of minority carriers becomes $1/e = 0.37$ of their original value in the p-type and n-type regions, respectively. Associated with these lengths are the times τ_n and τ_p, the *excess minority carrier lifetimes* required for the minority carriers to decrease to the fraction $1/e$ of their original concentration due to recombination. Finally, p_{n_0} and n_{p_0} are the minority carrier concentrations at equilibrium in the n-type and p-type regions, respectively. Physically, L_p and L_n range from 10^{-4} to 10^{-2} cm, and τ_p and τ_n range from 10^{-8} to 10^{-6} s. Note that I_s is entirely a function of the physical characteristics of the minority carriers.

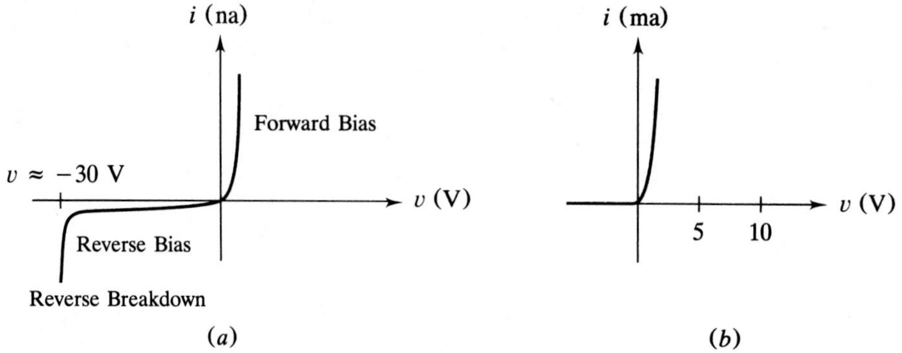

FIGURE 4-7
Diode response curves.

An extremely readable account of this material is given in Hodges and Jackson.[3]

The general appearance of the *iv*-relationship given previously is depicted in Fig. 4-7, with an indication of operating regions. The actual appearance, of course, depends on the scale being used. The general appearance (Fig. 4-7*a*) prevails when nanoamperes are used for the ordinate. In milliamperes, the curve has the form shown in Fig. 4-7*b*. The inclusion of nonlinear elements in circuits complicates their analysis, in particular, since superposition is now no longer valid. It is thus common to idealize the behavior of these devices in some fashion. First, however, we illustrate the inclusion of a diode as a nonlinear circuit element and derive governing equations.

Example 4-2. Obtain the governing equations for the two circuits in Fig. 4-8.

Solution. Clearly, the derivation of governing equations for a circuit is the same, whether or not nonlinear elements are included. The linear circuit simply serves as a review of the procedure.

(*a*) The current i and the voltage drops v_L and v_R are to be determined. The application of KVL yields

$$-v + v_L + v_R = 0$$

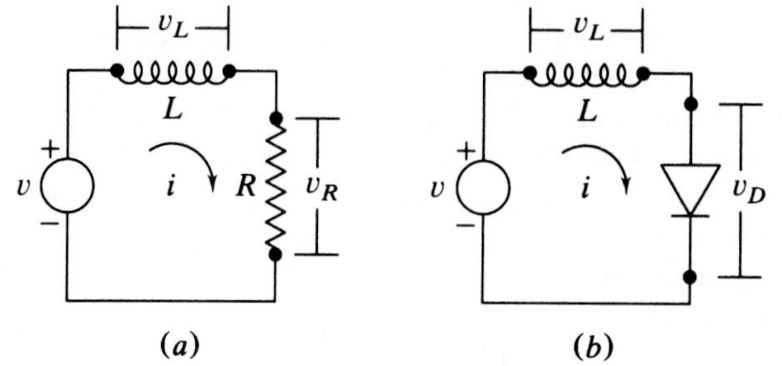

FIGURE 4-8
Linear and nonlinear circuits.

This is one equation for three unknowns. The remaining equations are given by the *iv*-characteristics of the devices

$$v_R = iR \qquad \text{and} \qquad v_L = L\frac{di}{dt}$$

These are the governing equations. To solve, we substitute these relationships into the loop equation to obtain

$$L\frac{di}{dt} + Ri = v$$

Once $i(t)$ has been obtained, the voltages may then be calculated from the device relationships.

(*b*) We now treat the inclusion of nonlinear elements in precisely the same manner. To be sure, this is a relatively academic exercise, since it is far more common in practice to use piecewise linear approximations of the *iv*-relationships within specific operating ranges. The unknowns for the nonlinear circuit are i, v_L, and v_D. The loop equation is

$$-v + v_L + v_D = 0$$

and the device characteristics are given by

$$v_L = L\frac{di}{dt} \qquad \text{and} \qquad i = I_s(e^{v_D/V_T} - 1)$$

$$\text{or} \qquad v_D = V_T \ln\left(\frac{i + I_s}{I_s}\right)$$

These equations are the governing equations. Again, we begin with the solution for the unknowns by substituting the *iv*-relationships into the loop equation to obtain the nonlinear differential equation

$$L\frac{di}{dt} + \frac{kT}{q}\ln\left(\frac{i + I_s}{I_s}\right) = v$$

Once $i(t)$ has been obtained, the calculation of v_L and v_D is straightforward.

Example 4-3 Load line analysis. Consider the simple circuit in Fig. 4-9, involving a resistance and a diode. The current i and the voltage drops v_R and v_D are to be determined for a given constant applied voltage v.

Solution. From an application of KVL the loop equation is obtained as

$$v_R + v_D = v$$

The common current i is related to the voltage drop v_D by

$$i(v_D) = I_s(e^{v_D/V_T} - 1)$$

Substitution in the loop equation then yields

$$Ri(v_D) + v_D = v$$

This equation is satisfied for some $v_D = v_D^*$. The solution v_D^* may be obtained

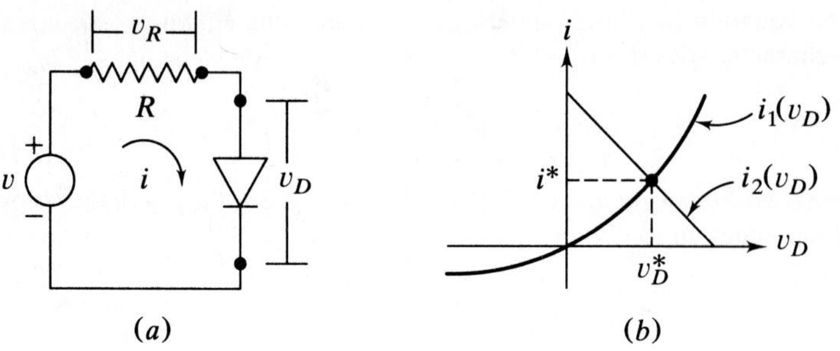

FIGURE 4-9
Load line analysis.

graphically by viewing the pair (v_D^*, i^*) as the intersection of the two curves

$$i_1(v_D) = I_s(e^{v_D/v_T} - 1)$$

$$i_2(v_D) = \frac{1}{R}(v - v_D)$$

as shown in Fig. 4-9*b*. That is,

$$i_1(v_D^*) = i_2(v_D^*) = i^*$$

Load line analysis of simple resistance circuits, including nonlinear devices, is one of the few routine approaches for nonlinear circuit problems. As mentioned, it is far more common to introduce piecewise linear approximations for the *iv*-relationships of the devices.

As a first approximation the diode may be viewed as a rectifier, a device that passes current in only one direction. That is,

$$i \geq 0 \quad \text{for} \quad v = 0$$
$$i = 0 \quad \text{for} \quad v < 0$$

as shown in Fig. 4-10*a*. This model is often an oversimplification since it neglects the forward voltage drop. In many real situations the range of currents

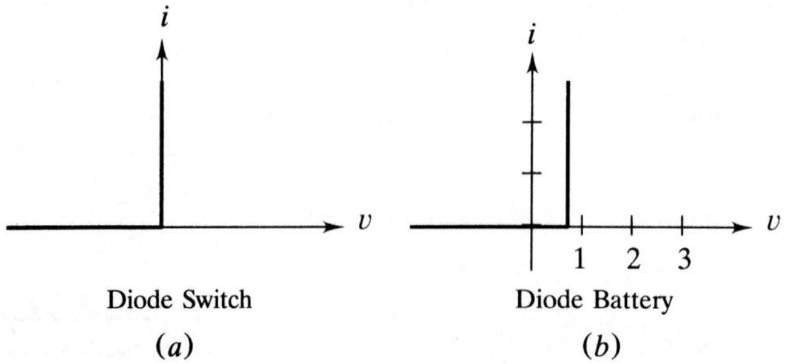

FIGURE 4-10
Diode idealizations: (*a*) diode switch; (*b*) diode battery.

is such that this forward voltage drop realistically lies between 0.6 and 0.8 V. Consequently, one also uses the approximation in Fig. 4-10b, with

$$i \geq 0 \quad \text{for} \quad v = 0.7 \text{ V}$$
$$i = 0 \quad \text{for} \quad v < 0.7 \text{ V}$$

Example 4-4

(a) Derive the governing differential equations for the nonlinear circuit in Fig. 4-11a with i_D and i_C as the unknowns. Assume that the iv-characteristic for the diode is given by $i = I_s(e^{v/V_T} - 1)$.

(b) Suppose the diode characteristics are idealized as shown in Fig. 4-11b. Draw the circuit corresponding to each idealization and determine which situation will prevail with $v(t) = e^{-t}$, $v_C(0) = -10$ V, $R = 100\ \Omega$, and $C = 10^{-3}$ F.

Solution

(a) The nodal equation is

$$i = i_D + i_C$$

The loop equations are

$$iR + v_D = v$$
$$v_D = v_C$$

In terms of the currents, these latter two equations are

$$(i_D + i_C)R + V_T \ln\left(\frac{i_D}{I_s} + 1\right) = v$$

$$V_T \ln\left(\frac{i_D}{I_s} + 1\right) = v_C(0) + \frac{1}{C}\int_0^t i_C(\tau)\, d\tau$$

These are the governing equations for the circuit. Note that at $t = 0$ we must

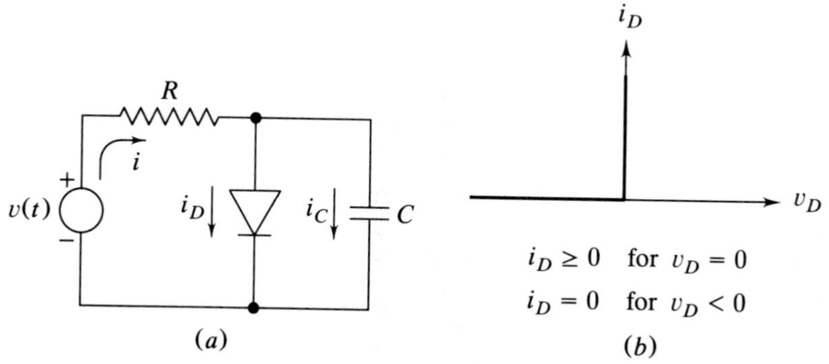

FIGURE 4-11
Circuit with idealized diode.

satisfy the conditions

$$i(0)R + V_T \ln\left(\frac{i_D(0)}{I_s} + 1\right) = v(0)$$

$$V_T \ln\left(\frac{i_D(0)}{I_s} + 1\right) = v_C(0)$$

so that only one condition may be arbitrarily specified, the remainder being determined by these equations.

(*b*) Because of the initially specified voltage across the capacitance, the initial idealized circuit can only have the form shown in Fig. 4-12*a*. Thus, with the diode as an open circuit, the use of KVL yields

$$iR + v_C(0) + \frac{1}{C}\int_0^t i(\tau)\,d\tau = e^{-t}$$

implying the initial condition

$$i(0) = 100 - 10 = 1 \quad \Rightarrow \quad i(0) = \frac{11}{100}$$

Differentiation of the integral equation results in

$$\frac{di}{dt} + 10i = -\frac{1}{100}e^{-t}$$

whose solution subject to the initial conditions is given by

$$i(t) = \frac{1}{9}e^{-10t} - \frac{1}{900}e^{-t}$$

It remains to check the condition $v_D = v_C < 0$.

An integration of the current yields

$$v_C(t) = v_C(0) + \frac{1}{10^{-3}}\int_0^t i(\tau)\,d\tau$$

$$= \frac{10}{9}(e^{-t} - 10e^{-10t})$$

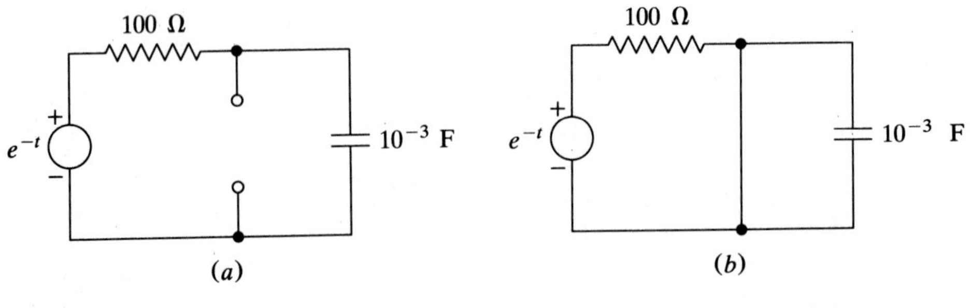

FIGURE 4-12
Idealized circuits.

The required inequality thus has the form

$$\frac{10}{9}e^{-t}(1 - 10e^{-9t}) \leq 0$$

and it follows that $v_D < 0$ for

$$0 \leq t < \bar{t} = \frac{1}{9}\ln 10$$

At $t = \bar{t}$, $v_C(\bar{t}) = 0$ and $i(\bar{t}) = 0$. At this point the diode begins to conduct current and the idealized circuit is the one of Fig. 4-12*b*, with the diode presented as a short circuit. The loop equation for this circuit is

$$e^{-t} = iR \quad \Rightarrow \quad i(t) = \frac{1}{100}e^{-t}$$

and the circuit continues in this state for the remainder of its operation.

Remark 4-1. Note carefully that the switch of the diode from one idealized state to the other entailed a current jump by an amount

$$\begin{aligned}[i] &= \lim_{t\to\bar{t}^+} i(t) - \lim_{t\to\bar{t}^-} i(t) \\ &= \frac{1}{100}\frac{1}{(10)^{1/9}}\end{aligned}$$

This jump is due to the piecewise linear approximation of the actual diode iv-characteristics. The actual nonlinear circuit does not exhibit such an abrupt jump. Finally, from a physical point of view, any sharp increase in current would not occur instantaneously but would require a finite amount of time.

4-3-3 The Depletion Region

In our context the depletion region is a well-defined region at the junction of n- and p-type materials. Within the region electrons and holes achieve a sort of diffusive equilibrium state which ideally depicts the region as being totally devoid of mobile charges. An understanding of the concept is essential, since depletion regions are the pipelines for current flow in semiconductor devices, such as MOSFETs and charge transfer devices.

There are two major phenomena that contribute to current flow in a conductor: drift and diffusion. Particles in a conductor always exhibit a more or less random thermal motion for which the individual currents tend to cancel so that no net current is produced. When an electric field is applied to the conductor, the charges tend to move along the field lines, resulting in a net current flow. This phenomenon is known as *drift*.

For the evaluation of the drift current in a conductor, consider the bar in Fig. 4-13, for definiteness. Suppose that the average velocity of the charge carrier within the region is v and the carrier charge is q. For simplicity, assume furthermore that the average *transit time* is τ, for a carrier to move from one end of the bar to the other. With n being the intrinsic *carrier concentration* per

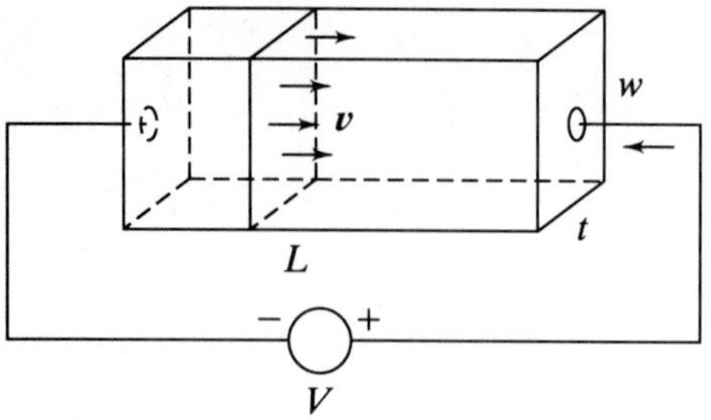

FIGURE 4-13
Drift current depicted for electron carriers.

unit volume, the total charge in the piece is

$$Q = nq(Lwt)$$

The average current is then given by

$$I = \frac{Q}{\tau} = nq(wt)\frac{L}{\tau} = nq(wt)v$$

In this context one also defines a current density in amperes per unit area with

$$J = \frac{I}{wt} = nqv$$

Diffusion, by contrast, is a process that occurs in any medium in an effort to overcome inequities in concentration. Suppose that there are different concentrations of particles in a given medium; then there is a tendency for particles to strive toward an equal concentration within the medium. This process—of the flow of particles from regions of high concentration to regions of low concentration—is called *diffusion*. When charged particles are involved, the process again gives rise to a current flow with

$$I = Dq(wt)\left(-\frac{dn}{dx}\right)$$

where dn/dx is the concentration gradient in the x-direction; D is called the *diffusion constant*. The diffusion current density is defined as before with

$$J = -Dq\frac{dn}{dx}$$

Suppose now that an n-type material and a p-type material have been placed in contact with one another, as shown in Fig. 4-14a, with no external field applied to the junction. Now, the concentration of holes is high on the p-side and low on the n-side, and the concentration of electrons is high on the n-side and low on the p-side, giving rise to diffusion. The holes would thus like to diffuse from the p-side to the n-side, leaving a net concentration of negatively $(-)$ ionized acceptor atoms on the p-side. The electrons would like to diffuse from the n-side to the p-side, leaving a net concentration of $(+)$ ionized

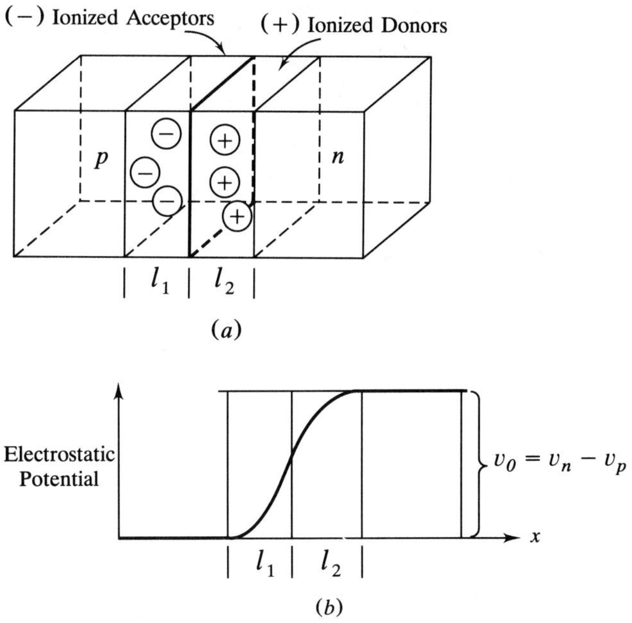

FIGURE 4-14
The depletion region.

donor atoms. The positively ionized group on the right will attract the electrons that are attempting to diffuse, and the negatively ionized atoms on the *p*-side will attract the holes that are attempting to diffuse. Eventually, the diffusion due to the concentration gradients and the attraction due to the electrostatic potentials will cancel, and equilibrium will be established with *no* net current flow. The two regions with ionized atoms and a total length of $l_1 + l_2$ are termed the *depletion region*, since the region is essentially depleted of mobile carriers.

The concentration of positive ions on the right side of the junction and of negative ions on the left side of the junction results in a corresponding potential drop from the *n*-side to the *p*-side, as shown in Fig. 4-14*b*. The potential drop may be written as

$$v_0 = v_n - v_p = v_{F_p} - v_{F_n}$$

where v_{F_p} and v_{F_n} are the Fermi potentials of the *p*-type material and the *n*-type material, respectively. We term v_0 the *contact potential* between the *n*-type material and the *p*-type material. It is also called the built-in potential of the junction.

Following Tsividis,[4] we finally provide equations that allow a quantitative evaluation of the lengths l_1 and l_2 comprising the depletion region. Subject to some simplifying assumptions, these lengths are given by

$$l_2 = \sqrt{\frac{2k_s\epsilon_0}{qN_A}}\sqrt{\frac{v_0}{1+\left(\frac{N_A}{N_D}\right)}}$$

$$l_1 = \frac{N_A}{N_D}l_2$$

where N_A and N_D are the acceptor and donor concentrations per unit volume, respectively, k_s is the dielectric constant of the material, and $\epsilon_0 = 8.854 \times 10^{-12}$ F/m is the permittivity of free space.

The application of external potentials to the junction will compress or expand the depletion region in accordance with Kirchhoff's voltage law. For example, if a forward bias v is applied to the junction, the depletion region will be reduced with v_0 replaced by $v_0 - v$ in the equations for l_1 and l_2, making it easier for the carriers to diffuse across the boundary. Conversely, the application of a reverse bias extends the depletion region, making it virtually impossible for diffusion to occur from one side to the other.

Subject to all of the simplifying assumptions made here for our one-dimensional case, the depletion region was merely compressed or expanded. In general, the application of a variety of potentials is used to deform the depletion region in a manner suited to the regulation of current flow.

4-3-4 The MOS Transistor

For charge-coupled devices (CCDs), which are used extensively in imaging technology, the MOS capacitor is the basic building block, both as image sensor and as charge transfer device. It is thus of interest to discuss this capacitor in some detail. We begin with a discussion of its basic structure and operation, followed by its circuit characterization. Additional and similar discussions may be found in basic electronics texts such as Carlson and Gisser[5] and Belanger, Adler, and Rumin.[6]

The MOS capacitor is available as a two-, three- or four-terminal device. However, the basic structure is that of a capacitor as shown in Fig. 4-15*a*. The construction generally starts with a substrate or body which is an *n*- or *p*-type semiconductor; it is taken to be *p*-type silicon here. This is followed by an oxide insulating layer, which we take to be SiO_2 (silicon dioxide). Finally, there is a polysilicon or metal layer, called the *gate*. Reading these from the top down, we devise the acronym MOS (metal-oxide-silicon). If an external voltage v is applied across the MOS capacitor, then the equivalent small signal capacitance is the same as that of two capacitors C_s and C_o connected in series, with resulting capacitance

$$\frac{1}{C} = \frac{1}{C_s} + \frac{1}{C_o}$$

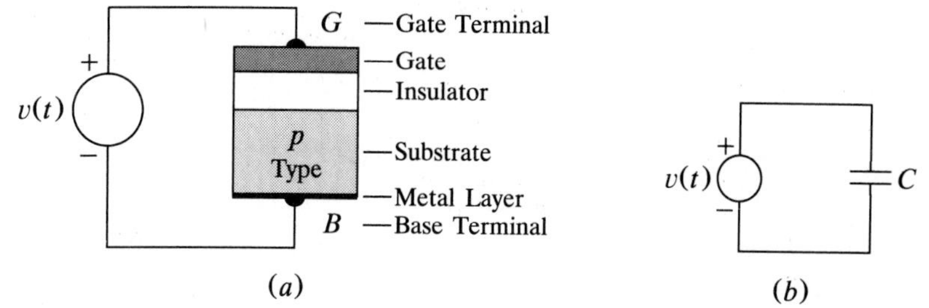

FIGURE 4-15
The MOS capacitor.

where C_s is the capacitance across the substrate and C_o is the capacitance of the oxide layer. For a theoretical estimate of the values, see Tsividis.[4] Thus the small signal equivalent circuit for the simplest MOS capacitor is the one shown in Fig. 4-15*b*.

The charge in the capacitor resides in the substrate, in a region adjacent to the silicon oxide layer. Depending on the applied voltage v, three types of charge balances prevail in the capacitor when a *p*-type substrate is assumed. In the following, we define the *flat-band* voltage v_{FB} as the externally applied voltage that would be needed to keep the semiconductor everywhere neutral. We then have:

$v = v_{\mathrm{FB}}$. *Flat-band condition*. Total neutrality of the semiconductor is maintained.

$v < v_{\mathrm{FB}}$. *Accumulation*. Holes accumulate in the region near the surface.

$v > v_{\mathrm{FB}}$ (v only slightly higher than v_{FB}). *Depletion*. The positive potential at the surface will drain holes away from the surface, leaving a depletion region similar to that encountered for the *pn*-junction.

$v > v_{\mathrm{FB}}$. *Inversion*. Electron-hole generation in the depletion region continues until, for sufficiently high v, the number of electrons exceeds the number of holes in the region near the surface. This state is then termed *surface inversion*.

It is this inversion layer that is of greatest interest in practical applications of the semiconductor. Its richness in electrons makes it useful for conducting current sideways, and the amount of current that flows in this channel can be regulated by the potential applied at the gate G.

THE *n*-CHANNEL MOS TRANSISTOR. The flow of current in the inversion layer just mentioned is achieved by including channel stops of heavily doped (n^+-type) material at each edge of the capacitor sandwich, as shown in Fig. 4-16. The terminals attached to these channel stops are labeled source (S) and drain (D).

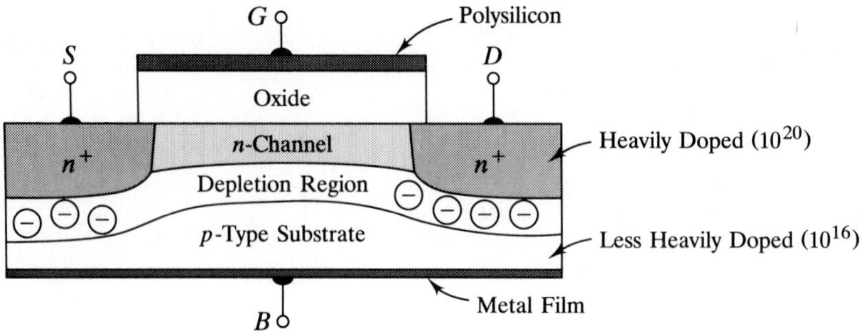

FIGURE 4-16
The four-terminal *n*-channel MOS transistor.

More formally, the introduction of the n^+ material results in a depletion region similar to that for the usual *pn*-junction. When a voltage is applied to the gate G, the usual inversion layer forms near the surface. This layer is then termed a channel—in the present case, an *n*-channel which forms in the *p*-type substrate. The application of a voltage across S and D causes a current to flow in the channel. The gate voltage may then be used to regulate the amount of current flow, or it may be used to turn the device "on" or "off." The remaining objective is to determine the drain current i_D for the possible combinations of terminal voltages.

These possible combinations are restricted by some basic necessities and assumptions (see also Tsividis[4]):

1. The substrate is uniformly doped.
2. The channel is sufficiently long and wide so that edge effects may be neglected.
3. Both *pn*-junctions are reverse biased. That is, $v_{SB} \geq 0$ and $v_{DB} \geq 0$ (see Fig. 4-17*a*).
4. The gate current is negligible. Because of the metal oxide layer, this is generally the case.
5. The direct current in the reverse-biased *pn*-junction may be taken to be 0.

There are two major types of MOSFETs (MOS field effect transistors): the enhancement type and the depletion type. A physical channel exists in the depletion type, differentiating it from the enhancement type, where such a channel must be created by the application of a gate voltage of proper magnitude and polarity. In addition, either polarity is acceptable for the depletion type.

Finally, we remark on the source and the drain. The terminal with the higher potential is termed the drain, with the result that the drain current i_D flows from the drain to the source.

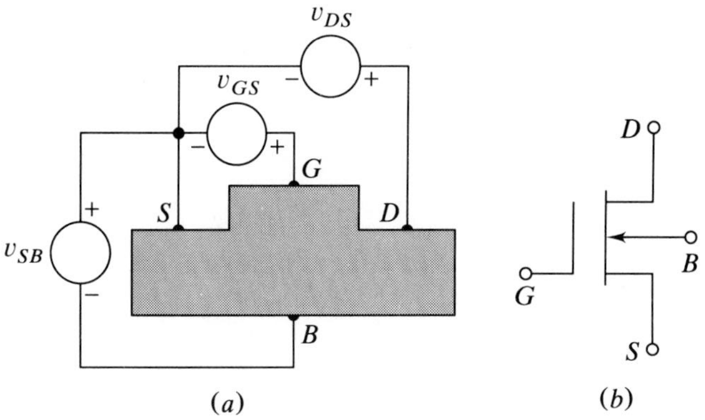

FIGURE 4-17
(*a*) Source-referenced voltages; (*b*) *n*-channel depletion MOSFET.

Just as it was for the diode, the actual current-voltage relationship again is nonlinear, with the additional complication that the current is now a function of two variables; that is, $i_D = f(v_{GS}, v_{DS})$ for a fixed value of v_{SB}. For a given device, the plot of i_D versus v_{DS} is usually obtained experimentally. An analytical expression may be obtained from a use of Poisson's equation (Tsividis[4]).

For practical purposes, one thus has graphical representations like the one shown in Fig. 4-18, a plot of i_D versus v_{DS} for different values of v_{GS}. In interaction with a resistance circuit, the actual static operating point for the circuit would again be obtained from a load line analysis, taking into account the particular value of v_{GS}.

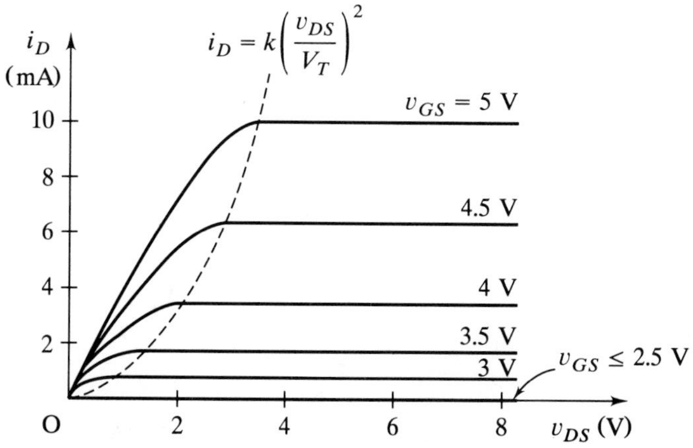

FIGURE 4-18
Plot of i_D versus v_{DS} for a given v_{GS}.

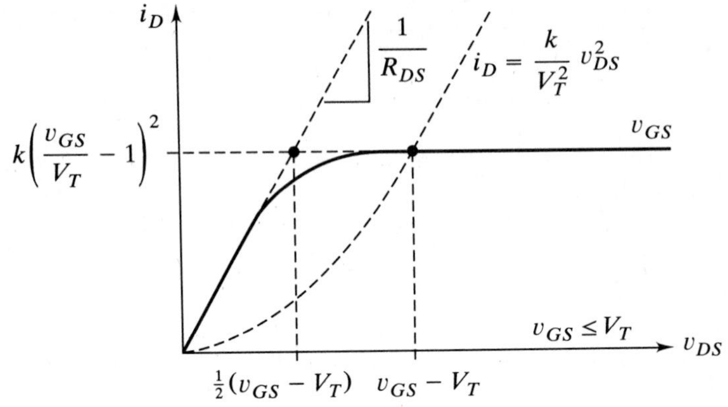

FIGURE 4-19
Approximate operating regions.

In actual design work, however, it is useful to provide approximate analytic expressions valid in certain operating regions. These expressions may be defined in terms of a number of characteristic parameters and a general i_D versus v_{DS} curve for fixed v_{GS} as shown in Fig. 4-19. For a given threshold voltage $V_T < 0$, and provided the body effect coefficient is small, the three operating regions for the n-channel depletion MOS may be classified in the following manner:

$v_{GS} \leq V_T$. *Cuttoff mode*. The drain current

$$i_D = 0 \qquad \text{for all} \quad v_{DS} \geq 0$$

$v_{GS} > V_T$ and $0 \leq v_{DS} \leq v_{GS} - V_T$. *Triode mode*. In this region the current

$$i_D \propto \left[(v_{GS} - V_T)v_{DS} - \tfrac{1}{2}v_{DS}^2\right]$$

For small v_{DS} we may ignore v_{DS}^2 and write

$$i_D = \frac{1}{R_{DS}} v_{DS}$$

where

$$R_{DS} = \frac{V_T}{2k} \frac{1}{\left(\dfrac{V_{GS}}{V_T} - 1\right)}$$

and the MOS transistor then behaves like a voltage-controlled resistor.

$v_{GS} > V_T$ and $v_{GS} - V_T \le v_{DS}$. *Pinch-off mode.* As is evident from Fig. 4-19, the drain current in this region is nicely approximated by

$$i_D = k\left(\frac{v_{GS}}{V_T} - 1\right)^2$$

a constant independent of v_{DS}.

We finally note that the boundary between the triode and the pinch-off regions was defined by $v_{DS} = v_{GS} - V_T$ or

$$\frac{v_{DS}}{V_T} = \frac{v_{GS}}{V_T} - 1$$

so that this boundary may also be expressed in the form

$$i_D = k\left(\frac{v_{DS}}{V_T}\right)^2 = \frac{k}{V_T^2} v_{DS}^2$$

4-4 BINARY VARIABLES AND LOGIC

Logic circuits play an essential role in all computer-directed activity, and robots totally depend on such circuits to allow them to function in the desired fashion. Analog-to-digital converters (ADCs) and digital-to-analog converters (DACs) are essential to the communication between digital controllers and analog sensor drive systems. Yet they generally have not been covered, even by juniors in electrical engineering. Furthermore, encoders play a fundamental part in sensing devices. We thus present enough fundamental material to be able to devise and understand simple encoders. As one desk reference for this material, we shall use Mano,[7] a standard text on this topic, and we shall adhere to the notation therein insofar as possible. We begin with a discussion of number systems.

4-4-1 Number Bases and Codes

Any decimal number with n digits in front of the decimal and m digits following the decimal may be written in the form

$$a_{n-1}10^{n-1} + a_{n-2}10^{n-2} + \cdots + a_1 10^1 + a_0 10^0$$
$$+ a_{-1}10^{-1} + a_{-2}10^{-2} + \cdots + a_{-m}10^{-m}$$

By convention, only the coefficients a_i are generally included in the number, with their position in the sequence denoting the implied powers of 10; that is, we write

$$a_{n-1}a_{n-2} \cdots a_1 a_0 \cdot a_{-1}a_{-2} \cdots a_{-m}$$

Example 4-5. Write the decimal number 5323.31 in expanded form.

Solution. There are four digits before the decimal and two digits that follow it; hence $n = 4$, $m = 2$. The resultant expanded form is

$$5 \times 10^3 + 3 \times 10^2 + 2 \times 10^1 + 3 \times 10^0 + 3 \times 10^{-1} + 1 \times 10^{-2}$$

or

$$5000 + 300 + 20 + 3 + 0.3 + 0.01 = 5323.31$$

The decimal number system is said to be of *base* or *radix* 10 because it is based on the 10 digits $(0, 1, 2, \ldots, 9)$, and the coefficients are multiplied by corresponding powers of 10. When the basis of a particular number is not evident, we indicate it with an appropriate subscript [e.g., $(5323.31)_{10}$].

The same approach is used in the binary system. In this system there are only two coefficients, 0 and 1, and the coefficients are multiplied by powers of 2. Again, with n digits before and m digits after the decimal, we have

$$a_{n-1}2^{n-1} + a_{n-2}2^{n-2} + \cdots + a_1 2^1 + a_0 2^0$$
$$+ a_{-1}2^{-1} + a_{-2}2^{-2} + \cdots + a_{-m}2^{-m}$$

and we abbreviate with

$$(a_{n-1}a_{n-2} \cdots a_1 a_0 \cdot a_{-1}a_{-2} \cdots a_{-m})_2$$

with the position again indicating the appropriate power of 2.

Example 4-6. Write the decimal equivalent of $(1001.101)_2$.

Solution. Here, $n = 4$, $m = 3$, and the result is given by

$$1 \times 2^3 + 0 \times 2^2 + 0 \times 2^1 + 1 \times 2^0 + 1 \times 2^{-1} + 0 \times 2^{-2} + 1 \times 2^{-3}$$
$$= 8 + 1 + \tfrac{1}{2} + \tfrac{1}{8} = 9\tfrac{5}{8} = 9.625$$

Thus, in general, the decimal equivalent of a number with radix r is given by

$$a_{n-1}r^{n-1} + a_{n-2}r^{n-2} + \cdots + a_1 r^1 + a_0 r^0 + a_{-1}r^{-1} + \cdots + a_{-m}r^{-m}$$

As we have seen, it is a straightforward matter to obtain the decimal equivalent of a number of any given radix. Naturally, it is also of interest to express decimal numbers in terms of other bases.

Example 4-7. Obtain the binary expression corresponding to the decimal expression 53.

Solution. The most obvious approach is to arrive at 53 by simply adding powers of 2. We have

$$2^5 + 2^4 + 2^2 + 2^0 = 53$$

Since 2^5 is the highest power of 2 present, we have six digits, and

$$\underline{1}\,\underline{1}\,\underline{0}\,\underline{1}\,\underline{0}\,\underline{1}$$

is the desired binary equivalent.

There is a more formal approach which allows a quick conversion from a decimal number to the corresponding number in another basis. If the decimal number contains a decimal point, it is necessary to first convert the number into an integer plus decimal fraction, since the conversion procedure differs for the two.

Example 4-8. Write the decimal number 365.24 as a base 5 number with decimal.

Solution. We first separate the fractional decimal from the integral part with 365 plus 0.24.

To convert the integral part, the number is first divided by the base r, leaving an integer quotient and a remainder of the form p/r, $p < r$; $p = a_0$, the least significant digit, in the base r expansion of the number. The integer quotient is again divided by r, yielding a_1, and the process continues until the integer quotient is 0. In this manner we obtain the following coefficients:

Ratio		Integer quotient		Remainder	Coefficient
$\frac{365}{5}$	=	73	+	$\frac{0}{5}$	$a_0 = 0$
$\frac{73}{5}$	=	14	+	$\frac{3}{5}$	$a_1 = 3$
$\frac{14}{5}$	=	2	+	$\frac{4}{5}$	$a_2 = 4$
$\frac{2}{5}$	=	0	+	$\frac{2}{5}$	$a_{n-1} = a_3 = 2$

For the integral part of the conversion, we thus have the equivalence

$$(365)_{10} = (2430)_5$$

a result that may easily be checked with

$$2 \times 5^3 + 4 \times 5^2 + 3 \times 5^1 + 0 \times 5^0 = 365$$

To convert the decimal fraction, we multiply by r rather than dividing. We first multiply the fraction by r to yield an integer part and a remainder; the integer part is the coefficient a_{-1}. The remainder is again multiplied by r, eventually yielding a_{-2}. The process continues until the remainder is 0, or until a sufficient decimal accuracy has been reached. The fractional base 5 coefficients for 0.24 are

Product		Integer part		Decimal part	Coefficient
$0.24 \cdot 5$	=	1	+	0.20	$a_{-1} = 1$
$0.20 \cdot 5$	=	1	+	0	$a_{-2} = 1$

Consequently, we have the equivalence

$$(365.24)_{10} = (2430.11)_5$$

In digital computers numbers are represented either in binary or in coded decimal form. Indeed, all of the identification and manipulation of items in a computer is carried out by assigning a binary code to each item. Thus there is a direct analogy between binary circuit elements and binary digits. A binary circuit element may represent 0 when off and 1 when on. Binary digits are also called *bits*. An array of n bits may be used to represent (code) 2^n distinct binary elements.

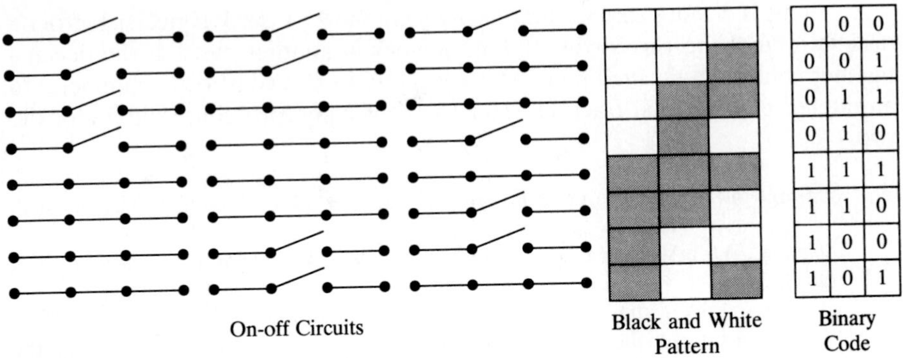

FIGURE 4-20
Three-bit information.

Example 4-9. Suppose we have 3 bits. Then these may be used to produce or represent the distinct patterns and binary codes shown in Fig. 4-20. Three bits thus allow the representation of $2^3 = 8$ distinct elements. To distinguish among a group of 10 elements, such as the decimal digits, requires at least 4 bits, since 3 bits allow 8 and 4 bits allow $2^4 = 16$ distinct elements. Six possible additional assignments remain unused.

There are numerous different codes that can be obtained by arranging 4 or more bits in 10 distinct combinations. One of the most common such assignments is the binary coded decimal, or BCD code. Each position in the four-digit code may be assigned a weight in such a way that those multiplied by 1 add up

Decimal Digit	BCD 8421
0	0000
1	0001
2	0010
3	0011
4	0100
5	0101
6	0110
7	0111
8	1000
9	1001

FIGURE 4-21
BCD decimal equivalent.

to the corresponding digit between 0 and 9. The most common weights for the BCD code are 8421, as shown in Fig. 4-21.

Example 4-10. Express the decimal number 290 in binary form and in terms of the BCD code.

Solution. The binary expression is obtained most easily from

$$2^8 + 2^5 + 2^1 = 290$$

implying

$$(290)_{10} = (100100010)_2$$

As a decimal expressed in terms of the BCD code, we have

0010	1001	0000
2	9	0

A computer must have a way of storing on/off information, that is, of storing individual bits. A *binary cell* is a device capable of storing one bit of information. Such a cell can occupy only one of two stable states at a time. The most common binary cells in standard use are electronic flip-flop circuits.

A *register* is a group of binary cells, with each cell storing either a 1 or a 0. A *memory unit* is a collection of thousands of registers used for storing digital information. All computer operations essentially reduce to interregister transfer operations.

4-5 BINARY LOGIC AND LOGIC CIRCUITS

By now it is evident that all discrete information can be identified with corresponding binary codes. The formal manipulation of such codes and binary calculations require an organizational logic that allows them to be shifted and stored in an orderly fashion. All of the logic statements are ultimately reduced to a yes/no structure. All of the statements are formulated mathematically in terms of variables which are called Boolean variables, in honor of the English mathematician George Boole. Since the variables can take on only the values 0 and 1, it becomes necessary to establish rules for the usual arithmetic operations. We shall define only the three basic operations: AND, OR, and NOT. We give the formal definitions of the operations, some simple circuits for their implementation, the symbols that are in use for their manipulation, and the truth tables that establish each identity.

The AND Operation

(*a*) *The operation*. We write $Z = X \cdot Y$ and read this statement as "Z equals X AND Y." The statement is defined by: $Z = 1$ if and only if $X = 1$ and $Y = 1$; otherwise, $Z = 0$.

(*b*) *The simple circuit*. See Fig. 4-22.

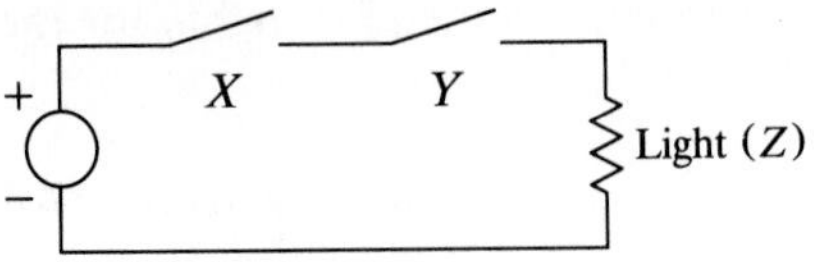

FIGURE 4-22
A simple AND circuit.

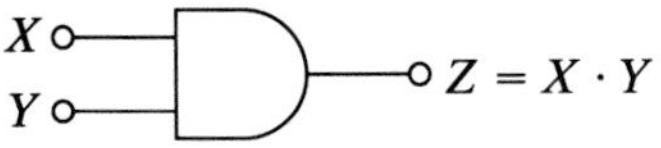

X	Y	Z
1	0	0
0	1	0
0	0	0
1	1	1

FIGURE 4-23
The AND symbol (left) and truth table (right).

(c) *The AND gate symbol and truth table.* See Fig. 4-23. We have shown a gate with only two input terminals. The definition and operation easily extend to n input terminals.

The OR Operation

(a) *The operation.* We write $Z = X + Y$ and read this statement as "Z equals X OR Y." The statement is defined by: $Z = 0$ if and only if $X = 0$ and $Y = 0$; otherwise, $Z = 1$.

(b) *The simple circuit.* See Fig. 4-24.

(c) *The OR gate symbol and truth table.* See Fig. 4-25. The extension to an n-input terminal gate is straightforward.

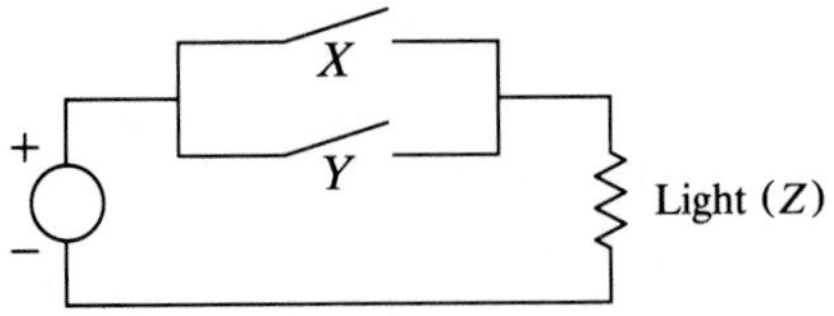

FIGURE 4-24
A simple OR circuit.

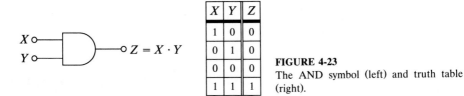

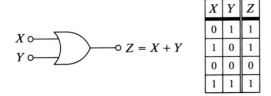

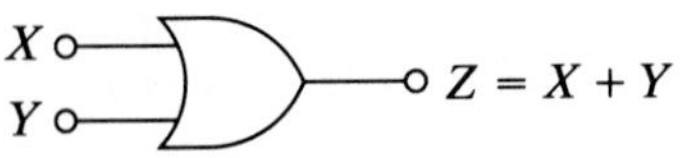

X	Y	Z
0	1	1
1	0	1
0	0	0
1	1	1

FIGURE 4-25
The OR symbol (left) and truth table (right).

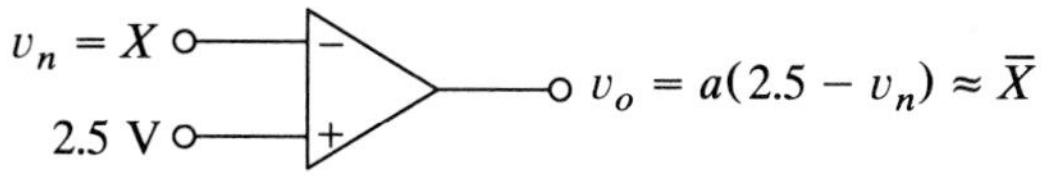

FIGURE 4-26
A simple NOT circuit.

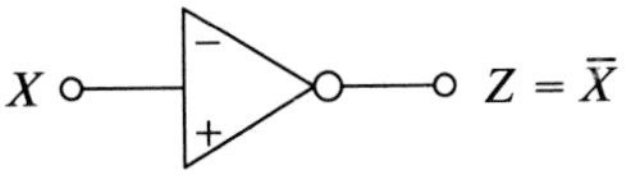

X	Z
0	1
1	0

FIGURE 4-27
The NOT gate symbol (left) and truth table (right).

The NOT Operation

(*a*) *The operation.* We write an overbar over a Boolean variable to denote the NOT operation; that is, $Z = \overline{X}$. We read this statement as "Z equals NOT X." The statement is defined by: $Z = 1$ if and only if $X = 0$, and $Z = 0$ if and only if $X = 1$.

(*b*) *The simple circuit.* See Fig. 4-26. Let logic "0" be $X = 0$ V and logic "1" be $X = 5$ V.

(*c*) *The NOT gate symbol and truth table.* See Fig. 4-27.

One of the tasks structured in terms of logic circuits is that of reducing the number of variables required for the identification of a specified number of items. For example, suppose we have a 3-bit code to identify four items. There then is a waste of four codes, since a 2-bit code actually suffices to identify the items.

Example 4-11. Construct a 2-bit output code for the given 3-bit input code (see Fig. 4-28) by using an appropriate reducing logic circuit.

Solution. There is no unique approach to the this kind of problem. Usually, the best approach is to simply produce one logic circuit that works and subsequently to reduce the number of needed components by using Boolean algebra. One circuit that produces the desired output is given in Fig. 4-29.

C_1	C_2	C_3	x	y
0	0	0	0	0
1	0	0	0	1
1	1	0	1	1
1	1	1	1	0

FIGURE 4-28
Three-bit input code.

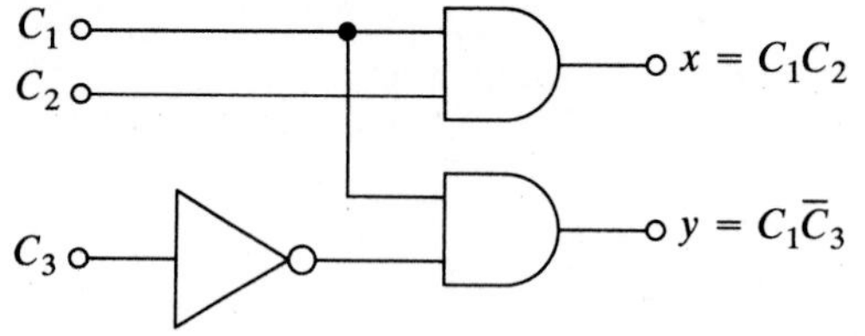

FIGURE 4-29
A simple encoder.

The intent of this brief introduction to logic circuits was to provide just enough information for an understanding of the possible use and purpose of logic circuits, for example, the encoder in connection with the analog-to-digital converter in the next section.

We close this section with a summary of some basic and some more esoteric identities in Boolean algebra (see Table 4-1).

TABLE 4-1

$X + 0 = X$	$X \cdot 1 = X$	$\overline{X + Y} = \bar{X} \cdot \bar{Y}$
$X + 1 = 1$	$X \cdot 0 = 0$	$\overline{X \cdot Y} = \bar{X} + \bar{Y}$
$X + X = X$	$X \cdot X = X$	$X + YZ = (X + Y)(X + Z)$
$X + \bar{X} = 1$	$X \cdot \bar{X} = 0$	

4-6 DIGITAL-TO-ANALOG CONVERTERS

Digital-to-analog converters (DACs or D/As) appear whenever a computer is used to control machinery. In this context their purpose is to convert the computer's digital code output into an analog signal capable of driving the machinery. There are a number of ways in which this task can be achieved. Here, we shall again present only the most straightforward configuration—the weighted-resistor DAC. The reader is referred to Franco[1] for a detailed treatment of the subject.

The weighted-resistor DAC is simply an invertor-summer with judicious choices for the input resistors, which may be switched on or off in accordance with some binary code.

Example 4-12. Analyze the weighted-resistor DAC shown in Fig. 4-30. Determine the output and discuss its possible values.

Solution. In the sketch v_R is a reference voltage that may be adjusted to produce a normalized output, the b_i are 0 or 1 ("off" when connected to ground and "on" when connected to v_R), and the remaining circuit is that of the usual summer-invertor.

Summing currents at the summing junction yields

$$i_1 + i_2 + \cdots + i_N = i_n + i_F$$

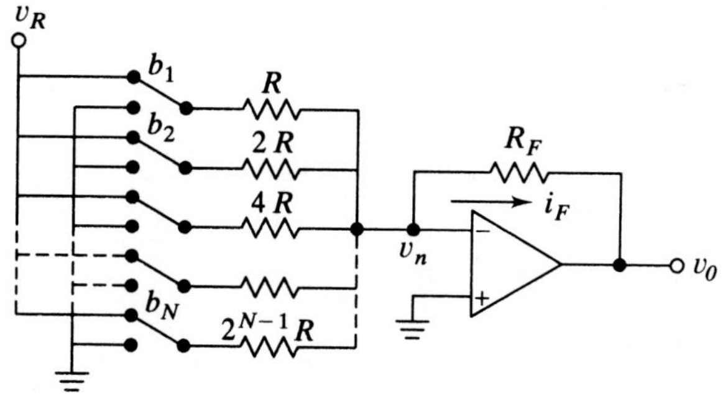

FIGURE 4-30
The weighted-resistor DAC.

The use of Ohm's law then results in

$$b_1\frac{v_R - v_n}{R} + b_2\frac{v_R - v_n}{2R} + \cdots + b_N\frac{v_R - v_n}{2^{N-1}R} = i_n + \frac{v_n - v_0}{R_F}$$

As usual for nonsaturated operation with $v_p = 0$, we have $v_n = 0$, with the result

$$v_R\left(\frac{b_1}{R} + \frac{b_2}{2R} + \cdots + \frac{b_N}{2^{N-1}R}\right) = -\frac{v_0}{R_F}$$

and hence

$$v_0 = -\frac{2R_F v_R}{R}\left(\frac{b_1}{2} + \frac{b_2}{2^2} + \cdots + \frac{b_N}{2^N}\right)$$

In this context we term b_1 the most significant bit (MSB), b_2 the next significant bit, and so on, with b_N as the least significant bit (LSB).

Some additional terminology is used in connection with some of the extremal values of the DAC:

(*a*) The LSB output corresponds to 00...01 with the result

$$v_{0\,\mathrm{LSB}} = -2\frac{R_F v_R}{R}\frac{1}{2^N}$$

(*b*) The MSB output corresponds to 10...00 with the result

$$v_{0\,\mathrm{MSB}} = -2\frac{R_F v_R}{R}\frac{1}{2} = -\frac{R_F v_R}{R}$$

(*c*) The maximum output occurs when all of the bits are equal to 1, for 11...11, resulting in

$$v_{0\,\max} = -2\frac{R_F v_R}{R}\left(\frac{1}{2} + \left(\frac{1}{2}\right)^2 + \cdots + \left(\frac{1}{2}\right)^N\right)$$

$$= -2\frac{R_F v_R}{R}\left(\frac{2^N - 1}{2^N}\right)$$

(*d*) The *nominal full-scale* output is defined to be

$$v_{0\ \mathrm{FS}} = 2v_{0\ \mathrm{MSB}} = -2\frac{R_F v_R}{R}$$

(*e*) It is common to normalize the nominal full-scale output to be either -2.5 V, -5.0 V, or -10.0 V; for example,

$$2\frac{R_F v_R}{R} = -10.0$$

resulting in a general output voltage

$$v_0 = 10\left(\frac{b_1}{2} + \frac{b_2}{4} + \cdots + \frac{b_N}{2^N}\right)$$

Note that the expression in parentheses is simply a decimal equivalent of the binary number $b_1 b_2 \ldots b_N$. For obvious reasons we thus term this an N-bit DAC.

The greater the number of bits used, the greater is the refinement of intervals into which the overall range is separated.

Definition 4-1 Resolution of the *N*-bit DAC. Let the nominal full-scale reading of the DAC be $2R_F v_R/R$. Then the resolution of the DAC is

$$r = \frac{1}{2^N}\frac{2R_F v_R}{R}$$

Note that the nominal full scale serves as the basis for defining the resolution. The full-scale value itself is generally not attainable for a finite number of bits; the maximum attainable level is $v_{0\ \mathrm{FS}}(1 - 1/2^N)$.

There are a number of difficulties with this kind of DAC; we mention only two of them here. Note that the resistance ratio of maximum to minimum resistance is 2^{N-1}. Large resistance ratios, say $N \geq 8$, are difficult to establish in practice. The difficulty can be eliminated by using cascaded resistor networks (see Franco[1]).

Another detrimental aspect is the *settling time*, the time required for the output voltage to settle within a specific error band of the steady-state output voltage for a specified digital input change, usually corresponding to a worst case condition from 00...00 to 11...11.

4-7 ANALOG-TO-DIGITAL CONVERTERS

Although there are some sensors that provide a digital output, most of them produce an analog output. In order to process and manipulate this output, it is generally necessary to change it to digital form. Again, there is a variety of analog-to-digital converters (ADCs or A/Ds) available. We shall base our discussion on a most straightforward approach—the parallel comparator ADC, or flash ADC, so-called because of its operational speed.

Formally, an ADC converts a given analog signal to a digital number or code. A given number of available code bits provides a corresponding number

Input Voltage	Code
$0 < v_i < 1$	0 0 0
$1 < v_i < 2$	0 0 1
$2 < v_i < 3$	0 1 0
$3 < v_i < 4$	0 1 1
$4 < v_i < 5$	1 0 0
$5 < v_i < 6$	1 0 1
$6 < v_i < 7$	1 1 0
$7 < v_i$	1 1 1

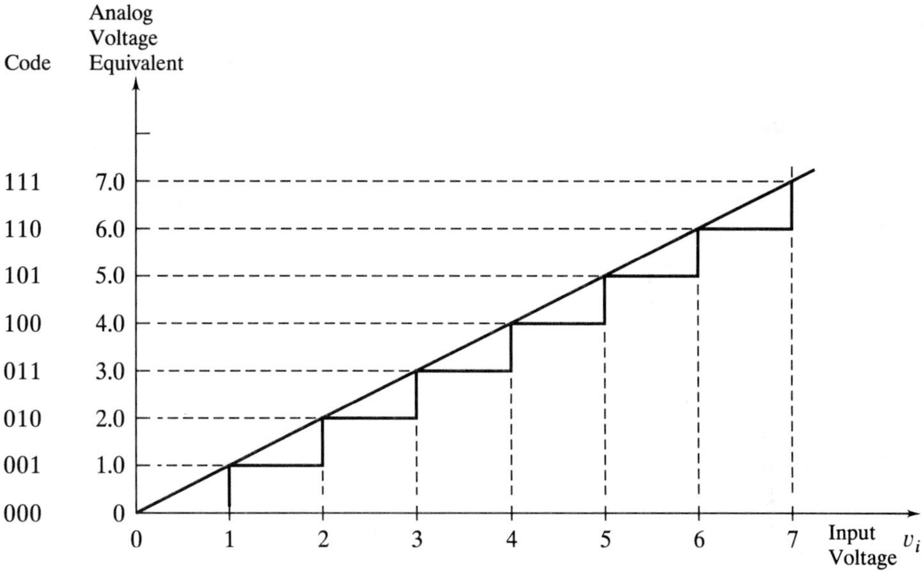

FIGURE 4-31
ADC: analog intervals to binary code.

of levels to which a code may be assigned; for example, 3 bits would provide $2^3 = 8$ levels. Although not required, it is usual to space the coded levels at equal intervals. To provide a specific example, suppose we consider a 3-bit code for a 7-V input range. (We leave a similar 2-bit ADC as an exercise.) A common set of code assignments to the different voltage levels (the least significant bit switches at each level change) is given by those in Fig. 4-31.

Definition 4-2 Resolution of the *N*-bit ADC. For the digitization of a given voltage range $[v_0, v_1]$, assume that the interval has been normalized to $[0, v_A]$ with $v_A = v_1 - v_0$. Let the code $00\ldots0$ correspond to 0 and the code $11\ldots1$ to 1.

Then the resolution of the ADC is given by

$$r = \frac{v_A}{2^N - 1}$$

For our previously illustrated ADC, the resolution thus is

$$r = \frac{7}{8 - 1} = 1 \text{ V}$$

that is, any changes in analog input involving less than 1 V will not be noted in the digital output. This unavoidable error between the analog input and the digital output is termed the *quantization error*.

Definition 4-3 Quantization error. The quantization error is the difference between the actual voltage implied by the diagonal in Fig. 4-31 and the quantized voltage level assigned. The maximum quantization error is equal to the resolution.

The quantization error relevant to our previous example has been plotted in Fig. 4-32. For example, if the analog input is $v_i = 5.4$ V, it will be quantized as 5.0 V with code assignment 1 0 1 and with a quantization error of -0.4 V. (Note that the quantization error is always negative.)

Based on the standard code used, with a jump in the LSB for every level change, the maximum quantization error may also be viewed as -1 LSB. All of the previous terminology applies when the so-called truncation approach to analog-to-digital conversion is used.

The maximum quantization error may be reduced to $\pm \frac{1}{2}r$, r being the resolution, by using a voltage offset from 0 equal to one-half of the resolution, with the remaining intervals the same length as before. This is also termed the round-off approach to A/D conversion.†

Now, to the flash ADC. The basic layout of the ADC is shown in Fig. 4-33. It has a three-state structure: a voltage divider to split the full range into equal comparison intervals; comparators to provide a primary digitalization of the analog signal; and, finally, an encoder to assign final (hopefully, minimal) codes to the intervals. A somewhat more detailed discussion of the three stages follows.

For the voltage divider segment, we have the usual analysis; for example,

$$v_R = i(7R) \qquad \text{and} \qquad v_0 = i\left(\frac{13}{2}R\right)$$

with the result

$$v_0 = \frac{13}{14}v_R$$

†See Exercise 4-18 and Franco[1] for further discussion of this topic.

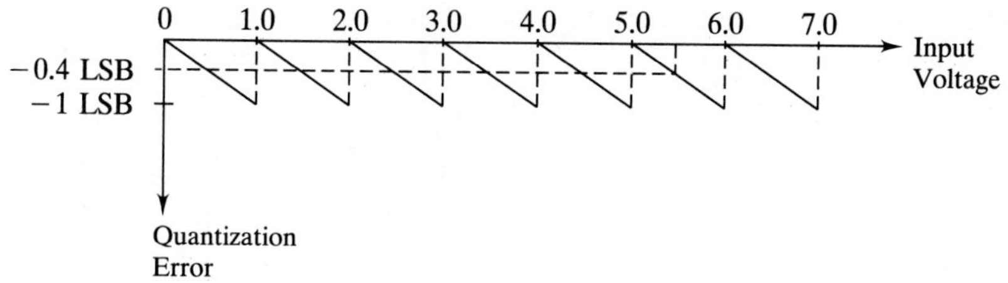

FIGURE 4-32
The quantization error.

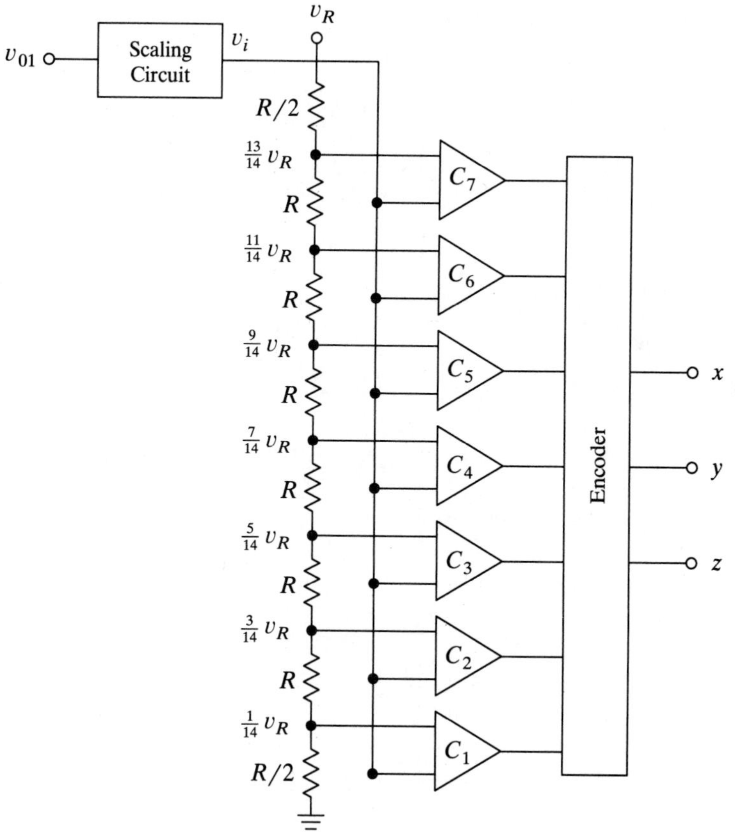

FIGURE 4-33
A flash ADC.

for the uppermost branching. When the analog voltage input is not within the required range set by v_R, it is necessary to precede the converter with an appropriate scaling circuit. Since the major advantage of the flash ADC is its speed, any additional circuitry provides delays that detract from this advantage. Of course, the scaling should take full advantage of the available range.

As an example of the ADC conversion process, suppose the analog input is $v_i = 0.57v_R$. Then the comparators yield the following primary code:

$$
\begin{aligned}
C_1 &= 1 \quad \text{since} \quad v_1 = a\left(0.57 - \tfrac{1}{14}\right)v_R > 0 \\
C_2 &= 1 \quad \text{since} \quad 0.57 - \tfrac{3}{14} > 0 \\
C_3 &= 1 \quad \text{since} \quad 0.57 - \tfrac{5}{14} > 0 \\
C_4 &= 1 \quad \text{since} \quad 0.57 - \tfrac{7}{14} > 0 \\
C_5 &= 0 \quad \text{since} \quad 0.57 - \tfrac{9}{14} < 0 \\
C_6 &= 0 \quad \text{since} \quad 0.57 - \tfrac{11}{14} < 0 \\
C_7 &= 0 \quad \text{since} \quad 0.57 - \tfrac{13}{14} < 0
\end{aligned}
$$

where the comparator high has been taken to be equivalent to logic 1. The encoder, finally, is a logic circuit that reduces the seven-digit code to a

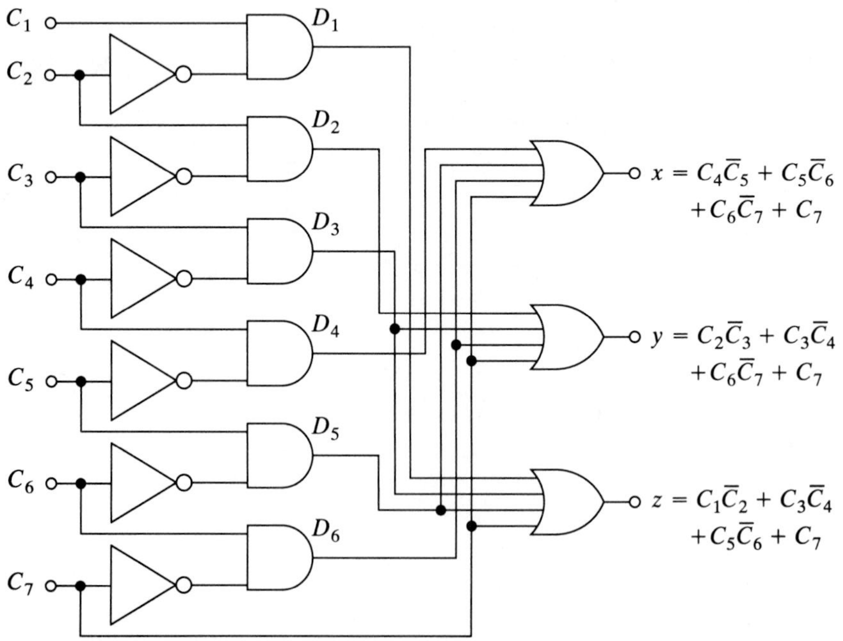

FIGURE 4-34
Encoder for a three-bit ADC.

C_1	C_2	C_3	C_4	C_5	C_6	C_7	D_1	D_2	D_3	D_4	D_5	D_6	D_7	x	y	z
1	0	0	0	0	0	0	1	0	0	0	0	0	0	0	0	1
1	1	0	0	0	0	0	0	1	0	0	0	0	0	0	1	0
1	1	1	0	0	0	0	0	0	1	0	0	0	0	0	1	1
1	1	1	1	0	0	0	0	0	0	1	0	0	0	1	0	0
1	1	1	1	1	0	0	0	0	0	0	1	0	0	1	0	1
1	1	1	1	1	1	0	0	0	0	0	0	1	0	1	1	0
1	1	1	1	1	1	1	0	0	0	0	0	0	1	1	1	1

FIGURE 4-35
Truth table for a three-bit ADC.

three-digit code; here, the reduction takes the primary code 1 1 1 1 0 0 0 into the minimal code 1 0 0. The encoder logic circuit and its truth table are shown in Figs. 4-34 and 4-35, respectively. By and large the encoder configuration depicted here is deduced from a similar reduction encoding given in Mano.[7]

Because of its speed, variations of the flash ADC are used in electronic vision systems and in other applications requiring real-time performance. We have only touched upon the extensive possibilities available for digital-to-analog and analog-to-digital conversion. However, it is an understanding of how the various concepts can be implemented that ultimately gives robotics engineers the confidence needed in what they are doing, and it provides them with some of the limitations that they might encounter due to present technology.

EXERCISES

4-1. Determine the input-output relationships for the circuits in Fig. E4-1; name the devices and obtain the corresponding system functions for them under the assumption of ideal operations of the op amps.

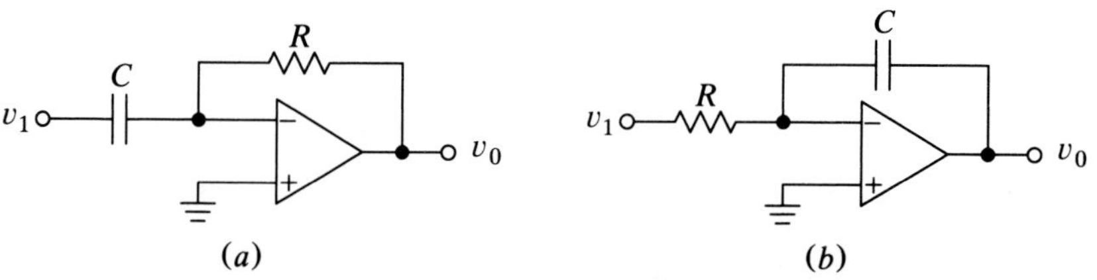

FIGURE E4-1

4-2. Consider again the inverting summer shown in Fig. 4-3 with input voltages v_1 and v_2. Suppose that the power supply voltages to the op amp are symmetric at ± 15 V. Obtain a constraint on the input voltages that will assure proper (nonsaturated) operation of the circuit.

4-3. Consider an ideal op amp in proper (nonsaturated) operation. In this case both of the input currents $i_n \approx 0$ and $i_p \approx 0$ and the current at the output may flow either into or out of the op amp, depending on the additional feedback circuitry and loads (see Fig. E4-3). Explain how this is possible in light of Kirchhoff's current law, which must always be satisfied.

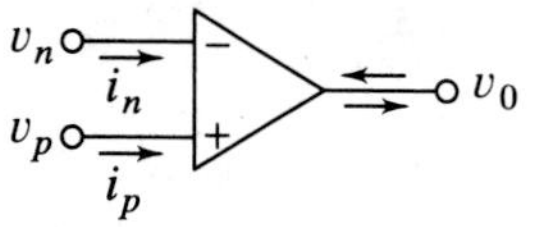

FIGURE E4-3

4-4. Consider the ideal diode equation and suppose that the *pn*-junction is a typical low-power *pn*-junction.

(*a*) Calculate V_T at room temperature.

(*b*) Suppose that the cross-sectional area of the junction is $A = 2000\ (\mu\text{m})^2$. The equilibrium concentrations of the minority carriers in each region are given by $n_{p_0} = 2 \times 10^2/\text{cm}^3$ and $p_{n_0} = 2 \times 10^4/\text{cm}^3$; the excess minority carrier lifetimes are $\tau_n = 5 \times 10^{-8}$ s and $\tau_p = 2.5 \times 10^{-8}$ s, with corresponding diffusion lengths $L_n = 12\ \mu$m and $L_p = 7\ \mu$m. Calculate the saturation current I_s.

4-5. Consider the circuit in Fig. E4-5. Suppose that the diode is viewed as an ideal rectifier and assume that the applied voltage is $v = A \sin \omega t = 10 \sin 2t$ and that $R = 1000\ \Omega$. Graph the voltage v_R versus time and draw the circuits that correspond to the idealized diode representations. That is, replace the diode by a short circuit for positive v and by an open circuit for negative v. Draw the iv-curve for the diode and resistor circuit for the "on" condition.

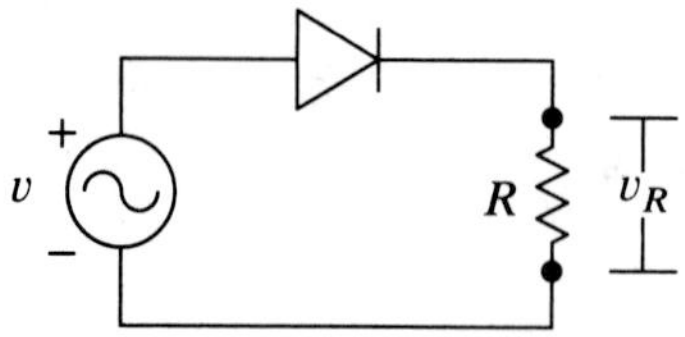

FIGURE E4-5
(The $\pm$ for the input is included to attain uniformity in the derivation.)

4-6. Consider the circuit in Fig. E4-6. The voltage drop across R_2 and the current flowing through R_2 are to be determined. Assume a constant voltage source $v_1 = 10$ V and use $R_1 = 300\ \Omega$ and $R_2 = 500\ \Omega$. Determine the exact solution by using the iv-characteristic

$$i = 10^{-12}(e^{40v} - 1)$$

and an approximate solution based on the approximation

$$i > 0 \quad \text{for} \quad v_D = 0.7\text{ V}$$

$$i = 0 \quad \text{for} \quad v_D < 0.7\text{ V}$$

Calculate the percentage error introduced by using the approximation.

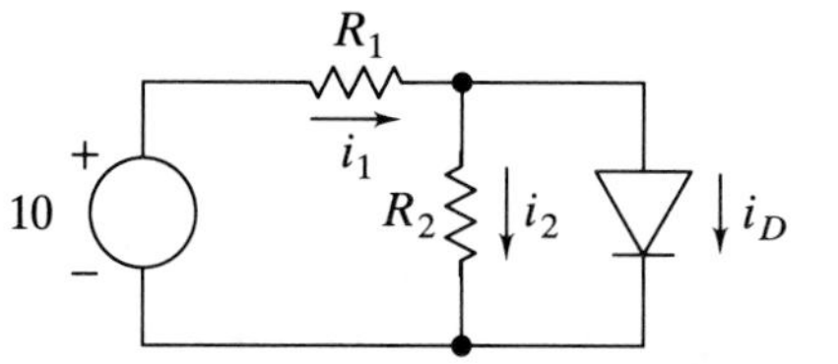

FIGURE E4-6

4-7. For relatively large voltages v_D across a diode, the iv-characteristic of the diode may be approximated by $i_D \cong I_s e^{v_D/V_T}$. Show that the op-amp circuit in Fig. E4-7*a* is a logarithmic amplifier and that the circuit in Fig. E4-7*b* is an exponential amplifier. Be sure to indicate clearly where the op-amp operating assumptions are used.

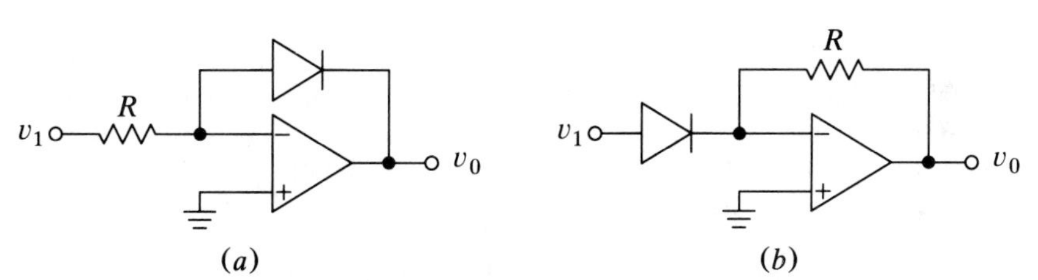

FIGURE E4-7

4-8. Obtain the decimal equivalent of the following numbers:
(*a*) $(5420.21)_6$.
(*b*) $(754.02)_8$.
(*c*) $(1010.001)_2$.

4-9. (*a*) Write $(321)_{10}$ in binary form.
(*b*) Write $(2221)_{10}$ in octal form.

4-10. Express the decimal number 542 in binary form and in terms of BCD code.

4-11. Design an encoder (logic circuit) to convert the given 3-bit code $C_1\,C_2\,C_3$ into the specified binary code xy (Fig. E4-11).

C_1	C_2	C_3	x	y
0	0	0	0	0
0	0	1	1	0
0	1	1	1	1
1	1	1	0	1

FIGURE E4-11

4-12. Prove the De Morgan identities

(*a*) $$\overline{X+Y} = \overline{X} \cdot \overline{Y}$$

b) $$\overline{X \cdot Y} = \overline{X} + \overline{Y}$$

by constructing appropriate truth tables. That is, evaluate both sides of each expression for all possible combinations of X and Y.

4-13. Perform the following calculations for a 4-bit DAC. Assume a nominal full-scale voltage of − 5.0 V:

(*a*) Calculate $v_{0\ \mathrm{MSB}}$, $v_{0\ \mathrm{LSB}}$, and $v_{0\ \max}$.

(*b*) Calculate the output voltage for the binary combination (1 0 0 1).

4-14. Perform the following calculations for an 8-bit DAC. Assume a nominal full-scale voltage of − 10.0 V:

(*a*) Calculate $v_{0\ \mathrm{MSB}}$, $v_{0\ \mathrm{LSB}}$, and $v_{0\ \max}$.

(*b*) Calculate the output voltage for the binary combination (1 0 0 1 1 0 0 1).

(*c*) Calculate $v_{0\ \mathrm{MSB}}$, $v_{0\ \mathrm{LSB}}$, and $v_{0\ \max}$ as the number of bits in the DAC tends to ∞.

4-15. In the discussion of the flash ADC, we mentioned the need of scaling circuits to place the analog input within the range of the ADC. For the following, assume $v_R = 10$ V and that v_{i_0} is within the given ranges. Design appropriate op-amp scaling circuits with the prescribed input range and with output $0 \leq v_i \leq 10$ V. For definiteness, assume that ± 10 V is available when needed. Use all op amps in their inverting configuration and specify all required resistance ratios.

(*a*) Suppose the unscaled analog input is in the range $0 \leq v_{i_0} \leq 15$ V.

(*b*) Suppose the unscaled analog input is in the range $-5 \leq v_{i_0} \leq 7$ V.

4-16. Suppose that the output of the scaling circuit preceding the flash ADC of Sec. 4-7 is $v_0 = 0.43 v_R$. Determine the corresponding 3-bit code.

4-17. Recall the 3-bit ADC presented in Sec. 4-7. Carry out a similar analysis for a 2-bit analog-to-digital converter. That is, produce all of the figures and tables that were carried out for the 3-bit ADC.

4-18. In Sec. 4-7 it was suggested that the quantization error could be reduced to $\pm \frac{1}{2} r$. An indication of the appropriate division of levels about the diagonal is shown in Fig. E4-18. Consider again the specific numerical example used in the text, with an analog voltage range of $v_A = 7$ V.

(*a*) Complete the voltage level assignment sketch and provide the corresponding interval-code table.

(*b*) Plot the corresponding quantization error and determine the quantization error for an analog input of $v_i = 5.4$ V.

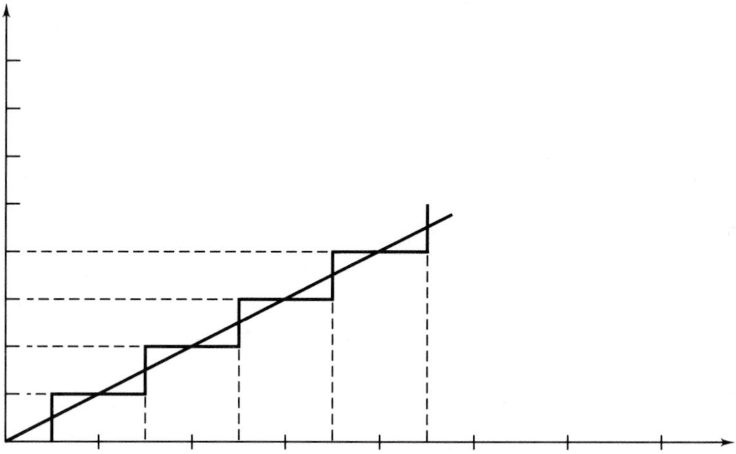

FIGURE E4-18

4-19. The encoder in Fig. E4-19 is a BCD to excess three-code converter. Determine the output Boolean variables x, y, z, and w as functions of the input variables A, B, C, and D.

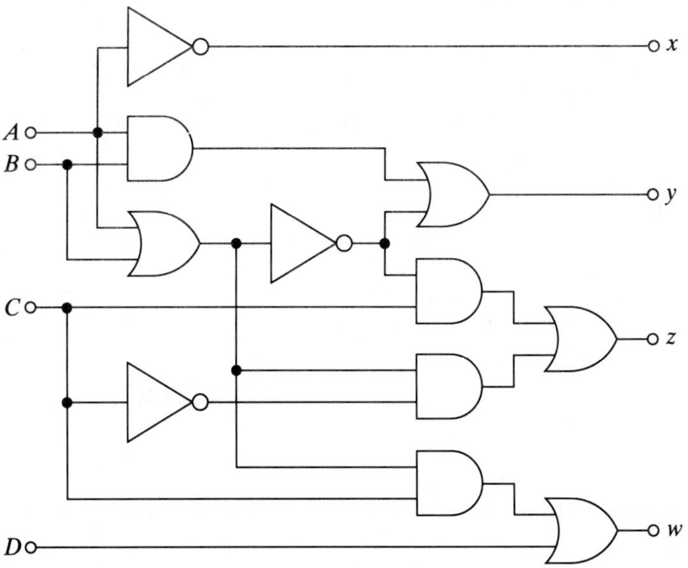

FIGURE E4-19

4-20. Consider the logic diagram in Fig. E4-20a. Determine the outputs F_1 and F_2 in terms of A, B, and C and $\bar{A}$, $\bar{B}$, and $\bar{C}$. Complete the truth table given in Fig. E4-20b. Name the device represented by this diagram.

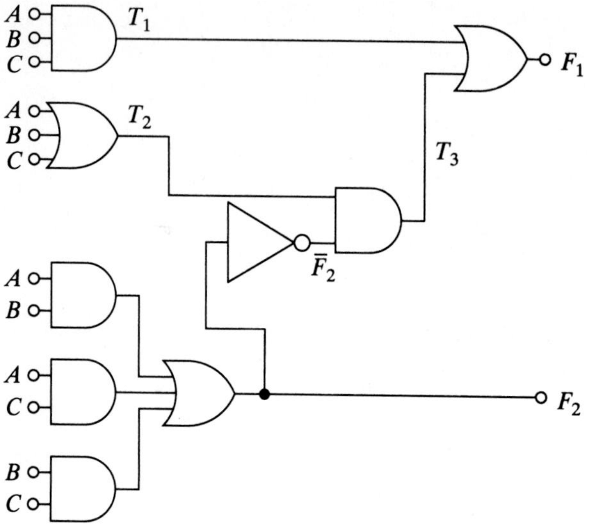

(*a*)

A	B	C	F_2	$\bar{F}_2$	T_1	T_2	T_3	F_1
0	0	0						
0	0	1						
0	1	0						
0	1	1						
1	0	0						
1	0	1						
1	1	0						
1	1	1						

(*b*)

FIGURE E4-20

4-21. Suppose that the nominal full-scale reading of a DAC has been normalized to -10 so that

$$v_0 = 10\left(\frac{b_1}{2} + \frac{b_2}{2^2} + \cdots + \frac{b_N}{2^N}\right)$$

Show that the maximum output that can be obtained is given by $v_{\max} = 10 - r$, where r is the resolution of the DAC.

REFERENCES

1. Franco, S.: *Design with Operational Amplifiers and Analog Integrated Circuits*, McGraw-Hill, New York, 1988.
2. Kittel, C.: *Introduction to Solid State Physics*, 5th ed., Wiley, New York, 1976.
3. Hodges, D. A., and H. G. Jackson: *Analysis and Design of Digital Integrated Circuits*, McGraw-Hill, New York, 1988.
4. Tsividis, Y. P.: *Operation and Modeling of the MOS Transistor*, McGraw-Hill, New York, 1987.
5. Carlson, A. B., and D. G. Gisser: *Electrical Engineering (Concepts and Applications)*, Addison-Wesley, Reading, Mass., 1981.
6. Belanger, P. R., E. L. Adler, and N. C. Rumin: *Introduction to Circuits with Electronics*, CBS College Publishing, New York, 1985.
7. Mano, M. M.: *Computer Engineering (Hardware Design)*, Prentice-Hall, Englewood Cliffs, N.J., 1988.

CHAPTER

FIVE

SENSORS AND INSTRUMENTATION

5-1 INTRODUCTION

One way to measure a robot's sophistication is in terms of its independent interaction with its environment—more specifically, in terms of its capability to sense the environment and its programmed skill to interpret it. Nowhere is the gap between these two aspects more evident than in computer vision, where it is relatively simple to obtain the image but extremely difficult to interpret it and act upon the information in a timely fashion. In all sensing tasks time is of the essence, since the reaction of the robot should be quick and accurate.

Virtually all measuring devices contain one or all of the elements indicated in Fig. 5-1, where the output of the measured medium, $f(t)$, serves as the input into the measuring device, and the quantity $y(t)$ is what the observer eventually is obliged to accept. Generally, the primary sensing device may be a transducer of some sort (e.g., pressure to voltage), whose output is a more suitable variable than that describing the actual medium. This variable may then be amplified or manipulated in some fashion to ready it for transmission, since the readout element, which provides the final data presentation, is virtually always removed from the measurement location.

Measuring devices are classified as static if the data variables vary slowly with time or not at all, and as dynamic if the measured variables vary rapidly. In addition, we distinguish between digital and analog instrumentation. A standard adjunct to measurement is the communication of the data to a computer requiring an A/D converter and, subsequently, a D/A converter to pass instructions from the computer to an analog driving device.

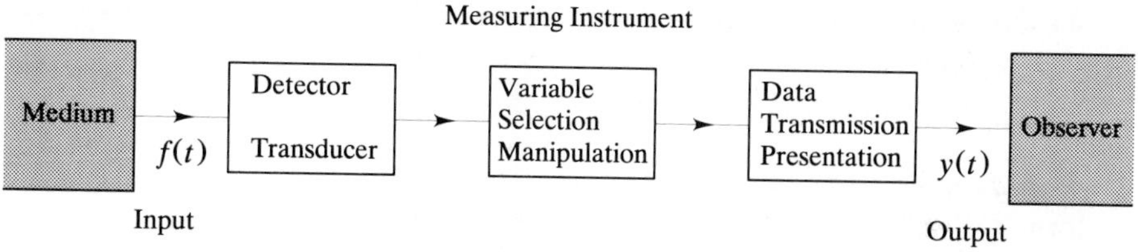

FIGURE 5-1
Schematic of a measuring device.

The manner in which the output $y(t)$ is presented to the observer also provides limitations to accuracy. While a device with a digital output may provide a voltage reading to virtually any desired degree of accuracy, an analog readout device such as a dial or gauge may be inherently limited to three or four significant figures. It is for this reason that devices with a direct digital readout, such as the optical encoder, are particularly desirable, since they avoid one conversion process and provide an output whose refinement depends only on the design of the device itself.

It is clear that we never measure or sense what we set out to measure; we always sense the system together with the device we have introduced to measure it. Hence care should be taken to introduce measuring devices in such a way as to least disturb the original system. The fine tuning of a system consists of adjusting the combination of system and measuring devices. In the derivation of mathematical models for the combined system, the separate mathematical models of the devices are needed. For linear devices, this is usually a linear differential equation and corresponding system function. It is common to classify only zero-, first-, and second-order devices, depending on whether the system is governed by a linear algebraic equation or a first- or second-order differential equation.

1. *Zeroth-order instrument.* In the time domain the equation has the form

$$y(t) = Kf(t)$$

The constant K is called the static sensitivity of the instrument. The corresponding equation in the frequency domain is, of course,

$$Y(s) = KF(s) \qquad \text{with} \quad G_0(s) = K$$

for the system function.

2. *First-order instrument.* The time domain equation has the form

$$\tau \frac{dy}{dt} + y = Kf(t)$$

Here, τ is called the time constant, and K is again termed the static sensitivity. The corresponding system function is

$$(\tau s + 1)Y(s) = KF(s) \quad \Rightarrow \quad G_1(s) = \frac{K}{\tau s + 1}$$

3. *Second-order instrument.* The standard equation in the time domain has the form

$$\frac{d^2y}{dt^2} + 2\zeta\omega_n\frac{dy}{dt} + \omega_n^2 y = Kf(t)$$

Here, ω is called the natural circular frequency of the device in radians per second, ζ is the nondimensional damping ratio, and K is once more the static sensitivity of the instrument. The corresponding system function has the form

$$G_2(s) = \frac{K}{s^2 + 2\zeta\omega_n s + \omega_n^2}$$

Much of the additional discussion of this classification and design of measuring devices deals with the amount of distortion of idealized inputs $f(t)$, such as ramp and step functions, and the corresponding adjustments of the device constants. An excellent discussion of this traditional treatment may be found in Doebelin.[1]

With the advent of robotics, there has been a virtual explosion of sensor design, ranging from tactile to proximity sensors, and from the sensing of sound to vision. Entire conferences and books are devoted to the subject. Clearly, only a selection can be presented here, hopefully a balance between the traditional and the modern.

Our first treatment will include some of the standard measuring devices such as potentiometers and tachometers, as well as the more exotic Hall sensors and charge-coupled vision systems. The description of vision systems is particularly detailed, since they are the most sophisticated sensors in use. We begin with some of the more traditional sensors, whose versatility and robustness are likely to assure their continued use.

5-2 THE STRAIN GAUGE

Strain gauges are still the mainstay for use in transducers where a connection between a small displacement and a voltage is the objective. Strain gauges are not a recent development. The possibility of a strain gauge was first noted by Lord Kelvin in 1856. In describing experimental results to the Royal Philosophical Society, he demonstrated that the resistance of copper or iron wire changes when subject to strain.

In what follows, it will be our aim to measure strain in terms of a voltage readout. We begin with a derivation of the change in resistance due to changes in the physical configuration of a wire segment. The segment (strain gauge) is

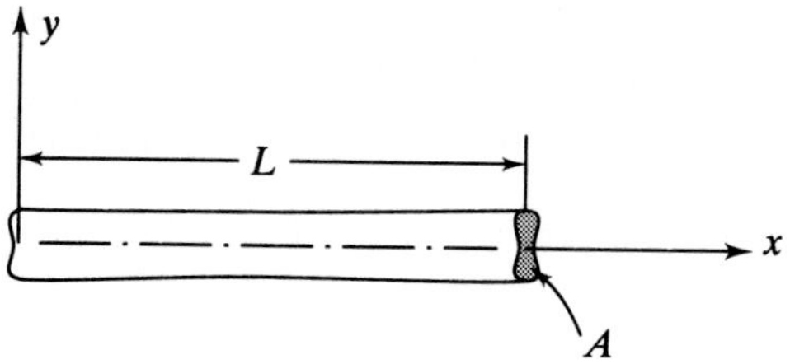

FIGURE 5-2
A wire segment.

then used as part of a bridge circuit in order to measure this small change of resistance in terms of a voltage.

We take the uniform wire segment in Fig. 5-2 as the framework for the first part of our discussion. We suppose that the segment has an unstretched length L and a uniform cross-sectional area A. If ρ is the resistivity of the material, the total resistance of the segment in ohms is given by

$$R = \rho \frac{L}{A} \tag{5-1}$$

For the remainder, we take $A = kD^2$, where k is a proportionality constant depending on the section shape and D is some characteristic dimension. For a circular cross section, for example, D may be the diameter and $k = \pi/4$.

If the segment is now strained and we assume that all quantities change, then the total change in resistance may be expressed as the differential

$$dR = \frac{1}{kD^2}\left[\rho\, dL + L\, d\rho - 2\rho L \frac{dD}{D}\right] \tag{5-2}$$

which we write in the form

$$\frac{dR/R}{dL/L} = \left[1 + \frac{d\rho/\rho}{dL/L} - 2\frac{dD/D}{dL/L}\right] \tag{5-3}$$

The average longitudinal and lateral strains are defined by

$$\frac{dL}{L} = \epsilon_x \qquad \text{average axial strain}$$

$$\frac{dD}{D} = \epsilon_y \qquad \text{average lateral strain}$$

Poisson's ratio is given by

$$\mu = -\frac{\epsilon_y}{\epsilon_x}$$

With these definitions the bracketed quantity in (5-3) may be written in the form

$$G = 1 + \frac{d\rho/\rho}{\epsilon_x} + 2\mu \tag{5-4}$$

which is now termed the gauge factor. Consequently,

$$\epsilon_x = \frac{1}{G}\frac{dR}{R} \tag{5-5}$$

In practice, finite rather than infinitesimal changes are considered, and we then consider an average strain

$$\epsilon = \frac{1}{G}\frac{\Delta R}{R} \tag{5-6}$$

We have thus expressed the average strain in the wire segment in terms of the change in resistance of the segment. If we assume that the resistivity of the material does not change during the deformation and if we take Poisson's ratio equal to $\frac{1}{2}$, then we obtain a commonly used value $G = 2$ for the gauge factor. If the total resistance of the undeformed wire is $R = 100\ \Omega$ and we have a strain of $\epsilon = 10^{-6}$ cm/cm, then

$$\Delta R = GR\epsilon = (2)(100)(10^{-6}) = 0.0002\ \Omega$$

Such small changes in resistance are difficult to measure directly, and one thus resorts to an indirect approach, using a bridge circuit.

We continue our discussion by incorporating the strain gauge as one of the resistances in a bridge circuit and relating the output voltage of the circuit to the change in resistance experienced by the wire segment constituting the strain gauge. It is common to combine the bridge circuit with a differential amplifier; the resultant circuit is depicted in Fig. 5-3. For definiteness in the following, suppose that R is the resistance of the strain gauge in its unstressed stage, as before, and that R_1 is a variable resistance that has been adjusted to the value R_1 in order to yield $v_0 = 0$ for the unstressed gauge. At this value of R_1 the bridge is termed *balanced*. Throughout, the reference voltage v_R is taken as positive.

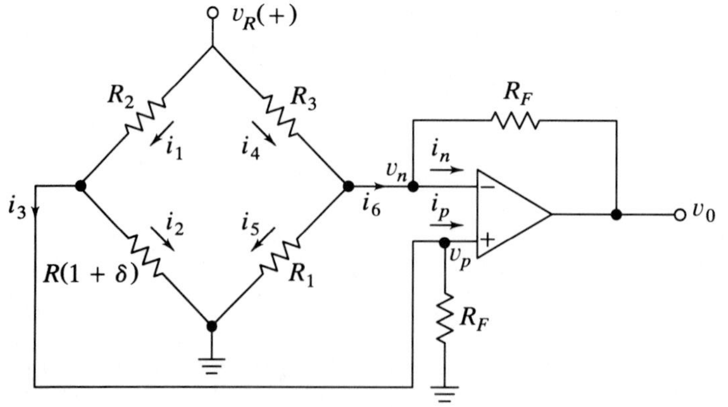

FIGURE 5-3
Strain gauge bridge circuit with differential amplifier.

This balance is then disturbed by the deformation of the strain gauge changing the resistance by an amount ΔR with corresponding change in output voltage given by v_0. To determine this voltage as a function of ΔR, we shall first solve for v_n and v_p and eventually set $v_p - v_n \approx 0$, for proper nonsaturated operation of the op amp and hence to solve for v_0 in terms of $\delta = \Delta R/R$.

The use of KCL at the two bridge junctions in Fig. 5-3 yields

$$i_1 = i_2 + i_3 \qquad \text{and} \qquad i_4 = i_5 + i_6 \tag{5-7}$$

The use of Ohm's law across each device, together with $i_n \approx 0$ and $i_p \approx 0$, eventually yields the equations

$$\begin{aligned} \frac{v_R - v_p}{R_2} &= \frac{v_p - 0}{R(1+\delta)} + \frac{v_p - 0}{R_F} \\ \frac{v_R - v_n}{R_3} &= \frac{v_n - 0}{R_1} + \frac{v_n - v_0}{R_F} \end{aligned} \tag{5-8}$$

These result in

$$\begin{aligned} v_p &= \frac{v_R}{R_2} \frac{R(1+\delta)R_2R_F}{R_2R_F + R(1+\delta)(R_F + R_2)} \\ v_n &= \left(\frac{v_R}{R_3} + \frac{v_0}{R_F}\right) \frac{R_1R_FR_3}{R_FR_3 + R_1R_3 + R_1R_F} \end{aligned} \tag{5-9}$$

Equating these two expressions yields v_0 in the form

$$v_0 = \frac{v_RR_F}{R_1R_3}\left[\frac{R(1+\delta)(R_FR_3 + R_1R_3 - R_1R_2) - R_1R_2R_F}{R_2R_F + R(1+\delta)(R_F + R_2)}\right] \tag{5-10}$$

The expression simplifies considerably when two or more of the resistances are chosen as equal. Thus a choice of $R_1 = R$ and $R_2 = R_3 = R_0$ yields

$$v_0 = \frac{v_RR_F}{R}\left[\frac{\delta}{\dfrac{R_0}{R} + (1+\delta)\left(1 + \dfrac{R_0}{R_F}\right)}\right] \tag{5-11}$$

For $R_F \gg R_0$ and $\delta \ll 1$, the expression takes on the form

$$v_0 \approx \frac{v_RR_F}{R}\left[\frac{\delta}{\dfrac{R_0}{R} + 1}\right] \tag{5-12}$$

a linear relationship between v_0 and δ. A still more simplified expression is achieved when all of the bridge resistances are equal to R. The result then is

$$v_0 = \frac{v_R R_F}{R}\left[\frac{\delta}{1 + (1+\delta)\left(1 + \dfrac{R}{R_F}\right)}\right] \tag{5-13}$$

With $R_F \gg R$ and $\delta \ll 1$, the result becomes

$$v_0 \approx \frac{v_R R_F}{R}\left(\frac{\delta}{2}\right) \tag{5-14}$$

a particularly simple linear relationship between v_0 and δ. Finally, the use of $\epsilon = (1/G)\delta$ yields

$$v_0 = \left(\frac{v_R R_F}{2R} G\right)\epsilon$$

a direct measure of the strain in terms of voltage.

This result can, of course, be used to measure a variety of quantities. Indirectly, we may measure any quantity that can be related to strain, such as force, pressure, and displacement.

Example 5-1. Suppose a homogeneous metal bar of length L_0, elastic modulus $E = 200$ GPa, and uniform cross-sectional area $A_0 = 2\ \text{cm}^2$ is being stretched by an axial load P_0. Use a strain gauge with a resistance $R = 500\ \Omega$, with all bridge resistances equal to R, with $R_F = 800\ \text{k}\Omega$, with a gauge factor $G = 2$, and with a reference voltage $v_R = 10$ V to provide a measure of the force P applied to the end of the bar (see Fig. 5-4).

Solution. In view of the uniform cross section and the homogeneity of the material, we may assume that the strain is constant throughout the elastic rod. We thus have

$$\epsilon = \frac{2R}{v_R R_F G} v_0 = \frac{1}{E}\sigma = \frac{1}{E}\frac{P_0}{A_0}$$

or

$$P_0 = \frac{2REA_0}{v_R R_F G} v_0 = 2500 v_0$$

Note carefully that the units of area had to be put in terms of square meters to conform with those of E and that the constant thus has units newtons/volt. For example, a reading of 2 V would indicate a force of 5000 N.

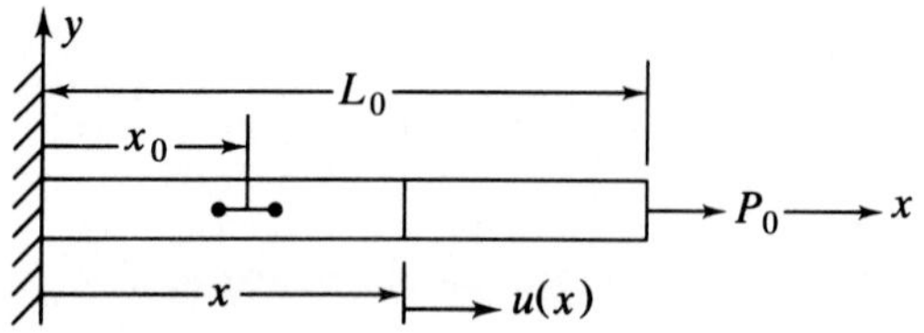

FIGURE 5-4
Measurement of axial load.

Strain gauges are here to stay; they are a classical measuring device. (They are covered in a great deal more detail in texts such as Doebelin.[1]) The strain gauge is clearly a zeroth-order instrument so that its system function is

$$v_0(t) = k\epsilon(t) \quad \Rightarrow \quad G(s) = k$$

when the strain is taken as the input and the voltage as the output.

5-3 USED SENSORS

In the previous section we developed a linear relationship between strain and voltage. Of particular interest in that development was the fact that the linearity depended on mechanical as well as electrical "smallness" assumptions. Virtually all electromechanical transducers involve such interactive assumptions within their linear operating ranges.

We now provide a brief discussion of some additional "well-used" sensors in their linear ranges. We begin the discussion with the potentiometer when used as a linear or angular position sensor. We briefly introduce the tachometer as an angular velocity sensing device, and we close this section with the discussion of the linear variable differential transformer.

5-3-1 Resistive Potentiometers

Sliding contact resistive transducers are used to express linear or angular displacements in terms of voltage. The best resolution is obtained when the potentiometer consists simply of a wire and a sliding contact connected to the object whose displacement is to be measured. Because of strength and wear considerations, there are limitations to the stroke length for single resistance devices. To overcome these, one also uses resistive elements constructed by wrapping wire around a "card." The turns around the card are insulated from one another to prevent shorting, and the contact (brush) moves across the turns from one turn to the next. The main detriments of this approach are that the resistance is no longer a continuous function of the brush movement since the slider moves from one turn to the next and that the transducer is no longer linear. The smallest increment into which the whole length of such a wound conductor may be divided is called the *potentiometer resolution*. For a resistance winding, this resolution is equal to the reciprocal of the number of turns. For example, if 1500 turns are used and we assume that the winding is linear, then the resolution would be $1/1500$, or .067%. In line with our emphasis on concepts rather than technological finesse, we now discuss the single resistance element.

Consider the displacement potentiometers with some output device shown in Fig. 5-5. The reference voltage is v_R, R is the total resistance of the element whose total stroke length is L, and R_0 is an output resistance as in a voltmeter. The objective is to obtain an expression (preferably linear) for the displacement x in terms of the output voltage v_0. In a straightforward manner one then

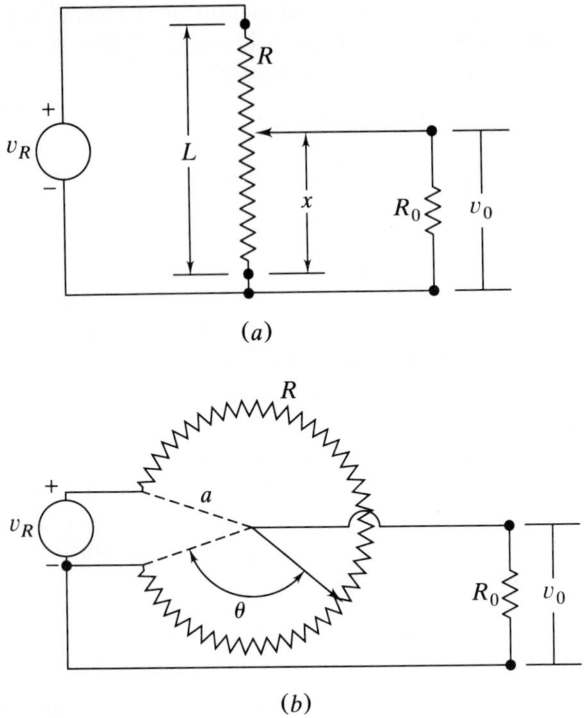

FIGURE 5-5
Linear and rotary potentiometers.

obtains

$$v_0 = \frac{v_R x}{L}\left[1 + \frac{R}{R_0}\left(\frac{x}{L}\right)\left(1 - \frac{x}{L}\right)\right]^{-1}$$

$$= \frac{v_R x}{L}\left[1 - \frac{R}{R_0}\left(\frac{x}{L}\right)\left(1 - \frac{x}{L}\right) + \cdots\right]$$

Thus, for $R_0 \gg R_1$, the expression may be taken to be linear in x.

The analysis of the rotary potentiometer proceeds in the same fashion, with x replaced by $a\theta$, a being the radius of the circular resistance element.

5-3-2 Tachometers

Tachometers are essentially generators with an output voltage proportional to the angular velocity of the rotor. Most tachometers used in control systems are of the DC variety and they serve as velocity indicators and provide a shaft speed readout, or they are used to provide velocity feedback for speed control or stabilization. For example, in position control systems, velocity feedback is often used to improve the stability or the overall damping of the system. However, the most traditional use of a DC tachometer is as a visual speed readout of a rotating shaft.

The basic characteristic of all tachometers is that the output voltage is proportional to the rotor speed. The governing equation in the time domain is

$$v_0(t) = K\omega(t) = K\frac{d\theta}{dt}(t)$$

where $v_0(t)$ is the output voltage, K is the tachometer constant in volts/radian/second, and where either the rotor velocity $\omega(t)$ in radians/second or the rotor angular displacement $\theta(t)$ in radians serves as the input. In catalog representations K is usually given in volts per 1000 rpm (V/krpm). A typical value for K is 6 V/krpm.

With $\theta(t)$ as the input, the system function for the tachometer is

$$G(s) = Ks$$

obtained in the usual fashion.

5-3-3 The Linear Variable Differential Transformer

A section on sensors probably would not be complete without mentioning yet another classical displacement sensor: the linear variable differential transformer, or LVDT. It is one of the most used displacement transducers, particularly when high accuracy is needed.

The basic concept is that of a ferrous core moving in a magnetic field, the field being produced in a manner similar to that of a standard transformer. Thus we have a central core surrounded by two identical secondary coils and one primary coil, as shown in Fig. 5-6. As a consequence of the core displacement, the mutual inductance between the primary coil and the secondary coils becomes a linear function of the displacement over a considerable segment of the transducer. As is the case with all such magnetic phenomena, the linearity breaks down near the boundaries of the transducer. We briefly review the underlying physics of the transducer.

Recall that when two coils of wire (inductors) are placed next to each other and one of them has a current flowing in it, then there exists a mutual inductance between the coils in accordance with the formula

$$M_{21} = \frac{N_2\Phi_{21}}{i_1}$$

where M_{21} is the mutual inductance in coil 2 due to a current i_1 in coil 1, N_2 is the number of turns in coil 2, and Φ_{21} is the magnetic flux in coil 2 due to the current in coil 1. As usual, the flux is defined by

$$\Phi_{21} = \oint \boldsymbol{B}_1 \cdot d\boldsymbol{A}_2$$

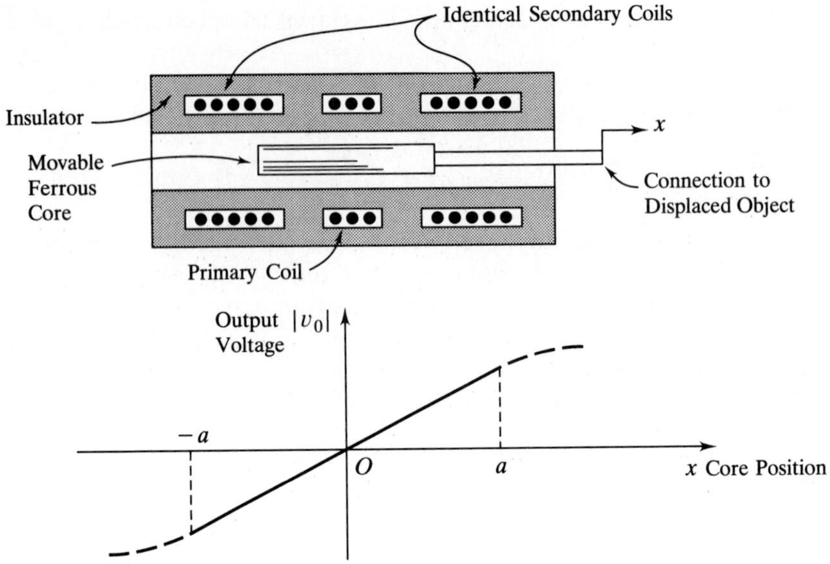

FIGURE 5-6
Basic LVDT structure.

where $\boldsymbol{B}_1$ is the magnetic field as it extends from coil 1 to coil 2, as shown in Fig. 5-7, and the integral is extended over the surface area (or section of coil 2) penetrated by the flux lines of $\boldsymbol{B}_1$. If the field $\boldsymbol{B}_1$ is time dependent so that Φ_{21} is a function of time, then this changing flux produces a reverse electromotive force (emf) in a turn given by Faraday's law

$$\epsilon = -\frac{d\Phi_{21}}{dt}$$

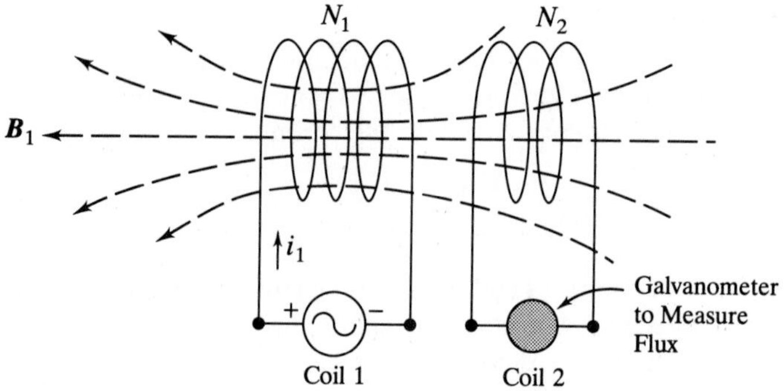

FIGURE 5-7
Mutual induction.

Since the coil has N_2 turns, the total induced emf will be

$$\epsilon_2 = -N_2 \frac{d\Phi_{21}}{dt} = -M_{21} \frac{di_1}{dt}$$

That is, a change in the current in coil 1 produces the emf in coil 2. The argument may be repeated, with the roles of coil 1 and coil 2 interchanged; furthermore, it may then be shown that $M_{12} = M_{21} = M$.

With this brief review of the concepts, we now take a look at the specific mutual inductance circuit that governs the LVDT. The defining equations for the basic mutual inductance circuit (Fig. 5-8a) are:

$$v_1 = L_1 \frac{di_1}{dt} + M \frac{di_2}{dt}$$

$$v_2 = M \frac{di_1}{dt} + L_2 \frac{di_2}{dt}$$

where L_1 and L_2 denote the self-inductances of the coils and M is the mutual inductance between them. (Recall that a black dot at the end of a coil is used to denote the polarity of v_2 with respect to v_1; i.e., if the dots are at the same end, v_1 and v_2 have the same polarity.)

For a fixed core position, the circuit equations for the circuit in Fig. 5-8b, modeling the LVDT, are given by

$$v_p = L_p \frac{di_p}{dt} + R_p i_p + (M_2 - M_1) \frac{di_s}{dt}$$

$$v_0 = -L_s \frac{di_s}{dt} - R_s i_s + (M_2 - M_1) \frac{di_p}{dt}$$

The subscripts p and s refer to primary and secondary, respectively. The two secondary coils are identical and they are connected in series opposition; this assures the existence of a null position for the core at which the output voltage $v_0(t) = 0$. The primary coil is driven by a precise sinusoidal input voltage v_p at frequencies ranging from 100 Hz to 10 kHz with strong amplitude stability. The constants M_1 and M_2 denote the mutual inductance between the primary coil and the two secondary coils, L_p and L_s are the self-inductances, and R_p and R_s are the winding resistances.

To obtain the system function relating $v_p(t)$ as input and $v_0(t)$ as output, we take the Laplace transform of both equations with all initial conditions set equal to 0, resulting in

$$V_p = (L_p s + R_p) I_p + Ms I_s$$

$$V_0 = -(L_s s + R_s) I_s + Ms I_p$$

where we have taken $M = M_2 - M_1$. If the output port is taken as an open

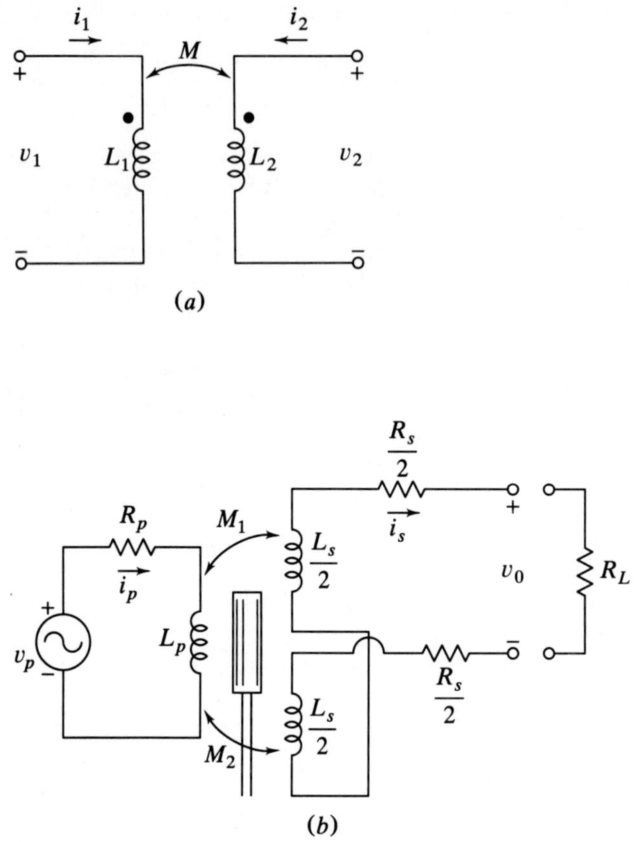

FIGURE 5-8
(*a*) Basic mutual inductance circuit; (*b*) LVDT mutual inductance circuit. (The $\pm$ with v_p indicates the polarity used for the derivation.)

circuit, then $i_s(t) = 0$, and the corresponding system function is given by

$$G_0(s) = \frac{V_0(s)}{V_p(s)} = \frac{Ms}{L_p s + R_p} \tag{5-15}$$

If an output load—say, some measuring device—is included as a resistance R_L, then a current will flow in the secondary with $v_0(t) = R_L i_s(t)$. The corresponding system function of the loaded circuit is given by

$$G_L(s) = \frac{MsR_L}{(M^2 + L_p L_s)s^2 + (L_p R_L + L_p R_s + R_p L_s)s + R_p(R_L + R_s)} \tag{5-16}$$

The preceding discussion was based on a fixed core position. For a fixed input voltage $v_p(t)$, it is clear that only M can change with the core position. Indeed, it is M that is a linear function of the core displacement x as long as $|x| \leq a$. Since x itself may generally be a function of time, such a quasi-static analysis can be applied only if the current changes are considerably faster than changes in the core motion. Usually, this requires a carrier frequency ω at least 10 times larger than the highest expected modulation frequency of the core motion.

With this in mind, suppose we now consider an open output circuit or an essentially infinite load resistance R_L. Let $v_p(t) = A \sin \omega t$, a fixed primary voltage. At $s = j\omega$, the system function for the LVDT is

$$G_0(j\omega) = \frac{Mj\omega}{L_p j\omega + R_p}$$

Since M is a linear function of x, there is a sign change in $G_0(j\omega)$ when x passes through the null position—a 180° jump in the phase. In addition, the output phase is shifted by the amount

$$\phi(\omega) = 90^\circ - \text{Arctan}\, \frac{L_p\omega}{R_p}$$

Within this same framework, we may view $v_p(t)x(t)$ as a combined input, $v_0(t)$ as output, yielding a system function

$$G(s) = \frac{Ks}{L_p s + R_p}$$

As a consequence, the output of the LVDT in the time domain is a sine wave whose amplitude is proportional to the core motion; that is,

$$v_0(t) = \frac{KA\omega x(t)}{\sqrt{(L_p\omega)^2 + R_p^2}} \sin(\omega t + \phi)$$

The discussion we have given here presents an idealized viewpoint intended to provide an understanding of the process. For guidance in practical applications, the reader is referred to additional discussions in Kennedy[2] and Alloca and Stuart.[3] For a review of the physics aspects, see Halliday and Resnick.[4]

This concludes our discussion of displacement measuring devices. Naturally, one may use differentiators to obtain velocity and acceleration data. However, it is generally more desirable to begin with the measurement of acceleration and then to use integrators to obtain velocity and displacement data. The main reason for this is that integrators tend to suppress noise. Our next section concerns the accelerometer.

5-4 THE PIEZOELECTRIC ACCELEROMETER

We shall structure the discussion pretty much in the same manner used for other, more complex sensors. Here, we begin with the discussion of the behavior of the piezoelectric crystal that forms the basic transducer from deformation to voltage. We follow this with the dynamic equations of the accelerometer and its seismic mass. These, together with the related contact and amplification circuit, will form the accelerometer.

Consider then a piezoelectric crystal in axial compression under a stress σ_{33}, as shown in Fig. 5-9. The pertinent material constant in this case is given by

$$g_{33} \triangleq \frac{\text{electric field produced in direction 3}}{\text{stress applied in direction 3}}$$

$$= \frac{e/t}{\sigma_{33}} \qquad \sigma_{33} = \frac{f_3}{ab}$$

where the first subscript generally refers to the direction of the electrical effect, and the second subscript, to that of the mechanical effect. For the remainder, we shall restrict ourselves to a quartz crystal and values of constants that pertain thereto: for quartz, $g_{33} = 50 \times 10^{-3}$ (V/m)/(N/m^2). For a given crystal, the output voltage is thus related to the deformation by

$$\sigma_{33} = E\epsilon_{33} = E\frac{du_{33}}{dx_3} \quad \Rightarrow \quad \frac{du_{33}}{dx_3} = \frac{\sigma_{33}}{E} \quad \Rightarrow \quad u_{33} = \frac{\sigma_{33}t}{E}$$

$$\Rightarrow \quad e = gEu$$

where we have dropped the subscripts for convenience. The elastic modulus of quartz is $E = 8.6 \times 10^{10}$ N/m^2.

The crystal may also be viewed as a capacitor. In this case the relevant constant is

$$d = \frac{\text{charge generated in the vertical direction}}{\text{force applied in the vertical direction}}$$

$$= \epsilon g$$

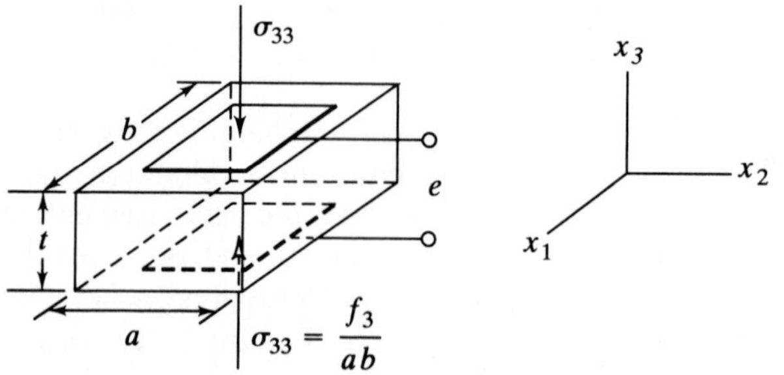

FIGURE 5-9
Crystal in compression.

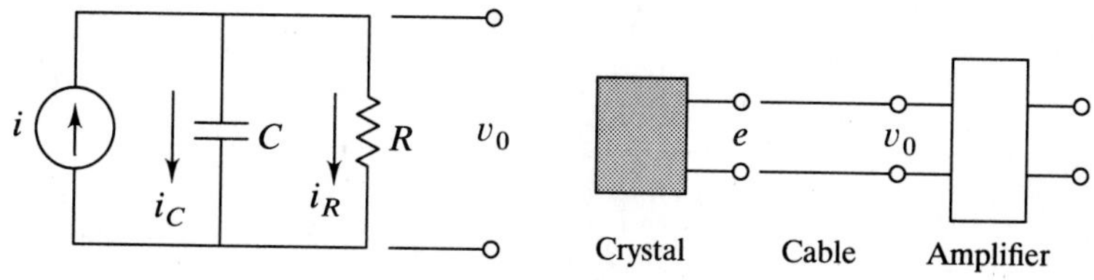

FIGURE 5-10
Output circuit.

where ϵ is the dielectric constant of the material; for quartz, $\epsilon = 4.06 \times 10^{-11}$ F/m. The total capacitance of the crystal is

$$C_{\text{cr}} = \frac{\epsilon ab}{t}$$

The output voltage thus may also be written in the form

$$e = \frac{q}{C_{\text{cr}}} = gEu \quad \Rightarrow \quad q = C_{\text{cr}} gEu$$

or, in terms of the current,

$$i = \frac{dq}{dt} = C_{\text{cr}} gE \frac{du}{dt} = K_q \frac{du}{dt}$$

It must be emphasized that e and i are the voltage and current generated at the crystal. Generally, there is a cable connection to an amplifier, and the input voltage at the amplifier, v_0, can be represented in connection with the circuit shown in Fig. 5-10. Here,

$$C \triangleq C_{\text{cr}} + C_{\text{cable}} + C_{\text{amp}}$$

$$R \triangleq \frac{R_{\text{amp}} R_{\text{leak}}}{R_{\text{amp}} + R_{\text{leak}}} \approx R_{\text{amp}}$$

With the nodal equation

$$i = i_C + i_R = C \frac{dv_0}{dt} + \frac{1}{R} v_0 = K_q \frac{du}{dt}$$

we eventually obtain the system function

$$G_1(s) = \frac{V_0(s)}{U(s)} = \frac{\tau K_1 s}{\tau s + 1}$$

where $\tau = RC$ is the time constant for the instrument in seconds and $K_1 = K_q/C$ is the sensitivity in volts/meter. We now have the ingredients for the construction of the piezoelectric accelerometer.

The standard configuration of the piezoelectric accelerometer, as well as its simplified physical model, is shown in Fig. 5-11. A construction schematic is

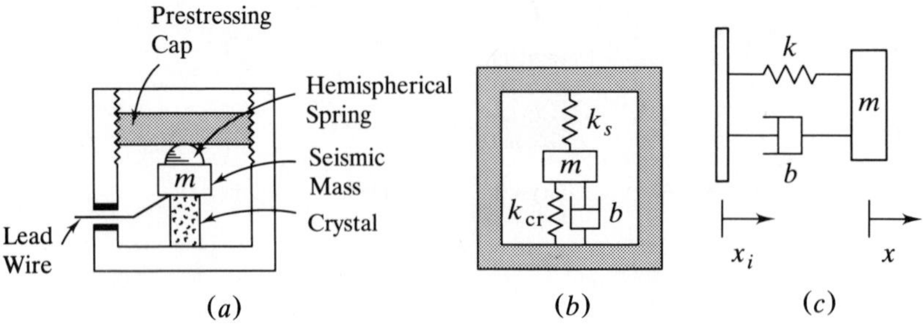

FIGURE 5-11
(*a*) Accelerometer construction; (*b*) simplification in terms of springs and dashpot; (*c*) seismic mass on a massless platform.

depicted in Fig. 5-11*a*. The prestressing cap is adjustable to set the stress range in which the crystal is to operate. The hemispherical cap serves to distribute the load due to tightening of the cap over the crystal surface. For small deformations the spherical cap acts like a linear spring with equivalent spring constant k_s; the equivalent spring constant for the crystal is k_{cr}. The seismic mass ultimately provides the input that allows the measurement of the motion of the casing and hence the body to which it is attached.

Figure 5-11*b* is a simplified physical model of the accelerometer, and Fig. 5-11*c* is the model for the derivation of the equation of motion—a damped oscillator on a moving massless base. For this latter configuration let x_i and x be the absolute displacements of the massless base and the seismic mass, respectively. The equation of motion of the system is then given by

$$-k(x - x_i) - b(\dot{x} - \dot{x}_i) = m\ddot{x}$$

or

$$m\ddot{u} + b\dot{u} + ku = -m\ddot{x}_i$$

where we have taken $u = x - x_i$, the relative displacement of the seismic mass (as well as the deformation of the crystal), and where $k = k_{cr} + k_s$. Division by m yields the standard form

$$\ddot{u} + 2\zeta\omega_n\dot{u} + \omega_n^2 u = -\ddot{x}_i$$

where $\zeta = \dfrac{b}{2\sqrt{mk}}$ and $\omega_n^2 = \dfrac{k_s + k_{cr}}{m}$

With the acceleration $\ddot{x}_i(t)$ as input and the relative displacement as output, the system function is given by

$$G_2(s) = \frac{U(s)}{s^2 X_i(s)} = \frac{-1}{s^2 + 2\zeta\omega_n s + \omega_n^2} \tag{5-17}$$

The block diagram for the combined system, consisting of accelerometer and

amplifier, is given by

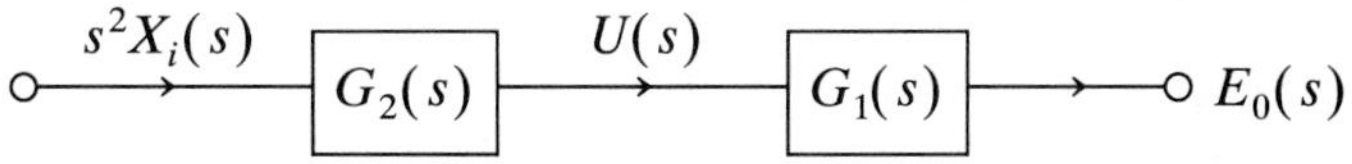

The combined system function thus is

$$G(s) = \frac{E_0(s)}{s^2X_i(s)} = -\frac{\tau K_1 s}{\tau s + 1}\frac{1}{s^2 + 2\zeta\omega_n s + \omega_n^2} \tag{5-18}$$

and the governing differential equation for the combined system is

$$\tau\frac{d^3e_0}{dt^3} + (2\tau\zeta\omega_n + 1)\frac{d^2e_0}{dt^2} + \left(\tau\omega_n^2 + 2\zeta\omega_n\right)\frac{de_0}{dt} + \omega_n^2 e_0 = -K_1\tau\frac{da_i}{dt} \tag{5-19}$$

Remark 5-1. In essence, the amplifier output voltage here is the same as the input voltage $E_0(s)$. In the present context the amplifier is usually a high-impedance cathode follower used mainly for isolation purposes rather than voltage gain.

In connection with piezoelectric accelerometers, there are several advantages to using charge amplifiers rather than the usual voltage amplifiers. The main advantage will be evident upon derivation of the circuit equations. The circuit with the crystal as a current source, as before, and with amplifier output $e_0(t)$ is shown in Fig. 5-12. At the summing junction for the op amp, we have the current balance

$$i = i_n + i_C + i_F$$

In accordance with the usual assumptions for op amps in their operating range, we set $i_n \approx 0$ and $v_p - v_n \approx 0$, which implies $i_C \approx 0$. We thus have

$$\begin{aligned} i = i_F &= i_{R_F} + i_{C_F} \\ &= \frac{v_n - e_0}{R_F} + C_F\frac{d}{dt}(v_n - e_0) \\ &= -\frac{1}{R_F}e_0 - C_F\frac{de_0}{dt} = K_q\frac{du}{dt} \end{aligned}$$

With u as input and e_0 as output, the system function is

$$G_3(s) = \frac{E_0(s)}{U(s)} = -\frac{K_2\tau s}{\tau s + 1} \tag{5-20}$$

where $K_2 = K_q/C_F$ is the sensitivity in volts/meter and $\tau = R_F C_F$ is the time constant in seconds.

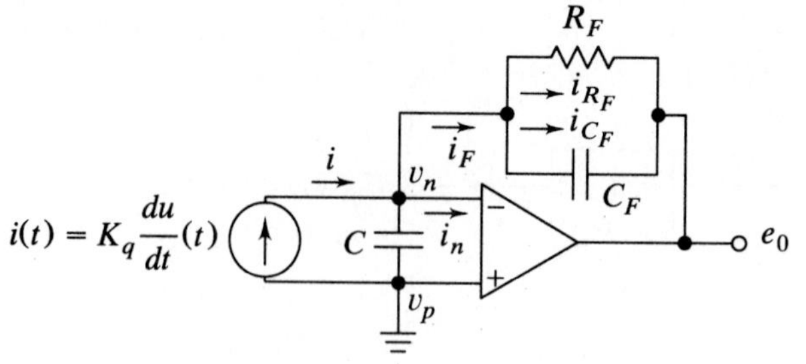

FIGURE 5-12
Charge amplifier circuit.
$i(t) = K_q \frac{du}{dt}(t)$

Remark 5-2. Note that the inclusion of R_F prevents the small leakage current coming from the capacitor from saturating the operational amplifier.

The combined system equation is the same as (5-18), with K_2 replacing K_1, with the new definition of time constant and sensitivity, and the minus signs cancel. The advantage of using a charge amplifier should now be apparent—namely, the crystal capacitance and the cable capacitance are no longer involved in the system function. Thus often used long connecting cables do not affect either the sensitivity or the time constant of the system. Note carefully that $e_0(t)$ here is what we actually see displayed as the measured acceleration.

Accelerometers, in conjunction with electronic integrators, of course, may also be used to measure velocity and displacement. Much of the preceding discussion is based on the material of Doebelin.[1] The reader who wishes to delve further into the details of accelerometers is referred to pages 291–305 of that reference.

5-5 HALL EFFECT SENSORS

In robotics, the Hall effect makes a frequent appearance as an indicator of ferromagnetic proximity. Its inclusion in a discussion of traditional sensors is intellectual necessity. For a mechanicist, the discussion of a fundamental effect in physics is a return to roots; and for the sometime historian, a digression into the history of the effect and its discoverers is unavoidable. The historical comments are based on an article by O. Hannaway,[5] a science historian at Johns Hopkins University.

So that we may all know what we are about, we begin the discussion with a description of Hall's own experiment (see Hannaway[5]):

> Edwin Hall's experiment, performed almost exactly one hundred years ago, had an elegant simplicity to it. A current from a carbon-zinc battery was passed through a strip of gold foil (2 cm × 9 cm) fixed firmly on a glass plate by means of brass clamps. The plate bearing the gold leaf was placed between the poles of an electromagnet in such a way that the lines of magnetic force passed perpendicularly through the horizontal plane of the foil. Opposite edges at the midpoint of the

> gold foil strip were tapped to a high-resistance galvanometer in order to detect any influence of the strong magnetic field on the current flowing through the gold foil. The results indicated the existence of an electromotive force at right angles to the direction of the primary current and perpendicular to the magnetic field. It was this transverse potential, produced by the action of an external magnetic field on a permanent current, which became known as "the Hall effect!"

Hall, then a second-year graduate student in physics at Johns Hopkins University, quickly established priority in a paper entitled, "On a New Action of the Magnet on Electric Currents," published before the end of 1879 in the *American Journal of Mathematics*.[6] The experiment eventually became Hall's Ph.D. thesis and was published in a second paper, in 1880, in the *American Journal of Science*.[7]

Hall completed his undergraduate studies at Bowdoin College, graduating at the top of his class in 1875. Upon graduation, he became a schoolteacher; two years later he entered graduate study in physics, studying with Henry Augustus Rowland at Johns Hopkins. He eventually became a professor at Harvard.

Rowland, Hall's mentor, was a similarly interesting individual. He graduated as a civil engineer from Rensselear Technological Institute in 1870. In his sophomore year, however, he had already decided that he would devote himself to "pure science." He built up an extensive private physics library, conducting experiments based on Faraday's text, *Experimental Researches in Electricity*, and in five years transformed himself into a theoretical physicist of international standing. Based on this emerging reputation, he was recruited to Johns Hopkins by its president, Daniel Coit Gilman. Rowland is best known for his famous experiment, conducted at Helmholtz's laboratory in Berlin, which demonstrated that a moving electrostatic charge produced a magnetic effect similar to that of a current moving in a conductor.

With this lofty digression, we now return to the more mundane world of our discussion of sensors. In particular, we now give a presentation of the Hall effect within the context of modern physics. Recall that a vector field may be viewed simply as a vector-valued function of a scalar variable, a vector variable, or both. For example, a magnetic field in $\mathbb{R}^3$ might be written as $\boldsymbol{B}(x, y, z; t)$, indicating that the field strength at point P in some region depends on both the location (x, y, z) and the time t. In component form one might thus write

$$\boldsymbol{B}(\boldsymbol{x}; t) = B_x(\boldsymbol{x}; t)\hat{\imath} + B_y(\boldsymbol{x}; t)\hat{\jmath} + B_z(\boldsymbol{x}; t)\hat{\boldsymbol{k}}$$

with $\boldsymbol{x} = (x, y, z)$ for short. In the following, we shall use the mks (meter-kilogram-second) system of units. Since few students in engineering seem to be well acquainted with electrodynamic quantities and their units, we precede the discussion with a relevant list:

- q charge (coulombs)
- B magnetic flux density (webers/square meter, or teslas)
- E electric field strength (newtons/coulomb)

F force (newtons)
I current (coulombs/second, or amperes)
J current density (amperes/square meter)
V potential difference (volts); also termed the electromotive force

along with the constants

$$e = 1.602 \times 10^{-19}\ \mathrm{C} \qquad \text{the electron charge}$$

$$m = 9.107 \times 10^{-31}\ \mathrm{kg} \qquad \text{the electron mass}$$

A generalized Ohm's law for an isotropic material is given by

$$\boldsymbol{J} = \sigma \boldsymbol{E}$$

where σ (mhos/meter) is the conductivity of the material and $\rho = 1/\sigma$ (ohm · meter) is the resistivity.

With these, albeit somewhat sparse, preliminaries, we now derive an expression for the Hall potential beginning with the Lorentz force on an electron.

Suppose an isotropic conducting material is subjected to an electric field $\boldsymbol{E}$ and a magnetic field $\boldsymbol{B}$. Suppose, further, that the material contains n majority charge carriers per unit volume, each of them having charge q. Collectively, the group of carriers in such a unit volume is assumed to have drift velocity (average carrier velocity) $\boldsymbol{v}$.

Then the Lorentz force per unit volume acting on such a group is given by

$$\boldsymbol{F} = qn(\boldsymbol{E} + \boldsymbol{v} \times \boldsymbol{B})$$

In addition, the group is taken to be subject to a drag force given by

$$\boldsymbol{f} = -nm\frac{1}{\tau}\boldsymbol{v}$$

where τ is the collision time (in essence, the mean free time of the group between collisions). With these forces the classical Newtonian momentum balance for the system becomes

$$mn\frac{d\boldsymbol{v}}{dt} = \boldsymbol{F} + \boldsymbol{f} = qn(\boldsymbol{E} + \boldsymbol{v} \times \boldsymbol{B}) - nm\frac{1}{\tau}\boldsymbol{v}$$

For steady-state motion (zero acceleration), this equation becomes

$$qn(\boldsymbol{E} + \boldsymbol{v} \times \boldsymbol{B}) - nm\frac{1}{\tau}\boldsymbol{v} = \boldsymbol{0}$$

The introduction of a current density

$$\boldsymbol{J} = qn\boldsymbol{v}$$

results in

$$qn\boldsymbol{E} + \boldsymbol{J} \times \boldsymbol{B} = \frac{m}{q\tau}\boldsymbol{J}$$

or

$$\boldsymbol{J} - \frac{q\tau}{m}\boldsymbol{J} \times \boldsymbol{B} = \frac{q^2 n\tau}{m}\boldsymbol{E}$$

This expression has the form of a generalized Ohm's law, and we accordingly define a conductivity

$$\sigma = \frac{q^2 \tau n}{m}$$

resulting in

$$\boldsymbol{J} - \frac{\sigma}{qn}\boldsymbol{J} \times \boldsymbol{B} = \sigma\boldsymbol{E}$$

We now introduce

$$R_H = \frac{1}{qn}$$

and write the equation in the final form

$$\boldsymbol{J} - \sigma R_H \boldsymbol{J} \times \boldsymbol{B} = \sigma\boldsymbol{E}$$

The negative term in this expression is called the Hall effect, and R_H is called the Hall constant.

Remark 5-3. This derivation has been based on majority carriers with positive charge q. If electrons are the majority carriers, then $q = -e$, and if carriers of both signs are present, the equations must be altered. Note that the Hall constant is also positive or negative, depending on the charge of the majority carrier.

Consider now the specific example of an n-type semiconductor in which the electrons are the majority carriers. Assume that the material is in the shape of a parallelopipedon with width w, length L, and thickness t, as shown in Fig. 5-13. Traditionally, a direct current is then applied in the x-direction and a magnetic field $\boldsymbol{B}$ in the z-direction. Specifically, we take constant fields

$$\boldsymbol{B} = B_z\hat{\boldsymbol{k}} \quad \text{and} \quad \boldsymbol{J} = J_x\hat{\boldsymbol{\imath}}$$

where we have defined a current density

$$J_x = \frac{I}{tw}$$

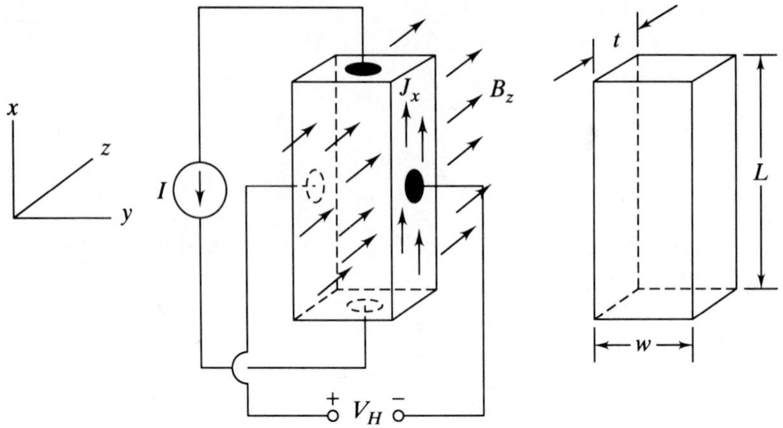

FIGURE 5-13
Sample with Hall potential.

In these terms the final governing equation becomes

$$\frac{1}{\sigma}\frac{I}{tw}\hat{\imath} - \sigma R_H\left(\frac{I}{tw}\hat{\imath}\right) \times \left(B_z\hat{k}\right) = \boldsymbol{E}$$

or

$$\boldsymbol{E} = \frac{1}{\sigma}\frac{I}{tw}\hat{\imath} + R_H\frac{IB_z}{tw}\hat{\jmath}$$

The transverse field

$$E_y = R_H\frac{IB_z}{tw}$$

is called the Hall field, and

$$V_H = E_y w = R_H\frac{IB_z}{t}$$

is called the Hall voltage. For example, if electrons are the majority carriers, then

$$R_H = -\frac{1}{ne}$$

and

$$V_H = -\frac{1}{ne}\frac{IB_z}{t}$$

with resulting polarity as indicated in Fig. 5-13.

Remark 5-4. The experiment may be conducted by applying an alternating current source. In this case it is usual to use B_z^{peak}, I^{rms}, and V_H^{rms} in the calculations.

The Hall effect may also be explained in a somewhat more direct, although heuristic, manner. Suppose that we have an n-type material in the shape of a rod, as shown in Fig. 5-13. The Lorentz force per unit volume on the group of electrons is

$$\boldsymbol{F} = \boldsymbol{J} \times \boldsymbol{B}$$

forcing the electrons toward the left face of the specimen. Since not all of them can get to the left face, they get as close as they can, and this distribution of the electrons gives rise to the corresponding potential distribution collectively equal to the voltage drop V_H.

We now turn briefly to the use of the Hall effect in measurement. Traditionally, the effect has been used to measure the carrier density in materials. This density is given by

$$n = \left| \frac{IB_z}{V_H q t} \right|$$

the number of carriers per unit volume. Rather than measuring n directly, it is usual to measure the Hall constant with

$$R_H = \left| \frac{V_H t}{IB_z} \right|$$

Remark 5-5. Hurd[8] mentions that the applied current should be as high as possible for increased accuracy in Hall constant measurements. He cites $10^6\ \mathrm{A/m^2}$ as a typical value for the current density in a high-conductivity sample.

Remark 5-6. As indicated in Kittel[9], there can be considerable differences between the theoretical value of the Hall constant as obtained from $R_H = -1/nq$ with an assumed carrier concentration and the measured values as obtained from $R_H = (V_H t/IB_z)$. Furthermore, the experimental values differ when taken at room temperature and when taken at 4 K, for example.

When the Hall voltage V_H is used as a proximity sensor, one generally measures it as a function of the magnetic field changes. In order to determine proximity in terms of a distance x, the magnetic field density B_z must be known as a function of x. We illustrate the idea by means of a simple example.

Example 5-2. Suppose that a metal strip of width w, length L, and thickness t is moving through a magnetic field $\boldsymbol{B}$ (pointing into the page as shown in Fig. 5-14) and with velocity $\boldsymbol{v}$ as indicated. If the potential difference across the strip is measured to be V, calculate the speed v.

Solution. The situation is essentially the one depicted in Fig. 5-13. Suppose we consider electrons to be the majority carriers. A differential of charge in the direction x is given by

$$dq = (wt)ne\,dx$$

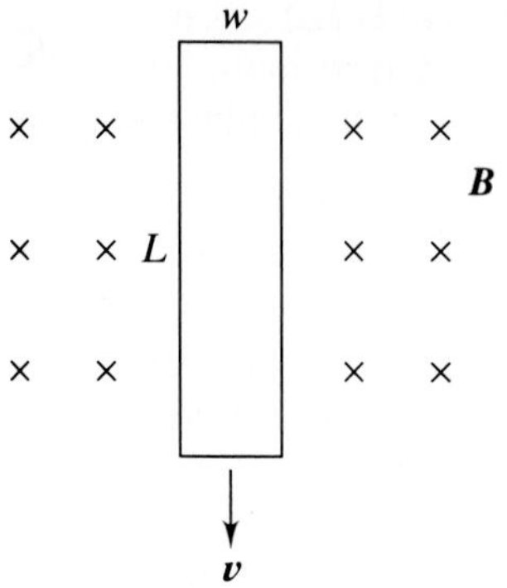

FIGURE 5-14
Moving metal strip in a magnetic field.

so that the current flowing through the magnetic field is given by

$$I = \frac{dq}{dt} = \frac{dq}{dx}v = wtnev$$

The previous expression for the carrier density was

$$n = \left|\frac{IB_z}{V_H qt}\right| = \left|\frac{IB}{Vet}\right|$$

The substitution of the expression for I in n yields

$$v = \frac{V}{wB}$$

which, as the reader should verify, indeed has the units of meters per second.

5-6 OPTICAL ENCODERS

Optical encoders are typically used as shaft angle encoders in rotating systems; naturally, the approach works equally well in measuring lineal displacement. Since the device output is in digital form, it is often cited as one of those fortunate devices that does not require a subsequent analog-to-digital conversion of the output. One may argue, however, that only the manner in which the analog-to-digital conversion is carried out here is different—one still measures a continuous motion and simply provides the data in digital form. Because of the interaction with computers that is usually required, every motion measuring device ultimately is an analog-to-digital transducer, and it becomes irrelevant when and how the analog-to-digital conversion occurs.

It is evident from Doebelin[1] that optical encoders have been around at least since the 1960s. Traditionally, position encoders consisted of a pattern impressed upon a part of the system which characterized the motion and a subsequent readout of the pattern by capacitative, magnetic, or contact means. Here, the readout is accomplished by optical means. An optical encoder typically consists of five components, as illustrated in Fig. 5-15: (1) a light source, (2) a scaled pattern of opaque and translucent segments attached to the

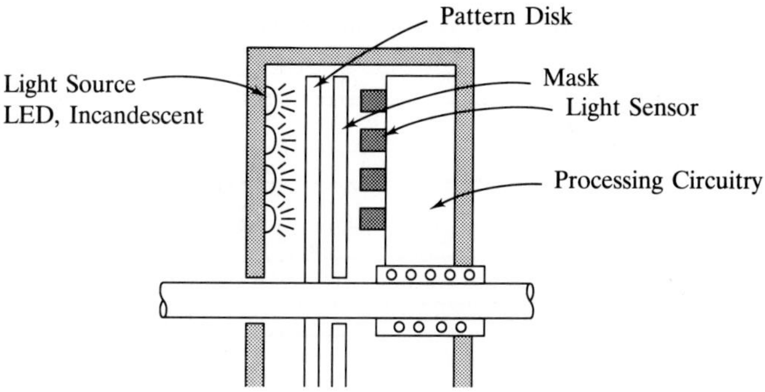

FIGURE 5-15
Schematic of an optical encoder.

moving body and located between the light source and its associated light sensor, (3) a stationary mask for high-resolution encoders (to block extraneous light), (4) the light sensor, and (5) circuitry for data processing.

The light source used most often is a light-emitting diode (LED) or an incandescent lamp. The pattern is created on thin disks or lineal elements, most often made of thin glass. The light sensor may be a phototransistor or a photovoltaic transducer. And the circuitry serves to present the data in a computer communicative form.

There are two main classifications of such devices: absolute encoders and incremental encoders. When velocity is the desired readout, then incremental encoders are used exclusively. Most of our discussion shall deal with rotary encoders, since they are by far the most common.

5-6-1 Absolute Encoders

For the absolute or "whole word" encoder, the main element is the transparent disk with 2 to 30 separate, equally spaced tracks. Segments of these tracks are either transparent or opaque, forming a pattern on the disk. Light may pass through the transparent sections and activate a light sensor. As the disk rotates the light sensor is alternately on or off, depending on whether or not light hits it. Correspondingly, the sensors produce a sequence of pulses, as shown in Fig. 5-16.

We have chosen a 4-track disk, indicating 16 positions, based on the 16 wedges with apex angle $360°/16 = 22.5°$. By identifying powers of 2 with each track (the outer track serves as the LSB, and the innermost track, as the MSB), the pattern on the disk may be used to produce an output in code. The light sensor output is usually a relatively weak sinusoidal or triangular signal. This is then amplified and passed through a comparator to obtain a signal compatible with digital logic. The pulses on the right represent the sensor output in digital code for a quarter turn of the disk, with 0 for the opaque (black) segments and 1

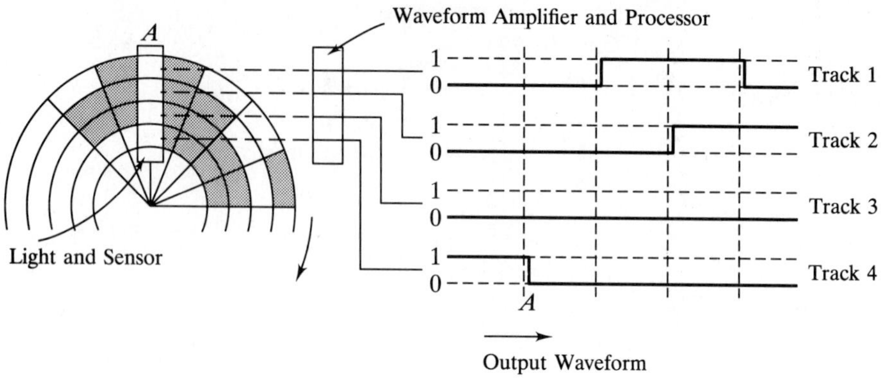

FIGURE 5-16
Output waveform for the absolute encoder.

for the transparent (white) segments. In essence, each track provides the bit of a code word.

In Fig. 5-16 we have used gray code to encode the 16 positions of the disk. The same 16-segment disk with an output in BCD code would thus require 8 separate tracks. The advantage of gray code, of course, is that each position advance requires only one change in the digital code. This assures that the maximum possible error in the output is one unit; by comparison, using standard binary code allows for the possibility of larger errors.

Clearly, absolute encoders may be turned off without losing track of the position; indeed, they need only be powered when a reading is desired.

Encoders are not only used for position measurement. Special codes are routinely created for other purposes such as altimeters and various types of inspection equipment.

5-6-2 Incremental Encoders

The incremental encoder excels through its simplicity. It generally has only one or two output channels and thus has fewer components and a less complex code disk. The incremental encoder output is a pulse train representing the number of increments that the code disk has rotated. While this, in essence, suffices to obtain velocity data, the determination of position requires an external digital counter that keeps track of the number of pulses. In case of a power failure, the counter may reset, resulting in loss of the position information; similarly detrimental is the fact that if an error does occur it is propagated to all subsequent information.

Thus both incremental steps and the direction of motion can be sensed. This may be accomplished in at least two ways—by using either two encoder tracks and two photocells or one track and two photocells. We shall discuss the

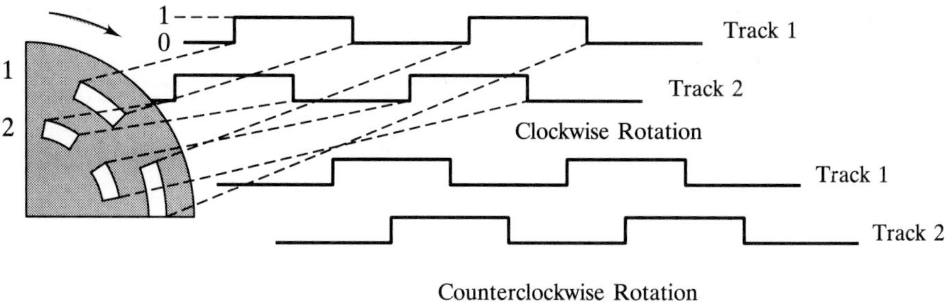

FIGURE 5-17
Sense of rotation.

operation for the case of two tracks and two photocells; the one-track case operates in virtually the same fashion.

When using two tracks, the direction of rotation is sensed by offsetting the slots in the tracks with respect to one another. The "leading" track then implies a corresponding direction of rotation. Suppose that the encoder disk has two tracks as shown in Fig. 5-17, the outer track being labeled "track 1," and the inner one, "track 2." Again, the white areas are taken to be transparent, the black areas are opaque, with outputs 1 and 0, respectively. The opaque and the transparent intervals are taken to be of equal length. We let the slots of track 1 be set half a slot length ahead of those of track 2. For a clockwise rotation, the photocells of the outer track are activated first, then both cells are on, and, finally, only the inner cell is on. This is the procedure that yields the square wave pattern shown in Fig. 5-17, with the outer track leading the inner track. For counterclockwise rotation, the inner track leads.

The following example illustrates some of the calculations that might be involved.

Example 5-3. Suppose that the output of the two-track incremental encoder of a rotating shaft is the one shown in Fig. 5-18. The output is being sampled at 10 MHz, and it is known that the photocell for the outer track is on for 5×10^4 sampling pulses (see Fig. 5-18a). The track contains 200 slots evenly distributed around the circumference. Determine the sense of rotation and the angular speed of the shaft.

Solution. Since the inner track is leading, the shaft is rotating in the counterclockwise direction. A sampling rate of 10 MHz results in a "slot length" (see Fig. 5-18b) of 5×10^4 sampling pulses. Consequently,

$$\frac{10 \times 10^6}{5 \times 10^4} \frac{\text{pulses} \cdot \text{slots}}{\text{sec} \cdot \text{pulses}} = 2 \times 10^2 \frac{\text{slots}}{\text{sec}}$$

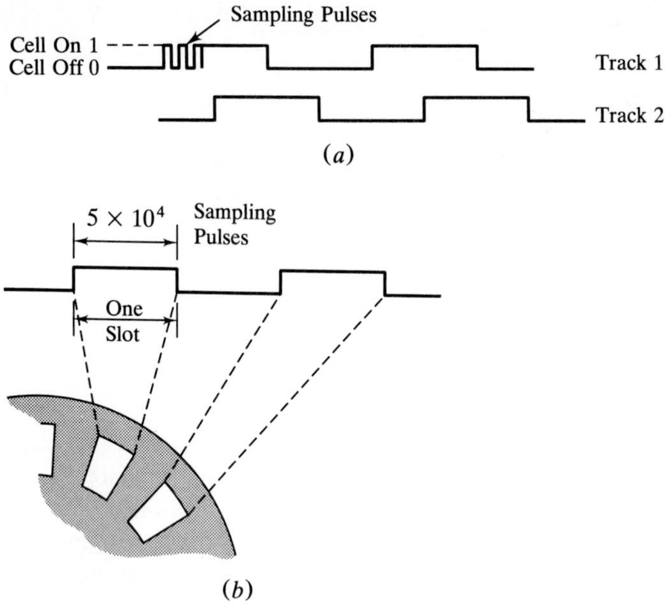

FIGURE 5-18
Specific encoder output.

With 200 slots per revolution, we then have

$$\frac{2 \times 10^2}{200} \frac{\text{slots rev}}{\text{sec slots}} = 1 \frac{\text{rev}}{\text{sec}} \cdot 60 \frac{\text{sec}}{\text{min}} = 60 \text{ rpm}$$

5-6-3 Encoder Quality

We shall only briefly touch upon encoder quality. Clearly, an encoder can only be as good as its peripherals—the mechanical parts and processing electronics. The size and weight of the encoder, the shaft loading and end play of the shaft, and the external counter for the incremental encoder all play a part in the quality of the encoder output. The basic quality of the encoder itself, however, is its resolution: in essence, the smallest unit of measurement it can provide or, equivalently, the smallest input increment that still provides a measurable change in output.

Definition 5-1 Resolution of encoders. The resolution of the *absolute encoder* is

$$r = 2^n$$

where n is the number of tracks of the encoder. The corresponding angular resolution is

$$r_\theta = \frac{360°}{2^n} \sim \frac{2\pi}{2^n}$$

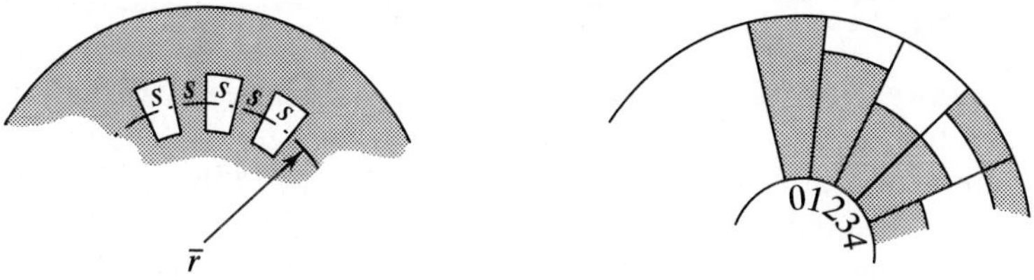

FIGURE 5-19
Encoder resolution.

The resolution of the *incremental encoder* is simply the number of slots per revolution

$$N = \frac{\pi \bar{r}}{s}$$

where $\bar{r}$ is the radial distance from the center to the middle of the encoder slot, and s is the width of the slot (and the opaque segment as well) at the same distance.

The concepts are illustrated in Fig. 5-19.

Example 5-4. Suppose an incremental encoder has a resolution of $N = 2000$. Determine the period and the frequency, in hertz, of the square wave output of the encoder if the shaft is rotating at 500 rpm.

Solution. Half of the period T of the square wave is given by the length of time for which the light cell is on. This results in

$$\bar{r}\omega \frac{T}{2} = s \quad \Rightarrow \quad T = \frac{2s}{\bar{r}\omega} \text{ sec}$$

where ω is the angular velocity of the shaft in radians/second. Furthermore,

$$s = \frac{2\pi \bar{r}}{4000} \text{ cm} \qquad \text{and} \qquad \omega = \frac{500 \cdot 2\pi}{60} = \frac{100\pi}{6} \frac{\text{rad}}{\text{sec}}$$

Substitution in the expression for T yields the period

$$T = \frac{2}{\bar{r}} \frac{2\pi \bar{r}}{4000} \frac{6}{100\pi} = 6 \times 10^{-5} \text{ sec}$$

and a frequency

$$f = \frac{1}{T} = 16.7 \text{ kHz}$$

The output circuits, including counters, of incremental encoders are extensively discussed in Snyder.[10] An additional detailed, somewhat more applied discussion of optical encoders may be found in the handbook by the Electro-Craft Corporation.[11]

5-7 TACTILE AND FORCE SENSORS

Particularly in robotics, no chapter on sensors would be complete without a discussion of force, torque, and tactile sensors. They play an essential role in the nondestructive interaction of the robot with its surroundings—in the avoidance of either excessive or insufficient force. Today's robot, when presented with a marble egg and a real one, is still as likely to drop the one and break the other as not.

However, the technology in these areas is evolving rapidly. We thus confine our presentation to two relatively well-established approaches: a *wrist sensor*, which senses the forces and moments experienced by a robot hand in its interaction with its environment; and a *tactile array*, based on the pressure sensitivity of a conductive elastomer. The term *wrist sensor* already implies that the sensor is usually installed at the robot wrist, just prior to the gripped object, whose maximal six degrees of freedom would require a measure of the forces and moments needed to fully sustain such a motion. Tactile sensors are placed at the contact surface, usually on the "fingers" of the robot end effector. The term *tactile* derives from the Latin word *tangere*—to touch. We take tactile sensing to provide a measure of the amount of contact pressure that is being exerted. The word *contact* also derives from *tangere*; and within the present context, we shall use *touch* to indicate the presence or absence of contact.

According to Dr. Warnecke, head of the Fraunhofer Institute, the first integration of tactile sensors with gripping surfaces occurred at Nagoya University, Japan, in 1972. An adaptive force control that gripped workpieces with a minimum of force was produced there. The standard problem (always dutifully mentioned in this context)—that of introducing a bolt into a hole automatically—was first carried out by Hitachi with its Hi-T-Hand. The procedure has been continuously improved upon since then. It has become the benchmark of compliant manipulation.

For further reading in tactile sensing, we recommend Webster[12] and Russell.[13] An extensive survey and analysis of nonvisual sensors is presented in Diesing and Schmucker.[14]

5-7-1 The Wrist Sensor

We emphasize the wrist sensor as the present mainstay of force and moment sensing in robotic workpiece manipulation. The central idea is that a collection of "beams" is oriented in such a way that their bending within a rigid frame may be used to deduce force and moment information. We shall precede our main discussion with a somewhat simplified alternative.

Forces and moments by their very nature cannot be measured directly. One way of measuring is through compensation, by using an apparatus to match an unknown force, such as the weighing of an object on a scale. Another method is the deduction of force as a result of the deformation of some transducer that is in contact with the force-producing element. The measurement of dynamic force will not be considered within the present context. The standard transducer is still the strain gauge, and it serves as the main transducer here.

Example 5-5. The built-in cantilevered beam of length L and rectangular cross section is loaded by an unknown force P at the free end, as shown in Fig. 5-20. Use strain gauges mounted on the beam surface at a distance e from the fixed end to deduce the magnitude and direction of P. Furthermore, use a potentiometric circuit to obtain a voltage readout instead of the usual bridge circuit. Assume a voltage source of 5 V. Express P in terms of the problem geometric and material parameters which you may take as given with the gauge factor $G = 2$.

Solution. We shall first obtain an expression for the strain at O. With the usual sign convention for the internal resultants, the internal moment M at the point O is given by

$$-M - P(L-e) = 0 \quad \Rightarrow \quad M = -P(L-e)$$

In the remainder of the discussion, we shall use only the absolute value of this expression. The corresponding axial stress at the gauge locations is given by the usual formula

$$\sigma = \frac{Mc}{I} = \frac{P(L-e)\frac{b}{2}}{\frac{1}{12}ab^3} = \frac{6P(L-e)}{ab^2}$$

and the corresponding axial strain is

$$\epsilon = \frac{1}{E}\sigma = \frac{6P(L-e)}{Eab^2}$$

Equation (5-6) yields the desired relationship between strain and resistance change, with positive strain (elongation) indicating a positive change in resistance

$$\epsilon = \frac{1}{2}\frac{\Delta R}{R} \quad \Rightarrow \quad \Delta R = 2R\epsilon = \frac{12PR(L-e)}{Eab^2}$$

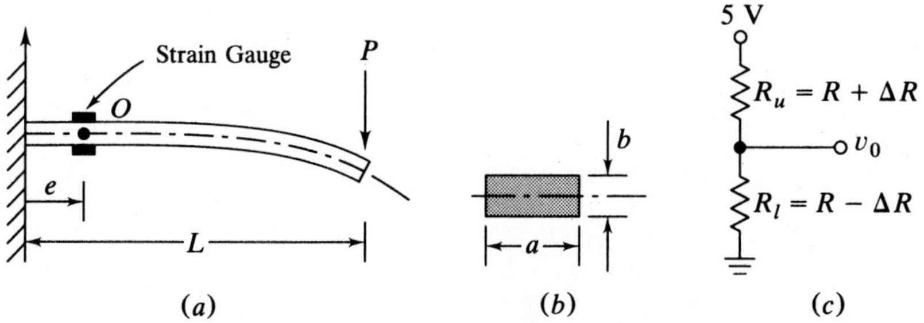

FIGURE 5-20
(*a*) The beam configuration; (*b*) the cross section; (*c*) the circuit.

where we have used $G = 2$ and where R is the resistance of the unstrained gauge wire. The result is

$$P = \frac{Eab^2}{12R(L-e)}\,\Delta R$$

It remains to express ΔR in terms of a voltage readout. Suppose we wire the two strain gauges in series with an applied voltage of 5 V, as shown in Fig. 5-20*c*. For this situation the output of the circuit is given by

$$v_0 = (R - \Delta R)\frac{5}{2R} \quad \Rightarrow \quad \Delta R = R\left(1 - \frac{2}{5}v_0\right)$$

so that

$$P = \frac{Eab^2}{12(L-e)}\left(1 - \frac{2}{5}v_0\right)$$

With the strain gauges connected in the given order, a positive P is a downward force.

We now turn to the description of a particular wrist sensor.

Wrist sensors for robots are generally located just prior to the hand itself, as shown in Fig. 5-21. The hand here is attached to the hub of the sensor, while the rigid rim of the sensor is connected to the remaining part of the robot arm. The deformation of the inner cross section then serves to identify the desired forces and moments.

THE MALTESE CROSS. The Maltese cross, used in medieval times as an emblem by the knights of Malta, consisted of four arrowheads pointing toward a common center. The concept of a Maltese cross was first used in a sensor developed by V. Scheinman.[15] Scheinman's company, Vicarm, Inc., which was later acquired by Unimation, produced a refined version for Jet Propulsion Laboratories. (For more details, refer to Bejczy.[16]) The term *Maltese cross* is an excellent mnemonic device and has helped in publicizing the type of sensor configuration shown in Fig. 5-22. But bear in mind that a slight stretch of the imagination will be required to apply the term to the sensor depicted.

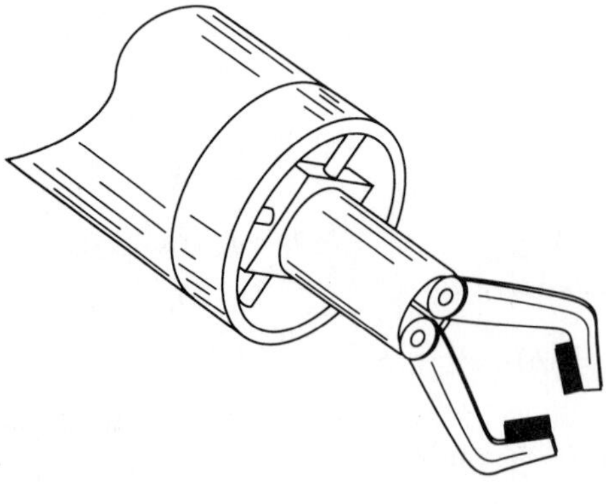

FIGURE 5-21
Wrist sensor connection.

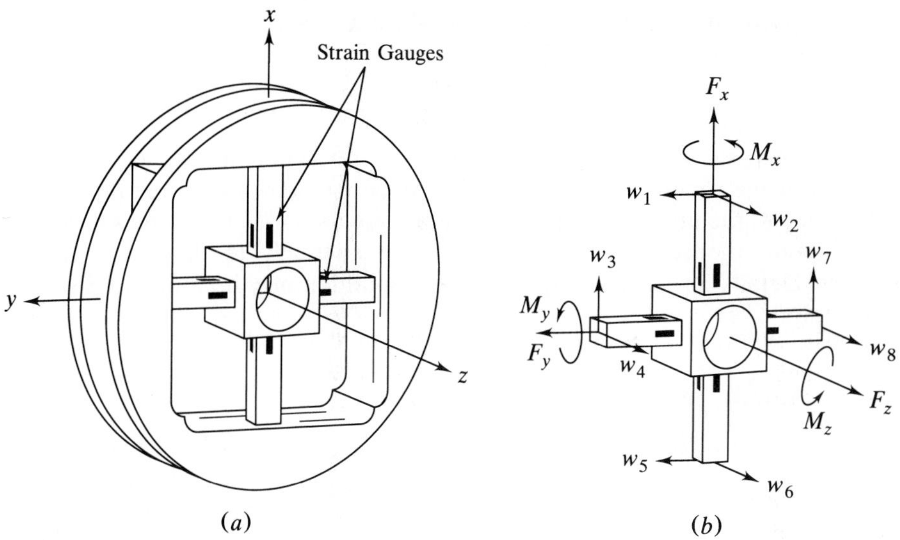

FIGURE 5-22
The Maltese cross: (*a*) general configuration machined from a single piece of aluminum; (*b*) raw data and force and moment resultants.

The sensor shown in Fig. 5-22 is machined from a single piece of aluminum. Measurements are obtained from pairs of strain gauges mounted on the four sides of each of the four spokes (slender beams). The spokes are attached to the relatively flexible rim on one side and to the square hub at the center, approximating a simple support and a rigid support, respectively.

Each pair of strain gauges—eight pairs in all—is connected to a potentiometric circuit like the one used in Example 5-5. Insofar as the support conditions given previously are satisfied, we may assume that the deformations are uncoupled and that the output voltages v_i of the potentiometric circuits are proportional to the corresponding forces w_i at the ends of the spokes, as shown in Fig. 5-22*b*. These raw data are related to the orthogonal force and moment components via the matrix equation

$$\mathbf{F} = \mathbf{R}\mathbf{w}$$

where

$$\mathbf{F} = (F_x \quad F_y \quad F_z \quad M_x \quad M_y \quad M_z)^T \qquad \text{and} \qquad \mathbf{w} = (w_1\, w_2 \ldots w_z)^T$$

and where the 6×8 matrix

$$\mathbf{R} = [r_{ij}]$$

is called the *resolved force matrix*. When the readings are uncoupled, as assumed previously, the matrix is sparse, since we have

$$F_x = r_{13}w_3 + r_{17}w_7$$

for example, with no other contributions to F_x.

Clearly, the preceding system is only approximately uncoupled, since the support at the rim always produces some resisting moments. When the inaccuracies due to the uncoupling assumption become too large, it becomes necessary to calibrate the resolved force matrix experimentally to determine the 48 entries. Details for such an experimental calibration may be found in Shimano and Roth.[17]

5-7-2 Tactile Sensors

We shall take a touch sensor to simply measure the presence or absence of contact, something that may be accomplished by simple limit switches, for example (i.e., a switch closes or opens the instant contact is established). We shall use the term *tactile* in connection with sensors that measure the pressure distribution over contact surfaces. We shall adopt the following formal definition, a mix of previous ones in the literature.

Definition 5-2 Tactile sensing. The continuous sensing of variable contact stress.

We have used the word *stress* here to indicate that force per unit area is to be sensed in a continuous fashion. Sometimes, tactile sensors are constructed as arrays of load cells termed *taxels* (or *tactels*), in analogy to the discretization introduced for vision systems. Tactile sensors may also consist of continuous pressure-sensitive films, from which the pressure information could be extracted without the introduction of an array of taxels.

Overall, such sensors are an attempt at mimicking a human sense of touch, particularly in connection with the human finger. Thus we are trying to imitate skin. Harmon[18] queried 47 researchers and manufacturers concerning desirable attributes of such sensors, based, in part, on physiological information on the human sense of touch. The survey prompted the following requirements:

1. The sensor should have a spatial resolution of 1 to 2 mm, about that of the human sense of touch at the fingertips. This amounts to about 16 taxels per square centimeter.
2. The sensitivity of individual load cells should be about 0.01 N/m^2, with an upper limit of about 10 N/m^2, corresponding to a dynamic range of 1000 : 1, preferably with a logarithmic characteristic.
3. Nonlinear behavior is acceptable; hysteresis of the sensor is not acceptable, since good repeatability is extremely desirable.
4. The sensor should be robust, allowing it to function well within harsh environmental conditions.

5. Each sensor element should have a response time ranging from 1 to 10 ms. A typical scanning range for a 16×16 sensor is 4 kHz, implying that individual taxels are being scanned at 1 MHz.

It may not be desirable to copy the human sensory system too closely. With respect to the sense of touch, M. H. E. Larcombe[19] writes:

> These sensors are liberally distributed over the entire skin surface. With such multiplicity of sensors, we might expect some superb pattern recognition abilities. In fact, the system by itself is almost devoid of pattern processing. Over large areas, the ability to discriminate between two points requires a spatial separation of two centimeters or more. In addition, we find that many groups of sensors share common "data channels" even when the groups are widely separated—leading to some bizarre signal confusions such as an injury in the foot giving a sensation in the mouth.

We now turn to some specific sensorial capabilities. The first level of selection concerns the choice of an active or a passive sensor. The active sensor would attain its energy from the deformation; the passive sensor would require a separate energy source. The former thus measures change almost exclusively; the latter is also capable of measuring static phenomena.

Most sensing cells use a deformation transducer of some sort with corresponding measurable changes in resistance, capacitance, or magnetic field. Optical means have also been used for the measure of deformation.

One of the classical means for the construction of a load cell or taxel is, of course, the use of a capacitor. An extensive article by Seow[20] deals with just such a capacitative sensor array. The article indicates that these sensors are more sensitive than other types, have a lower temperature coefficient, and exhibit better long-term stability than piezoresistive sensors. Specifically, "The capacitative sensor is 20 times more sensitive than the piezoresistive sensor, has a smaller package, consumers less power, and has long-term stability. However, the circuitry needed for buffering a capacitative sensor introduces temperature dependency that can be as large as 1.3 kPa/°C."

The efficient measurement of capacitance is fundamental to the process. The following simple example deals with the measurement of capacitance and hence pressure, a process that is repeated n^2 times in an $n \times n$ sensoral array with individually addressable load cells.

Example 5-6. Design a capacitive force sensor and provide an expression for the compressive force P in terms of an output voltage v_0 of some measuring circuit and in terms of relevant material and geometric parameters.

Solution. For definiteness, suppose the basic capacitive cell has the structure shown in Fig. 5-23*a*. A dielectric of thickness d is sandwiched between two electrodes, all with cross-sectional area A; the dielectric has elastic modulus E and permittivity ϵ.

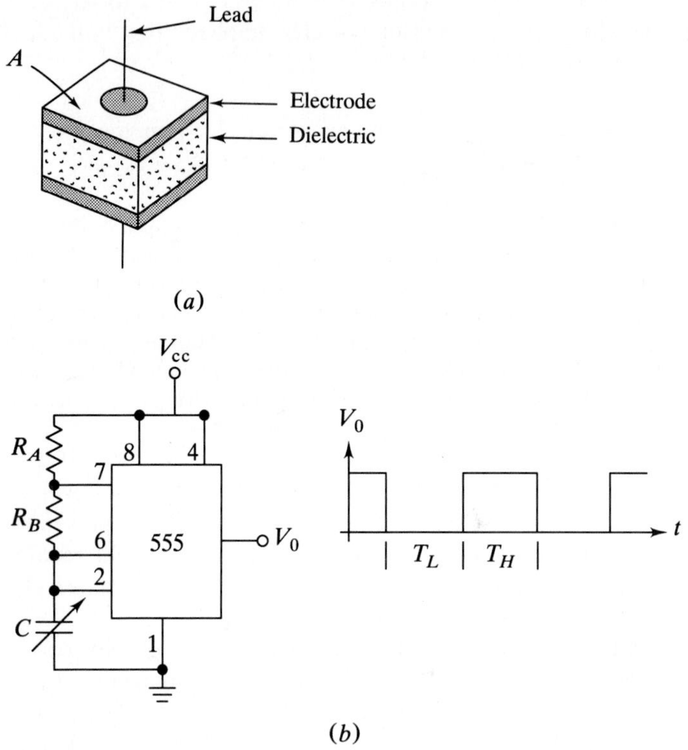

FIGURE 5-23
Capacitor and measuring circuit.

We first derive an expression for the force P in terms of the presumably variable capacitance C. The standard formula for the compression u of a bar of length d in terms of P is

$$u = \frac{Pd}{AE}$$

so that the thickness of the dielectric is

$$d_1 = d\left(1 - \frac{P}{AE}\right) \qquad \text{with} \quad C_1 = \frac{\epsilon A}{d_1}$$

yielding

$$P = AE\left(1 - \frac{\epsilon A}{C_1 d}\right)$$

Of course, division by A would provide a pressure relationship.

The simplest way to measure a capacitance C_1 is with a timing circuit involving a 555 timer, as shown in Fig. 5-23*b*. The output of the timer is a square wave with

$$T_L = R_B C_1 \ln 2 \qquad \text{and} \qquad T_H = (R_A + R_B) C_1 \ln 2$$

resulting in the frequency

$$f = \frac{1}{T_L + T_H} = \frac{1}{C_1(2R_B + R_A) \ln 2}$$

The standard linear frequency-to-voltage converter is governed by

$$v_0 = kf \quad \Rightarrow \quad C_1 = \frac{k}{v_0(2R_B + R_A) \ln 2}$$

so that

$$P = EA\left[1 - \frac{\epsilon A v_0 (2R_B + R_A) \ln 2}{dk}\right]$$

In a capacitive tactile array, this measurement is carried out for each taxel. For additional detail concerning timers and frequency-to-voltage converters, the reader is referred to Franco.[21]

We close this section with a description of the structure and output of a simple tactile array. One way of providing a semblance of an elastic skin is with conductive *elastomers*, rubberlike materials whose electrical conductivity changes locally when pressure is applied. This change in resistance can be used to measure the pressure. One of the first to build such a sensor was Larcombe.[22] Her approach was then further refined and developed by Snyder and St. Clair[23]; our discussion is based on their approach.

The sensor itself consists of three layers and circuitry, as shown in Fig. 5-24: a protective covering, a sheet of conductive elastomer, and a printed circuit board, plus the data acquisition circuitry. The printed circuit board consists of two rows of two "bullseyes," each with conductive inner and outer rings. These comprise the taxels of the sensor. The outer rings of each column are connected together and to a column-select transistor switch T. The center rings of each bullseye are connected to diodes D.

Once a column has been selected, a 5-V source provides a current which first flows through a fixed 1-kΩ resistance and through the diode to the inner ring connection at the cathode of the diode. The current then continues through the elastomer to the outer ring and thence through the transistor to ground. Current flows in both of the parallel branches connected to the "high" transistor switch.

We note that it generally is not possible to excite just a single taxel, since any pressure applied to one taxel causes some depression in neighboring taxels. This unavoidable elastic interaction is one type of so-called cross-talk. Electronic cross-talk would arise in neighboring columns when a particular column is activated (they would become part of the circuit); this cross-talk is eliminated by the diodes.

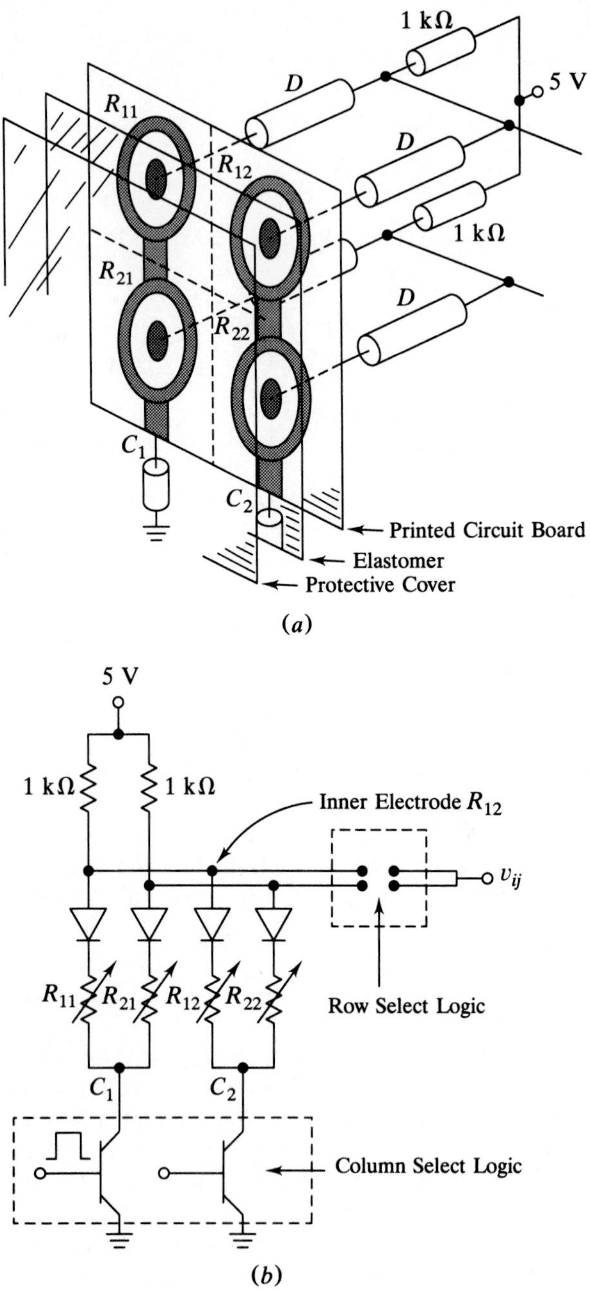

FIGURE 5-24
(*a*) The taxel array; (*b*) acquisition circuit.

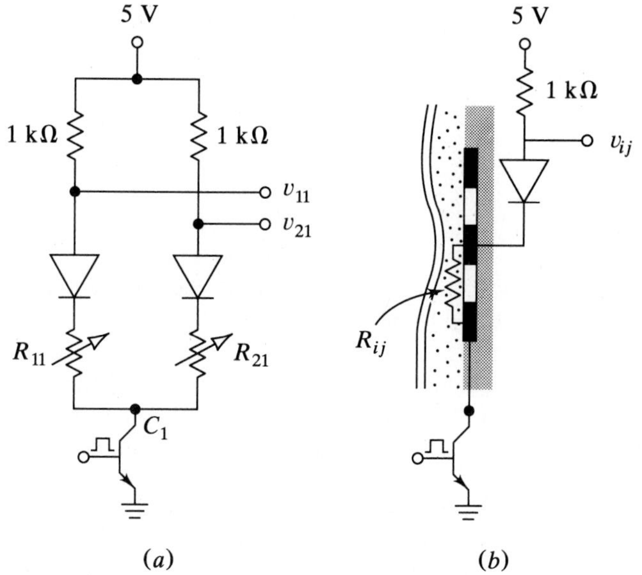

FIGURE 5-25
(*a*) Selection of column 1; (*b*) the general circuit.

With this general scheme in mind, we now turn to the specific analysis of the circuit shown in Fig. 5-24*b* and the pressure array derived from it. No matter which column is chosen, the corresponding activated circuit has the form shown in Fig. 5-25*a*. Each separate branch is simply a voltage divider, as shown in Fig. 5-25*b*, where the dark segments denote a side view of the printed circuit rings. Keeping in mind that the variable resistances are what we wish to measure, we eventually obtain

$$R_{ij} = \frac{1000 v_{ij}}{5 - v_{ij}}$$

where v_{ij} is the voltage output from a particular selected voltage divider. (For the analysis, we remind the reader that the transistor conducts current when the base voltage—the pulse—is greater than the transistor threshold voltage and the diode admits current only in its forward direction.)

Once the resistances have been calculated, they may be converted to pressures by making use of the conduction curve for the given elastomer. A calibrated version of this curve is taken to have the form shown in Fig. 5-26. The final result is a sensor stress matrix

$$\mathbf{P} = \begin{bmatrix} p_{11} & p_{12} \\ p_{21} & p_{22} \end{bmatrix}$$

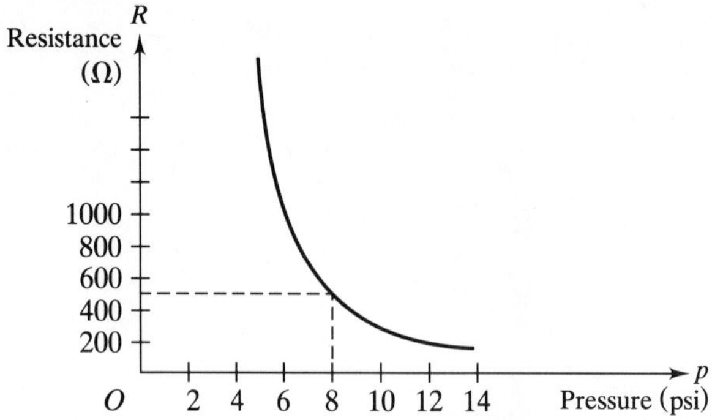

FIGURE 5-26
Typical elastomer conduction curve.

The entries of this matrix are analog values and they may be converted to digital levels by a suitable A/D conversion. This process and the subsequent analysis are carried out in much the same way as for the image matrix which we obtain for computer image analysis in Chap. 6.

Although elastomers may seem ideal for use in elastic skins, they do have some drawbacks. Standard elastomers are sensitive to rough surfaces and may wear out easily, sometimes with a lifetime of only a few hundred cycles. They may also exhibit considerable amounts of hysteresis, and even when there is no permanent deformation they may be slow to return to their original shape. Both of these latter types of behavior seriously worsen the repeatability of the sensor.

As in the optimal design of composite materials, the use of carbon fibers can remedy a number of these effects. For instance, Larcombe reports that a sensor with a carbon fiber fabric as its contact surface has been operated for more than 500,000 cycles as a presence sensor on an overhead monorail track.

This concludes our discussion of what might be termed "traditional sensors"—namely, those that have been in use for some time and quite likely will continue to be used. We have only touched the surface of this very active research area. The principles we have exhibited to achieve force and tactile sensing are likely to remain for some time, although the details may vary. The robotics literature is well stocked with sensors and conferences on sensors and articles about sensors, often of the variety "Look at What My Sensor Can Do," with very little revealed about how they do what they do.

The following chapter is devoted to a detailed treatment of the most sophisticated sensor in use, the CCD vision sensor.

EXERCISES

5-1. Recall that a first-order instrument has the governing equation

$$\tau \frac{dy}{dt} + y = Kf(t).$$

(*a*) Determine the time response of a first-order instrument to a step input $f(t) = f_0 u(t)$, where $u(t)$ is the unit step function. Plot the normalized response of the system with t/τ as abscissa and $y(t)/Kf_0$ as ordinate.

(*b*) Determine the range of the ratio t/τ for which the nondimensional system response is within 5% of its steady-state value. Obtain the range of the time constant τ for which the system settling time, $t_1 \leq 3$. [The settling time is the amount of time needed by the instrument to reach and stay within a specified $\pm$ percentage error band of the steady-state value $y(t) = f_0$.]

5-2. Consider again the first order instrument with the governing equation as given in Problem 5-1.

(*a*) Draw straight line approximations for the Bode magnitude and phase plots. For definiteness, use $K = 10$, $\tau = 0.02$ and four-cycle semilog paper.

(*b*) Suppose the input into the instrument is

$$f(t) = 2 \sin 75t$$

so that the ideal output with gain $K = 10$ is given by

$$y(t) = 20 \sin 75t$$

Discuss the distortion, attenuation, and phase shift of the output signal for $\tau_1 = 0.02$ and $\tau_2 = 0.002$.

5-3. The circuit in Fig. E5-3 is a difference amplifier. Use Kirchhoff's laws and the usual assumptions for the operation of nonsaturated operational amplifiers to derive an expression for v_0 in terms of the input voltages v_1 and v_2. All specified voltages are referenced to ground.

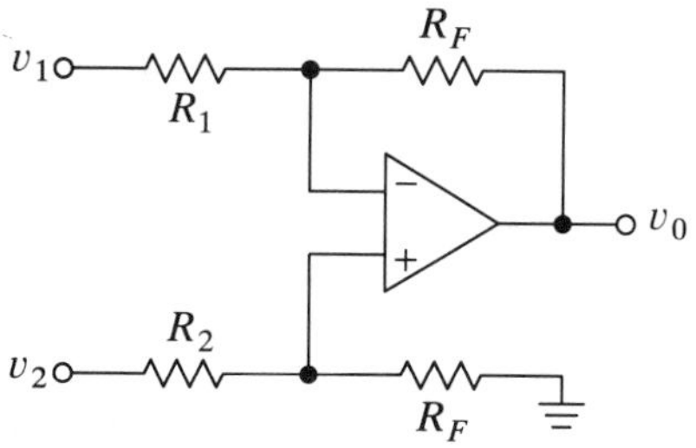

FIGURE E5-3
A difference amplifier.

5-4. The output of a bridge circuit generally needs to be amplified with the most common choice being an IA (instrumentation amplifier). The simplest circuit

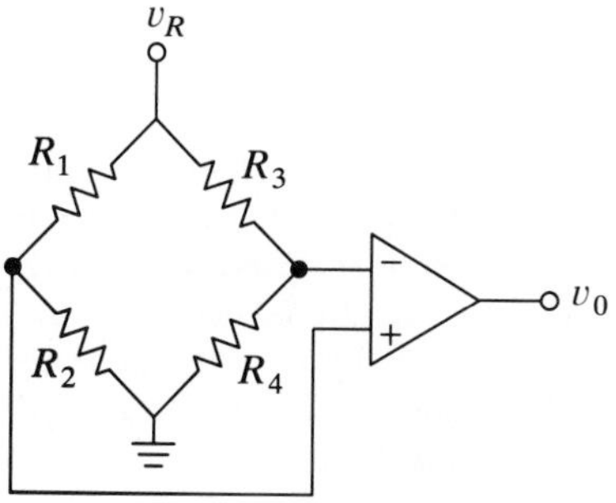

FIGURE E5-4
Bridge circuit with op amp.

involves only an operational amplifier. For the circuit in Fig. E5-4:

(*a*) Derive an expression for the output v_0 in terms of the resistances R_1, R_2, R_3, and R_4. Assume that the equation for the open loop operation of the op amp is $v_0 = K(v_p - v_n)$.

(*b*) Suppose $R_1 = R_2 = R_3 = R$ and $R_4 = R(1 + \delta)$. Derive an expression for the output v_0 under the assumption $\delta \ll 1$.

5-5. Suppose some arbitrary surface is bounded by a closed loop. The "number" of magnetic lines that pass through the surface within the loop is called the magnetic flux Φ for that surface. It is defined by

$$\Phi = \oint \boldsymbol{B} \cdot d\boldsymbol{A}$$

where $\boldsymbol{B}$ is the magnetic field and $d\boldsymbol{A}$ is the element of surface area, and the integration is being carried out over the entire surface. More specifically, consider a plane surface bounded by a circle of radius R, as shown in Fig. E5-5. Assume that the magnetic lines are all perpendicular to the surface (pointing into the page) and that the magnetic field strength is a function of r, with $\boldsymbol{B} = -\alpha r \hat{\mathbf{k}}$. Calculate the magnetic flux Φ for this region.

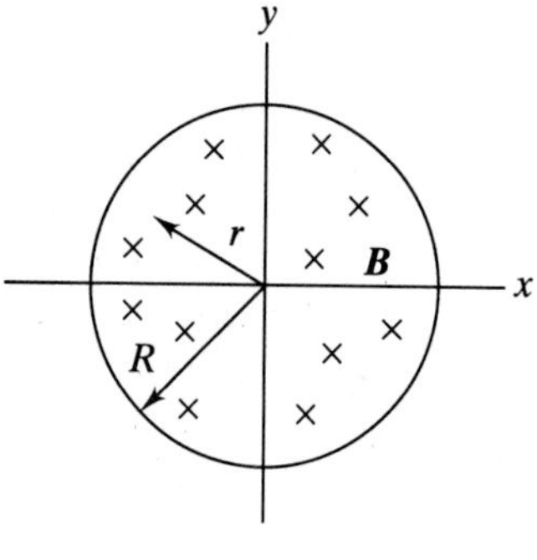

FIGURE E5-5

5-6. (*a*) Derive the expressions $G_0(s)$ and $G_L(s)$ as given by (5-15) and (5-16), respectively.

(*b*) The phase shift of $v_0(t)$ with respect to the voltage $v_p(t)$ of the LVDT is given by $\phi(\omega) = \operatorname{Arg} G(j\omega)$. Determine the phases $\phi_0(\omega)$ and $\phi_L(\omega)$ and those ω for which these phase shifts are zero.

5-7. The phase shift of $v_0(t)$ with respect to the voltage $v_p(t)$ of the LVDT is often undesirable (see also Exercise 5-6). Manufacturers thus specify the frequency or frequencies at which the phase shift is 0. Various circuits are used to allow the phase shift to be 0 for finite ω. Determine the frequency (or frequencies) at which each of the circuits in Fig. E5-7 exhibits zero phase shift. [*Hint:* Determine the governing equations in s-space, deduce the system function $G(s)$, calculate the phase shift $\operatorname{Arg} G(j\omega)$, and solve for that ω which makes it 0.]

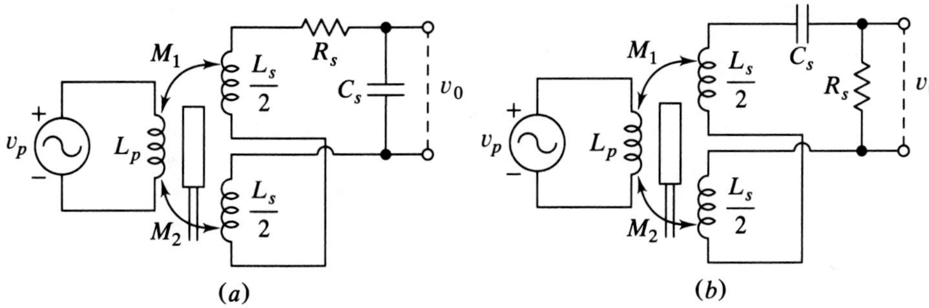

FIGURE E5-7
(*a*) Retardation of a leading phase angle; (*b*) advancing a lagging phase angle. (The ± with v_p indicates the polarity to be used in the derivation.)

5-8. Assume that a piezoelectric accelerometer is being used in conjunction with a charge amplifier so that (5-18) and (5-19) describe the overall system. For most practical applications, the damping constant of the crystal may be considered to be zero. Furthermore, suppose that a quartz crystal with $a = b = 1$ cm and $t = 3$ mm is being used and that the charge amplifier dials have been set at $C_F = 100{,}000$ pF and $R_F = 10^{14}\ \Omega$. Assume $\omega_n = 20$ kHz.

(*a*) Suppose a Fourier analyzer screen displays $e_0(t)$ as shown in Fig. E5-8, one period of a sine wave. Determine the acceleration, including units; that is, determine $a_i(t)$. Note that a linear relationship between a_i and e_0 is generally desirable. What approximations would you have to make for this to be the case here?

(*b*) Suppose $a_i(t) = c = \text{const}$. Obtain the exact voltage output $e_0(t)$ of the system, assuming zero initial conditions.

(*c*) Draw the Bode magnitude and phase plots for $G(s)$, the system function of the combined system, using the usual straight-line approximations.

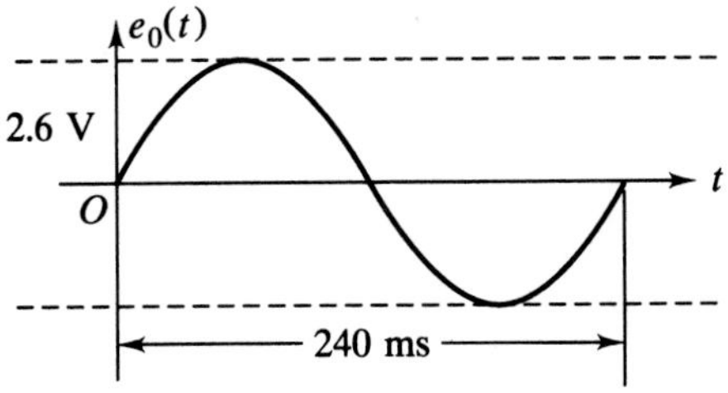

FIGURE E5-8

5-9. Consider again the system function describing the crystal output, together with the charge amplifier

$$G_3(s) = \frac{\tau K_2 s}{\tau s + 1} = \frac{E_0(s)}{U(s)}$$

with the minus sign omitted.

(*a*) Suppose the input into the circuit is given by

$$u(t) = \begin{cases} kt & 0 \le t < T \\ 0 & t \ge T \end{cases}$$

and calculate the system response $e_0(t)$ for both $t \in [0, T]$ and $t \ge T$, assuming zero initial conditions.

(*b*) Calculate $e_0(T^-)$ and obtain the error introduced by the circuit,

$$E\left(\frac{T}{\tau}\right) = u(T^-) - e_0(T^-)$$

(*c*) Determine the range of T/τ which will assure that the error is less than or equal to 5%. The exact determination of the critical ratio T/τ will require the solution of a transcendental equation involving T/τ and $\exp(-T/\tau)$. You may obtain an approximate solution by expanding the exponential in a power series with truncation at $(T/\tau)^2$.

5-10. (From Halliday and Resnick[4]) In a Hall effect experiment, a current of 3.0 A lengthwise in a conductor 1.0 cm wide, 4.0 cm long and 10 μm thick produces a transverse Hall voltage (across the width) of 10 μV when a magnetic field of 1.5 T (tesla) is passed perpendicularly through the thin conductor. From these data:

(*a*) Find the drift velocity of the charge carriers.

(*b*) Find the density of the charge carriers.

(*c*) Show, on a diagram, the polarity of the Hall voltage with given current and magnetic field direction, assuming that the charge carriers are (negative) electrons. Recall that 1 T = 1 Wb/m^2 = 10^4 G.

5-11. In Section 5-6-2 we introduced incremental encoders for the measurement of position and velocity. The raw output of an encoder is sinusoidal, with frequency determined by the encoder resolution. To make the signal suitable for digital signal processing, a pulse shaping circuit is required.

Suppose the raw output of an encoder has the form $e_1 = A \sin \omega t$. Design a signal processing circuit which will produce a square wave related to the original sinusoid as shown in Fig. E5-11.

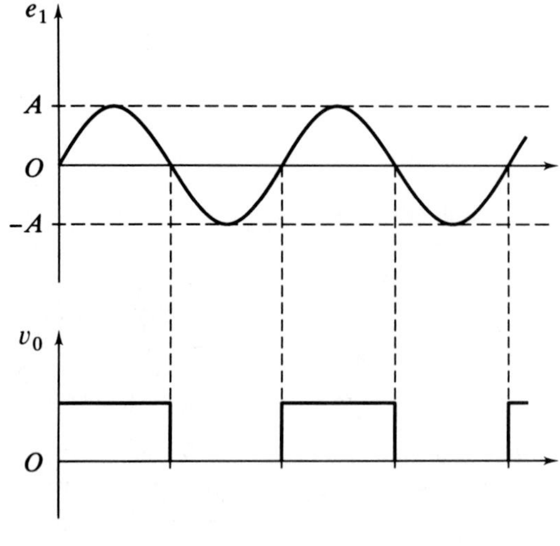

FIGURE E5-11

Proceed as follows:

(*a*) Suppose you were to use a simple comparator powered by ± 15 V. Discuss the corresponding output, using a reference voltage $v_R = v_P = 0$. Is the result adequate? Why or why not?

(*b*) Use an op amp with a Zener diode feedback and a suitably adjusted input and reference voltage to condition the signal to obtain a 0 to 5 V logic transition. You may assume noise margins of one volt at the upper and lower ends; that is, "0" requires an output in the range $0 \le v_0 \le 1$ V and "1" requires $4 \le v_0 \le 5$ V.

5-12. Optical encoders frequently use the gray scale rather than the straight binary scale in the representation of decimal digits for counting. The likelihood of an erroneous reading is smaller for the gray scale than for the binary scale. Furthermore, when an erroneous reading does occur, the corresponding digital error generally is less when the gray scale is used. Compare the two scales for the digits 0 to 9. Discuss the gray scale advantage in terms of both the bit arrangements and the manner in which the most severe error may occur for the two scales.

5-13. Determine the angular resolution of an absolute encoder with 10 tracks.

5-14. Suppose BCD 8421 code is to be used on an eight-track optical encoder. Determine the angular resolution of this encoder and the coded output if the shaft angle is 1 rad. Sketch the relevant encoder segment.

5-15. To further convey the workings of the Maltese cross wrist sensor, consider a simply supported beam of length L, to which a moment M has been applied. The beam has a rectangular cross section, and the moment M is applied at the center of the beam in its plane of symmetry, as shown in Fig. E5-15. Assume that four strain gauges have been mounted a distance e from the center. Use voltage dividers to obtain the requisite voltages, as was done in Example 5-5. Use $G = 2$ and derive an expression for the moment M in terms of the output voltage of one of the strain gauge pairs. Explain why it does not matter which set of strain gauges is used to deduce the result.

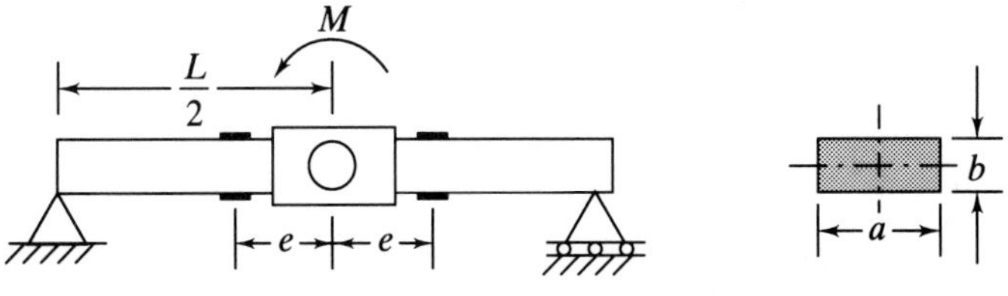

FIGURE E5-15

5-16. Suppose that the resistances R_1 and R_2 of the potentiometric circuit in Fig. E5-16 are changed by the same amount ΔR. Show that the system output v_0 remains the same if and only if $R_1 = R_2$.

5-17. Derive the expression

$$v_0 = \frac{v_R x}{L}\left[1 + \frac{R}{R_0}\left(\frac{x}{L}\right)\left(1 - \frac{x}{L}\right)\right]^{-1}$$

the output of the linear potentiometer shown in Fig. 5-5.

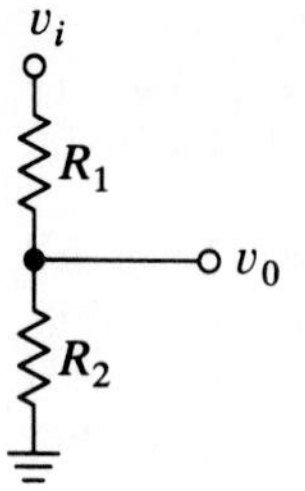

FIGURE E5-16

5-18. A planar two-arm manipulator is loaded with a weight W at its end effector. Suppose that the joint motors are to provide enough holding torque to maintain static equilibrium. One way of measuring the required torque is by measuring the individual joint torques via the current requirements. Suppose that the DC motors here have separate fields and armatures (see Chap. 7), so that the motor torques are proportional to the armature currents with $T = k_T i$, where k_T is the torque constant. If the current requirements are known to be i_1 and i_2 for the position shown in Fig. E5-18, determine the weight being held. What relationship, if any, exists between i_1 and i_2? Neglect the weight of the manipulator arms and motors.

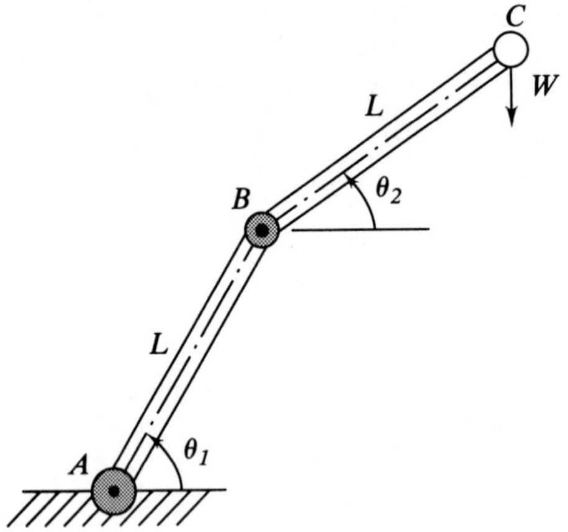

FIGURE E5-18

5-19. Provide the details for the derivation of the expression

$$R_{ij} = \frac{1000 v_{ij}}{5 - v_{ij}}$$

governing the circuits examplified in Fig. 5-25.

5-20. (From Gaillet and Reboulet[24]) There is a considerable variety of wrist sensors. One of the simplest (conceptually) is the one shown in Fig. E5-20. Six rods connect two disks. The end effector is connected to the upper plate. The six forces in the rods are measured with strain gauges and the results are then used to deduce force and moment resultants with respect to the *xyz*-frame. Suppose both disks have radius R and that they are separated by a height h. Let L denote the length of the rods.

(*a*) Write the forces $F_1, F_2, \ldots, F_6$ in vector form in terms of the unit vectors $\hat{\imath}$, $\hat{\jmath}$, and $\hat{k}$ along the *xyz*-axes. Write the vectors as emanating from the lower plate and terminating on the upper plate.

(*b*) Deduce the entries c_{ij} in the conversion matrix **C** in

$$\begin{pmatrix} F_x \\ F_y \\ F_z \end{pmatrix} = \mathbf{C} \begin{pmatrix} F_1 \\ \vdots \\ F_6 \end{pmatrix}$$

Use the abbreviations $a = R/2L$ and $b = h/L$.

(*c*) Discuss the possible advantages and disadvantages of this sensor.

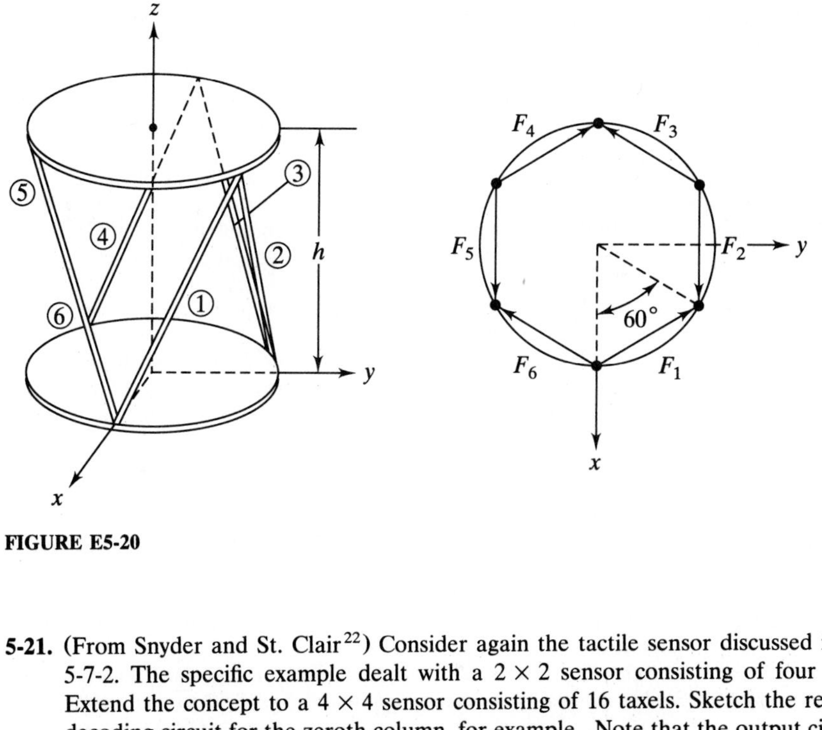

FIGURE E5-20

5-21. (From Snyder and St. Clair[22]) Consider again the tactile sensor discussed in Sec. 5-7-2. The specific example dealt with a 2×2 sensor consisting of four taxels. Extend the concept to a 4×4 sensor consisting of 16 taxels. Sketch the required decoding circuit for the zeroth column, for example. Note that the output circuitry must again allow for the addressing of the individual taxels.

5-22. In Sec. 5-7-1 we mentioned that the resolved force matrix **R** was sparse as long as the basic data were uncoupled measurements. Suppose they are uncoupled; deduce the basic structure of the matrix **R**. That is, you need not obtain specific expressions for the r_{ij}; you need only indicate which of them are generally nonzero. (*Hint:* View the basic data w_i in Fig. 5-22*b* as if they were forces.)

REFERENCES

1. Doebelin, E. O.: *Measurement Systems*, rev. ed., McGraw-Hill, New York, 1975.
2. Kennedy, E. J.: *Operational Amplifier Circuits: Theory and Applications*, Holt, Rinehart and Winston, New York, 1988.
3. Alloca, J. A., and A. Stuart: *Transducers: Theory and Applications*, Reston, Reston, Va., 1984.
4. Halliday, D., and R. Resnick: *Fundamentals of Physics*, 3rd ed., Wiley, New York, 1988.
5. Hannaway, O.: "E. H. Hall and Physics at Hopkins: The Background to Discovery," in C. L. Chien and C. R. Westgate (Eds.), *The Hall Effect and Its Applications*, Plenum, New York, 1980.
6. Hall, E. H.: "On a New Action of the Magnet on Electric Currents," *American Journal of Mathematics*, vol. 2, p. 287, 1879.
7. Hall, E. H.: "On the New Action of Magnetism on a Permanent Electric Current," *American Journal of Science*, ser. 3, vol. 20, p. 161, 1880.
8. Hurd, C. M.: *The Hall Effect in Metals and Alloys*, Plenum, New York, 1972.
9. Kittel, C.: *Introduction to Solid State Physics*, 5th ed., Wiley, New York, 1976.
10. Snyder, W. E.: *Industrial Robots: Computer Interfacing and Control*, Prentice-Hall, Englewood Cliffs, N.J., 1985.
11. Electro-Craft Corporation: *DC Motors, Speed Controls, Servo Systems, An Engineering Handbook*, 5th ed., Electro-Craft Corporation, Hopkins, Minn., 1980.
12. Webster, J. G. (Ed.): *Tactile Sensors for Robotics and Medicine*, Wiley, New York, 1988.
13. Russell, R. A.: *Robot Tactile Sensing*, Prentice-Hall, Englewood Cliffs, N.J., 1990.
14. Diesing, H., and K.-U. Schmucker: "Nonvisual Sensors for Industrial Robots" (in German), Dissertation submitted to the Academy of Sciences of the [former] German Democratic Republic, Institute of Automation, Berlin, 1990.
15. Scheinman, V. D.: "Design of a Computer Manipulator," Artificial Intelligence Laboratory Memo AIM-92, Stanford University, Palo Alto, Calif., 1969.
16. Bejczy, A. K.: "Smart Sensors for Smart Hands," *Proceedings of AAIA/NASA Conference on "Smart Hands*," November 1978, and *Progress in Astronautics and Aeronautics*, p. 67, 1980.
17. Shimano, B. E., and B. Roth: "On Force Sensing Information and Its Use in Controlling Manipulators," *Proceedings of the 9th International Symposium on Industrial Robots*, Washington, D.C., pp. 119–126, 1979.
18. Harmon, L. D.: "Automated Tactile Sensing," *International Journal of Robotics Research*, vol. 1, no. 2, pp. 1–32, 1982.
19. Larcombe, M. H. E.: "Tactile Sensing," Chapter 9 in *Robotic Engineering* (IEEE Control Engineering Series 23), edited by A. Pugh, Peter Peregrinus, London, 1983, pp. 97–102.
20. Seow, K. C.: "Capacitative Sensors," Chapter 10 in *Tactile Sensors for Robotics and Medicine*, edited by J. G. Webster, Wiley, New York, 1988, pp. 197–222.
21. Franco, S.: *Design with Operational Amplifiers and Analog Integrated Circuits*, McGraw-Hill, New York, 1988.
22. Larcombe, M. H. E.: "Tactile Sensing Using Digital Logic," *Proceedings, Shop Floor Automation Conference*, Birniehill Institute, National Engineering Laboratory, East Kilbride, Glasgow, December 11–13, 1973.
23. St. Clair, J., and W. E. Snyder: "Conductive Elastomers as a Sensor for Industrial Parts Handling Equipment," *IEEE Transactions on Instrumentation and Measurement*, vol. IM-27, no. 1, pp. 94–99, March 1978.
24. Gaillet, A., and C. Reboulet: "An Isostatic Six Component Force and Torque Sensor," *Proceedings of the 13th International Symposium on Industrial Robots*, Chicago, pp. 18-102–18-111, 1983.

CHAPTER

SIX

FROM PHOTON TO IMAGE IDENTIFICATION

6-1 INTRODUCTION

Computer—or, synonymously, "robotic"—vision systems are among the most complex electronic sensors in use. (They are also extremely compact and robust image acquisition systems for video recorders.) Although there are numerous texts and articles on image processing in general, little seems to have been written concerning the actual image acquisition process. The intent here is to guide the student through that process, from the emission of light to the interpretation of an acquired image.

We begin with a review of the general behavior of light, basically to define light intensity for quanta and waves. (As before, other basic concepts are reviewed when appropriate.) We continue with discussions of geometric optics, leading into the lensmaker's equation. The CCD (charge-coupled device) image sensor is then treated in considerable detail. The last part of the chapter provides an introduction to image processing and consideration of the camera's role in robotics systems.

We use some standard texts as desk references. For the electronic aspects of the area image sensor, we turn to the work by Sequin and Tompsett.[1] Some of the technological aspects are based on the Fairchild-Weston-Schlumberger 1987 databook.[2] The material concerning image processing is relatively standard material; we mention only Gonzalez and Wintz.[3] For much of the basic physics, the text by Halliday and Resnick[4] serves as the main source.

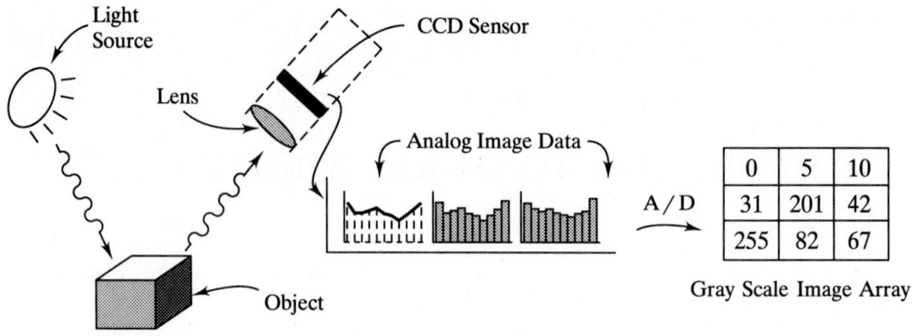

FIGURE 6-1
The image acquisition process.

A schematic of the process leading from the light source to an algebraic image array is depicted in Fig. 6-1. Photons are first emitted to illuminate an object. Next, the intensity of the reflected light is sensed, then registered as a part of some analog voltage array in the line readout of a single frame. Finally, the voltage array is converted to an algebraic array which can then be manipulated as an "image." Hopefully, this chapter will shed more light on the sensory procedure, giving the reader a clearer picture of computer vision systems.

6-2 SOME LIGHT REVIEW

In engineering it is generally assumed that a second course in college physics gives a student sufficient background on light and that memory will serve the student as needed. (In my case, neither held true.) It seems worthwhile to present a brief sketch of some basics.

Both the wave interpretation and the quantum interpretation are relevant. In the wave interpretation light is viewed as an electromagnetic wave governed by Maxwell's equations. In the quantum interpretation light is a stream of particles. Commonly, experiments may pin down one or the other aspect of light; both cannot be detected simultaneously. We have Bohr's principle of complementarity (as quoted in Halliday and Resnick[4]):

> The wave and particle aspects of a quantum entity are both necessary for a complete description. However, both aspects cannot be revealed in a single experiment. The aspect that is revealed is determined by the nature of the experiment being done.

Both aspects enter our "experiment"—to illuminate the objects and to measure light intensity. For the illumination the light is viewed as a wave. In the CCD sensor photon bundles are identified in terms of the corresponding amounts of charge.

How do we get light? Recall that the external electrons in an atom can arrange themselves only in certain energy states, each with its own energy E_i. The lowest of these levels is called the ground state E_0, and this state is arbitrarily taken as the datum with $E_0 = 0$.

When the energy state of an electron changes from a higher to a lower level, light is emitted in the process in accordance with Bohr's formula

$$E_2 - E_1 = h\nu \tag{6-1}$$

where ν is the frequency of the emitted light in hertz and where

$$h = 4.14 \times 10^{-15} \text{ eV} \cdot \text{s}$$

is Planck's constant. Typically, such a light emission takes about 10^{-8} s, and we may view the emitted light as a wave train several meters in length (Fig. 6-2). For simplicity, suppose we take light to be the electric component of the electromagnetic field vector, in the form of a moving sinusoidal wave (the E_m have nothing to do with the energy levels just mentioned):

$$E(x,t) = E_m \sin(kx - \omega t)$$

where the standard terminology is in use. That is,

$$\lambda = \frac{2\pi}{k} \text{ (m)}$$

is the *wavelength*, k is the *angular wave number* in radians/meter, and

$$\kappa = \frac{1}{\lambda} \text{ (m}^{-1}\text{)}$$

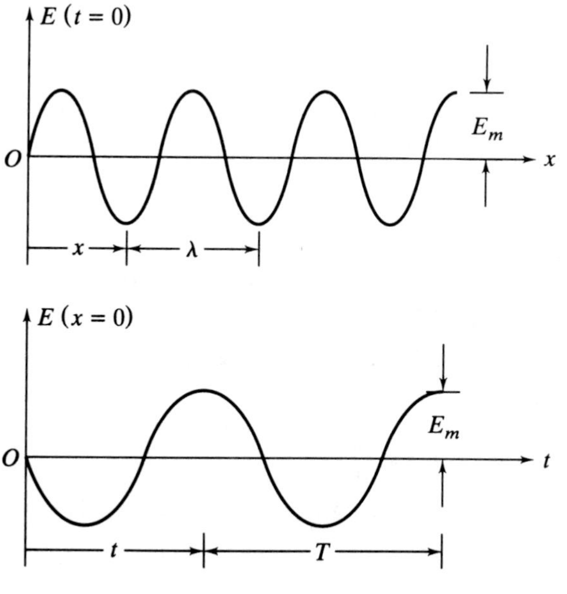

FIGURE 6-2
Light wave terminology.

is the *wave number*. Furthermore, with respect to the time domain, one has the *period*

$$T = \frac{2\pi}{\omega} \text{ (s)}$$

where ω is the *angular frequency* in radians/second, and

$$\nu = \frac{1}{T} \text{ (s}^{-1}\text{)}$$

is the frequency in hertz. In this context the *wave speed* is simply the speed of light, and we thus have

$$c = \frac{\omega}{k}$$

Remark 6-1. It is important to note that these concepts and terminology apply not only to the visible spectrum, but also to the whole electromagnetic spectrum (see Fig. 6-3). Note also that the visible spectrum is only a tiny fraction of the whole.

Recall that we are interested in measuring light intensity. We define the intensity of a light wave to be the average rate per unit area at which energy is transmitted by the wave. For an electromagnetic wave this energy transport is given by the Poynting vector

$$\boldsymbol{S} = \frac{1}{\mu_0}\boldsymbol{E} \times \boldsymbol{B} \left(\frac{\text{W}}{\text{m}^2}\right) \tag{6-2}$$

where $\boldsymbol{E}$ and $\boldsymbol{B}$ are the electric and magnetic field components, respectively, and

$$\mu_0 = 4\pi \times 10^{-7} \text{ H/m}$$

The direction of $\boldsymbol{S}$ at a point indicates the direction of energy transport at that point. The corresponding rate is given by the magnitude of $\boldsymbol{S}$,

$$|\boldsymbol{S}| = S(x,t) = \frac{1}{\mu_0}E(x,t)B(x,t)$$

when the wave is a plane wave, for example. The electric and magnetic field amplitudes are related by

$$c = \frac{E_m}{B_m} = \frac{E(x,t)}{B(x,t)}$$

so that

$$S(x,t) = \frac{1}{c\mu_0}E^2(x,t)$$

is the energy flow rate for a plane wave.

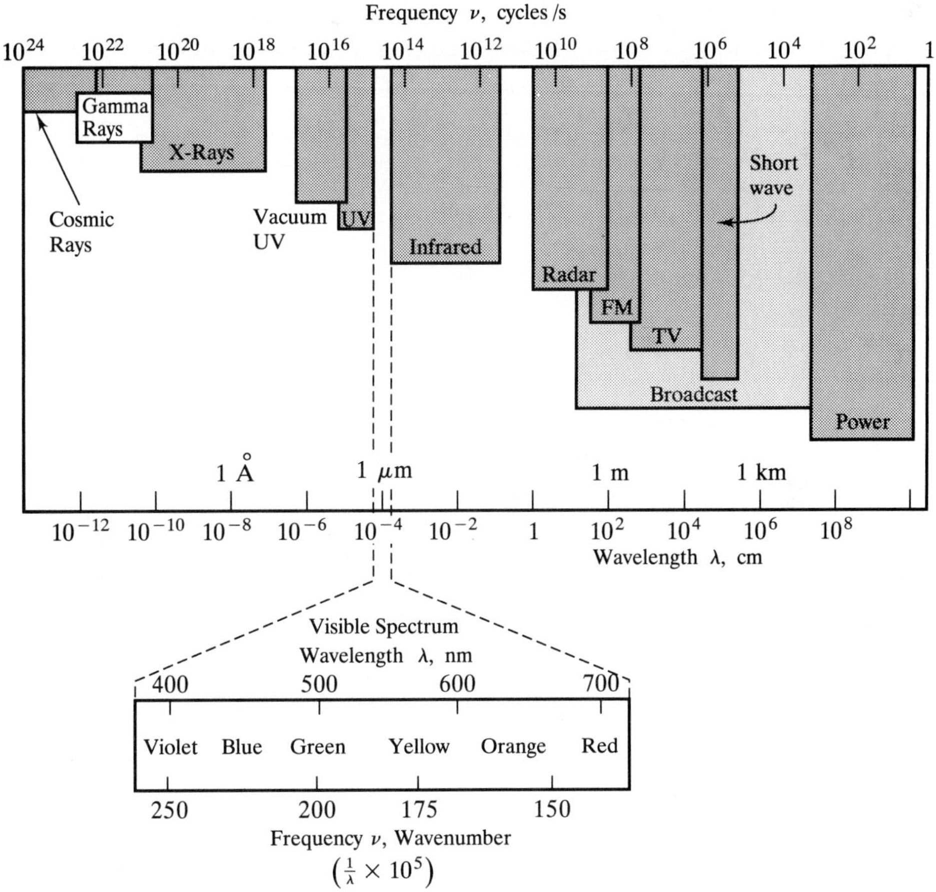

FIGURE 6-3
The electromagnetic spectrum. (*Source:* Martin D. Levine, *Vision in Man and Machine*, McGraw-Hill, New York, 1985. Reproduced with permission of McGraw-Hill.)

Definition 6-1 Intensity. The intensity I of an electromagnetic wave is given by the time average of the magnitude of the Poynting vector over a period T. That is, at the point P,

$$I(P) = \frac{1}{T}\int_0^T |S(P,t)|\,dt \left(\frac{\mathrm{W}}{\mathrm{m}^2}\right)$$

For the plane wave given previously, the intensity at a location x is given by

$$I(x) = \frac{1}{2}\frac{1}{c\mu_0}E_m^2$$

Since CCD imaging devices are essentially quantum detectors, the quantum view of light is of particular interest. In accordance with Einstein's hypothesis, one assumes that light behaves as if its energy were concentrated in discrete bundles called *light quanta* or *photons*. The energy in a single photon is given by

$$E = E_2 - E_1 = h\nu \tag{6-3}$$

The corresponding wavelength λ of the emitted light is determined from the relationship

$$c = \lambda \nu$$

Now, if E_s (photons/s · m^2) is the photon flux at some surface and if we take $h\nu$ to be the energy per photon, then the rate of energy transmitted per unit area is given by

$$N_s = E_s h\nu \left(\frac{\mathrm{W}}{\mathrm{m}^2}\right) \tag{6-4}$$

which we take to be the intensity for the quantum case.

As mentioned earlier, the photons striking the sensor are measured there in terms of the charge they generate. Such a photon-induced charge generation is called the *photoelectric effect*. When a photon of energy $h\nu$ hits an electron in some metal plate (or, for that matter, in some other body), then the maximum kinetic energy the electron may acquire is

$$K = h\nu - \phi \tag{6-5}$$

where ϕ is the *work function* for the metal—that is, the minimum amount of energy required to surmount the potential barrier that exists at the metal surface. Let V_0 be the potential that will stop the fastest electron emitted in this manner; then

$$K = eV_0$$

or

$$V_0 = \left(\frac{h}{e}\right)\nu - \frac{\phi}{e}$$

Since we require $V_0 \geq 0$, there clearly exists a minimum frequency ν_0 below which no electron will be knocked loose,

$$\nu_0 = \frac{\phi}{h}$$

Photons with insufficient energy will not free any electrons and hence generate no charge. This provides a lower bound for the sensor; no electromagnetic wave with frequency $\nu \leq \nu_0$ can be sensed.

We close our discussion with an estimation of the charge generated within the sensor cell by the incident photon flux. In accordance with Pinson,[6] we take this charge to be given by

$$Q_s = E_s \eta \tau q(ab) \text{ (C)} \tag{6-6}$$

where η is the detector quantum efficiency (charge carriers per photon; a work function of sorts), τ (seconds) is the charge carrier's mean lifetime, q is the electronic charge (coulombs), and ab is the sensor surface area.

We have presented only the simplest possible discussion, enough for a fundamental understanding of the behavior of light. In particular, we have omitted any discussion of the reflection and absorption of light by illuminated objects, and all of the discussion involved only light at a single wavelength. Generally, a whole band of wavelengths is present and an integration over λ is needed to account for the total effect.

6-3 LENSES

In dealing with solid-state vision sensors, it is easy to get so involved in the sensor electronics and the image analysis that we tend to forget that *the image we capture is only as good as the optics we use*! The solid-state sensor is located in the focal plane of the camera assembly. Only when the object is of the order of magnitude of the sensor (about 1 cm^2) may we obtain an image without the optics. In this section we briefly review the lensmaker's equation and some of the related terminology of geometric optics.

Geometric optics is just another treatment of light—namely, its treatment in applications where light may be considered as rays represented by straight lines. Recall that in analytic geometry we define a parabola as the set of points (x, y) which are equidistant from a point (the focus of the parabola) and a fixed line (the directrix of the parabola). In addition, if we construct a mirror in the form of a parabola, then the reflections of all light rays *parallel* to the axis of the parabola pass through the *focus* of the parabola (see Fig. 6-4*a*).

It is this ideal situation that is used to define the focal distance for the reflection and refraction of light rays on other surfaces, in particular, spherical surfaces. For such surfaces a focus will exist only in an approximate fashion, the approximation usually being based on the assumption of small angles of incidence, reflection, and refraction (see Fig. 6-4*b*). For example, for the spherical mirror (see Fig. 6-4*c*), let P_o be a point object or light source, and let P_i be an image formed at the approximate focus. Then the inner rays will reflect from the mirror's surface and pass through the image point, while rays farther out will not. Those rays that pass through the image point are called *paraxial* rays. Those that do not produce a blurring of the image called *spherical aberration*. For a spherical mirror the object distance s_o, the focal distance f, and the image distance s_i are related by

$$\frac{1}{s_o} + \frac{1}{s_i} = \frac{1}{f} \tag{6-7}$$

where $f = \frac{1}{2}r$ (see Exercise 6-6); F is the focal point, and C is the center of curvature. As a sign and image convention, we term images "behind" the mirror as virtual, and we take the corresponding image distance to be negative. The plane perpendicular to the axis and passing through F is termed the *focal plane*. We have mentioned spherical mirrors here to lead up to lenses and because they could conceivably serve to focus an object on the sensor.

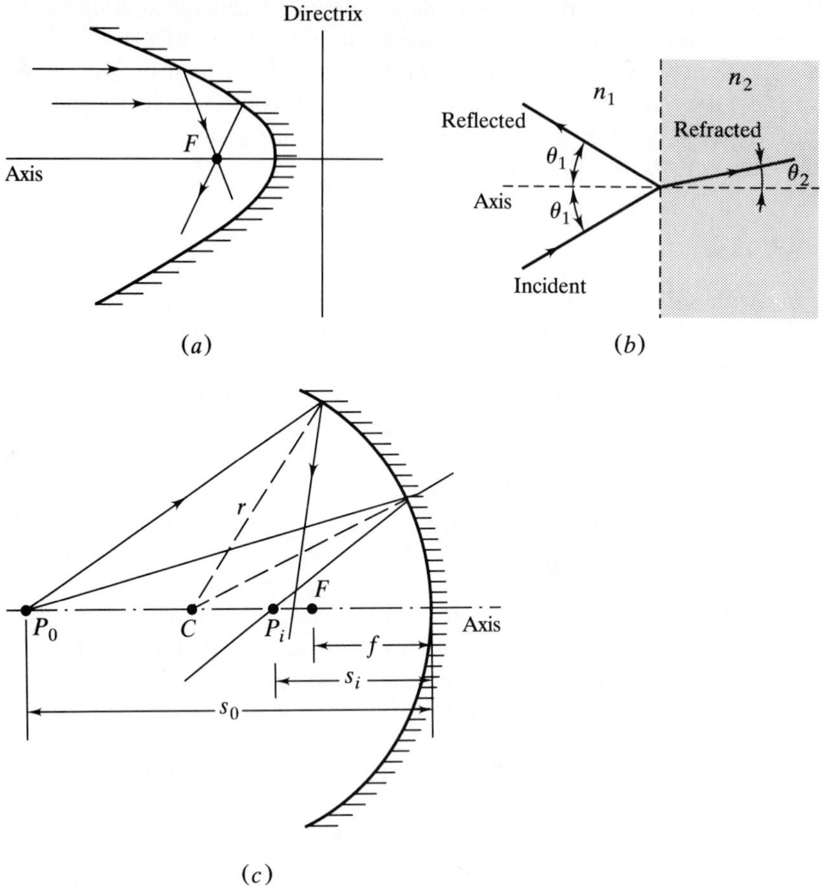

FIGURE 6-4
Basic reflection and refraction.

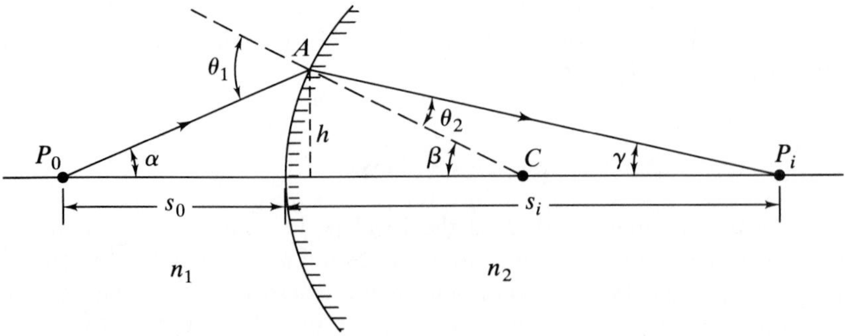

FIGURE 6-5
Refraction at a spherical surface.

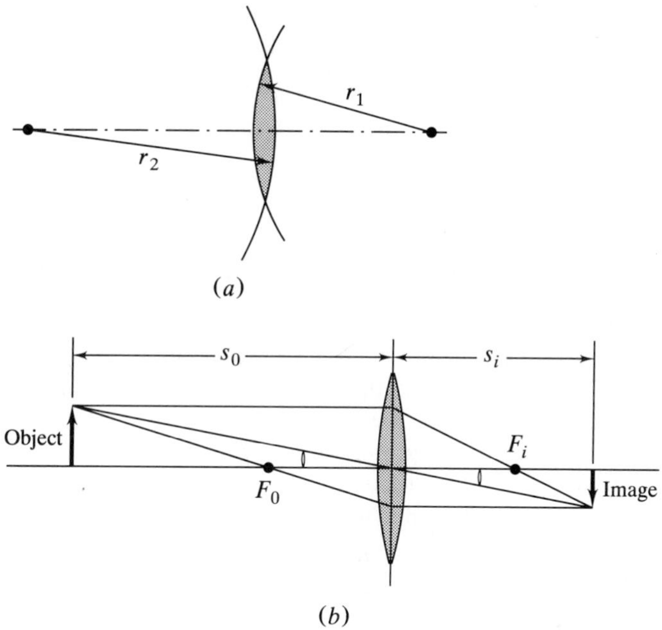

FIGURE 6-6
The thin, doubly convex lens.

Our main concern, however, is the lensmaker's equation. The equation is developed from the refraction of light rays in a spherical surface separating two media with refraction indices n_1 and n_2 (Fig. 6-5). Snell's law,

$$n_1 \sin \theta_1 = n_2 \sin \theta_2$$

together with the assumption of "small" angles, may be used to derive the equation

$$\frac{n_1}{s_o} + \frac{n_2}{s_i} = \frac{n_2 - n_1}{r} \tag{6-8}$$

where s_o is the object distance, s_i is the image distance, and r is the radius of the spherical surface. The primary use of (6-8) is made in the derivation of the lensmaker's equation.

To derive this equation for thin lenses, (6-8) is used twice, once for each surface, with the image resulting from the first use taken as the object for the second. The ultimate result (see Fig. 6-6) is the equation

$$\frac{1}{s_o} + \frac{1}{s_i} = (n - 1)\left(\frac{1}{r_1} - \frac{1}{r_2}\right) \tag{6-9}$$

where s_o and s_i are the object and image distances, respectively, n is the refraction index of the lens material, and r_1 and r_2 are the radii of curvature of the lens surfaces. The *focal* distance for a thin lens is defined to be the image distance corresponding to a large object distance. Thus, with $s_o = \infty$ and $s_i = f$, we have

$$\frac{1}{f} = (n - 1)\left(\frac{1}{r_1} - \frac{1}{r_2}\right) \tag{6-10}$$

For the thin, doubly convex lens in Fig. 6-6, r_1 is considered to be a positive radius and r_2 is taken as negative because the center of curvature of the second surface lies on the left, or virtual, side of the surface.

In calculations with lenses it is useful to set up a ray diagram based on the definition of the focal lengths. One obtains the two focal points by assuming parallel rays either from the right or from the left. The points on the left and right of the lens, a distance f_o and f_i from the lens, are denoted by F_o and F_i and are called the first and the second focal points, respectively (see Fig. 6-6*b*). Planes through F_o and F_i and perpendicular to the axis of the lens are again called focal planes.

6-4 THE VIDICON TUBE

The eyes of a robot vision system are television cameras, which provide a real-time image of the surroundings of the robot. Since the early 1980s, solid-state cameras have been used almost exclusively for this purpose. Prior to their introduction, the vidicon camera was in extensive use, and we present it here because it still serves as an excellent introduction to terminology, concepts, and industry standards.

The vidicon tube is an optoelectronic transducer. It takes optical data and presents them in the form of electrical output. The basic structure of the tube is illustrated in Fig. 6-7.

The image is first formed on the glass *faceplate* which lies in the focal plane of the optical lens. There are two additional layers attached to the faceplate. The first layer is a transparent conducting metal film which serves as the electrode, providing the video signal. The second layer, the *target layer*, is a thin film of photosensitive material deposited on the metal layer. It consists of densely packed segments whose electrical resistance decreases with increasing photon intensity. Thus the amount of current that can flow through such a conductive segment is a function of the light intensity. Following the target layer, there is a positively charged fine wire mesh. The cathode ray gun on the left emits a low-velocity electron beam which is focused and directed by the corresponding coils. Upon arrival at the target layer, the electrons are slowed to zero velocity by the positively charged wire mesh. This arrangement is used to generate the electronic image.

A positive potential is applied to the metal layer. The electron beam scans the target layer. The target layer then behaves like a dielectric and becomes a

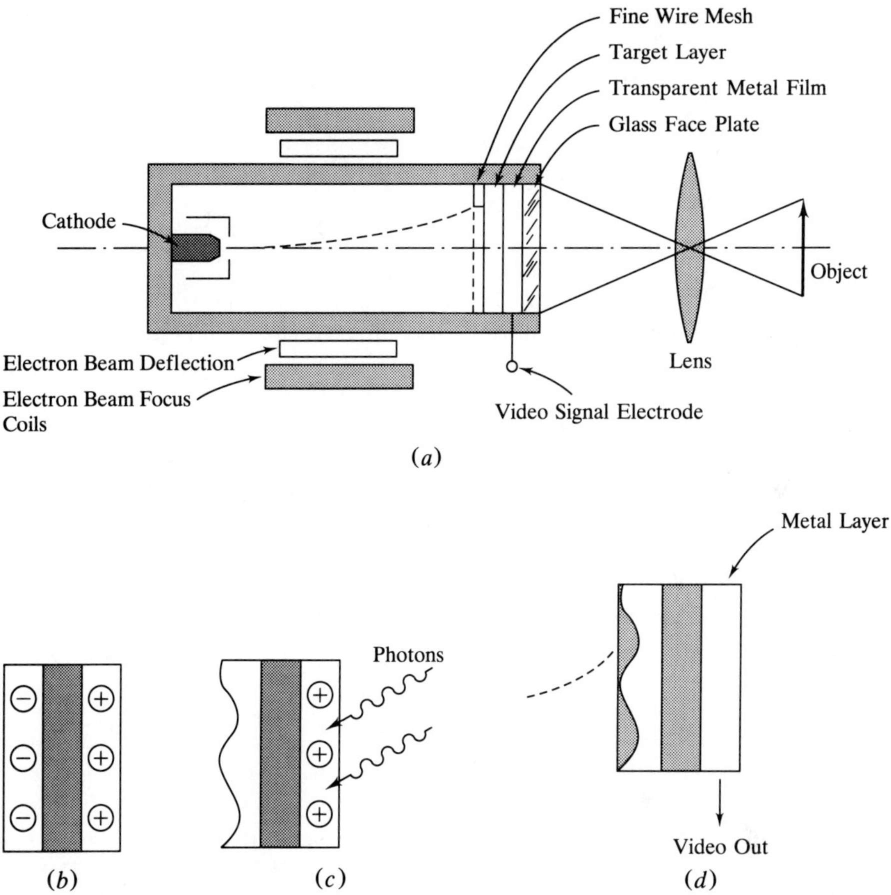

FIGURE 6-7
The vidicon tube: (*a*) schematic of vidicon tube; (*b*) target layer as capacitor; (*c*) electron image profile; (*d*) replenishment and video.

capacitor, with the positive potential on the right just matched by the negative electrons deposited on the left. We now allow light to hit the target layer, all the while keeping the metal layer at a constant positive potential. The local light intensity then produces a reduction in the resistance of the corresponding segment of the target layer. Enough current flows to leave an electron potential proportional to the light intensity. The process eventually produces an electron distribution on the left of the target layer which is proportional to the light intensity at each point—that is, an electronic image.

Now, when the electron beam again scans the target layer, it replaces the lost charge, causing a corresponding current to flow in the metal layer which serves as the video signal electrode. After suitable processing and amplification, this produces a voltage train whose pulse magnitudes are proportional to the light intensity and whose order mimics the scanning sequence. The repeated scanning process is carried out in accordance with the conventions described later in this section.

It is difficult to provide a theoretical quantification for the image acquisition process just described. Suffice it to say that the potential field representing the image consists of a charge accumulation

$$q(x, y; t_F) = \int_0^{t_F} kN(x, y; t)\, dt$$

where $q(x, y; t)$ is the charge intensity in coulombs/square meter, $q(x, y; 0) = 0$, k (coulombs/joule) is a constant depending on the film composition, $N(x, y; t)$ is the incident light intensity implying that both the photon flux E and the frequency ν may now vary with position and time, and where t_F is the *frame time* (see the following discussion). If the frame time is short enough, it may suffice to take $q(x, y; t_F) = t_F kN(x, y; \bar{t})$ for some $\bar{t} \in [0, t_F]$ for a continuously (in t) distributed N. Thus the charge intensity is proportional to the light intensity.

More generally, one may take an output video signal $I(x, y)$ to be related to the input image (either reflected or transmitted light) by the equation (Levine[5])

$$I(x, y) = kN(x, y)^{\gamma}$$

where k is again a constant and γ is a parameter, depending on the particular photoelectric transducer chosen. Thus $\gamma \approx 1.0$ for the silicon-based sensor which will be considered here, whereas $\gamma = 0.65$ for the vidicon tube.

With this approach it is clearly not possible to scan all points on the screen, nor is it possible to know the precise location of the electron beam. One therefore subdivides the screen into a grid of rectangles, with centers (x_i, y_i) serving as the coordinates of the charge accumulated over the particular rectangle. That is, we take $q(x_i, y_i; t_F) = t_F kN(x_i, y_i; \bar{t})$ as the charge distribution for the whole rectangle (called a *pixel*, an acronym derived from "picture elements"). The screen may now be subdivided into lines and columns of pixels. The number of pixels per line (i.e., the number of columns) is the *horizontal resolution*, and the number of lines per faceplate is the *vertical resolution*. The total number of pixels per faceplate is sometimes termed the *sensor resolution*.

These conventions and terms are illustrated in Fig. 6-8. There, the horizontal resolution is 12, the vertical resolution is 9, and the sensor resolution is $9 \times 12 = 108$. We have chosen the axes to conform with $(x, y) \sim$ (row, column) for ease in identifying the elements of the image matrix, which we shall subsequently introduce.

To assure the compatibility of the many different types of television cameras and monitors, they are constructed in accordance with the RS-170 standard as prescribed by the American Electronics Industry Association (EIA).

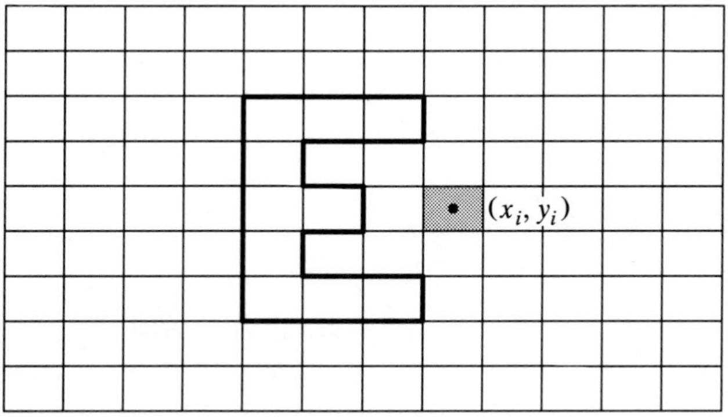

FIGURE 6-8
Image resolution and orientation.

In the United States the total field (faceplate) consists of 525 horizontal lines, 40 of which are used for timing and synchronization information, with 300 to 512 samples taken per line. (By comparison, European television has a vertical resolution of 625 lines.)

The image field is scanned in two segments from top to bottom and from left to right. The scanning electron beam first scans the odd field consisting of lines $1, 3, 5, \ldots, 523, 525$, and then it scans the even field consisting of lines $2, 4, 6, \ldots, 522, 524$. The beam is *blanked* between lines (horizontal blanking), that is, as it moves from the end of one line to the beginning of the next. It is blanked once more as the beam moves from one field to the next (vertical blanking). The scanning of each field requires 1/60th of a second, the *field time*, with the whole image being scanned in 1/30th of a second, commonly termed the *frame time* t_F.

For each pixel location, the output from the camera is an analog voltage, so that the image lines are essentially continuous voltage distributions separated by blanking and synchronization pulses, as shown in Fig. 6-9. This type of video signal is termed *composite video*; when the synchronization pulses are omitted, the video is termed *noncomposite*.

A common sensor size used in robotics is 512 × 512. Note also that the system resolution is actually the dominant concept, since it limits the amount of information that can be processed and displayed. Thus it is possible to use a 1024 × 1024 camera on a 510 × 484 system; however, all that the user ever sees is 510 × 484.

We have used this limited discussion of the vidicon tube to introduce the basic image acquisition process and related standard operating procedures. As mentioned earlier, our emphasis is on the solid-state vision sensor. We now turn to a relatively detailed analysis of this sensor, followed by some of the most fundamental concepts and ideas of image processing.

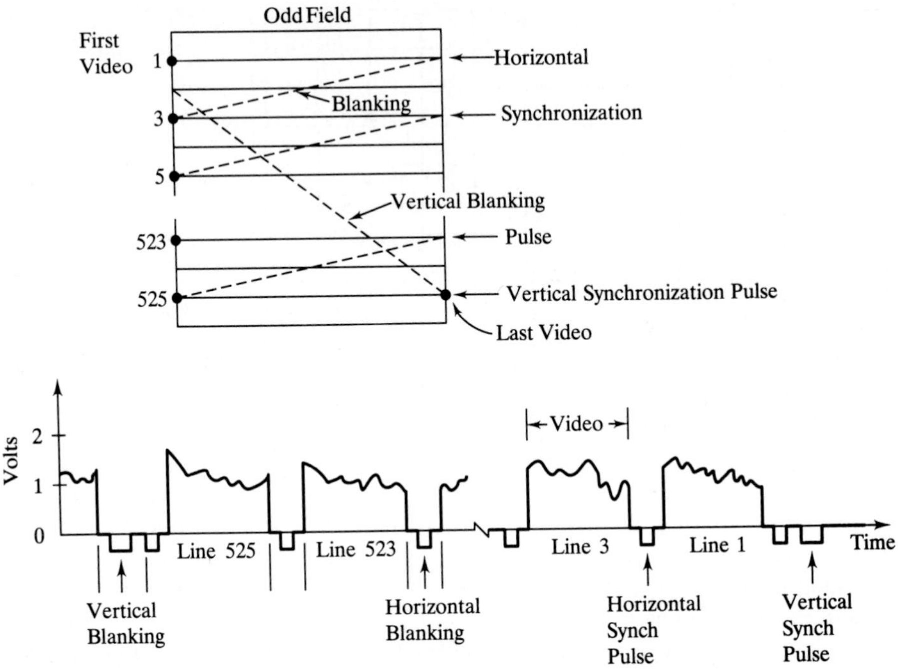

FIGURE 6-9
Odd field video signal.

6-5 SOLID-STATE VISION SYSTEMS

Solid-state vision sensors are used almost exclusively. Their advantages are many and their faults are likely to be resolved in the near future. Image sensors with high resolution are taken to be among the most challenging problems of very large scale integration (VLSI) technology.

No previous discussion was found that presented imaging fundamentals from photon to image identification, including all of the electronics relevant to image acquisition. What we present here is based on the reading and study of numerous articles as well as material stemming from Sequin and Tompsett,[1] the Fairchild-Weston-Schlumberger 1987 databook,[2] and Pinson.[6] Two tutorial articles (one by Gilbert F. Amelio and another by Frank H. Bower in the Fairchild-Weston-Schlumberger 1987 databook[2]) and survey articles by R. H. Dyck[7,8] were also useful.

The figures are generally schematics, and sketches of the actual device construction are sometimes also included. Theoretical models and quantitative estimates are included only when the basics of the modeling effort do not exceed the level of the presentation.

For solid-state imaging devices, the pixels, which previously were simply a subdivision of a continuous imaging field, are individual sensors arranged on a single chip, with resolutions equalling and exceeding those found in the usual television image acquisition systems. In summary, solid-state imaging devices consist of three components: (1) a photosensitive array of pixels, (2) a scanning structure to collect the information recorded by the individual sensors, and (3) a charge-sensing preamplifier which provides the video output.

There are two basic approaches to solid-state image acquisition: charge injection devices (CIDs) and charge-coupled devices (CCDs). For CIDs, each pixel location contains two adjacent MOS capacitors which may be independently addressed. They may be used separately or together to form a potential well in which a photogenerated charge may collect. By pulsing them individually, the charge may be shifted between them without signal degradation, or they may be set to 0 simultaneously, resulting in dumping of the charge into the substrate, where it may then be detected as current. There are now many variations of this approach.

Charge-coupled devices may also be classified by the manner in which local light intensity is registered. One approach uses photodiodes as the individual sensors. The photocurrent is integrated and the resulting charge is capacitatively stored on the diode. Charge-coupled shift registers are then used to scan the array and to provide the video output. The result is called a charge-coupled photo diode (CCPD) device. The second approach uses photosensitive CCDs to sense the image, again in terms of charge; CCD shift registers are used to scan the image array.

The advantages and disadvantages of these approaches are extensively discussed in Sequin and Tompsett.[1] Our emphasis here will be on CCDs, and we shall thus provide only a brief comparison of the latter two methods mentioned previously.

The low-output capacitance of the CCD imager simplifies the low-level signal extraction; the higher-output capacitance of the photodiodes makes this more difficult. The major drawback of the CCD imagers, of course, is the semitransparent electrode that covers the sensing area. It produces optical interference throughout the visible spectrum. In particular, the strong absorption at short wavelengths drastically limits the blue response. According to Dyck[7]:

> The fundamental limitations on spectral response are these internal response limitations: the long wavelength-limiting response set by the thickness of the silicon chip, and the short wavelength limit set by the onset of photoemission into the oxide.

Effectively, then, the silicon detector response is limited to wavelengths between 200 and 1100 nm.

A historical sketch of the discovery of photoconductivity in different materials is given by Schroder.[9] He notes that the photoconductive effect was first observed by Smith[10] in 1873 when he experimented with selenium as an insulator for submarine cables. A thallous sulfide detector using this effect was first demonstrated in 1917. A serious effort to develop infrared detectors was mounted in Germany and in the United States just prior to World War II. Photoconductivity in silicon was first reported by Burstein et al.[11] in 1951. The CCD was invented by William Boyle and George Smith[12] in 1969 at Bell Laboratories.

6-5-1 The CCD Shift Register

We begin the more detailed discussion of the monolithic image sensor array with the shift register. We chose to do so since the arrangement of the photocells depends on the manner in which the charge packets are removed from the array of photocells. In brief, we have the following description of an analog shift register (Sequin and Tompsett[1]):

> A charge transfer device is essentially an assembly of transfer electrodes interconnected in a periodic manner which, when properly pulsed, produce a moving array of potential wells.

This charge transfer is made possible by coupling and shaping the depletion regions of adjacent MOS devices. There are a number of different device structures that can be used to shift charge packets, such as surface channel, bulk channel, or bucket brigade devices. Within imaging arrays two-phase bulk channel CCDs appear to be most prevalent. Our discussion is limited to this type of device.

The potential well concept is a great aid in visualizing charge transfer. We introduce the concept by means of the simple MOS capacitor depicted in Fig. 6-10a, consisting of a metal gate, an oxide layer, two p^+ channel stops

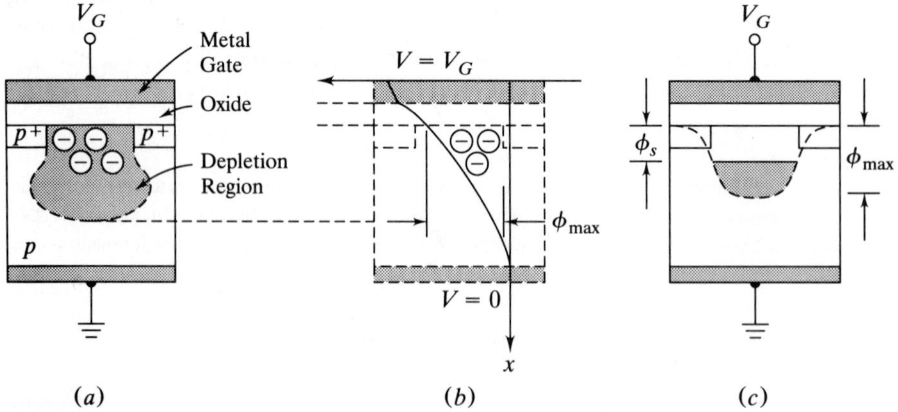

FIGURE 6-10
(a) MOS capacitor and depletion region; (b) potential distribution across the capacitor; (c) potential well.

(which shape the depletion region and keep charge from leaking into an adjacent device), a p-type substrate, and a metal electrode at the bottom. A voltage V_G is applied across this junction. The result is a potential distribution ranging from 0 to V_G, as shown in Fig. 6-10b. The shaded depletion region is assumed to be initially free of minority carriers (electrons). Because of the potential distribution, any electrons that are generated in the depletion region (either by injection or by incident photons) tend to gather at the interface between the oxide and the substrate in a "potential well." It is common and suggestive to depict this potential well as shown in Fig. 6-10c, where ϕ_s is taken as increasing with the distance from the interface, ϕ_{max} being the maximum potential difference attained within the depletion region. As the charge Q_s collected in the well increases, the interface potential decreases. This eventually leads to the collapse of the depletion region.

When these "capacitors" are connected in sequence, the charges may be made to move from well to well by proper pulsing of suitably connected electrodes. Of course, the electrons do not really move from well to well; in fact, they move along the $Si–SiO_2$ interface. This leads to certain performance limitations, among them surface trapping (see Sequin and Tompsett[1]). These limitations may be avoided by moving the potential well deeper into the substrate, an approach taken in buried channel or equivalently bulk channel CCDS. The implantation of an intermediate layer of opposite polarity to that of the substrate (Fig. 6-11a) yields the shifted potential distribution shown in Fig. 6-11b and hence lowers the well to the position shown in Fig. 6-11c. Rather than traveling along the $Si–SiO_2$ interface, the charge now always moves within the doped region, which allows more rapid charge transfer.

To obtain a proper shift register, n of these "capacitors" are now lined up in sequence in contact with one another, with judiciously attached transfer

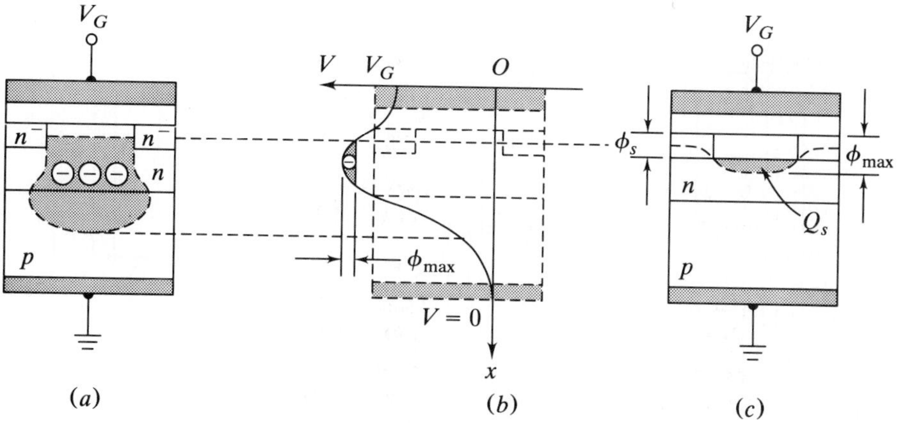

FIGURE 6-11
(a) MOS capacitor with n-implant; (b) potential distribution; (c) potential well.

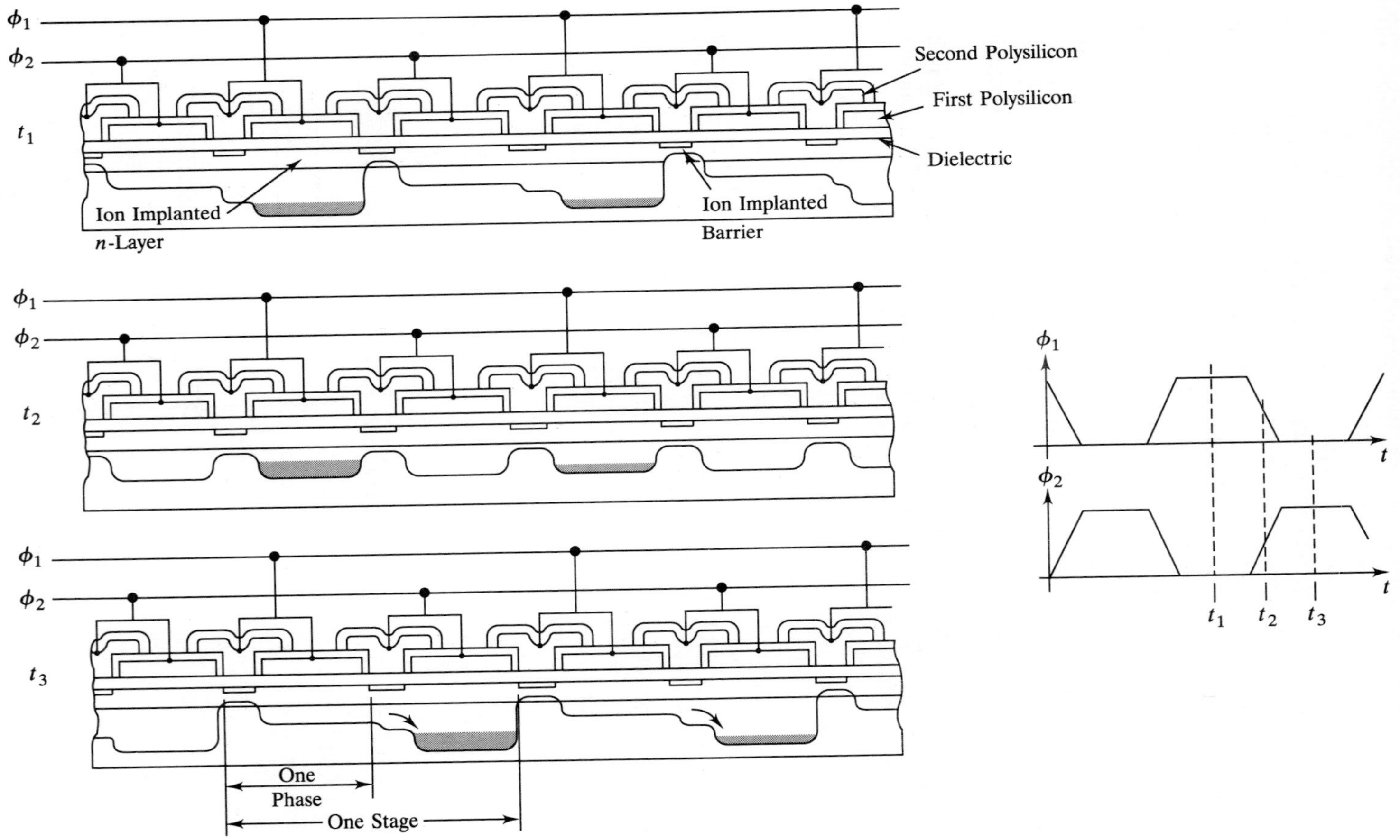

FIGURE 6-12
Two-phase charge transfer. (Used with permission of Loral Fairchild Imaging Sensors.)

electrodes. Placed closely enough together, the depletion regions of any two adjacent "capacitors" will overlap and the potential wells will couple. Charge will then "flow" to the deepest part of the combined well.

There are many arrangements of transfer electrodes which, when pulsed, will produce such a flow of charge. An electrode arrangement for two-phase transfer is depicted in Fig. 6-12. Again, there are a number of ways in which such a two-phase system may be pulsed. (One such pulsing sequence is shown at the right of the figure.) The figure exhibits the three stages of charge locations corresponding to the three times indicated in the clocking diagram. Note that only half a clocking cycle is required to shift the charge from one phase to the next.

Remark 6-2. Note that the implanted barriers produce an asymmetric potential well profile. This asymmetry has two consequences. It makes the two-phase transfer possible, and the charge can be made to move only to the right no matter what clocking cycle combination is used. Without this built-in asymmetry, a minimum of three clock phases would be required.

In essence, a shift register functions like a discretized Archimedean screw. To continue the mechanical analogy, suppose we consider the asymmetrical piston arrangement shown in Fig. 6-13. The fluid is obviously equivalent to the charge, the piston shapes provide the asymmetric potential distribution, and the crankshaft and connecting rods provide the timing for the fluid transfer.

Finally, to allow the reader to become aware of the actual complexity of the monolithic chip, including the required manufacturing difficulties, a realistic cross section of a chip segment is shown in Fig. 6-14.

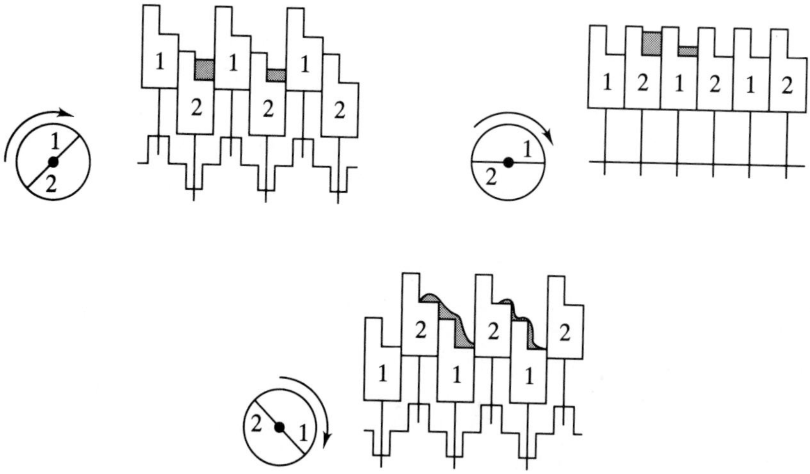

FIGURE 6-13
Asymmetric pistons as a mechanical analogy to two-phase charge transfer. (Used with permission of Loral Fairchild Imaging Sensors.)

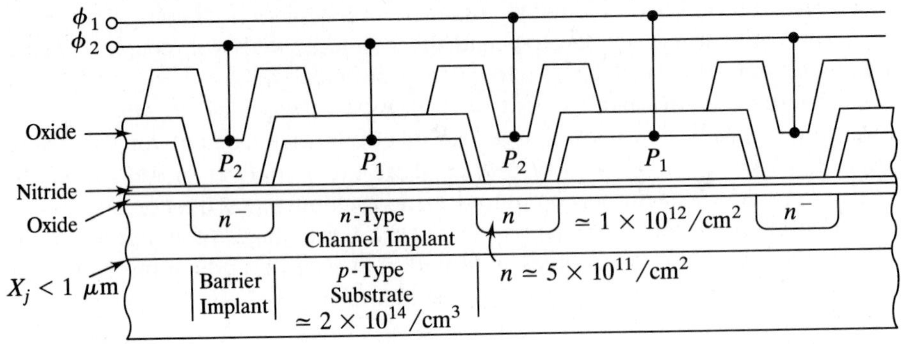

FIGURE 6-14
Two-phase implanted barrier CCD structure. (*Source:* R. H. Dyck, "VLSI Imagers," in *VLSI Handbook*, Academic Press, New York, 1985. Used with permission of Academic.)

At this point, the reader might have the impression that the speed of charge transfer depends only on the chosen clock timing. In fact, there is an upper and a lower frequency limit to charge transfer. In addition to the desirable charge accumulation, such as photon-induced charge, there exists another ever-present source of charge called *dark current*. Typically, this restricts operation to about 2 kHz minimum, since the dark current then tends to become the dominant signal generator. At the upper limit there is a certain amount of "charge inertia" to be overcome, for example, the amount of time it takes the charge to move from one storage site to the next. In addition, there is a limit on the possible rise time for a clock pulse. Generally, these provide for an upper limit of about 20 MHz (Dyck[7].)

When the CCD shift register is used as part of an imaging device, the charge input is due to the photon flux at the photosites. These photon-generated charge packets are then transferred to the register. Usually, several registers are interconnected in order to provide an image output at some final collection point. This interconnection is generally accomplished by joining the depletion regions of two adjacent storage cells and applying appropriate transfer voltage pulses.

Figure 6-15 depicts schematics of some standard image acquisition arrangements. In the sketches the shift registers are shaded and the photosites are left white. The arrows indicate the direction of charge transfer.

It was noted earlier that the image is acquired in two segments for television usage. The odd field is read out first, followed by the even field. Subsequently, the full image is again displayed on a television monitor. It is common to recreate the image by first "writing out" the odd field in 1/60 s; the even field is then written in between in another 1/60 s. This process is called *interlacing*; it reduces the apparent flicker of a television image. In order to be compatible with such monitors, the same interlaced format is used with CCD images.

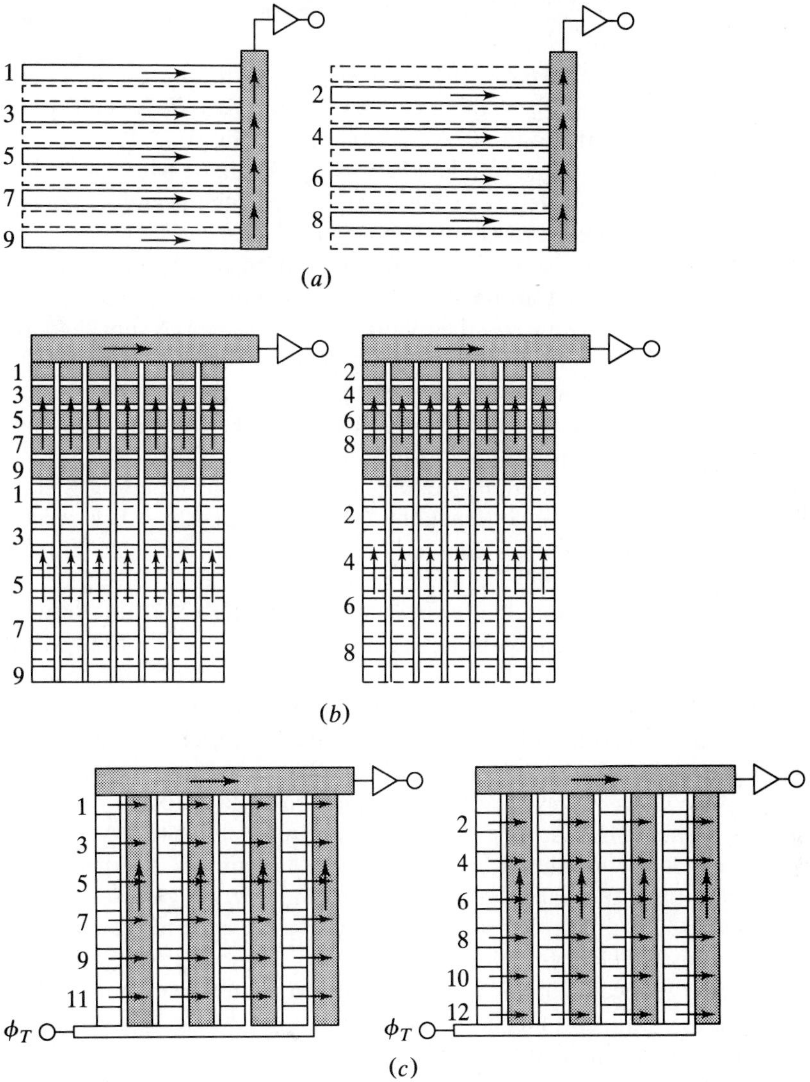

FIGURE 6-15
Array structures: (*a*) line-by-line transfer CCD; (*b*) frame transfer CCD; (*c*) interline transfer CCD.

We shall exhibit three image acquisition arrangements: a line-by-line transfer CCD, a frame transfer CCD, and an interline transfer CCD. In each case we provide a pair of sketches, one for each field transfer.

For the line-by-line transfer CCD, each field is first shifted horizontally, line by line, then transferred to the vertical shift register, where they are shifted in sequence to the video output. To maintain proper spacing at the video output, each line transfer must be timed to account for the different times needed to get to the output.

For the frame transfer device, the photosites and the storage cells are arranged in vertical columns. The wells under rows 1 and 2, 3 and 4, and so on are coupled. To acquire the odd field, the photosites in rows $1, 3, \ldots$ are activated; that is, wells are formed under these rows. At the frame integration time t_F, the whole field is shifted vertically and stored in the shielded storage area. The photosites in the even rows are then activated. During the exposure of the even field, the previously stored odd rows are shifted one by one into the horizontal shift register and transferred to the video output. For two-phase registers the alternate exposure of the photosites is easily accomplished by setting ϕ_1 and ϕ_2 to form the wells under the appropriate photosites. The process is, of course, analogous for the even field.

For the devices we have just discussed, the shift registers (shaded segments) are shielded from light. The photosites, however, operate in the staring mode. That is, no shuttering is employed while the photosites operate as shift registers; charge continues to be generated by the incident photons. This results in what is termed *image smearing*—charge is being added to the signal from a particular site while it passes under another exposed site.

This image smearing is avoided in the interline transfer CCD. In essence, each photosite has associated with it a corresponding storage site. More precisely, one storage cell is used for two photosites, since we again need to store only the odd or the even field at a given time. Thus photosites 1 and 2 in the first column are coupled and one storage cell in the adjacent vertical shift register is set to receive the accumulated charge under site 1 for the odd field and that under site 2 for the even field. To acquire the odd field, for example, potential wells are established under all of the odd-row photosites. At $t = t_F$, *all* of the photosites are shuttered by an appropriate setting of the *photogate* voltage ϕ_p, preventing the accumulation of charge; the *transfer gate* voltage ϕ_T is simultaneously set to allow the field of charges to transfer to wells in the vertical shift registers. The even field is then exposed. During this exposure the odd field is shifted vertically line by line and transferred to the horizontal shift register one line at a time and thence to the video output. Again, all of the shift registers are, of course, shielded.

Some of this discussion will be expanded upon in our more detailed presentation of the photosites as segments of the monolithic two-phase interline transfer CCD imager.

We now turn briefly to some of the inherent performance limitations for these devices. Frequency bounds and image smearing have already been mentioned; a more quantitative treatment of others follows. Extensive discussions of these topics may be found in Sequin and Tompsett.[1]

DARK CURRENT. The main cause of electron generation is the incident photon flux. A lesser, though more ubiquitous cause is thermal generation. The current that flows during the unillumined time is called the *dark current*, and we write

$$i(t) = i_p(t) + i_d(t)$$

(p—photon; d—dark) for the total current. The dark current assures that the potential well will eventually fill up after some time t_{sat}.

When this happens the depletion region capacitance discharges, the voltage across the region decreases, and the width of the region narrows. The voltage drop across the region ultimately decreases to the amount needed to maintain the potential well at equilibrium where the flow of electrons into the well is balanced by the outward diffusion of electrons back into the p-type substrate. This equilibrium voltage is generally 500 to 700 mV, and the corresponding saturation time, t_{sat}, at which this happens lies between 3 and 30 s. Generally, the integration time t_F should be such that the charge due to the dark current is no more than 1% of Q_{sat}, the total charge at saturation.

Example 6-1. Consider an individual photosite when viewed as a capacitor (see Fig. 6-16). Use this model to obtain an estimate of the saturation time t_{sat}. For a gate oxide thickness of 1000 Å, the capacitance between the gate electrode and the n-type surface inversion layer is 3.4×10^{-8} F/cm^2. Assume a dark current density of 100 nA/cm^2 and a gate voltage of 10 V.

Solution. The total capacitance for the pixel is

$$C = 3.4 \times 10^{-8} \frac{\text{F}}{\text{cm}^2} \times \frac{10^4 \text{ cm}^2}{\text{m}^2} \times (13 \times 10^{-6})(17 \times 10^{-6}) \text{ m}^2$$

$$= 0.07514 \text{ pF}$$

For a 10-V gate voltage, the charge at saturation is

$$Q_{sat} = CV = 0.7514 \text{ pC}$$

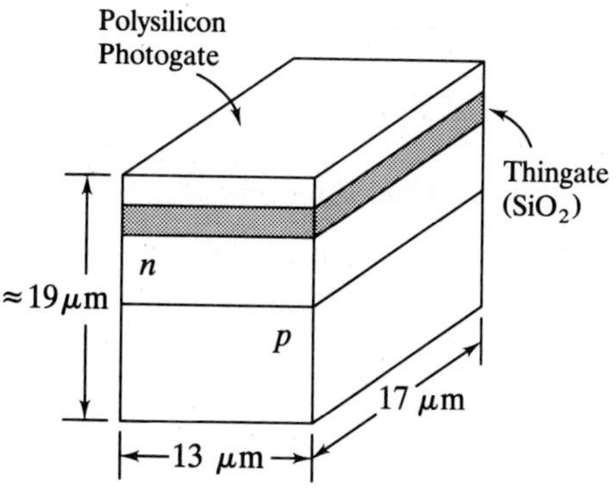

FIGURE 6-16
Photosite.

For the given dark current density, we have

$$i_d = 100 \frac{\text{nA}}{\text{cm}^2}(13 \times 10^{-6})(17 \times 10^{-6})\ \text{m}^2 \frac{10^4\ \text{cm}^2}{\text{m}^2}$$

$$= 0.221\ \text{pA}$$

The saturation time may then be taken to be

$$t_{\text{sat}} = \frac{Q_{\text{sat}}}{i_d} = \frac{0.7514\ \text{pC}}{0.221\ \text{pA}} = 3.4\ \text{s}$$

In line with our earlier comments, the frame time should be 1% of this time, or $t_F = 0.034$ s = 34 ms.

TRANSFER INEFFICIENCY. Ideally, one visualizes an immediate and total charge transfer. Generally, such a complete charge transfer is achieved only asymptotically in an infinite amount of time. In practice, charge transfer is never complete; neither is it instantaneous. Indeed, there is always a trade-off between transfer speed and the amount of charge left behind. Relatively detailed discussions of the physics of charge transfer may be found in Sequin and Tompsett[1] and Pinson.[6] Here, we shall be content with characterizing the efficiency of charge transfer in terms of the fraction of charge left behind, or, conversely, the fraction of charge transferred.

Definition 6-2 Charge transfer inefficiency. The fractional amount of charge lost in transferring charge from one potential well to the next is termed the *charge transfer inefficiency*. It is denoted by ϵ. The quantity $\eta = 1 - \epsilon$ is termed the charge transfer efficiency.

We assume that ϵ is constant. It may be a function of the time and of the amount of charge. The types of voltage pulses used in achieving charge transfer are an additional strong influence. In particular, trapezoidal pulses can provide a considerable improvement in transfer efficiency when compared to the use of square pulses.

Suppose now that Q_0 is the charge at the first site. During the transfer of charge from the first to the second site, ϵQ_0 is lost. The amount of charge left at the second site is

$$Q_1 = Q_0 - \epsilon Q_0 = Q_0(1 - \epsilon)$$

After the second transfer, the amount of charge in the third site is

$$Q_2 = Q_1 - \epsilon Q_1 = (1 - \epsilon)Q_0(1 - \epsilon)$$

$$= Q_0(1 - \epsilon)^2$$

and after k transfers the amount of charge in the $(k + 1)$th site is

$$Q_k = Q_0(1 - \epsilon)^k$$

The total amount of charge lost after k transfers is

$$\Delta Q_k = Q_0 - Q_k = Q_0\left[1 - (1 - \epsilon)^k\right]$$

and if ϵ is small this may be approximated by

$$\Delta Q_k \approx k\epsilon Q_0$$

or, the amount of charge lost is a linear function of the number of transfers.

In the previous two subsections we have quantified some of the performance limitations of charge transfer devices. The comments are meant to make the student aware of the limitations rather than to provide a full discussion. A whole chapter is devoted to this topic in Sequin and Tompsett.[1] The discussion there is basic to the structure of the device and thus will remain current in spite of changes in technology.

This concludes our discussion of shift registers. The next two sections deal with the photosensitive elements and the interactive structure between photosite and shift register.

6-5-2 The Photodiode

The basic diode structure was discussed in Sect. 4-3-2. We now extend this discussion to include photosensitivity.

When a photon of sufficient energy is absorbed by a semiconductor, it creates a hole-electron pair. These then move to their respective regions in accordance with the electric potential e which exists across the depletion region (Fig. 6-17*a*). The electrons move to the n-side and the holes to the p-side. Photons of different wavelengths penetrate to different depths. Those of short wavelength tend to be absorbed in the p-region, those of medium wavelength in the depletion region, and those of long wavelength can penetrate all the way to the n-layer. To obtain a broad spectral response, it thus becomes desirable to make the depletion region as wide as possible. It is for this reason that the photodiode is reverse biased, for the resistivity of the depletion region and the magnitude of the reverse bias determine the thickness of the region. A schematic of the photodiode is shown in Fig. 6-17*b*. In accordance with Jones,[13] we take the ideal optical current density to be

$$J_{\text{op}} = qE_s$$

where q is the carrier charge and E_s is the photon flux in photons/square meter · second, as before. The basic idealness assumptions are that the internal quantum efficiency is unity and that zero amount of light is reflected. Thus the total current density for the diode is given by

$$J = J_s(e^{qV/kT} - 1) - qE_s$$

where J_s is the saturation current, V is the applied voltage, defined to be positive when it makes the p-side more positive than the n-side, and J_{op} is a

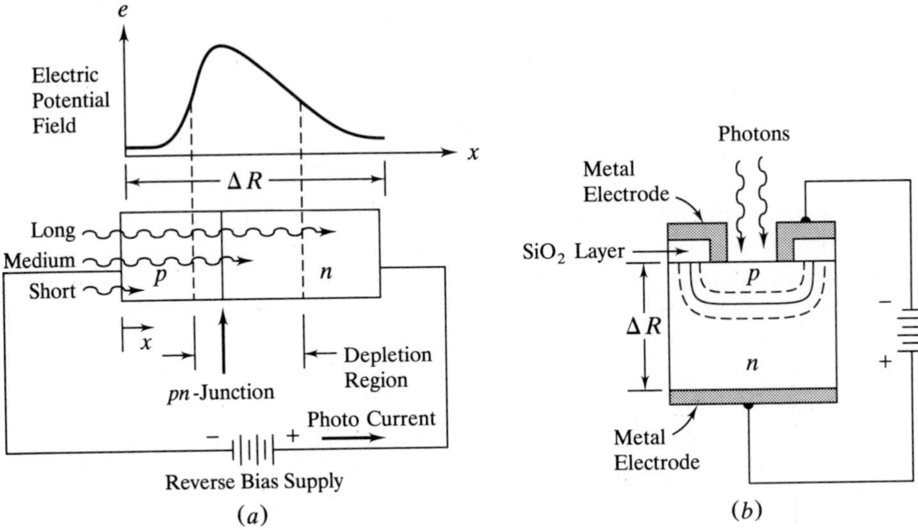

FIGURE 6-17
(*a*) Wavelength penetration; (*b*) Photodiode schematic.

negative current. Finally, the photocurrent is intergated and stored as charge on the diode.

6-5-3 The CCD Photosite

As mentioned earlier, the photosite design is strongly influenced by the manner in which the accumulated information is to be processed off the chip. Interlacing is almost uniformly employed to conform with standard television usage; among the possible shift register arrangements, one of the most desirable, from an overall point of view, is the interline transfer arrangement. This latter arrangement serves as the basis for our discussion of CCD photosites.

As always, the manipulation of the depletion region of a given site plays an essential role in actuating charge collection or charge transfer to the shift registers. Also, the two-phase transfer for shift registers and the interline transfer arrangement appear to be made for each other. Thus a single shift register site has two transfer electrodes, each controlling a well. Across from them are two photosites. Each such combination is called an *imaging cell*. Figure 6-18*a* depicts the overall dimensions of such a cell, while Fig. 6-18*b* depicts the cell layout, including some of the layer structure and the channel stops needed to separate cells and sites. Figure 6-18*c* provides a schematic of the surface layer structure of such a a cell.

Although the photosites remain in a staring mode, a shuttering of sorts is going on. It is governed by two voltages, V_p and V_t, the photogate voltage and

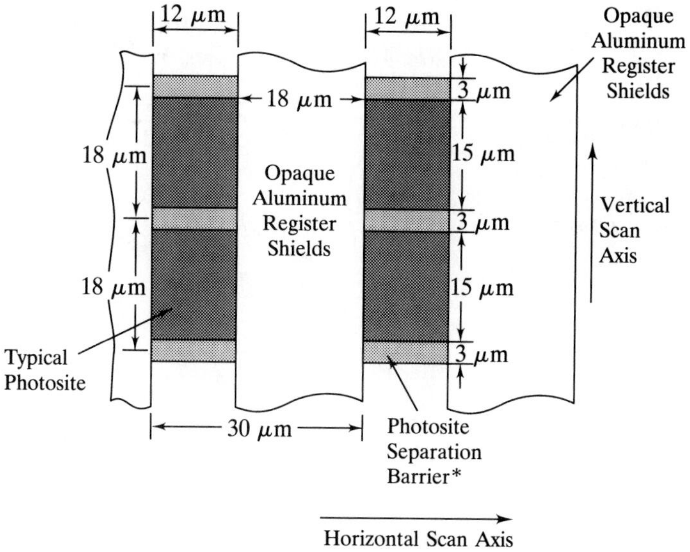

(*a*)

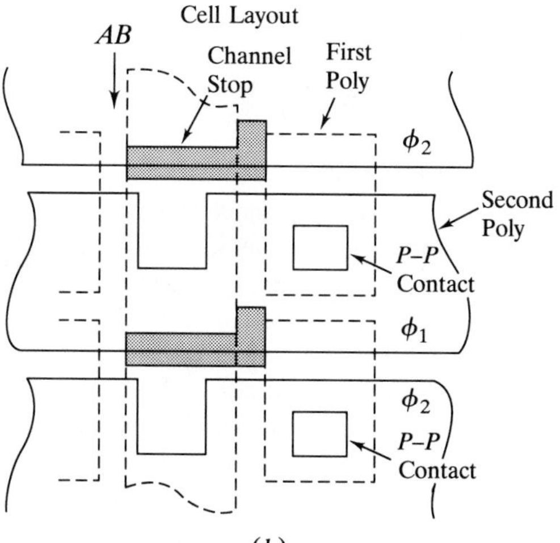

(*b*)

FIGURE 6-18
Sketches are characteristic for the Fairchild-Weston-Schlumberger CCD 222 Area Imaging Sensor. (Used with permission of Loral Fairchild Imaging Sensors.) (*a*) Typical image cell dimensions; (*b*) cell layout; (*c*) dead layer structure (next page).

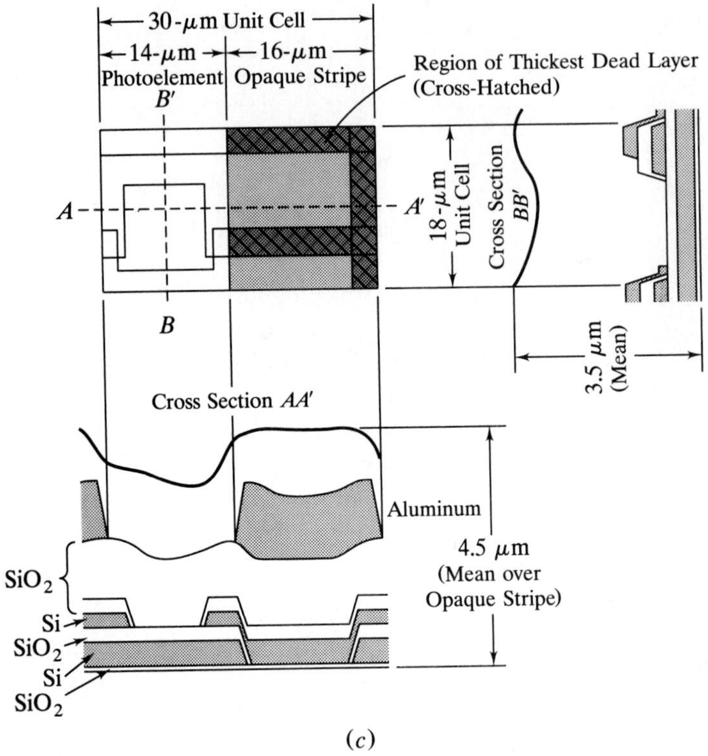

FIGURE 6-18 (*Continued*).

the transfer gate voltage, respectively. While this photogate voltage V_p is held high, charge proportional to the incident photon intensity is collected in the storage walls under the photosensors. During this time the transfer gate voltage V_t is held low. At the end of the integration time t_F, the transfer gate voltage V_t is raised and the shift register electrodes adjacent to the photosensor elements are also brought to high. Lowering the photogate voltage then results in a charge transfer of the accumulated photocharge to the adjacent shift register storage wells. The return of V_t and V_p to their usually low and high states, respectively, then sets the stage for the next charge transfer.

The preceding process is eloquently summarized in the following statement from Sequin and Tompsett[1]:

> The individual photosensors are isolated from the readout register by a transfer gate. When this gate is opened, all the charges integrated in the photosensors, normally depleted MOS capacitors, transfer in parallel into the readout register which has one complete transfer cell opposite to each photosensor. After the gate is closed, the photosensors immediately start integrating the next line, while the previous line is read out along the transfer register, which is shielded from incident light.

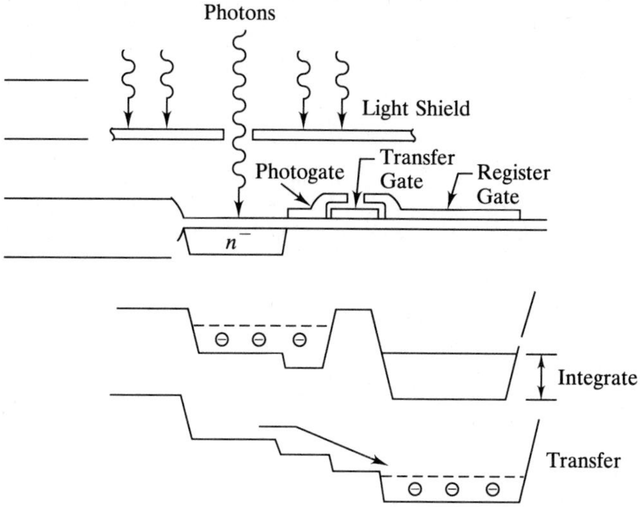

FIGURE 6-19
Charge transfer from photosite to shift register. (Used with permission of Loral Fairchild Imaging Sensors.)

The essentials of the charge transfer arrangement from photosite to shift register are depicted in Fig. 6-19.

6-5-4 The Video

At this point the electronic part of the image acquisition process is nearly complete. We still need to process the charges that are currently piling up at the output of the horizontal shift register. Two things need to be accomplished there: The size of the charge packets must be determined, and the information must be supplied in terms of a suitable voltage change for further computational processing.

There are many ways in which such a charge output detection can be accomplished. In line with previous practice, we present one of the simplest possible concepts and subsequently point out practical extensions and refinements. Our simple output circuit is the one shown in Fig. 6-20 (Navon[14])

A positively pulsed MIS (metal-insulator-semiconductor) sandwich element is introduced at the end of the shift register. It produces an electric field in the silicon, which drives holes entering the field to ground. When holes from the last CCD in the shift register drift toward this output electrode, they are repelled into the substrate. There they generate a current i_0 to ground, which is detected as a voltage drop v_1 across the resistor R_0 when v_0 is held at some given value. More specifically, assume that v and v_0 are given fixed voltages. We

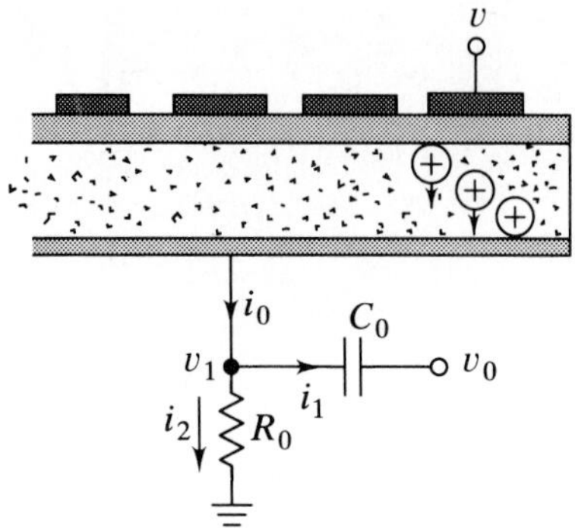

FIGURE 6-20
A simple charge detection circuit.

then have

$$i_0 = i_1 + i_2$$

$$= C_0 \frac{d}{dt}(v_1 - v_0) + \frac{1}{R_0} v_1$$

$$= C_0 \frac{dv_1}{dt} + \frac{1}{R_0} v_1$$

since v_0 is constant. Thus the response v_1 may be used to identify i_0.

This simple approach was essentially the first one used in demonstrating the possibility of charge-coupled devices, an approach which is also reminiscent of the change detection in the vidicon tube. There are two major problems with this simplified approach: Charge is measured destructively, and the signal may be too weak without additional amplification.

It is now more common to use floating gate amplifiers, preferably included on the imaging chip itself. The signal charge packet is then measured nondestructuviely by its image charge in this gate. It can thus be sampled several times as it passes several amplifiers. The result is high sensitivity and a high signal-to-noise ratio. Additional discussion of charge detection, including further referenes, may be found in Sequin and Tompsett.[1]

We close our presentation of electronic image acquisition with two brief comments about a common performance limitation and a performance specification.

According to Tompsett, "To a certain extent all image sensors demonstrate blooming, which is an apparent increase in the size of an image of a bright object under overload conditions." In simple terms, the well of a particular photosite fills up and starts spilling over into adjacent wells, giving the appearance of a larger object image. All of the remedies seem to employ some sort of excess charge drain.

A common specification of an image sensor is its *dynamic range*—the ratio of the saturation output voltage to the rms noise in the dark. Other currently used definitions of the term include: the range of input signals over which the camera operates successfully, and the number of bits of RAM used in a digital image representation. In view of this multiplicity of meanings, some care must be exercised in using the term.

6-6 IMAGE PROCESSING

At this point, we have covered only the first 1/30th of a second in the image identification process, and even this time span is prescribed only in deference to television usage. Actually, all of the preceding activity can be made to happen in about 4 ms, and many nonstandard frame times are now commercially available. Indeed, most vision systems can now be programmed to acquire a frame in 1/60th of a second (the odd field, for example), if vertical resolution is not required. All of the remaining time is then taken up by image processing.

Unfortunately, in most texts on computer vision or machine vision, about the same proportion of time is allocated to the electronics of the acquisition process. These terms have even become synonymous with digital image processing. There are some good reasons for this. To understand the fundamental concepts, for example, not much more mathematics is required than that obtainable in engineering education. Not even a background in electronics is required. There are a number of exhaustive texts on image processing and identification. Our objective here is to introduce the reader to some relatively straightforward image processing concepts.

In the preceding section the image had attained the sequential form suggested in Fig. 6-9. If we take 512 samples per line and assume a maximum signal output of 5.0 V, then one line has the form shown in Fig. 6-21.

Our discussion now deals with the way this information may be stored and processed.

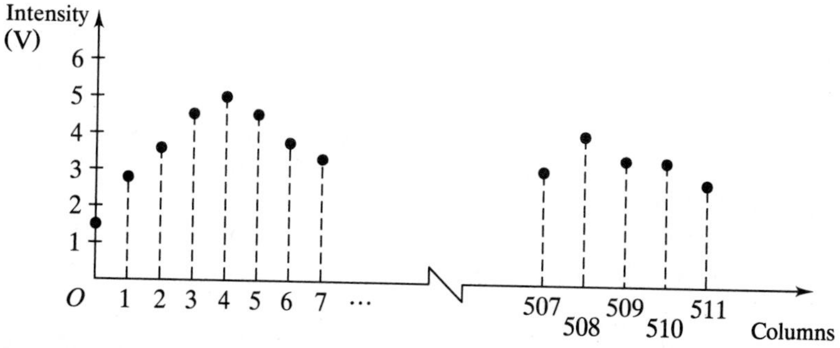

FIGURE 6-21
Analog video.

6-6-1 Digitizing the Image

For the solid-state sensor, the image field itself is already digitized in terms of the pixel locations. The voltage output from the sensor, however, is still in analog form; that is, with each pixel there is associated a voltage $0 \leq v \leq 5$ V. The first step in processing the image thus consists of subdividing the interval [0, 5] into a finite set of subintervals, with a specified intensity for each interval. Based on practical present technology, this subdivision can range from a crude binary subdivision, which assigns only 0 or 1 to each pixel, to a 128 gray level quantification. Although a full gray level quantification assigns 8 bits per pixel, the last bit is simply treated as noise. Naturally, the more levels used, the greater the amount of computer memory needed. For a binary image only 1 bit per pixel is required to store the image—in this case, $512 \times 512 = 262{,}144$ bits of information. The use of a full gray scale would require 8 bits (1 byte) of memory per pixel, resulting in a total of 2,097,152 bits of RAM per frame.

Image digitization is easily accomplished by using an ADC. The best results are obtained when the camera and ADC are synchronized. Mathematically, analog-to-digital conversion may be viewed as a process of mapping integer intervals into the integers by using the greatest integer function, and then encoding these intensity levels. The greatest integer function is a mapping $f(\cdot): \mathbb{R}^+ \rightarrow \mathbb{R}^+$ defined by

$$f(x) = [x]$$

where the heavy brackets indicate that only the greatest integral part of a number is to be retained. Thus, for

$$0 \leq x < 1 \qquad f(x) = 0 \qquad \text{e.g., } f(0.5) = 0$$

$$1 \leq x < 2 \qquad f(x) = 1.0 \qquad \text{e.g., } f(1.25) = 1.0$$

and so on. Subsequently, these integral levels may then be encoded in some fashion.

The details of such a conversion are illustrated with the following, albeit somewhat academic, example.

Example 6-2. A 5-V maximum signal ($0 \leq v \leq 5$) is to be converted into a four-level gray scale digitized output. Design an ADC to perform this task.

Solution. As illustrated earlier, we begin with a voltage divider, followed by a set of comparators, as shown in Fig. 6-22*a*. For the first comparator, we have the situation depicted in Fig. 6-22*b*, with

$$v_0 = a\left(v - \frac{3}{4}v_R\right) = v_{0H} \qquad \text{for} \quad v > \frac{3}{4}v_R = \frac{15}{4}$$

As is usually done, the reference voltage has been set to the maximum expected input voltage; that is, $v_R = 5$ V. Conventionally, we identify $v_0 = v_{0H}$ as logic 1 and $v_0 = v_{0L} < 0$ as logic 0. We shall designate these outcomes by writing $C_i = 0$ or 1. The outcomes of this process are summarized in Fig. 6-22*c*.

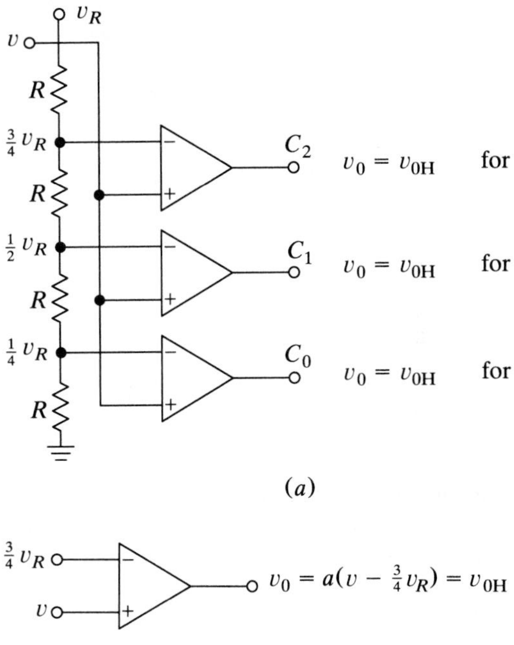

Interval	C_0	C_1	C_2
$0 \le v < \frac{5}{4}$	0	0	0
$\frac{5}{4} \le v < \frac{5}{2}$	1	0	0
$\frac{5}{2} \le v < \frac{15}{4}$	1	1	0
$\frac{15}{4} \le v < 5$	1	1	1

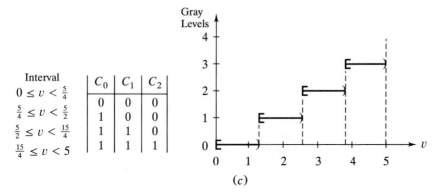

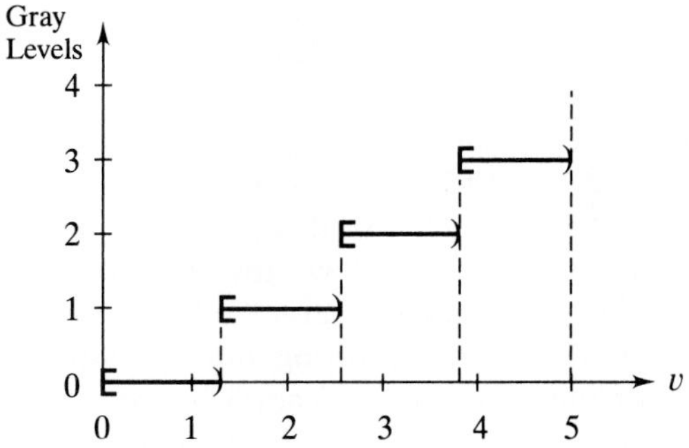

(c)

FIGURE 6-22
(*a*) A simple ADC; (*b*) the first comparator; (*c*) gray levels and primary coding.

To attain the present subdivisions, the greatest integer function has been taken in the form

$$f(v) = \left[\frac{v}{1.25}\right]$$

resulting in

$$0 \le v < 1.25 \qquad \text{and} \qquad f(v) = 0$$

$$1.25 \le v < 2.5 \qquad \text{and} \qquad f(v) = 1$$

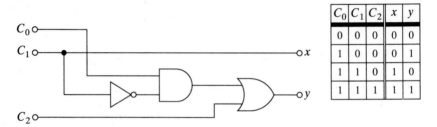

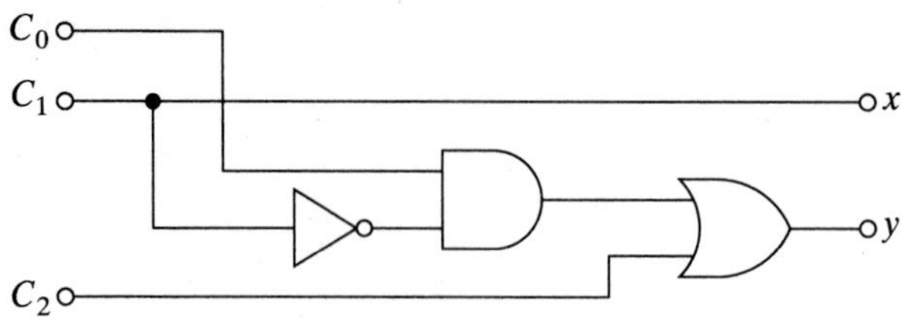

C_0	C_1	C_2	x	y
0	0	0	0	0
1	0	0	0	1
1	1	0	1	0
1	1	1	1	1

FIGURE 6-23
Encoder and truth table.

and so on. Note that the use of the flash ADC has already produced a primary binary code, as indicated by the Boolean variables C_i; this code would require 3 bits of storage space. It is usual, however, to allocate the minimum number of bits needed to store a given amount of information. Here, we have four levels of gray scale which properly should require only 2 bits of RAM. Hence the use of an encoder reduces the four pieces of information to 2-bit binary. The simple encoded shown in Fig. 6-23 accomplishes the task.

Once the video has been digitized in this manner, it remains to store the image in the computer in a way that facilitates further manipulation of the image. The obvious approach is to store the image as a mathematical array. We summarize the preceding discussion and the final image representation in terms of a very simplified 3×4 area image sensor.

In order to properly locate each pixel in an *xy*-roster, we assume the following: (1) square pixels (though they are not; the previous ones were 12×18 μm) and (2) no gaps between pixels (when there are actually fairly large gaps—the shielded shift registers). In addition, we take the pixel width as our unit length. We then have the situation shown in Fig. 6-24*a*. The *xy*-axes may be chosen among the sensor edge or, as we have done here, through the centers of the pixels, implying that all integral coordinates are also at the centers of the pixels. This location becomes important when absolute position measurement is an objective. Furthermore, we have chosen our ordered pair (x, y) so as to eventually correspond to (row, column).

Initially associated with each pixel was an analogy voltage proportional to the incident light intensity. That voltage may be plotted as a "mountain" over the pixel array (see Fig. 6-24*b*). Based on Example 6-2, the corresponding digitized mountain has the four gray levels shown in Fig. 6-24*c* (binary codes not indicated). In a more abbreviated form, each gray level may simply be noted at the appropriate location, and we finally introduce the 3×4 image matrix

$$\mathbf{F}_g = \begin{bmatrix} 2 & 1 & 0 & 1 \\ 3 & 3 & 2 & 3 \\ 2 & 1 & 1 & 1 \end{bmatrix} = \begin{bmatrix} F(0,0) & F(0,1) & F(0,2) & F(0,3) \\ F(1,0) & F(1,1) & F(1,2) & F(1,3) \\ F(2,0) & F(2,1) & F(2,2) & F(2,3) \end{bmatrix}$$

which provides the basis for all further calculations.

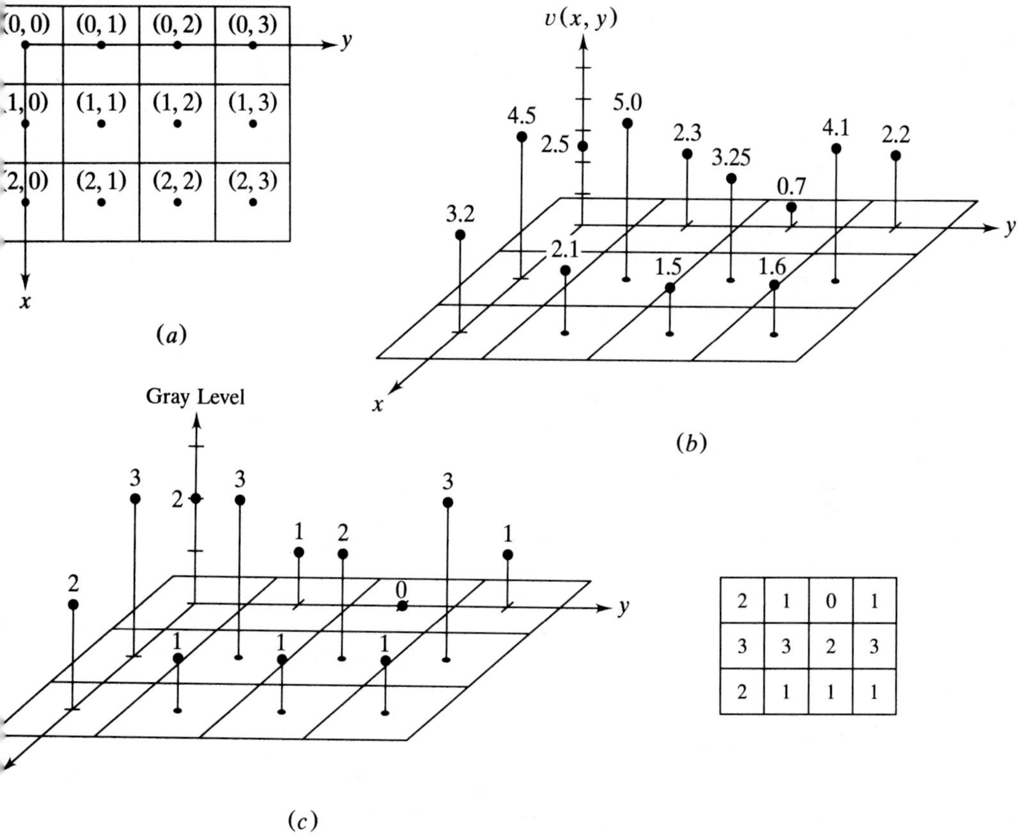

2	1	0	1
3	3	2	3
2	1	1	1

FIGURE 6-24
(*a*) Sensor coordinates; (*b*) analog video; (*c*) gray scale video; (*d*) image array.

Remark 6-3. The number of gray levels used generally depends on the gray scale resolution capabilities of the receiver. If human visual perception is the ultimate goal, then there is no point in going beyond $2^6 = 64$ gray levels, since this is all that the human eye can perceive.

Finally, we note that 0 corresponds to black and 255 to white, with the remaining shades of gray in between.

6-6-2 Thresholding

We have just shown how to fully digitize the image. Although gray scale image analysis is a popular area of endeavor, we shall do very little more of it. Our main objective is to provide an understanding of the possible extraction of information from images, rather than the details of sophisticated image analysis.

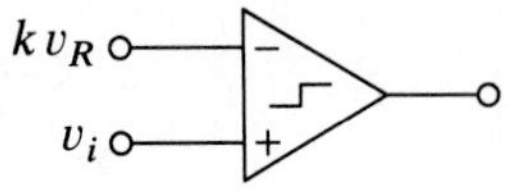

$$v_0 = a(v_i - kv_R) \Rightarrow \begin{array}{ll} v_0 = v_{0H} & \text{for } v_i > kv_R \\ v_0 = v_{0L} & \text{for } v_i < kv_R \end{array}$$

FIGURE 6-25
The voltage comparator.

We shall thus restrict ourselves to a few, relatively common topics in binary image analysis.

The choice of a *threshold* is a voltage v_T which is used to separate the video into two disjoint regions—one with $v > v_T$, labeled logic 1, and the other with $v < v_T$, labeled logic 0. We take the former as the *dark object*, and the latter as the light background—just the opposite of the gray scale extremes. Obviously, the roles may easily be reversed. The simplest way to implement such a threshold electronically is by means of a voltage comparator, a 1-bit ADC, an op amp in an open loop configuration (see Fig. 6-25). For a given reference voltage v_R, we may adjust k to achieve any desired threshold.

Example 6-3. Suppose the maximum possible analog voltage of a video is $v_{max} =$ 5.0 V. Set up a comparator for a threshold voltage $v_T = 0.5$ V. That is, provide logic 1 for $v_i > v_T$ and logic 0 for $v_i < v_T$. More specifically, determine k, if the reference voltage is chosen to be $v_R = v_{max} = 5.0$ V.

Solution. We want

$$\begin{array}{lll} v_i > 0.5 & \Rightarrow & \text{logic 1} \\ v_i < 0.5 & \Rightarrow & \text{logic 0} \end{array}$$

We need only set

$$kv_R = 0.5 \quad \Rightarrow \quad k = \frac{0.5}{5.0} = 0.1$$

Consequently, we then have

$$\begin{array}{llll} v_i > kv_R = 0.1 \times 5.0 = 0.5 & \Rightarrow & v_0 = v_{0H} & \text{(logic 1)} \\ v_i < 0.5 & \Rightarrow & v_0 = v_{0L} & \text{(logic 0)} \end{array}$$

Example 6-4. Suppose the 10-sample video in the sketch is to be thresholded at $v_T = 2.5$ V. Deduce the binary image corresponding to the analog image in Fig. 6-26.

Solution. The comparator output is shown in Fig. 6-27*a*. The corresponding pixel row on a monitor image would have the form shown in Fig. 6-27*b*. We have taken logic 0 as the white background and logic 1 as the black object.

Remark 6-4. Repeated thresholding of an image may be used to construct a gray scale image. Recall that gray levels corresponded to voltage intervals for the analog image. We may thus begin with a threshold voltage corresponding to, say,

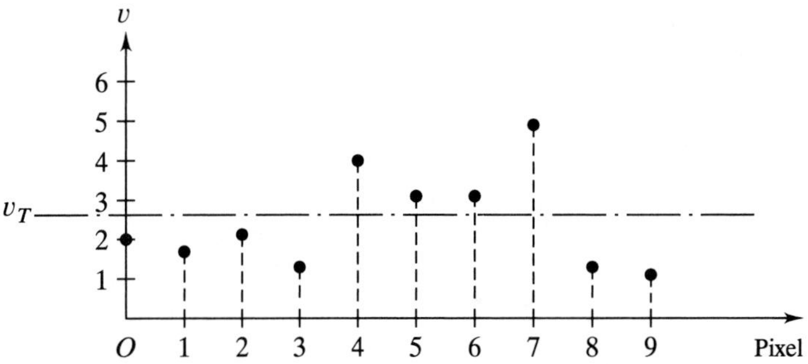

FIGURE 6-26
A row of analog video.

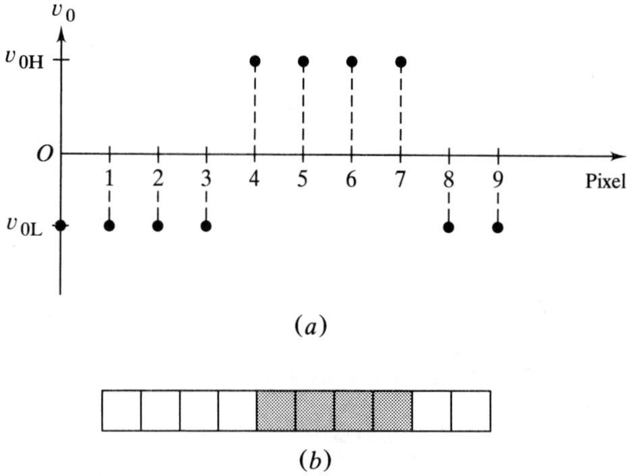

FIGURE 6-27
(*a*) Comparator output;
(*b*) monitor image.

gray level 2, and construct a corresponding "binary" image with the "object" identified by the particular gray (rather than black) tone. The threshold is then stepped to the next gray level. The new object points are now adjusted to this new gray level, while the background points are simply maintained at their previous gray levels. This process continues until all desired gray levels have been considered.

Because of its enormous data reduction capabilities, this repeated thresholding is a powerful tool in image processing and analysis; thus the judicious choice of a threshold is important. One way to select the appropriate contrast and delineation of a binary image is to "step" through successive threshold levels and to view the results on a television monitor until a desired contrast is achieved. This approach is suitable, for example, when opaque objects are placed on an illuminated background. For more complex situations with three-dimensional objects and irregular illumination, a more formal approach may be required.

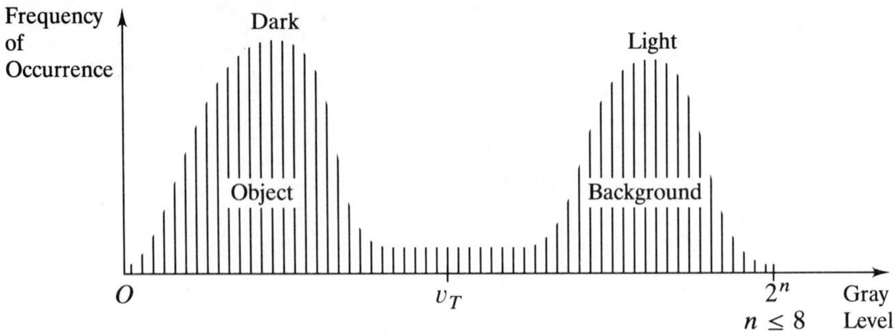

FIGURE 6-28
Gray level histogram.

More specifically, the choice of threshold may be taken to be a function

$$v_T = v_T(x, y; p(x, y), v(x, y))$$

reflecting the dependence on location and varying image intensity. The most complex situation is a dependence on the location (x, y); in accordance with Gonzalez and Wintz,[3] this is termed a *dynamic* threshold.

The next possibility, termed a *local* threshold, concerns segmented thresholding, where the threshold remains constant over subsets of the image, the subset selection being described by $p(x, y)$. The simplest situation occurs when the threshold is *global*, that is, when it is a function only of the image intensity. The subsequent image analysis based on $v_T = v_T(v(x, y))$ is called *low-level* vision analysis. Here, we shall consider only some aspects of this latter case.

The most common approach to the selection of this global threshold is based on a *histogram* of the image. To construct the histogram, the image is first digitized into gray levels, and the histogram itself then is a plot of the frequency of occurrence of a particular gray level versus the available gray levels. In situations where there is essentially a dark-light contrast, such a histogram will have the general appearance indicated in Fig. 6-28. The "best" object-to-background separation is then obtained for a threshold corresponding to the valley between the frequency peaks.

There are additional methods for obtaining good thresholds. For example, if it is known that an image will have two peaks, then the two elevated regions may be considered to be brightness probability density functions. One may then calculate the total probable error in discerning background and object pixels. The optimal threshold then is one that minimizes this error.

6-7 BINARY IMAGE ANALYSIS AND IDENTIFICATION

Obviously, when an image contains many shades of gray, it may not be possible to determine a reasonable threshold and thus reduce the image to a binary one.

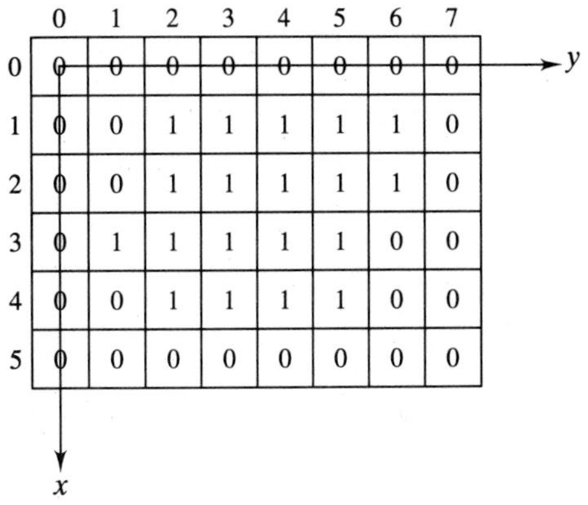

FIGURE 6-29
Binary image array.

For the remainder of this chapter, we shall assume that an optimal threshold has been established and that object and background are clearly separated. We shall discuss the detection of separating boundaries, using edge-finding algorithms, and the identification of what they surround, accomplished by associating characteristic numbers with given objects.

For definiteness, suppose we focus our attention on the binary array given in Fig. 6-29. Generally, one of the first steps in distinguishing something in the image array is to determine the object boundary. We shall make use of the following concepts of neighbors of a pixel p (Gonzalez and Wintz[3]).

Definition 6-3 Neighbors of a pixel p. The 4-neighbors of a pixel p located at (x,y) are given by

$$(x-1, y), (x, y+1), (x+1, y), (x, y-1)$$

These, together with

$$(x-1, y+1), (x+1, y+1), (x+1, y-1), (x-1, y-1)$$

constitute the 8-neighbors of p.

Remark 6-5. The neighbors of a pixel are illustrated in Fig. 6-30. With each 8-neighbor of a pixel p, we have also associated a number indicating its direction

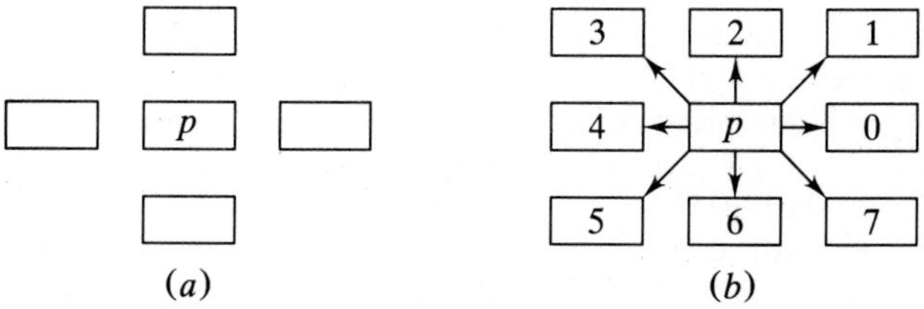

FIGURE 6-30
(a) 4-neighbors of pixel p; (b) 8-neighbors of pixel p.

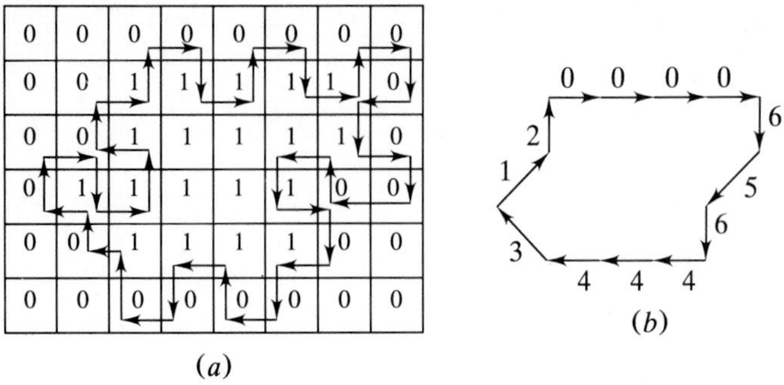

FIGURE 6-31
(*a*) Finding the edge; (*b*) coding the edge.

from the pixel p. These directional codes may then be used to describe or encode the boundary of an object. That is, as we move along the boundary, the direction of each "step" is indicated by the appropriate numerical code.†

6-7-1 An Edge-Finding Algorithm

We shall take pixel intensity values of 0 and 1 to denote background and object pixels, respectively.

Step 1. Do a line-by-line scan until an object pixel is encountered.

Step 2. "Stand" in the object pixel, "turn left," and "step" one pixel.

Step 3. If the new pixel encountered is another object pixel, "turn left" and "step."

Step 4. If a background pixel is encountered, "turn right" and "step."

Step 5. Stop when the first object pixel is encountered a second time.

Example 6-5. Consider the binary image given previously (see Fig. 6-29).

(*a*) Use arrows to illustrate the steps of edge-finding algorithm given previously.

(*b*) Use the chain code illustrated in Fig. 6-30 to encode the boundary of the object.

Solution. The result of the edge-finding algorithm is shown in Fig. 6-31*a*. The x- and y-axes have been omitted for clarity.

Once the boundary pixels have been established, they may be encoded with the chain code illustrated in Fig. 6-31*b*. The corresponding computer entry would be the string of figures 0000656444312. Clearly, this code depends on the starting point and thus cannot be used as a unique identifier for an object. Additional processing may be used to eliminate this difficulty.

†According to Gonzalez and Wintz,[3] such chain codes were first mentioned in Freeman.[15]

6-7-2 Descriptors

In order to repetitively identify a given object or region in an image, one attempts to associate a (hopefully) unique number with the object. There is a large variety of descriptors—the number of holes, arcs, corners, or straight-line segments, for example, or the diameters of best inscribed or best circumscribing ellipses. We shall introduce only some of the more obvious ones, such as area perimeter, and other basic geometric concepts.

Obviously, the area by itself would not be a good descriptor, since it does not take into account the actual shape of the region. Other descriptors suffer from a similar lack of uniqueness. However, if several descriptors are used simultaneously for a given object, then one may reach good statistical confidence levels for having properly identified the object.

Definition 6-4 Characteristic function. Let the universal set be S and let $O \subseteq S$. Then

$$\mu(x, y) = \begin{cases} 1 & (x, y) \in O \\ 0 & (x, y) \notin O \end{cases}$$

is called the characteristic function of O.

This is the same function used in mathematics for the construction of a measure. Here, the function is useful in the construction of object descriptors. Throughout the remainder of this discussion, we shall assume that O, the object, is simply connected—that is, there are no holes.

We take the universal set S to be given by the pixel array

$$S = \{(i, j): (i, j) \in I \times J\}$$

where I and J are the sets of nonnegative integers denoting the rows and columns, respectively, of the image array. An object, then, is a subset O of S given by

$$O = \{(i, j): i \in I' \subseteq I \text{ and } j \in J' \subseteq J\}$$

The discrete characteristic function of O is

$$\mu(i, j) = \begin{cases} 1 & (i, j) \in O \\ 0 & (i, j) \notin O \end{cases}$$

Definition 6-5 Object descriptors. We introduce the following object descriptors:

(*a*) *Area*

$$A = \sum_{\substack{i \in I' \\ j \in J'}} \mu(i, j)$$

(*b*) *Centroid*

$$x_G = \frac{1}{A} \sum_{\substack{i \in I' \\ i \in J'}} i\mu(i, j) \qquad y_G = \frac{1}{A} \sum_{\substack{i \in I' \\ j \in J'}} j\mu(i, j)$$

(*c*) *Perimeter*. A boundary pixel is any pixel p whose 4-neighbors have intensity values of both 0 and 1. The perimeter is simply the sum of all boundary pixels.

(*d*) *Major diameter*. Let $p_i = (x_i, y_i)$ and $p_j = (x_j, y_j)$ be pixels in the perimeter of the object O. Then the major diameter D of O is given by

$$D = \max_{i,j}\left\{\sqrt{(x_j - x_i)^2 + (y_j - y_i)^2}\right\}$$

(*e*) *Compactness*

$$C = \frac{P^2}{A}$$

(*f*) *Thinness*

$$T = \frac{D}{A}$$

We shall illustrate the calculation of these descriptors for the image array of Fig. 6-29.

Example 6-6. Calculate the descriptors (*a*) through (*f*) for the binary array in Fig. 6-29.

Solution

(*a*) The object area is given by $A = 19$.

(*b*) For the location of the centroid we have

$$x_G = \frac{1}{A}\Big[\underbrace{3\cdot 1}_{\text{col. 1}} + \underbrace{1\cdot 1 + 2\cdot 1 + 3\cdot 1 + 4\cdot 1}_{\text{col. 2}}$$
$$+ \underbrace{1\cdot 1 + 2\cdot 1 + 3\cdot 1 + 4\cdot 1}_{\text{col. 3}} + \underbrace{1\cdot 1 + 2\cdot 1 + 3\cdot 1 + 4\cdot 1}_{\text{col. 4}}$$
$$+ \underbrace{1\cdot 1 + 2\cdot 1 + 3\cdot 1 + 4\cdot 1}_{\text{col. 5}} + \underbrace{1\cdot 1 + 2\cdot 1}_{\text{col. 6}}\Big]$$
$$= \frac{46}{19} = 2.42$$

$$y_G = \frac{1}{A}[(2 + 3 + 4 + 5 + 6) + (2 + 3 + 4 + 5 + 6)$$
$$+ (1 + 2 + 3 + 4 + 5) + (2 + 3 + 4 + 5)]$$
$$= \frac{69}{19} = 3.53$$

(*c*) The perimeter is given by $P = 13$.

(*d*) The major diameter obviously is given by the distance between the pixels located at (3, 1) and (1, 6), with

$$D = \sqrt{(3-1)^2 + (1-6)^2} = \sqrt{29} = 5.39$$

(*e*) The compactness is

$$C = \frac{P^2}{A} = \frac{169}{19} = 8.89$$

(*f*) The thickness is

$$T = \frac{D}{A} = \frac{\sqrt{29}}{19} = 0.283$$

Remark 6-6. Note carefully that all of the results here are given in "pixel units." For example, the actual area is given by $A \cdot a$, where a is the mean area (including gaps) of a pixel. If the individual pixels are rectangular, these pixel units may be different for each of the coordinate directions. In addition, the actual object outline may cover fractions of pixels, a fact not considered in the analysis. Similarly, the actual perimeter may differ considerably from the number computed previously, depending, for example, on how one deals with corner pixels. Finally, the centroid location clearly is not independent of the placement of the object.

6-8 THE CAMERA TRANSFORMATION

The final discussion of this chapter is intended to provide the connection between the image and the real world it is meant to depict. There are two aspects to this connection: The flat image should provide information about the three-dimensional world, and we must know where the sensor is. We can locate the sensor itself in the same way we determined other aspects of the robot configuration. The primary relationship between image plane and object is contained in the perspective transformation.

CAMERA LOCATION. There are a number of reference frames that may be used in the specification of camera position and orientation. We shall use the ones illustrated in Fig. 6-32. The frame $(0xyz)_0$, as always, denotes the frame fixed in space, so that (x_0, y_0, z_0) are the world coordinates of some physical object point. The frame $(0xyz)_c$ we term the camera frame, with its origin at some swivel mechanism or gimbal. Finally, we take the sensor reference frame to be given by $(0xyz)$, without a subscript. A specific pixel location in this frame is given by $(x, y, 0)$, and we note that the frame is offset with respect to the frame used earlier for the location of pixels in the image plane. The camera is usually allowed two orientations: One is panning, a rotation about the z_c-axis by angle θ; the other is tilting, which is a rotation about the x_c-axis by an angle α. The location of O_c relative to O_0 is given by $\boldsymbol{c}_c$, and the location of O relative to O_c is given by $\boldsymbol{c}$. As in Chap. 2, our objective now is to express the world coordinates of a point in terms of those of the "moving" reference frame; in the present case, to express $\boldsymbol{r}_0$ in terms of $\boldsymbol{r}$, the location of the image point.

Here, it would lead too far to deal with both a moving camera as well as a moving object point P_0. We shall thus consider a fixed camera position and a

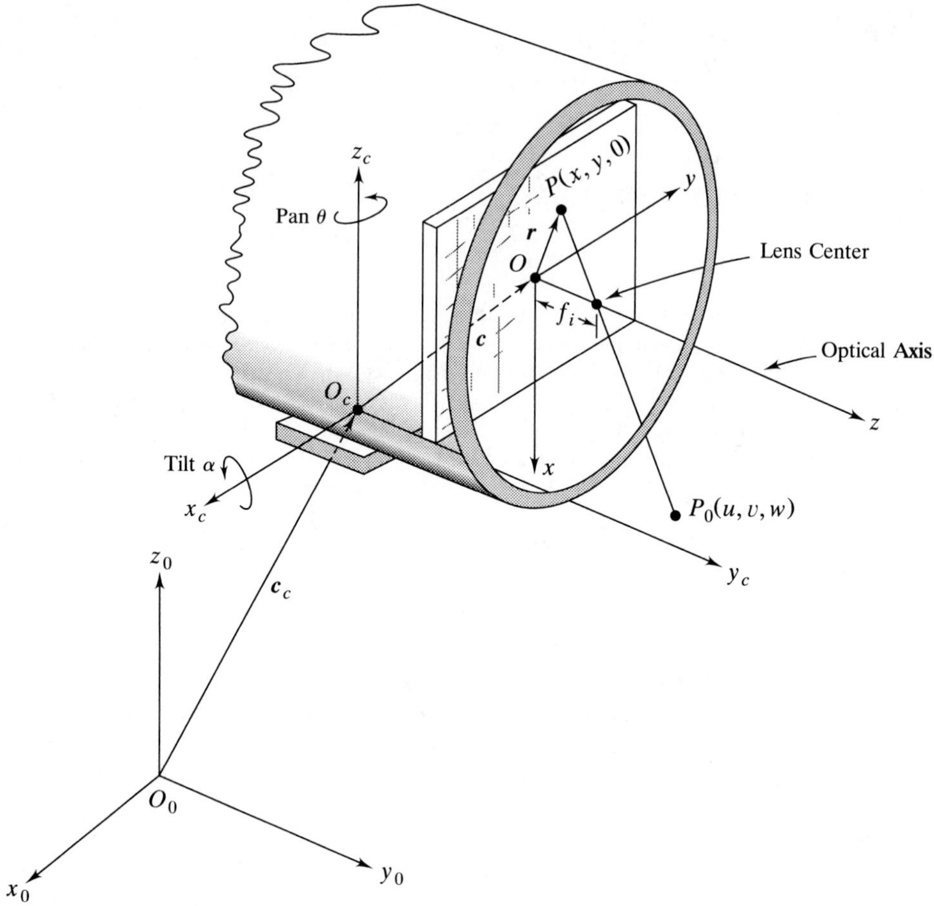

FIGURE 6-32
The camera model.

fixed object point P_0. With this in mind, the absolute position vector is given by

$$\boldsymbol{r}_0 = \boldsymbol{c}_c + \boldsymbol{c} + \boldsymbol{r}$$

A more useful expression is obtained when this is written in the form

$$\mathbf{r}_0 = \mathbf{C}\mathbf{r}$$

in terms of homogeneous coordinates. We shall call $\mathbf{C}$ the *camera transformation matrix*. To construct $\mathbf{C}$, we simply think of a rigid body motion for the sensor from coincidence with the fixed frame to its final position in space. We shall use the following positioning sequence: a translation from O_0 to O_c, a panning by an angle θ, followed by a tilt angle α, and, finally, a reorientation and translation to O.

For the first translation we have

$$\mathbf{B}_1 = \begin{bmatrix} 1 & 0 & 0 & a_0 \\ 0 & 1 & 0 & b_0 \\ 0 & 0 & 1 & c_0 \\ 0 & 0 & 0 & 1 \end{bmatrix} \qquad \text{and} \qquad \mathbf{r}_0 = \mathbf{B}_1 \mathbf{r}_c$$

The panning is given by

$$\mathbf{B}_2 = \begin{bmatrix} C\theta & -S\theta & 0 & 0 \\ S\theta & C\theta & 0 & 0 \\ 0 & 0 & 1 & 0 \\ 0 & 0 & 0 & 1 \end{bmatrix} \qquad \text{and} \qquad \mathbf{r}_c = \mathbf{B}_2 \mathbf{r}_c^1$$

The tilting is given by

$$\mathbf{B}_3 = \begin{bmatrix} 1 & 0 & 0 & 0 \\ 0 & C\alpha & -S\alpha & 0 \\ 0 & S\alpha & C\alpha & 0 \\ 0 & 0 & 0 & 1 \end{bmatrix} \qquad \text{and} \qquad \mathbf{r}_c^1 = \mathbf{B}_3 \mathbf{r}_c^2$$

The translation to the sensor origin is given by

$$\mathbf{B}_4 = \begin{bmatrix} 1 & 0 & 0 & a \\ 0 & 1 & 0 & b \\ 0 & 0 & 1 & c \\ 0 & 0 & 0 & 1 \end{bmatrix} \qquad \text{and} \qquad \mathbf{r}_c^2 = \mathbf{B}_4 \mathbf{r}_c^3$$

Finally, we rotate the frame to obtain the orientation of the sensor reference. A 90° rotation about the z-axis

$$\mathbf{B}_5 = \begin{bmatrix} 0 & -1 & 0 & 0 \\ 1 & 0 & 0 & 0 \\ 0 & 0 & 1 & 0 \\ 0 & 0 & 0 & 1 \end{bmatrix} \qquad \text{and} \qquad \mathbf{r}_c^3 = \mathbf{B}_5 \mathbf{r}_c^4$$

is followed by a 90° rotation about the y-axis

$$\mathbf{B}_6 = \begin{bmatrix} 0 & 0 & 1 & 0 \\ 0 & 1 & 0 & 0 \\ -1 & 0 & 0 & 0 \\ 0 & 0 & 0 & 1 \end{bmatrix} \qquad \text{and} \qquad \mathbf{r}_c^4 = \mathbf{B}_6 \mathbf{r}$$

The camera matrix $\mathbf{C}$ is thus given by

$$\mathbf{C} = \prod_{i=1}^{6} \mathbf{B}_i$$

$$= \begin{bmatrix} -S\theta S\alpha & -C\theta & -S\theta C\alpha & aC\theta - bS\theta C\alpha + cS\theta S\alpha + a_0 \\ C\theta S\alpha & -S\theta & C\theta C\alpha & aS\theta + bC\theta C\alpha - cC\theta S\alpha + b_0 \\ -C\alpha & 0 & S\alpha & bS\alpha + cC\alpha + c_0 \\ 0 & 0 & 0 & 1 \end{bmatrix} \qquad (6\text{-}11)$$

Remark 6-7. In the derivation we took $\mathbf{c}$ to have the general form $\mathbf{c} = (a \; b \; c)^T$, which would be used, for example, when $(0xyz)$ is the previously introduced image frame. However, when used in accordance with Fig. 6-32, the vector always has the form $\mathbf{c} = (0 \; b \; c)^T$.

The preceding transformation establishes the world coordinates of a particular point on the surface of the image sensor. The ultimate aim, of course, is to be able to use the camera to determine the location of a physical object point P_0. This can be done, once we know how the points P on the image sensor are related to the real-world points P_0. In essence, knowing the location of an object within the image frame should be sufficient to locate the actual object in the world frame.

THE PERSPECTIVE TRANSFORMATION. It is clear that the two-dimensional image of a three-dimensional scene will result in some loss of information, the most obvious being depth. To achieve our previously stated goal, we would have to replace this information in some fashion. We shall stop somewhat short of this goal.

Once more, we should like to locate points in space by using the camera, or, rather, what we know about a point based on the camera image. We shall assume that a relatively distant image is to be found on the image sensor. The sensor is thus taken to be located in the focal plane, a focal distance f_i away from the center of the lens. In terms of a ray passing through the lens center, a world point (u, v, w) has a corresponding image point $(x, y, 0)$, as illustrated in Fig. 6-32. Based on the proportional triangles in the figure, we may easily write

$$y = \frac{f_i v}{f_i - w} \qquad \text{and} \qquad x = \frac{f_i u}{f_i - w} \tag{6-12}$$

for the relationship between $P_0(u, v, w)$ and $P(x, y)$ in the image plane.

Suppose we consider the special, somewhat simplified situation shown in Fig. 6-33. The camera location and orientation are taken to be specified by $a_0 = 0$, $b_0 = 0$, $c_0 = 30$ cm, $a = 0$, $b = 4$, and $c = 2$, along with $\alpha = \theta = 0$ and a focal length of $f_i = 2$ cm. Suppose, furthermore, that it has somehow been established that the perpendicular distance from P_0 to the image sensor is $w = 8$ cm, and we have determined that the image point is located at $x = 0$ and $y = 1$ cm, for simplicity. This information is to be used to determine the world coordinates of P_0.

We begin by using the transformation equations (6-12) to obtain the coordinates (u, v, w) based on what we know about the image coordinates (x, y). Together with the known distance w, we then obtain $u = 0$, $v = -3$, and $w = 8$, and hence

$$\mathbf{r}_0 = \begin{bmatrix} 0 & -1 & 0 & 0 \\ 0 & 0 & 1 & 4 \\ -1 & 0 & 0 & 32 \\ 0 & 0 & 0 & 1 \end{bmatrix} \begin{pmatrix} 0 \\ -3 \\ 8 \\ 1 \end{pmatrix} = \begin{pmatrix} 3 \\ 12 \\ 32 \\ 1 \end{pmatrix}$$

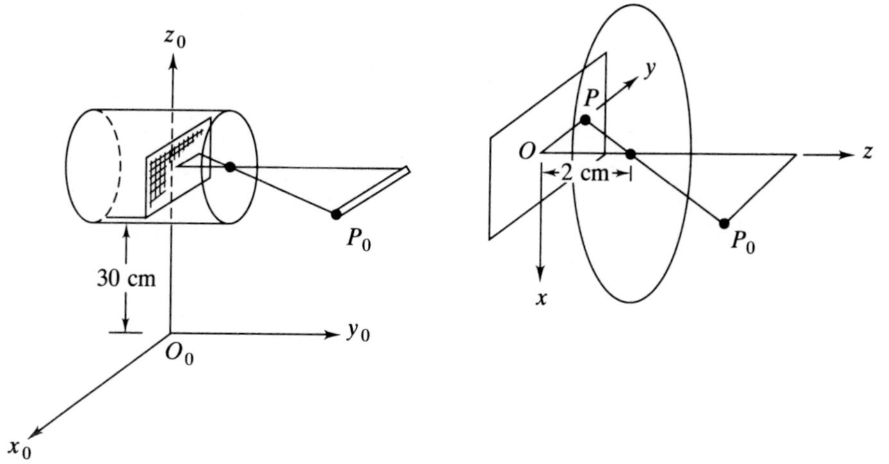

FIGURE 6-33
Location of a point from its image.

as the world coordinates of P_0. These calculations seem deceptively simple and quick. In reality, this approach can be quite time consuming. We leave it to the reader to deduce where we have buried most of the time needed for carrying out these calculations.

The transformation equations (6-12) may be obtained in a compact form by introducing a homogeneous perspective transformation matrix **P** relating the image coordinates and the coordinates of the object point with respect to the sensor reference frame. There is a slight deviation from our earlier use of homogeneous coordinates, where we simply set the scaling factor equal to 1 to obtain an immediate identification with the physical coordinates. Here, the retrieval of the transformation equations from a simple matrix multiplication is based on a suitable choice of scale factor. In order to determine this proper choice, we introduce arbitrary scale factors with both the image point coordinates and the object point coordinates. We thus write

$$\begin{pmatrix} k_0 x \\ k_0 y \\ k_0 z \\ k_0 \end{pmatrix} = \begin{bmatrix} 1 & 0 & 0 & 0 \\ 0 & 1 & 0 & 0 \\ 0 & 0 & 1 & 0 \\ 0 & 0 & -\dfrac{1}{f_i} & 1 \end{bmatrix} \begin{pmatrix} ku \\ kv \\ kw \\ k \end{pmatrix} = \begin{pmatrix} ku \\ kv \\ kw \\ -\dfrac{k}{f_i} w + k \end{pmatrix}$$

The square matrix in this equation is termed the perspective transformation matrix **P**. The division of both sides of the equation by the scale factor

$$k_0 = k\left(-\frac{w}{f_i} + 1\right)$$

then yields the following relationships between the physical coordinates

$$x = \frac{uf_i}{f_i - w} \qquad y = \frac{vf_i}{f_i - w} \qquad z = \frac{f_i w}{f_i - w}$$

Only the first two relationships are relevant within the present context, since $z = 0$ always for points in the image plane, while w clearly is nonzero. Mathematically, $z = 0$ is simply the image of all points P_0 which lie on the ray that passes through the lens center. We deal with this discrepancy by simply ignoring the z-coordinate transformation.

This concludes our discussion of vision systems. We have concentrated on solid-state devices, since they are superior to traditional systems in most respects and it is clear that they will eventually supplant them for image acquisition. Computer vision is an extremely rich area which is only in its infancy. Image analysis and pattern recognition are still the most time-consuming part in any application of computer vision. In the problem given previously—determining the location of an object by using its image—nearly all of the computational time is used in locating the point in the image plane. Current capabilities do not yet even approximate human vision.

When used in a more narrow context or in a surrounding specifically designed for computer vision, with proper lighting and object presentation, computer vision can be a powerful and quick sensor for providing decision information. The list of where it is being used successfully is long and ranges from grocery store checkout counters to electronic assembly lines, for proper alignment of electrical connections. At present, however, by the time a robot's vision system analyzes the source of an annoying buzz, the fly will be gone.

EXERCISES

6-1. Recall that for a plane light wave we have

$$E(x,t) = E_m \sin(kx - \omega t) \qquad E_m > 0$$

Show that the root mean square (rms) value for the wave is given by

$$E_{\text{rms}} = \left[\frac{1}{T}\int_0^T E^2(x,t)\,dt\right]^{1/2} = \frac{1}{\sqrt{2}}E_m$$

6-2. The expression for the relativistic relationship between the momentum p and the total energy E of a particle, such as a proton or electron, is given by

$$E^2 = (pc)^2 + (mc^2)^2$$

Assume $m = 0$ and obtain an expression for the linear momentum of a photon in terms of the wavelength λ. Include units with your answer.

6-3. A sodium vapor lamp emits yellow light at an effective wavelength of 589 nm. Determine the energy of an emitted photon and its momentum. Include units with your answer.

6-4. Shown in Fig. E6-4 is a graph of the stopping potential V_0 versus the frequency ν for sodium. Determine the work function ϕ for the sodium. Include units with your answer.

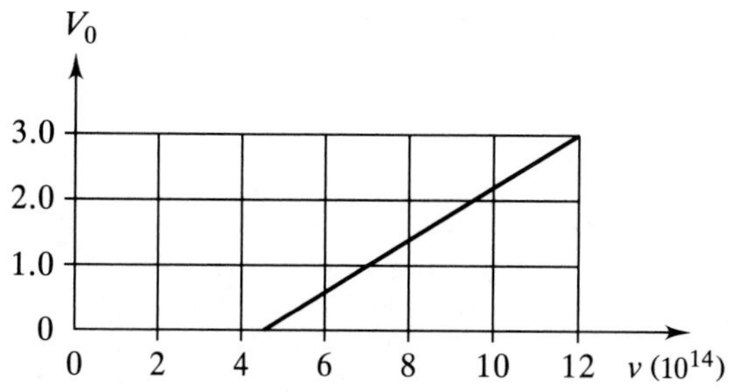

FIGURE E6-4

6-5. Calculate the angle α between the tangent line to the curve $y^2 = 2px$ at an arbitrary point $P(x, y)$ on the curve and the line PF connecting P and the focus F of the parabola (see Fig. E6-5).

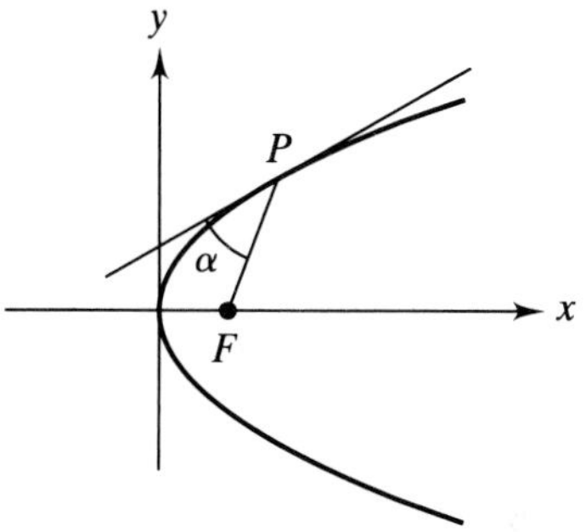

FIGURE E6-5

6-6. Show that for small θ the focal distance f for the spherical mirror is given by $f = \frac{1}{2}r$, where r is the radius of curvature of the mirror (see Fig. E6-6).

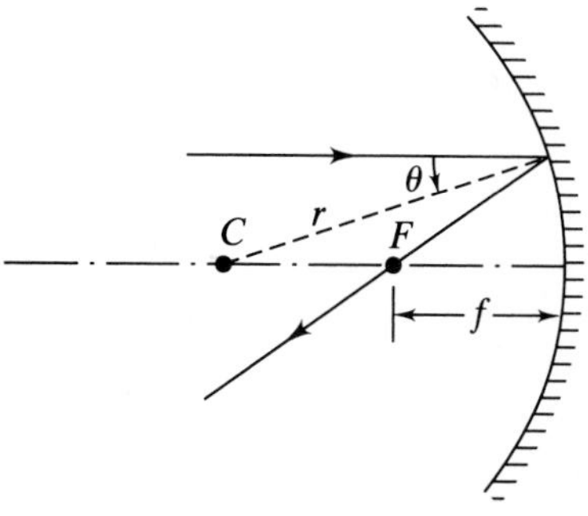

FIGURE E6-6

6-7. Carry out the details of the derivation of (6-8).

6-8. A doubly convex thin glass lens with index of refraction $n = 1.5$ has both radii of curvature of magnitude 20 cm. An object 2 cm high is placed 10 cm from the lens. Find the focal length of the lens; locate the image and find its size. Is the final image virtual or real? Explain.

6-9. The cathode ray tube (CRT) is still the most desirable display device for both monochrome and color video. As in the vidicon tube, electrons are boiled off from a heated cathode, contracted to a beam, and directed to a phosphor coating on the front surface of the tube. Suppose an electron with mass m is emitted at C with initial velocity v_0. It then passes between the vertical deflection plates of length w, where it is subjected to a vertical force of magnitude qV/d, where q is the electron charge, V is the applied voltage across the plates, and d is the distance between the plates. After clearing the plates, the electron travels in a straight line through a vacuum and strikes the phosphorescent screen at P. Determine the deflection s in terms of the dimensions of the voltage plates and tube as illustrated in Fig. E6-9. You may neglect the weight of the electron.

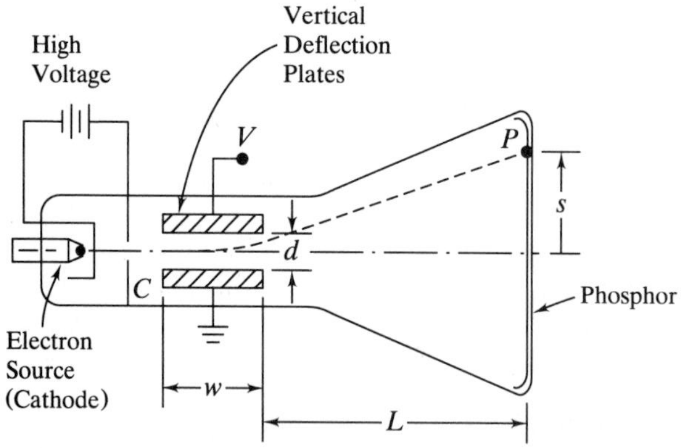

FIGURE E6-9

6-10. Consider a shift register with $n + 1$ photosites labeled $0, 1, 2, \ldots, n$. Suppose that a charge Q_0 is placed into the photosite O and that the charge transfer inefficiency for the register is ϵ. Show that the amount of charge at the kth site after n charge transfers is given by

$$Q_n(k) = \binom{n}{k} Q_0 \epsilon^{n-k} (1 - \epsilon)^k$$

where $\binom{n}{k}$ is the binomial coefficient. Sketch this result for a shift register with four photosites with $Q_0 = 1$ and $\epsilon = 0.1$.

6-11. For those who are mathematically inclined, use mathematical induction to show that the statement $Q_n(k)$ in Exercise 6-10 identifies the charge at the kth site for every n, $k \leq n$. Recall that there are three steps to such a proof:

1. Show that the statement holds for $n = 0$. That is, show that $Q_0(0) = Q_0$.
2. Assume that the statement holds for $n = r$—that is, that $Q_r(k)$ is true, $k \leq r$.
3. Show that if $Q_r(k)$ is true, this implies that the statement holds for $Q_{r+1}(k)$.

6-12. Consider the charge detection scheme mentioned in Sec. 6-5-4. Assume that the charge packet produces a current blip $i_0(t) = I_0\,\delta(t)$.

(*a*) Calculate the corresponding response $v_1(t)$ if $v_1(0) = 0$.
(*b*) Sketch the response.
(*c*) Calculate the time t_1 at which $v_1(t_1)$ is 5% of its initial value.

(*d*) Recall that the impulse response method for the determination of the system function uses a δ-function input, the response of system in s-space being the desired system function. Use this result and the convolution theorem to determine the time responses of the circuit to inputs $i_0(t) = u(t) - u(t-1)$, where $u(\cdot)$ is the unit step function. Use $v_1(0) = 0$ and sketch the response.

6-13. Suppose that the comparator output of some ADC device is given by the 4-bit code identified with the C_i shown in Fig. E6-13. Construct an encoder that will translate this 4-bit code into the indicated 2-bit xy-code.

C_0	C_1	C_2	C_3	x	y
0	0	0	1	0	0
0	0	1	0	0	1
0	1	1	0	1	0

FIGURE E6-13

6-14. Evaluate the camera matrix $\mathbf{C}$ [Eq. (6-11)] and sketch the situation for the following two special cases:

(*a*) The panning angle $\theta = 90°$, the tilt angle $\alpha = 0°$, $\mathbf{c}_c = (0\ b_0\ c_0)^T$, and $\mathbf{c} = (0\ b\ c)^T$. Use $\mathbf{r}_0 = \mathbf{Cr}$ with $\mathbf{r} = (0\ y\ 0)^T$ and sketch your result.

(*b*) Take the panning angle $\theta = 0°$ and the tilt $\alpha = 90°$. Let $\mathbf{c}_c = (a_0\ 0\ c_0)^T$ and $\mathbf{c} = (0\ b\ c)^T$. Use $\mathbf{r}_0 = \mathbf{Cr}$ with $\mathbf{r} = (x\ y\ 0)^T$ and sketch your result.

6-15. Suppose you have a 6×12 pixel area image sensor and a 4-bit gray scale which is evenly divided over the voltage interval $0 \le v_i \le 5$.

(*a*) Calculate the total number of storage bits needed to digitize the frame.

(*b*) How many gray scale levels are there? What specific voltage intervals do they correspond to? State the greatest integer function that will map these intervals into the integers.

(*c*) Assume that the digitized image has the gray scale entries shown in Fig. E6-15. Draw the histogram of the image and thus determine an appropriate (best) threshold voltage for a binary image. Sketch the binary image array based on your choice of threshold. The gray level image depicts a light object on a dark background.

	0	1	2	3	4	5	6	7	8	9	10	11
0	1	4	4	3	3	4	4	3	8	3	12	12
1	1	4	2	9	2	2	2	11	4	8	4	12
2	1	3	4	3	11	11	2	2	2	2	12	7
3	5	4	3	3	3	10	10	11	11	12	12	13
4	3	3	9	3	2	10	10	11	6	12	12	13
5	5	9	10	10	10	10	11	11	11	11	13	13

FIGURE E6-15

6-16. The digitized output of a CCD camera has resulted in the gray scale array shown in Fig. E6-16.

(*a*) Draw a corresponding histogram based on an eight-gray-level subdivision.

(*b*) Choose an optimal threshold v_T, using $v \geq v_T$ as logic 1, and $v < v_T$ as logic 0, and sketch the corresponding binary image array.

(*c*) Calculate the object area, the compactness, and the thinness parameter for the image obtained in part (*b*).

(*d*) If the total operating voltage is 6 V, indicate what voltage intervals map into what gray levels and mark the threshold voltage v_T.

0	2	3	2	3	2	3	2	2
1	2	3	6	6	6	5	2	1
2	2	3	6	7	7	5	2	1
3	1	3	3	6	6	5	2	1
4	1	3	2	0	4	4	2	1
5	1	2	1	2	2	3	3	1

FIGURE E6-16

6-17. Recall that in the discussion of the perspective transformation it was mentioned that the distance w, for example, had to be known in order to carry out the remaining calculations. The present problem illustrates how panning of the camera may be used to determine w. Suppose the camera model has the following parameter values: $a_0 = b_0 = c_0 = 0$, $a = 0$, $b = 6$ cm, and $c = 4$ cm. The focal length $f_i = 4$ cm. It is furthermore known from the image analysis that the image of the object point P_0 for $\theta = 0$ is at $(0, 1, 0)$ and that after panning by $-30°$ the image point is at $(0, -4, 0)$, where the sensor coordinates $(0xyz)$ have been used.

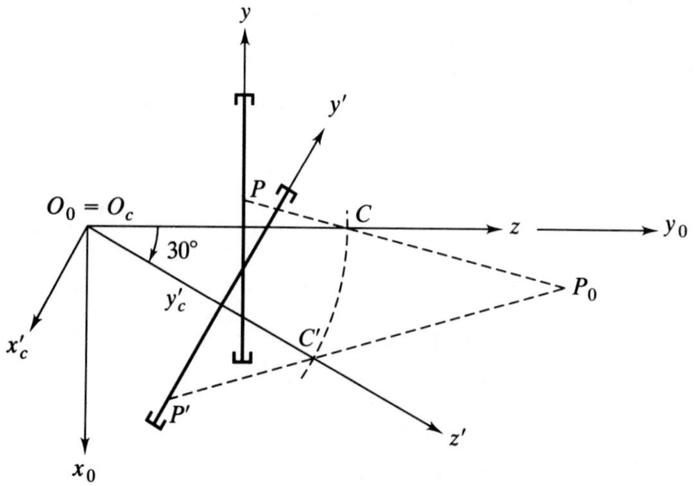

FIGURE E6-17

Use this information to determine the absolute location of P_0 in space as well as its perpendicular distance to the sensor in its initial position. The situation is illustrated in Fig. E6-17.

REFERENCES

1. Sequin, C. H., and M. F. Tompsett: *Charge Transfer Devices*, Academic Press, Inc., New York, 1975.
2. Fairchild-Weston-Schlumberger: *1987 CCD Databook (CCD Solid State Imaging Technology)*, Fairchild Weston Systems, Inc., CCD Imaging Division, 810 West Maude Avenue, Sunnyvale, California 94086. Current company address: Loral Fairchild Imaging Sensors, 1801 McCarthy Boulevard, Milpitas, California 95035.
3. Gonzalez, R. C., and P. Wintz: *Digital Image Processing*, Addison-Wesley, Reading, Mass., 1987.
4. Halliday, D., and R. Resnick: *Fundamentals of Physics*, extended 3rd ed., Wiley, New York, 1988.
5. Levine, M. D.: *Vision in Man and Machine*, McGraw-Hill, New York, 1985.
6. Pinson, L. J.: *Electro-Optics*, Wiley, New York, 1985.
7. Dyck, R. H.: "Design, Fabrication and Performance of CCD Images," Chapter 3 in *VLSI Electronics: Microstructure Science*, vol. 3, Academic, New York, 1982.
8. Dyck, R. H.: "VLSI Imagers," in *VLSI Handbook*, Academic, New York, 1985.
9. Schroder, D. K.: "Extrinsic Silicon Focal Plane Arrays," in *Charge-Coupled Devices* (D. F. Barbe, Ed.), *Topics in Applied Physics*, vol. 38, Springer, New York, 1980.
10. Smith, W.: [no title available], *Journal of the Society of Telegraph Engineers*, vol. 2, p. 31, 1873.
11. Burstein, E., et al.: [no title available], *Physical Reviews*, vol. 82, p. 764, 1951.
12. Boyle, W. S., and G. E. Smith: [no title available], *Bell Systems Technical Journal*, vol. 49, pp. 587–593, 1970.
13. Jones, K. A.: *Introduction to Optical Electronics*, Harper and Row, New York, 1987.
14. Navon, D. H.: *Electronic Materials and Devices*, Houghton Mifflin, Boston, 1975.
15. Freeman, H.: "On the Encoding of Arbitrary Geometric Configurations," *IEEE Transactions on Electronics and Computers*, vol. EC-10, pp. 260–268, 1961.

CHAPTER
SEVEN

ACTUATORS AND POWER TRANSMISSION DEVICES

In this chapter we treat the muscle and tendons of robots. In earlier chapters we provided the basic kinematics, including prescribed motions, and we determined the forces and moments required to sustain these motions. For implementation we simply assumed that there were rotary and linear actuators available to supply the forces and moments. Here, we shall discuss some implements.

There are two major classes of actuators: Those that are powered by a pressurized fluid or gas, and those that are based on electrical power. Of these two groups, pneumatic and hydraulic systems are still used far more in robotics than are electric motors. There are a variety of reasons for this.

In load carrying capacity, for example, the robot driven by electrical motors generally has the least capability, say 0 to 5 lb, compared with the pneumatic robot's payload of 5 to 10 lb, while the hydraulic robot has load carrying capacities of up to 2000 lb. For electric motors the power-to-weight and torque-to-weight ratios are major disadvantages. However, they can easily be supplied with power and are portable; they also operate cleanly and can be precisely controlled.

Because of weight and inertia considerations, power sources are often located at some distance from their point of actual application, or they may supply their power in an unmodulated form. This necessitates the use of power transmission devices. We shall discuss only three such implements—belts, spur gears, and power screws—all of which are frequently used in robotics.

As in previous chapters we shall often use a "just in time" approach to treat some of the well-known basics in some detail, including a review of topics when needed.

7-1 PNEUMATIC AND HYDRAULIC ACTUATORS

We shall give a combined treatment of these two devices because of their many similarities. From an analytical point of view, the hydraulically driven robot is the more interesting of the two; we thus emphasize its analysis. Prior to their separate discussions, it is useful to provide a comparison of the advantages and disadvantages of the two systems as well as a contrast in terms of use.

Pneumatically powered robot components generally move at full speed from one mechanical stop to the next, with no intermediate motion control except for a possible damping of the impact at each stop. The mechanical stops may be changed to "reprogram" the robot. For these reasons such robots are also called "bang-bang," with reference to their noise of operation, and "pick-and-place," with reference to their main use. Some continuous control has been accomplished with pneumatically operated systems. By comparison, hydraulic robots may—and generally do—provide continuous control of the motion.

Both air and fluid are provided to the systems in pressurized form—air usually at about 100 psi or 7 to 8 bars (1 bar = 1 atm = 14.7 psi); oil, in the hydraulic system, is at about 2000 psi or about 14 MPa (1 psi = 6895 Pa).

Air is a relatively clean operating medium and may be released to the surroundings with little negative effect (if you do not mind the constant pfft, pfft). For the hydraulic system at 2000 psi, even a pinhole leak can wreak havoc: Oil can quickly soil a large area, and the nearly invisible high-pressure stream can damage equipment and injure human operators. Also, oil is flammable, which requires extreme caution and necessitates continuous cooling to maintain proper operating temperatures, whereas pneumatic systems are relatively indifferent to temperature changes.

The compressibility of air allows compliance with outside forces. Oil is essentially incompressible, allowing no compliance with the outside system once the main flow valve has been closed. The hydraulic system thus has high positioning stiffness. System response depends on the amount of time taken by a disturbance to propagate through the system; the propagation speed in oil is about four times faster than in air.

In contrast with oil, which automatically lubricates the system, air provides virtually no lubrication; therefore dry friction tends to be a problem in pneumatic systems. In addition, pneumatic systems tend to be less damped than hydraulic systems because air is not highly viscous, as oil is. However, unlike air which requires no cleaning, oil must be continuously filtered and cleaned since even very small particles of the order of 1/5000 can cause a hydraulic system to lock up.

These are some of the major advantages and disadvantages of the two systems. We now turn to some of the governing fluid equations that they have in common.

7-1-1 Description of Fluid Behavior

Mechanical engineers taking this course have probably had a basic course in fluids. However, electrical engineers quite likely have not, what with the trend toward "all-encompassing specialization"; and they probably thought they would never have to deal with such systems anyway. The former may take comfort in the fact that we are not really using any hard fluid concepts; and the latter, that all of the system stuff remains the same. Any basic text in fluid mechanics may be used for further study. We take White[1] as our desk reference.

Fluid systems may operate in one of two basic modes: static and dynamic. In the static case, fluid flow effects are negligible, and force and torque are taken to be proportional to the pressure. This is the prevalent case in robotics. Since the fluid generally acts on moving parts (e.g., a piston), we consider a pressure difference $p_2 - p_1$ and take the *force* to be given by

$$F = A_0(p_2 - p_1) \tag{7-1}$$

where A_0 is an area, and take the *moment* to be

$$M = V_0(p_2 - p_1) \tag{7-2}$$

where V_0 is some characteristic volume.

For the dynamic operating mode, fluid flow at high speed is used to drive some rotating device, such as a turbine.

For the remaining fluid equations, we consider a steady-state flow at low velocity. All of the flows may be considered one dimensional, in that the fluid properties will be a function of only one spatial variable. If the cross-sectional areas at two ends of a tube are A_1 and A_2 (see Fig. 7-1), then the expression of *conservation of mass* takes on the form

$$\rho_1 A_1 v_1 = \rho_2 A_2 v_2 \tag{7-3}$$

The quantity ρAV is termed the *mass flux*, which may also be denoted in an abbreviated fashion by $\dot{m}$. When the mass density ρ is constant, we have

$$A_1 v_1 = A_2 v_2 \tag{7-4}$$

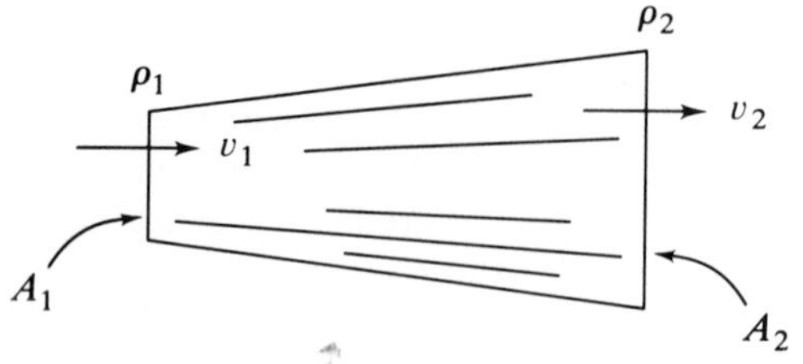

FIGURE 7-1
Flow through a stream tube.

and we simply define $q = Av$ as the *volumetric flow rate* of the liquid. Observing the conservation of mass in the derivation of basic governing equations is important, since a violation of the condition will generally produce totally useless results.

For steady frictionless incompressible flow, the total energy in the flow is conserved. The classical expression for the conservation of the total energy along a stream line is the Bernoulli equation,

$$\frac{p}{\rho} + \frac{1}{2}v^2 + gz = \text{const.} \tag{7-5}$$

where (p, ρ, v) are the fluid properties at a point on the stream line and z is the corresponding elevation above some chosen datum. Furthermore, if we assume that these properties are uniform across a stream tube with cross section A, then we may also write the equation in terms of the volumetric flow rate as

$$p + \frac{1}{2}\rho\frac{q^2}{A^2} + \rho gz = \text{const.} \tag{7-6}$$

All liquids are nearly incompressible; however, even gases may behave as if they were incompressible at low speeds (say, at speeds less than one-third the speed of sound in the gas). In high-performance hydraulic systems, the effect of oil compressibility must be included.

Consider a reservoir of constant volume V containing a fluid at a uniform pressure p. Then, if q_1 and q_2 are the incoming and outgoing volumetric flows, respectively, the conservation of mass for the volume may be expressed as

$$\rho q_1 - \rho q_2 = \frac{d}{dt}(\rho V) = V\frac{d\rho}{dt}$$

or

$$q_1 - q_2 = \frac{V}{\rho}\frac{d\rho}{dt} \tag{7-7}$$

It is also often useful to express this equation in terms of the pressure change rather than the density change. A relationship between pressure and density is a *constitutive* relationship for a *particular* fluid. For most liquids a good first-order approximation relating differential pressure and density is given by

$$d\rho = \frac{\rho}{B}\,dp \tag{7-8}$$

where B (in newtons per square meter or pounds per square inch) is termed the *bulk modulus* or the *compressibility modulus* of the liquid. With (7-8) the mass conservation equation (7-7) may be written in the form

$$q_1 - q_2 = \frac{V}{B}\frac{dp}{dt} \tag{7-9}$$

Remark 7-1. It is also common to simply define the bulk modulus by

$$B = -V\frac{\partial p}{\partial V} = \rho\frac{\partial p}{\partial \rho}$$

the partials being taken with the entropy held constant. The bulk modulus of a liquid thus is strongly dependent on the local temperature and pressure. In an operating system these can change rapidly, and an effort must be made at intermediate points to reestablish operating values. For example, if cavitation develops in a hydraulic liquid (air bubbles form), then the bulk modulus could drop virtually to 0 at such a location. At the other extreme, the ideal case of complete incompressibility corresponds to an infinite bulk modulus.

We now provide a few examples so that the student may regain familiarity with fluid theoretic concepts.

Example 7-1. Suppose a cylindrical reservoir with cross section A has liquid flowing into it at a rate q_i and liquid exiting at a flow rate of q_0 as shown in Fig. 7-2. The flow exits through a valve whose pressure-flow relationship may be approximated by $p = Rq_0$, where p is the pressure drop across the valve. Assume that all openings are at atmospheric pressure.

(a) Derive the governing differential equation for this system with the input flow rate as input and the height h of the liquid as output.

(b) Determine the corresponding system function.

Solution

(a) Since the flows are volumetric flows, we have the volume time rate of change

$$\frac{d}{dt}(Ah(t)) = q_i(t) - q_0(t) \tag{7-10}$$

where the respective time dependence has been emphasized. The pressure at the tank outlet prior to the valve is related to the head by

$$p(t) = \rho g h(t)$$

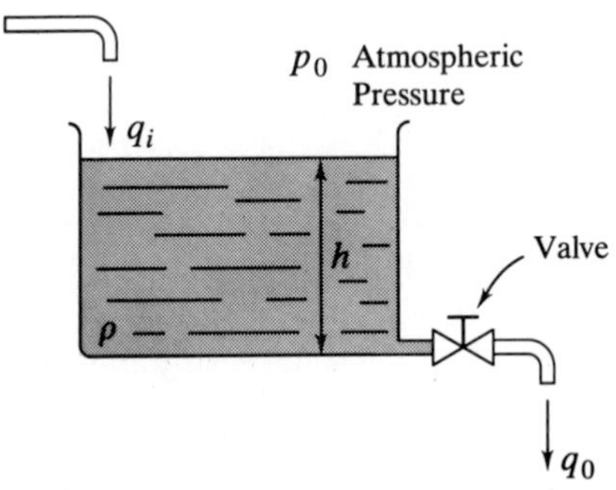

FIGURE 7-2
Tank filling with liquid.

Together with the relationship for the valve, we thus have

$$q_0(t) = \frac{\rho g}{R} h(t) \tag{7-11}$$

Substitution of (7-11) into (7-10) yields

$$\frac{dh}{dt} + \frac{\rho g}{RA} h = \frac{1}{A} q_i(t) \tag{7-12}$$

as the governing differential equation for the system.

(*b*) The system function is obtained by taking the Laplace transform of *both* sides of the equation with all initial conditions set equal to 0,

$$\left(s + \frac{\rho g}{RA}\right) H(s) = \frac{1}{A} Q_i(s)$$

or

$$G(s) = \frac{H(s)}{Q_i(s)} = \frac{R}{\rho g} \frac{1}{\tau s + 1} \qquad \tau = \frac{RA}{\rho g} \tag{7-13}$$

with τ being the *time constant* of this first-order system.

Example 7-2. The radius of a horizontal circular duct changes gradually from a segment 1 with radius r_1 to a segment 2 with radius $r_2 < r_1$ as shown in Fig. 7-3. Obtain an expression for the mass flux in the narrowed section as a function of the pressure difference between segments 1 and 2.

Solution. Based on a use of the Bernoulli equation (7-5) for the center (stream) line, we have

$$\frac{p_1}{\rho} + \frac{1}{2} v_1^2 + g z_1 = \frac{p_2}{\rho} + \frac{1}{2} v_2^2 + g z_2$$

Since the tube is horizontal, $z_1 = z_2$, and

$$\frac{p_1}{\rho} + \frac{1}{2} v_1^2 = \frac{p_2}{\rho} + \frac{1}{2} v_2^2$$

or

$$v_2^2 - v_1^2 = \frac{2}{\rho}(p_1 - p_2)$$

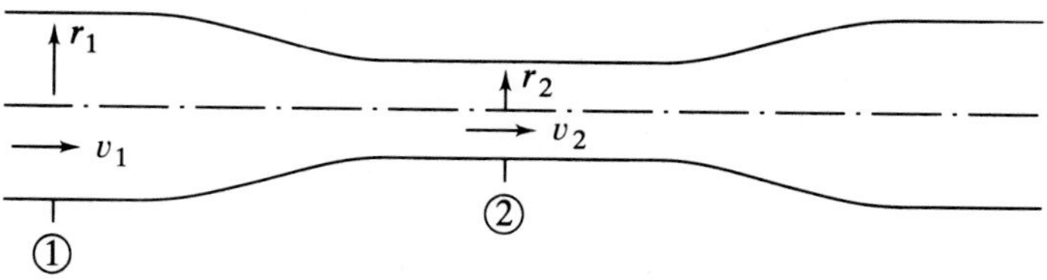

FIGURE 7-3
A venturi tube.

As always, the incompressible continuity equation (7-4) must hold

$$A_1 v_1 = A_2 v_2 \quad \Rightarrow \quad v_1 = r^2 v_2 \qquad r = \frac{r_2}{r_1}$$

This equation may be substituted into the previous equation to obtain

$$v_2 = \left[\frac{2(p_1 - p_2)}{\rho(1 - r^4)} \right]^{1/2}$$

The mass flux is then given by

$$\dot{m} = \rho A_2 v_2 = \pi r_1^2 \left[\frac{2\rho(p_1 - p_2)}{1 - r^4} \right]^{1/2}$$

7-1-2 Fluid Flow Through a Small Orifice

The following discussion is relevant for the modeling of flow through a valve, an essential component of controlled fluid flow. The same theory is also used in the design of fluid metering devices which are used in the measurement of head loss, for example. Collectively, these are termed *Bernoulli-type devices*, and the corresponding theory is called *Bernoulli obstruction theory*.

Recall that the Reynolds number R for a flow is given by

$$R = \frac{\rho v D}{\mu}$$

where ρ is the fluid mass density, μ is the dynamic viscosity, v is the average flow velocity, and D is a characteristic length (e.g., a pipe diameter). The Reynolds number is a nondimensional parameter that characterizes flow behavior. In particular, we distinguish between *laminar flow*, a flow dominated by viscosity forces, and *turbulent flow*, which is dominated by inertia forces. The former generally occurs for $R < 2000$, and the latter for $R \geq 2000$. For the modeling of flow in hydraulic systems, turbulent flow at high Reynolds number is the most relevant.

There are two types of sudden flow changes that may occur: a sudden expansion or a sudden contraction. In the former, the flow loss due to shear stresses arising in the separated flow at the exit corners is negligible, and a control volume analysis suffices to obtain a theoretical estimate of the losses (White[1]). In the latter, the flow separation in the downstream section causes the main stream to contract through a minimum diameter called the *vena contracta* (see Fig. 7-4). We shall analyze this flow in some detail.

The Bernoulli equation and the continuity equation are the basic equations for the flow between locations 1 and 2; that is, we have

$$\frac{v_1^2}{2} + \frac{p_1}{\rho} + g z_1 = \frac{v_2^2}{2} + \frac{p_2}{\rho} + g z_2$$

and

$$v_1 A_1 = v_2 A_2$$

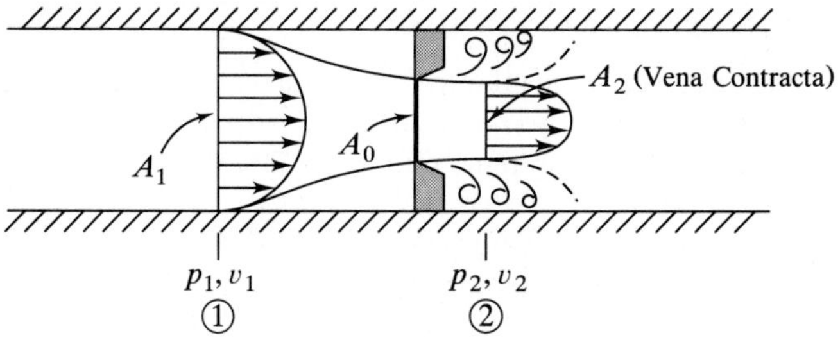

FIGURE 7-4
Small orifice flow.

With $z_1 = z_2$, their simultaneous solution yields the volumetric flow rate at location 2,

$$v_2 A_2 = \frac{A_2}{\sqrt{1 - (A_2/A_1)^2}} \sqrt{\frac{2}{\rho}(p_1 - p_2)}$$

To avoid having to measure the *vena contracta*, we now assume that A_2 is nearly equal to A_0, and we introduce the contraction ratio $C_c = A_2/A_1$, with the result

$$v_2 A_2 = \frac{A_0}{\sqrt{1 - C_c^2}} \sqrt{\frac{2}{\rho}(p_1 - p_2)}$$

Another inaccuracy still present in the expression is due to the neglect of friction in duct flow, where it is known to have a strong effect. To account for it, we introduce an experimentally determined dimensionless *discharge coefficient* C_d and thus obtain the flow rate

$$q = C_d A_0 \frac{1}{\sqrt{1 - C_c^2}} \sqrt{\frac{2}{\rho}(p_1 - p_2)}$$

We then introduce a *flow coefficient* (experimentally determined)

$$c = \frac{C_d}{\sqrt{1 - C_c^2}}$$

to write the flow rate in the final form

$$q = cA_0 \sqrt{\frac{2}{\rho}(p_1 - p_2)} \tag{7-14}$$

7-1-3 Hydraulic Actuators

Hydraulic actuators do not exist in a vacuum. Valves are essential for their controlled operation, and they have little purpose without loads. The mathematical model must consider the combined system. The main aim of this section is to arrive at a suitable model, although we shall also provide a discussion of other items essential to the proper operation of a hydraulic system. In the arrangement and discussion of the material in this section, the author benefitted from the considerably more detailed treatment given in Dransfield[2] and Ogata.[3] Part of the effort will be directed toward helping the student gain a foothold in the area of hydraulic control systems, including some of the standard symbols used in hydraulic system design.

Hydraulic systems power the strongest and the stiffest robots available. Hydraulic robots have handled payloads of up to 2000 lb. Hydraulic systems can produce flow rates ranging from 2 to 500 gal/min, ultimately encompassing a power range of 3 to 700 hp. It is generally recommended that hydraulics be used for systems requiring more than 5 to 7 hp.

For proper operation of a hydraulic system, the compliance and hence the bulk modulus of the oil are extremely important attributes to be selected. A high bulk modulus implies a stiff, quickly responding system with a corresponding quick pressure buildup, while a low bulk modulus may result in a system that is too loose because of the high compressibility of the oil.

We shall use the following physical parameter values for computational purposes.† We shall assume that the operating fluid is a light mineral oil with a bulk modulus of 100,000 psi in its operational state, a mass density of $\rho = 1.60\ \text{slug/ft}^3$, a *kinematic viscosity* of $\nu = 0.00035\ \text{ft}^2/\text{sec}$, and a *dynamic* or *absolute viscosity* of $\mu = \rho\nu = 0.00056\ \text{slug/(ft}\cdot\text{sec)}$. We take 2000 psi to be a reasonable operating pressure.

Remark 7-2. We again remind the reader that the material parameters are local values or average values for the system. For example, the viscosity of some fluids can vary widely with operating temperature. Thus, if wide temperature fluctuations are expected, the fluid must be appropriately chosen.

With these preliminaries, we now turn to a discussion of hydraulic system components. Rather than making some arbitrary selection, we shall base our discussion on the specific hydraulic system depicted in Fig. 7-5*a*.

Similar to the symbols used in logic circuits and in electric circuits, there are a variety of symbols used in hydraulic circuit design. We have made use of these symbols in the figure. Descriptions are also included, to ease the student into the acceptance and routine use of these symbols. We shall describe each component in turn; however, our mathematical system model will comprise only

†The actual values in use vary too widely to be able to specify some common or average value.

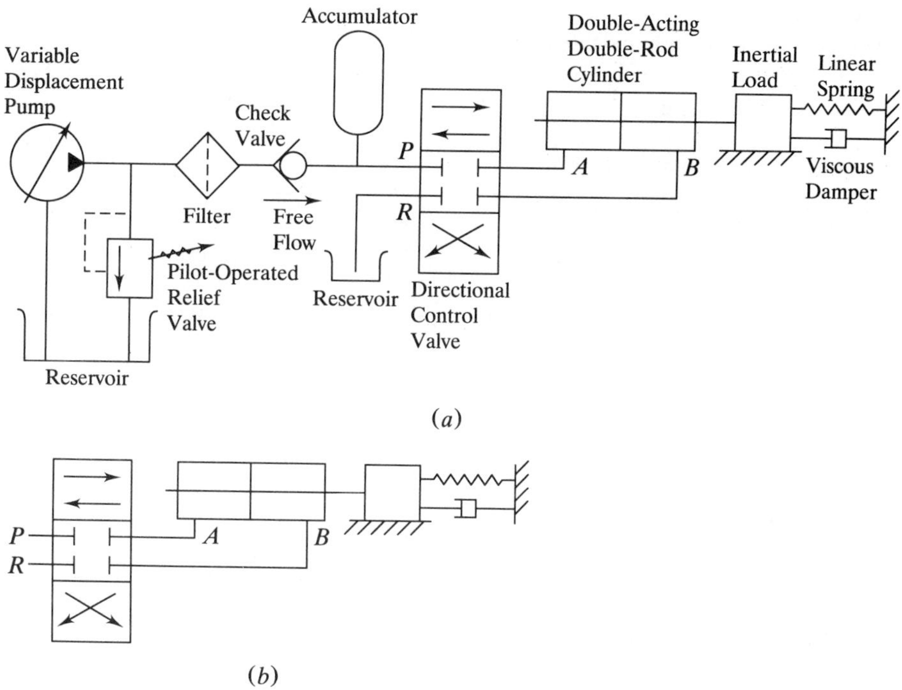

FIGURE 7-5
(*a*) Complete hydraulic circuit; (*b*) system components to be mathematically modeled.

the components shown in Fig. 7-5*b*. A sample tabulation of the symbols used for hydraulic system components is given in Table 7-1.

Hydraulic systems or circuits always contain four essential components: a reservoir to hold the fluid and pumps to move it, valves to control the flow, and an actuator to carry out the dictates of the fluid on some load. In the component descriptions that follow, we shall make use of the symbol identifications used in Fig. 7-5 and Table 7-1.

RESERVOIR. The reservoir holds the fluid used in hydraulic operation and should contain ample fluid for all system operations. That is its obvious function. The reservoir serves to cool and clean the returning hydraulic fluid and, in addition, to prevent turbulence, which tends to introduce air bubbles into the fluid. (It is important to remember that the mixture of air into the system can drastically alter the fluid properties and may damage system components.)

VARIABLE DISPLACEMENT PUMP. Hydraulic pumps may be classified as *positive displacement* and *nonpositive displacement* pumps. The main distinction is that a positive displacement pump is sealed between inlet and outlet, preventing

TABLE 7-1
Symbols for hydraulic system components

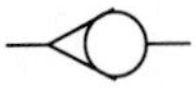	Check valve; flow is free to the right, blocked to the left	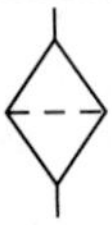	Filter
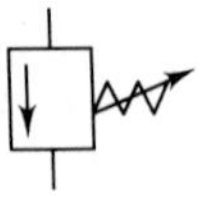	Simple relief valve	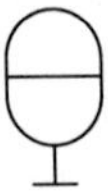	Accumulator
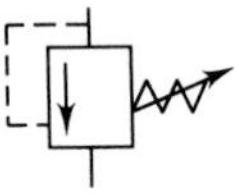	Pilot-operated relief valve	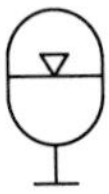	Gas-pressurized accumulator
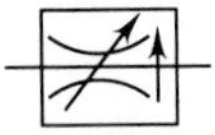	Pressure-compensated flow control valve		Variable displacement pump
	Needle valve with variable restrictor		Pressure-compensated variable displacement pump
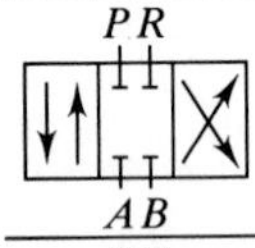	Directional control valve closed port–closed center	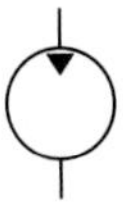	Gear motor
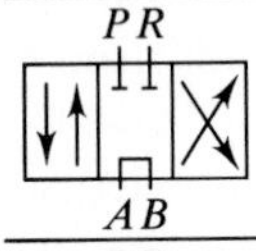	Directional control valve closed center–open port		Variable displacement motor
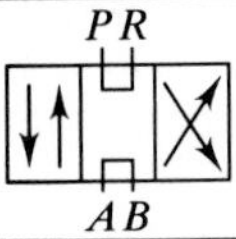	Directional control valve open center–open port	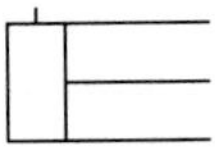	Single-action cylinder
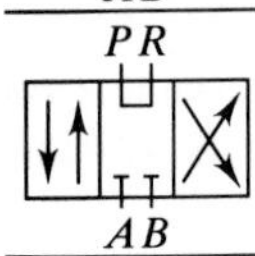	Directional control valve open center–closed port	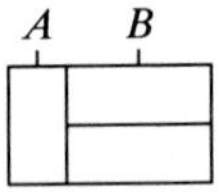	Double-action single-rod cylinder
	Hydraulic reservoir	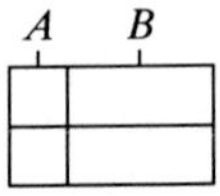	Double-action double-rod cylinder

the backflow of liquid; whereas a nonpositive displacement pump has no such seal. In the case of the latter type, when the output is constricted in some fashion, part of the liquid will be forced back into the pump. The pump will continue to operate, and the pressure will build up, with a maximum pressure reached when the pump is completely blocked. A positive displacement pump creates flow rather than pressure; it maintains a constant flow rate even though the outlet may be constricted. Since both controlled flow and pressure are essential to the proper operation of a hydraulic system, nonpositive displacement pumps are of little use for such systems.

Pump volume is the amount of fluid discharged or moved by the pump in one minute. Virtually all hydraulic pumps double as hydraulic motors and hence as rotary hydraulic actuators.

FILTER. Filters, strainers, and magnetic plugs remove particles from the fluid. Fluid contamination accelerates system wear and, if severe, may block system operation. Filters are rated in accordance with allowed pressure and the size of the particles trapped.

ACCUMULATOR. Accumulators serve two functions. For a given flow supplied to a hydraulic line, they can provide a suddenly required increase in fluid; or, conversely, they can serve as shock absorbers, accepting fluid which is forced back into the system due to an increase in load, for example. In other words, they cope with sudden fluid requirements or restrictions and facilitate the fluid flow to subsequent system points.

PILOT-OPERATED RELIEF VALVE. A hydraulic system simply cannot operate without valves. If fluid were to be pumped at a constant rate in a closed system, pressure would build up until some orifice is created to provide an outlet for the fluid. A relief valve provides a noncatastrophic outlet. Valves respond to pressure. As long as the operating pressure is normal, the fluid flows toward the system load. If the pressure becomes too great, the relief valve opens and reroutes some of the fluid back to the reservoir until pressure returns to normal. The response pressure of the valve may or may not be adjustable.

A valve acts like a flow restrictor: As more fluid tries to pass through the valve opening, the system pressure tends to build up. As more and more fluid is returned to the reservoir, the pressure drops below the *cracking pressure* of the valve, and the valve closes. This opening and closing of the valve sends shocks through the system. One way to avoid them is to include a pilot valve. The primary valve, secured by a fixed spring, has a hole through which fluid may flow into a chamber which is secured by the adjustable pilot valve. As pressure builds up in this chamber, the pilot valve opens and allows some fluid to return to the reservoir. Eventually, this reduction of pressure in the chamber will cause the opening of the main valve due to the system pressure. More fluid will return to the reservoir, until the pressure in the chamber again overwhelms the system pressure and forces the main valve closed. Thus the main valve moves only enough to maintain system pressure.

CHECK VALVE. A check valve simply allows fluid to flow in only one direction. Flow in the other direction is blocked.

ACTUATORS. We have already mentioned that hydraulic pumps also serve as rotary actuators. There are three main types of linear actuators: single-action pistons, double-action pistons, and differential pistons. For a cylinder and piston, we distinguish between the *rod end* and the *blind end*. For a single-action cylinder, fluid is pumped into the blind end only; the piston is returned by a spring or by the load. For the double-action cylinder, fluid is pumped into both ends of the cylinder. Since the piston rod is on the rod side, the piston areas exposed to the fluid are different, and different amounts of pressure are required to produce a given force. This asymmetry can be overcome by using piston rods on both sides of the cylinder—a double-action piston with a double shaft. In the case of the differential piston, a fixed pressure is maintained in the rod end, while the blind end functions as before.

DIRECTION CONTROL VALVES. Depending on the desired motion of the piston, fluid must be directed either to the rod end or the blind end. This directing of the fluid flow is accomplished by directional control valves. Generally, this requires two outlets, or *control ports*, to supply the piston ends with fluid, and two valve inlets, one for the hydraulic fluid supply and the other to return fluid to the reservoir. These inlets are termed the *center*. The various ways in which the inlets and outlets can be connected form "tracks" in a valve, with the fluid being switched to different tracks by an appropriate displacement of the *valve spool*.

A valve is classified in accordance with the tracks that exist when the spool is in its neutral position. Thus the valve may be a *closed-center–open-port* valve, for example, meaning that the valve spool completely blocks fluid supply and drain and that fluid is free to flow between the two ports at the piston ends. In essence, all of the actuators mentioned require four such tracks, with the exception of the differential piston, whose valve need only supply three tracks. Control over the flow and, hence, over the actuator motion, is thus achieved by positioning the spool, either manually or by means of electrical servos.

Collectively, the four-track valves are called four-way spool valves, and it is this type of valve, together with the linear actuator and load, that we shall now model mathematically.

We shall develop governing equations for each segment in turn. Recall that the governing equations of a physical system are unique, in that their differences can derive only from admissible (admitting the same solution) mathematical manipulations. Because of this uniqueness it suffices to assume some possible state of the system and to base our derivation on that assumption.

Figure 7-6 illustrates the consecutive free bodies, drawn in accordance with the assumed system state. Figure 7-6*a* shows the four-way spool valve with

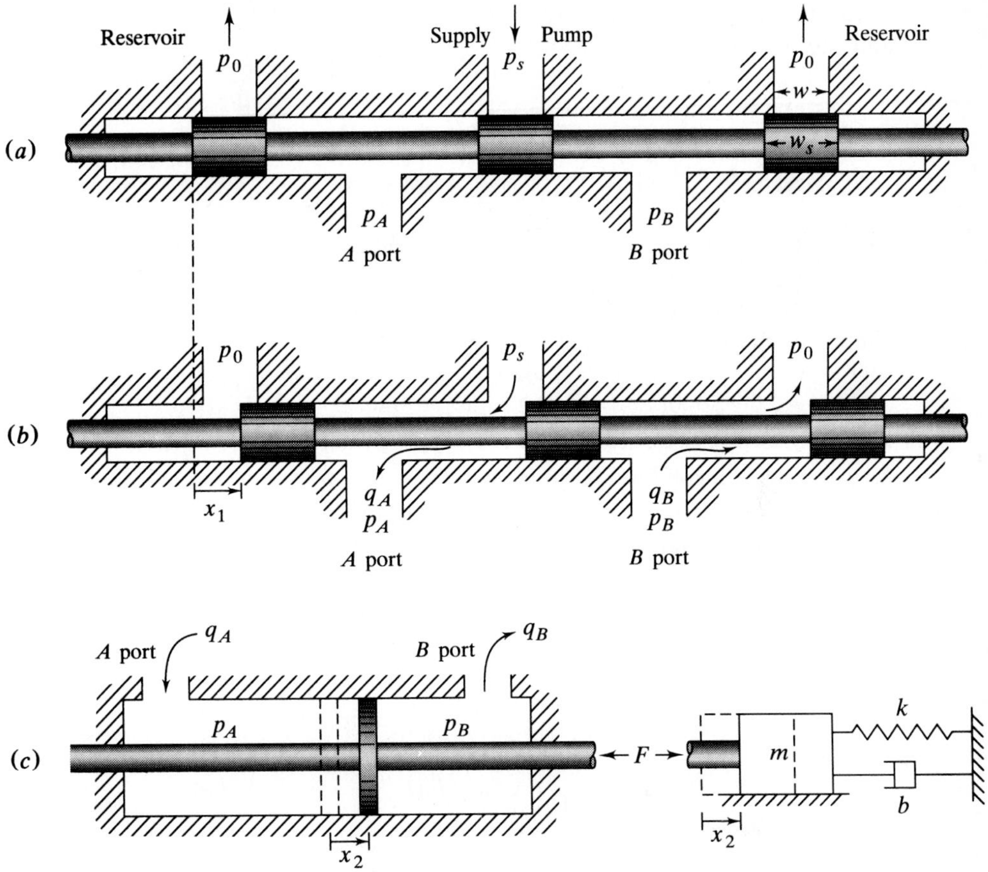

FIGURE 7-6
Free-body diagrams for the valve-actuator-load combination.

its spool in the neutral position blocking all inlets and outlets (closed-center–closed-port valve). Corresponding to this neutral position, we take the piston to be in static equilibrium with equal pressure on both sides of the piston and with zero spring and damper force.

We now assume that the spool is at some displacement $x_1(t)$ from its neutral position, allowing fluid to flow as indicated in Fig. 7-6*b*. The pressures are:

- p_0 the reservoir or sump pressure (sometimes assumed to be negligible, but we shall not make this assumption);
- p_s the supply pressure (it is assumed that the pump supplies fluid at a constant pressure);
- p_A, p_B the actuator pressures at the respective control port locations.

Furthermore, the flows depend on the relationship between the spool width w_s and the port width w. We say that a spool valve

is line on line	if $w = w_s$
underlaps	if $w > w_s$
overlaps	if $w < w_s$

In realistic situations one generally has a slight overlap in order to avoid leakage in the neutral position of the valve.

In the mathematical model for the valve flow, we shall make the following simplifying assumptions:

1. $w = w_s$, the spool and ports are line on line.
2. The reservoir pressure p_0 and the supply pressure p_s are constant.
3. The flow is incompressible, so that $q_A = q_B = q$.
4. The flow areas to the supply and return ports are proportional to the spool displacement; that is, $A_0 = k_0 x_1$ and $A_s = k_s x_1$.

In accordance with (7-14), the flow rates are given by

$$q_A = c_s A_s \sqrt{\frac{2}{\rho}(p_s - p_A)} = C_s x_1 \sqrt{p_s - p_A}$$

and

$$q_B = c_0 A_0 \sqrt{\frac{2}{\rho}(p_B - p_0)} = C_0 x_1 \sqrt{p_B - p_0}$$

where

$$C_s = c_s k_s \sqrt{\frac{2}{\rho}} \qquad \text{and} \qquad C_0 = c_0 k_0 \sqrt{\frac{2}{\rho}}$$

We now suppose that $C_s = C_0$ and equate the flow rates, yielding

$$p_s - p_A = p_B - p_0$$

With the positive pressure differences

$$p = p_A - p_B \qquad \text{and} \qquad \Delta p = p_s - p_0$$

the flow rate may be written in the form

$$q = C_s x_1 \sqrt{\frac{1}{2}(\Delta p - p)} = f(x_1, p)$$

Thus the flow rate is a nonlinear function of the valve displacement and the pressure drop across the piston, since Δp is constant. Our ultimate aim is to obtain a system function, an inherently linear approach, and we shall thus use a linearized version of the relationship around some operating values $(\bar{x}_1, \bar{p})$ of x_1 and p. The usual approach is to expand $f(x_1, p)$ in a Taylor series for several independent variables and to keep only the linear terms. For a function $f(\cdot)\colon \mathbb{R}^n \to \mathbb{R}$ in a neighborhood of the point $\boldsymbol{x}_0$ in $\mathbb{R}^n$, Taylor's formula with remainder is given by†

$$f(\boldsymbol{x}) = f(\boldsymbol{x}_0) + \sum_{i=1}^{n} \frac{\partial f}{\partial x_i}(\boldsymbol{x}_0) h_i + \frac{1}{2!} \sum_{i=1}^{n} \sum_{j=1}^{n} \frac{\partial^2 f}{\partial x_i \, \partial x_j}(\boldsymbol{x}_0) h_i h_j + R_3(\boldsymbol{x})$$

where $h_i = x_i - x_{i0}$ and where the remainder after two terms is given by

$$R_3(\boldsymbol{x}) = \frac{1}{3!} \sum_{i=1}^{n} \sum_{j=1}^{n} \sum_{k=1}^{n} \frac{\partial^3 f}{\partial x_i \, \partial x_j \, \partial x_k}(\boldsymbol{x}_0 + \theta \boldsymbol{h}) h_i h_j h_k$$

with $\theta \in (0, 1)$. Relative to some general operating point, the flow may thus be written in the form

$$q = f(x_1, p) = f(\bar{x}_1, \bar{p}) + \frac{\partial f}{\partial x_1}(\bar{x}_1, \bar{p})(x_1 - \bar{x}_1) + \frac{\partial f}{\partial p}(\bar{x}_1, \bar{p})(p - \bar{p})$$

or

$$q - \bar{q} = k_1(x_1 - \bar{x}_1) - k_2(p - \bar{p}) \tag{7-15}$$

where

$$\bar{q} = f(\bar{x}_1, \bar{p})$$

$$k_1 = \frac{\partial f}{\partial x_1}(\bar{x}_1, \bar{p}) = C_s \sqrt{\frac{1}{2}(\Delta p - \bar{p})}$$

$$k_2 = \frac{\partial f}{\partial p}(\bar{x}_1, \bar{p}) = C_s \left(\frac{1}{2}\right)^{3/2} \frac{\bar{x}_1}{(\Delta p - \bar{p})^{1/2}}$$

Suppose we now specialize the equation to the common operating point $(\bar{x}_1, \bar{p}) = (0, 0)$. Then the flow is given by

$$q = k_1 x_1$$

since $f(0, 0) = 0$ and $k_2 = 0$. This is the linearized flow produced by the valve for a given valve opening x_1. Next, we look at the phenomena that contribute to this required flow rate.

There are three effects that contribute to the flow rate. We assume that these effects are additive, so that

$$q = q_v + q_c + q_L$$

the contributions being due to the volume change, the compression of the fluid, and its leakage around the piston.

---

†For notational convenience we present only terms up to a cubic remainder, based on Fleming.[4]

The contribution due to the volume change is given by

$$q_v = A\frac{dx_2}{dt}$$

where A is the piston cross-sectional area. The contribution due to the compression of the oil in the piston chamber is given by

$$q_c = \frac{V}{B}\frac{dp}{dt}$$

where B is the bulk modulus in the fluid, V is the volume of fluid under compression (about half the cylinder volume), and p, of course, is the net pressure experienced by the fluid. The final contribution is due to the fluid leakage around the piston; we take it to be proportional to the pressure difference across the piston,

$$q_L = k_L p$$

where k_L may be determined experimentally by using the blocked piston test, for example.

We have thus arrived at the following equation relating the valve displacement, the piston displacement, and the pressure drop across the piston:

$$k_1 x_1 = A\frac{dx_2}{dt} + \frac{V}{B}\frac{dp}{dt} + k_L p \tag{7-16}$$

We finally come to the free bodies of piston and load. A straightforward application of Euler's law of linear momentum to the motion of the mass (which we take to include that of the piston and rod) yields

$$m\frac{d^2x_2}{dt^2} + b\frac{dx_2}{dt} + kx_2 = Ap \tag{7-17}$$

Equations (7-16) and (7-17) are the governing differential equations for the system.

The appropriate system functions may now be obtained in the usual fashion. Note that there are two of them. With $x_1(t)$ as the input, we may consider either the pressure difference $p(t)$ or the displacement $x_2(t)$ as the output. The Laplace transform of both equations, with all initial conditions set equal to 0, yields the simultaneous equations

$$\begin{aligned} AsX_2(s) + \left(s\frac{V}{B} + k_L\right)P(s) &= k_1 X_1(s) \\ (ms^2 + bs + k)X_2(s) - AP(s) &= 0 \end{aligned} \tag{7-18}$$

Their simultaneous solution yields the system functions

$$G_x(s) = \frac{X_2(s)}{X_1(s)} = \frac{Ak_1}{(ms^2 + bs + k)\left(s\frac{V}{B} + k_L\right) + A^2 s} \tag{7-19}$$

$$G_p(s) = \frac{P(s)}{X_1(s)} = \frac{k_1(ms^2 + bs + k)}{(ms^2 + bs + k)\left(s\frac{V}{B} + k_L\right) + A^2 s} \tag{7-20}$$

These system functions provide essential segments for the feedback control of the actuator-load combination to be treated in a later section.

7-1-4 Gas Flow Through a Small Orifice

Although we shall take a somewhat more sketchy approach to pneumatic systems than we did to hydraulic ones, we shall maintain the same order of presentation. Again, we begin with small orifice flow essential to the description of gas flow through valves. More often than not, pneumatic actuators are used in a bang-bang fashion with valves either on or off and no settings in between. The open valve acts much like a nozzle, and we shall view it as such in our derivation of the mass flow and pressure relationship for the flow through such a contraction.

Pneumatic systems are generally operated at room temperature and at pressures of around 100 psi. In this range the behavior of air deviates little from that of a perfect gas. We shall ultimately assume isentropic flow, an assumption that is justified for adiabatic flow with negligible friction effects (e.g., the flow through a nozzle). As a desk reference in this context, we have used Streeter and Wylie.[5]

VELOCITY AS A FUNCTION OF AREA. The use of Euler's equation for one-dimensional flow at constant elevation

$$v\,dv + \frac{dp}{\rho} = 0 \tag{7-21}$$

with velocity v, density ρ, and pressure p, together with the differential form of the continuity equation,

$$\frac{d\rho}{\rho} + \frac{dv}{v} + \frac{dA}{A} = 0 \tag{7-22}$$

yields

$$v\,dv + c^2\frac{d\rho}{\rho} = 0 \tag{7-23}$$

where $c^2 = kRT$ is the speed of sound in the gas; k is the ratio of specific heats, R is the gas constant, and T is the absolute temperature. The elimination of

$d\rho/\rho$ between these last two equations and the introduction of the Mach number $M = v/c$ yield

$$\frac{dA}{dv} = \frac{A}{v}(M^2 - 1) \tag{7-24}$$

as the equation governing area change with respect to velocity change. We shall limit our discussion to subsonic flow, since shock waves are not likely to be desirable in pneumatic systems. With $M < 1$, $dA/dv < 0$ is the case, and we conclude that the cross-sectional area must decrease to achieve an increase in velocity.

VELOCITY AS A FUNCTION OF THE DOWNSTREAM PRESSURE. We begin again with Euler's equation

$$v\,dv + \frac{dp}{\rho} = 0$$

For isentropic flow in an ideal gas, we have

$$\frac{p}{\rho^k} = \text{const.} \quad \Rightarrow \quad p = C\rho^k$$

yielding
$$v\,dv + Ck\rho^{k-2}\,d\rho = 0$$

This equation may be integrated to obtain

$$\frac{1}{2}v^2 + \frac{k}{k-1}\frac{p}{\rho} = \text{const.} \tag{7-25}$$

With this in mind, the velocity difference between an upstream station 1 and a downstream station 2 may be written as

$$v_2^2 - v_1^2 = \frac{p_1\rho_1}{\rho_2^2}\frac{2k}{k-1}\left[1\left(\frac{p_2}{p_1}\right)^{2/k} - \left(\frac{p_2}{p_1}\right)^{(k+1)/k}\right] \tag{7-26}$$

To obtain a simplified expression for v_2 as a function of p_2, we may take two different views. We may assume flow from a reservoir with $v_1 = 0$ or we may use the continuity equation to write

$$v_2^2 - v_1^2 = v_2^2\left[1 - \left(\frac{A_2}{A_1}\right)\left(\frac{p_2}{p_1}\right)^{2/k}\right]$$

and neglect the second term in the brackets. In either case we then obtain the following expression for the velocity:

$$v_2 = \frac{1}{\rho_2}\sqrt{\frac{2k}{k-1}p_1\rho_1}\sqrt{\left(\frac{p_2}{p_1}\right)^{2/k} - \left(\frac{p_2}{p_1}\right)^{(k+1)/k}} \tag{7-27}$$

MAXIMUM VELOCITY. It is clear that the velocity cannot be increased indefinitely simply by changing p_2; indeed, there is a maximum attainable velocity. A necessary condition for a maximum of v_2 with respect to p_2 (with all else considered as specified constants) is $dv_2/dp_2 = 0$, which yields

$$\frac{p_c}{p_1} = \left(\frac{2}{k+1}\right)^{k/(k+1)} \tag{7-28}$$

where we have used the subscript c to denote values at the critical point. Since $p_2 < p_1$ is always implied, the previous expression for the velocity [Eq. (7-26)] is valid in the range

$$p_c \leq p_2 \leq p_1$$

The corresponding critical (maximum) velocity is given by

$$v_c = \sqrt{\frac{2k}{k+1}\frac{p_1}{\rho_1}} = \sqrt{kRT_c} \tag{7-29}$$

the speed of sound for the gas at section 2. That is, if we take the downstream pressure $p_2 = p_c$, then the flow will attain its maximum speed at that point, the speed of sound.

This maximum velocity is the transition of the flow from sonic to supersonic with $M = 1$, a shock at the throat. At this point, the flow upstream of the throat also becomes independent of flow conditions downstream of the throat. Note, however, that actually achieving supersonic flow in the tube would require a subsequent expansion of the nozzle in accordance with the implications of (7-24).

FLOW OF AIR THROUGH AN ORIFICE. The preceding discussion provides a general background which we now put to use. We turn to the modeling of an air flow through an orifice, as illustrated in Fig. 7-7. We shall concern ourselves only with the subsonic flow regime corresponding to

$$p_c = 0.53p_1 \leq p_2 \leq p_1$$

Throughout, we take $R = 1717$ ft · lb/slug °R and $k = 1.4$ for air. Furthermore, A_1 and A_0 are taken to be known cross-sectional areas with $A_2 = C_c A_0$, where C_c is the contraction coefficient.

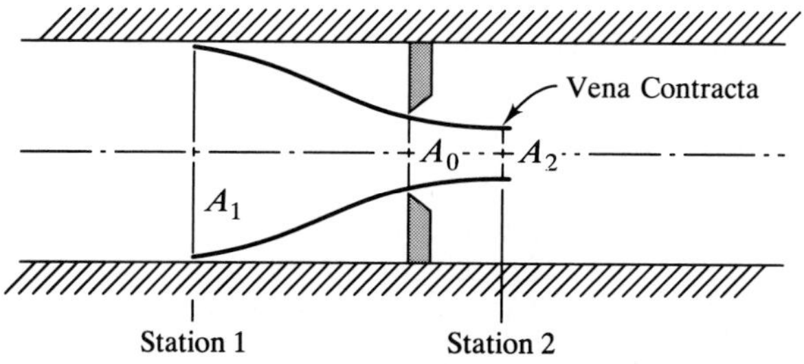

FIGURE 7-7
Air flow through a small orifice.

The *volumetric flow rate* for air in cubic feet per second is given by

$$q = A_2 v_2 = 109.63 C_d A_0 \sqrt{T_1} \sqrt{\left(\frac{p_2}{p_1}\right)^{2.85} - \left(\frac{p_2}{p_1}\right)^{3.14}} \tag{7-30}$$

where C_d is an experimentally determined discharge coefficient combining both the contraction coefficient and the previously neglected effects of friction.

The *mass flow rate* in slugs per second is given by

$$w = \rho_2 A_2 v_2 = 109.63 C_d A_0 \rho_1 \sqrt{T_1} \sqrt{\left(\frac{p_2}{p_1}\right)^{1.43} - \left(\frac{p_2}{p_1}\right)^{1.71}} \tag{7-31}$$

For the sharp-edged orifice depicted in Fig. 7-7, a discharge coefficient of 0.68 is generally assumed. For the ports encountered in valves, it is reduced somewhat to about 0.63. Care must be taken to maintain consistent units in these expressions—for example, feet, slugs, and degrees Rankine.

As before, we strive to obtain a linearized expression relating mass flow and pressure for specific operating ranges. We shall follow the approach used in Ogata[3] to obtain such an expression.

Accordingly, we introduce an expansion factor

$$\epsilon = \sqrt{\frac{k}{k-1} \frac{p_1^2}{p_2(p_1 - p_2)} \left[\left(\frac{p_2}{p_1}\right)^{2/k} - \left(\frac{p_2}{p_1}\right)^{(k+1)/k}\right]} \tag{7-32}$$

which yields

$$w = C_d A_0 \epsilon \sqrt{\frac{2}{RT_1}} \sqrt{p_2(p_1 - p_2)} \tag{7-33}$$

For $p_c \le p_2 \le p_1$, we have $0.97 \le \epsilon \le 1.0$. Splitting the difference, we use $\epsilon = 0.985$ to write

$$\begin{aligned} w &= 0.034 C_d A_0 \frac{1}{\sqrt{T_1}} \sqrt{p_2(p_1 - p_2)} \\ &= 0.034 C_d A_0 \frac{1}{\sqrt{T_1}} \sqrt{(p_1 - p)p} \end{aligned} \tag{7-34}$$

where $p = p_1 - p_2$ is the pressure drop across the contraction. Suppose we now consider p_1 and T_1 as given constants. Then we may write

$$w = K\sqrt{(p_1 - p)p}$$

or

$$\frac{w^2}{\left(\frac{1}{2}p_1 K\right)^2} + \frac{\left(p - \frac{1}{2}p_1\right)^2}{\left(\frac{1}{2}p_1\right)^2} = 1 \tag{7-35}$$

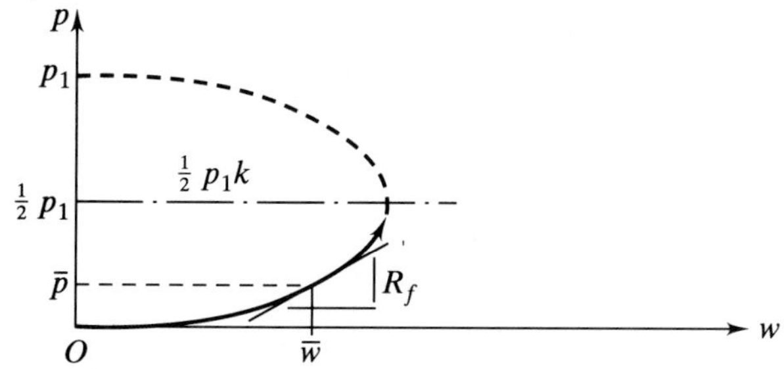

FIGURE 7-8
The simplified *wp*-relationship.

which plots as the ellipse shown in Fig. 7-8. In this figure the maximum flow rate corresponds to $p = \frac{1}{2}p_1$ or $p_2 = \frac{1}{2}p_1$. This maximum flow rate is not attainable, since $0.53p_1 \le p_2 \le p_1$ or, equivalently, $0 \le p \le 0.47p_1$, is required.

On this admissible segment, we may now linearize in the usual fashion around some operating point $(\bar{w}, \bar{p})$. The result is

$$w - \bar{w} = \frac{1}{R_f}(p - \bar{p}) \tag{7-36}$$

where the *fluid resistance* R_f is given by

$$R_f = \frac{dp}{dw} = \frac{2}{K}\frac{\sqrt{(p_1 - \bar{p})\bar{p}}}{p_1 - 2\bar{p}}$$

Thus the deviation of the flow from some mean flow is a linear function of the pressure drop across the throat in a neighborhood of the mean pressure drop $\bar{p}$. As before, the valve position could be worked into the analysis by considering the mass flow to be a function of x_1 and p, x_1 again denoting the valve displacement.

7-1-5 Pneumatic Actuators

A comparison of the advantages and disadvantages of pneumatic and hydraulic systems was given earlier. Thus we shall develop and discuss the components of pneumatic systems in much the same way as was done for hydraulic systems. As there are symbols similar to those used in hydraulic system design, we thus begin the discussion with a symbolic schematic of an actuator in which all of the essential components are clearly indicated. A somewhat reduced table of symbols is also included. We then follow with a brief description of the function and purpose of each item, and we complete the section with the derivation of a system function.

The descriptions will follow the order of components as illustrated in Fig. 7-9. The first major component is generally a compressor to provide compressed air. It is preceded by a filter at the air intake, to start the air through the system in as clean a state as possible. We shall begin our discussion with the compressor and discuss the filter at the point of its second occurrence.

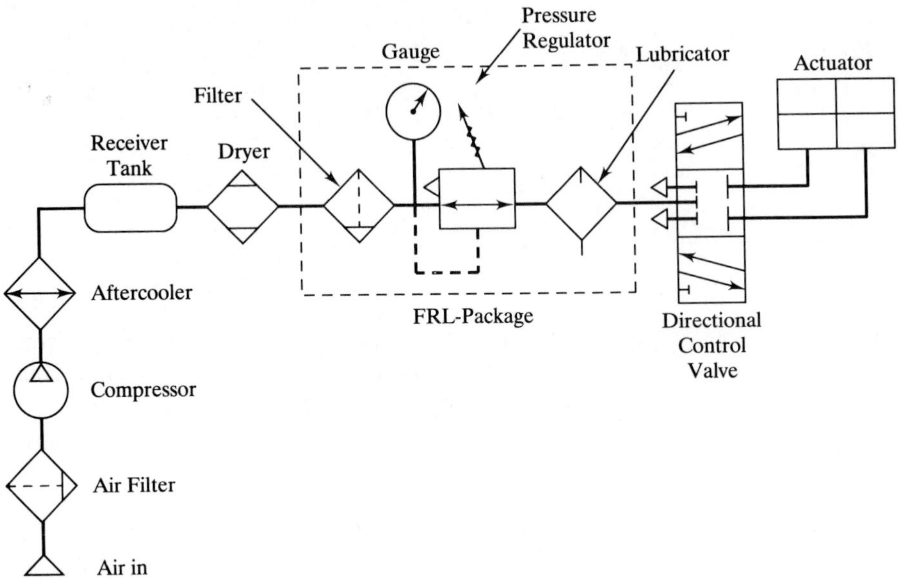

FIGURE 7-9
The pneumatic actuator.

COMPRESSOR. Its function is to compress air. There are a number of types of compressors in use, such as diaphragm compressors and multistage compressors, which use intermittent cooling of the air. The most common type of compressor is the reciprocating piston compressor, consisting of a piston and chamber. The piston is driven by a rod and crankshaft. The air chamber at the opposite end of the cylinder contains an intake valve and an outlet valve. When the piston motion increases the size of the air chamber, it creates a low-pressure region, and air is admitted through the intake valve. During the opposite motion, the volume of the air chamber is decreased, the air is compressed, and the compressed air is exhausted through the outlet valve when the air chamber volume is at its smallest. The compressed air may be fed directly into the line or it may be cooled first, or, as is more common, it may be stored in a pressurized storage tank.

AFTERCOOLER. It cools the air after it has been compressed. Hot air can contain a considerable amount of water vapor, which causes corrosion of metal system components. Cooling the air removes the water vapor and, furthermore, helps to maintain downstream pressure, since the pressure may otherwise decrease due to the subsequent cooling of the air in the line. Cool air thus improves the efficiency of operation.

STORAGE TANK. Storage or receiver tanks are always included in pneumatic systems. They serve the same purpose accumulators do in hydraulic systems—namely, to supply a constant flow of high-pressure air to the system components. The compressor alone cannot deal with the normal demand fluctuation present in a pneumatic system. In addition, the fluctuations introduced by intermittent pressurization are detrimental to the system. There is a simple feedback loop with the compressor, where the compressor is turned off and on based on a maximum and minimum pressure prescribed for the tank. In addition, the tank, with a normal operating pressure of 100 psi, has a safety valve.

DESICCANT DRIERS. Obviously, driers are used to remove moisture. In the pneumatic system the air stream passes through chemicals that remove moisture from the air. In some systems two chemical filters operate alternately, with some of the dried air being used to dry the chemicals of the inactive part of the chemical bed.

FILTERS. Filters remove oil droplets, water droplets, and particles from the air stream. There are two types. In surface filters the air simply passes through a screen, with little resultant pressure drop. The size of the mesh determines the filter rating, guaranteeing the removal of particles ranging in size from 5 to 70 μm. In depth filters the air passes through a region of sintered beads, with a consequent loss of pressure. The size of the beads determines the rating, which ranges from 5 to 50 μm. In both types of filters there are provisions for the removal of trapped matter.

PRESSURE REGULATORS. Because different actuators in the system usually require different operating pressures, pressure regulators are used throughout the system. The simplest kind is a poppet valve, where the poppet is moved up or down by a spring-loaded diaphragm. When the back pressure from an actuator reaches a set level, it acts on the diaphragm, closing the poppet and thus stopping the air flow. When there is a pressure drop due to a movement of the load, for example, then the spring force overcomes the resultant pressure, displacing the diaphragm and opening the poppet, and air flow resumes.

LUBRICATORS. The dryness of the air can cause problems in pneumatic actuators. Lubricators inject atomized oil into the air stream to lubricate the motion of the actuator. A filter-regulator-lubricator combination is often supplied in what is termed an FRL package.

DIRECTIONAL CONTROL VALVES. As in hydraulic systems, these valves control the direction of air flow—in essence, the direction and, to some extent, the speed of the actuator motion. There are two types: slide valves and spool valves. Their basic operation is much the same as that of hydraulic spool valves (see Sec. 7-1-3). An alternative is provided by solenoid-operated, spring-loaded, magnetic valves, used only in on-off operations.

Slide valves are simple and relatively inexpensive. Spool valves are precision instruments and thus are quite sensitive to contamination. Slide valves may be built quite small, and it can be quite difficult to align the proper holes by sliding or rotating a valve segment; whereas it generally requires little force to bring a spool valve into proper alignment to connect the desired pipe segments. Here, too, spool valves are classified in accordance with their flow characteris-

TABLE 7-2
Symbols for pneumatic system components

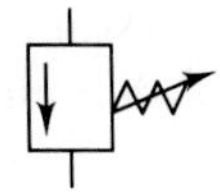	Reliefvalve	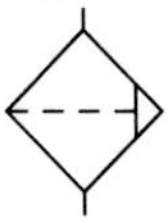	Filter
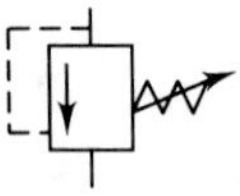	Pilot-operated relief valve	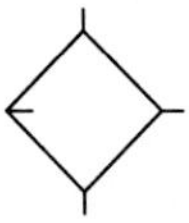	Lubricator
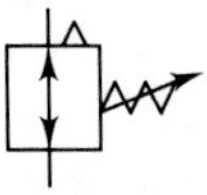	Regulator	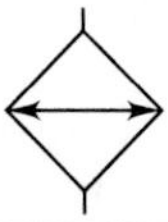	Aftercooler
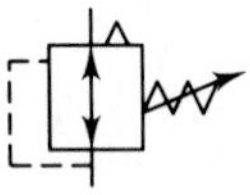	Pilot-operated regulator	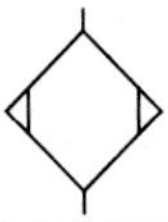	Drier
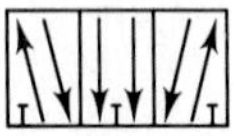	Directional control valve exhaust center		Compressor
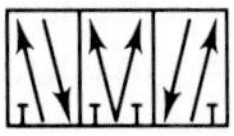	Directional control valve pressure center		Motor
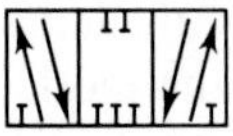	Directional control valve blocked center	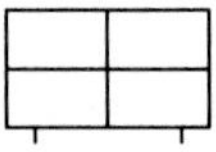	Double-action double-rod cylinder
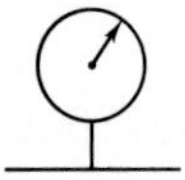	Gauge	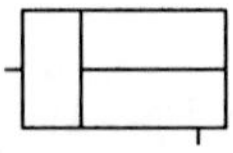	Double-action single-rod cylinder
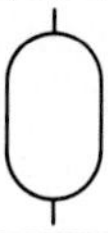	Receiver tank	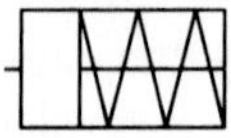	Single-action spring return cylinder

tics when the spool is in its neutral position. For example, in Fig. 7-9, a *blocked center* spool valve indicates that the two exhausts leading to the actuator—the pressure line and the two pneumatic lines—are blocked when the spool is in the neutral position.

ACTUATORS. Linear and rotary actuators are classified more or less as before. That is, pistons may be single or double action, and pumps may also serve as motors. One of the main differences between linear and rotary actuators is that the air is usually exhausted to the atmosphere rather than being returned to some reservoir. Some of the component symbols used in the design of pneumatic systems are shown in Table 7-2.

A pneumatic system need not contain all the components shown in Fig. 7-9. Only the air intake, compressor, and actuator are essential; the other components serve mainly to improve the system operation.

The reader who wants to pursue the subject of pneumatic and hydraulic systems can refer to Ogata,[3] which includes many component schematics and treats control theoretical aspects, and Hoekstra[6] and Holzbock,[7] which contain more technically detailed descriptions, technical data, and operational details of components.

We close this section with an example of the derivation of the governing equations of a pneumatically actuated valve.

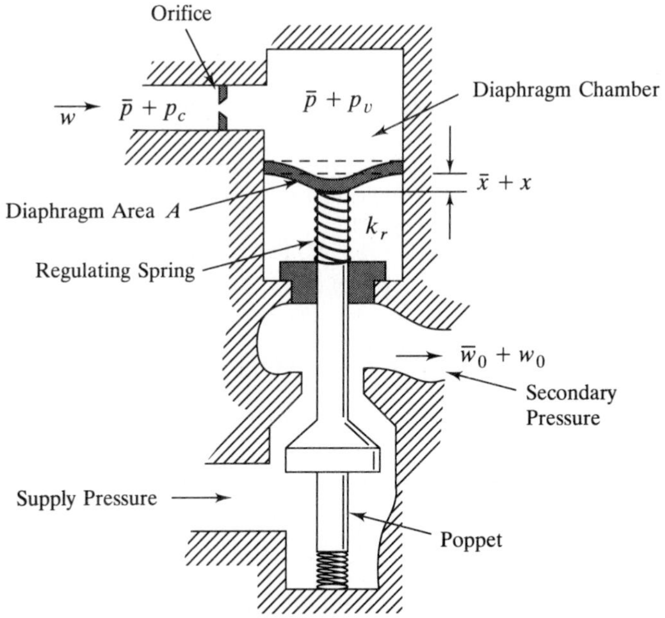

FIGURE 7-10
Schematic of diaphragm valve.

Example 7-3 A diaphragm valve. (A schematic of the valve is shown in Fig. 7-10.) At steady-state operation, the valve is set at some operating point designated by a control pressure $\bar{p}$, which is also the pressure in the diaphragm chamber; the corresponding valve displacement is $\bar{x}$. The steady-state secondary flow from the valve is $\bar{w}_0$.

(*a*) If the control pressure changes by an amount p_c, determine the corresponding additional displacement x of the valve and the system function with p_c as input and x as output.

(*b*) Determine the system function with the additional secondary mass flow rate w_0 as output. Neglect the masses of the diaphragm and the poppet.

Solution

(*a*) For the orifice flow at the input to the diaphragm chamber, we take a resistance R_i and a pressure drop $p_c - p_v$ so that the mass flow w is given by

$$w = \frac{1}{R_i}(p_c - p_v)$$

In accordance with (7-9), the flow rate is related to the gas pressure by

$$w = V\frac{d\rho}{dt} = \frac{V\rho}{B}\frac{dp}{dt}$$

where B is the bulk modulus for air (in this example). For a gas with frictionless adiabatic compression, the bulk modulus is given by $B = kp$, k being the ratio of specific heats, and we then write

$$w = C_i\frac{dp_v}{dt}$$

where we have defined a fluid capacitance by $C_i = V/(kRT)$. Because of the small diaphragm displacement, this capacitance is virtually constant. The combination of the previous equations yields

$$\frac{1}{R_i}(p_c - p_v) = C_i\frac{dp_v}{dt} \tag{7-37}$$

When the diaphragm and poppet masses are neglected, equilibrium at the diaphragm requires

$$p_v A = k_r x \tag{7-38}$$

where k_r is the combined spring constant for the two springs acting on the poppet and diaphragm.

The Laplace transform of (7-37) and (7-38) with zero initial conditions is

$$\frac{1}{C_i R_i}(P_c(s) - P_v(s)) = sP_v(s)$$

$$P_v(s)A = k_r X(s)$$

so that the corresponding system function is given by

$$G_x(s) = \frac{X(s)}{P_c(s)} = \frac{A}{k_r}\frac{1}{C_iR_is + 1}$$

(*b*) If we furthermore incorporate the primary and secondary valve flow with

$$w_0 = K_v x$$

then

$$G_q(s) = \frac{W_0(s)}{P_c(s)} = \frac{W_0(s)}{X(s)}\frac{X(s)}{P_c(s)} = \frac{K_v A}{k_r}\frac{1}{C_iR_is + 1}$$

7-1-6 Electrical Analogs to Fluid Flow

By way of transition to electrical systems, we now take a brief look at electrical systems whose behavior is analogous to the fluid systems discussed previously. Our discussion centers on linear and linearized systems. Suppose we begin with a literal, rather than a mathematically precise, definition of analogous systems.

Definition 7-1 Analogous systems. Two physical systems are *analogous* if and only if they have the same mathematical model.

In our context this will generally mean that the systems have the same system function or the same governing equation(s), with different physical interpretations of constants and variables. It is common to construct electrical analogs for other physical systems, since it is then possible to actually build an analogous circuit and thus study the system behavior. The analog computer is the culmination of this approach. However, analogs also serve interdisciplinary understanding of phenomena, and it is perhaps in this respect that they are the most useful.

Example 7-4. The damper and mass shown in Fig. 7-11*a* execute rectilinear motion under the action of the force $f(t)$.

(*a*) Obtain the equation of motion of the system and the system function.

(*b*) Construct a device-by-device analogous electrical system and list the equivalences of the analogy.

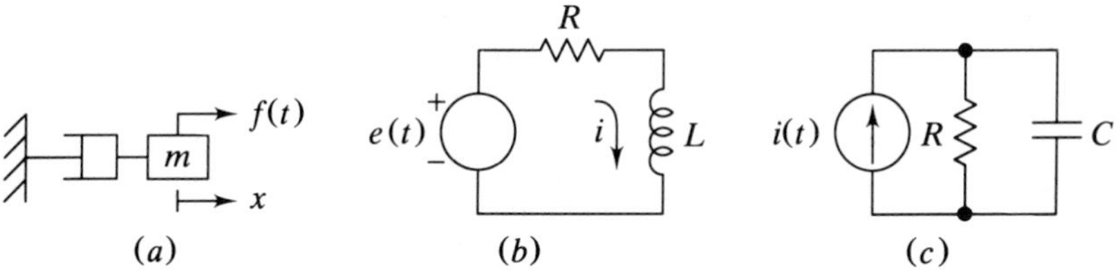

FIGURE 7-11
Analogous systems.

Solution

(*a*) Newton's second law yields the equation

$$m\frac{d^2x}{dt^2} + b\frac{dx}{dt} = f(t)$$

The system function is

$$G(s) = \frac{X(s)}{F(s)} = \frac{1}{ms^2 + bs}$$

(*b*) Kirchhoff's voltage law applied to the loop in Fig. 7-11*b* yields

$$L\frac{d^2q}{dt^2} + R\frac{dq}{dt} = e(t)$$

with system function

$$G(s) = \frac{Q(s)}{E(s)} = \frac{1}{Ls^2 + Rs}$$

The equivalences of the analogy† are given by

$$m \sim L \qquad x \sim q$$
$$b \sim R \qquad f \sim e$$

The mathematical symbol $\sim$ denotes equivalence rather than equality, since the quantities are generally numerically equal with different physical units.

Indeed, consider the circuit in Fig. 7-11*c* with a current source $i(t)$. The application of Kirchhoff's laws yields

$$\frac{1}{R}v + C\frac{dv}{dt} = i(t)$$

or

$$C\frac{d^2v}{dt^2} + \frac{1}{R}\frac{dv}{dt} = \frac{di}{dt} = h(t)$$

with system function

$$G(s) = \frac{V(s)}{H(s)} = \frac{1}{Cs^2 + \dfrac{1}{R}s}$$

The equivalences of this analogy are

$$m \sim C \qquad x \sim v$$
$$b \sim \frac{1}{R} \qquad f \sim \frac{di}{dt}$$

Although the first analogy may appear to be more natural, the second is also a perfectly good analogous system. Thus analogs are certainly not unique.

†This analogy is sometimes called a force-voltage analogy because of the equivalence of force and voltage. We shall refrain from naming analogies.

When constructing electrical analogs to linear systems, it is common to use *RLC* circuits. Since fluid inductance (inertiance) plays mainly a detrimental role here, we shall restrict our discussion to fluid resistance and fluid capacitance.

FLUID RESISTANCE. In electrical systems a *pure* resistor is an electrical device for which the current i through the device is a function of the voltage drop v across the device; that is,

$$i = f(v)$$

An *ideal* resistor is one for which this relationship is linear with

$$i = \frac{1}{R} v$$

where R (in ohms) is the resistance. The linear expression also serves as the approximation of the nonlinear process in the neighborhood of some operating point.

The choice of analogous concepts in fluid flow is relatively obvious. We take the volumetric flow or the mass flow to be equivalent to the current, and we take the pressure drop to be equivalent to the voltage drop. We shall deal only with the linearized case. We thus write

$$R_f = \frac{\text{differential change in pressure difference}}{\text{differential change in flow}}$$

or, equivalently,

$$q = \frac{1}{R_f} p \qquad \text{or} \qquad w = \frac{1}{R_f} p \tag{7-39}$$

for hydraulic and pneumatic flows, respectively.

Example 7-5. Write the resistive flow equations for pneumatic and hydraulic flows through a small orifice (valve).

Solution. In accordance with (7-36), we have

$$w - \bar{w} = \frac{1}{R_f}(p - \bar{p})$$

where $(\bar{w}, \bar{p})$ is the operating point for the system and where

$$R_f = \frac{2}{K} \frac{\sqrt{(p_1 - \bar{p})\bar{p}}}{p_1 - 2\bar{p}} \left(\frac{\text{N} \cdot \text{s}}{\text{kg} \cdot \text{m}^2} \right) \tag{7-40}$$

p_1 is the given constant upstream pressure.

For hydraulic flow the fluid resistance is obtained from (7-14) as

$$R_f = \frac{dp}{dq} = \frac{\sqrt{2\bar{p}\rho}}{cA_0} \left(\frac{\text{N} \cdot \text{s}}{\text{m}^5} \right) \tag{7-41}$$

so that the valve flow in the neighborhood of an operating point $(\bar{q}, \bar{p})$ can be represented by

$$q - \bar{q} = \frac{1}{R_f}(p - \bar{p})$$

FLUID CAPACITANCE. We deal with fluid capacitance in a similar fashion. From the electrical point of view, a *pure* capacitor is an electrical device for which the accumulated charge q is a function of the potential drop v across the device; that is,

$$q = g(v)$$

An *ideal* capacitor is one for which this relationship is linear with

$$q = Cv$$

or, more commonly, with

$$i = C\frac{dv}{dt}$$

where C (in farads) is the capacitance.

We now take the total mass m of the liquid to be equivalent to the charge and the pressure difference p to be equivalent to the potential drop. We thus write

$$C_f = \frac{\text{differential change in mass}}{\text{differential change in pressure difference}}$$

with

$$w = \frac{dm}{dt} = C_f\frac{dp}{dt} \tag{7-42}$$

for the linearized relationship.

We now treat two specific cases. The first is a reservoir or tank in which fluid is stored and where the pressure within the fluid is due to its weight. The second will deal with a fluid under pressure in a tank of fixed volume. In both cases we take p_1 to be the atmospheric pressure and use $p = p_2 - p_1$ to be the pressure difference, with p_2 as the pressure indicated in Fig. 7-12.

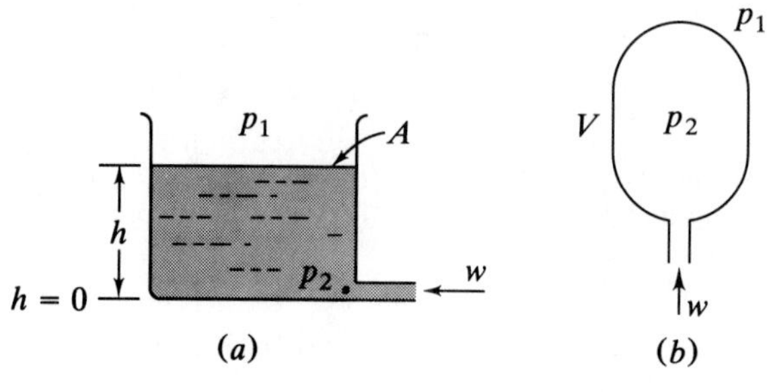

FIGURE 7-12
Fluid capacitance.

For the reservoir in Fig. 7-12a, we consider an incompressible fluid and we neglect acceleration and inertia effects within the tank. The pressure at the inlet is p_2. We take the inlet to be small enough to consider all of it to be located at $h = 0$, where h denotes the fluid head, the elevation of the fluid level. The tank has constant cross section A.

The continuity equation yields

$$w = \frac{dm}{dt} = \frac{d}{dt}(\rho h A) = \rho A \frac{dh}{dt}$$

The pressure p_2 is related to the head by the equation

$$p_2 = p_1 + \rho g h \quad \Rightarrow \quad p = \rho g h$$

so that

$$w = \rho A \frac{d}{dt}\left(\frac{p}{\rho g}\right) = \frac{A}{g}\frac{dp}{dt}$$

We define C_f in the obvious manner, with

$$C_f = \frac{A}{g} \ (\mathrm{m \cdot s^2}) \tag{7-43}$$

In this context it is also common to take the head to be equivalent to the potential, with a corresponding change in the definition of C_f.

The second example, shown in Fig. 7-12b, involves a pressurized tank of specified volume V filled with a compressible fluid, with more being added by an inflow w. We have

$$w = \frac{dm}{dt} = \frac{d}{dt}(\rho V) = V\frac{dp}{dt}$$

Assuming a constitutive relationship $\rho = \rho(p)$ allows us to write

$$\begin{aligned} w &= V\frac{d\rho}{dp}\frac{dp}{dt} \\ &= \frac{V\rho}{B}\frac{dp}{dt} \end{aligned}$$

where we have made use of (7-8), the definition of the bulk modulus B. We thus define

$$C_f = \frac{V\rho}{B} \tag{7-44}$$

Example 7-6. Consider the piston-mass combination shown in Fig. 7-13. Air is allowed to flow into the left chamber of the cylinder and the valve is then closed. At that instant the pressure in the left chamber is $\bar{p}_2$, the volume of the chamber is $\bar{V}$, and the spring is compressed by an amount $\bar{x}$; we take p_1 to be a constant

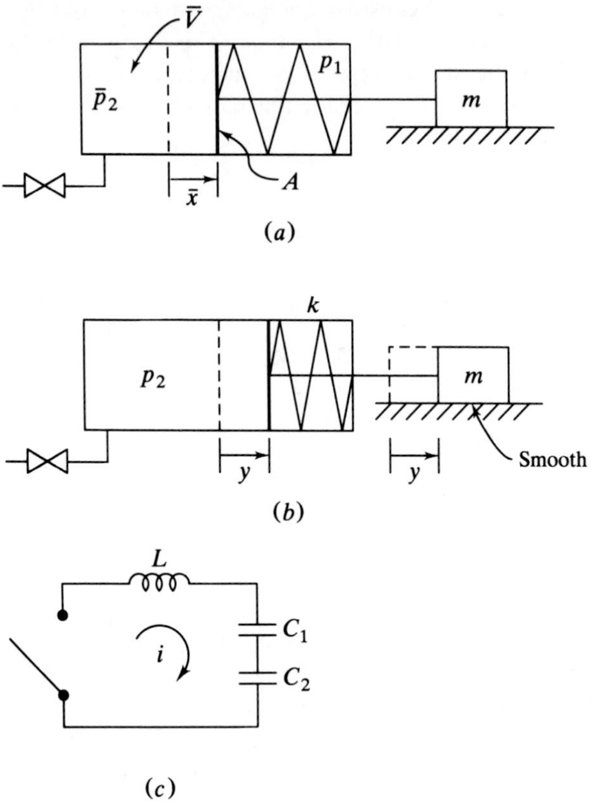

FIGURE 7-13
Pneumatic oscillator.

pressure, say, atmospheric pressure. Suppose the mass m is now given a small displacement y_0 to the right.

(*a*) Determine the governing equation(s) for the ensuing motion and obtain the general solution for y as a function of t.

(*b*) Determine the system function with a force $f(t)$ acting on the mass as input and with $y(t)$ as the output for the system.

(*c*) Determine an analogous electrical system and list all of the equivalences of the analogy.

Solution

(*a*) Figure 7-13*a* depicts the static equilibrium state of the system characterized by

$$A\bar{p}_2 = Ap_1 + k\bar{x} \tag{7-45}$$

For the derivation of the governing equations, we consider the possible system state shown in Fig. 7-13*b*, where y is the displacement of the piston measured from the static equilibrium state. For the displaced state we have

$$p_2 = \bar{p}_2 - p \qquad \text{and} \qquad V = \bar{V} + Ay$$

Since the mass of air in the blind chamber is constant, we have

$$0 = \frac{d}{dt}(\rho V) = \rho\frac{dV}{dt} + V\frac{d\rho}{dt} = \rho A\frac{dy}{dt} + V\frac{d\rho}{dp_2}\frac{dp_2}{dt}$$

With $V \approx \bar{V}$ this results in

$$A\frac{dy}{dt} - \frac{\bar{V}}{B}\frac{dp}{dt} = 0 \tag{7-46}$$

For the motion of the mass m, the application of Newton's second law yields

$$Ap_2 - Ap_1 - k(\bar{x} + y) = m\frac{d^2y}{dt^2}$$

In view of (7-45) and the expression for p_2, this becomes

$$-Ap = ky + m\frac{d^2y}{dt^2} \tag{7-47}$$

Equation (7-46) may be integrated to obtain

$$p(t) = \frac{AB}{\bar{V}}y(t)$$

since $p(t_1) = 0$, where t_1 is the time at which $y = 0$. Substitution of this expression into (7-47) yields

$$m\frac{d^2y}{dt^2} + \left(k + \frac{A^2B}{\bar{V}}\right)y = 0 \tag{7-48}$$

whose general solution is given by

$$y(t) = C_1 \cos \omega t + C_2 \sin \omega t$$

where
$$\omega^2 = \frac{1}{m}\left(k + \frac{A^2B}{\bar{V}}\right)$$

(*b*) The system function corresponding to an input $f(t)$ at the mass is given by

$$G(s) = \frac{Y(s)}{F(s)} = \frac{1}{m}\frac{1}{s^2 + \omega^2}$$

(*c*) An analogous electrical system is the one shown in Fig. 7-13*c*, whose governing equation is given by

$$L\frac{d^2i}{dt^2} + \left(\frac{1}{C_1} + \frac{1}{C_2}\right)i = 0$$

The equivalences of the analogy thus are

$$m \sim L \qquad \frac{A^2 B}{\bar{V}} \sim \frac{1}{C_2}$$

$$k \sim \frac{1}{C_1} \qquad y \sim i$$

Remark 7-3. Note that there were two analogs involved in the preceding example: the compressed air acting like a linear spring and the linear spring being equivalent to capacitance.

This relatively short discussion of analogs is extremely important from a conceptual point of view in electromechanical systems. It provides some understanding of the interaction of system components whose mathematical models derive from different engineering backgrounds.

7-2 ELECTRICAL ACTUATORS

As mentioned earlier, less than half of the robots in existence are driven by electrical actuators. This is likely to change as electrical motors decrease in cost and their weight-to-power ratio is improved with the development of lighter permanent magnets. The motors in use are almost exclusively DC servos or stepper motors, and they are the ones we will emphasize. Their greatest advantage is that they are well suited to continuous speed control—so essential to the continuous motion control often required for the end effector of a robot. (In essence, the speed may be varied from 0 to the rated rpm of the motor simply by adjusting the applied voltage. These control capabilities may be used to maintain a given motion, even for extensive load variations, which is a distinct advantage over fluid actuators.) Often, too, the decisive advantages are their superior cleanliness and lesser system complexity. In the final analysis, there clearly is a place for all three systems: for pneumatic actuators, because of their inherent simplicity; for hydraulic actuators, because of their strength; and for electrical actuators, because of their refined control capabilities and cleanliness.

We shall take what, by now, is an ingrained approach. We begin with some relevant concepts in magnetism, progress to a simple motor, and from there to some rudimentary DC machines and their circuit representations. The section closes with a discussion of stepper motors.

7-2-1 Relevant Magnetism

Any basic physics text presents the necessary magnetic topics; here, we again take Halliday and Resnick[8] as our desk reference. We begin with a recollection of some of the terminology used in magnetism. To avoid confusion, we shall use

SI units exclusively. Our interest centers on the forces that magnets exert on charge and on the magnetic fields produced by moving charges together with the interactive forces that are created.

Any magnet produces around itself a magnetic field. The *amount* of magnetism present in the region occupied by the magnet and its surroundings is described by the magnetic flux ϕ (in webers). The density of the flux and its direction at a given point in space is termed the magnetic flux density $\boldsymbol{B}$ (in webers/square meter), a vector field. Although viewpoints differ on this, we shall simply refer to $\boldsymbol{B}$ as the magnetic field.

CONDUCTOR AT REST IN A MAGNETIC FIELD. A charged particle with charge q, moving along a curve C with velocity $\boldsymbol{v}$ in a magnetic field $\boldsymbol{B}$, is subject to an induced force given by

$$\boldsymbol{F} = q\boldsymbol{v} \times \boldsymbol{B}$$

(see Fig. 7-14). Instead of a single charged particle moving through a magnetic field, suppose now that a current-carrying conductor traverses a magnetic field. The identity

$$i = \frac{dq}{dt} = \frac{dq}{ds}\frac{ds}{dt} = \frac{dq}{ds}v$$

may be extended to three dimensions to yield the differential statement

$$i\,ds = dq\,v$$

and hence the force differential

$$d\boldsymbol{F} = dq\,\boldsymbol{v} \times \boldsymbol{B} = i\,ds \times \boldsymbol{B} \tag{7-49}$$

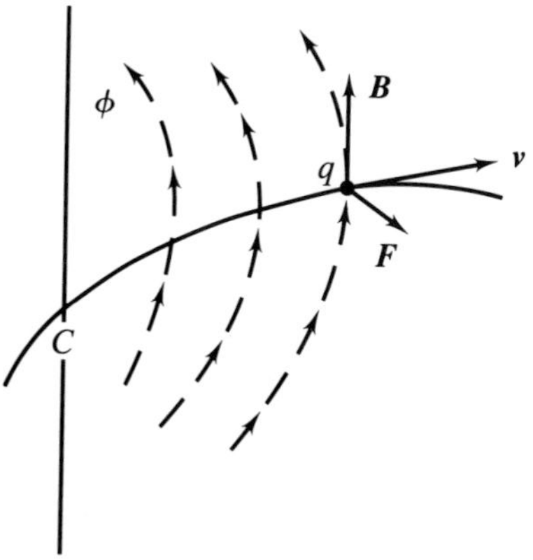

FIGURE 7-14
Force on a charged particle.

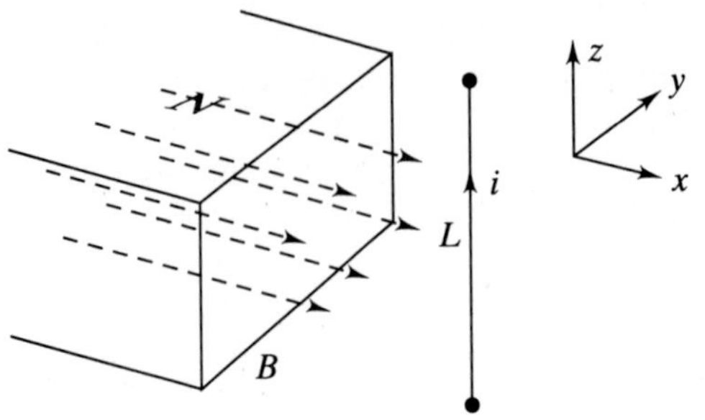

FIGURE 7-15
Force on a conductor.

Example 7-7. A conductor of length L, carrying a constant current i, is immersed in a constant (independent of position) field $\boldsymbol{B}$ as shown in Fig. 7-15. Calculate the resultant force $\boldsymbol{F}$ exerted by the field $\boldsymbol{B}$ on the conductor.

Solution. We have

$$\boldsymbol{F} = \int_0^L i\, d\boldsymbol{s} \times \boldsymbol{B}$$

$$= \int_0^L i(dz\,\hat{\boldsymbol{k}} \times B\hat{\imath})$$

$$= iB\hat{\jmath}\int_0^L dz$$

$$= iBL\hat{\jmath}\ (\mathrm{N})$$

Note that the current always flows in a closed loop, so that we have simply shown only a segment of such a circuit.

The previous discussion dealt with a fixed magnetic field $\boldsymbol{B}$ traversed by a current $\boldsymbol{i}$, where $\boldsymbol{B}$ and $\boldsymbol{i}$ are considered to be separate entities. We now turn to the generation of magnetic fields due to a current.

A current flowing through a wire produces a magnetic field in the surrounding space. This phenomenon was first noted by the Danish physicist Hans Christian Oersted in 1820. The basic law that is used to deduce the strength of the field at a given radial distance r from the conductor is the Biot-Savart law

$$d\boldsymbol{B} = \frac{\mu}{4\pi}\frac{i\, d\boldsymbol{s} \times \boldsymbol{r}}{r^3} \tag{7-50}$$

where
$$\mu = \mu_0\mu_r$$

with SI units of tesla · meters/ampere (T · m/A) is the *permeability* of the medium in which the field exists; $\mu_0 = 4\pi \times 10^{-7}$ T · m/A is the permeability of a vacuum or the *permeability constant*, and μ_r is the *relative permeability*. In essence, the permeability of a medium is its capacity for sustaining a magnetic field. For many ordinary materials, including air, $\mu_r \approx 1$; for ferromagnetic materials μ_r may be 1000 or more.

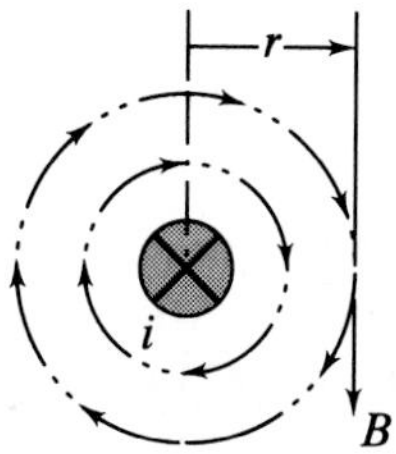

FIGURE 7-16
Field due to a conductor.

For a long (infinite) straight wire, for example, the flux density at a perpendicular distance r from the wire is given by

$$B = \frac{\mu i}{2\pi r} \tag{7-51}$$

obtained by integrating $d\mathbf{B}$ over the full length of the wire (see Fig. 7-16).

Of more specific interest for electromagnets is the flux density sustained in a cylinder, with the wire wound around the cylinder in a helical coil of radius r and height h (see Fig. 7-17). With $h \gg r$ the flux density inside the cylinder is approximately

$$B = \frac{\phi}{A} = \frac{\mu N i}{h},$$

where N is the number of turns in the coil. Such a helical coil is also called a solenoid.

CONDUCTOR MOVING IN A MAGNETIC FIELD. The motion of a conducting loop through a magnetic field produces a current in the loop. No motion, no current. Suppose, then, we consider a conductor of length L (the horizontal

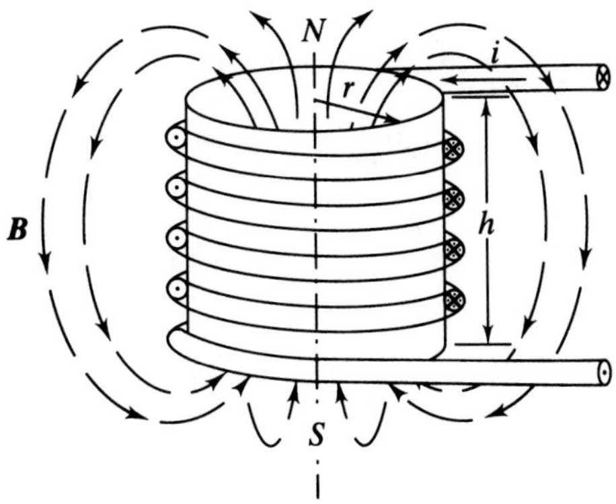

FIGURE 7-17
A solenoid.

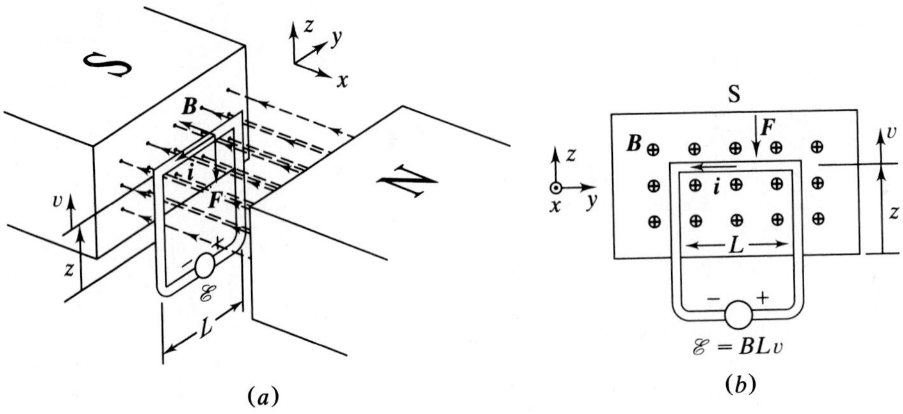

FIGURE 7-18
Electromotive force (emf).

segment of the loop) moving through a constant magnetic field $\boldsymbol{B}$ with a constant vertical velocity $\boldsymbol{v}$, as shown in Fig. 7-18a. According to Lenz's law (Ref. 8):

> An induced current in a closed conducting loop will appear in such a direction that it opposes the change that produced it.

This statement allows us to deduce the direction of the induced current. Experimentally, we are well aware that there is an opposing force when we attempt to move a conducting loop through a magnetic field. If we thus interpret the change that produces the current as the motion of the loop, then the current must be induced so as to provide the opposing force in accordance with (Figure 7-18b).

$$\boldsymbol{F} = -F\hat{\boldsymbol{k}} = (iL\hat{\jmath}) \times (-B\hat{\imath}) = iLB\hat{\boldsymbol{k}}$$

so that

$$i = -\frac{F}{LB}$$

indicating a current flowing to the left, produced by a potential $\mathscr{E}$ with the indicated polarity.

In accordance with Faraday's law, this potential is also given by

$$\mathscr{E} = \frac{d\phi}{dt}.$$

The defining expression for the magnetic flux is

$$\phi_B = \oint \boldsymbol{B} \cdot d\boldsymbol{A}$$
$$= BA$$

if the magnetic field is everywhere constant and perpendicular to the area A. Hence, we now have

$$\phi_B = BLz \qquad \text{and} \qquad \mathscr{E} = BLv.$$

If R is the total resistance of the loop material, then we furthermore have

$$\mathscr{E} = iR = BLv$$

so that the magnitude of the current is

$$i = \frac{BLv}{R}.$$

with corresponding force magnitude

$$F = iLB = \frac{B^2L^2v}{R}.$$

These seeming parlor effects are the essence of DC motors.

7-2-2 Faraday's Motor

The student may or may not have encountered the previous material in physics, and he or she may have discussed Faraday's motor at the same time and then, possibly once more, in a basic circuits course. In any case it is safe to assume that the student has not been inundated with the topic, and the present discussion will serve nicely either as a review or as an introduction. To some extent, we rely on repetition to create the desirable familiarity with the material.

With the exception of a few added refinements, the machine we shall discuss here is essentially the one built by Faraday in the 1880s. We consider the simple arrangement shown in Fig. 7-19, consisting of a *stator*, which may be a permanent magnet or an electromagnet, and the *rotor*, which we take to consist of a nonferromagnetic material with $\mu_r = 1$ and a coil consisting of two turns of a conductor. Such a combination of a core and current-carrying coil is also called an *armature*. Here, then, we have a rotating armature. (Note that, with this definition in mind, the stator and rotor may be armatures, although the present arrangement, with a permanent magnet stator and armature rotor, is the most common for DC motors used in robotics.)

With some simplifying assumptions, we may take the field $\boldsymbol{B}$ due to the permanent magnet to be radial. Based on the indicated direction of current flow, the resultant torque exerted on the rotor is then given by

$$T = 2(2rF) = 4riLB = 2ABi = k_T i$$

where A is the area surrounded by the coil (see Fig. 7-19). We term k_T the torque constant.

Of course, with the ensuing motion, we now also have the situation of a moving conductor in a magnetic field, and a current opposing this motion will be induced. Suppose that the armature is rotating with angular speed ω so that the speed of the conductor through the field is $v = r\omega$. It then follows that the

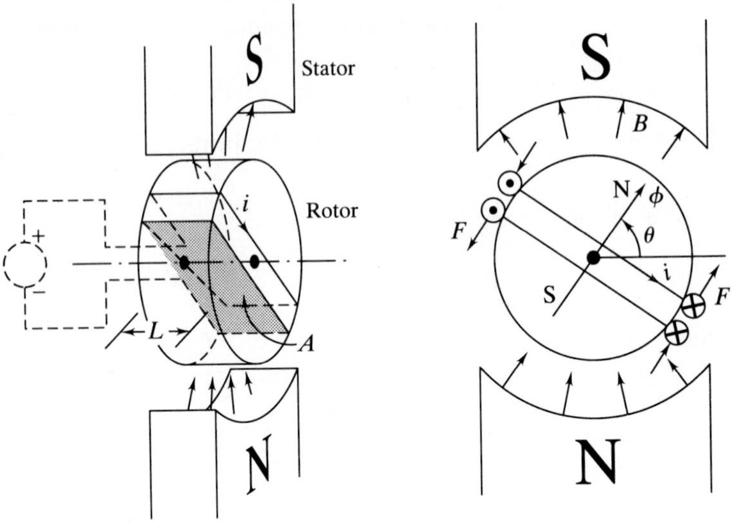

FIGURE 7-19
Stator and rotor for Faraday's motor.

induced potential, the so-called "back emf" or "counter emf" is given by

$$\mathscr{E} = e_b = BLr\omega$$

for a single conductor, or by

$$e_b = 4BLr\omega = 2AB\omega = k_b\omega$$

for the four that we have. This potential is often specified in the form

$$\mathscr{E} = -\frac{d\phi}{dt}$$

with the minus sign included to emphasize that this potential will act to oppose the primary potential applied to produce the rotation.

The actual angular speed ω of the rotating armature may now be determined in a relatively straightforward manner. From a mechanical point of view, we have a rigid body in plane rotation about a fixed point. The application of Euler's second law yields

$$T = k_T i = J\frac{d\omega}{dt}$$

where J is the polar mass moment of inertia of the rotor about its axis of rotation and where we have neglected friction and damping.

For the determination of the current, we now have the circuit equation for the rotating armature. Since the armature is a current-carrying coil, there is a self-inductance, an emf, given by

$$e_L = L\frac{di}{dt}$$

With total resistance R for the coil wire, externally applied potential $e(t)$ and the back emf $e_b(t)$, we then have the *KVL* equation

$$e(t) - e_L(t) - e_b(t) = iR$$

or

$$L\frac{di}{dt} + Ri = e(t) - k_b\omega$$

The governing equation for ω as a function of the externally applied potential thus is

$$\frac{LJ}{k_T}\frac{d^2\omega}{dt^2} + \frac{RJ}{k_T}\frac{d\omega}{dt} + k_b\omega = e(t)$$

At this point, of course, all of this is really valid only within the field B generated by the two stator poles.

The torque $T = k_T i$ will be exerted only until the north pole of the armature produced magnetic field (indicated by ϕ in Fig. 7-19) coincides with the south pole of the stator, at which point the torque becomes zero. For a DC motor, however, we want a continuously applied torque to provide a smooth rotation of the rotor. One way this can be accomplished is by switching the current direction as the coil passes through the horizontal position, as indicated in Fig. 7-20.

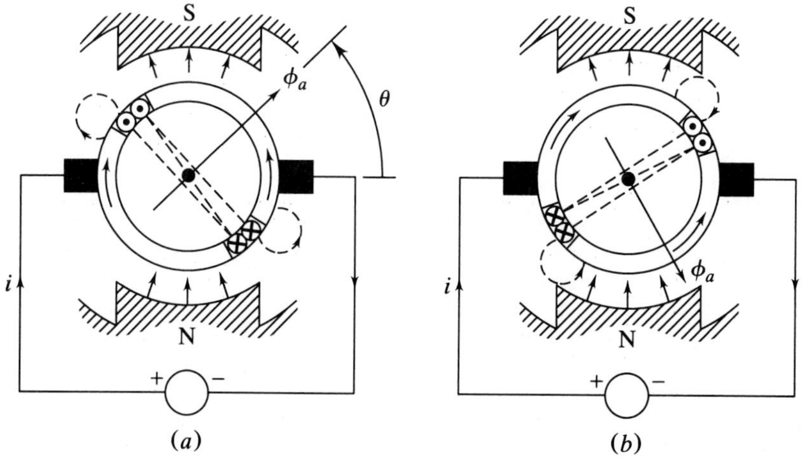

FIGURE 7-20
A simple commutator: (*a*) just before switching; (*b*) just after switching (assume ccw rotation).

As a possible implementation of such a switching arrangement, suppose we take two copper semicircular cylinders mounted on a nonconducting core and insulated from one another at the coil. For the previous coil consisting of two turns, we connect the coils to the copper segments as shown in Fig. 7-20. The segments are supplied with current by external brushes as indicated. With this arrangement, the direction of the current flow in the coil changes each time the armature flux resultant ϕ_a passes through vertical alignment and the direction of the resultant is flipped by 180°, as shown in Figs. 7-20*a* and *b*. Such a switching device is called a *commutator*.

7-2-3 More of a Motor

We now turn to a slightly more realistic model which will illustrate most of the operational aspects required for an understanding of DC motors. In anticipation of the discussion of the particular commutator used in Slemon and Straughen,[9] we shall use a rotor with six single turn coils, as shown in Fig. 7-21. Figure 7-21*a* shows a somewhat realistic relatively common motor configuration, and Fig. 7-21*b* shows the schematic we shall use in the remaining discussion. Note that six coils would normally require 12 slots around the circumference. They may be wound in six slots, however, provided that the slots "double up"—that is, each slot accommodates two coil sides—a situation that will become clearer during our discussion of the commutator.

Again, we first consider the situation where we simply maintain the specific current flow illustrated in Fig. 7-21*b*. At the instant depicted, the armature flux resultant has the direction indicated. If we assume an essentially radial field $\boldsymbol{B}$ and we take the current in each turn to be i, then a torque

$$
\begin{aligned}
T &= 3(2F)(2r) \\
&= 6ABi
\end{aligned}
$$

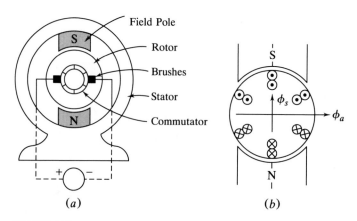

FIGURE 7-21
(*a*) DC motor; (*b*) six single-turn coils schematic.

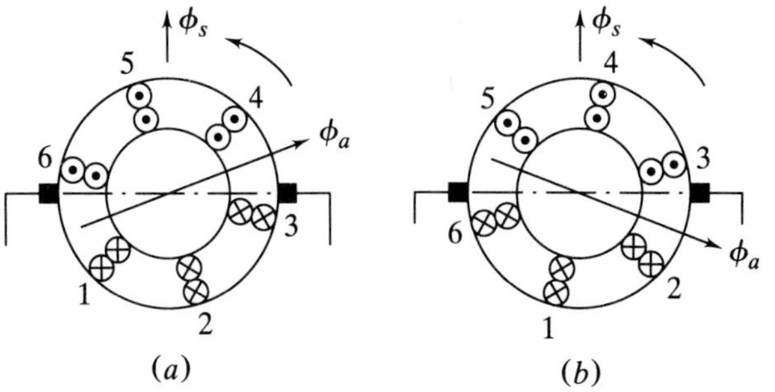

FIGURE 7-22
The switch: (*a*) just before; (*b*) just after.

will be developed until ϕ_a becomes aligned with the stator resultant. The motor then stops. This is an extremely desirable attribute for stepper motors, but it is somewhat less so when continuous rotation is the objective. A continuously acting torque is obtained by using a commutator.

As before, we assume that the segments between the coils are insulated from one another, so that switching occurs just as a coil passes through the horizontal position. Figure 7-22 illustrates the current configuration just before and just after switching. With this switching the rotor flux resultant ϕ_a will rotate one-sixth of a revolution and jump back to the position shown in Fig. 7-22*b*, just after the current direction was switched in slot 3. Clearly, the greater the number of coils, the smaller is the displacement of the flux resultant. With a further increase in the number of coils, one eventually attains an armature field virtually fixed in space, with the stator and the rotor field mutually perpendicular.

As before, the actual switching is carried out by a commutator. One way would be to provide a separate commutator for each coil. The following arrangement shows that a single commutator may be used to accomplish the result.

A commonly used commutator is a copper cylinder, consisting of equal segments which are insulated from one another—there being as many segments as there are coils (see Fig. 7-23). Figure 7-23*a* shows the armature together with the commutator, with segments 4 and 1 in contact with the positive and negative brush, respectively. The "flattened" version of commutator and coil winding shown in Fig. 7-23*b* indicates how the particular current pattern shown in Fig. 7-23*a* can be obtained. It is apparent that there are two parallel paths, each containing half of the turns that make up the winding. Thus, if the current supplied by the DC source is i, then $\frac{1}{2}i$ flows from commutator segment 4 to both slots 1 and 3. The remaining current flow in the left branch has the slot sequence 1 4 2 5 3 6; that in the right branch has the slot sequence 3 6 2 5 1 4, with both of these currents combining and exiting at commutator segment 1 and thence through the negative brush. As the motor rotates the commutator segments move past the brushes, two coils at a time. (For example, turns passing through slots 1 and 3 are transferred from one parallel path to the other.) As a

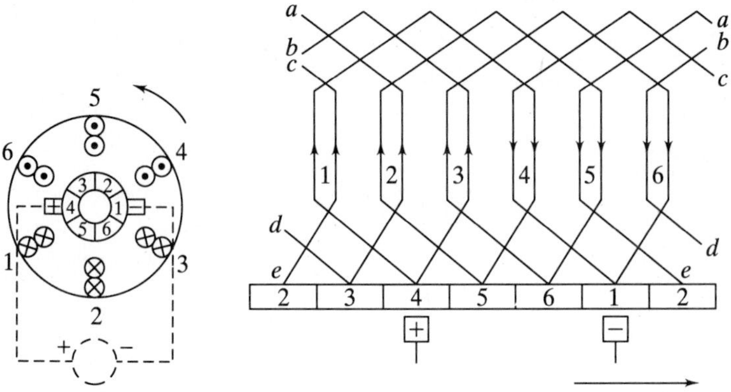

(*a*) (*b*)

FIGURE 7-23
(*a*) Rotor from the commutator side; (*b*) winding diagram for the six coils.

consequence, the resultant flux axis (also termed the *rotor magnetomotive force axis*) is maintained in a nearly fixed position. Note that this axis is determined by the location of the brushes and for this reason is often also called the *brush axis*. If the motor is to have the same operating characteristics for both directions of rotation, this axis must be at 90° with respect to the stator field. This position is therefore also referred to as the *neutral axis*.

We close this part of our motor discussion with an expression for the total torque developed. Let n be the number of conductors moving through the field, let p be the number of poles, each with constant flux ϕ, and let m be the number of parallel conducting paths in the armature. Then, for an armature current i, the total developed torque is given by

$$T = \frac{n\phi p}{2\pi m} i = k_T i \tag{7-52}$$

and we term k_T the *torque constant*.

We now turn to the circuit models for DC motors and the corresponding system functions.

7-2-4 Circuit Models and System Functions

In order to incorporate DC motors into systems analysis, one develops circuit models for the motors. The corresponding behavioral characteristics may be linear or nonlinear, depending on the manner in which the field and armature of the motor are powered and connected.

There are several classifications and subclassifications of DC motors. In terms of power, DC motors are classified into two categories: those with power ratings of 1 hp or more and those with fractional horsepower. The latter are prevalent in robotics, if for no other reason than weight.

In addition, motors may be classified as variable flux or constant flux motors. Variable flux is provided by external sources; constant flux, generally by permanent magnets. The manner in which variable flux is provided gives rise to a final subclassification of variable flux motors.

We shall refer to the stationary stator field simply as the "field" and to the rotor field as the "armature." We then distinguish the following: (1) field and armature separately excited, (2) field and armature in series, (3) field and armature in parallel, and (4) field and armature connected in a mixed fashion. We shall now discuss some of the corresponding circuit models.

Since inductance plays such an essential role, it behooves us to take a quick look at its basic definition. Recall that an inductor is an electrical device which may be used to set up a known magnetic field within some specified region. A solenoid is an obvious configuration for such a device. Quite generally, inductance may be defined as

$$L = \frac{N\phi}{i} \tag{7-53}$$

with units of tesla · meters squared/ampere ($T \cdot m^2/A$), now termed a *henry*. Here, i is the current in the device, N is the number of turns in the coil, and ϕ is the flux. Every coil of conducting wire with current produces such an inductance.

Example 7-8. Calculate the inductance L for a "long" circular cylindrical solenoid of length h. Assume that the interior of the solenoid is air (see Fig. 7-24). Assume the solenoid has N turns.

Solution. In accordance with the definition [Eq. (7-53)] given previously, we have

$$L = \frac{NAB}{i}$$

where $A = \pi r^2$ is the cross-sectional area of the solenoid. The magnetic field B outside the solenoid is 0; in the interior—more specifically in a central region—the field is given by

$$B = \mu_0 i \frac{N}{h}$$

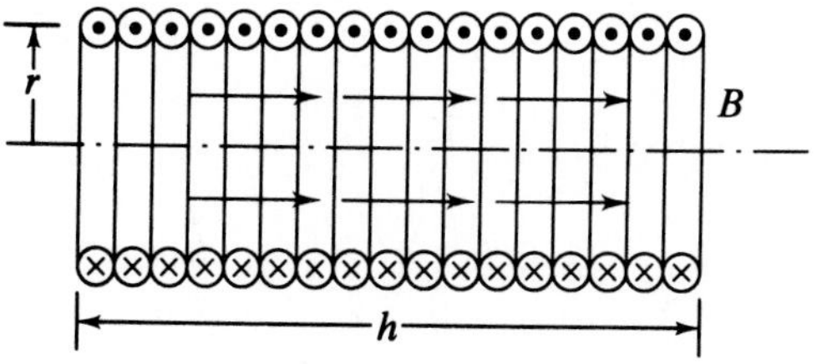

FIGURE 7-24
A "long" solenoid.

where μ_0 is the permeability constant and i is the current in the solenoid windings. Consequently, the final expression for the inductance is given by

$$L = \mu_0 \pi r^2 \frac{N^2}{h}$$

Our discussion of motors will be illustrated with two separate schematics: one indicating the field and armature connections; the other, the corresponding circuit diagram. The armature and field symbols to be used are depicted in Fig. 7-25. In addition, the armature symbol will also be used within the circuit to emphasize the source of the back emf.

FIGURE 7-25
(*a*) Armature; (*b*) field.

All of the following circuit models will have some basic equations in common. The field flux will always be taken to be proportional to the field current $i_f(t)$ with

$$\phi(t) = k_f i_f(t) \tag{7-54}$$

The corresponding motor torque is proportional to the field flux and the armature current $i_a(t)$. Thus

$$T_m(t) = k_m \phi(t) i_a(t) \tag{7-55}$$

The back emf, generated by the motion of the conductors through the magnetic field, is proportional to the flux and the angular velocity of the motor, $\omega_m(t)$, so that

$$e_b(t) = k_b \phi(t) \omega_m(t) \tag{7-56}$$

Finally, we shall always take the load on the motor to consist of the polar mass moment of inertia of the rotor, some viscous resistance proportional to the angular velocity of the rotor, and a torque T_L due to the presence of some external load.

Let J_m denote the mass moment of inertia of the rotor, ω_m its angular velocity, T_m the magnetic torque applied to the rotor, and b_m the damping coefficient. Then the equation of motion of the rotor in accordance with Euler's second law is given by (see Fig. 7-26)

$$T_m - T_L - b_m \omega_m = J_m \frac{d\omega_m}{dt} \tag{7-57}$$

With this general background in mind, we shall now discuss some of the particular field-armature combinations.

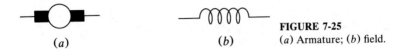

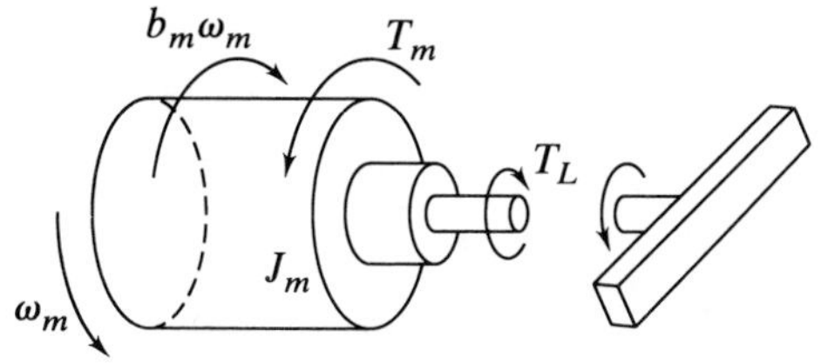

FIGURE 7-26
Rotor and loads.

ARMATURE AND FIELD IN SERIES. This kind of DC motor is usually employed when large start-up torques are required. The required current then decreases with an increase in angular velocity, with a corresponding decrease in magnetic flux. Since the field winding carries the full armature current, it generally consists of only a few turns of heavy gauge wire. Theoretically, this kind of motor would "run away" in a no-load condition; friction and losses, however, keep it in a safe operating range.

The field and armature configuration and the corresponding circuit model are shown in Fig. 7-27. Here, the field current is the same as the armature current, $i_a = i_f = i$. As always, the air gap flux is proportional to the field current, with

$$\phi(t) = k_f i(t)$$

from which the motor torque follows as

$$\begin{aligned} T_m(t) &= k_m \phi(t) i_a(t) \\ &= k_s i^2(t) \end{aligned}$$

where k_s is the torque constant for the series motor. For the basic emf we write

$$e_b = k_c i(t) \omega_m(t)$$

with the subscript c designating the "counter" as in counter emf, an often-used, alternate term for back emf. Note that both the torque and the back emf are nonlinear relationships. The law of moment of momentum, [Eq. (7-57)] then

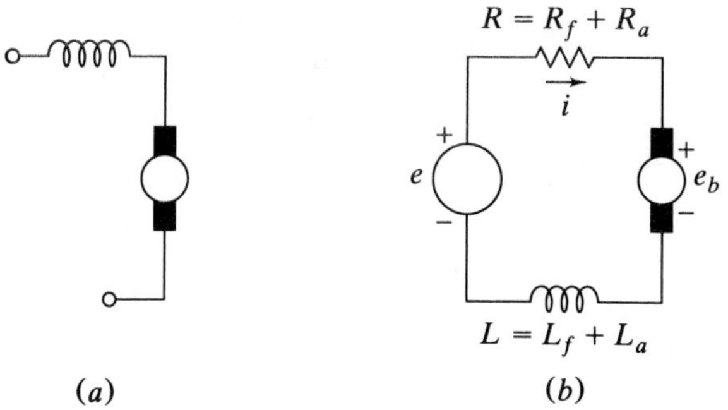

FIGURE 7-27
Series motor: (*a*) configuration schematic; (*b*) circuit diagram.

takes on the form

$$J_m \frac{d\omega_m}{dt} + b_m \omega_m = k_s i^2 - T_L. \tag{7-58}$$

The circuit equation is

$$L\frac{di}{dt} + Ri = e - e_b = e - k_c i \omega_m \tag{7-59}$$

where $R = R_a + R_f$ and $L = L_a + L_f$ are the combined field and armature resistance and inductance, respectively, and where e_b is the back emf generated in the armature. Equations (7-58) and (7-59) are the governing equations for the motor.

ARMATURE AND FIELD IN PARALLEL. This type of motor is termed a *shunted* DC motor. It has found wide use for both fixed and variable speed applications. The configuration schematic and the corresponding circuit are shown in Fig. 7-28.

Again, the air gap flux is given by

$$\phi(t) = k_f i_f(t)$$

and the corresponding torque by

$$T_m(t) = k_p i_f(t) i_a(t)$$

where k_p is the torque constant for the shunted (parallel) case. The back emf has the form

$$e_b(t) = k_c i_f(t) \omega_m(t).$$

We emphasize that the expressions for the torque and the back emf are nonlinear.

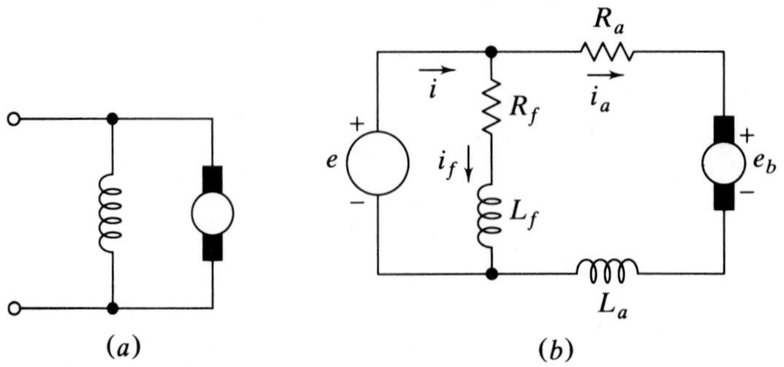

FIGURE 7-28
Shunted motor: (*a*) configuration schematic; (*b*) circuit diagram.

Euler's second law for the rotor has the form

$$J_m\frac{d\omega_m}{dt} + b_m\omega_m = k_p i_f i_a - T_L \tag{7-60}$$

and the corresponding circuit equations are given by

$$\begin{aligned} L_f\frac{di_f}{dt} + R_f i_f &= e \\ L_a\frac{di_a}{dt} + R_a i_a &= e - k_c i_f \omega_m \end{aligned} \tag{7-61}$$

Equations (7-60) and (7-61) are the governing equations for the shunted DC motor.

Remark 7-4. Note that the coupling terms in this problem—the motor torque and the back emf—are nonlinear. The idealized equations above become linear only when steady-state conditions corresponding to constant field and armature currents and a constant applied potential are considered. (In this connection, see also Exercises 7-13 and 7-14.)

SEPARATE ARMATURE AND FIELD. Since this case is most suited to linear systems analysis, we shall develop the corresponding mathematical model in more detail. As indicated, two separate potentials are used to power the armature and field. It is common to fix one potential and use the other to control the motor. We shall consider a fixed field current and use the armature current as our control. The configuration schematic and corresponding circuit are shown in Fig. 7-29.

We begin with the model for the field whose circuit equation is

$$e_f = i_f R_f + L_f\frac{di_f}{dt}$$

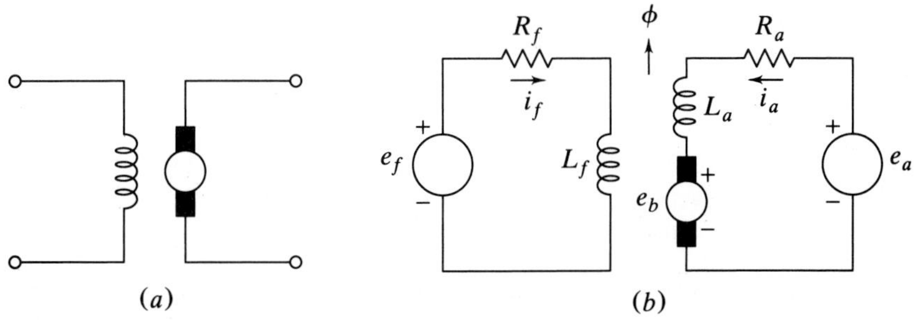

FIGURE 7-29
Separate field and armature: (*a*) configuration schematic; (*b*) circuit diagram.

We shall assume a constant potential E_f and assume that the circuit is operating at steady state so that $E_f = I_f R_f$, yielding a constant field current I_f.

From this it follows immediately that the air gap flux is constant with

$$\phi(t) = k_f I_f$$

and that the motor torque

$$\begin{aligned} T_m(t) &= k_m k_f I_f i_a(t) \\ &= k_T i_a(t) \end{aligned}$$

is proportional to the armature current with k_T denoting the torque constant.

The moment of momentum equation for the rotor is given by

$$J_m \frac{d\omega_m}{dt} + b_m \omega_m = k_T i_a - T_L \tag{7-62}$$

The circuit equation for the armature is given by

$$L_a \frac{di_a}{dt} + R_a i_a = e_a - k_b \omega_m \tag{7-63}$$

Equations (7-62) and (7-63) are the governing equations for this motor. It is common to write these equations in the standard first-order form

$$\dot{\mathbf{x}} = \mathbf{Ax} + \mathbf{Bu}$$

The result here has the form

$$\begin{pmatrix} \dfrac{d\omega_m}{dt} \\ \dfrac{di_a}{dt} \end{pmatrix} = \begin{bmatrix} -\dfrac{b_m}{J_m} & \dfrac{k_T}{J_m} \\ -\dfrac{k_b}{L_a} & -\dfrac{R_a}{L_a} \end{bmatrix} \begin{pmatrix} \omega_m \\ i_a \end{pmatrix} + \begin{bmatrix} -\dfrac{1}{J_m} & 0 \\ 0 & \dfrac{1}{L_a} \end{bmatrix} \begin{pmatrix} T_L \\ e_a \end{pmatrix} \tag{7-64}$$

Finally, we may also consider the separately excited DC motor as a linear systems component with system function $G(s)$. With $e_a(t)$ as the input and $\omega_m(t)$ as the output, this system function is given by

$$G(s) = \frac{\Omega_m(s)}{E_a(s)} = \frac{k_T}{(L_a s + R_a)(J_m s + b_m) + k_T k_b} \tag{7-65}$$

a result we shall make use of in a later section, in discussing joint control.

Remark 7-5. This same model is, of course, applicable to permanent magnet DC motor, with the exception that the constant air gap flux ϕ is that case is provided by the permanent stator magnets.

Remark 7-6. It can be shown in a relatively straightforward fashion that $k_T = k_b$ when appropriate units are used for the two constants. In the SI system, k_T is in newton · meters/ampere and k_b is taken to have the units newtons/radian/second. An appropriate conversion constant appears when English units are used.

It is difficult to know when to desist and to end this discussion of the basic concepts and operation of electric motors. There are many additional topics that could be treated, ranging from power dissipation to various motor specifications. The reader will have to pursue these in other texts, of which we particularly recommend Slemon and Straughen[9], the Electrocraft Handbook[10] and Kuo.[11]

7-2-5 Stepper Motors

According to Takashi,[12] stepper motors (also called stepping motors) were first used for the remote control of the direction indicators of torpedo tubes and guns in British warships and later, for a similar purpose, in the U.S. Navy. A variable reluctance stepper motor was first patented in 1919 by C. L. Walker, a Scottish civil engineer; however, commercial production of such devices did not commence until 1950. Industrial use increased rapidly in the 1970s, with improved dynamic performance, and stepper motors are now widely used in the computer industry.

Reluctance plays an essential part in this discussion, and we shall thus take a closer look at the meaning of this term. Magnetic reluctance is the analog of electrical resistance. Just as current occurs only in a closed loop, so magnetic flux occurs only around a closed path, although that path may be more varied than that of current.

Figure 7-30 illustrates the analogy. The flux in the ferromagnetic core depends on the number of turns N of the coil around the core and on the current in the wire. Analogous to electric potential, we define the magnetomotive force by

$$\mathcal{F} = Ni$$

and the magnetic reluctance in the circuit by

$$\mathcal{F} = \Re\phi$$

Continuing the analogy for a core with cross section $A(s)$ and permeability $\mu(s)$, we define

$$\Re = \oint \frac{ds}{\mu(s)A(s)} = \sum \frac{l_i}{\mu_i A_i}$$

the latter term referring to a core with piecewise constant cross-sectional area A_i and permeability μ_i.

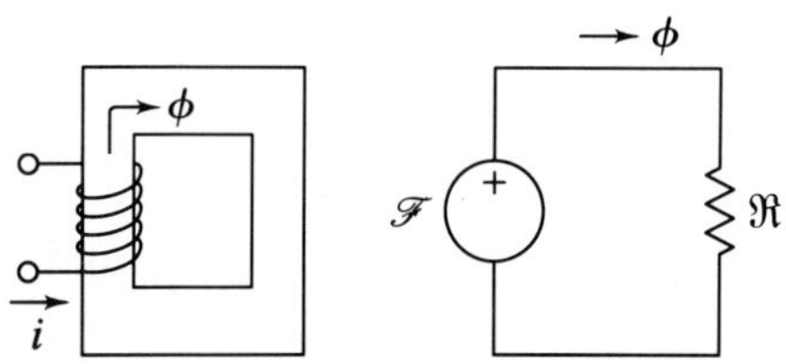

FIGURE 7-30
A flux loop.

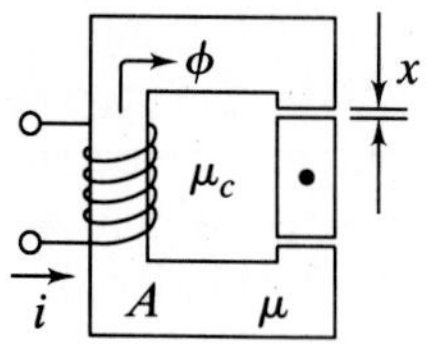

FIGURE 7-31
Magnetic reluctance.

Example 7-9. Calculate the total magnetic reluctance for the core configuration shown in Fig. 7-31. The gaps are air gaps, and the core material is ferromagnetic with relative permeability μ_r. Take the length of the ferromagnetic core section (including the rotor segment) to be L and assume a constant cross-sectional area A throughout.

Solution. The total reluctance is

$$\Re = \frac{L}{\mu_0 \mu_r A} + \frac{2x}{\mu_0 A} = \frac{1}{\mu_0 A}\left(\frac{L}{\mu_r} + 2x\right)$$

Clearly, the reluctance decreases considerably with a decrease in air gap. For example, if $L = 10$ cm, $x = \frac{1}{2}$ mm, and $\mu_r = 1000$, then $L/\mu_r = 0.01$ and $2x = 1$, so that the reluctance of the whole core is only $1/100$ of that of the air gap.

Remark 7-7. Because of the high reluctance of the air gap, it is obviously desirable to make the air gap as small as possible. Furthermore, a smaller gap also results in a higher flux density in the gap. According to Takashi,[12] modern motors have gaps ranging from 30 to 100 μm.

In contrast to the continuously turning motors discussed previously, a stepper motor is designed to turn through a specific number of steps and then stop. For each current pulse transmitted to an electronic motor driver, the rotor rotates through a fixed angle θ_s, called the step angle, in degrees. In this connection one defines the *resolution* or step number for a stepper motor as

$$S = \frac{360°}{\theta_s}$$

The prominent features of the stator are several pole pairs which are arranged at equal intervals around the stator, as shown in Fig. 7-32. Each pole pair is called a phase; thus the motor in Fig. 7-32 has three phases, the minimum number of phases required to permit rotation in either direction.

The coils for a pole pair are connected either in series or in parallel. When excited by a DC current, the coils produce a radial field in the pole pair. The poles are also referred to as stator teeth. There are six teeth in Fig. 7-32, with opposing teeth belonging to the same phase. We shall use a rotor with four teeth to show the manner in which rotation is produced.

When one of the phases, say AA', is excited, the rotor eventually positions itself to complete the flux path shown in Fig. 7-32. Note that there is a main flux

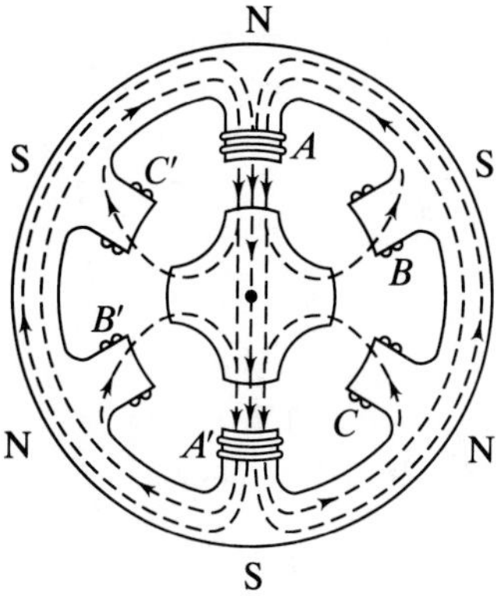

FIGURE 7-32
Basic configuration of stepper motor.

path through the aligned rotor and stator teeth, with secondary flux paths occurring as indicated. When rotor and stator teeth are aligned in this manner, the reluctance is minimized and the rotor is at rest in this position. This minimizing of the reluctance is the defining feature of the *variable reluctance stepper motor* (or, simply, VR motor). The remainder of our discussion will emphasize this common type of stepper motor.

To rotate the motor counterclockwise, phase AA' is turned off and phase BB' is excited. At that point the main flux path has the form indicated in Fig. 7-33*a*. Note that the lesser number of teeth in the rotor prepositions the next pair of rotor teeth to be drawn into alignment by the oppositely polarized phase BB'. The Maxwell stress in the flux path (the "tension" in the flux lines) again acts to minimize the reluctance expressed in a decreasing of the air gap between rotor and stator tooth. This tension in the lines produces a counter-

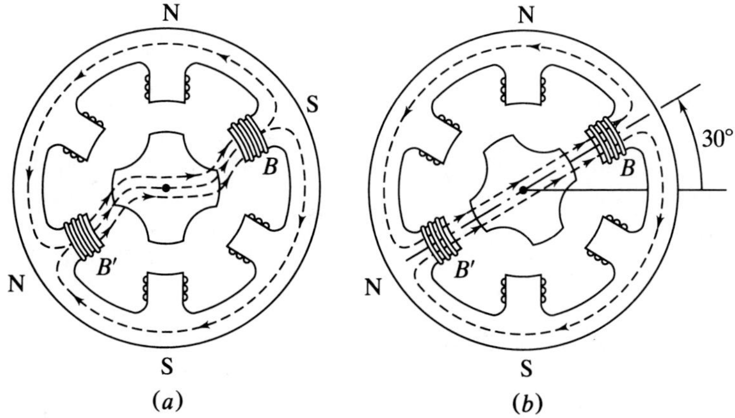

FIGURE 7-33
(*a*) Beginning of step; (*b*) completed loop.

clockwise torque until the rotor is again aligned with the stator poles, now corresponding to phase BB'. At the completion of this process, the rotor has executed one step, as shown in Fig. 7-33*b*.

With this process in mind, the resolution of the motor may be expressed in terms of the number of phases p and the number of rotor teeth n_r. The result is

$$S = pn_r$$

The motor in Fig. 7-32 thus has a resolution of $3 \times 4 = 12$ steps per revolution, or a step angle of 30°. This discussion of rotation was based on the excitation of one phase at a time and is thus termed single-phase excitation.

STATIC HOLDING TORQUE. Generally, stepper motors drive some kind of load, however small it may be. When the motor stops, the load may remain as a static load on the motor. This always causes an angular deviation from the desired equilibrium position, no matter how small the load torque and no matter how large the motor's restoring torque. The plot of this static restoring torque versus the angular deviation is called the motor's static torque/rotor position characteristic.

Suppose a load torque T_L has caused an angular deviation θ as shown in Fig. 7-34*a*. An approximation to the static restoring or holding torque is given by the sine wave in Fig. 7-34*b*. At static equilibrium we have $T_r = -T_L$. Consequently, with n_r being the number of rotor teeth, the static positioning error is given by

$$\theta_e = \frac{1}{n_r} \sin^{-1}\left(\frac{T_L}{T_{\text{rp}}}\right)$$

Clearly, whenever $T_L > T_{\text{rp}}$, the rotor will rotate to the next position (or more) and a positioning error will result.

SINGLE-STEP DYNAMIC RESPONSE. Our desk reference for this discussion is Takashi.[12] He, in turn, bases much of his theoretical treatment of the dynamics and stability of stepper motors on the fundamental work by P. J. Lawrenson and A. Hughes at the University of Leeds, England. Our discussion will be restricted to the single-phase operation of the VR motor.

To be specific, we suppose that phase AA' is being excited and is drawing the rotor into alignment after leaving phase BB'. Let the rotor be an angular distance θ (take ccw as positive) from alignment with phase AA', as shown in Fig. 7-35. Then, if the current in phase AA' is i_A, the torque exerted on the rotor by phase AA' is

$$T = \frac{1}{2} i_A^2 \frac{dL_A}{d\theta}$$

where L_A is the self-inductance of the coils comprising phase AA'. This inductance is a maximum when the rotor teeth are aligned with the stator teeth. It is a minimum when the AA'-axis is midway between the rotor teeth. If we assume that the variation between these extremes is sinusoidal in θ, as is

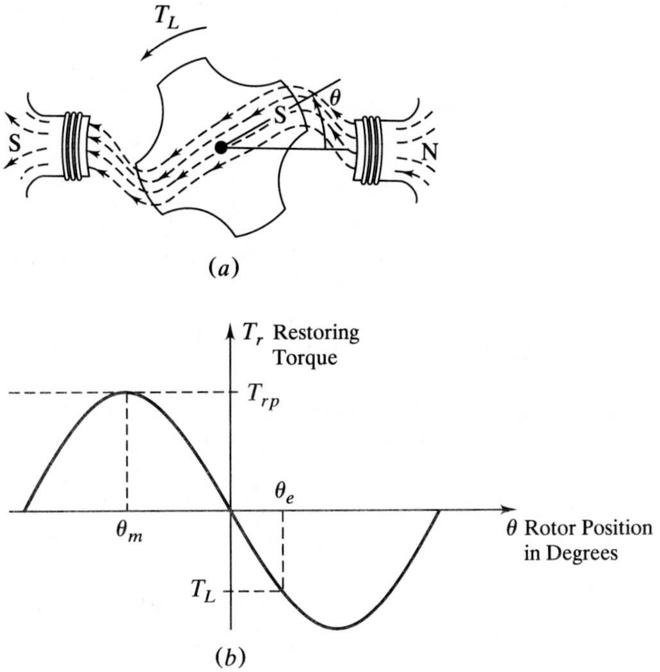

FIGURE 7-34
(*a*) Rotor deviation; (*b*) restoring torque.

commonly done, then

$$L_A = L_0 + L \cos n_r\theta$$

where n_r is the number of teeth in the rotor, as before. With this in mind, the exerted torque becomes

$$T = -\frac{1}{2} i_A^2 L n_r \sin n_r\theta$$

Note that the torque and θ always have opposite signs. Suppose then that a load torque T_L is applied to the motor, that J_m is the polar mass moment of inertia,

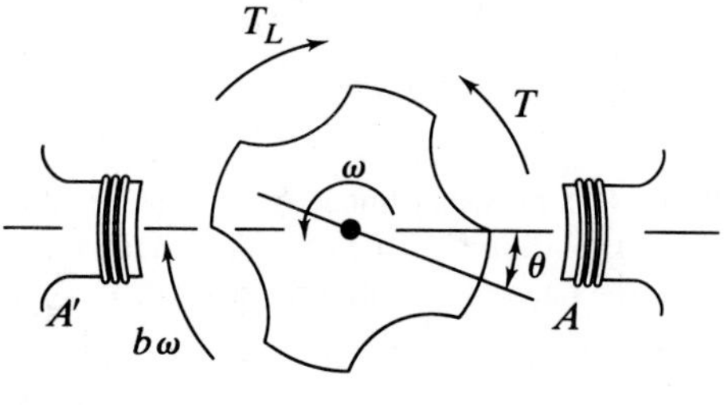

FIGURE 7-35
Dynamic response of the rotor.

and that viscous damping of the type $b\omega$ is present. The application of Euler's second law yields

$$-T_L + T - b\omega = J_m \frac{d\omega}{dt}$$

or

$$J_m \frac{d^2\theta}{dt^2} + b\frac{d\theta}{dt} + \frac{1}{2} i_A^2 L n_r \sin n_r \theta = -T_L \tag{7-66}$$

If we assume a constant voltage v_0 across the windings for phase AA' and we take them in series, then the attendant circuit equation is given by

$$v_0 - i_A R - \frac{d}{dt}(L_A i_A) = 0 \tag{7-67}$$

Equations (7-66) and (7-67) are the nonlinear governing equations for single-phase excitation. We shall now linearize these equations.

Toward this purpose, let $\beta(t)$ be the small deviation of the actual angle $\theta(t)$ from the desired constant step angle θ_i; that is,

$$\beta(t) = \theta_0(t) - \theta_i$$

Correspondingly, we take the current $i_A(t)$ to be given by

$$i_A(t) = i_0 + y(t)$$

where i_0 is the constant stationary current required to maintain the angle θ_i and $y(t)$ is the small deviation in current corresponding to the deviation $\beta(t)$. The substitution of these two expressions into (7-66) and (7-67) with $\theta(t) = \beta(t)$, $T_L = 0$, and neglecting all products of "small" terms, yields the linearized equations

$$J_m \frac{d^2\beta}{dt^2} + b\frac{d\beta}{dt} + \frac{1}{2} i_0^2 L n_r^2 \beta = 0 \tag{7-68}$$

and

$$(L_0 + L)\frac{dy}{dt} + Ry = 0 \tag{7-69}$$

Thus the linear equations are uncoupled.

Next, we turn to the derivation of an appropriate system function. Suppose we simply identify the phase AA' with the desired step angle θ_i in the equation

$$\beta(t) = \theta_0(t) - \theta_i \tag{7-70}$$

Substitution in (7-68) yields

$$J_m \frac{d^2\theta_0}{dt^2} + b\frac{d\theta_0}{dt} + \frac{1}{2} i_0^2 L n_r^2 \theta_0 = \frac{1}{2} i_0^2 L n_r^2 \theta_i \tag{7-71}$$

Remark 7-8. Some care is required here. The previous linearization implies that the equation applies only for small angles. Equation (7-70), however, requires only that the difference of the angles be small. We have thus added the assumption that all of the quantities in (7-70) be small. This is no great restriction, since it is common to have stepping angles of 15° or less.

To continue, we write (7-71) in a standard form by dividing by J_m. The resulting equation is the standard equation for the harmonic oscillator with damping,

$$\frac{d^2\theta_0}{dt^2} + 2\zeta\omega_n\frac{d\theta_0}{dt} + \omega_n^2\theta_0 = \omega_n^2\theta_i \tag{7-72}$$

where we have introduced the *natural circular frequency*

$$\omega_n = i_0 n_r \sqrt{\frac{L}{2J_m}} \left(\frac{\text{rad}}{\text{s}}\right)$$

and the *damping factor*

$$\zeta = \frac{b}{b_{cr}} = \frac{b}{i_0 n_r}\frac{1}{\sqrt{2LJ_m}}$$

The corresponding system function with output θ_0 and input θ_i is

$$G(s) = \frac{\Theta_0(s)}{\Theta_i(s)} = \frac{\omega_n^2}{s^2 + 2\zeta\omega_n s + \omega_n^2} \tag{7-73}$$

Systems are often compared in terms of their response to a unit step input. The use of an input $\theta_i\ (t) = u(t)$, the unit step function, along with the specification of zero initial conditions and $0 < \zeta < 1$, subcritical damping, leads to the response

$$\theta_0(t) = 1 - \frac{1}{\sqrt{1-\zeta^2}}e^{-\zeta\omega_n t}\sin\left(\omega_d t + \text{Arctan}\,\frac{\sqrt{1-\zeta^2}}{\zeta}\right) \tag{7-74}$$

where $\omega_d = \omega_n\sqrt{1-\zeta^2}$ is the damped frequency; one also defines a damped period $T_d = 2\pi/\omega_d$, although the response clearly is not periodic.

A sketch of this response is shown in Fig. 7-36. We use the figure to illustrate some specific system parameters which are used in the comparison of system performance. Generally, these terms are used in connection with under-damped systems:

1. *Maximum overshoot*. This is simply the difference between the first peak and the intended value. The intended value here is 1.0.
2. *Rise time*. The time required for the response to go from 0 to its first intersection with the intended value. The range from 10% to 90% of the intended value is also in use.
3. *Settling time*. The time required for the system to reach a stage where the oscillations remain within a specified interval about the intended value. Two

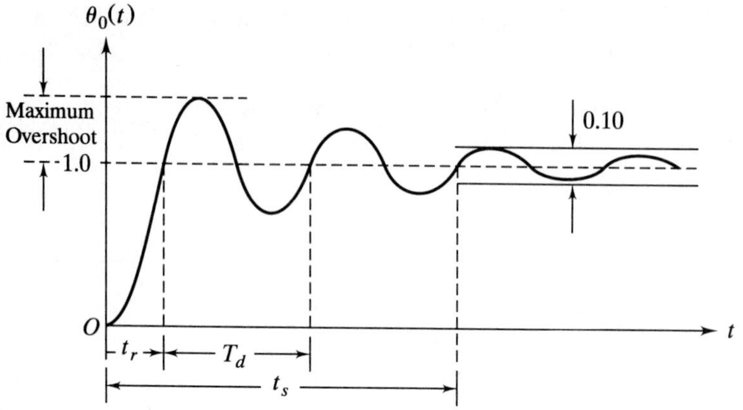

FIGURE 7-36
The unit step response.

ranges are in common use, an interval of $\pm 2\%$ or $\pm 5\%$, centered on the intended value.

This overshooting of the rotor position and the accompanying oscillation are obviously undesirable features. Unfortunately, phenomena such as viscous friction, which increase system damping, also tend to contribute to rotor wear. Suffice it to say that there are a variety of mechanical and electronic remedies, among them the use of dampers and a judicious pulsing of the motor.

There is another detrimental operational aspect which bears mentioning in this context. Because of these oscillations, the successive stepping of the motor has the form shown in Fig. 7-37. It seems clear that if the pulsing which urges the rotor from position to position is poorly chosen, it may amplify the oscillations until a step is skipped.

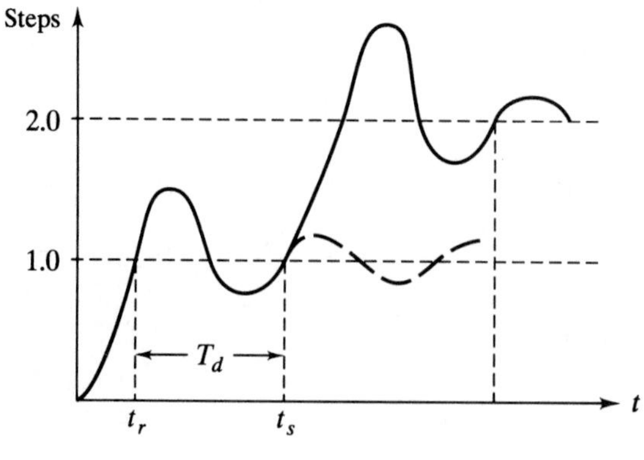

FIGURE 7-37
Sequential stepping.

We shall illustrate this phenomenon with the following idealized situation involving a sequence of step inputs into a harmonic oscillator with damping.

Example 7-10. Consider the sequential stepping of a rotor, one phase at a time. The response of the rotor at each step is given by

$$\theta_0(t) = 1 + Ae^{-\zeta\omega_n t}\sin(\omega_d t + \phi)$$

where $\omega_n^2 = k/m$, $\omega_d = \omega_n\sqrt{1-\zeta^2}$, and where A and ϕ are determined from initial conditions (generally the conditions prevailing at the end of the preceding step). Take $\zeta = 0.1$ and $\omega_n = 4$ rad/s for the numerical illustrations.

(*a*) Determine the rise time t_{r0} and the maximum overshoot for the first step.
(*b*) Assume that the next step input is applied at $t = t_s$, as shown in Fig. 7-37, and determine the rise time t_{r1} and peak overshoot for this response.
(*c*) Carry out a third step and hence estimate a critical pulsing frequency at which a loss of synchronism could result.

Solution. We shall consider each step to be a separate step, matching only the velocities at each step.

(*a*) For the first step, the initial conditions are taken to be $\theta_0(0) = 0$ and $\dot{\theta}_0(0) = 0$. The response of the rotor then is

$$\theta_0(t) = 1 - \frac{1}{\sqrt{1-\zeta^2}}e^{-\zeta\omega_n t}\sin\left(\omega_d t + \text{Arctan}\,\frac{\sqrt{1-\zeta^2}}{\zeta}\right)$$

$$= 1 - 1.005e^{-0.4t}\sin(3.98t + 1.47)$$

The rise time is given by the time t_{r0} for which $\theta_0(t_{r0}) = 1$ for the first time. The result is

$$\omega_d t_{r0} = \pi - \text{Arctan}\,\frac{\sqrt{1-\zeta^2}}{\zeta}$$

$$\Rightarrow \quad t_{r0} = \frac{1}{\omega_n\sqrt{1-\zeta^2}}\left(\pi - \text{Arctan}\,\frac{\sqrt{1-\zeta^2}}{\zeta}\right)$$

$$= 0.42 \text{ s}$$

To determine the time at which the first peak occurs, we note that the first zero slope occurs at $t = 0$, a minimum. The first maximum occurs half a damped period later, with $t_{m0} = \pi/\omega_d$. The corresponding maximum overshoot is

$$\theta_0\left(\frac{\pi}{\omega_d}\right) = 1 + e^{-\zeta\pi/\sqrt{1-\zeta^2}} = 1.729$$

(*b*) We assume that the next pulse occurs a damped period after the first rise time —that is, at

$$t_{p0} = t_{r0} + T_d$$
$$= \frac{1}{\omega_d}\left(3\pi - \operatorname{Arctan}\frac{\sqrt{1-\zeta^2}}{\zeta}\right)$$
$$= 2.0 \text{ s}$$

The velocity at that time is given by

$$\dot{\theta}_0(t_{p0}) = -\frac{\omega_n}{\sqrt{1-\zeta^2}} e^{-\zeta\omega_n t}\left(\sqrt{1-\zeta^2}\cos(\omega_d t + \phi) - \zeta\sin(\omega_d t + \phi)\right)\Big|_{t=t_{p0}}$$
$$= \omega_n \exp\left[-\frac{\zeta}{\sqrt{1-\zeta^2}}\left(3\pi - \operatorname{Arctan}\frac{\sqrt{1-\zeta^2}}{\zeta}\right)\right]$$
$$= 1.80 \text{ rad/s}$$

This provides the initial conditions for the second step: $\theta_0(0) = 0$ and $\dot{\theta}_0(0) = v_0 = 1.80$ rad/s. The corresponding response to a step input is

$$\theta_0(t) = 1 + \sqrt{\frac{1 - 2\zeta\dfrac{v_0}{\omega_n} + \left(\dfrac{v_0}{\omega_n}\right)^2}{1-\zeta^2}}\, e^{-\zeta\omega_n t}\sin\left(\omega_d t + \operatorname{Arctan}\frac{\sqrt{1-\zeta^2}}{\zeta - \dfrac{v_0}{\omega_n}}\right)$$
$$= 1 + 1.06e^{-0.4t}\sin(3.98t - 1.23)$$

The rise time for this response is given by

$$t_{r1} = -\frac{1}{\omega_d}\operatorname{Arctan}\frac{\sqrt{1-\zeta^2}}{\zeta - \dfrac{v_0}{\omega_n}}$$
$$= 0.31 \text{ s}$$

The initial velocity helps. The peak overshoot occurs when $\dot{\theta}_0(t_{m1}) = 0$ or

$$\omega_d t_{m1} = -\operatorname{Arctan}\frac{\sqrt{1-\zeta^2}}{\zeta - \dfrac{v_0}{\omega_n}} + \operatorname{Arctan}\frac{\sqrt{1-\zeta^2}}{\zeta}$$
$$t_{m1} = 0.68 \text{ s}$$

This peak is given by

$$\theta_0^1(t_{m1}) = 1 + 1.06e^{-0.27}\sin 1.47 = 1.805 \text{ rad}$$

(*c*) The third pulse is again applied at the point of maximum positive velocity,

$$t_{p1} = t_{r1} + T_d$$
$$= 0.31 + 1.578 = 1.889 \text{ s}$$

The initial velocity for the third step is $\dot{\theta}_0(t_{p1}) = 1.98$ rad/s. The corresponding response is

$$\theta_0(t) = 1 + 1.08e^{-\zeta\omega_n t}\sin(\omega_d t - 1.19)$$

The rise time for the third step is $t_{r2} = 0.30$ s. The peak overshoot is attained at $t_{m2} = 0.668$, with $\theta_0(t_{m2}) = 1.822$ rad.

A period $t_r + T_d$ would result in a positive initial velocity at each step, with a consequential buildup of the overshoot. A pulsing frequency of, say, $f = 1/(0.3 + 1.578)$ Hz should thus be avoided.

We have just provided a reasonably accurate picture of the manner in which driving frequencies might resonate with rotor setting oscillations. There are a variety of similar problems. Indeed, the torque versus stepping rate diagram of a typical stepper motor is fraught with "dips and islands" representing ranges in which the motor simply will not operate. Our final item for discussion is the drive system for a stepper motor.

OPEN LOOP DRIVE SYSTEM. A simple DC motor with appropriate voltage and current rating will run even when simply plugged into an outlet. Not so the stepper motor; only the proper sequential excitation of the phases will produce motion. We shall discuss this motion in terms of the three-phase stator and four-tooth rotor depicted in Fig. 7-33. The motion of the rotor there was explained in terms of simply turning off the phase with which the rotor was aligned and turning on the next phase to attract the next opposing set of rotor teeth. This kind of control is called one-phase-on sequencing, and we shall restrict ourselves to this case.

We begin the discussion with a schematic of the required drive system components as shown in Fig. 7.38. (For brevity, we have referred to phase AA' as phase A, for example, and we shall continue to do so in the remainder of this section.) The logic sequencer simply assures that the phases are powered in proper sequence, and the driver provides the current needed.

It is common to depict the proper sequencing of the phrases by means of a diagram such as the one shown in Fig. 7-39. We take phase A to be the reset (R) or home position of the rotor from where the steps are counted. Together with the schematic we show the first three phase actuations and the corresponding rotor position, as indicated by the darkened rotor tooth. Observe that a

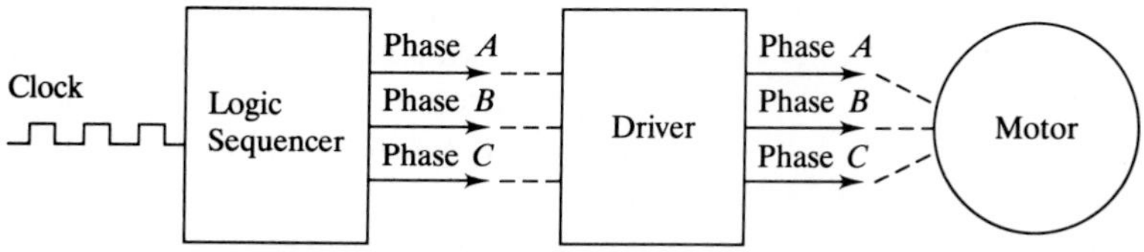

FIGURE 7-38
Schematic of drive system.

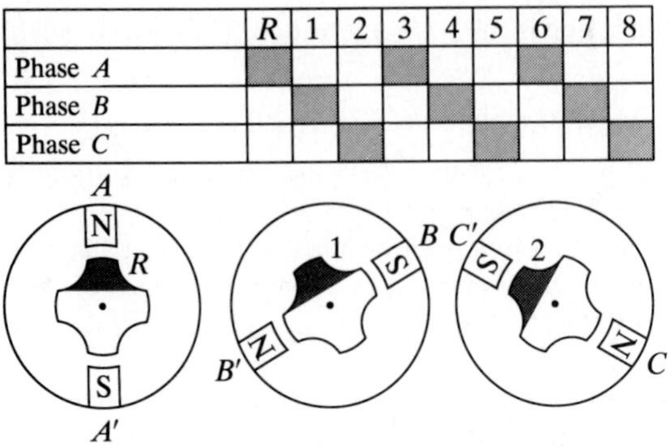
R
1
2
3
4
5
6
7
8
Phase A
Phase B
Phase C
A
N
R
S
A′
1
S
N
B′
B
C′
S
2
N
C

FIGURE 7-39
Phase sequencing for counterclockwise rotor rotation.

clockwise sequencing of the phases results in a counterclockwise rotor rotation. For a clockwise rotation the sequence is simply reversed, and we shall thus restrict ourselves to just the counterclockwise rotation.

We now turn to a logic sequencer which may be used to produce the switching sequence.

Flip-flops are central to this logic circuit. Since they were omitted in our earlier potpourri of logic concepts, we shall at least partially rectify this omission with a brief description of their function. Our discussion previously was limited to combinatorial circuits, whose outputs depend only on the current inputs. By contrast, a sequential circuit consists of both combinatorial circuitry and storage elements that can store binary information. Thus the output of a sequential circuit depends on both the circuit input and the current state represented by the storage elements.

Flip-flops are the storage elements employed in *clocked* sequential circuits. Since changes in such circuits are initiated by clock pulses, these circuits are also called synchronous sequential circuits. A flip-flop receives input from both the clock pulses and the combinatorial circuit; however, the state of the flip-flop may change *only* at instants determined by the clock pulses. Consequently, the output of a sequential circuit can only change in time with the clock pulses. Flip-flops are characterized, in part, by the way in which they receive binary information; that is, the way in which they can change state. One way of assuring proper operation is to have no changes in the output while the input is changing. Another way is to admit changes (triggering) only during the transition of the clock signal (0 to 1 or 1 to 0), with no changes occurring for a constant signal. The latter type are termed edge-triggered flip-flops. Since data reach the output only for specific changes in the clock signal, and since these do not happen instantaneously, the input must be presented (set up) and maintained (held) sufficiently long for the flip-flop circuit to be able to respond without ambiguity. This imposes a limitation on the frequency of signal change.

In our motor driver we shall make use of *JK* negative transition flip-flops (changes in state occur when the clock pulse changes from 1 to 0). A standard graphic symbol for such a flip-flop and its characteristic table are shown in

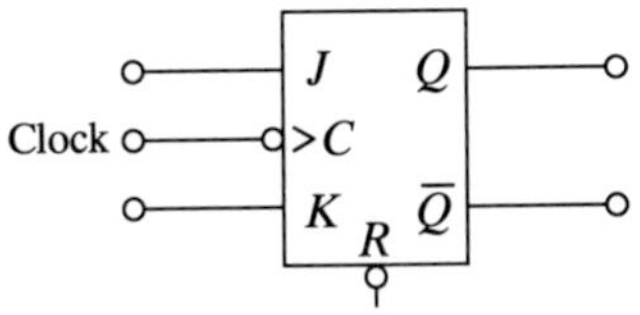

(*a*)

J	K	$Q(t+1)$	Operation
0	0	$Q(t)$	No Change
0	1	0	Reset
1	0	1	Set
1	1	$\overline{Q}(t)$	Complement

(*b*)

FIGURE 7-40
(*a*) Negative transition *JK* flip-flop; (*b*) characteristic table.

Fig. 7-40. (We adhere to the notation and symbology of our desk reference on logic circuits, Mano.[13])

A brief description of the meaning and purpose of the particular terminals is useful. Q and $\overline{Q}$ are the outputs of the flip-flop, and we generally describe the state of the flip-flop in terms of Q. Thus we say that the flip-flop is "off" or in the reset state when $Q = 0$ and that it is "on" or in the set state when $Q = 1$. $\overline{Q}$, of course, is the complement of Q. The input C receives the clock pulses. The arrowhead at the C input indicates that the input is dynamic or edge-triggered, and the adjacent circle indicates negative edge triggering. The J and K terminals are binary inputs; the J input serves to set the flip-flop, and K to reset. The R input may be used to clear the flip-flop asynchronously; that is, it simply turns the flip-flop "off" independent of any clock pulses.

An appropriate, relatively standard logic sequencer is provided by the sequential circuit in Fig. 7-41*a*. It consists of a shift register and three AND gates; more simply put, it counts from 0 to 2 over and over. We illustrate the operation of the sequencer by stepping through one of its 0-to-2 sequences.

First, note that $K1$ and $K2$ are always at logic 1. We take the initial position to be the reset position R, with $Q1$ and $Q2$ at 0 and $\overline{Q1}$ and $\overline{Q2}$ at 1. Thus phase A is activated. With $\overline{Q2} = 1$, the feedback produces $J1 = 1$, resulting in $K1 = 1$ *and* $J1 = 1$. The next clock pulse thus yields $Q1(t+1) = \overline{Q1(t)} = 1$, which forces $\overline{Q1(t+1)} = 0$; $Q2(t+1)$ and $\overline{Q2(t+1)}$ remain at 0 and 1, respectively. Thus phase A is turned off and phase B is activated. Meanwhile, $Q1(t+1) = 1$ results in $J2 = 1$ so that $J2$ *and* $K2$ are now equal to 1. At the next clock pulse we then get $Q1(t+2) = \overline{Q1(t+1)} = 0$, along with $\overline{Q1(t+2)} = 1$, since $J1$ and $K1$ are still at 1, and $Q2(t+2) = \overline{Q2(t+1)} = 1$ with $\overline{Q2(t+2)} = 0$. This shuts off phase B and activates phase C. The feedback from $\overline{Q2}$ yields $J1 = 0$, and $Q1 = 0$ yields $J2 = 0$, so that both $J1$ and $J2$ are now at 0. As a consequence, both flip-flops return to the "off"position at the next clock pulse with $Q1(t+3) = Q2(t+3) = 0$, and we are back to the R state. This continues ad infinitum as long as clock pulses are applied. This logic sequence is illustrated in the truth table (Fig. 7-41*b*).

The outputs from the AND gates activate the respective phase drivers. The simplest "driver" is a direct connection of the logic circuit to the base of

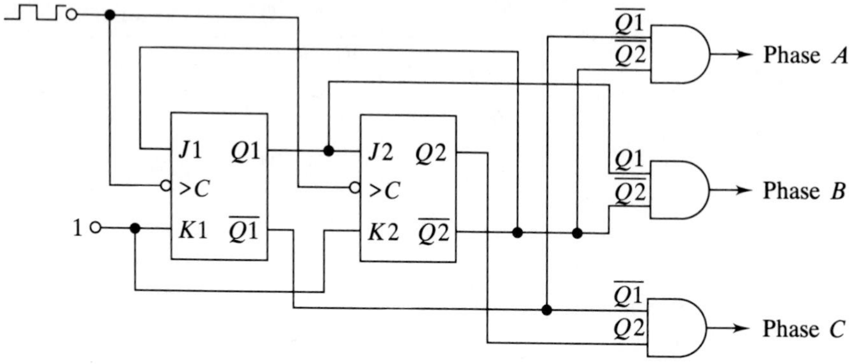

(*a*)

	t	*t* + 1	*t* + 2	*t* + 3	*t* + 4	*t* + 5
	R	1	2	3	4	5
*Q*1	0	1	0	0	1	0
$\overline{Q1}$	1	0	1	1	0	1
*Q*2	0	0	1	0	0	1
$\overline{Q2}$	1	1	0	1	1	0

(*b*)

FIGURE 7-41
(*a*) Logic sequencer; (*b*) truth table.

the transistor switch. The resulting current may not be enough to saturate the transistor and the driver would then include some current amplifiers. Once the switch is saturated, the full constant phase voltage V_p is applied across the phase circuit, since the voltage drop across the transistor is negligible. Usually, V_p will be high enough to supply the rated phase current.

Typical phase circuits for one-phase-on operation have been included in Fig. 7-42. The circuit includes the self-inductance of the winding L_w and the winding resistance R_w. It also includes an external (external to the winding) resistance R_s and a diode. The presence of L_w and R_w is unavoidable, and there is a simple explanation for the inclusion of the other two.

When a particular phase is turned on, the current flows through the winding as indicated in the first loop, since the diode prevents the flow in the other direction. The applied voltage V_p is generally high enough so that the current that flows is the rated current for the winding. Without the diode segment of the circuit, turning off the phase would produce a sudden change in current and hence a large voltage drop $L_w(di/dt)$ which could be high enough to damage the power transistor. The inclusion of the diode in parallel with the

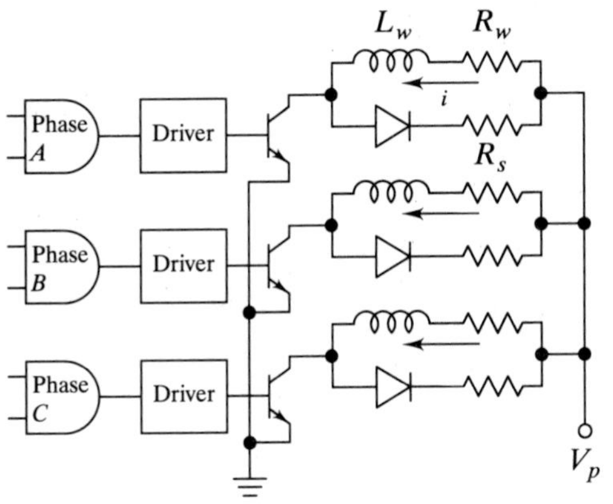

FIGURE 7-42
Phase circuits and drivers.

winding allows the current to continue to flow and to die out slowly. The resulting current loop and diode are termed the freewheeling circuit and freewheeling diode, respectively. The main disadvantage of this remedy is that the continuing flow of current produces a lingering magnetic field and hence a drag on the rotor motion. The external resistance R_e is included to decrease the time constant of the freewheeling circuit and thus to speed up the current decay.

CONCLUDING REMARKS. We have given a detailed discussion of the basic principles involved in the production of motion in stepper motors. All are based on the pulsed excitation of magnetic fields, and there is a variety of ways in which this pulsing is accomplished, each approach with advantages and disadvantages. The principles were illustrated with a common, though minimal configuration for a variable reluctance motor. We illustrated the one-phase-on operation of the VR motor. Depending on the pulsing intervals, this operation may produce overshoot and oscillation about the final equilibrium position. These undesirable phenomena may be considerably reduced with two-phase-on operation, involving the simultaneous excitation of two phases at a time. In essence, the rotor is then stepped in half-step intervals.

The number of steps available in a stepper motor is essentially limited only by the technological refinement that can be achieved in providing individually wound phases. To an extent, this is accomplished simply by increasing the number of teeth on both rotor and stator, thus increasing the resolution of the motor. In this context the stator teeth will usually appear grouped on larger wound poles, so that all the teeth connected to the pole will exhibit the same polarity at any given moment.

Finally, as is the case with virtually all electronic and electrical devices which are on and off sequentially, the time constants of the relevant circuits play a crucial role in limiting the operating speeds. Here, we are referring to the speed at which excitation changes in the phases can take place. It is common to consider speeds of 100 steps/s or less as low, and speeds of more than 100 steps/s as high. In addition to these general limitations and refinements, we now cite a few common variants of steeper motors. For a more detailed treatment of these variants, the reader is referred to Takashi[12] and Acarnley.[14] (The latter is particularly readable.)

STACKED VARIABLE RELUCTANCE MOTORS. The individual VR motor was discussed in some detail. Here, as the term implies, several of these motors are "stacked" along the motor axis as magnetically and electrically isolated sections. All of the stators are aligned; the rotors are not. Thus the offset of each rotor with respect to its predecessor may be used to refine the step size somewhat in the manner of a micrometer adjustment. In general, VR motors are used when several revolutions are desired at step sizes of 15° or more.

PERMANENT MAGNET MOTORS. Rather than having only electrically produced magnetic poles, these motors have permanent magnets in the rotor. They are usually manufactured without rotor teeth and for step sizes larger than 30°, since it is difficult to provide very many permanent magnetic poles in the rotor. Their advantages include a somewhat increased torque for a given size and coming to rest in a fixed position because of the presence of torque, even when the motor is off. On the negative side, the permanent magnets tend to be costly and the flux density is limited by the magnetic remnance of the magnet.†

HYBRID MOTORS. In both permanent magnet motors and hybrid motors, the torque is proportional to the current and a holding torque exists when the motor is off. Hybrid motors may include permanent magnets either in the stator or in the rotor. Their operational characteristics combine those of VR and PM motors. They are used when high resolution is required and a step angle of 1.8° is common. Their torque-to-weight ratio is high.

Stepper motors are not suited to operations with heavy loads. However, if open loop accurate position control at low torque is the objective, as it is in microrobotics and for printers and plotters, then stepper motors are the ideal actuators.

7-3 POWER TRANSMISSION

All of the preceding devices produced power of one form or another, either supplying torque at a given angular speed or force at some specified translational speed. However, the location at which the power was produced was not

†In ferromagnetic materials there are two measures of magnetic effects: the magnetic flux density $\boldsymbol{B}$ and the magnetic intensity $\boldsymbol{H}$. A plot of B versus H is a constitutive relationship for a given material. When a ferromagnetic material exhibits hysteresis, the limit as H tends to 0 will result in a residual magnetic flux density B_r; this is termed the *magnetic remnance*.

necessarily where it was needed. Hence we need power transmission devices to deliver torque or motion from some actuator output to a removed point where it is used. There are numerous such devices. We shall discuss three which find frequent use in robotics: belts, gear trains, and lead screws.

Since the concept of power lies at the center of our discussion, a brief review of the concept in this context may be useful. For the formal definition, we suppose that a force $\boldsymbol{F}(t)$ is acting on a point whose velocity is $\boldsymbol{v}_p(t)$. We have included the subscript to emphasize that the velocity in the definition is that of the point and not that of the force vector.

Definition 7-2 Power. The *instantaneous* power provided by the force $\boldsymbol{F}$ is

$$P(t) = \boldsymbol{F}(t) \cdot \boldsymbol{v}_p(t)$$

The *time average* power over the time interval $[t_0, t_1]$ is

$$P_{\text{av}} = \frac{1}{t_1 - t_0} \int_{t_0}^{t_1} \boldsymbol{F}(t) \cdot \boldsymbol{v}_p(t)\, dt$$

Definition 7-3 Work. The work done by the force $\boldsymbol{F}(t)$ over the time interval $[t_0, t_1]$ is

$$W = \int_{t_0}^{t_1} \boldsymbol{F}(t) \cdot \boldsymbol{v}_p(t)\, dt$$

Remark 7-9. The velocity of the tip of the force vector is, in general, different from the velocity of the point on which the force acts at a given instant. This distinction disappears when the force acts on the same point throughout the motion, as is the case in particle dynamics.

Example 7-11. Suppose a man weighing 150 lb is running up an escalator with a constant speed of 9 ft/s relative to the escalator as shown in Figure 7-43. The

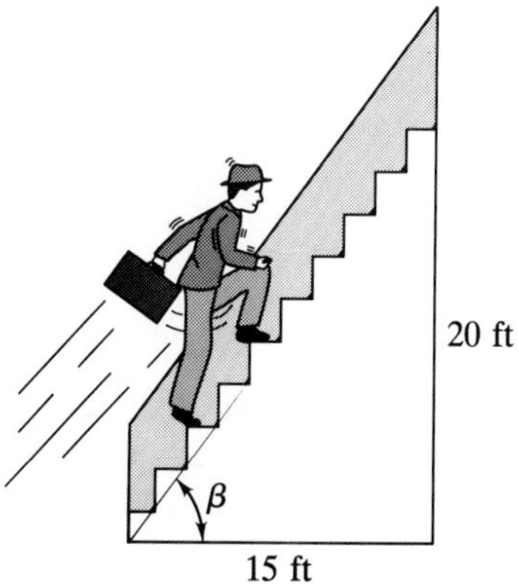

FIGURE 7-43
Man running up an escalator.

escalator is moving at a constant speed of 6 ft/s. Take the man to be at rest just before he steps on and just after he steps off.

(*a*) Calculate the instantaneous power supplied by the escalator in moving the man.

(*b*) Calculate the work done by the escalator in moving the man to the top.

(*c*) Compare your result in part (b) to the work that would be done by the escalator in moving the man to the top if he were to remain at rest with respect to the escalator.

Solution. The only force which allows the man to move relative to the escalator is the friction force between the escalator and the man's feet. For the analysis, suppose we let the man take infinitely small steps and remain in constant contact with the escalator which we view as an inclined moving walkway. With unknown friction force F, an application of Newton's second law yields

$$F = mg \sin \beta$$

in view of the postulated constant velocity.

(*a*) The instantaneous power produced by this force is

$$\begin{aligned} P(t) &= F \cdot v_p \\ &= (150)\left(\tfrac{4}{5}\right) \cdot 15 = 1800 \text{ ft} \cdot \text{lb/sec} \end{aligned}$$

Note that we are using the absolute speed of the man.

(*b*) At the speed of 15 ft/s it takes the man $t_1 = \frac{25}{15} = \frac{5}{3}$ sec to reach the top. The work done by the escalator thus is

$$W = \int_0^{t_1} P(t)\, dt = \int_0^{5/3} 1800\, dt = 3000 \text{ ft} \cdot \text{lb}$$

precisely the potential energy acquired by the man due to his change in elevation.

(*c*) If the man remains at rest with respect to the escalator, the only thing that changes is the man's absolute velocity which now is $v_p = 6$ ft/s. The instantaneous power provided by the escalator is

$$P(t) = 120 \cdot 6 = 720 \text{ ft} \cdot \text{lb/s}$$

The time it takes the man to get to the top is $t_2 = \frac{25}{6}$ sec and the work done by the escalator is

$$W = \int_0^{t_2} 720\, dt = 3000 \text{ ft} \cdot \text{lb}$$

Thus the total work done by the escalator on the man is the same no matter whether the man stands still or moves relative to the escalator.

In essence, we have used the work-energy theorem to arrive at this result. Clearly, in a colloquial sense, the running man puts in "work" to get to the top in a shorter time. However, these calories that the man expends, this biscuit work, is not accounted for in the mechanical theory of work. There is, however, some evidence of it in that the instantaneous power required from the escalator is considerably more in the first case. When viewed in terms of the motor torque required to drive the escalator, the required torque in the first case is more than double that needed in the second.

Remark 7-10. As a final comment on the use of power, we note that power in a rotational context is defined by

$$P(t) = \mathbf{T}(t) \cdot \boldsymbol{\omega}(t)$$

where $\mathbf{T}(t)$ denotes an applied torque and $\boldsymbol{\omega}(t)$ is the angular velocity of the body to which the torque is applied. Note that both work and power are scalar concepts.

For more detailed discussions of the following topics, we recommend the desk references on machine component design by Juvinall[15] and Burr.[16]

7-3-1 Belts

Flat belts were in extensive use not too many years ago. I still remember seeing a rather cavernous shop where various machines were driven by leather belts connected to a row of different-sized pulleys, all mounted on a hefty rod driven by a waterwheel. The reason we begin our discussion with belts is that they are the most likely to have been part of the student's more recent experience. They are often discussed in statics in connection with a treatment of friction.

Robotics applications generally involve V-belts; however, highly tensioned flat steel belts are also in use. Our treatment of V-belts will adhere to the traditional treatment of flat belts, since only a slight adjustment of the latter's descriptive equations will be necessary.

The basic configuration of a flat belt drive is shown in Fig. 7-44.† In the figure F_1 is the *tight side tension*, and F_0 is the *slack side tension*. The difference $F_1 - F_0$ is termed the *net belt pull*. The smaller pulley is usually called the driver pulley, and the larger one the driven pulley—a relationship that is also apparent from the labeling of the torques with driving torque T_0 and load torque T_L. Since the belt action on the smaller pulley is the critical one, the remainder of this discussion will be cast in this framework, with obvious analogs for the larger pulley.

The angle θ over which the belt is in contact with the pulley is the *angle of wrap*, as illustrated in Fig. 7-45*a*. The angular velocity of the pulley at steady-state operation is taken to be a constant ω. The normal pressure distribution between the belt and the pulley around the circumference is denoted by $p(\phi)$, with $p(0) = p_0$, and we take the friction coefficient between the belt and the pulley to be μ. The mass per unit length of the belt is ρ and we neglect the belt thickness

†The notation used in the following derivation is relatively standard; for the most part, we adhere to the notation and terminology used in Burr.[16]

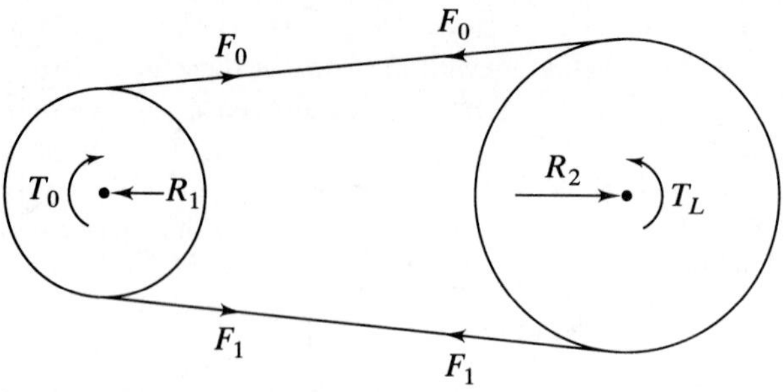

FIGURE 7-44
Flat belt drive.

in comparison to the pulley radius r so that the belt is taken to be collinear with the pulley circumference. The resultant force in the belt at a section ϕ is denoted by $F(\phi)$, all as shown in Fig. 7-45b. The width of the belt is b.

A summation of forces in the radial direction yields

$$pbr\,d\phi - F\frac{d\phi}{2} - (F + dF)\frac{d\phi}{2} = -(\rho r\,d\phi)r\omega^2$$

Neglecting higher-order terms in the differentials and canceling $d\phi$ leaves the equation

$$\begin{aligned} F &= pbr + \rho r^2\omega^2 \\ &= pbr + F_c \end{aligned} \tag{7-75}$$

A summation of moments about the point O (with counterclockwise as positive) yields the equation

$$(F + dF)r - Fr - r(pbr\,d\phi)\mu = 0 \quad \Rightarrow \quad dF = \mu pbr\,d\phi \tag{7-76}$$

since the belt is moving at constant speed. To obtain both F and p as functions

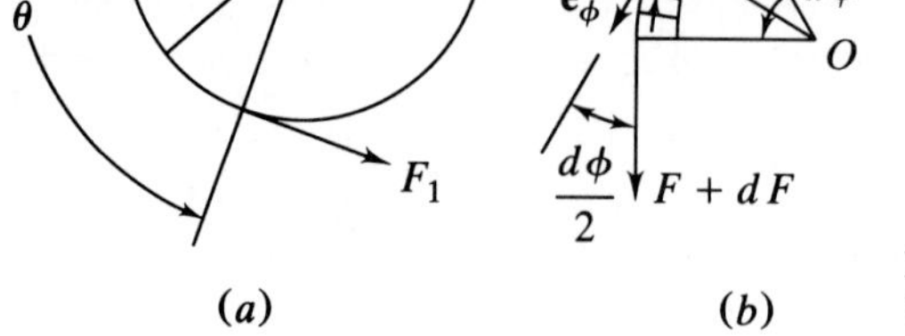

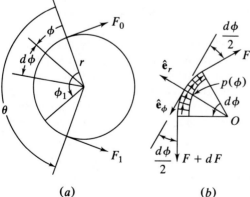

FIGURE 7-45
Free bodies of belt and pulley.

of ϕ, we take the differential of (7-75),

$$dF = br\,dp$$

and substitute this into (7-76), with the result

$$dp = \mu p\,d\phi$$

$$\int_{p_0}^{p} \frac{dp}{p} = \int_0^{\phi} \mu\,d\phi$$

$$p = p_0 e^{\mu\phi} \tag{7-77}$$

The minimum pressure occurs at the slack end ($\phi = 0$) with $F = F_0$. Equation (7-75) may thus be used to obtain

$$F_0 = p_0 br + F_c \qquad \text{or} \qquad p_0 = \frac{F_0 - F_c}{br} \tag{7-78}$$

The torque developed by a pulley is the net belt pull times the pulley radius, or

$$T_0 = (F_1 - F_0)r \tag{7-79}$$

In turn, this torque must be generated by the maximum available friction force. We thus have

$$T_0 = \int_0^{\phi_1} \mu p(\phi) br^2\,d\phi$$

$$= \mu p_0 br^2 \int_0^{\phi_1} e^{\mu\phi}\,d\phi$$

$$= p_0 br^2[e^{\mu\phi_1} - 1]$$

where ϕ_1 is the *active angle* and $\phi_1 \le \theta$ is the angle of wrap. Substitution of the expression for p_0 from (7-78) yields

$$T_0 = (F_0 - F_c)r[e^{\mu\phi_1} - 1] \tag{7-80}$$

The elimination of T_0 between (7-79) and (7-80) finally results in the useful relationship between the tight force F_1 and the slack force F_0,

$$\frac{F_1 - F_c}{F_0 - F_c} = e^{\mu\phi_1} \tag{7-81}$$

When the pulley is rotating slowly or when only the static holding torque is to be considered, the relationship reduces to

$$\frac{F_1}{F_0} \approx e^{\mu\phi_1} \tag{7-82}$$

The ratio clearly attains its maximum for $\phi_1 = \theta$, which also yields the maximum driver torque.

For $0 \le \phi \le \phi_1$, the belt force is a function of ϕ, and F changes from F_0 to F_1; thereafter, in the belt segment from ϕ_1 to θ, F_1 remains constant so that

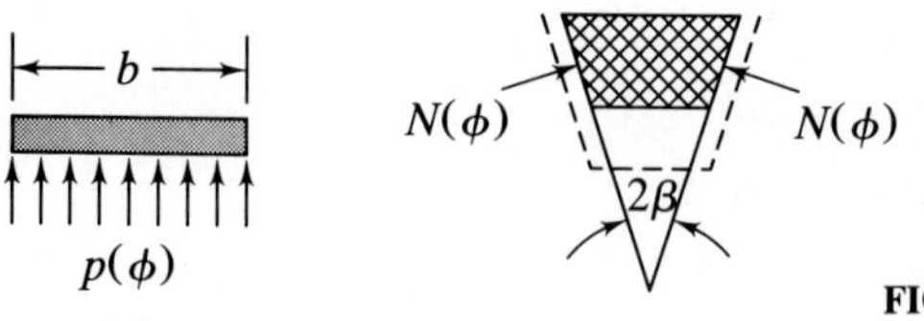

(a) (b)

FIGURE 7-46
(*a*) The flat belt; (*b*) the V-belt.

this segment contributes nothing to the available torque. As a consequence of the changing belt tension, a corresponding strain is developed in the interval $0 \leq \phi \leq \phi_1$ and, collectively, a relative displacement between the belt and the pulley. This displacement, termed *belt creep*, results in a slight loss in belt speed and hence a loss in the transmitted power. These losses are generally considered to be negligible, and all calculations are performed by taking the belt velocity to be equal to the surface velocity of the pulley.

The previous equations were derived for flat belts. As mentioned earlier, only a slight alteration is necessary to make these equations applicable to V-belts. For the flat belt discussion we considered a normal pressure $p(\phi)$ distributed over the contact area, as illustrated in the sectional view of Fig. 7-46*a*. A V-belt rides in a groove, as indicated by the heavy dashed lines in Fig. 7-46*b*. There is a clearance space between the bottom of the belt and the pulley, and only the slanted sides of the belt maintain contact. For this analysis we represent the interaction pressure between the belt and the pulley by a resultant normal force $N(\phi)$ per unit length. Strictly speaking, this resultant acts at a distance $r + h$ from the center; as before, we take h to be negligible. With these preliminaries in mind, (7-75) becomes

$$\begin{aligned} F &= 2rN(\phi)\sin\beta + \rho r^2\omega^2 \\ &= 2rN\sin\beta + F_c \end{aligned}$$

where 2β is the groove angle, as shown in Fig. 7-46*b*. Equation (7-76) becomes

$$dF = 2\mu N r\,d\phi$$

Continuation of the analysis as before yields (7-77) in the form

$$N = N_0 e^{\mu_0\phi_1} \qquad \mu_0 = \frac{\mu}{\sin\beta}$$

where μ_0 is termed the *effective friction coefficient*. Equation (7-78) can now be written as

$$F_0 = 2rN_0\sin\beta + F_c \quad \Rightarrow \quad N_0 = \frac{F_0 - F_c}{2r\sin\beta}$$

and the subsequent expression for the torque is given by

$$\begin{aligned} T_0 &= 2r^2 N_0 \sin\beta(e^{\mu_0\phi_1} - 1) \\ &= 2r^2 \sin\beta \frac{F_0 - F_c}{2r\sin\beta}(e^{\mu_0\phi_1} - 1) \\ &= (F_0 - F_c)r[e^{\mu_0\phi_1} - 1] \end{aligned}$$

The elimination of T_0, as before, provides

$$\frac{F_1 - F_c}{F_0 - F_c} = e^{\mu_0\phi_1}$$

Effectively, then, all of the previously derived equations are applicable to V-belts as long as we replace the friction coefficient μ by the effective friction coefficient

$$\mu_0 = \frac{\mu}{\sin\beta}$$

Example 7-12. Show that the tight side tension is a minimum for $\phi_1 = \theta$, the wrap angle, when a specified power $\mathscr{P}$ is to be supplied at a belt velocity v.

Solution. When belt creep is neglected, the total power supplied by the driver pulley is

$$\mathscr{P} = T_0\omega = (F_1 - F_0)r\omega = (F_1 - F_0)v$$

where v is the surface velocity of the driver pulley. The simultaneous solution of this equation and (7-81) yields F_1 as a function of ϕ_1,

$$F_1(\phi_1) = F_c + \frac{\mathscr{P}}{v}\left(\frac{e^{\mu\phi_1}}{e^{\mu\phi_1} - 1}\right)$$

The derivative of this expression with respect to ϕ_1 is

$$\frac{dF_1}{d\phi_1} = -\mu\frac{\mathscr{P}}{v}e^{\mu\phi_1}$$

so that F_1 is monotonically decreasing with ϕ_1, $0 \le \phi_1 \le \theta$. Thus

$$(F_1)_{\min} = F_c + \frac{\mathscr{P}}{v}\left(\frac{e^{\mu\theta}}{e^{\mu\theta} - 1}\right)$$

In robotics, belts are most often used with fixed center drives. To function properly in loaded operation, they must be mounted with a sufficient initial or *standing tension* F_s. This required standing tension is related to the tight side tension by

$$F_1 = F_s + \frac{\mathscr{P}}{2v}$$

where $\mathscr{P}$ and v have the same meaning as in Example 7-12. The corresponding minimum possible standing tension is related to the minimum tight side tension by

$$(F_1)_{\min} = (F_s)_{\min} + \frac{\mathscr{P}}{2v}$$

attained for $\phi_1 = \theta$.

Example 7-13. Suppose a motor with a 4-in pulley supplies $\frac{3}{4}$ hp at 1500 rpm to a SCARA joint with a 6-in pulley at a fixed center distance of 10 in from the driver pulley. The V-belt connecting the two pulleys has a groove angle of 36° and the belt weighs 0.012 lb/in. The coefficient of friction is $\mu = 0.15$.

(*a*) Calculate the minimum possible tight side tension capable of supporting this power supply.

(*b*) Calculate the corresponding minimum standing tension.

(*c*) It is common to include a safety factor in the design standing tension to account for the subsequent gradual stretching of the belt with use. Suppose the design value of the standing tension is taken to be one-third more than the minimum. Calculate the corresponding initial action angle ϕ_1 and the initial tight side and slack side tensions F_1 and F_0, respectively.

Solution. We first calculate some needed quantities and convert given ones to proper units. For a given fixed center distance c and radii r and R, the corresponding angles of wrap may be obtained from the expression

$$\sin\alpha = \frac{R-r}{c}$$

based on the illustration in Fig. 7-47. Here, the wrap angle for the driver pulley is thus given by

$$\theta = 180 - 2\sin^{-1}\frac{R-r}{c} = 168.52° \approx 2.94 \text{ rad}$$

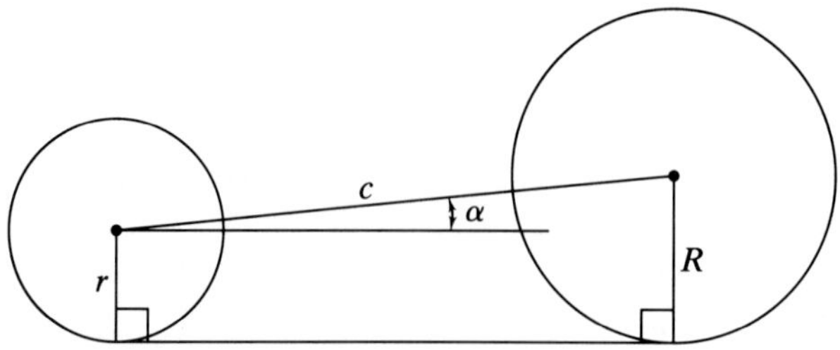

FIGURE 7-47
Toward the calculation of the wrap angle.

The power supply is

$$\mathscr{P} = 0.75 \cdot 550 = 412.50 \text{ ft} \cdot \text{lb}$$

The angular velocity of the driver pulley is

$$\omega = 1500 \cdot \frac{2\pi}{60} = 157.08 \text{ rad/sec}$$

resulting in a velocity

$$v = r\omega = \left(\frac{1}{6}\right) \cdot 157.08 = 26.18 \text{ ft/sec}$$

The application of the analysis to V-belts requires

$$\mu_0 = \frac{\mu}{\sin\beta} = \frac{0.15}{\sin 18°} = 0.49$$

The mass per unit length of the V-belt is

$$\rho = 0.012 \cdot \frac{12}{32.2} = 0.0045 \text{ slugs/ft}$$

These are the ingredients for the calculations of the required quantities.

(*a*) The belt force F_c resulting from the centripetal acceleration is

$$F_c = \rho r^2\omega^2 = (0.0045)(26.18)^2 = 3.08 \text{ lb}$$

This yields the possible minimum tight side tension

$$\begin{aligned}(F_1)_{\min} &= F_c + \frac{\mathscr{P}}{v}\left(\frac{e^{\mu_0\theta}}{e^{\mu_0\theta} - 1}\right) \\ &= 3.08 + \frac{412.50}{26.18}\left[\frac{4.23}{4.23 - 1}\right] \\ &= 23.71 \text{ lb}\end{aligned}$$

(*b*) The standing tension is given by

$$(F_s)_{\min} = 23.71 - \frac{412.50}{2 \cdot 26.18} = 15.83 \text{ lb}$$

(*c*) Our final design is based on the inclusion of a safety factor, and we thus take the design standing tension to be given by

$$F_s = 1.33(F_s)_{\min} = 21.05 \text{ lb}$$

This yields a tight side tension

$$F_1 = F_s + \frac{\mathscr{P}}{2v} = 21.05 + 7.88 = 28.93 \text{ lb}$$

and a slack side tension

$$F_0 = F_s - \frac{\mathscr{P}}{2v} = 13.17 \text{ lb}$$

The active angle is finally given by

$$\phi_1 = \frac{1}{\mu_0} \ln\left(\frac{F_1 - F_c}{F_0 - F_c}\right) = \frac{1}{0.49} \ln\left(\frac{28.93 - 3.08}{13.17 - 3.08}\right)$$

$$= 1.92 \text{ rad} \approx 110.01°$$

Remark 7-11. It is common to use multiple belt drives. For an N belt drive, one would then have N times any required force; for example, the total tight side tension would be NF_1, F_1 being the tight side tension sustained by an individual belt.

The previous calculations and analysis serve as the basis for the selection of suitable drive belts from manufacturers' data and catalogs. As in all things, some occasional belt-tightening is beneficial.

7-3-2 Spur Gears

Gears have been in use for a long time. According to Juvinall,[15] the Chinese are known to have used complex gear systems in their chariots as long ago as 2600 B.C., Aristotle wrote about gears as commonplace objects in 4 B.C., and most engineers may (or may not) be aware of the many types of gears used by Leonardo da Vinci in his designs. They have lost none of their appeal.

We shall only touch upon some of the details of spur gears—the simplest and perhaps most common type of gear, used to transmit rotary motion between parallel shafts with gear teeth that are parallel to these shafts. Typically, there is also an umbrella society that watches over, establishes, and maintains standards for tolerance and precision in gears: AGMA, the American Gear Manufacturers Association.

We shall merely whet the appetite for those who may really wish to "gear up." We begin our discussion with much of the standard terminology, followed by a relatively detailed presentation of a specific gear profile, and eventually, a kinematic and kinetic analysis of spur gears. As our desk references we shall use Juvinall,[15] Burr,[16] and Wilson, Sadler, and Michels.[7]

We reiterate that the purpose of gears is the transmission of rotary motion. This transmission should occur as smoothly and with as little noise as possible, and, most importantly, the transmitted motion should be uniform. Clearly, the gear profile—that is, the shape of the individual gear teeth and their density on the circumference—plays the decisive role in attaining these goals. In particular, the term *uniform motion* here has the very specific meaning that this shape must be such that when the driving gear is rotating with a constant angular velocity, the driven gear must move with a *constant* angular velocity also. This basic requirement of the uniformity of transmitted motion is enshrined in the so-called law of conjugate gear tooth action.

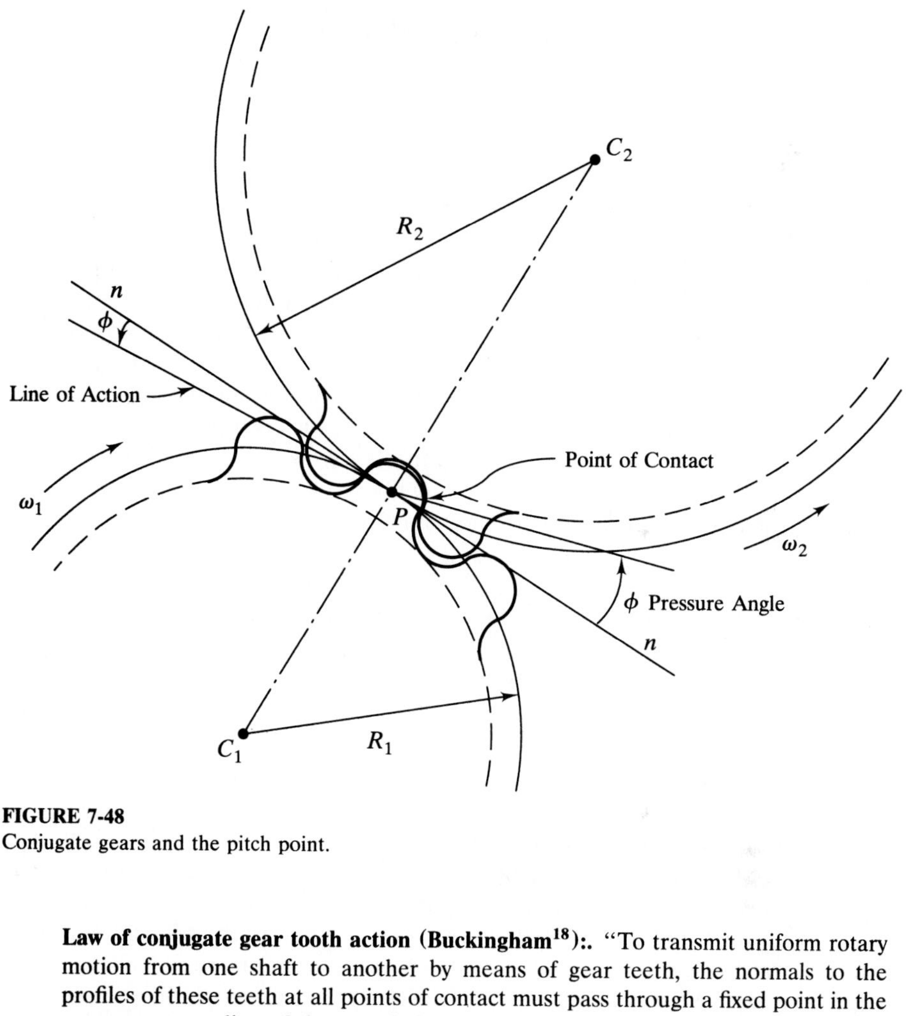

FIGURE 7-48
Conjugate gears and the pitch point.

Law of conjugate gear tooth action (Buckingham[18]):. "To transmit uniform rotary motion from one shaft to another by means of gear teeth, the normals to the profiles of these teeth at all points of contact must pass through a fixed point in the common center line of the two shafts."

This fixed point is called the *pitch* point; in Fig. 7-48 the pitch point is indicated as P. In this common configuration the word *gear* serves as both a generic term for all types of gears, as well as the specific designation of the larger of the two gears. The smaller gear is termed the *pinion*. Furthermore, in all of the following, we shall take the pinion to be the driving gear (with all terms related thereto give a subscript 1), and the gear to be driven (with all related terms given a subscript 2).

The introduction of the pitch point P gives rise to two *pitch circles* with radii (diameters) $R_1(D_1)$ and $R_2(D_2)$, as shown. Kinematically, the interaction of the two gears then is the same as that which would occur if the two circles were simply rolling upon each other without slipping; that is, with angular velocities ω_1 and ω_2, we have the relationship

$$R_1\omega_1 = -R_2\omega_2 \qquad \text{or} \qquad \omega_2 = -\frac{R_1}{R_2}\omega_1 \tag{7-83}$$

the minus sign indicating that the senses of rotation of the two gears are opposite to one another.

At a point of contact of two gear profiles, we have a common tangent plane. For conjugate gear profiles the line normal to this plane and passing through the point of contact (as well as through the pitch point) is termed the *line of action*. The angle ϕ between the line of action and the common tangent nn to the pitch circles is called the *pressure angle*. The locus of the points of contact is called the *path of contact*. In general, the orientation of the line of action and hence the pressure angle are different for each point of contact.

For a given conjugate gear profile, it is, of course, desirable that gears of different sizes and thus with different numbers of teeth mesh properly. This desideratum is met only if the path of contact of the two gears is symmetric with respect to the pitch point.

There are an infinite number of conjugate tooth profiles; for any chosen one, the conjugate profile for a mating gear may be developed. Among this infinite number of possibilities, one profile stands out clearly and has so many desirable properties that it is now used almost exclusively in gear design: the profile whose shape is the involute of a circle. We precede the detailed discussion of involute gears with a closer look at the curve itself.

THE INVOLUTE OF A CIRCLE. Boyer (in *A History of Mathematics*) indicates that an outline of evolutes was already provided by Appolonius (262–200 B.C.) in a purely theoretical work on conics. Perhaps the most celebrated use of involutes and evolutes occurred with Christiaan Huygens, who discovered that the involute of a cycloid was another cycloid congruent to the original one. This, together with his discovery that the cycloid was the tautochrone,† allowed him, the inventor of the pendulum clock, to construct one for which the period of the pendulum swing was independent of the height from which it was released (see Fig. 7-49). As subsequently discovered by Jakob Bernoulli and others, this curve was also the brachistochrone. Thus the cycloid was an extremely fascinating curve to 17th-century geometers, and it is therefore not surprising that early gear profiles were cycloidal. However, virtually all gear profiles today are involutes of a circle. We briefly present some of the attending mathematical description.

Involutes are generated from a given curve C by an imaginary string which is wound on the curve and then unwound while holding it taut. The taut end of

---

†A curve such that no matter where on the curve a particle, subject to the action of gravity, was released, it would require the same time to reach the bottom. Hence *tauto* ~ "same" and *chronos* ~ "time."

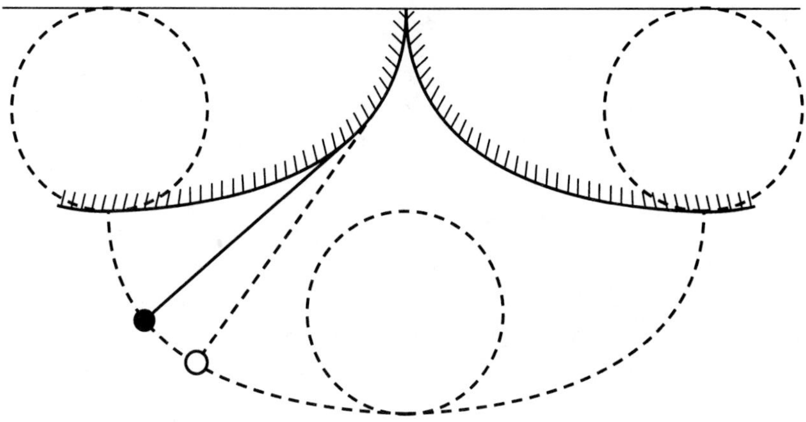

FIGURE 7-49
Christiaan Huygens' pendulum.

the string then generates a curve, as shown in Fig. 7-50a. More formally, we have the following definition.

Definition 7-4 Involute. Consider a given plane curve C. Then the involute C_1 of C is traced out by the end P of a taut string P_1P unwound from C.

We now restrict ourselves to the involute of a circle as shown in Fig. 7-50b. The circle C used to generate the involute is termed the *base circle* with radius r_1. In polar coordinates some fundamental relationships are immediately evident.

We have

$$r = \frac{r_1}{\cos(\beta - \theta)} \tag{7-84}$$

where β and θ are related by

$$\tan(\beta - \theta) = \beta \tag{7-85}$$

An additional relationship is obtained from the Pythagorean theorem as

$$\beta = \sqrt{\left(\frac{r}{r_1}\right)^2 - 1} \tag{7-86}$$

To illustrate their use, we note that the tangent to the involute at P is given by

$$\tan\psi = \frac{1}{r}\frac{dr}{d\theta} = \frac{r_1}{r}\sec(\beta - \theta)\tan(\beta - \theta)\left(\frac{d\beta}{d\theta} - 1\right)$$
$$= \frac{1}{\beta} = \frac{1}{\sqrt{\left(\frac{r}{r_1}\right)^2 - 1}}$$

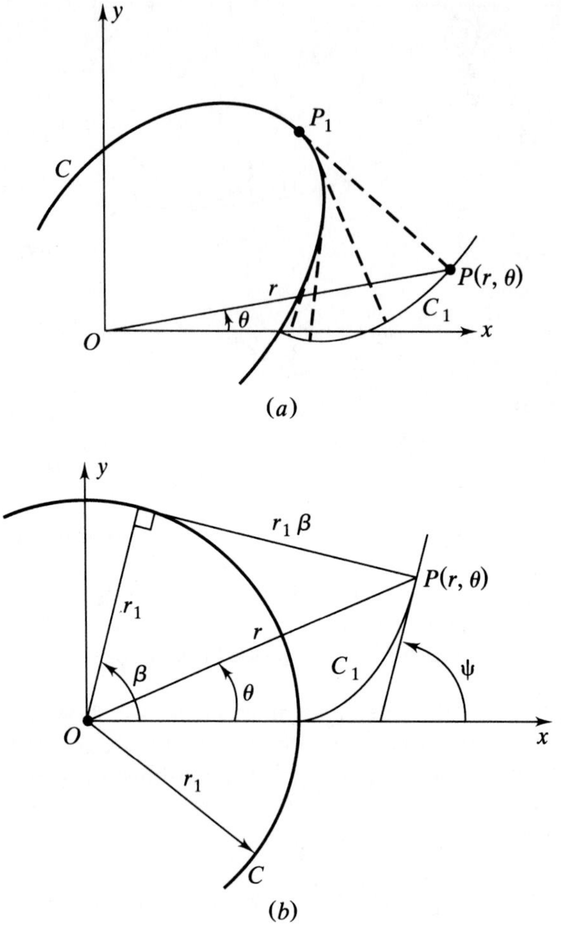

FIGURE 7-50
(*a*) Involute of a curve *C*; (*b*) involute of a circle.

Some of the mathematical properties of the involute are summarized in the following theorem.

Theorem 7-1. Let C_1 be the involute of the base circle with radius r_1.

(*a*) All lines normal to C_1 are tangent to the base circle.
(*b*) The radius of curvature of the involute at a point $P(r, \theta)$ is given by $\rho = r_1\beta$. Thus the base circle is the locus of the centers of curvature of the involute.

With this short mathematical review we now return to the discussion of gears.

KINEMATICS OF CONJUGATE INVOLUTE GEARS. We first illustrate the manner in which the involute gear profile is generated. We simply subdivide the

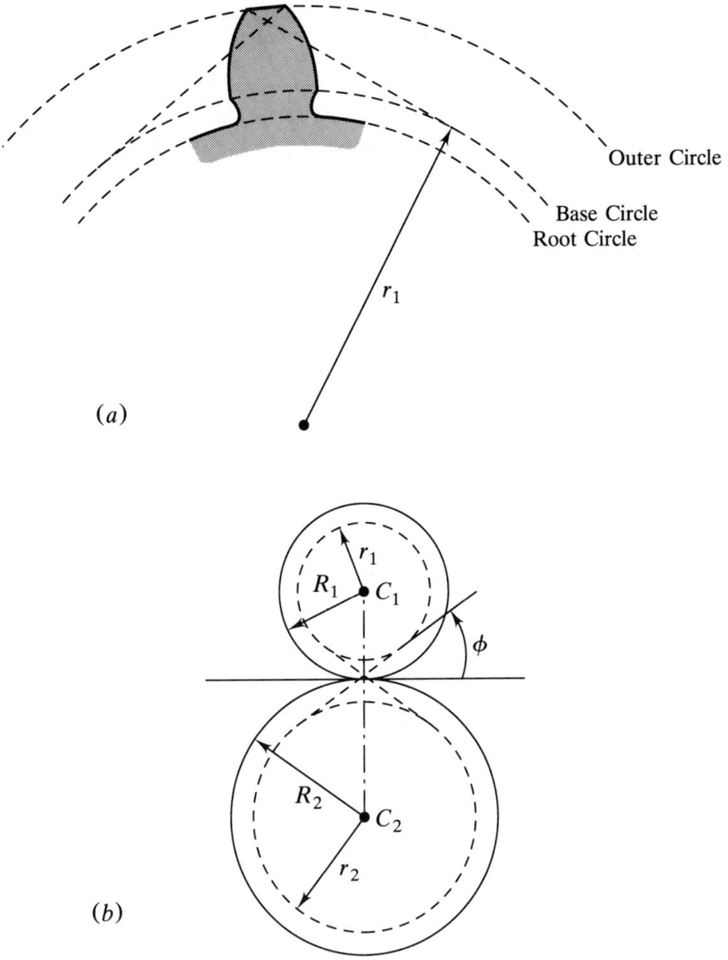

FIGURE 7-51
Generation of the involute tooth profile.

circumference of a suitable base circle into equal intervals corresponding to the desired number of teeth. Figure 7-51*a* shows the construction of a tooth.

The previously stated mathematical properties translate into a number of highly desirable practical attributes for gears. We emphasize that most of these properties must be viewed in the context of two conjugate involute gears. For example, a single involute gear has no base circle, no pitch circle, no line of action, and so on, until it is brought into contact with another gear. Based on the mathematical analysis of the involute, we may now make the following statements concerning two conjugate meshing involute gears (see Fig. 7-51*b*):

1. Their path of contact is a straight line.
2. The common tangent between the two base circles is the line of action as well as the path of contact.
3. The pressure angle ϕ is the same for all points of contact. It is the angle between the common tangent to the two base circles and the normal to the center line.

Until now, we have slowly introduced the student to some of the extensive terminology that has evolved in connection with gears. Since it is standard and is used in connection with the analysis, we provide a collection of these terms in Fig. 7-52. We emphasize once more that most of the illustrated terms make sense only within the context of a matching gear and they are duplicated on that gear. (This gear mate has been omitted here.)

We have already made extensive use of base circle and pitch circle. The *addendum* is the distance from the pitch circle to the outside edge of the tooth, and the *dedendum* is the distance from the pitch circle to the root of the tooth. The teeth thus lie between addendum and dedendum circles. For standard pressure angles of 20° and 25°, the dedendum equals 1.25 × addendum. There are three types of pitch in use, all defined with reference to the pitch circle:

1. The *circular pitch* is the sum of the tooth space and the tooth thickness. It is given by

$$p = \frac{\pi D}{N}$$

where D (in inches or millimeters) is the *pitch diameter* and N is the number of gear teeth.

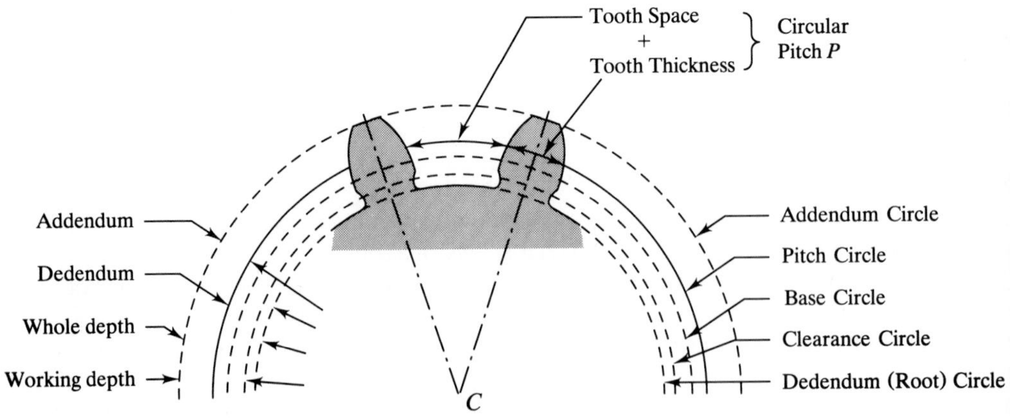

FIGURE 7-52
Gear terminology.

2. The *diametral pitch*, in most common use in the U.S. system, is given by

$$P = \frac{N}{D}$$

where D is measured in inches only. We define $P < 20$ as *coarse pitch* and $P \geq 20$ as *fine pitch*.

3. The *module* is given by

$$m = \frac{D}{N}$$

used in the SI system only, with both m and D in millimeters.

Based on this terminology, there are some frequently used kinematic relationships. For the velocity ratio we have

$$\frac{\omega_2}{\omega_1} = -\frac{R_1}{R_2} = -\frac{D_1}{D_2} = -\frac{r_1}{r_2} = -\frac{N_1}{N_2} \tag{7-87}$$

For two matched gears, the pitch is, of course, the same. The equality of the ratio of base radii and pitch radii follows easily from similar triangles.

The distance between gear centers is given by

$$c = R_1 + R_2 = \frac{1}{2P}(N_1 + N_2) \tag{7-88}$$

As our final kinematic comment, we mention that the clearance for, say, the pinion, is simply the difference between the dedendum of the pinion and the addendum of the matching gear. We illustrate the use of all of the terms with a simple example from gear design.

Example 7-14. Suppose a spur gear has 30 teeth and a diametral pitch of 5 teeth per inch. The gear is rotating at 500 rpm. Determine:

(*a*) The circular pitch.

(*b*) The pitch line velocity—that is, the velocity of a point on the pitch circle.

Solution

(*a*) The circular pitch is related to the diametral pitch by

$$p = \pi\frac{D}{N} = \frac{\pi}{P} = \frac{\pi}{5} = 0.6283 \text{ in}$$

(*b*) The radius of the pitch circle is given by

$$R = \frac{D}{2} = \frac{Np}{2\pi} = \frac{30 \cdot \dfrac{\pi}{5}}{2\pi} = 3 \text{ in}$$

The velocity of a point on the pitch circle is thus given by

$$v = R\omega = 3 \cdot 500 \cdot \frac{2\pi}{60} = 50\pi = 157.08 \text{ in/sec}$$

There are a number of important kinematic concepts we have not touched upon, such as interference, contact length, contact ratio, and the like. For these refinements, the reader is again referred to Juvinall,[15] Burr,[16] Wilson, Sadler, and Michels,[17] and Buckingham.[18]

FORCE ANALYSIS FOR GEARS. We shall continue our discussion of spur gears with some comments about gear design based on the expected or required load carrying capacity of the individual gear tooth. A basic static analysis is straightforward, in that the tooth is simply viewed as a cantilevered beam with a load at the free end. This type of analysis is thus also referred to as the beam strength of gear teeth.

At a point of contact of the two gears, the contact force acts along the normal to the common tangent plane, that is, along the line of action. The situation is depicted in Fig. 7-53. Note immediately that the line of action always passes through the pitch point P. For the overall analysis, it is common to resolve the force F into a component F_t which does work and a component F_n which tends to push the gears apart. For the strength analysis of the gear tooth itself, a conservative approach is used by assuming that the total load between the gears is applied at the tip of a single tooth. Realistically, the load is distributed over more than one tooth, with the major portion of the load acting at some intermediate point on the tooth.

For the details we take t to be the tooth width at the root circle and h to be the whole depth of the tooth. We take the gear *face width* to be b. The maximum bending stress at the root is given by

$$\sigma = \frac{Mc}{I} = \frac{6F_t h}{bt^2}$$

for the rectangular cross section. This formula is accurate for the pure bending of a uniform beam. It does not account for nonuniformity. To account for the differences in geometry of a tooth, one introduces the *Lewis form factor*, which allows the comparison of different tooth profiles and pitches. The shape factor introduced by Lewis is based on the similar triangles in Fig. 7-53. We have

$$\frac{x}{t/2} = \frac{t/2}{h} \quad \Rightarrow \quad \frac{t^2}{h} = 4x$$

so that the stress may now be written in the form

$$\sigma = \frac{3}{2}\frac{F_t}{bx}$$

At this point we introduce the form factor

$$y = \frac{2x}{3p} \quad \Rightarrow \quad \sigma = \frac{F_t}{bpy}$$

where p is the circular pitch. By defining $Y = \pi y$ the stress may be written in

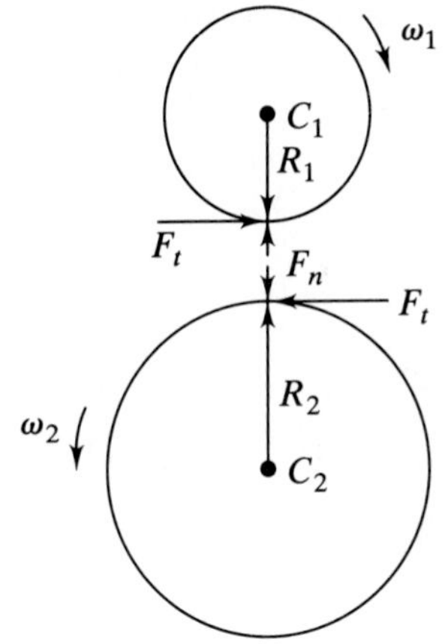

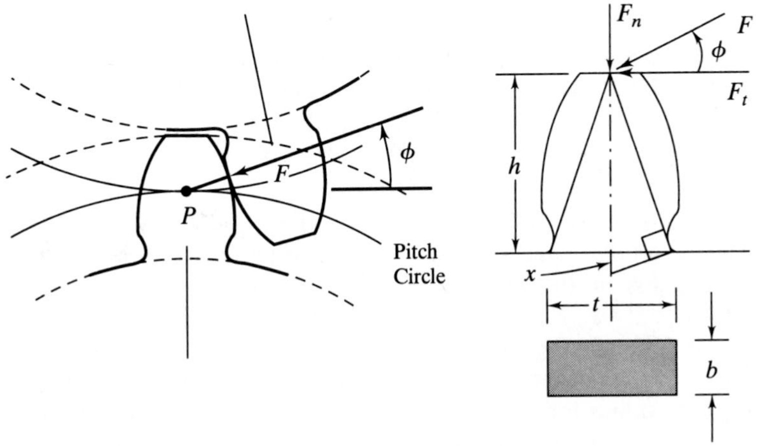

FIGURE 7-53
Gear interaction forces.

terms of the diametral pitch as

$$\sigma = \frac{F_t P}{bY} \tag{7-89}$$

(This was the first stress analysis of a gear tooth as presented to the Philadelphia Engineers Club in 1892. All in all, this seems a somewhat belated stress analysis, since the formula for the maximum stress had already been accurately stated by Coulomb in 1776.)

The AGMA has subsequently introduced a combined shape and stress concentration factor J in terms of which the maximum stress is given by

$$\sigma = \frac{F_t P}{bJ} \tag{7-90}$$

where J is termed the *spur gear geometry factor*. It is common to further embellish this stress expression with additional multipliers to account for the omitted dynamic effects, for possible overloads, and for different mounting conditions. Here, we shall add only the dynamic correction factor to write

$$\sigma = K_v \frac{F_t P}{bJ} \tag{7-91}$$

where

$$K_v = \frac{50 + \sqrt{v}}{50} \qquad \text{for} \quad v < 4000 \text{ ft/min}$$

for gears produced by shaping and hobbing, and

$$K_v = \sqrt{\frac{78 + \sqrt{v}}{78}} \qquad \text{for} \quad v < 7500 \text{ ft/min}$$

for high precision gears; v is the pitch line velocity in feet per minute.

In actual gear design it is usual to write (7-91) in the form

$$P = \frac{\sigma_a J b}{F_t K_v} \tag{7-92}$$

where σ_a is the allowable stress for the gear. In this expression only the allowable stress is generally given a priori. One obtains an accurate combination by iteration. We guess at the number of teeth and the pitch diameters to determine the values for J, F_t, and K_v. Usually, the Brinell hardness number (BHN) is given for the desired gear, and σ_a is then determined from Fig. 7-54*a*. The guess for the number of teeth is used to determine J from Fig. 7-54*b*, and we finally determine values for F_t and K_v from our guess at the pitch diameter D. The end result is a guess for the diametral pitch P. If our guess was a good one, then $N = PD$; if not, we need to repeat the process. All of this is illustrated with the following gear design problem.

Example 7-15. The simple manipulator in Fig. 7-55 is to be able to move a weight of 200 lb in the vertical plane at a speed of 80 ft/sec. The task is to be accomplished by a gear-and-pinion combination with a velocity ratio of 1:4. With respect to the gears, it is assumed that the whole dynamic load is applied at the tip of the gear tooth and that the whole width of the tooth is engaged. The gear is to be hardened to 250 BHN, while the pinion is to be treated to a hardness of 350 BHN, both conforming to Grade 1 manufacturing requirements. The remaining treatment of the gears is to be such that the previously stated expressions for K_v are applicable. Use a 20° gear system with a $\frac{3}{4}$-in face width b.

(*a*) Determine the horsepower required to achieve this task if the motor is directly connected to the pinion.

(*b*) Choose the appropriate gear pitch, number of teeth, and tooth size capable of carrying the applied load.

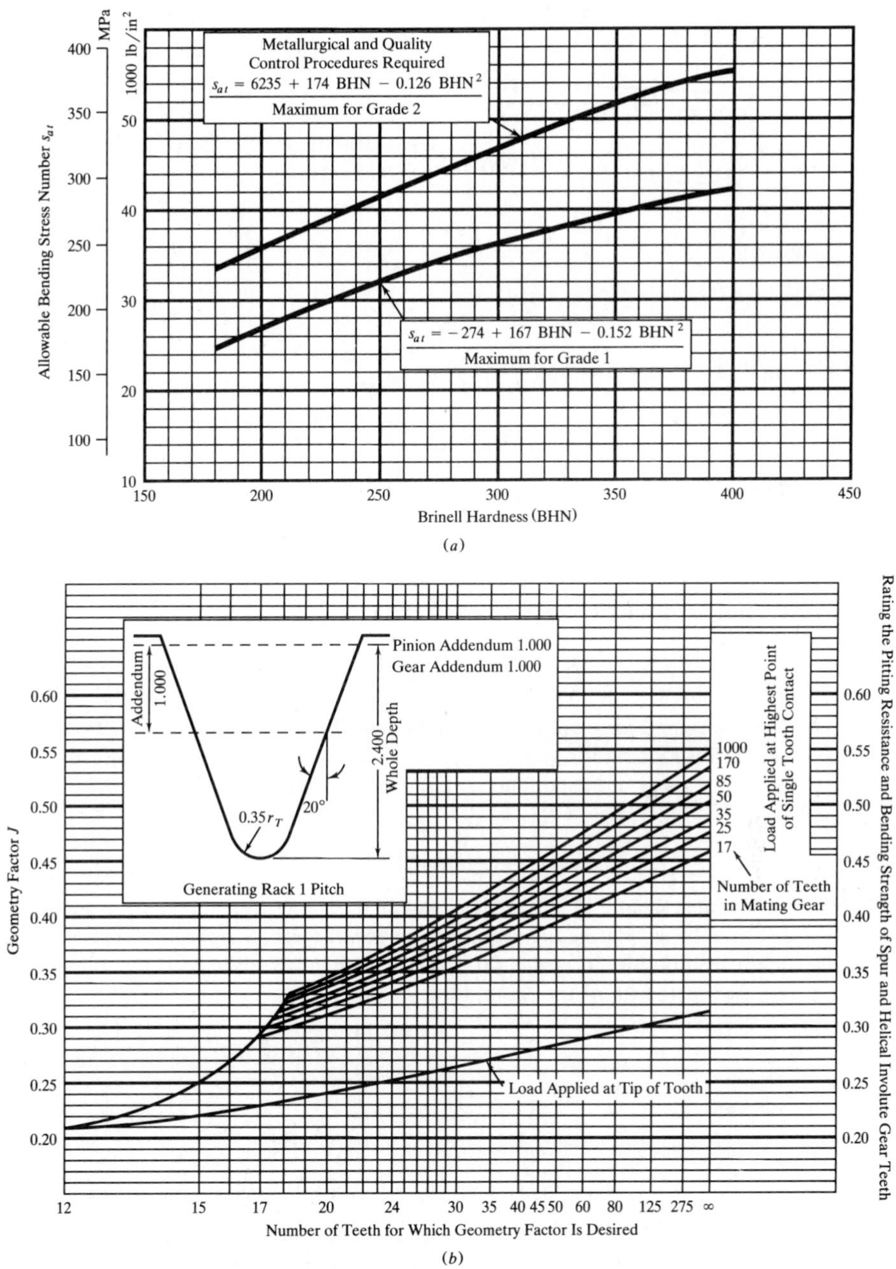

FIGURE 7-54
Empirical data in gear design. (*a*) Allowable bending stress number for steel gears, s_{at}; (*b*) geometry factor *J* for 20° spur gears (standard addendum). [*Source:* American Gear Manufacturers Association, Standard 218.01 (December 1982) for Rating the Pithing Resistance and Bending Strength of Spur and Helical Involute Gear Teeth (extraction from Fig. B1) and Standard 2001-B88 (May 1988) for Fundamental Rating Factors and Calculation Methods for Involute Spur and Helical Gear Teeth (extraction from Fig. 14.2). Used with permission of AGMA, 1500 King Street, Suite 201, Alexandria, Virginia 22314.]

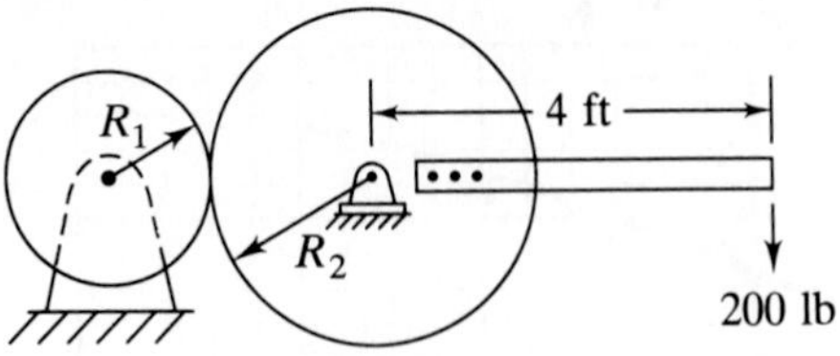

FIGURE 7-55
A simple gear train.

Solution

(a) The torque on the gear is

$$T_2 = 4 \times 200 = 800 \text{ ft} \cdot \text{lb}$$

The speed of the extreme point is to be 80 ft/sec or

$$\omega_2 = \frac{80}{4} = 20 \text{ rad/sec}$$

The corresponding power requirement (assuming no power loss) thus is

$$\begin{aligned}\mathscr{P} &= T_2\omega_2 \\ &= 800 \times 20 = 16{,}000 \text{ ft} \cdot \text{lb} = 29.09 \text{ hp} \approx 30 \text{ hp}\end{aligned}$$

or, since the velocity ratio is 1 : 4, implying

$$\omega_1 = 4\omega_2 = 80 \text{ rad/sec} \approx 764 \text{ rpm}$$

The motor must supply 30 hp at 764 rpm.

(b) Next, we need to select a gear system capable of transmitting this power with the corresponding torques and speeds. Toward this end we first note that the critical stresses corresponding to the given Brinell numbers are

$$\sigma_1 = 39{,}556 \text{ psi}$$
$$\sigma_2 = 31{,}976 \text{ psi}$$

as obtained from Fig. 7-54a. Next, we obtain a tentative value for the geometry factor J by estimating the required number of teeth. Suppose we take $N_1 = 20$ teeth resulting in $N_2 = 4 \times 20 = 80$ teeth. Figure 7-54b, read for the load as applied to the tip of the tooth, then yields

$$J_1 = 0.24$$
$$J_2 = 0.293$$

We thus have

$$\sigma_1 J_1 = (0.24)(39{,}556) = 9493$$
$$\sigma_2 J_2 = (0.293)(31{,}976) = 9369$$

From (7-92) it follows that choosing a smaller pitch is a conservative choice. Since F_t and K_v are the same for both gears, we shall complete the computation of our first guess with $\sigma_2 J_2 = 9369$.

Suppose we now assume $D_2 = 20$ in (implying $D_1 = 5$ in). Then

$$\begin{aligned}v_2 &= \omega_2 R_2 = 20 \cdot 10 = 200 \text{ in/sec} \\ &= 1000 \text{ ft/min}\end{aligned}$$

For this speed the first of the two expressions for K_v applies. Thus

$$K_v = \frac{50 + \sqrt{v_2}}{50} = 1.63$$

For a total torque $T_2 = 800$ ft · lb, we then have

$$F_t = \frac{800}{10/12} = 960 \text{ lb}$$

Our first estimate for the diametral pitch with $b = \frac{3}{4}$ in follows as

$$P = \frac{9369 \times 3}{4 \times 960 \times 1.63} = 4.49$$

Again, a conservative choice is $P = 4$ and

$$N_1 = 4 \cdot D_1 = 4 \cdot 5 = 20$$

$$N_2 = 4 \cdot D_2 = 4 \cdot 20 = 80$$

so that we have a consistent pitch. Our first guesses were lucky indeed (really!). If this computation for the gear teeth had not checked out, we would have had to repeat the process with new guesses. With this choice the actual maximum stress at the tooth root will be

$$\sigma_{\text{max}} = K_v \frac{F_t P}{b J_2} = 1.63 \frac{960 \cdot 4}{0.75 \cdot 0.293}$$

$$= 28{,}483 < \sigma_a = 31{,}976 \text{ psi}$$

Clearly, much of the realistic gear design is empirical, and we have touched on only a few of these pragmatic corrective factors to the fundamental theory. What we have provided is an outline of the standard approach to spur gear design. For the interested student the references cited previously will provide the added depth needed.

With respect to our trend to linear systems analysis, we note that all of the relevant gear system functions are linear and thus lend themselves nicely to incorporation into linear systems models. For example, if we view the gear train as an ideal mechanical transformer (no power loss), then we may write

$$T_2\omega_2 = T_1\omega_1 \quad \Rightarrow \quad T_2 = T_1\frac{\omega_1}{\omega_2} = T_1\frac{R_2}{R_1} = kT_1$$

for the relationship between the torque magnitudes.

7-3-3 Power Screws

In machine design power screws are sometimes referred to as linear actuators. In a robotics context we always take actuators to be machines that provide power to power-transmission devices. Power screws belong to this category. Their main use is as linear-to-rotary-motion transducers. A special type of power screw, the ball screw, is frequently used because of its virtually frictionless linear movement.

Once the thread terminology has been established, the kinematics of power screws are straightforward. The subsequent kinetic analysis deals with the transformation of torque to axial load, mainly when thread friction is taken into account. Our final discussion deals with length and speed limitations based on the analysis of the screws as columns and rotating shafts.

TERMINOLOGY. There is some similarity to gear terminology, and, as before, there are national and international agencies to maintain and revise established standards. (Two such agencies are the International Standards Organization (ISO), for the metric versions, and the American National Standards Institute (ANSI).) Juvinall[15] is a sufficient desk reference in this context.

We begin with a short list and some comments on the standard thread forms in use:

Acme screw threads—earliest standardized screw threads developed for use in machine tools.

Stub Acme screw threads—used in applications where coarse pitch and shallow depth are needed.

Modified square screw threads—most efficient type of sliding friction screw.

Buttress screw threads—designed to resist loads in only one direction.

As with gears different amounts of precision are required, depending on the intended use. The screws are then classified in terms of their fits and tolerances, which are determined by the amount of clearance provided between internal and external threads, for example.

The following characteristic terms and measurements are used in the thread classifications:

1. The pitch p. Its units are length. It is the axial distance along the pitch cylinder measured between adjacent edges of the thread.
2. The lead ℓ. Its units are inches per revolution. It is the axial displacement of a nut along the pitch cylinder per revolution of the screw.
3. The lead angle α. It is the angle of a thread formed by the intersection of a plane tangent to the pitch helix and one which is normal to the axis of the screw. The helix angle ψ is given by $\psi = 90° - \alpha$.
4. The thread angle λ. It is measured from a line normal to the axis of the screw to the thread slant.
5. The thread height h. It is measured from the minor radius and some tolerance to the outer radius of the screw.
6. The thread thickness t. It is the width of the internal thread. Generally, t is given as a fraction of the pitch; the location of this width on the thread serves to locate the basic pitch line.

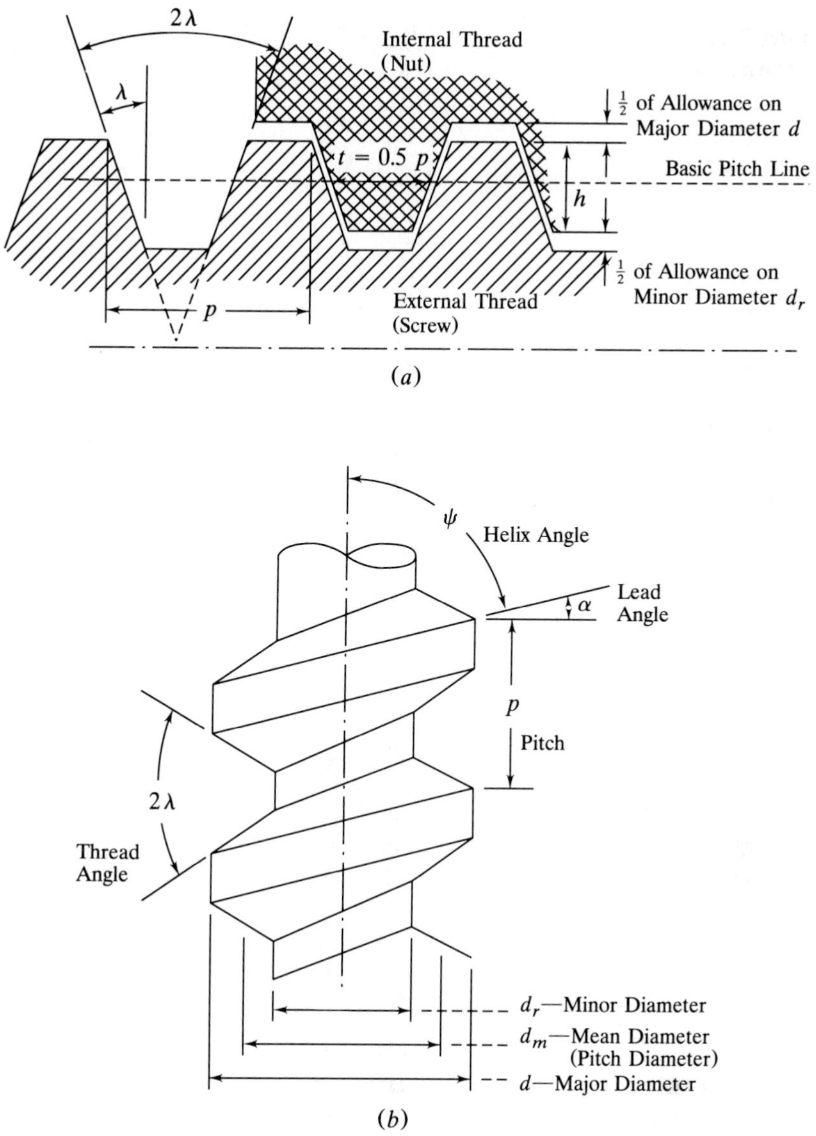

FIGURE 7-56
Standard thread terminology.

Figures 7-56*a* and *b* depict the standard thread terminology. Figure 7-57 shows the specific dimensions of one Acme power screw thread. The difference between the lead and the pitch is apparent from Fig. 7-58. Power screw threads are wrapped around a circular cylinder as opposed to cones for fasteners, for example.

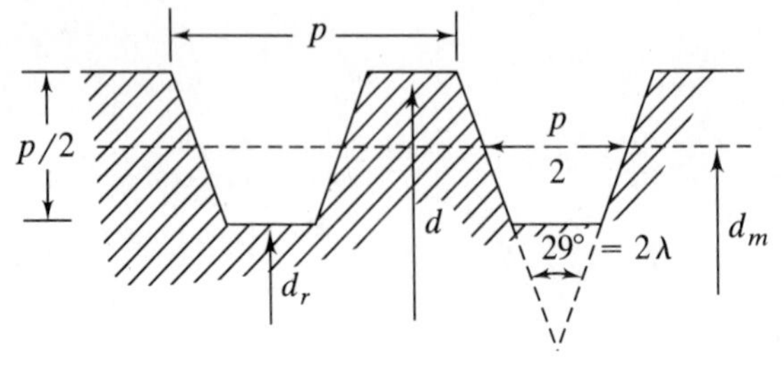

FIGURE 7-57
Standard Acme screw thread.

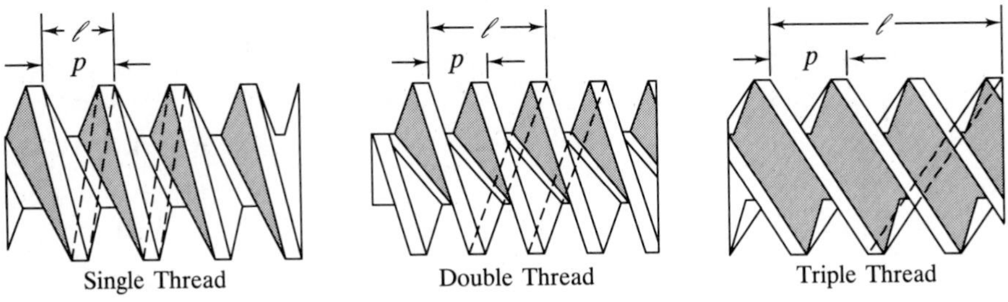

FIGURE 7-58
Pitch and lead.

KINEMATICS OF THE POWER SCREW. Fortified with this terminology, we shall now take a look at the kinematics of the screw. Based on Fig. 7-58, it is clear that the lead of the screw may be written in the form

$$\ell = np \text{ (in/rev)} \tag{7-93}$$

where ℓ is the lead of the screw in inches per revolution, n denotes the number of threads per revolution, and the pitch p is the number of inches per thread. We emphasize that "threads" and "revolutions" are nonunits, like radians; we have included them here for clarity of the combination. In this context we also define $N = 1/p$, the number of threads per inch. In addition, we have used inches simply because they are in common use in this context. With inches as our dimension of definition, it then follows that

$$\ell = \frac{1}{24\pi} np \left(\frac{\text{ft}}{\text{rad}} \right)$$

The total screw advance corresponding to a rotation by an amount θ in radians (Fig. 7-59) is given by

$$z(t) = \ell\theta(t) = k_1\theta(t)$$

when the usual time dependence is also taken into account. The corresponding system function for the advancing unit on a power screw is then given by

$$G(s) = \frac{Z(s)}{\Theta(s)} = k_1$$

if we take the linear displacement as the output.

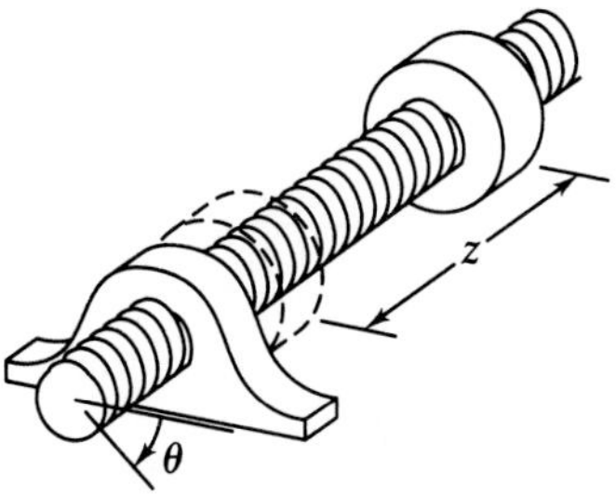

FIGURE 7-59
Nut advance.

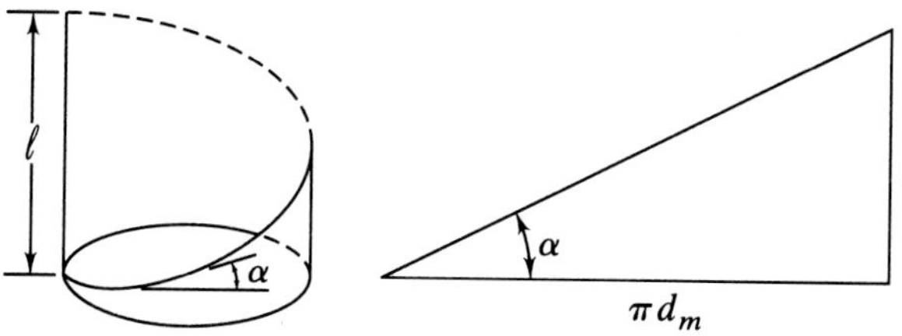

FIGURE 7-60
The lead angle.

Remark 7-12. Note specifically that the nut speed for a given angular speed increases with pitch and thread multiplicity.

There is an additional useful geometric relationship between lead angle and lead. Suppose we consider a triangular segment of a plane wrapped around the screw in such a way that the slanted edge lies along the helix and follows it for one revolution, as illustrated in Fig. 7-60. We obviously have

$$\tan \alpha = \frac{\ell}{\pi d_m} = \frac{np}{\pi d_m} \tag{7-94}$$

or

$$\alpha = \operatorname{Arctan}\left(\frac{\ell}{\pi d_m}\right)$$

KINETICS OF THE POWER SCREW. In order to raise a weight or to move a load horizontally, a certain amount of torque must be applied to the screw. The required torque depends on the amount of thread friction present in the system, the lead angle, and the thread angle.

Suppose we consider the situation depicted in Fig. 7-61, where a torque T is applied to a right-handed screw which, in turn, is to move a load to the right.

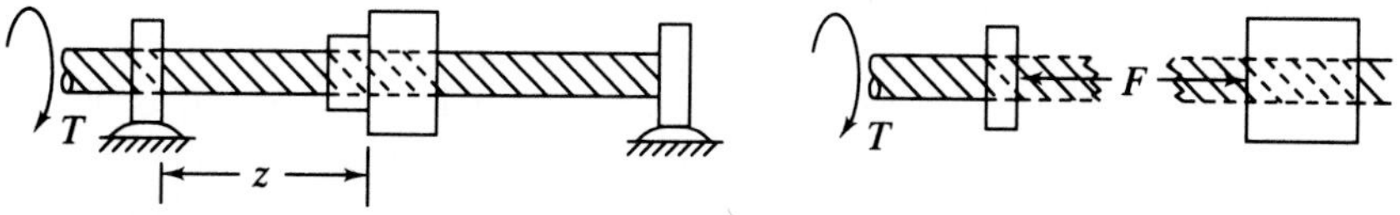

FIGURE 7-61
The loaded screw.

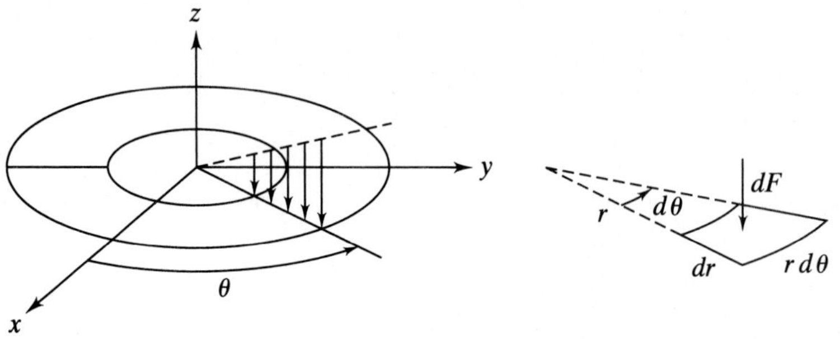

FIGURE 7-62
Resultant of a stress distribution.

Strictly speaking, the force F acting on the nut is distributed over the screw thread in contact with the nut, and we have to integrate over the thread surface to obtain the stress resultants. The following example provides a simplified review of this integration process.

Example 7-16. The thread surface to be idealized by a ring of minor diameter d_r and major diameter d is shown in Fig. 7-62. Let the normal stress distribution be given by

$$\tau_{zz}(r, \theta) = kr$$

as a function of the polar coordinates (r, θ). Calculate the stress resultant in the z-direction.

Solution. The resultant on an elemental area dA is given by

$$dF = -\tau_{zz} r \, dr \, d\theta$$

The total force is thus given by

$$F = \int_0^{2\pi} \int_{d_r/2}^{d/2} -\tau_{zz} r \, dr \, d\theta = -k \int_0^{2\pi} \int_{d_r/2}^{d/2} r^2 \, dr \, d\theta$$

$$= \frac{\pi k}{12} (d_r^3 - d^3)$$

With some symmetry assumptions, we may use a similarly simplified analysis to obtain an expression relating the applied torque T to the load F for impending motion (of screw advance against the load F). Our approach will consist of equilibrating the stress vectors at a point of the contact surface between the nut and the screw. Toward this purpose we first introduce a reference frame whose triad is tangent to the helix, normal to the thread surface, and aligned with the thread angle as viewed in a cross section normal to the helix.

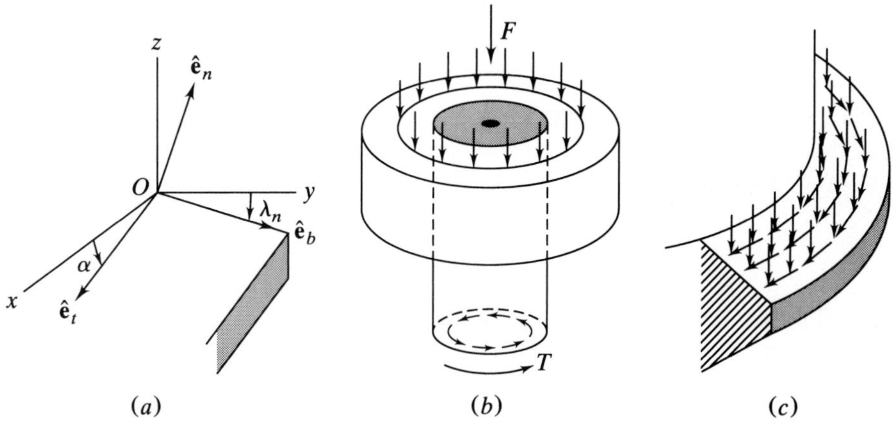

FIGURE 7-63
The loading of the screw.

To obtain this triad of unit vectors as a rotation from a standard $(0xyz)$ frame whose z-axis is parallel to the screw axis, we shall simply do two successive rotations: a rotation about the y-axis by the helix angle α, followed by a rotation around the x'-axis by an angle λ_n, as illustrated in Fig. 7-63. The resultant rotation matrix is

$$\mathbf{A} = \mathbf{A}(y, \alpha)\mathbf{A}(x', -\lambda_n)$$

$$= \begin{bmatrix} C\alpha & 0 & S\alpha \\ 0 & 1 & 0 \\ -S\alpha & 0 & C\alpha \end{bmatrix} \begin{bmatrix} 1 & 0 & 0 \\ 0 & C\lambda_n & S\lambda_n \\ 0 & -S\lambda_n & C\lambda_n \end{bmatrix}$$

$$= \begin{bmatrix} C\alpha & -S\alpha S\lambda_n & S\alpha C\lambda_n \\ 0 & C\lambda_n & S\lambda_n \\ -S\alpha & -C\alpha S\lambda_n & C\alpha C\lambda_n \end{bmatrix}$$

The desired unit vectors in the rotated frame described in terms of $\hat{\imath}$, $\hat{\jmath}$, and $\hat{k}$ are then given by

$$\hat{\mathbf{e}}_t = \mathbf{A}\begin{pmatrix} 1 \\ 0 \\ 0 \end{pmatrix} = \begin{pmatrix} C\alpha \\ 0 \\ -S\alpha \end{pmatrix} \quad \Rightarrow \quad \hat{\mathbf{e}}_t = \cos\alpha\hat{\imath} - \sin\alpha\hat{k}$$

and, similarly,

$$\hat{e}_n = \sin\alpha\cos\lambda_n\,\hat{\imath} + \sin\lambda_n\hat{\jmath} + \cos\alpha\cos\lambda_n\,\hat{k}$$

We shall have no need for $\hat{e}_b$ since the stresses in the $\hat{e}_b$-direction are simply internal reaction stresses.

The nut has on it a distributed load equivalent to

$$\boldsymbol{F} = -F\hat{\boldsymbol{k}}$$

as shown in Fig. 7-63*b*. We assume that the load is borne by a single thread and that this stress, as well as the remaining stresses, is uniformly distributed over the thread area. The result is a stress vector

$$\boldsymbol{f} = -\frac{F}{A}\hat{\boldsymbol{k}}$$

parallel to the screw axis, as shown in Fig. 7-63*c*.

The resistance to the load is represented by the torque applied to the screw. This torque ultimately is taken to result in a Coulomb friction stress at a point P given by the stress vector

$$\boldsymbol{f}_t = \mu f_n(\cos\alpha\,\hat{\boldsymbol{\imath}} - \sin\alpha\,\hat{\boldsymbol{k}})$$

Finally, there is a reactive stress vector normal to the thread surface,

$$\boldsymbol{f}_n = f_n\left(\sin\alpha\cos\lambda_n\,\hat{\boldsymbol{\imath}} + \sin\lambda_n\,\hat{\boldsymbol{\jmath}} + \cos\alpha\cos\lambda_n\,\hat{\boldsymbol{k}}\right)$$

The action of these stresses on elements of the nut and thread is shown in Fig. 7-64*a*. The external torque provides the friction necessary to maintain the

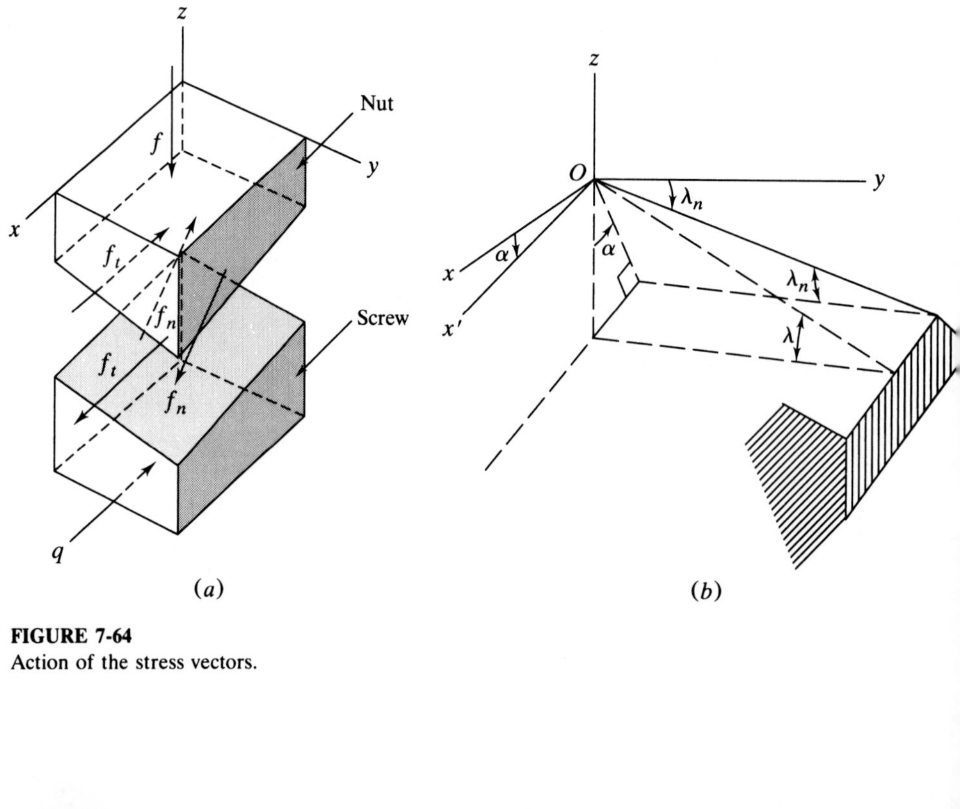

FIGURE 7-64
Action of the stress vectors.

equilibrium

$$T = \int\int_A rq\, dA$$

The stress vector f_t is obtained from the enforcement of static equilibrium in the $\hat{k}$-direction (with impending advance) on the nut element

$$f_n \cos\alpha \cos\lambda_n - f + \mu f_n \sin\alpha = 0$$

$$\Rightarrow \quad f_n = \frac{f}{\cos\alpha \cos\lambda_n + \mu \sin\alpha}$$

and in the $\hat{\imath}$-direction on the screw element, resulting in

$$-q + \mu f_n \cos\alpha - f_n \sin\alpha \cos\lambda_n = 0$$

$$\Rightarrow \quad q = f\frac{\mu \cos\alpha - \sin\alpha \cos\lambda_n}{\cos\alpha \cos\lambda_n + \mu \sin\alpha}$$

The needed applied torque is thus given by

$$T = \int\int_A rq\, dA = q\int\int_A r\, dA = qr_m A$$

$$= \frac{d_m}{2}F\frac{\mu \pm \tan\alpha \cos\lambda_n}{\cos\lambda_n \mp \mu \tan\alpha} \tag{7-95}$$

where the elevated signs simply correspond to the case where the direction of impending motion has been reversed.

Recall that the thread angle λ_n used previously was based on a thread cross section with normal $\hat{e}_t$. This angle is related to λ, the usual thread angle based on a cross section passing through the screw axis, by the formula (see Fig. 7-64*b*)

$$\tan\lambda_n = \cos\alpha \tan\lambda \tag{7-96}$$

which may be taken to be

$$\tan\lambda_n \approx \tan\lambda$$

for small lead angles α.

Remark 7-13. Although our analysis is based on a static approach, the result applies equally well for a moving nut, as long as inertial effects can be neglected.

We thus take

$$T(t) = k_2 F(t)$$

and, consequently,

$$T(s) = k_2 F(s)$$

where
$$k_2 = \frac{d_m}{2}\frac{\mu \pm \tan\alpha \cos\lambda_n}{\cos\lambda_n \mp \mu \tan\alpha}$$

OVERHAULING. Although not explicitly stated, one generally views the torque as the input and the force as the output. Suppose now that a load F is applied and that the applied torque $T = 0$. Then, due to friction, a certain limiting value of F must be reached before the screw will start rotating and allow the nut to move. If F is large enough to produce this motion, then the screw is said to be *overhauling*.

Example 7-17. Suppose the screw is loaded by a load F, as shown in Fig. 7-63*b*. Obtain a condition based on the geometric parameters and the coefficient of friction which will guarantee that the screw will be *self-locking*—that is, a condition sufficient to disallow overhauling. Take $T = 0$.

Solution. Suppose we first assume that the system remains at rest. In this case the friction "force" will simply be enough to maintain static equilibrium. The stress vectors on the nut element are

$$\mathbf{f}_n = f_n\left(\sin\alpha\cos\lambda_n\,\hat{\imath} + \cos\alpha\sin\lambda_n\,\hat{\jmath} + \cos\alpha\cos\lambda_n\,\hat{k}\right)$$

$$\mathbf{f}_t = f_t(-\cos\alpha\,\hat{\imath} + \sin\alpha\,\hat{k})$$

where we again ignore the $\mathbf{f}_b$ component, since it will not affect the computation. To maintain the system at rest, we must have

$$\hat{k}: \qquad f_n\cos\alpha\cos\lambda_n + f_t\sin\alpha = f$$

$$\hat{\imath}: \qquad f_n\sin\alpha\cos\lambda_n - f_t\cos\alpha = 0$$

with the result

$$f_t = f\sin\alpha$$

$$f_n = f\frac{\cos\alpha}{\cos\lambda_n}$$

The condition for no overhauling is that

$$|f_t| < f_{t,\max} = \mu f_n$$

This implies

$$\sin\alpha < \mu\frac{\cos\alpha}{\cos\lambda_n}$$

$$\tan\alpha < \frac{\mu}{\cos\lambda_n} \tag{7-97}$$

EFFICIENCY. The efficiency of a power screw is determined by comparing it with the ideal situation where no friction is present in the system. In this case the torque required to produce a force F is given by

$$T_0 = \frac{d_m}{2} F \tan \alpha = \frac{F\ell}{2\pi}$$

since $\mu = 0$. The efficiency then is the ratio of the torque required to produce a force F without friction to the torque required with friction—that is, the efficiency e is given by

$$e = \frac{T_0}{T} = \frac{\cos \lambda_n \mp \mu \tan \alpha}{\mu \cot \alpha \pm \cos \lambda_n} \tag{7-98}$$

Similarly, if the efficiency is provided, the torque required to produce a force F may be written in the form

$$T = \frac{1}{e} T_0 = \frac{\ell F}{2\pi e}$$

It is common to plot the efficiency versus the lead angle α. For a given μ the maximum efficiency is achieved for a lead angle of about 45°.

BALL SCREWS. Ball screws were first developed by the Saginaw Steering Division of General Motors Corporation, to be used in the steering mechanism of automobiles. Beaver Precision was the first company to design and manufacture ball screws for numerically controlled machines in the early 1950s. Today, there are a variety of manufacturers producing ball screws for use throughout the world in virtually all areas involving rotary-to-linear-motion transducers.

A ball screw is simply a screw that runs on bearing balls, as illustrated in Fig. 7-65. The screw thread is a hardened ball race. The nut consists of an array of bearing balls that circulate in a similar race. The inactive bearing balls are carried from one end of the nut to the other by return tubes. In this manner the sliding friction usually present is replaced by rolling friction. Because of this lowered friction, ball screws have efficiencies of 90% or higher.

Obviously, the kinematics remain unchanged. The torque-force relationship may be written in the form

$$T = \frac{\ell F}{2\pi e}$$

with an average efficiency of 92.5%.

At first glance the nirvana of power screws seems to have been attained. However, along with the advantages of ball screws, there are a number of disadvantages. We summarize:

ADVANTAGES

1. High efficiency.
2. Predictable life expectancy.

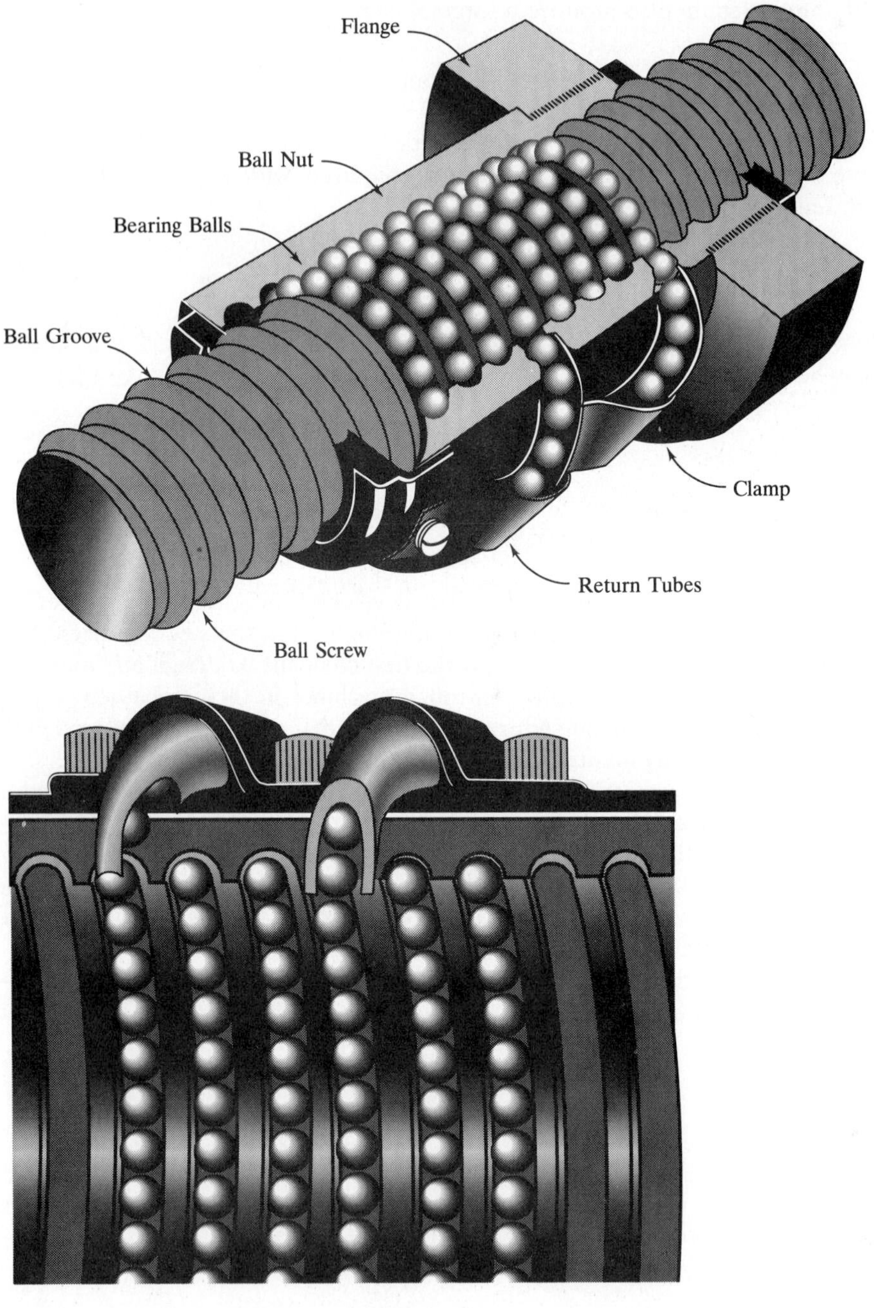

Ball Recirculation System

FIGURE 7-65
Ball screws. (*Source:* Warner Electric/Dana Catalog; used with permission.)

3. Precise positioning and positioning repeatability.
4. Low starting torque.
5. Easily preloaded to eliminate backlash.

DISADVANTAGES

1. Ball screws tend to overhaul.
2. Ball screws tend to require periodic overhauling to maintain their efficiency.
3. The intrusion of dirt or foreign matter can reduce their life or terminate it.
4. Ball screws are not as "stiff" as other power screws; thus deflection and critical speeds can cause difficulties.

STABILITY CONSTRAINTS. We shall briefly touch upon some stability constraints encountered when using power screws: the Euler buckling of the screw as a column and the whirling of the screw as a rotating shaft. The analysis is by no means exact or complete; its intent is to alert the designer to the consideration of these phenomena.

Virtually any book on the strength of materials (e.g., a standard text such as Popov, Nagarajan, and Lu[19]) includes a derivation of the Euler buckling load of a column which arises when a column is subject to compressive loads. The phenomenon may sometimes be avoided by redesigning the structural configuration to assure that the screw is always in tension. When such a redesign is not possible, this buckling load must be taken into consideration.

Suppose a column is axially loaded by a load P as shown in Fig. 7-66*a*. As long as $P < P_{\text{cr}}$, the Euler load for the column, internal elastic forces will return

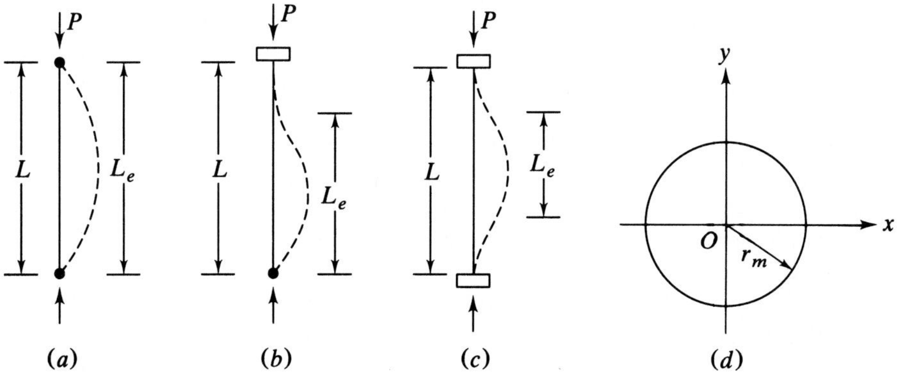

FIGURE 7-66
Euler buckling loads: (*a*) hinged-hinged $L_e = L$; (*b*) clamped-hinged $L_e = 0.707L$; (*c*) clamped-clamped $L_e = 0.5L$; (*d*) area moment of inertia.

the column to its vertical position when displaced from this position (indicated in the figure by dashed lines). However, for $P \geq P_{\text{cr}}$, the column will remain in the disturbed position or it will fail. The critical load depends on the support conditions for the column, on the cross-sectional shape, and on the elastic modulus of the material. In all cases the Euler critical load may be written in the standard form

$$P_{\text{cr}} = \frac{\pi^2 EI}{L_e^2} \tag{7-99}$$

where E is the elastic modulus, I is the minimum area moment of inertia of the column, and L_e is an equivalent column length depending on the support conditions; L is the actual length in all cases. Figure 7-66 includes some support conditions and equivalent lengths which are likely to be encountered in mounted power screws. The equivalent lengths generally connect hinge points and inflection points for the deflected column shape.

Within the present context the cross section will always be circular, and the area moment of inertia of the section is the same about any diameter (the column thus is equally likely to buckle in any direction). Based on the configuration in Fig. 7-66d, the area moment of inertia about the x-axis is given by

$$I_{xx} = \iint_A y^2\, dA = \int_0^{2\pi}\int_0^{r_m} r^2 \sin^2\theta \; r\, dr\, d\theta = \frac{\pi r_m^4}{4}$$

for example. The critical load then becomes

$$P_{\text{cr}} = \frac{\pi^3 E d_m^4}{64 L_e^2} \tag{7-100}$$

Realistically, the theoretical rigidity of the supports is rarely met in practice, and some fudging is required in the selection of the equivalent lengths; the arch-conservative would simply always design for the hinged-hinged case.

Most engineers are aware of the possibility of Euler buckling and will consider it in their design. There is a lesser awareness of the various critical running speeds of a screw. At certain rotational speeds a rotating shaft may bow out elastically, as illustrated in Fig. 7-67a, and continue to move in some orbit about its straight (aligned with the z-axis) equilibrium position (as shown by the dashed-line configuration). This behavior is called whirling of the shaft, and the critical rotational speed at which it happens is called the whirling speed of the shaft.

There are a variety of causes for this phenomenon: unbalance of an attached rotor, gyroscopic forces, oil friction in journal bearings, and so on. Problems associated with rotating shafts had already been noted by W. A. Rankine in 1869, and they were subsequently discussed by others. Numerous experiments on high-speed rotors were carried out by the Swedish engineer

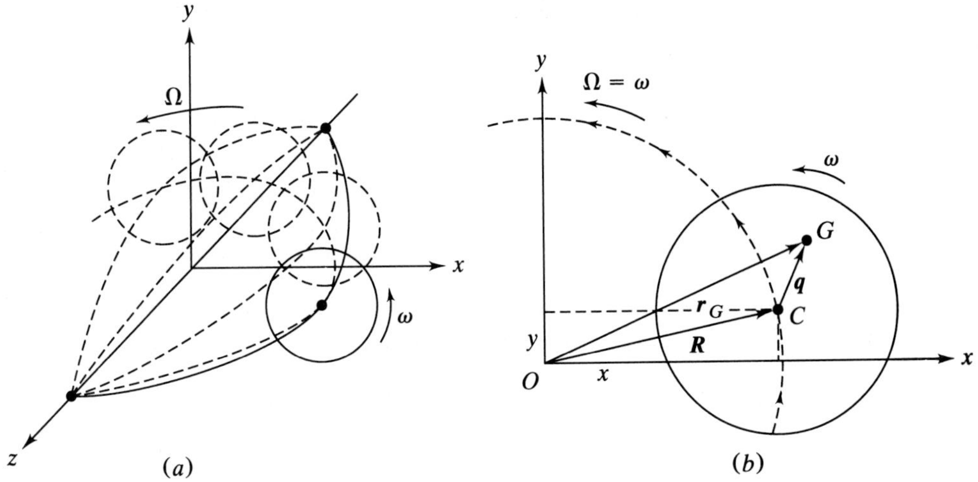

FIGURE 7-67
Whirling of a shaft.

C.-G. P. de Laval; the first to present a satisfactory theory and solve the problem was August Föppl, a professor of mechanics in Munich, who presented his solution in 1885 (Föppl[20]).

We shall focus on the case where an unbalanced rotor attached to the shaft gives rise to whirling. We begin our analysis by considering the shaft in some displaced position, as shown in Fig. 7-67*b*. The shaft passes through the center C of the rotor, whose center of mass is at a distance u from C; that is, the rotor has an eccentricity q. We assume that the rotor remains parallel to the xy-plane and that the movement of the shaft away from its straight position is opposed by two forces: a "spring force"

$$\boldsymbol{F}_s = -k\boldsymbol{R} = -k(x\hat{\imath} + y\hat{\jmath})$$

and a "viscous damping force"

$$\boldsymbol{F}_d = -b\dot{\boldsymbol{R}} = -b(\dot{x}\hat{\imath} + \dot{y}\hat{\jmath})$$

produced by the elastic and viscoelastic properties of the shaft itself.

The motion of the mass center G is given by

$$\boldsymbol{r}_G(t) = (x(t) + q\cos\omega t)\hat{\imath} + (y(t) + q\sin\omega t)\hat{\jmath}$$

with corresponding acceleration

$$\boldsymbol{a}_G(t) = (\ddot{x}(t) - q\omega^2\cos\omega t)\hat{\imath} + (\ddot{y}(t) - q\omega^2\sin\omega t)\hat{\jmath}$$

The use of Euler's first law on the rotor yields the vector equation of motion

$$\boldsymbol{F}_s + \boldsymbol{F}_d = m\ddot{\boldsymbol{r}}_G$$

where m is the mass of the rotor. The component equations of motion are

$$\begin{aligned} \hat{\imath}: &\quad m\ddot{x} + b\dot{x} + kx = mq\omega^2 \cos \omega t \\ \hat{\jmath}: &\quad m\ddot{y} + b\dot{y} + ky = mq\omega^2 \sin \omega t \end{aligned} \tag{7-101}$$

We shall treat the solution of these equations in a combined fashion by introducing the complex variable

$$z = x + jy$$

Multiplication of the second equation of (7-101) by j, addition to the first, and division of the result by m yield the standard damped oscillator equation

$$\ddot{z} + 2\zeta\omega_n\dot{z} + \omega_n^2 z = q\omega^2 e^{j\omega t} \tag{7-102}$$

where $\omega_n = \sqrt{k/m}$ is the natural circular frequency in radians per second and $\zeta = b/2\sqrt{km}$ is the damping factor. The assumption

$$z(t) = Ae^{j\omega t}$$

in (7-102) yields

$$A = \frac{qr^2}{(1 - r^2) + j2\zeta r} \qquad r = \frac{\omega}{\omega_n}$$

and hence the steady-state solution

$$z(t) = Re^{j(\omega t - \phi)} \tag{7-103}$$

where

$$R = \frac{qr^2}{\sqrt{(1 - r^2)^2 + (2\zeta r)^2}}$$

$$\phi = \begin{cases} \operatorname{Arctan} \dfrac{2\zeta r}{1 - r^2} & \omega < \omega_n \\ \dfrac{\pi}{2} & \omega = \omega_n \\ \pi + \operatorname{Arctan} \dfrac{2\zeta r}{1 - r^2} & \omega > \omega_n \end{cases}$$

Note that R attains its maximum for

$$\omega^* = \frac{\omega_n}{\sqrt{1 - 2\zeta^2}}$$

with

$$R_{\max} = \frac{q}{2\zeta\sqrt{1 - \zeta^2}}$$

and only for $\zeta = 0$ does this "maximum" occur for $\omega = \omega_n$.

Note, furthermore, that for a specified ω, the phase angle ϕ is constant. The relative location of C and G for the different frequency ranges is depicted in Fig. 7.68. For $\omega \ll \omega_n$, ϕ is small and Fig. 7-68a applies; for $\omega = \omega_n$, $\phi = \pi/2$ and $R \approx R_{\max}$; and, for $\omega = \omega^*$, $\phi \approx \pi/2$, $R = R_{\max}$, and Fig. 7-68b applies. Finally, for $\omega \gg \omega_n$, $\phi \to \pi$ and $R \to q$, so that the shaft is almost whirling about the mass center of the rotor, as depicted in Fig. 7-68c.

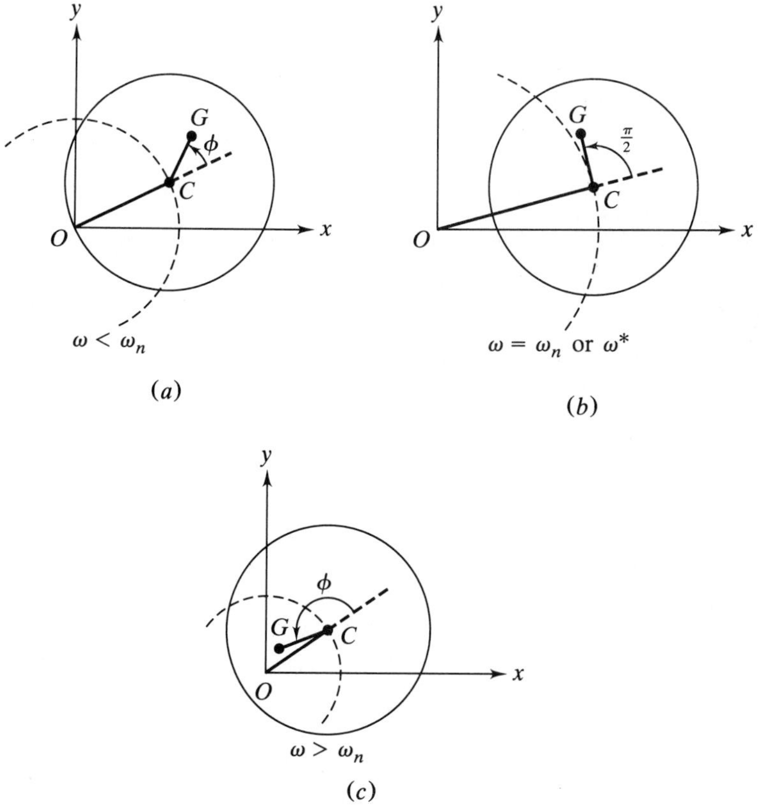

FIGURE 7-68
Rotor configuration in different frequency ranges.

Since the calculations are not quite as straightforward as they may appear here, we include the following example.

Example 7-18. Suppose a rotor weighing 1 lb is located at the center of a $\frac{1}{2}$-in-diameter steel shaft with 20 in between bearings. The eccentricity is $q = 0.0002$ in and the damping is given by $\zeta = 0.05$. The end points of the shaft are simply supported. The elastic modulus of steel is $E = 30 \times 10^6$ psi.

(a) Determine the critical speed ω^* for this screw.

(b) Determine the whirling amplitude for a rotor speed of 5000 rpm.

Solution. We first determine the problem parameters. To obtain the spring constant k, we consider a simply supported uniform beam loaded by a concentrated load P at its midpoint. The deflection v of the beam at the midpoint is given by

$$v = \frac{PL^3}{48EI} \quad \Rightarrow \quad P = \frac{48EI}{L^3}v$$

$$\Rightarrow \quad k = \frac{48EI}{L^3} = \frac{48 \times 30 \times 10^6 \times \pi}{20^3 \times 4^5} = 552 \frac{\text{lb}}{\text{in}}$$

$$= 6624 \frac{\text{lb}}{\text{ft}}$$

To obtain the total mass, we must include the effective weight of the shaft with a concentrated weight at its midpoint. Note that the natural fundamental lateral frequency of the beam in Fig. 7-69 is given by

$$\bar{\omega}_n = \sqrt{\frac{48EIg}{(W + 0.486w)L^3}}$$

where W is the concentrated weight at the midpoint and w is the weight per unit volume of the beam. This is the same as if we had considered a weightless beam and simply added $0.486w$ to the lumped weight W. We thus term $0.486w$ the effective weight of the beam with respect to a midpoint location. With a steel weight of 0.283 lb/in^3, the effective weight of the shaft is

$$W_e = 0.486 \times \frac{\pi}{4}\left(\frac{1}{2}\right)^2 \times 20 \times 0.283 = 0.540 \text{ lb}$$

Thus the total mass used at the midpoint is

$$m = \frac{1.54}{32.2} = 0.0478 \text{ slugs}$$

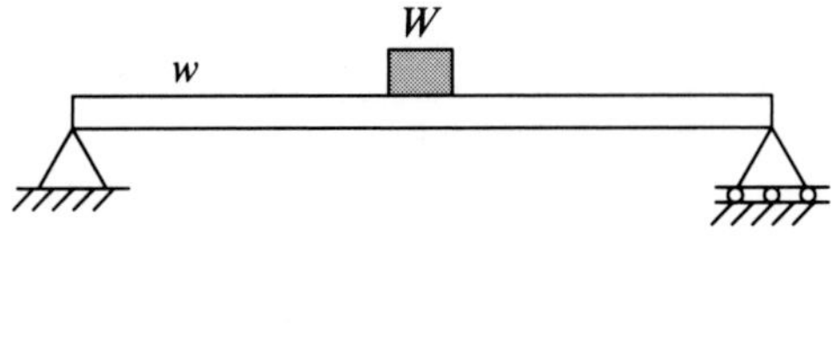

FIGURE 7-69
Simply supported beam with lumped weight at the midpoint.

(*a*) The critical speed is thus given by

$$\omega^* = \frac{\omega_n}{\sqrt{1 - 2\zeta^2}} = \sqrt{\frac{6624}{0.0478 \cdot 0.995}} = 373 \frac{\text{rad}}{\text{sec}}$$

$$\cong 3564 \text{ rpm}$$

In view of the low damping, this is virtually the same as the natural frequency of lateral vibration of the shaft with a weight at the middle, $\omega_n = 3555$ rpm.

(*b*) At 5000 rpm, the amplitude R is given by

$$R = \frac{0.0002 \cdot 1.98}{\sqrt{(1 - 1.98)^2 + 4 \times 0.0025 \times 1.98}} = 0.0004 \text{ in}$$

Remark 7-14. We ignored the shaft mass in our derivation, using the shaft only to provide a spring constant and damping. An equivalent mass depending on the rotor location may be included in the preceding manner or it may be omitted if it is negligible in comparison to the rotor mass. Note that in the previous example the effective mass of the shaft was of the same order of magnitude as that of the rotor so that its omission would have introduced a considerable error.

EXERCISES

7-1. The time required for a signal to pass through a tube of length L (m) filled with a fluid of mass density ρ (kg/cm^3) and having a bulk modulus B (bars) is given by

$$\tau = L\sqrt{\frac{\rho}{B}}$$

Provide a comparison of these times for pneumatic and hydraulic systems for the standard values mentioned in the text.

7-2. For a given cross section of a physical tube or a stream tube, the volumetric flow through a cross section of area A_0 is given by

$$q = \iint_{A_0} (\boldsymbol{v} \cdot \boldsymbol{n})\, dA$$

where $\boldsymbol{v}$ is the local velocity and $\boldsymbol{n}$ is the unit outward normal for the cross section. An average velocity, v_{av}, resulting in the correct volumetric flow, is given by

$$v_{\text{av}} = \frac{1}{A_0} \iint_{A_0} (\boldsymbol{v} \cdot \boldsymbol{n})\, dA$$

Suppose an approximate axial velocity profile for viscous flow through a circular tube is given by

$$u = u_0\left(1 - \frac{r}{R}\right)^m$$

where R is the outer radius of the tube and r measures the radial distance from the center of the cross section. Assume a constant density and compute the average velocity v_{av} for this flow.

7-3. Consider an ideal gas governed by $p = \rho RT$, where T is the absolute temperature in kelvins, R is the corresponding gas constant, and p is the absolute pressure. For such a case the constitutive relationship between ρ and p is given by $p = C\rho^n$, where

$$n = \begin{cases} 1 & \text{for isothermal processes} \\ \dfrac{c_p}{c_v} & \text{for adiabatic frictionless processes} \end{cases}$$

and where c_p and c_v are the specific heats at constant pressure and constant volume, respectively. Calculate the bulk modulus for an adiabatic frictionless process in an ideal gas. Express the speed of sound in the gas in terms of the bulk modulus and estimate the bulk modulus for air at sea level at 60°F.

7-4. Consider the cascaded system of tanks shown in Fig. E7-4. The flow q_1 into the first tank is controlled by a valve position x with $q_1 = k_1 x$; the corresponding supply line is maintained at a constant pressure p_0. The flow q_2 is related to the head h_1 of tank 1 by the "resistance" R_1 with $q_2 = R_1 h_1$. The exit flow q_0 is governed by the relationship $q_0 = R_2 h_2$. The tanks have constant cross sections A_1 and A_2, respectively.

(*a*) Write the governing equations for the system in standard first-order form

$$\dot{\mathbf{h}} = \mathbf{Ah} + \mathbf{Bx} \quad \text{and} \quad \mathbf{q} = \mathbf{Ch}$$

(*b*) Determine the overall system function for this system with $x(t)$ as the input and $q_0(t)$ as the output.

(*c*) Draw the corresponding block diagram for this system.

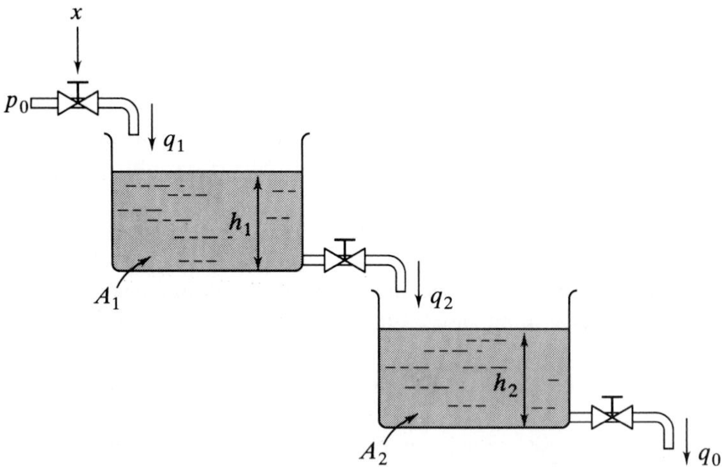

FIGURE E7-4

7-5. In the text we introduced suitable computational values for the material parameters and operating pressure of hydraulic fluid. We gave these values in the English system of units. Convert all of the values to the proper SI units.

7-6. In Sec. 7-1-3 we derived the expression

$$q = Cx_1\sqrt{\frac{1}{2}(\Delta p - p)} = f(x_1, p)$$

for the fluid flow through a valve opening subject to the assumption that the area of the opening was proportional to the spool displacement x_1. Furthermore, we used Taylor's theorem with remainder for functions of several variables to obtain a linearized equation for q in a neighborhood of $(\bar{x}_1, \bar{p}) = (0, 0)$. Obtain an estimate for the remainder $|R_2(x_1, p)|$ introduced by this approximation for $0 \le x_1 \le \epsilon$ and $0 \le p \le \epsilon$ for $\epsilon > 0$.

7-7. In the derivation of the system function for the hydraulic actuator, one of the assumptions made was that the orifice cross-sectional area was proportional to the valve displacement. Thus, if the valve spool and the supply line are square (Fig. E7-7*a*), then it is obvious that the total area of the opening is $A = hx_1$, so that the proportionality is exact. Consider now a circular supply line opening of radius R with a square valve spool moving from the central diameter toward each side (see Fig. E7-7*b*). Derive a linear approximation for the area as a function of y, based on a Taylor series expansion of the exact expression for $A(y)$.

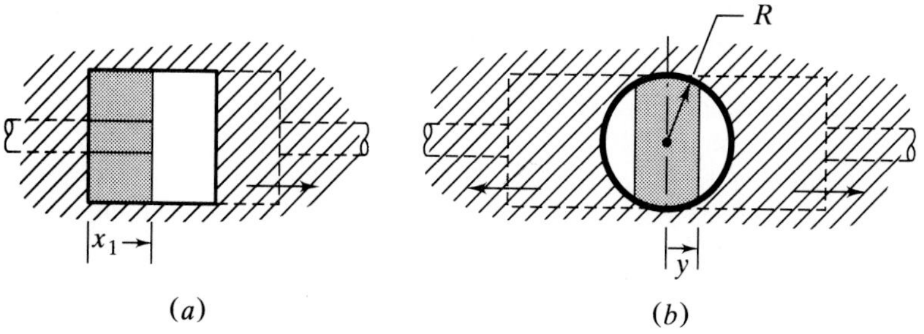

FIGURE E7-7

7-8. Provide the details in the derivations of the following equations. Be sure to indicate any specific equations used in the process.
(*a*) Begin with (7-25) and derive (7-26).
(*b*) Begin with (7-27) and derive (7-29).

7-9. Consider again the approximate expression obtained for the mass flow rate by the introduction of ϵ [Eq. (7-32)].
(*a*) Show that the maximum flow rate implied by (7-35) yields a maximum flow velocity at station 2 of $v_c = \sqrt{1.59RT_2}$.
(*b*) Show that the use of the maximum *allowable* flow rate yields $v_c = \sqrt{1.44RT_2}$.
In each case calculate the percentage error with respect to the exact maximum velocity.

7-10. In Sec. 7-1-6 we dealt with electrical analogs to fluid flow. Consider again the mass flow from/to a reservoir as a function of the pressure drop.

(*a*) Obtain an expression for the capacitance for an ideal gas and state its metric units.

(*b*) Calculate the capacitance for the specific case when the gas is air, the volume is 1 m^3, and the expansion process is adiabatic and frictionless at a temperature of 60 K.

(*c*) Do part (*b*) for an isothermal process.

7-11. Two circular cylindrical tanks are filled with water to heights h_1 and h_2, respectively. The bases of the tanks have a diameter of 0.5 m and the tanks are connected by a 2-cm-diameter pipe 1 m in length. Suppose $h_1 = 0.55$ m and $h_2 = 0.15$ m initially and that the flow in the pipe is laminar at a temperature of 30°C.

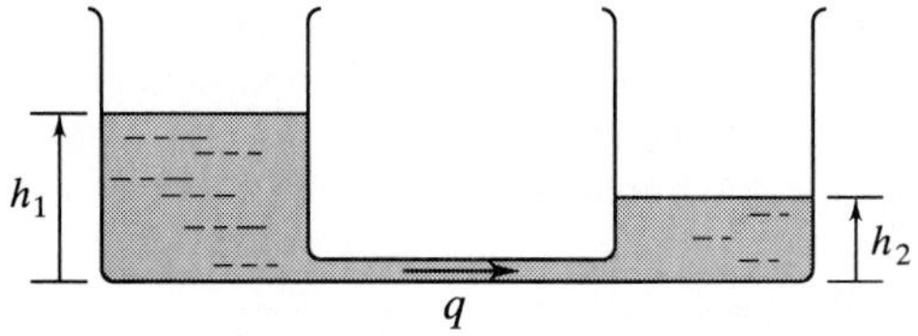

FIGURE E7-11

Determine:

(*a*) The fluid resistance R_f for the flow between the tanks.

(*b*) The volumetric flow q.

(*c*) The amount of time needed for the water level in the two tanks to equalize.

(*d*) An equivalent electrical system.

The configuration is illustrated in Fig. E7-11. (*Hint:* For laminar flow in a pipe the Hagen-Poiseuille formula applies.)

7-12. Suppose a current i is flowing through an infinitely long conductor. This current will then produce a magnetic field $\boldsymbol{B}$ in the vicinity of the wire. The differential field $d\boldsymbol{B}$ at a point P, at a perpendicular distance r from the wire, is given by the Biot-Savart law

$$d\boldsymbol{B} = \frac{\mu_0}{4\pi} \frac{i d\boldsymbol{s} \times \boldsymbol{b}}{b^3}$$

where $i\,d\boldsymbol{s}$ is the element of current vector and $\boldsymbol{b}$ is the vector pointing from the current element to the point P, as shown in Fig. E7-12. Calculate the field $\boldsymbol{B}$ at P.

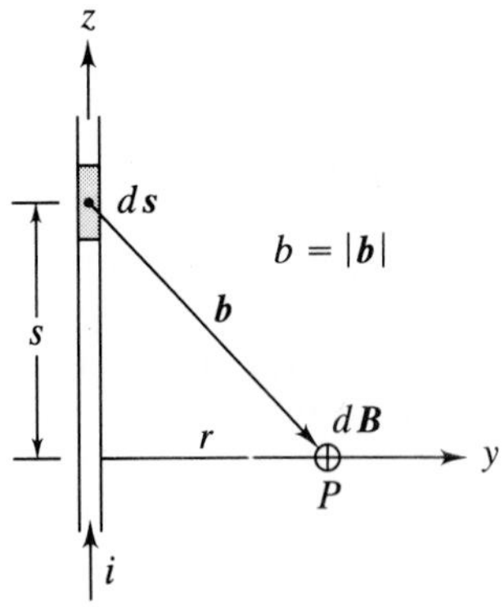

FIGURE E7-12

7-13. The following questions and graphs deal with the steady-state operation of DC motors. Take "steady-state" to refer to a system state when all of the state variables have reached constant values. Part of the following deals with the functional relations existing between these steady-state values. Consider field and armature in series with $T_L = T_f = 0$ and with zero damping.

(*a*) State the electro-mechanical governing equations for this system, including the expressions for T_m, ϕ and e_b.

(*b*) Set up the solution of these simultaneous nonlinear coupled equations by deriving the single nonlinear differential equation

$$Li\frac{d^2i}{dt^2} - L\left(\frac{di}{dt}\right)^2 + e\frac{di}{dt} + \frac{k_p k_s}{J_m}i^4 = 0$$

for the current supplying both armature and field. Assume a constant applied voltage e.

(*c*) Rewrite the governing electric circuit equations as they pertain to steady-state operation.

(*d*) Solve for i and ω_m as functions of T_m and show that the resulting functional relationships have the form shown in Fig. E7-13.

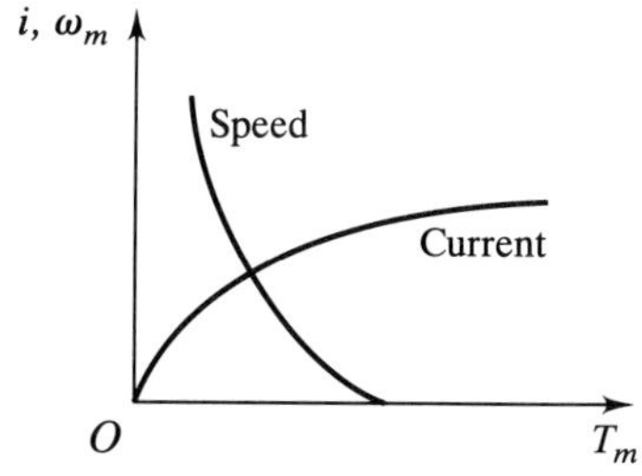

FIGURE E7-13

7-14. The following questions and graphs deal with the steady-state operation of DC motors. Take "steady-state" to refer to a system state where all of the state variables have reached constant values. Part of the following deals with the functional relations existing between these steady-state values. Consider field and armature in parallel with $T_L = T_f = 0$.

(*a*) State the governing equations for this system, including the expressions for T_m, ϕ and e_b.

(*b*) Set up the solution of these simultaneous nonlinear coupled equations by writing them in the standard first order form

$$\dot{\mathbf{x}} = \mathbf{A}\mathbf{x} + \mathbf{B}\mathbf{u} + \mathbf{f}(\mathbf{x})$$

with all nonlinearities contained in $\mathbf{f}(\mathbf{x})$; $\mathbf{A}$ is the linear state matrix, and $\mathbf{B}$ the input matrix. For the derivation, set $x_1 = i_f$, $x_2 = i_a$, $x_3 = \omega_m$, $u = e$.

(*c*) Rewrite the governing electrical circuit equations as they pertain to steady-state operation.

(*d*) Solve for i_a and ω_m as functions of T_m and show that the resulting functional relationships have the form shown in Fig. E7-14.

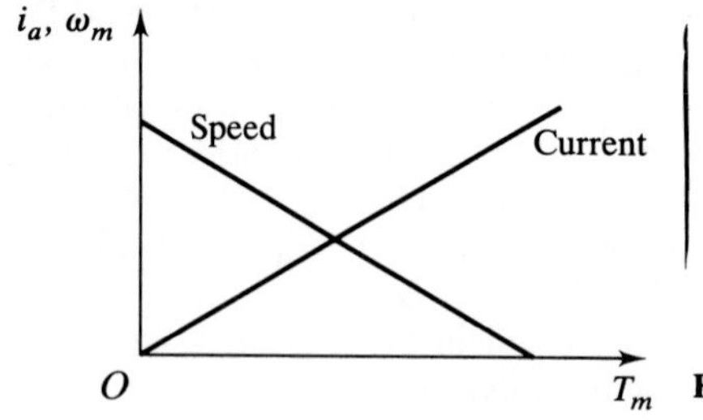

FIGURE E7-14

7-15. Suppose a VR stepper motor has an eight-phase stator and a rotor with 18 teeth. Calculate the resolution S of the stepper motor and the step angle θ_s.

7-16. Suppose the rotor of a VR stepper motor has 18 teeth around its circumference and that it can develop a maximum static holding torque of 0.6 N · m. Suppose a static load torque of 0.2 N · m is applied.

(*a*) Calculate the position error if a sinusoidal static torque-rotor characteristic is assumed.

(*b*) Suppose we take the sinusoidal representation in part (*a*) to be exact. Take a linear approximation around the 0° point and calculate the corresponding position error.

7-17. Consider the single step response of a stepper motor. Assume that ω_n is specified and that a unit step impulse has been applied to the rotor.

(*a*) Determine the condition on the damping factor ζ which will assure that the maximum overshoot of the rotor, $\theta_0(t_m)$, satisfies

$$|\theta_0(t_m) - 1| \leq 0.25$$

(*b*) Choose $\zeta = 0.5$ and $\omega_n = 4$ rad/s and calculate the corresponding rise time t_r and the settling time t_s for this rotor.

7-18. Consider the diode suppressor circuit of phase A in Fig. 7-42. Theoretically, steady-state conditions for the circuit are reached after an infinite amount of time —practically, in a time that is large compared to the system time constant. We may assume steady-state conditions have been attained in the coil just before it is turned off.

(*a*) Sketch the circuit for the time when the coil is on, derive the governing differential equation, and obtain the current $i(t)$ for a constant applied voltage V_p and subject to $i(0) = 0$. (You may neglect the voltage drop across the transistor.)

(*b*) At the instant when the transistor switch is turned off, calculate the energy stored in the inductance and the rate at which energy is being dissipated in the resistance R_w.

7-19. Suppose phase A in the circuit of Fig. 7-42 has just been turned off so that the circuit now is the freewheeling circuit.

(*a*) Sketch the circuit and derive the governing differential equation for this circuit.

(*b*) Show that the inclusion of R_s decreases the time constant for this circuit.

(*c*) Assume that the initial current $i(0)$ in this circuit derives from the energy stored in the inductance at turn-off. Obtain an expression for the (5%) settling time t_s of the circuit. That is, determine the time at which the current reaches $0.05i(0)$.

7-20. In our discussion of the drive system for the stepper motor, we presented a sequencer for counterclockwise rotation of the rotor. Design a corresponding sequencer for a clockwise rotor rotation. Keep the same coding for the phases so that the desired truth table for the phases has the form shown in Fig. E7-20.

(*a*) Draw the wiring diagram for the flip-flops. You may omit the phase connections.

(*b*) As was done in the text, discuss the changes of state with each input pulse. Begin with reset R and continue the discussion until this same system state is again reached.

Phase	Code	R	1	2	3	4
Phase A	$\overline{Q1}\ \overline{Q2}$	1	0	0	1	0
Phase B	$Q1\ \overline{Q2}$	0	0	1	0	0
Phase C	$\overline{Q1}\ Q2$	0	1	0	0	1

FIGURE E7-20

7-21. The division of the expression for $(F_1)_{\min}$ by the belt cross-sectional area yields the minimum belt stress for a given power $\mathscr{P}$. Conversely, for a given maximum allowable belt stress σ_{1a}, the expression may then be solved for maximum power per unit area.

(*a*) Show that this expression for the maximum power per unit area is given by

$$\frac{\mathscr{P}}{A} = v\left(\sigma_{1a} - \frac{\rho v^2}{A}\right)\frac{e^{\mu\theta} - 1}{e^{\mu\theta}}$$

(*b*) Determine the velocity v^* for which this power is a maximum and plot the maximum power versus the allowable stress σ_{1a}. (Use sufficient conditions to assure that you indeed have a maximum.)

7-22. Suppose a motor is to provide 20 hp at 2500 rpm by means of a multiple V-belt system. The driver pulley, attached directly to the motor, has a 5-in pitch diameter and the system geometry is such that the angle of wrap is 150°. The standard size 5 V-belts that are to be used have a groove angle of $\beta = 18°$ and a unit weight of 0.012 lb/in. The coefficient of friction is $\mu = 0.15$.

(*a*) Determine the number of belts that should be used if $(F_1)_{\min}$ is taken to be the critical load condition and $(F_1)_{\min}$ is not to exceed 200 lb tension, a conservative estimate.

(*b*) Suppose the choice is to include an additional safety factor of $\frac{1}{3}$ with respect to the active angle ϕ_1. That is, calculate F_1 corresponding to $\phi_1 = \frac{2}{3}\theta$. Will F_1 exceed the allowable tension? If so, what should be the number of belts based on this estimate?

7-23. Show that the Cartesian coordinates of the involute of the circle in Fig. 7-50*b* may be written in the form

$$x = r_1(\cos\beta + \beta\sin\beta)$$

$$y = r_1(\sin\beta - \beta\cos\beta)$$

7-24. Show that the radius of curvature of the involute of the circle in Fig. 7-50b at the point P is given by

$$\rho = \frac{1}{|\kappa|} = r_1\beta$$

where κ is the curvature of the involute at P. Consequently, the base circle is itself the locus of centers of curvature of the involute.

7-25. The velocity ratio of two spur gears is 1 : 5. The pinion has a module of 5 mm, 19 teeth, and rotates at 500 rpm.
(a) Determine the rpm of the gear.
(b) Determine the number of teeth for the gear.
(c) Determine the pitch line velocity.

7-26. Recall that the efficiency of an advancing power screw with load F opposite to the direction of motion is given by

$$e = \frac{\cos\lambda_n - \mu\tan\alpha}{\mu\cot\alpha + \cos\lambda_n}$$

Suppose $0 < \lambda < \pi/2$ and $0 < \alpha < \pi/2$. (a) Show that the efficiency is a decreasing function of the coefficient of friction for fixed λ_n and α.
(b) Let λ_n and μ be given. Show that the optimal efficiency with respect to α is obtained for that α which satisfies the condition

$$\tan 2\alpha = \frac{1}{\mu}\cos\lambda_n$$

Let α^* be the solution of this equation and show that the corresponding maximum efficiency is given by

$$e^* = \tan^2\alpha^*$$

You may base your results on necessary conditions only.
(c) Consider a thread angle $\lambda = 14.5°$ and $\mu = 0.10$ and calculate α^* and e^*.

7-27. Suppose that the power screw parameters are $d_m = 15$ mm, $\alpha = 10°$, and $\mu = 0.15$. Calculate the coefficient k_2 in the expression $T(t) = k_2F(t)$ with F such that it opposes the advancing screw. Assume an impending advance of the nut against the load and take $\lambda = 14.5°$.

7-28. Draw the screw efficiency curve corresponding to $\mu = 0.10$ and $\lambda = 14.5°$. That is, plot the screw efficiency versus the lead angle α (in degrees). Read off the value of α^* as specified in Exercise 7-26 and check the expression for the maximum efficiency as given in part (b) of the problem. Assume impending motion in the direction of the applied load.

7-29. A 175-kg rotor is located at one-quarter of the length of a 1.8-m shaft. The steel shaft has a diameter of 40 mm, and it is simply supported at its ends. You may assume that the effective mass of the shaft is negligible. The elastic modulus for steel is $E = 2.1 \times 10^{11}$ Pa. Calculate the natural frequency ω_n for the lateral motion of the shaft.

7-30. The simple manipulator in Fig. E7-30 is to support a weight of 2000 lb at one end, as shown. The arm is hinged at A and may be considered to be a uniform beam of weight 150 lb. The power screw BC is to raise the weight quasi-statically (i.e., the system dynamics may be neglected). The screw has a diameter of 0.5 in; it is made

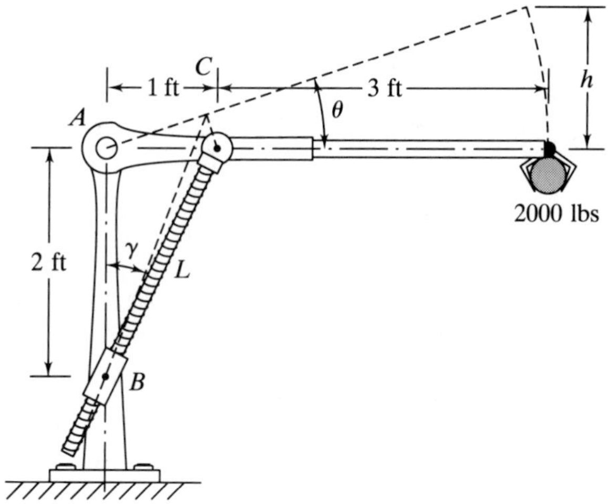

FIGURE E7-30

of steel with an elastic modulus of $E = 30 \times 10^6$ psi. You may assume that the screw is hinged at both B and C at a fixed distance of 1 ft from the hinge A. Determine the maximum height h to which the power screw can raise the weight before it fails.

REFERENCES

1. White, F. M.: *Fluid Mechanics*, McGraw-Hill, New York, 1979.
2. Dransfield, P.: *Hydraulic Control Systems—Design and Analysis of Their Dynamics*, no. 33, *Lecture Notes in Control and Information Sciences*, A. V. Balakrishnan and M. Thoma (Eds.), Springer, Berlin, 1981.
3. Ogata, K.: *System Dynamics*, Prentice-Hall, Englewood Cliffs, N.J., 1978; 2nd ed., 1992.
4. Fleming, W. H.: *Functions of Several Variables*, Addison-Wesley, Reading, Mass., 1965.
5. Streeter, L. V., and E. B. Wylie: *Fluid Mechanics*, 7th ed., McGraw-Hill, New York, 1979.
6. Hoekstra, R. L.: *Robotics and Automated Systems*, South-Western, Cincinnati, Ohio, 1986.
7. Holzbock, W. G.: *Robotic Technology, Principles and Practice*, Van Nostrand Reinhold, Wokingham, Berkshire, England, 1986.
8. Halliday, D., and R. Resnick: *Fundamentals of Physics*, extended 3rd ed., Wiley, New York, 1988.
9. Slemon, G. R., and A. Straughen: *Electric Machines*, Addison-Wesley, Reading, Mass., 1982.
10. Electro-Craft Corporation: *DC Motors, Speed Controls, Servo Systems, An Engineering Handbook*, Electro-Craft Corporation, Hopkins, Minn., 1980.
11. Kuo, B. C.: *Automatic Control Systems*, 5th ed., Prentice-Hall, Englewood Cliffs, N.J., 1987.
12. Takashi, K.: *Stepping Motors and Their Microprocessor Controls*, Clarendon, Oxford, 1984.
13. Mano, M. M.: *Computer Logic Design*, Prentice-Hall, Englewood Cliffs, N.J., 1972.
14. Acarnley, P. P.: *Stepping Motors: A Guide to Modern Theory and Practice*, 2nd ed., Peter Peregrinus, London, 1984; no. 19 in *IEEE Control Engineering Series*.
15. Juvinall, R. C.: *Fundamentals of Machine Component Design*, Wiley, New York, 1983.
16. Burr, A. H.: *Mechanical Analysis and Design*, Elsevier Science Publishing, New York, 1982.
17. Wilson, C. E., J. P. Sadler, and W. J. Michels: *Kinematics and Dynamics of Machinery*, Harper and Row, New York, 1983.

18. Buckingham, E.: *Analytical Mechanics of Gears*, McGraw-Hill, New York, 1949; Dover Publications, Mineola, N.Y., 1988.
19. Popov, E. P., S. Nagarajan, and Z. A. Lu: *Mechanics of Materials*, Prentice-Hall, Englewood Cliffs, N.J., 1978.
20. Föppl, A.: "Das Problem der De Laval'schen Turbinenwelle," *Civilingenieur*, vol. 61, pp. 333–342, 1895.

CHAPTER

EIGHT

TRAJECTORY PLANNING AND CONTROL

This is the chapter for which all of the others were written, for here we shall begin to look at the complete robot rather than at its components. This coming together of the individual concepts is, perhaps, best illustrated by the design project carried out by a group of three students—juniors with no previous experience in robotics. As has so often been the case, the capabilities and perseverance of these students were an example to me and expanded my understanding of robotics.

The available robot was a five-axis cable-driven Alphabot II, with all of its drives in the base of the robot. It had no sensory capabilities other than keeping track of incremental steps and its gripper activity. Its motion could be directed by teach pendant and by computer. The objective of the semester's project was to have the robot interact with me in some intelligent fashion without the introduction of sensors. By the end of the semester, through the students' accomplishments, the robot was playing tic-tac-toe.

The solution was actually simple. The students provided the robot with white wooden blocks, and I was given black cubes. The playing grid and the robot's blocks were arranged so that the robot knew where to pick up blocks and introduce them into play. At the beginning of each turn, the robot would determine which board position had been newly occupied by visiting each position in turn and closing its gripper. When a new block was encountered, the position was recorded and then the robot then made its move. This process continued, somewhat tediously, until termination of the game.

This simple interaction includes all the components that constitute a modern robot. There are three basic elements:

1. *Controller*. A mix of hardware and software that control the positioning and motion of the robot, as dictated by a teach pendant or computer.
2. *Sensors*. Monitor the robot's surroundings and behavior and provide the information, directly, either to the controller or the computer.
3. *Decision making*. Generally, software that provides the robot with decision-making capability. (The intelligence of the decisions made by the robot depends primarily on that of the programmer.)

The students combined these aspects beautifully in their robot, which was designed mainly to be taught by teach pendant, with a secondary programming capability. The gripper was used as a sensor, and the students used a commercially available tic-tac-toe program. The students' achievement lay in their understanding of the necessary interaction and in the writing of the software linking the individual components.

There was another aspect that played a part in each of the other aspects mentioned previously: the attempt to optimize the individual operation, from the path planning for the controller to the no-loss game theory comprising the tic-tac-toe program. This tacit requirement in all designs is, unfortunately, generally neglected in formal instruction. We have attempted to introduce optimization concepts throughout this book and will continue in this chapter as well.

Our discussion here will emphasize the first two robot components mentioned earlier—the controller and sensors. (We believe that computerized decision making, one of the basic robot components also mentioned, and artificial intelligence lend themselves more easily to separate treatment.) On a broad scale the discussion will be divided into kinematic aspects of robot control and the kinetic aspects embodied in the robot equations of motion. The kinematics will begin with a number of background concepts and will introduce the Denavit-Hartenberg parameters and Jacobian motion. This is followed by an Eulerian approach to the derivation of the robot equations of motion. The following section then deals with trajectory planning, overall motion control, and the feedback control used at the joints. We close the book with performance measures of the robot.

8-1 MANIPULATOR KINEMATICS

This section builds on the kinematic concepts we introduced in Chaps. 1 and 2, culminating in the kinematic treatment of actual manipulators. We shall provide analytical examples whenever possible, since these yield considerable insight into problems that may be dealt with only numerically in practical situations. As before, we shall include background material whenever needed.

8-1-1 Basic Kinematic Concepts

We shall use examples and discussion to outline problems which will receive a more realistic treatment in later sections.

All of the manipulator kinematics may be viewed as trajectory planning, since unplanned motion is clearly undesirable. Trajectory planning begins with the planning of an allowable, desirable, as well as possible *path* on which some characteristic point of the end-effector reference frame is to travel. The next step consists of an appropriate parametrization of the path, dictating the manner and speed with which it is to be traversed. This establishes the times at which the point is to be at particular coordinates; in essence, this establishes the so-called forward kinematics of the manipulator. We have now specified the world path, $\boldsymbol{r}(t)$, of the robot's motion. For a robot with a fixed base, the assumed coincidence of the reference frames $(0xyz)$ and $(0xyz)_0$ then provides $\boldsymbol{r}_0(t) = \boldsymbol{r}(t)$. The inverse kinematics deal with the determination of the robot variables that will yield the desired world path and traversal.

A simple example will firm up the required concepts and tasks. We shall strain the reader's credibility somewhat; however, this will allow us to carry out all of the operations in closed form—a useful attribute at this early juncture.

Example 8-1. The manipulator is that exemplary polar manipulator we introduced earlier, in Chaps. 2 and 3. Its work space without obstacles is depicted in Fig. 8-1*a*. The end effector E is to traverse a path—as yet unknown—between the points P_0 and P_3, as shown in Fig. 8-1*b*, at a constant speed v_E. Determine a smooth feasible path for the end effector E and the corresponding parametrization of the path in terms of the robot variables $(r(t), \theta(t))$ which will assure that the path is traversed at the constant speed V_E.

Solution. There are four steps that must be performed.

Step 1. Construction of a smooth path. We suppose that splining or some other interpolation procedure has yielded

$$y(x) = \tfrac{2}{3}x^{3/2}$$

as a smooth path which passes through all of the specified points.

Step 2. Path feasibility and access. Path feasibility requires that the path lie entirely within the robot's work space, as defined in Chap. 1. That is, it lies within the robot's work envelope while avoiding all permanent obstacles within. With this in mind we determine that the point P_0 is not feasible because it is not within the robot's work space. The first accessible point on the constructed path is the intersection of the two curves

$$x^2 + y^2 = 1 \qquad \text{and} \qquad y(x) = \tfrac{2}{3}x^{3/2}$$

or the point P (0.85, 0.52). The accessibility of the point P_3 is in question because of the obstacle. The straight-line path from the origin to P_3 is

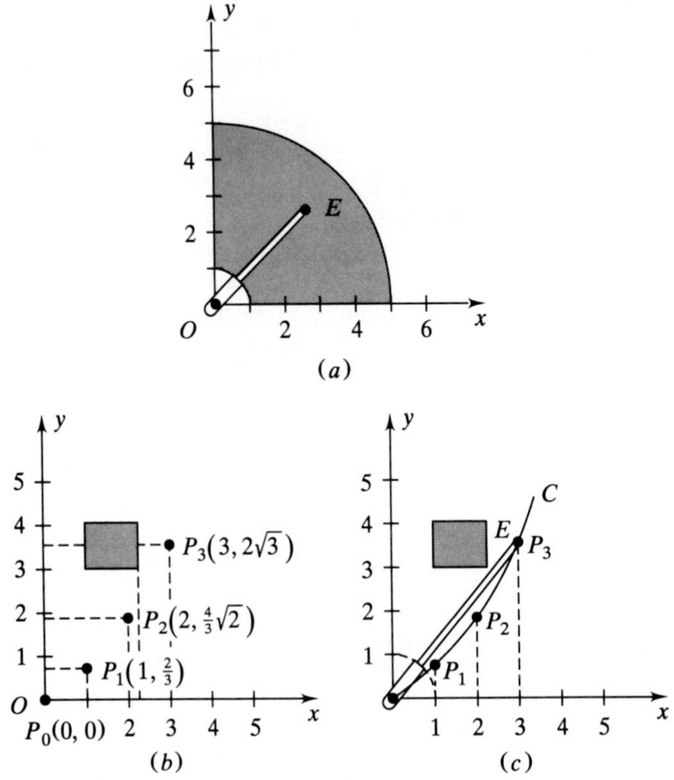

FIGURE 8-1
Basic trajectory planning.

given by

$$y(x) = \frac{2\sqrt{3}}{3}x$$

with $$y(2.2) = 2.79 < 3$$

and we conclude that the point is reachable for the robot, since the required reach is

$$\sqrt{3^2 + (2\sqrt{3})^2} = \sqrt{21} = 4.58 < 5$$

Step 3. The parametrization in world coordinates. We wish to parametrize the path in such a way that the speed of E along the path is constant. For a given curve C, there are an infinite number of parametrizations of the curve—in essence, all of the different ways in which the curve can be traversed. Examples 1-3 and 1-4 illustrated the crucial manner in which the choice of parametrization and path affected the acceleration of a point.

Here, we now have a curve C in the form

$$y = f(x)$$

and we are to determine the parametrization that will result in a specified speed along the curve. The motion of E on C is

$$\boldsymbol{r}(t) = x(t)\hat{\imath} + y(t)\hat{\jmath}$$

with

$$\boldsymbol{v}(t) = \dot{x}(t)\hat{\imath} + \dot{y}(t)\hat{\jmath}$$

and speed

$$v(t) = \sqrt{\dot{x}^2 + \dot{y}^2} = |\dot{x}(t)|\sqrt{1 + \left(\frac{df}{dx}(x(t))\right)^2}$$

With $\dot{x}(t) > 0$ and $x(t_0) = x_0$, the appropriate parametrization of the curve may be derived from the relationship

$$\int_{t_0}^{t} v(\tau)\, d\tau = \int_{x_0}^{x}\sqrt{1 + \left(\frac{df}{dx}(\xi)\right)^2}\, d\xi$$

Specifically, for the curve with $x(0) = 0.85$ and for a constant speed v_E, we require

$$\int_0^t v_E\, dt = \int_0^x \sqrt{1 + \xi}\, d\xi$$

$$\Rightarrow \quad v_E t = \tfrac{2}{3}(1 + \xi)^{3/2}\Big|_{0.85}^{x}$$

resulting in

$$1.5v_E t + 2.52 = (1 + x)^{3/2}$$

and hence

$$x(t) = (1.5v_E t + 2.52)^{2/3} - 1$$

$$y(t) = \tfrac{2}{3}\left[(1.5v_E t + 2.52)^{2/3} - 1\right]^{3/2}$$

Step 4. The inverse kinematics. The final step consists of the determination of the corresponding parametrization of the robot variables. This inverse determination is crucial. The speed with which this task can be accomplished characterizes the quality of the algorithm used in the calculation. Obviously, the task and its difficulty depend on the choice of basic robot configuration. Here, we simply have the transformation to polar coordinates given by

$$r(t) = \tfrac{1}{3}\left[b^{2/3}(t) - 1\right]\left[5 + 4b^{2/3}(t)\right]^{1/2}$$

$$\theta_1(t) = \text{Arctan}\,\tfrac{2}{3}\left[b^{2/3}(t) - 1\right]^{1/2} \qquad b(t) = 1.5v_E t + 2.52$$

Messy, but precisely what we had wished to accomplish.

This example illustrates the total analytical process concerned with the forward and inverse kinematics of the manipulator; it is not definitive. The standard definition of these terms is far more restrictive. For example, the homogeneous transformation matrix

$$\mathbf{H}_1(t) = \mathbf{H}_{01}(t) = \begin{bmatrix} C\theta_1 & -S\theta_1 & 0 & r(t)C\theta_1 \\ S\theta_1 & C\theta_1 & 0 & r(t)S\theta_1 \\ 0 & 0 & 1 & 0 \\ 0 & 0 & 0 & 1 \end{bmatrix}$$

would more commonly be termed the forward kinematics of this manipulator.

We shall reserve the more formal treatment of this topic until the Denavit-Hartenberg (DH) parameters have been introduced.

REPARAMETRIZATION. Suppose that the curve C is available in parametric form with parameter θ; that is, we have C in the form

$$\begin{aligned} x &= x(\theta) \\ y &= y(\theta) \\ z &= z(\theta) \end{aligned} \tag{8-1}$$

We wish to parametrize the curve C in terms of the time to obtain a desired velocity distribution. In robotics, we generally wish to attain a given velocity at a specified position (e.g., we program the position and the velocity at that position with a teach pendant). We thus take a circuitous route to our final parametrization: We first parametrize in terms of s and then in terms of the time t. The relationship between the arc length and θ is

$$s = \int_0^\theta \sqrt{\left(\frac{dx}{d\theta}(\xi)\right)^2 + \left(\frac{dy}{d\theta}(\xi)\right)^2 + \left(\frac{dz}{d\theta 2}(\xi)\right)^2}\, d\xi \tag{8-2}$$

a monotonically increasing function of θ. The inverse of this relationship provides $\theta(s)$. A suitable parametrization of the arc length in terms of t then yields $\theta(s(t)) = \theta(t)$. (See also Exercise 8-1 in this connection.) Again, we note that analytical solutions provide insight; they are rarely possible in practice.

MORE INVERSE KINEMATICS. We shall continue our discussion from Sec. 1-2. Clearly, the inverse trigonometric functions play a considerable role in the treatment of the inverse kinematics. We shall summarize the functions and their principal ranges and then use a simple example to illustrate some standard difficulties.

In listing the inverse trigonometric functions, it is customary to capitalize the first letter to indicate that the inverse function is to be constrained to its principal range:

Arctangent	$-\frac{\pi}{2} \le \text{Arctan } z \le \frac{\pi}{2}$
Arccosine	$0 \le \text{Arccos } z \le \pi$
Arcsine	$-\frac{\pi}{2} \le \text{Arcsin } z \le \frac{\pi}{2}$

When z characterizes the coordinates of a point that falls outside the principal range, we may add or subtract π to arrive at the corresponding angle. By convention, we shall always add π.

Example 8-2. Suppose a given point (x, y) is in the second quadrant as indicated in Fig. 8-2. Calculate the angle θ by using each of the previous inverse functions.

Solution. When the Arctan function is used to calculate θ, we have

$$\theta = \text{Arctan}\left(-\frac{y}{x}\right) + \pi = \pi - \text{Arctan}\left(\frac{y}{x}\right)$$

since the arctan function is an odd function. For the remaining functions we need to use

$$\theta = \text{Arccos}\left(\frac{-x}{\sqrt{x^2 + y^2}}\right)$$

$$\theta = \text{Arcsin}\left(\frac{-y}{\sqrt{x^2 + y^2}}\right) + \pi$$

$$= \pi - \text{Arcsin}\left(\frac{y}{\sqrt{x^2 + y^2}}\right)$$

We have already introduced one way in which to account for quadrant information in the calculation of the argument of a point in the plane. We formalize another approach frequently used, labeled the Atan 2 function.

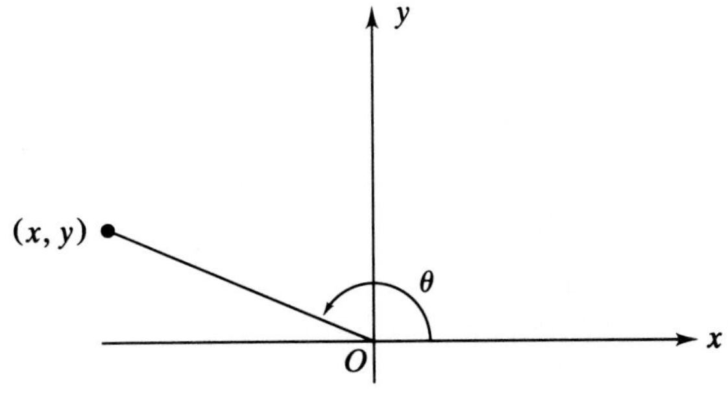

FIGURE 8-2
Point out of principal range.

Atan 2(y, x) and Atan 2(sin θ, cos θ). It is simply the Arctangent function incorporating quadrant information. It is a mapping

$$\text{Atan } 2(\cdot, \cdot): \mathbb{R}^2 \Rightarrow \mathbb{R}^1$$

with the first entry referring to the numerator, and the second, the denominator of the usual ratio in the Arctan function. The resultant angle is computed as follows: Suppose sin θ and cos θ and their signs have been specified. Let

$$\theta_0 = \text{Arccos}[\cos\theta]$$

If $\sin\theta \leq 0$, take

$$\theta = 2\pi - \theta_0$$

Otherwise, take $\theta = \theta_0$. For example, suppose we are given $\sin\theta = -\frac{1}{2}$ and $\cos\theta = -\sqrt{3}/2$. Then $\text{Arccos}(-\sqrt{3}/2) = 150°$. Since $\sin\theta < 0$, it follows that $\theta = 360° - 150° = 210°$, or

$$\text{Atan } 2\left(-\frac{1}{2}, -\frac{\sqrt{3}}{2}\right) = 210°$$

Thus equipped, we now take a look at a more relevant example which illustrates the type of problem that often must be solved at regular sampling intervals.

Example 8-3. Consider the simple two-link manipulator shown in Fig. 8-3*a*, with its end effector E located at the world point $(2\sqrt{3}, 0)$. Determine the corresponding values of the robot variables (θ_1, θ_2).

Solution. The transformation matrix $\mathbf{H}_2$ relating the end effector E to the base point O is given by

$$\mathbf{r}_0 = \mathbf{H}_{01}\mathbf{H}_{12}\mathbf{r}_2$$

$$= \begin{bmatrix} C\theta_1 & -S\theta_1 & 0 & 0 \\ S\theta_1 & C\theta_1 & 0 & 0 \\ 0 & 0 & 1 & 0 \\ 0 & 0 & 0 & 1 \end{bmatrix} \begin{bmatrix} C\theta_2 & -S\theta_2 & 0 & 2 \\ S\theta_2 & C\theta_2 & 0 & 0 \\ 0 & 0 & 1 & 0 \\ 0 & 0 & 0 & 1 \end{bmatrix} \begin{pmatrix} 2 \\ 0 \\ 0 \\ 1 \end{pmatrix}$$

$$= \begin{bmatrix} C\theta_1 C\theta_2 - S\theta_1 S\theta_2 & -C\theta_1 S\theta_2 - S\theta_1 C\theta_2 & 0 & 2C\theta_1 \\ S\theta_1 C\theta_2 + C\theta_1 S\theta_2 & -S\theta_1 S\theta_2 + C\theta_1 C\theta_2 & 0 & 2S\theta_1 \\ 0 & 0 & 1 & 0 \\ 0 & 0 & 0 & 1 \end{bmatrix} \begin{pmatrix} 2 \\ 0 \\ 0 \\ 1 \end{pmatrix}$$

$$= \mathbf{H}_2\mathbf{r}_2 \tag{8-3}$$

We preempt a precise definition here, in that we shall term the matrix $\mathbf{H}_2$ the *forward kinematics* of the simple two-link manipulator. We need to determine the values of (θ_1, θ_2) corresponding to the world point occupied by E in Fig. 8-3*a*.

We shall illustrate two relatively standard approaches for the solution of this inverse kinematics problem. The first is rather a piecemeal approach, based on the successive multiplication of (8-3) by the inverses of the relative transformation matrices comprising the forward kinematics of the manipulator, thus solving the

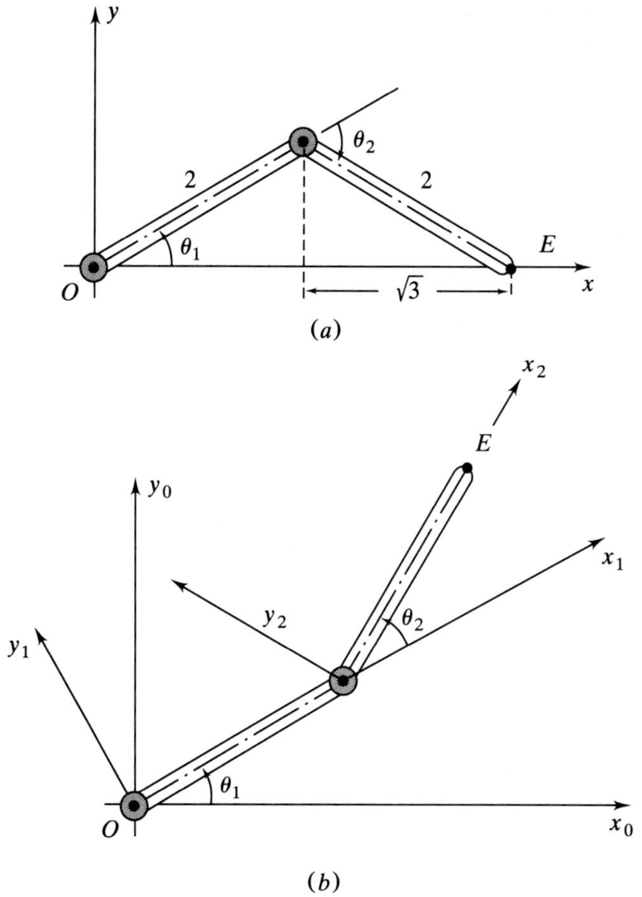

FIGURE 8-3
The simple two-link manipulator.

problem in stages. The second simply attempts to solve the final set of simultaneous equations implied by (8-3).

1. We first premultiply both sides of (8-3) by $\mathbf{H}_{01}^{-1}$ with the result

$$\mathbf{H}_{01}^{-1}\mathbf{r}_0 = \mathbf{H}_{12}\mathbf{r}_2$$

$$\begin{bmatrix} C\theta_1 & S\theta_1 & 0 & 0 \\ -S\theta_1 & C\theta_1 & 0 & 0 \\ 0 & 0 & 1 & 0 \\ 0 & 0 & 0 & 1 \end{bmatrix} \begin{pmatrix} 2\sqrt{3} \\ 0 \\ 0 \\ 1 \end{pmatrix} = \begin{bmatrix} C\theta_2 & -S\theta_2 & 0 & 2 \\ S\theta_2 & C\theta_2 & 0 & 0 \\ 0 & 0 & 1 & 0 \\ 0 & 0 & 0 & 1 \end{bmatrix} \begin{pmatrix} 2 \\ 0 \\ 0 \\ 1 \end{pmatrix}$$

This equality yields the simultaneous equations

$$\sqrt{3}\cos\theta_1 - \cos\theta_2 = 1$$

$$\sqrt{3}\sin\theta_1 + \sin\theta_2 = 0$$

With the substitution of

$$\cos\theta_1 = \sqrt{1-\sin^2\theta_1} \qquad \text{and} \qquad \cos\theta_2 = \sqrt{1-3\sin^2\theta_1}$$

we eventually obtain the single equation for $\sin\theta_1$,

$$1 - 3\sin^2\theta_1 = \tfrac{1}{4} \qquad \text{or} \qquad \sin\theta_1 = \pm\tfrac{1}{2}$$

In a straightforward manner we then deduce

$$\sin\theta_1 = \tfrac{1}{2} \quad \Rightarrow \quad \theta_1 = 30° \quad \text{and} \quad \theta_2 = -60°$$

$$\sin\theta_1 = -\tfrac{1}{2} \quad \Rightarrow \quad \theta_1 = -30° \quad \text{and} \quad \theta_2 = 60°$$

2. We consider (8-3) as it stands. This yields the simultaneous equations

$$\begin{aligned} \cos\alpha + \cos\theta_1 &= \sqrt{3} \\ \sin\alpha + \sin\theta_1 &= 0 \end{aligned} \qquad \alpha = \theta_1 + \theta_2$$

The substitution of

$$\cos\alpha = \sqrt{1-\sin^2\theta_1} \qquad \text{and} \qquad \cos\theta_1 = \sqrt{1-\sin^2\theta_1}$$

yields $$2\sqrt{1-\sin^2\theta_1} = \sqrt{3} \quad \Rightarrow \quad \sin\theta_1 = \pm\tfrac{1}{2}$$

These two possibilities result in

$$\sin\theta_1 = \tfrac{1}{2} \quad \Rightarrow \quad \theta_1 = 30° \quad \Rightarrow \quad \alpha = -30° \quad \Rightarrow \quad \theta_2 = -60°$$

$$\sin\theta_1 = -\tfrac{1}{2} \quad \Rightarrow \quad \theta_1 = -30° \quad \Rightarrow \quad \alpha = 30° \quad \Rightarrow \quad \theta_2 = 60°$$

Thus there are two possible robot configurations yielding the same world point. When the two links form part of an anthropomorphic robot, the two configurations are termed "above shoulder" and "below shoulder" configurations, respectively.

Rather than simply selecting one or the other configuration in some ad hoc fashion, a final selection is sometimes based on the imposition of additional criteria. For example, a comparison of the potential energies of the two configurations for links consisting of homogeneous rods of mass m yields

$$\theta_1 = 30° \qquad \text{and} \qquad V = m$$

$$\theta_1 = -30° \qquad \text{and} \qquad V = -m$$

with the x-axis as datum. Minimizing the potential energy thus would have served to select the below-shoulder configuration.

8-1-2 The Jacobian and the Jacobian Matrix

First and foremost, let us note that the Jacobian is the determinant of the Jacobian matrix, a distinction that is sometimes blurred in the robotics literature. Both are named for the 19th-century German mathematician Carl Gustav Jacob Jacobi (1804–1851), who first used Jacobians (the determinants) in 1829. Jacobi's crowning work devoted entirely to Jacobians was a long memoir in 1841, entitled "De determinantibus functionalibus," which appeared in *Crelle's Journal*, a prominent mathematical journal of the time. There it was pointed out that this determinant played much the same role for a function of several variables as the differential quotient does for a function of a single variable; for example, it provides a "tangent" to a function in n-dimensional space. Jacobi used it to determine whether a set of functions or equations is linearly dependent. In particular, he showed that if n functions in n variables are functionally related, then their Jacobian must vanish identically; if they are mutually independent, then their Jacobian cannot be identically 0. To a large extent, this is the way the concept will be used here.

A broader concept of function—that of a transformation (or mapping, or map)—is essential. For example, we may think of the linear matrix equation

$$\underset{(m\times 1)}{\mathbf{y}} = \underset{(m\times n)}{\mathbf{A}}\ \underset{(n\times 1)}{\mathbf{x}}$$

as a mapping $\mathbf{f}(\cdot)$: $\mathbb{R}^n \to \mathbb{R}^m$, from n-dimensional space $\mathbb{R}^n$ to m-dimensional space $\mathbb{R}^m$. Similarly, we view

$$x = x(r, \theta)$$

$$y = y(r, \theta)$$

or

$$\boldsymbol{r}(r, \theta) = x(r, \theta)\hat{\imath} + y(r, \theta)\hat{\jmath}$$

as a nonlinear transformation from $\mathbb{R}^2$ to $\mathbb{R}^2$. More generally, we define a transformation with

$$f(\cdot): \mathscr{D} \subset \mathbb{R}^n \quad \to \quad \mathscr{R} \subset \mathbb{R}^m$$

mapping a subset of $\mathbb{R}^n$ into a subset of $\mathbb{R}^m$; we shall take these subsets to be the domain and the range, respectively.

Recall (or note) that the differentiability of a scalar function of several variables requires more than the mere existence of the corresponding partial derivatives. That is, the partial derivatives may exist at a point and the function may not be differentiable there. The differential of a differentiable function at a point must also satisfy a certain approximation property there.

Suppose the function $g(\cdot)$: $\mathbb{R}^2 \to \mathbb{R}$ of the variables x and y is differentiable at the point (x_0, y_0). Then its differential at that point is given by

$$\begin{aligned} dz &= dg(x_0, y_0; dx, dy) \\ &= \frac{\partial g}{\partial x}(x_0, y_0)\, dx + \frac{\partial g}{\partial y}(x_0, y_0)\, dy \end{aligned}$$

where we have emphasized that the differential is a function of both the point (x_0, y_0) and the choice of the independent variables dx and dy. For any point (x, y) near (x_0, y_0), the expression

$$\Delta z = \frac{\partial g}{\partial x}(x_0, y_0)\,\Delta x + \frac{\partial g}{\partial y}(x_0, y_0)\,\Delta y$$

then furnishes a linear approximation to the difference $g(x, y) - g(x_0, y_0)$, which improves with the closeness of (x, y) to the point (x_0, y_0).

Example 8-4. Let $g(x, y) = x^2 + y^2$.

(*a*) Calculate the differential of $g(\cdot)$ at the point $(1, 1)$.

(*b*) Determine the approximate change in $g(x, y)$ when (x, y) changes from $(1, 1)$ to $(1.2, 0.9)$.

Solution

(*a*) The differential of $g(\cdot)$ at $(1, 1)$ is given by

$$dg(1,1) = \frac{\partial g}{\partial x}(1,1)\,dx + \frac{\partial g}{\partial y}(1,1)\,dy$$

$$= 2\,dx + 2\,dy$$

(*b*) With $\Delta x = x - x_0 = 1.2 - 1.0 = 0.2$ and $\Delta y = y - y_0 = 0.9 - 1.0 = -0.1$, we have

$$\Delta z = z - z_0 = 2\,\Delta x + 2\,\Delta y = 2(0.2) - 2(0.1) = 0.2$$

The actual change in the function is

$$g(1.2, 0.9) - g(1,1) = (1.44 + 0.81) - (1 + 1) = 0.25$$

We have illustrated this result in Fig. 8-4.

The extension of this concept of differentiability to transformations is straightforward. Suppose we have

$$f(x, y) = g(x, y)\hat{\imath} + h(x, y)\hat{\jmath}$$

or, equivalently,

$$\mathbf{f}(x, y) = \begin{pmatrix} g(x, y) \\ h(x, y) \end{pmatrix}$$

If this transformation is differentiable, then its differential of $\mathbf{f}(\cdot)$ at (x_0, y_0) is

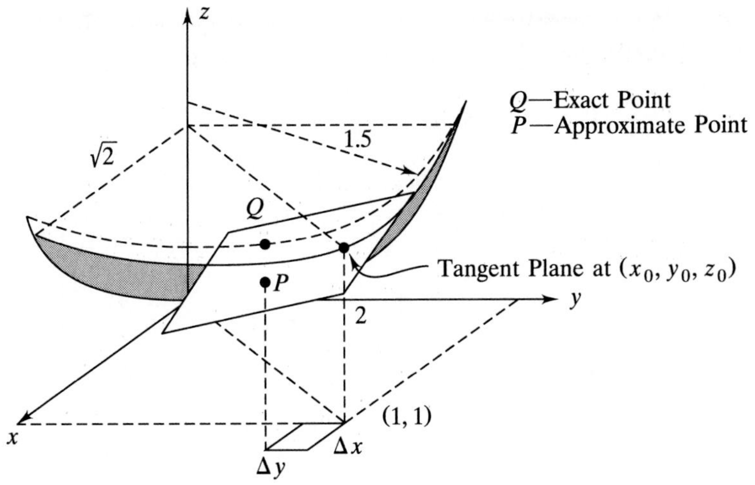

FIGURE 8-4
Tangent plane to a paraboloid.

given by

$$d\mathbf{f}(x_0, y_0) = \begin{pmatrix} dg(x_0, y_0) \\ dh(x_0, y_0) \end{pmatrix} = \begin{pmatrix} \dfrac{\partial g}{\partial x}(x_0, y_0)\,dx + \dfrac{\partial g}{\partial y}(x_0, y_0)\,dy \\ \dfrac{\partial h}{\partial x}(x_0, y_0)\,dx + \dfrac{\partial h}{\partial y}(x_0, y_0)\,dy \end{pmatrix}$$

$$= \begin{bmatrix} \dfrac{\partial g}{\partial x}(x_0, y_0) & \dfrac{\partial g}{\partial y}(x_0, y_0) \\ \dfrac{\partial h}{\partial x}(x_0, y_0) & \dfrac{\partial h}{\partial y}(x_0, y_0) \end{bmatrix} \begin{pmatrix} dx \\ dy \end{pmatrix}$$

For formal definitiveness we shall consider a transformation

$$\mathbf{f}(\cdot): \mathbb{R}^n \to \mathbb{R}^m$$

defined by

$$\mathbf{f}(\mathbf{z}) = \left(u_1(\mathbf{z})\, u_2(\mathbf{z}) \ldots u_m(\mathbf{z})\right)^T$$

$$\mathbf{z} = (x_1 \ldots x_n)^T$$

and we suppose that $\mathbf{f}(\cdot)$ is differentiable everywhere on its domain $\mathscr{D}$ with the possible exception of a finite number of isolated points.

Definition 8-1 Jacobian matrix and Jacobian. For the transformation $\mathbf{f}(\cdot)$, the $m \times n$ matrix of partial derivatives

$$\mathbf{J}(\mathbf{z}) = \frac{\partial(u_1, \dots, u_m)}{\partial(x_1, \dots, x_n)}(\mathbf{z}) = \begin{bmatrix} \dfrac{\partial u_1}{\partial x_1}(\mathbf{z}) & \dfrac{\partial u_1}{\partial x_2}(\mathbf{z}) & \cdots & \dfrac{\partial u_n}{\partial x_n}(\mathbf{z}) \\ \dfrac{\partial u_2}{\partial x_1}(\mathbf{z}) & \dfrac{\partial u_2}{\partial x_2}(\mathbf{z}) & \cdots & \dfrac{\partial u_2}{\partial x_n}(\mathbf{z}) \\ \vdots & & & \\ \dfrac{\partial u_m}{\partial x_1}(\mathbf{z}) & & \cdots & \dfrac{\partial u_m}{\partial x_n}(\mathbf{z}) \end{bmatrix}$$

is termed the *Jacobian matrix* of $\mathbf{f}(\cdot)$ at $\mathbf{z}$. For the case $m = n$, the determinant

$$J(\mathbf{z}) = |\mathbf{J}(\mathbf{z})| = \left| \frac{\partial(u_1, \dots, u_m)}{\partial(x_1, \dots, x_n)}(\mathbf{z}) \right|$$

is called the *Jacobian* of $\mathbf{f}(\cdot)$ at $\mathbf{z}$.

Definition 8-2 Singular point of the Jacobian. A point $\mathbf{z}_0$ is a singular point of the transformation $\mathbf{f}(\cdot)$ iff $J(\mathbf{z}_0) = 0$.

Example 8-5. Consider the transformation from polar to Cartesian coordinates as given by

$$x = x(r, \theta) = r \cos \theta$$

$$y = y(r, \theta) = r \sin \theta$$

(*a*) Calculate the differential of the transformation at the point $(2, \pi/4)$.
(*b*) Calculate the Jacobian of the transformation and determine all singular points.

Solution. Let $f(r, \theta) = x(r, \theta)\hat{\imath} + y(r, \theta)\hat{\jmath}$.

(*a*) The differential of $\mathbf{f}(\cdot)$ at the point $(2, \pi/4)$ is given by

$$d\mathbf{f}\left(2, \frac{\pi}{4}\right) = \left. \begin{bmatrix} \dfrac{\partial x}{\partial r} & \dfrac{\partial x}{\partial \theta} \\ \dfrac{\partial y}{\partial r} & \dfrac{\partial y}{\partial \theta} \end{bmatrix} \begin{pmatrix} dr \\ d\theta \end{pmatrix} \right|_{(r,\theta)=(2,\pi/4)}$$

$$= \begin{bmatrix} \cos\theta & -r \sin\theta \\ \sin\theta & r\cos\theta \end{bmatrix} \begin{pmatrix} dr \\ d\theta \end{pmatrix}$$

$$= \frac{\sqrt{2}}{2} \begin{bmatrix} 1 & 2 \\ 1 & 2 \end{bmatrix} \begin{pmatrix} dr \\ d\theta \end{pmatrix}$$

(*b*) The Jacobian of the transformation is

$$J(r, \theta) = \begin{vmatrix} \cos\theta & -r\sin\theta \\ \sin\theta & r\cos\theta \end{vmatrix} = r$$

and we conclude that $r = 0$ is the only singular point of the transformation, a fact we previously noted in Chap. 1.

We continued our discussion of Jacobians with some comments and definitions concerning the inverse of a transformation.

Definition 8-3 Univalence (one-to-oneness) of a Transformation. A transformation $\mathbf{f}(\cdot)$ is univalent on a domain $\mathscr{D} \subset \mathbb{R}^n$ iff distinct points of $\mathscr{D}$ have distinct images; that is, iff $\mathbf{f}(\mathbf{z}_1) = \mathbf{f}(\mathbf{z}_2)$ implies $\mathbf{z}_1 = \mathbf{z}_2$.

Definition 8-4 Inverse transformation. Suppose the transformation $\mathbf{f}(\cdot)$ is univalent on some domain $\mathscr{D}$. Let $\mathbf{f}(\mathscr{D}) = \mathscr{R}$ be the image of $\mathscr{D}$ in $\mathbb{R}^m$ under the mapping $\mathbf{f}(\cdot)$. Let $\mathbf{f}^{-1}(\cdot)$: $\mathbb{R}^m \to \mathbb{R}^n$ be the transformation whose value at $\mathbf{w} \in \mathscr{R}$ is the point $\mathbf{z} \in \mathscr{D}$ for which $\mathbf{f}(\mathbf{z}) = \mathbf{w}$. Then $\mathbf{f}^{-1}(\cdot)$ has the domain $\mathscr{R}$ and

$$\mathbf{f}^{-1}[\mathbf{f}(\mathbf{z})] = \mathbf{z} \qquad \text{and} \qquad \mathbf{f}\left[\mathbf{f}^{-1}(\mathbf{w})\right] = \mathbf{w}$$

for every $\mathbf{z} \in \mathscr{D}$ and every $\mathbf{w} \in \mathscr{R}$. The transformation $\mathbf{f}^{-1}(\cdot)$ is called the inverse of $\mathbf{f}(\cdot)$.

Remark 8-1. Note that the concepts of univalence and inverse do not require $m = n$.

At this point we are mathematically equipped to deal with a number of important theorems. We shall, however, proceed in a less formal fashion by simply stating some implications and properties.

For $m = n$ the inverse transformation also has an associated Jacobian. We shall denote this Jacobian by

$$j(\mathbf{w}) = \left| \frac{\partial(x_1, \ldots, x_n)}{\partial(u_1, \ldots, u_n)}(\mathbf{w}) \right| = \begin{vmatrix} \dfrac{\partial x_1}{\partial u_1}(\mathbf{w}) & \cdots & \dfrac{\partial x_1}{\partial u_n}(\mathbf{w}) \\ \vdots & & \vdots \\ \dfrac{\partial x_n}{\partial u_1}(\mathbf{w}) & \cdots & \dfrac{\partial x_n}{\partial u_n}(\mathbf{w}) \end{vmatrix} \tag{8-4}$$

It turns out that the Jacobian of the inverse transformation is the reciprocal of that of the transformation. We have

$$J(\mathbf{z}) = \frac{1}{j(\mathbf{w})}$$

where $\mathbf{w} = \mathbf{f}(\mathbf{z})$ must be kept in mind.

If a transformation $\mathbf{f}(\cdot)$ is differentiable at $\mathbf{z}_0 \in \mathscr{D}$ and the Jacobian $J(\mathbf{z}_0) \neq 0$, then the differential of the transformation $\mathbf{f}(\cdot)$ at $\mathbf{z}_0$ is given by

$$d\mathbf{f}(\mathbf{z}_0) = J(\mathbf{z}_0)\, d\mathbf{z}$$

As before, an implication of the existence of the differential is that it may serve as a linear transformation at $\mathbf{z}_0$, which may be used as an approximation to the change in the transformation itself; that is,

$$\Delta\mathbf{f} = \begin{pmatrix} \Delta f_1 \\ \Delta f_2 \\ \vdots \\ \Delta f_m \end{pmatrix} = J(\mathbf{z}_0) \begin{pmatrix} \Delta x_1 \\ \Delta x_2 \\ \vdots \\ \Delta x_n \end{pmatrix}$$

serves to approximate the difference $\mathbf{f}(\mathbf{z}) - \mathbf{f}(\mathbf{z}_0)$ for $\mathbf{z}$ close to $\mathbf{z}_0$.

Finally, we note that a transformation is said to be of class C^r (mathematicians have a penchant for using hearsay) if all of its component functions are of class C^r, where C^r is the space of all functions with continuous rth derivative. If a transformation $\mathbf{f}(\cdot)$ from an open set $\mathscr{D}$ into $\mathbb{R}^n$ is of class C^r, $r \geq 1$, and if $J(\mathbf{z}) \neq 0$ for every $\mathbf{z} \in \mathscr{D}$, then for any $\mathbf{z}_0 \in \mathscr{D}$ there exists a neighborhood of $\mathbf{z}_0$ at which (1) $\mathbf{f}(\cdot)$ is univalent and (2) the inverse of $\mathbf{f}(\cdot)$ exists and is also of class C^r. This is the essence of the infamous inverse function theorem.

Example 8-6. Consider again the transformation $\mathbf{f}(\cdot)$ defined by

$$x = x(r, \theta) = r \cos \theta$$

$$y = y(r, \theta) = r \sin \theta$$

and suppose we restrict our discussion to $x > 0$, to simplify the discussion.

(a) Determine the inverse transformation, state where it exists, and show that

$$\mathbf{f}^{-1}[\mathbf{f}(r, \theta)] = (r\ \theta)^T$$

(b) Show that the Jacobians of the transformations are reciprocals of one another.

Solution

(a) The inverse transformation is given by

$$r = r(x, y) = \sqrt{x^2 + y^2}$$

$$\theta = \theta(x, y) = \text{Arctan}\ \frac{y}{x}$$

or, we may write

$$\mathbf{f}^{-1}(x, y) = \begin{pmatrix} \sqrt{x^2 + y^2} \\ \text{Arctan}\ \dfrac{y}{x} \end{pmatrix}$$

We then have

$$\mathbf{f}^{-1}[\mathbf{f}(r,\theta)] = \mathbf{f}^{-1}[x(r,\theta), y(r,\theta)]$$

$$= \begin{pmatrix} \sqrt{(r\cos\theta)^2 + (r\sin\theta)^2} \\ \operatorname{Arctan}\dfrac{r\sin\theta}{r\cos\theta} \end{pmatrix} = \begin{pmatrix} r \\ \theta \end{pmatrix}$$

The inverse transformation exists everywhere for $x > 0$.

(*b*) The Jacobian of the inverse transformation is

$$j(x,y) = \begin{vmatrix} \dfrac{\partial r}{\partial x} & \dfrac{\partial r}{\partial y} \\ \dfrac{\partial \theta}{\partial x} & \dfrac{\partial \theta}{\partial y} \end{vmatrix} = \begin{vmatrix} \dfrac{x}{\sqrt{x^2+y^2}} & \dfrac{y}{\sqrt{x^2+y^2}} \\ \dfrac{-y}{x^2+y^2} & \dfrac{x}{x^2+y^2} \end{vmatrix} = \frac{1}{\sqrt{x^2+y^2}}$$

and we have

$$j(x,y) = \frac{1}{J(r,\theta)} = \frac{1}{r} = \frac{1}{\sqrt{x^2+y^2}}$$

Clearly, we have only touched upon this important topic of transformations and differential geometry. The treatment suffices for the intended applications in robot dynamics. For a more in-depth study of the topic, we recommend our desk references, Fleming[1] and Taylor,[2] which are well-nigh classics on this material.

8-1-3 The Denavit-Hartenberg Matrix

The basis for our discussion here is the paper by Denavit and Hartenberg previously cited in Chap. 2. The homogeneous rigid body motion matrices introduced there were informal DH matrices; we now formalize the concept.

The general framework is that of a kinematic chain, although such a broad generality is not needed in most practical applications. In essence, we simply have a sequence of links interconnected by various types of joints, two of which are in most common usage: *revolute joints*, which are hinges, and *prismatic joints*, which allow a link to slide in a sleeve. In this manner each joint either slides or rotates, as shown in Fig. 8-5. For a given manipulator there may be n links progressing from the base B to the end effector E. The objective is a unified notational approach presenting the motion of the end effector E with respect to the fixed base B—that is, the absolute motion of E.

We shall take the kinematic chain to consist of n joints and n links connected by revolute or prismatic joints. Although not actually a link, the base of the manipulator is taken to be the link "0" with link 1 connected to the base link by joint 1. This numbering continues until the tool point E, some characteristic point for the end effector, is reached.

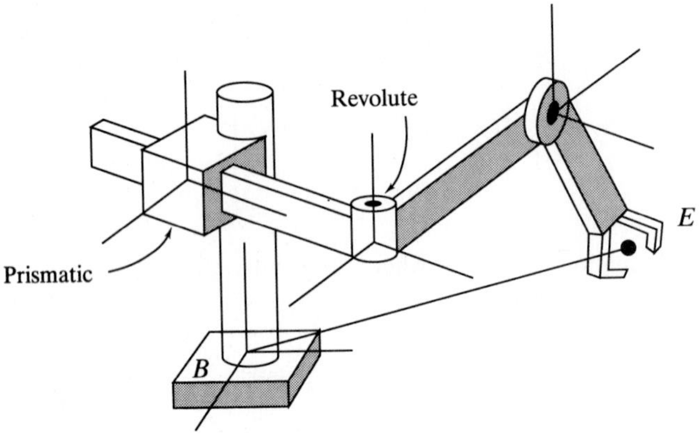

FIGURE 8-5
Revolute and prismatic joints.

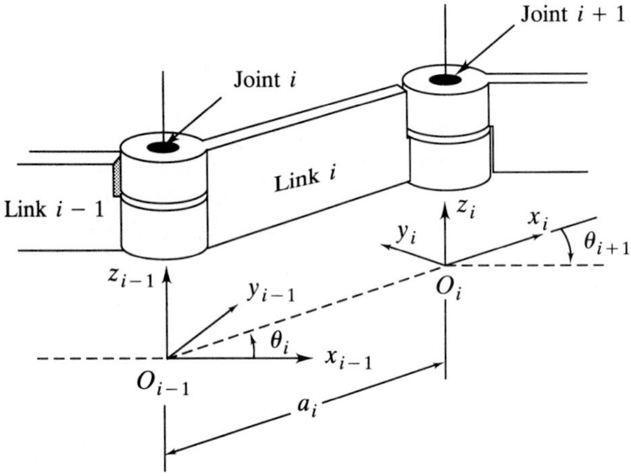

FIGURE 8-6
A succession of revolute joints.

We now define the Denavit-Hartenberg (DH) parameters for a given chain. We begin with a simple arrangement of revolute joints and then proceed to include prismatic ones. At joint i, we place the reference frame $(0xyz)_{i-1}$ with the z_{i-1}-axis as the joint axis, with x_{i-1} aligned with the link $i-1$, and with the y_{i-1}-axis simply chosen perpendicular to both of these in accordance with the right-hand rule. All of this is shown in Fig. 8-6. The length of the link i is denoted by a_i.

In this context the only actively controlled robot variables are the θ_i, the rotations of the links about the joint axes. The homogeneous transformations relating the successive reference frames are denoted by the matrices $\mathbf{H}_{i-1,i}$, as in Chap. 2. Based on Fig. 8-6, for example, the homogeneous relative rigid motion of $(0xyz)_i$ with respect to $(0xyz)_{i-1}$ is given by the matrix

$$\mathbf{H}_{i-1,i} = \begin{bmatrix} C\theta_i & -S\theta_i & 0 & a_i C\theta_i \\ S\theta_i & C\theta_i & 0 & a_i S\theta_i \\ 0 & 0 & 1 & 0 \\ 0 & 0 & 0 & 1 \end{bmatrix} \tag{8-5}$$

It is useful to keep in mind that this is the matrix of the linear transformation for which

$$\mathbf{r}_{i-1} = \mathbf{H}_{i-1,i}\mathbf{r}_i$$

is the case. These relative rigid motion matrices are eventually multiplied together to yield the absolute rigid motion matrix for the frame $(0xyz)_i$ with respect to the base frame $(0xyz)_0$. Indeed, we have

$$\mathbf{H}_i = \prod_{k=1}^{i} \mathbf{H}_{k-1,k} \qquad \text{with} \quad \mathbf{r}_0 = \mathbf{H}_i \mathbf{r}_i$$

We now expand our discussion to include the simple prismatic joint as shown in Fig. 8-7. The actively controlled variable for this joint is d_i, here the distance from O_{i-1} to O_i as measured along the z_{i-1}-axis. The corresponding relationship between vectors in the two reference frames is given by the pure

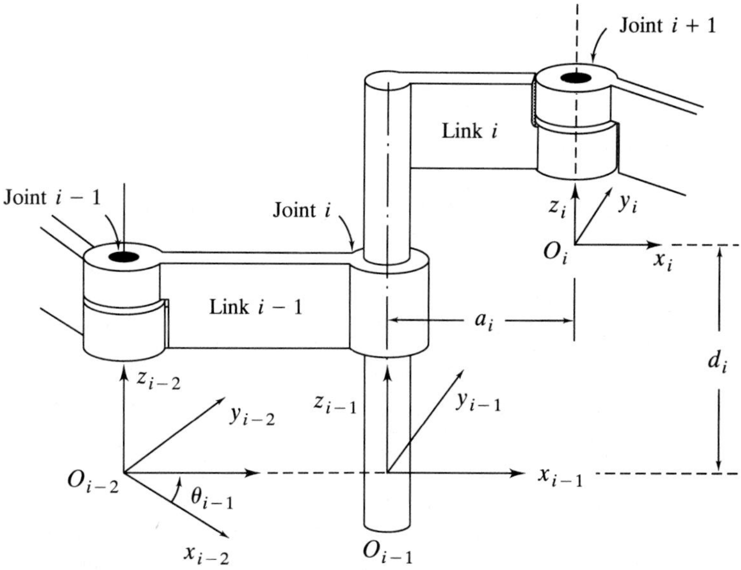

FIGURE 8-7
A prismatic joint.

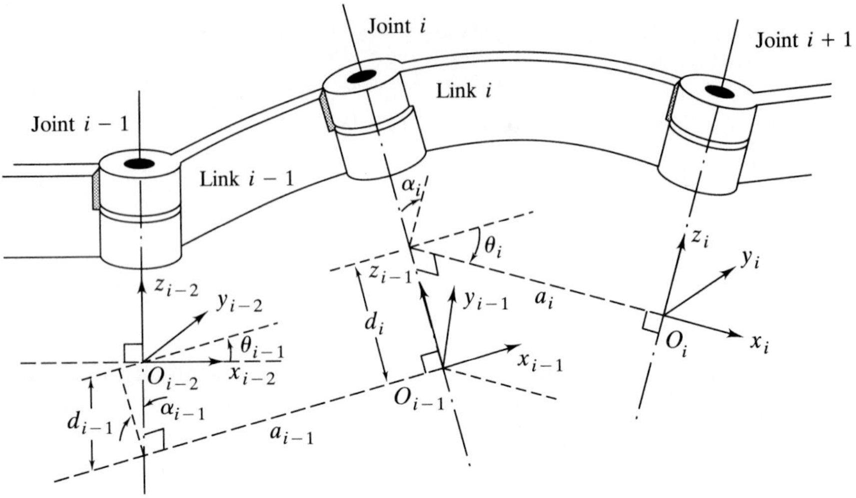

FIGURE 8-8
The DH parameters.

translation

$$\mathbf{H}_{i-1,i} = \begin{bmatrix} 1 & 0 & 0 & 0 \\ 0 & 1 & 0 & 0 \\ 0 & 0 & 1 & d_i \\ 0 & 0 & 0 & 1 \end{bmatrix} \tag{8-6}$$

The completely general case for the DH parameters and for the notation for kinematic chains is illustrated in Fig. 8-8. It is common to express the forward kinematics of a particular manipulator in terms of these parameters. We thus provide a short description of their use and evaluation. There are four DH parameters which we shall discuss in sequence:

θ_i the angle between links; the angle of link i is relative to link $i-1$; the rotation is a rotation about the z_{i-1}-axis with counterclockwise (as viewed along the z_{i-1}-axis toward the origin) as a positive rotation; it generally is the actively controlled variable for the revolute joint i.

a_i the "length" of the ith link; more precisely, in the general context which allows twisted links, it is the perpendicular distance from the joint axis $i-1$ to the joint axis i. Such a perpendicular distance always exists for nonintersecting lines. When two consecutive joint axes intersect, $a_i = 0$; the origins of the two reference frames are then taken to coincide at the intersection of the axes with the x_i-axis taken to be normal to the plane formed by z_i and z_{i-1}. When the joint axes $i-1$ and i are parallel, then the z_i- and z_{i-1}-axes are parallel, and we may place the origins anywhere on the joint axis, a common placement being one that aligns with a previous or subsequent normal distance.

d_i the "vertical" distance between links; more specifically, the distance between the x_{i-1}-axis and the x_i-axis as measured along the z_{i-1}-axis. For prismatic joints it may be the actively controlled variable.

α_i the twist of the ith link; the rotation of the z_i-axis relative to the z_{i-1}-axis measured as a rotation about the x_i-axis.

Figure 8-8, together with the descriptions, should provide a relatively clear picture of the meaning and purpose of the individual DH parameters. It may sound simple enough to specify a_i as the minimum distance between the joint axes (it is) and the alignment of the x-axis of the ith frame with this connecting line segment; this may, however, be rather messy and awkward in practice. We illustrate with an exercise from analytic geometry.

Example 8-7. The parametric equations of the two joint axes are

$$\begin{aligned} x &= 2t_1 - 4 \\ y &= -t_1 + 4 \\ z &= -2t_1 - 1 \end{aligned} \qquad \text{and} \qquad \begin{aligned} x &= 4t_2 - 5 \\ y &= -3t_2 + 5 \\ z &= -5t_2 + 5 \end{aligned}$$

all with respect to a common $(0xyx)$ frame.

(a) Determine the minimum distance between these two lines.

(b) Determine the location of this minimizing line segment and sketch the result.

Solution

(a) Suppose we simply take it for granted that the line segment perpendicular to both lines is the shortest line segment connecting the lines. The length of that line segment is given by

$$d = |\boldsymbol{r} \cdot \hat{\boldsymbol{n}}|$$

where $\boldsymbol{r}$ is any vector connecting the two lines and $\hat{\boldsymbol{n}}$ is a unit vector whose direction is perpendicular to both lines; that is,

$$\hat{\boldsymbol{n}} = \frac{\boldsymbol{a}_1 \times \boldsymbol{a}_2}{|\boldsymbol{a}_1 \times \boldsymbol{a}_2|}$$

with $\boldsymbol{a}_1$ and $\boldsymbol{a}_2$ parallel to the corresponding lines. We have

$$\boldsymbol{a}_1 = 2\hat{\imath} - \hat{\jmath} - 2\hat{k}$$

$$\boldsymbol{a}_2 = 4\hat{\imath} - 3\hat{\jmath} - 5\hat{k}$$

and hence

$$\hat{n} = \tfrac{1}{3}(-\hat{\imath} + 2\hat{\jmath} - 2\hat{k})$$

An obvious vector connecting the two lines is given by

$$r = -\hat{\imath} + \hat{\jmath} + 6\hat{k}$$

connecting the points with $t_1 = t_2 = 0$. From this follows

$$d = |r \cdot \hat{n}| = \left|(-\hat{\imath} + \hat{\jmath} + 6\hat{k}) \cdot (-\hat{\imath} + 2\hat{\jmath} - 2\hat{k})\tfrac{1}{3}\right|$$

$$= \tfrac{1}{3}|1 + 2 - 12| = 3$$

Note that this traditional approach has provided no direct information on the location of the minimizing line segment.

(*b*) We may now continue the traditional approach with

$$|\hat{a}_1 \times r_{12}(t_2)| = 3$$

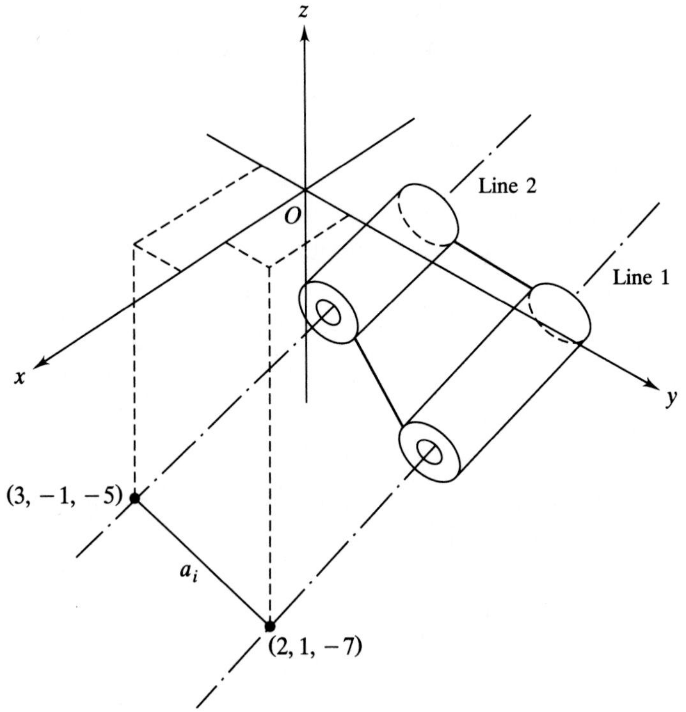

FIGURE 8-9
The shortest distance between two nonintersecting, nonparallel lines.

where $\hat{a}_1$ is a unit vector in the direction of the first line and $r_{12}(t_2)$ is a vector from an arbitrary fixed point on line 1 to any point (as a function of t_2) on line 2; t_1 may be similarly determined.

It is far more instructive to use an optimization approach, where the necessary conditions for optimality yield the desired values for t_1 and t_2 and hence for the corresponding x, y, and z's. We pose: Minimize

$$\begin{aligned} d(t_1, t_2) &= (x(t_1) - x(t_2))^2 + (y(t_1) - y(t_2))^2 + (z(t_1) - z(t_2))^2 \\ &= (2t_1 - 4t_2 + 1)^2 + (-t_1 + 3t_2 - 1)^2 + (-2t_1 + 5t_2 - 6)^2 \end{aligned}$$

with unconstrained (t_1, t_2). The use of standard first-order necessary conditions yields

$$\frac{\partial d}{\partial t_1}(t_1^*, t_2^*) = 0 \quad \Rightarrow \quad 9t_1^* - 21t_2^* = -15$$

$$\frac{\partial d}{\partial t_2}(t_1^*, t_2^*) = 0 \quad \Rightarrow \quad -21t_1^* + 50t_2^* = 37$$

with $t_1^* = 3$, $t_2^* = 2$, so that the intersection with line 1 is $(2, 1, -7)$ and that with line 2 is $(3, -1, -5)$. The results are illustrated in Fig. 8-9.

This background suffices to present some formal definitions of specific transformations used in connection with manipulators. All of them, of course, are ultimately equivalent to rigid body motions as defined in Chap. 2. We first define the Denavit-Hartenberg matrix which steps us from joint to joint, followed by the definition of the forward kinematics of a manipulator.

Definition 8-5 Denavit-Hartenberg matrix. The DH matrix consists of the following basic transformations taken in accordance with Fig. 8-8:

(i) Rotation by an amount θ_i about the z_{i-1}-axis:

$$\mathbf{A}_{i-1,i}(z_{i-1}, \theta_i)$$

(ii) Translation along the z_{i-1}-axis by the amount d_i:

$$\mathbf{T}(0, 0, d_i)$$

(iii) Twist about the x_i-axis by the amount α_i:

$$\mathbf{A}_{i-1,i}(x_i, \alpha_i)$$

(iv) Translation along the x_i-axis by the amount a_i:

$$\mathbf{T}(a_i, 0, 0)$$

The DH matrix then is given by (with some abuse of notation)

$$\mathbf{H}_{i-1,i} = \mathbf{A}_{i-1,i}(z_{i-1},\theta_i)\mathbf{T}(0,0,d_i)\mathbf{A}_{i-1,i}(x_i,\alpha_i)\mathbf{T}(a_i,0,0)$$

$$= \begin{bmatrix} C\theta_i & -S\theta_i & 0 & 0 \\ S\theta_i & C\theta_i & 0 & 0 \\ 0 & 0 & 1 & 0 \\ 0 & 0 & 0 & 1 \end{bmatrix} \begin{bmatrix} 1 & 0 & 0 & 0 \\ 0 & 1 & 0 & 0 \\ 0 & 0 & 1 & d_i \\ 0 & 0 & 0 & 1 \end{bmatrix}$$

$$\times \begin{bmatrix} 1 & 0 & 0 & 0 \\ 0 & C\alpha_i & -S\alpha_i & 0 \\ 0 & S\alpha_i & C\alpha_i & 0 \\ 0 & 0 & 0 & 1 \end{bmatrix} \begin{bmatrix} 1 & 0 & 0 & a_i \\ 0 & 1 & 0 & 0 \\ 0 & 0 & 1 & 0 \\ 0 & 0 & 0 & 1 \end{bmatrix}$$

$$= \begin{bmatrix} C\theta_i & -S\theta_i C\alpha_i & S\theta_i S\alpha_i & a_i C\theta_i \\ S\theta_i & C\theta_i C\alpha_i & -C\theta_i S\alpha_i & a_i S\theta_i \\ 0 & S\alpha_i & C\alpha_i & d_i \\ 0 & 0 & 0 & 1 \end{bmatrix}$$

Remark 8-2. It must be noted that it is sometimes convenient to introduce links of zero length a_i in this context, for example, in connection with some manipulator "wrists." The link twist α_i also is often 0. Finally, the robot variables θ_i and d_i may, of course, be identically 0 or may take on zero value for some specific time.

We continue with the description of the forward kinematics of the robot.

Definition 8-6 Forward kinematics. Suppose a manipulator consists of n ordered links and joints, beginning with joint 0 as the connection to the base reference frame $(0xyz)_0$. The joints are numbered consecutively with a reference frame $(0xyz)_i$ at each joint. The last reference frame $(0xyz)_n$ is located at the tool point E. Let $\mathbf{H}_{i-1,i}$ denote the DH matrix relating joint $i-1$ to joint i. Then the absolute motion matrix

$$\mathbf{H}_n = \prod_{i=1}^{n} \mathbf{H}_{i-1,i}$$

is termed the *forward kinematics* of the particular manipulator.

Until now we have taken E to be the end effector or tool point without making this terminology precise. It is common to take the origin of the nth reference frame to be located at some characteristic point of the end effector or gripper of the robot, as illustrated in Fig. 8-10. With the approach of a tool to a workpiece in mind, $\hat{k}_n$ is taken to be the approach vector $\hat{a}$ and $\hat{j}_n$ is the orientation vector $\hat{o}$; no special name is given to $\hat{n} = \hat{o} \times \hat{a}$. Collectively, $(0xyz)_n$ is also termed the hand frame. The usefulness of this viewpoint, of course, lies in our being able to define the tool orientation along with the specification of

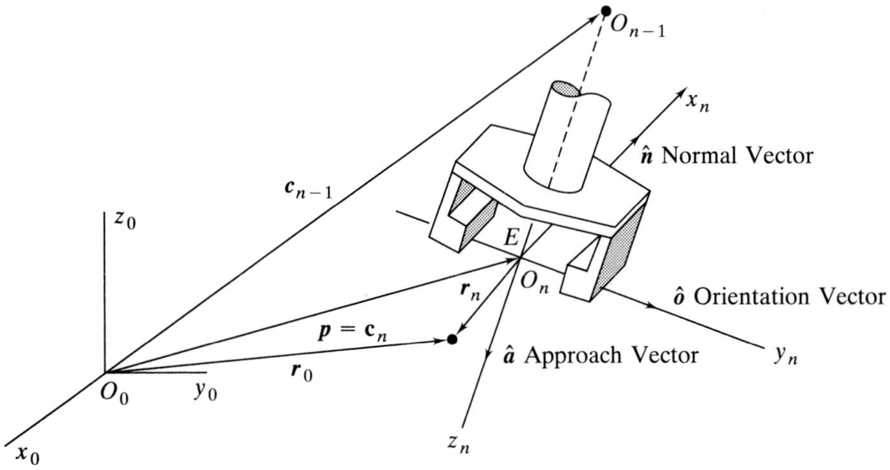

FIGURE 8-10
The hand frame.

the trajectory to be followed by the tool point E. All of our previous examples dealt only with the motion of the tool point.

The present terminology relates to the notation in Chap. 2 in the following manner. The vector $\boldsymbol{p}$ is the same as $\boldsymbol{c}_n$ so that

$$\boldsymbol{c}_n = \boldsymbol{p} = p_x\hat{\boldsymbol{\imath}}_0 + p_y\hat{\boldsymbol{\jmath}}_0 + p_z\hat{\boldsymbol{k}}_0$$

The remaining vectors have the form

$$\hat{\boldsymbol{n}} = n_x\hat{\boldsymbol{\imath}}_0 + n_y\hat{\boldsymbol{\jmath}}_0 + n_z\hat{\boldsymbol{k}}_0$$

$$\hat{\boldsymbol{o}} = o_x\hat{\boldsymbol{\imath}}_0 + o_y\hat{\boldsymbol{\jmath}}_0 + o_z\hat{\boldsymbol{k}}_0$$

$$\hat{\boldsymbol{a}} = a_x\hat{\boldsymbol{\imath}}_0 + a_y\hat{\boldsymbol{\jmath}}_0 + a_z\hat{\boldsymbol{k}}_0$$

locating the x_n-axis, y_n-axis, and z_n-axis with respect to $(0xyz)_0$. For example, since the components of $\hat{\boldsymbol{o}}$ locate the y_n-axis, they must correspond to the second column of the rotation matrix (2-19) with

$$b_{x_0y_n} = o_x \qquad b_{y_0y_n} = o_y \qquad b_{z_0y_n} = o_z$$

If we imagine $(0xyz)_n$ to be embedded in a rigid body, then the vectors $\boldsymbol{p}$, $\hat{\boldsymbol{n}}$, $\hat{\boldsymbol{o}}$, and $\hat{\boldsymbol{a}}$ completely specify the *position* and *orientation* of the body in 3-space.

Definition 8-7 Hand matrix. Let $\boldsymbol{p}$ be the position vector of the tool point E and let unit vectors $\hat{\boldsymbol{n}}$, $\hat{\boldsymbol{o}}$, and $\hat{\boldsymbol{a}}$ be defined as before. Then the matrix

$$\mathbf{H} = \begin{bmatrix} n_x & o_x & a_x & p_x \\ n_y & o_y & a_y & p_y \\ n_z & o_z & a_z & p_z \\ 0 & 0 & 0 & 1 \end{bmatrix}$$

is termed the *hand matrix* of the robot.

Typically, trajectory planning will provide the entries of this matrix as functions of time. The following example illustrates a possible specification for the hand matrix.

Example 8-8. Determine the hand matrix if the manipulator tool point in Fig. 8-11 is to move along the line

$$x = 0$$
$$y = y(t)$$
$$z = 2$$

and if the indicated gripper orientation is to be maintained.

Solution. We have

$$\hat{\boldsymbol{n}} = 1\hat{\boldsymbol{j}}_0 \qquad \hat{\boldsymbol{o}} = 1\hat{\boldsymbol{i}}_0 \qquad \hat{\boldsymbol{a}} = -1\hat{\boldsymbol{k}}_0$$

$$p_x = 0 \qquad p_y = y(t) \quad p_z = 2$$

The hand matrix is thus given by

$$\mathbf{H} = \begin{bmatrix} 0 & 1 & 0 & 0 \\ 1 & 0 & 0 & y(t) \\ 0 & 0 & -1 & 2 \\ 0 & 0 & 0 & 1 \end{bmatrix}$$

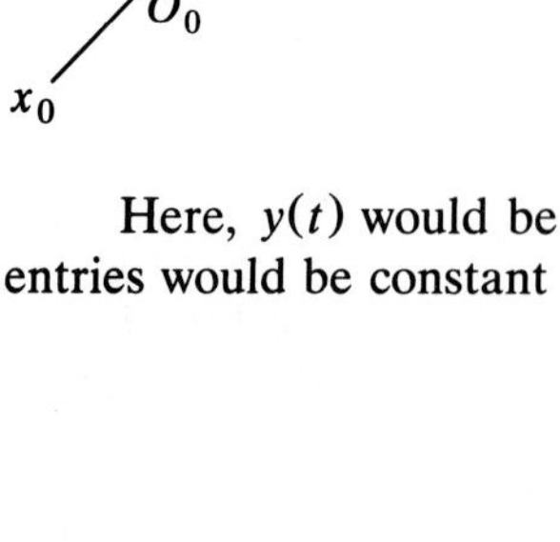

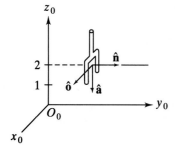

FIGURE 8-11
Specification of the hand matrix.

Here, $y(t)$ would be prescribed as a function of time, and the remaining entries would be constant throughout the motion. Since we generally require

$$\mathbf{H} = \mathbf{H}_n = \prod_{i=1}^{n} \mathbf{H}_{i-1,i}$$

these specified entries may be used to obtain relationships among the robot variables when solving the inverse kinematics problem.

We have simply illustrated the hand matrix as the last link orientation. This suppresses the fact that the last three links of manipulators generally serve to provide the wristlike action for the orientation of the hand frame. We shall not deal with this aspect here in order to reduce the algebraic complexity.

The next two examples illustrate the use of the DH matrices in writing the forward kinematics of manipulators. The first is an academic example; the second deals with a commercial SCARA model robot. Additional applications are provided in the exercises.

Example 8-9. You are given the manipulator in Fig. 8-12 with joint reference frames as shown. The placement of several reference frames along a given joint axis implies the coincidence of the origins unless appropriate DH parameters have been specified. Note also that the gripper orientation is fixed with θ_3 as the only controllable motion of the gripper.

(*a*) Establish the connecting DH matrices for the reference frames indicated.
(*b*) Determine the forward kinematics for the manipulator.
(*c*) Tabulate the DH parameters for this manipulator.

Solution

(*a*) The connecting DH matrices are easily established as

$$\mathbf{H}_{01} = \begin{bmatrix} C\theta_1 & 0 & S\theta_1 & RC\theta_1 \\ S\theta_1 & 0 & -C\theta_1 & RS\theta_1 \\ 0 & 1 & 0 & 0 \\ 0 & 0 & 0 & 1 \end{bmatrix} \qquad \mathbf{H}_{12} = \begin{bmatrix} C\theta_2 & -S\theta_2 & 0 & L_1C\theta_2 \\ S\theta_2 & C\theta_2 & 0 & L_1S\theta_2 \\ 0 & 0 & 1 & 0 \\ 0 & 0 & 0 & 1 \end{bmatrix}$$

$$\mathbf{H}_{23} = \begin{bmatrix} C\theta_3 & -S\theta_3 & 0 & L_2C\theta_3 \\ S\theta_3 & C\theta_3 & 0 & L_2S\theta_3 \\ 0 & 0 & 1 & 0 \\ 0 & 0 & 0 & 1 \end{bmatrix}$$

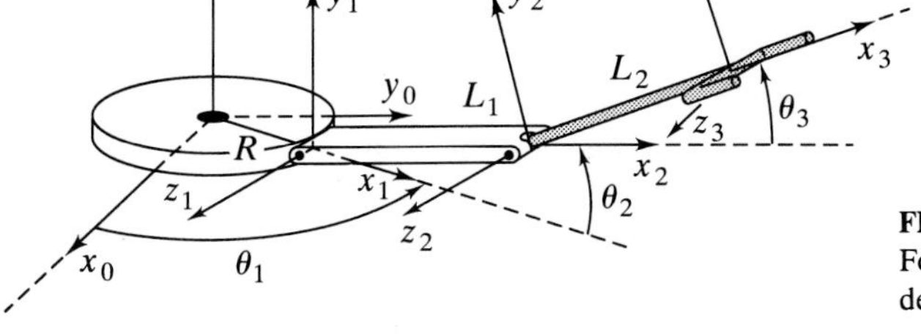

FIGURE 8-12
Forward kinematics for an academic manipulator.

TABLE 8-1

Link	Variable	θ_i	α_i	a_i	d_i
1	θ_1	θ_1	90°	R	0
2	θ_2	θ_2	0	L_1	0
3	θ_3	θ_3	0	L_2	0

(*b*) These may be multiplied together to yield the following forward kinematics for the manipulator:

$$\mathbf{H}_3 = \mathbf{H}_{01}\mathbf{H}_{12}\mathbf{H}_{23}$$

$$= \begin{bmatrix} C\theta_1 C(\theta_2+\theta_3) & -C\theta_1 S(\theta_2+\theta_3) & S\theta_1 & C\theta_1[L_2C(\theta_2+\theta_3)+L_1C\theta_2+R] \\ S\theta_1 C(\theta_2+\theta_3) & -S\theta_1 S(\theta_2+\theta_3) & -C\theta_1 & S\theta_1[L_2C(\theta_2+\theta_3)+L_1C\theta_2+R] \\ S(\theta_2+\theta_3) & C(\theta_2+\theta_3) & 0 & L_2S(\theta_2+\theta_3)+L_1C\theta_2 \\ 0 & 0 & 0 & 1 \end{bmatrix}$$

(*c*) Rather than multiplying together all of these matrices, it is common to simply tabulate the DH parameters for a particular robot in a table such as Table 8-1. The individual matrices may then be written down when needed.

Example 8-10 The AdeptOne. The AdeptOne is a five-axis SCARA configuration robot produced by Adept Technology, Inc. This particular industrial robot was selected because of the relative simplicity of its dynamics and its wide range of application, and—last, but not least—because of the company's geographical proximity. To some extent, we shall follow a paper by Goel[3] to allow the reader easy access to additional material about this particular robot.

Note that the robot exhibits the previously mentioned separation into sets of axes: those that provide the basic arm motion and those that serve to position and orient the gripper. The first two axes here accomplish the former task; the following three axes, the latter. For the specified joint frames shown in Fig. 8-13:

(*a*) Tabulate the DH parameters for this robot.

(*b*) Determine the forward kinematics of the robot.

Solution

(*a*) The DH parameters for the robot are shown in Table 8-2.

(*b*) We relegate the specification and multiplication of the relevant matrices to an exercise. Here, we only state the final result. The forward kinematics of the

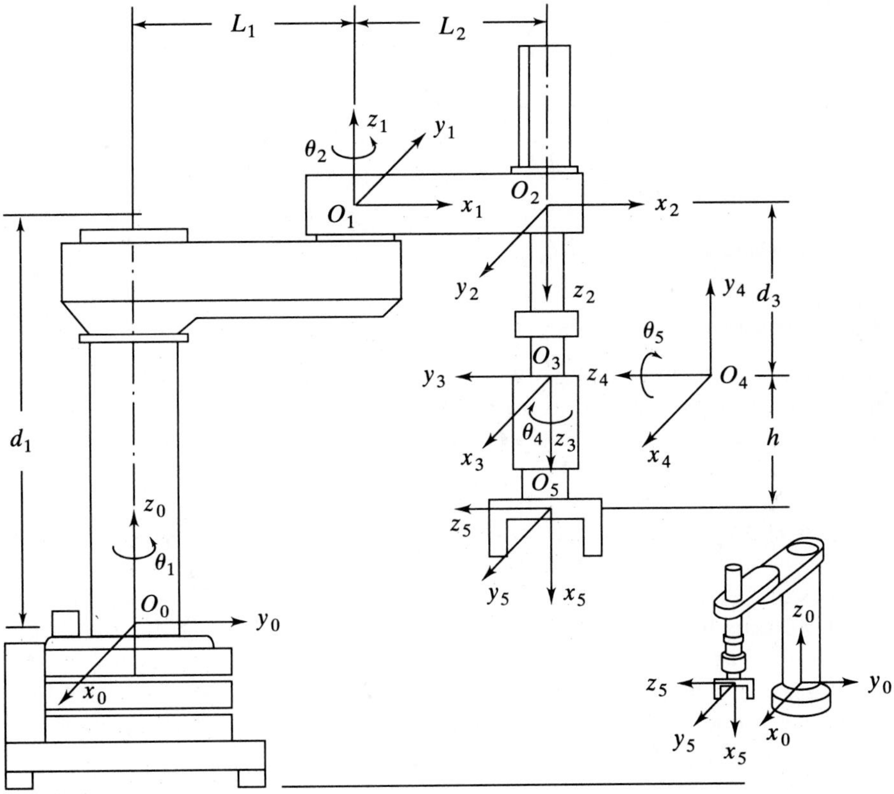

FIGURE 8-13
The AdeptOne. (The position in the bottom right corner corresponds to the robot variable values $\theta_1 = 0$, $\theta_2 = 0$, $\theta_4 = 0$, $\theta_5 = -90°$.)

TABLE 8-2

Link	Variable	θ_1	α_i	a_i	d_i
1	θ_1	θ_1	0	L_1	d_1
2	θ_2	θ_2	$-180°$	L_2	0
3	d_3	0	0	0	d_3
4	θ_4	θ_4	$-90°$	0	0
5	θ_5	θ_5	0	h	0

AdeptOne are

$$\mathbf{H}_5 = \mathbf{H}_{01}\mathbf{H}_{12}\mathbf{H}_{23}\mathbf{H}_{34}\mathbf{H}_{45}$$

$$= \begin{bmatrix} C\theta_5 C\psi & -S\theta_5 C\psi & S\psi & hC\theta_5 C\psi + L_2 C(\theta_1+\theta_2) + L_1 C\theta_1 \\ C\theta_5 S\psi & -S\theta_5 S\psi & -C\psi & hC\theta_5 S\psi + L_2 S(\theta_1+\theta_2) + L_1 S\theta_1 \\ S\theta_5 & C\theta_5 & 0 & hS\theta_5 - d_3 + d_1 \\ 0 & 0 & 0 & 1 \end{bmatrix} \tag{8-7}$$

where $\psi = \theta_1 + \theta_2 - \theta_4$.

8-1-4 Inverse Kinematics

As mentioned previously, the objective is the calculation of successive values of the robot variables required to maintain a specified trajectory and orientation of an object. For example, an object might have to be kept level while being transported from one point to another along some curve.

We summarize some of the viewpoints of this problem. In accordance with Chap. 1, we define the number of axes of a robot as the number of robot variables that are actively controlled. We recall that a rigid body in space has six degrees of freedom requiring six variables for their specification. For an n-axis robot we thus have a vector of n robot variables $\boldsymbol{\xi} = (\xi_1 \ldots \xi_n)^T$, a particular choice of which yields the object position and orientation designated by $\mathbf{w} = (x\,y\,z\,\alpha\,\beta\,\gamma)^T$, where α, β, and γ may be taken to be Eulerian angles for a reference frame with origin at (x, y, z) and embedded in the body. Formally, then, we may view the robot as a mapping

$$\mathbf{f}(\cdot): \mathbb{R}^n \to \mathbb{R}^6$$

such that

$$\mathbf{f}(\boldsymbol{\xi}) = \mathbf{w}$$

For the forward kinematics a choice of $\boldsymbol{\xi}$ yielded a corresponding world position and orientation $\mathbf{w}$.

Definition 8-8 Inverse kinematics. Given a trajectory $\mathbf{w}(t)$ in $\mathbb{R}^6$, the determination of a trajectory $\boldsymbol{\xi}(t)$ in $\mathbb{R}^n$ such that

$$\mathbf{f}(\boldsymbol{\xi}(t)) = \mathbf{w}(t)$$

is called the inverse kinematics problem for a specified manipulator.

We now make the meaning of this general statement more precise within the present context. Expressed in terms of the forward kinematics of a manipulator, we have the equation

$$\mathbf{r}_0(t) = \mathbf{H}_n(\boldsymbol{\xi}(t))\mathbf{r}_n(t)$$

relating the position of a point with respect to $(0xyz)_n$ to its position with respect to the base reference frame. When planning the robot's motion, it is common to specify the hand matrix of the robot, $\mathbf{H}(\mathbf{w}(t))$, as a function of time characterizing the position and orientation of the end effector. A specified hand matrix is then maintained with

$$\mathbf{H}_n(\boldsymbol{\xi}(t)) = \mathbf{H}(\mathbf{w}(t)) \tag{8-8}$$

and the entries of $\mathbf{H}_n$ are to be determined as a function of the entries of $\mathbf{H}$; in essence, we attempt to calculate $\boldsymbol{\xi}(\mathbf{w}(t))$.

Since $\mathbf{H}_n$ will differ from robot to robot, the solution of the inverse problem will generally require different approaches. Depending on the complexity of the robot configuration, this is often one of the most difficult aspects in the provision of a real-time response to the robot's sensory inputs. Closed form solutions to this problem will allow a considerably faster response than those obtained in some segmented fashion. For most practical manipulators such closed form solutions have been obtained.

Obviously, constraints may be imposed on either set of variables. Points $\mathbf{w}$ in space may be inaccessible because of obstructions; conversely, design restrictions on the robot variables $\boldsymbol{\xi}$ may result in corresponding limitations of the work space. In the end, however, once a *feasible* trajectory $\mathbf{w}(t)$ has been provided, the task consists of the determination of the corresponding $\boldsymbol{\xi}(t)$.

There are two relatively straightforward approaches to the solution of the problem, and we shall concentrate on these.

The first of these simply begins with (8-8). Theoretically, the equality provides 12 relationships between the matrix entries on both sides, not all of them independent. In some cases these equations suffice to obtain the desired closed form solutions.

The second method also begins with (8-8) in the expanded form

$$\mathbf{H}_n(\boldsymbol{\xi}) = \mathbf{H}_{01}(\xi_1)\mathbf{H}_{12}(\xi_2)\ldots\mathbf{H}_{n-1,n}(\xi_n) = \mathbf{H}(\mathbf{w})$$

The multiplication of both sides by $\mathbf{H}_{01}^{-1}(\xi_1)$ yields

$$\mathbf{H}_{12}(\xi_2)\ldots\mathbf{H}_{n-1,n}(\xi_n) = \mathbf{H}_{01}^{-1}(\xi_1)\mathbf{H}(\mathbf{w})$$

Hopefully, a comparison of selected entries on both sides will allow us to solve for ξ_1 in terms of the known entries of $\mathbf{H}(\mathbf{w})$ and the remaining variables ξ_i. Another premultiplication of the equation by the next inverse yields

$$\mathbf{H}_{23}(\xi_3)\ldots\mathbf{H}_{n-1,n}(\xi_n) = \mathbf{H}_{12}^{-1}(\xi_2)\mathbf{H}_{01}^{-1}(\xi_1)\mathbf{H}(\mathbf{w})$$

presumably allowing a solution for ξ_2 in terms of the known entries of $\mathbf{H}(\mathbf{w})$, $\xi_1(\mathbf{w}, \xi_i)$, and the remaining variables ξ_3 to ξ_n. The process continues until all of the inverses have been used or until all of the ξ_i have been obtained as functions of $\mathbf{w}$. The inverse DH matrix plays a prominent role in this approach. It is given by

$$\mathbf{H}_{i-1,i}^{-1} = \begin{bmatrix} C\theta_i & S\theta_i & 0 & -a_i \\ -S\theta_i C\alpha_i & C\theta_i C\alpha_i & S\alpha_i & -d_i S\alpha_i \\ S\theta_i S\alpha_i & -C\theta_i S\alpha_i & C\alpha_i & -d_i C\alpha_i \\ 0 & 0 & 0 & 1 \end{bmatrix} \tag{8-9}$$

In all of this algebraic formality, it is easy to lose sight of the geometric nature of this process. A visualization of the geometry is essential in gaining an understanding of these relationships.

Finally, how do we know that what we have computed is correct? We may spot-check by introducing some obvious configurations, or we may attempt to show directly that

$$\mathbf{H}_n(\boldsymbol{\xi}(\mathbf{w})) = \mathbf{H}(\mathbf{w})$$

We illustrate these methods with a continuation of our previous treatment of the AdeptOne robot.

Example 8-11. Obtain a closed form solution for the inverse kinematics problem of the AdeptOne robot using the approaches just discussed.

Solution. In line with our emphasis on geometric insight, we shall relate much of our discussion to the robot schematics shown in Fig. 8-14. In order to write the

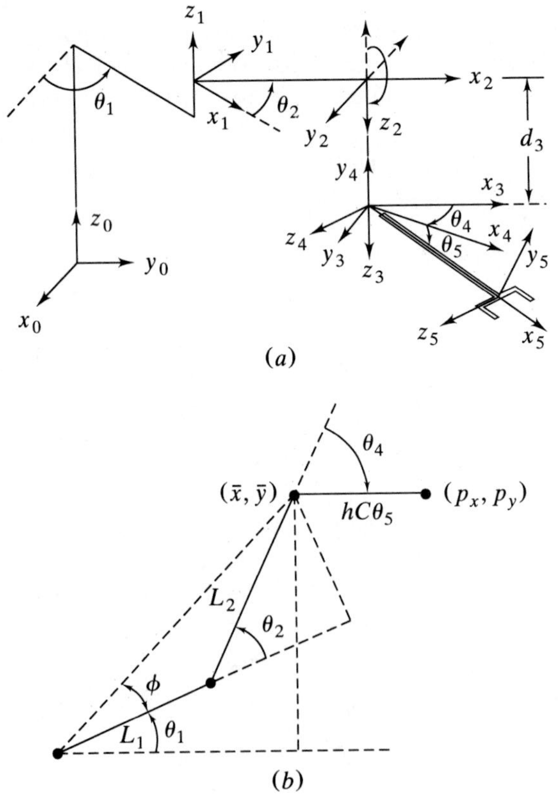

FIGURE 8-14
The stick AdeptOne: (*a*) overall configuration; (*b*) top view.

proper hand matrix for the manipulator, we first recall that the hand matrix as a rigid motion always has the form

$$\mathbf{H} = \begin{bmatrix} (x_n) & (y_n) & (z_n) & (p) \\ 0 & 0 & 0 & 1 \end{bmatrix}$$

where we have used (x_n) to denote the direction cosines of x_n, for example, and (p) to denote the coordinates of the tool point all with respect to $(0xyz)_0$. With reference to Fig. 8-14, we have the approach vector $\hat{a}$ along the x_5-axis, the orientation vector $\hat{o}$ along the z_5-axis, and the normal vector $\hat{n} = \hat{o} \times \hat{a}$ along the y_5-axis. In terms of this triad, the hand matrix thus has the form

$$\mathbf{H} = \begin{bmatrix} a_x & n_x & o_x & p_x \\ a_y & n_y & o_y & p_y \\ a_z & n_z & o_z & p_z \\ 0 & 0 & 0 & 1 \end{bmatrix}$$

We now suppose that the hand matrix has been specified (in general, as a function of time, although we shall suppress this dependence here).

We begin with the first approach, the direct comparison

$$\mathbf{H} = \mathbf{H}_5 \tag{8-10}$$

The result is the following set of simultaneous equations:

$$a_x = C\theta_5 C\psi \qquad n_x = -S\theta_5 C\psi \qquad o_x = S\psi$$

$$a_y = C\theta_5 S\psi \qquad n_y = -S\theta_5 S\psi \qquad o_y = -C\psi$$

$$a_z = S\theta_5 \qquad n_z = C\theta_5 \qquad o_z = 0$$

$$p = hC\theta_5 C\psi + L_2 C(\theta_1 + \theta_2) + L_1 C\theta_1$$

$$p_y = hC\theta_5 S\psi + L_2 S(\theta_1 + \theta_2) + L_1 S\theta_1$$

$$p_z = hS\theta_5 - d_3 + d_1$$

The easy ones are immediately obtained as

$$\theta_5 = \text{Atan}\,2(a_z, n_z) \qquad \text{and} \qquad d_3 = ha_z - p_z + d_1$$

and we note that the orientation vector $\hat{o}$ is always parallel to the x_0, y_0-plane ($o_z = 0$). It remains to solve for the angles θ_1, θ_2, and θ_4.

Suppose we define

$$\bar{x} = p_x + hn_z o_y \qquad \text{and} \qquad \bar{y} = p_y - hn_z o_x$$

where $(\bar{x}, \bar{y})$ denotes the end of the first two links of the top view (Fig. 8-14b). The relationships involving p_x and p_y then become

$$L_2C(\theta_1 + \theta_2) + L_1C\theta_1 = \bar{x}$$
$$L_2S(\theta_1 + \theta_2) + L_1S\theta_1 = \bar{y} \tag{8-11}$$

These equations may be solved for $C\theta_1$ and $S\theta_1$ in terms of θ_2 as

$$C\theta_1 = \frac{\bar{x}(L_2C\theta_2 + L_1) + \bar{y}(L_2S\theta_2)}{L_1^2 + L_2^2 + 2L_1L_2C\theta_2}$$
$$S\theta_1 = \frac{\bar{y}(L_2C\theta_2 + L_1) - \bar{x}(L_2S\theta_2)}{L_1^2 + L_2^2 + 2L_1L_2C\theta_2} \tag{8-12}$$

Squaring and summing these two expressions eventually yields

$$\theta_2 = \text{Arccos}\left(\frac{\bar{x}^2 + \bar{y}^2 - L_1^2 - L_2^2}{2L_1L_2}\right) \tag{8-13}$$

The geometric interpretation of this result is simple. It is immediate from an application of the law of cosines to links L_1 and L_2 (see Fig. 8-14*b*). Note that (8-13) generally provides two solutions for θ_2.

Based on the previous expressions for $C\theta_1$ and $S\theta_1$, we obtain

$$\theta_1 = \text{Atan}\,2(\bar{y}(L_2C\theta_2 + L_1) - \bar{x}(L_2S\theta_2), \bar{x}(L_2C\theta_2 + L_1) + \bar{y}(L_2S\theta_2)) \tag{8-14}$$

since the denominators of (8-12) are always greater than 0. Again, there are two possible values, depending on the choice made for θ_2. Based on a purely geometric viewpoint (see Fig. 8-14*b*), this may also be written in the form

$$\theta_1 = \text{Atan}\,2(\bar{y}, \bar{x}) - \text{Atan}\,2(L_2S\theta_2, L_1 + L_2C\theta_2) \tag{8-15}$$

The final variable θ_4 is most easily calculated by what might be termed sleight of hand. We have

$$\theta_4 = (\theta_1 + \theta_2) - (\theta_1 + \theta_2 - \theta_4) = (\theta_1 + \theta_2) - \psi$$

From (8-11) we obtain

$$\tan(\theta_1 + \theta_2) = \frac{\bar{y} - L_1S\theta_1}{\bar{x} - L_1C\theta_1}$$

and from the collective equations,

$$\tan\psi = -\frac{o_x}{o_y}$$

Consequently,

$$\theta_4 = \text{Atan}\,2(\bar{y} - L_1S\theta_1, \bar{x} - L_1C\theta_1) - \text{Atan}\,2(o_x, -o_y) \tag{8-16}$$

Of course, this first approach is the easiest—when it works. The second approach is also a relatively obvious one and is presented next. As mentioned, it consists of the successive premultiplication of both sides of (8-10) by the inverse DH matrices.

As before, the process begins with the comparison of $\mathbf{H}$ and $\mathbf{H}_5$; however, this time we select only the most obvious relationships, in the hope that similarly simple additional relationships will arise after the premultiplication by the inverses. The first comparison thus is taken to yield only

$$a_z = S\theta_5 \qquad n_z = C\theta_5 \quad \Rightarrow \quad \theta_5 = \text{Atan}\,2(a_z, n_z)$$

Again, we note that $o_z = 0$ always, and we equate the elements $(3,4)$ of the matrices to obtain

$$d_3 = ha_z - p_z + d_1$$

These are the obvious relationships.

Premultiplication by $\mathbf{H}_{01}^{-1}$. The premultiplication of both sides of (8-10) by $\mathbf{H}_{01}^{-1}$ results in a comparison of the matrices

$$\mathbf{H}_{01}^{-1}\mathbf{H} = \mathbf{H}_{01}^{-1}\mathbf{H}_5 = \mathbf{H}_{15}$$

That is,

$$\begin{bmatrix} C\theta_1 & S\theta_1 & 0 & -L_1 \\ -S\theta_1 & C\theta_1 & 0 & 0 \\ 0 & 0 & 1 & -d_1 \\ 0 & 0 & 0 & 1 \end{bmatrix}\begin{bmatrix} a_x & n_x & o_x & p_x \\ a_y & n_y & o_y & p_y \\ a_z & n_z & 0 & p_z \\ 0 & 0 & 0 & 1 \end{bmatrix}$$

$$= \begin{bmatrix} C\theta_5 C(\theta_2-\theta_4) & -S\theta_5 C(\theta_2-\theta_4) & S(\theta_2-\theta_4) & hC\theta_5 C(\theta_2-\theta_4) + L_2 C\theta_2 \\ C\theta_5 S(\theta_2-\theta_4) & -S\theta_5 S(\theta_2-\theta_4) & -C(\theta_2-\theta_4) & hC\theta_5 S(\theta_2-\theta_4) + L_2 S\theta_2 \\ S\theta_5 & C\theta_5 & 0 & hS\theta_5 - d_3 \\ 0 & 0 & 0 & 1 \end{bmatrix}$$

We shall opt for a comparison of the elements $(1,3)$ and $(2,3)$ to obtain expressions for $C\theta_1$ and $S\theta_1$ in terms of the remaining variables and parameters. The simultaneous solution of

$$o_x C\theta_1 + o_y S\theta_1 = S(\theta_2 - \theta_4)$$

$$o_y C\theta_1 - o_x S\theta_1 = -C(\theta_2 - \theta_4)$$

yields

$$\begin{aligned} C\theta_1 &= o_x S(\theta_2-\theta_4) - o_y C(\theta_2-\theta_4) \\ S\theta_1 &= o_x C(\theta_2-\theta_4) + o_y S(\theta_2-\theta_4) \end{aligned} \tag{8-17}$$

We continue the process by premultiplying with another inverse.

Premultiplication by $\mathbf{H}_{12}^{-1}$. Premultiplication by $\mathbf{H}_{12}^{-1}$ results in a comparison of

$$\mathbf{H}_{12}^{-1}\mathbf{H}_{01}^{-1}\mathbf{H} = \mathbf{H}_{12}^{-1}\mathbf{H}_{15} = \mathbf{H}_{25}$$

or

$$\begin{bmatrix} a_xC(\theta_1+\theta_2)+a_yS(\theta_1+\theta_2) & n_xC(\theta_1+\theta_2)+n_yS(\theta_1+\theta_2) & o_xC(\theta_1+\theta_2)+o_yS(\theta_1+\theta_2) & p_xC(\theta_1+\theta_2)+p_yS(\theta_1+\theta_2)-L_1C\theta_2-L_2 \\ a_xS(\theta_1+\theta_2)-a_yC(\theta_1+\theta_2) & n_xS(\theta_1+\theta_2)-n_yC(\theta_1+\theta_2) & o_xS(\theta_1+\theta_2)-o_yC(\theta_1+\theta_2) & p_xS(\theta_1+\theta_2)-p_yC(\theta_1+\theta_2)-L_1S\theta_2 \\ -a_z & -n_z & 0 & -p_z+d_1 \\ 0 & 0 & 0 & 1 \end{bmatrix}$$

$$= \begin{bmatrix} C\theta_4C\theta_5 & -C\theta_4S\theta_5 & -S\theta_4 & hC\theta_4C\theta_5 \\ S\theta_4C\theta_5 & -S\theta_4S\theta_5 & C\theta_4 & hS\theta_4C\theta_5 \\ -S\theta_5 & -C\theta_5 & 0 & -hS\theta_5+d_3 \\ 0 & 0 & 0 & 1 \end{bmatrix}$$

Our aim at this point will be to express both θ_1 and θ_4 in terms of θ_2 and to obtain an explicit expression for θ_2 itself.

A comparison of the elements (1, 3) and (2, 3) yields the equations

$$o_xC(\theta_1+\theta_2)+o_yS(\theta_1+\theta_2) = -S\theta_4$$

$$-o_yC(\theta_1+\theta_2)+o_xS(\theta_1+\theta_2) = C\theta_4$$

with solution

$$\begin{aligned} C(\theta_1+\theta_2) &= -o_xS\theta_4 - o_yC\theta_4 \\ S(\theta_1+\theta_2) &= o_xC\theta_4 - o_yS\theta_4 \end{aligned} \tag{8-18}$$

A comparison of the elements (1, 4) and (2, 4) yields

$$p_xC(\theta_1+\theta_2)+p_yS(\theta_1+\theta_2) = L_1C\theta_2+L_2+hn_zC\theta_4$$

$$-p_yC(\theta_1+\theta_2)+p_xS(\theta_1+\theta_2) = L_1S\theta_2+hn_zS\theta_4$$

The substitution of (8-18) results in

$$\begin{aligned} -AS\theta_4+BC\theta_4 &= L_2+L_1C\theta_2 \\ BS\theta_4+AC\theta_4 &= L_1S\theta_2 \end{aligned} \tag{8-19}$$

where

$$A = o_xp_x+o_yp_y \qquad \text{and} \qquad B = o_xp_y-o_yp_x-hn_z$$

Equations (8-19) may be solved to yield

$$\begin{aligned} S\theta_4 &= \frac{1}{A^2+B^2}[BL_1S\theta_2 - A(L_1C\theta_2+L_2)] \\ C\theta_4 &= \frac{1}{A^2+B^2}[AL_1S\theta_2 + B(L_1C\theta_2+L_2)] \end{aligned} \tag{8-20}$$

The summation of the squares of these two expressions yields

$$C\theta_2 = \frac{A^2 + B^2 - L_1^2 - L_2^2}{2L_1L_2} \tag{8-21}$$

with the same interpretation as that of (8-13). The corresponding value of $S\theta_2$ may then be easily calculated, followed by a determination of θ_4 from

$$\theta_4 = \text{Atan}\,2\left[BL_1S\theta_2 - A(L_1C\theta_2 + L_2),\, AL_1S\theta_2 + B(L_1C\theta_2 + L_2)\right] \tag{8-22}$$

For the calculation of θ_1 we now return to (8-17). The substitution of (8-20) for $S\theta_4$ and $C\theta_4$ yields

$$\begin{aligned} S\theta_1 &= \frac{1}{A^2 + B^2}\left[(o_yA + o_xB)(L_1 + L_2C\theta_2) + (o_yB - o_xA)L_2S\theta_2\right] \\ C\theta_1 &= \frac{1}{A^2 + B^2}\left[(o_xA - o_yB)(L_1 + L_2C\theta_2) + (o_xB + o_yA)L_2S\theta_2\right] \end{aligned} \tag{8-23}$$

with θ_1 obtained again from the evaluation of the modified arctangent function.

In view of the fact that the first approach already provided a geometrically appealing solution, this second approach may appear somewhat contrived. It is. It does, however, serve as a perfectly adequate illustration of this standard approach. Furthermore, the natural algebraic combinations of terms that arise in the derivation, such as A and B, differ from the natural geometric combinations and thus provide additional insight.

The solution of the inverse problem for the AdeptOne robot suffices as an introduction to this important area. The present approaches are standard first steps. Ultimately, the approach will generally differ for each robot configuration. The attendant trigonometric and algebraic dexterity is always relevant.

Still, it is not always possible to attain exact globally inverse solutions. Instead, it may only be feasible to obtain pointwise approximations. These are usually based on the differential and the defining Jacobian matrix. Such approximations are the topic of the next section.

8-1-5 Jacobian Motion

If the end effector experiences a small displacement and rotation, what are the corresponding required small changes in the robot variables? This is the question that will be addressed in this section. The answer lies in the approximation property satisfied by the differential of the coordinate transformation implicit in rigid body motion.

We shall take all such changes to be occurring for reference frames embedded in rigid bodies. These differential rigid body displacements thus consist of differential rotations and displacements. We first develop an understanding of each of these individually, and eventually build thereon to derive expressions for manipulator Jacobian matrices.

The statement of Chasles' theorem, a basic result in kinematics, is the assertion that the most general displacement of a rigid body may be separated into the translation of an arbitrary base point fixed in the body, followed by a rotational displacement about an axis through this base point. As before, for general rigid body motion, this possible separate treatment of motion again allows us to write a final result as a single homogeneous transformation matrix.

More precisely, we consider a differential change in the hand matrix $\mathbf{H}$ and the corresponding change in the robot variables. Symbolically, we had

$$\mathbf{H} = \mathbf{H}_n(\boldsymbol{\xi})$$

and, consequently,

$$d\mathbf{H} = \frac{d\mathbf{H}_n}{d\boldsymbol{\xi}}(\boldsymbol{\xi}) * d\boldsymbol{\xi}$$

where $*$ denotes some type of multiplication which will be clarified next. Suppose the elements of $\mathbf{H}$ are designated with h_{ij} and those of $\mathbf{H}_n$ with h_{ij}^n, where $i, j = 1, \ldots, 4$. Let the robot in question have r axes and let $\hat{e}_i$, $i = 1, \ldots, r$, be an orthonormal basis for $\mathbb{R}^r$. Introduce the notation

$$d\boldsymbol{\xi} = d\xi_1\hat{e}_1 + \cdots + d\xi_r\hat{e}_r \qquad \text{and} \qquad \frac{\partial h_{ij}^n}{\partial \boldsymbol{\xi}} = \frac{\partial h_{ij}^n}{\partial \xi_1}\hat{e}_1 + \cdots + \frac{\partial h_{ij}^n}{\partial \xi_r}\hat{e}_r$$

In terms of these our "product" takes on the following meaning:

$$d\mathbf{H} = \begin{bmatrix} dh_{11} & \cdots & dh_{14} \\ \vdots & & \vdots \\ dh_{41} & \cdots & dh_{44} \end{bmatrix} = \begin{bmatrix} \dfrac{\partial h_{11}^n}{\partial \boldsymbol{\xi}} \cdot d\boldsymbol{\xi} & \cdots & \dfrac{\partial h_{41}^n}{\partial \boldsymbol{\xi}} \cdot d\boldsymbol{\xi} \\ \vdots & & \vdots \\ \dfrac{\partial h_{41}^n}{\partial \boldsymbol{\xi}} \cdot d\boldsymbol{\xi} & \cdots & \dfrac{\partial h_{44}^n}{\partial \boldsymbol{\xi}} \cdot d\boldsymbol{\xi} \end{bmatrix} = \frac{d\mathbf{H}_n}{d\boldsymbol{\xi}} * d\boldsymbol{\xi} \tag{8-24}$$

an identity which we shall exploit later for the calculation of the manipulator Jacobian matrix. We shall again use a relatively detailed didactic approach by including a side by side development of the vector and matrix expressions. For ease of presentation, we shall make use of an embedded frame $(0xyz)_1$ with $(0xyz)_0$ as the usual base frame. We shall derive expressions for the differential $d\mathbf{r}_0$ when the rigid body $\mathscr{B}$ (the reference frame $(0xyz)_1$) has experienced a differential translation $d\mathbf{c}_1$ and a differential rotation $d\mathbf{A}_1$.

DIFFERENTIAL TRANSLATION. We begin with the vector notation because of its geometric appeal. Our first example consists of a differential translation from a position of coincidence of the two frames. In a straight-forward manner, we have

$$(\boldsymbol{r}_0 + d\boldsymbol{r}_0) - \boldsymbol{r}_0 = d\boldsymbol{r}_0 = (d\boldsymbol{c}_1 + \boldsymbol{r}_1) - \boldsymbol{r}_1 = d\boldsymbol{c}_1$$

where

$$d\boldsymbol{c}_1 = da_1\hat{\boldsymbol{i}}_0 + db_1\hat{\boldsymbol{j}}_0$$

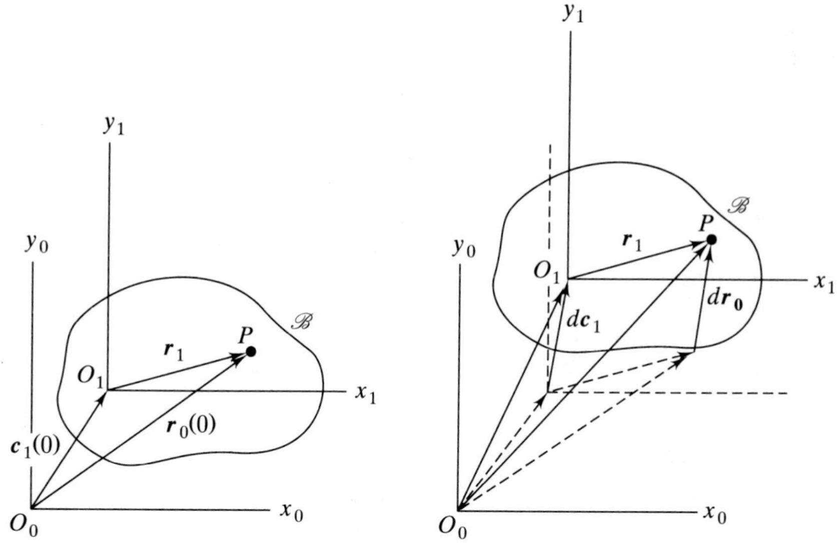

FIGURE 8-15
Translation from a noncoincident reference configuration.

A slightly more general case is depicted in Figure 8.15 where a differential translation is imposed upon an existing finite one. We have

$$\boldsymbol{r}_0 = \boldsymbol{c}_1 + \boldsymbol{r}_1$$

and

$$\boldsymbol{r}_0 + d\boldsymbol{r}_0 = \boldsymbol{c}_1 + d\boldsymbol{c}_1 + \boldsymbol{r}_1$$

with the result

$$d\boldsymbol{r}_0 = (\boldsymbol{r}_0 + d\boldsymbol{r}_0) - \boldsymbol{r}_0 = d\boldsymbol{c}_1$$

as before.

A matrix point of view is given by

$$\mathbf{r}_0 = \mathbf{c}_1 + \mathbf{E}\mathbf{r}_1$$

where $\mathbf{E}$ is the identity matrix in $\mathbb{R}^2$. The differential $\mathbf{r}_0$ is simply

$$d\mathbf{r}_0 = d\mathbf{c}_1$$

since $\mathbf{E}\mathbf{r}_1$ does not change.

Finally, with some care, we may carry out the calculations within the homogeneous representation and we shall do so for the general case

$$\mathbf{r}_0 = \left[\begin{array}{ccc:c} 1 & 0 & 0 & a_1 \\ 0 & 1 & 0 & b_1 \\ 0 & 0 & 1 & c_1 \\ \hdashline 0 & 0 & 0 & 1 \end{array}\right] \begin{pmatrix} x_1 \\ y_1 \\ z_1 \\ 1 \end{pmatrix}$$

Note that the differential change now only affects the physical components of the operator (the translation matrix). The scaling factor, essentially a bookkeeping device, must be maintained at 1. The result is

$$d\mathbf{r}_0 = \begin{bmatrix} 0 & 0 & 0 & \vdots & da_1 \\ 0 & 0 & 0 & \vdots & db_1 \\ 0 & 0 & 0 & \vdots & dc_1 \\ \cdots & \cdots & \cdots & \cdots & \cdots \\ 0 & 0 & 0 & \vdots & 1 \end{bmatrix} \begin{pmatrix} x_1 \\ y_1 \\ z_1 \\ 1 \end{pmatrix} = \begin{pmatrix} da_1 \\ db_1 \\ dc_1 \\ 1 \end{pmatrix}$$

as expected.

DIFFERENTIAL ROTATION. We begin with a discussion of some facts about rotations.

We have mentioned earlier that finite rotations do not commute. For example, a rotation about the x_1-axis followed by a rotation about the now rotated y_1-axis is generally not equal to a rotation about the y_1-axis followed by a rotation about the rotated x_1-axis. That is,

$$\begin{bmatrix} 1 & 0 & 0 \\ 0 & C\alpha & -S\alpha \\ 0 & S\alpha & C\alpha \end{bmatrix} \begin{bmatrix} C\phi & 0 & S\phi \\ 0 & 1 & 0 \\ -S\phi & 0 & C\phi \end{bmatrix} = \begin{bmatrix} C\phi & 0 & S\phi \\ -S\alpha S\phi & C\alpha & -S\alpha C\phi \\ -C\alpha S\phi & S\alpha & C\alpha C\phi \end{bmatrix}$$

$$\neq \begin{bmatrix} C\phi & 0 & S\phi \\ 0 & 1 & 0 \\ -S\phi & 0 & C\phi \end{bmatrix} \begin{bmatrix} 1 & 1 & 0 \\ 0 & C\alpha & -S\alpha \\ 0 & S\alpha & C\alpha \end{bmatrix}$$

$$= \begin{bmatrix} C\phi & S\phi S\alpha & S\phi C\alpha \\ 0 & C\alpha & -S\alpha \\ -S\phi & C\phi S\alpha & C\phi C\alpha \end{bmatrix}$$

If, however, we use small rotations $\delta\alpha$ and $\delta\phi$ and neglect higher-order (than linear) terms, with $\cos\delta\phi \approx 1$, $\sin\delta\phi \approx \delta\phi$, and $\delta\phi\,\delta\alpha \approx 0$, and both sides of the equation above reduce to the same matrix

$$\begin{bmatrix} 1 & 0 & \delta\phi \\ 0 & 1 & -\delta\alpha \\ -\delta\phi & \delta\alpha & 1 \end{bmatrix}$$

More generally, it can be shown that differential rotations in sequence have the same final position regardless of the order in which the rotations are carried out. In short, differential rotations are vectors and "adding" them thus is clearly commutative.

Furthermore, in accordance with Chasles' theorem, we may write the instantaneous angular velocity of the rigid body (and hence of the imbedded reference frame) as

$$\boldsymbol{\omega}_1 = \lim_{\Delta t \to 0} \frac{\Delta \boldsymbol{\kappa}_1}{\Delta t} = \frac{d\boldsymbol{\kappa}_1}{dt}$$

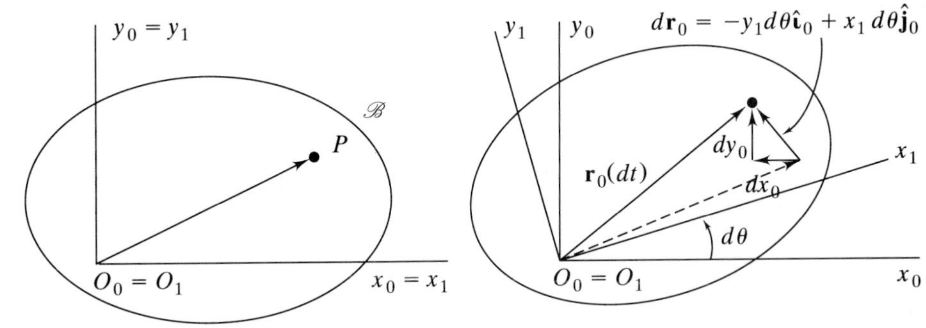

FIGURE 8-16
A differential rotation.

with an instantaneous axis as mentioned in the theorem. Viewed as a differential rotation expressed with respect to $(0xyz)_0$ we then have

$$\boldsymbol{\omega}_1 \, dt = d\boldsymbol{\kappa}_1 = d\alpha_1 \hat{\boldsymbol{\imath}}_0 + d\phi_1 \hat{\boldsymbol{\jmath}}_0 + d\theta_1 \hat{\boldsymbol{k}}_0$$

the direction being that of the axial vector mentioned in Chapter 2. Indeed we have the corresponding skew-symmetric matrix representation

$$d\boldsymbol{\kappa}_1 = \begin{bmatrix} 0 & -d\theta_1 & d\phi_1 \\ d\theta_1 & & -d\alpha_1 \\ -d\phi_1 & d\alpha_1 & 0 \end{bmatrix}$$

Suppose, we illustrate this result with a plane rotation about a fixed axis, assuming initially coincident reference frames as shown in Figure 8.16. We have

$$\boldsymbol{r}_0(t) = x_1 \hat{\boldsymbol{\imath}}_1(t) + y_1 \hat{\boldsymbol{\jmath}}_1(t)$$

so that

$$d\boldsymbol{r}_0 = x_1 d\hat{\boldsymbol{\imath}}_1 + y_1 d\hat{\boldsymbol{\jmath}}_1$$

where

$$d\hat{\boldsymbol{\imath}}_1 = (-\sin\theta_1 \hat{\boldsymbol{\imath}}_0 + \cos\theta_1 \hat{\boldsymbol{\jmath}}_0) d\theta_1$$
$$d\hat{\boldsymbol{\jmath}}_1 = (-\cos\theta_1 \hat{\boldsymbol{\imath}}_0 - \sin\theta_1 \hat{\boldsymbol{\jmath}}_0) d\theta_1$$

Substitution into the expression for $d\boldsymbol{r}_0$ yields

$$\begin{aligned} d\boldsymbol{r}_0 &= [(-x_1 \sin\theta_1 - y_1 \cos\theta_1)\hat{\boldsymbol{\imath}}_0 + (x_1 \cos\theta_1 - y_1 \sin\theta_1)\hat{\boldsymbol{\jmath}}_0] d\theta_1 |_{\theta_1 = 0} \\ &= (-y_1 \hat{\boldsymbol{\imath}}_0 + x_1 \hat{\boldsymbol{\jmath}}_0) d\theta_1 \end{aligned}$$

since we are considering a rotation from the coincident position of the reference frames. The matrix form of this expression is

$$d\mathbf{r}_0 = \begin{pmatrix} dx_0 \\ dy_0 \end{pmatrix} = \begin{bmatrix} 0 & -d\theta \\ d\theta & 0 \end{bmatrix} \begin{pmatrix} x_1 \\ y_1 \end{pmatrix}$$

Quite generally we may begin with

$$\boldsymbol{r}_0 = \boldsymbol{r}_1$$

and

$$\boldsymbol{v}_0 = \boldsymbol{\omega}_1 \times \boldsymbol{r}_1$$

to obtain

$$\begin{aligned}
d\boldsymbol{r}_0 &= d\boldsymbol{\kappa}_1 \times \boldsymbol{r}_1 = d\boldsymbol{\kappa}_1 \times \boldsymbol{r}_0 \\
&= \left(d\alpha\hat{\boldsymbol{\imath}}_0 + d\phi\hat{\boldsymbol{\jmath}}_0 + d\theta\hat{\boldsymbol{k}}_0\right) \times \left(x_0\hat{\boldsymbol{\imath}}_0 + y_0\hat{\boldsymbol{\jmath}}_0 + z_0\hat{\boldsymbol{k}}_0\right) \\
&= (z_0 d\phi - y_0 d\theta)\hat{\boldsymbol{\imath}}_0 + (x_0 d\theta - z_0 d\alpha)\hat{\boldsymbol{\jmath}}_0 + (y_0 d\alpha - x_0 d\phi)\hat{\boldsymbol{k}}_0
\end{aligned}$$

with the matrix representation

$$d\mathbf{r}_0 = \begin{pmatrix} dx_0 \\ dy_0 \\ dz_0 \end{pmatrix} = \begin{bmatrix} 0 & -d\theta & d\phi \\ d\theta & 0 & -d\alpha \\ -d\phi & d\alpha & 0 \end{bmatrix} \begin{pmatrix} x_0 \\ y_0 \\ z_0 \end{pmatrix}$$

This expression may be written in terms of $\mathbf{r}_1$ by using $\mathbf{r}_0 = \mathbf{A}_1\mathbf{r}_1$.

We close this part of our discussion with the homogeneous differential rotation. The basic identity is

$$\mathbf{r}_0 = \begin{bmatrix} \mathbf{A}_1 & \vdots & \mathbf{0} \\ \cdots & \cdots & \cdots \\ \mathbf{0} & \vdots & 1 \end{bmatrix} \mathbf{r}_1$$

where $\mathbf{A}_1$, of course, is the rotation matrix. A variation of only the physical components as before yields

$$\begin{aligned}
d\mathbf{r}_0 &= \begin{bmatrix} d\mathbf{A}_1 & \vdots & \mathbf{0} \\ \cdots & \cdots & \cdots \\ \mathbf{0} & \vdots & 1 \end{bmatrix} \mathbf{r}_1 \\
&= \begin{bmatrix} d\mathbf{A}_1\mathbf{A}_1^{\mathrm{T}} & \vdots & \mathbf{0} \\ \cdots & \cdots & \cdots \\ \mathbf{0} & \vdots & 1 \end{bmatrix} \mathbf{r}_0
\end{aligned}$$

As noted in Chapter 2, $d\mathbf{A}_1\mathbf{A}_1^{\mathrm{T}}$ is a skew symmetric matrix.

By combining the results for rotation and translation, we may obtain the homogeneous differential rigid body displacement.

With

$$\mathbf{r}_0 = \begin{bmatrix} \mathbf{A}_1 & \vdots & \mathbf{c}_1 \\ \cdots & \cdots & \cdots \\ \mathbf{0} & \vdots & 1 \end{bmatrix} \mathbf{r}_1 \quad \text{and} \quad \mathbf{r}_1 = \begin{bmatrix} \mathbf{A}_1^{\mathrm{T}} & \vdots & -\mathbf{A}_1^{\mathrm{T}}\mathbf{c}_1 \\ \cdots & \cdots & \cdots \\ \mathbf{0} & \vdots & 1 \end{bmatrix} \mathbf{r}_0$$

the homogeneous differential may be written in the form

$$d\mathbf{r}_0 = \begin{bmatrix} d\boldsymbol{\kappa}_1 & \vdots & d\mathbf{c}_1 - d\boldsymbol{\kappa}_1\mathbf{c}_1 \\ \cdots & \cdots & \cdots \\ \mathbf{0} & \vdots & 1 \end{bmatrix} \mathbf{r}_0$$

where $d\boldsymbol{\kappa}$ is the previously introduced skew symmetric differential rotation matrix. Accordingly, we now give the following definition for the general differential homogeneous rigid body displacement.

Definition 8-9. Differential homogeneous rigid body displacement. Let all of the reference frames of a manipulator be ordered and let $(0xyz)_i$ precede the frame $(0xyx)_j$ with the frames embedded in the rigid bodies $\mathscr{B}_i$ and $\mathscr{B}_j$, respectively. Then the homogeneous differential rigid body displacement of $\mathscr{B}_j$ relative to $\mathscr{B}_i$ is

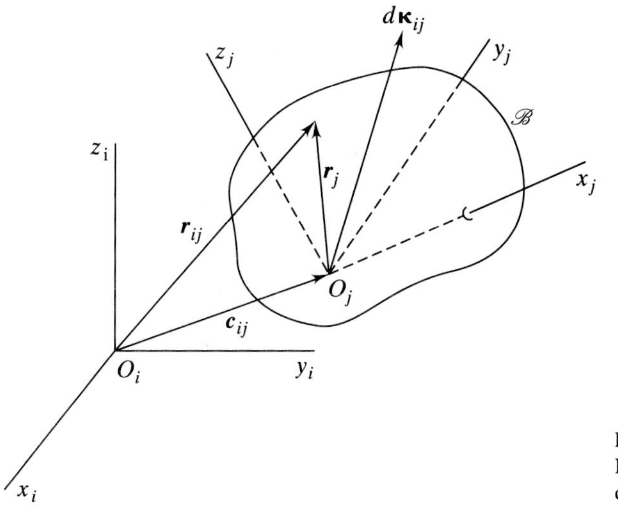

FIGURE 8-17
Notation for homogeneous differential displacement.

given by

$$d\mathbf{r}_{ij} = \begin{bmatrix} d\boldsymbol{\kappa}_{ij} & \vdots & d\mathbf{c}_{ij} - d\boldsymbol{\kappa}_{ij}\mathbf{c}_{ij} \\ \cdots & \cdots & \cdots \\ \mathbf{0} & \vdots & 1 \end{bmatrix} \mathbf{r}_{ij}$$

The situation is illustrated in Figure 8.17.

The collection of differentials

$$d\mathbf{D} = \left(da_{ij} db_{ij} dc_{ij} d\alpha_{ij} d\phi_{ij} d\theta_{ij}\right)^T$$

is indicative of the six degrees of freedom that a rigid body enjoys for unconstrained motion in three dimensions. We now have all of the terminology needed to return to the relationship between displacement and the differential changes in the robot variables required to produce it.

Subsequent examples will deal with the differential displacement of the end effector relative to the base frame. For simplicity in that discussion, we shall omit the subscripts and take

$$d\mathbf{r}_0 = \begin{bmatrix} 0 & -d\theta & d\phi & \vdots & da - bd\theta + cd\phi \\ d\theta & 0 & -d\alpha & \vdots & db + ad\theta - cd\alpha \\ -d\phi & d\alpha & 0 & \vdots & dc - ad\phi + bd\alpha \\ \cdots & \cdots & \cdots & \cdots & \cdots \\ 0 & 0 & 0 & \vdots & 1 \end{bmatrix} \mathbf{r}_0$$

to be the differential displacment of the end effector of an r-axes manipulator relative to the base frame.

The Jacobian matrix of a manipulator is defined in terms of the relationship between these basic differentials and the differentials of the robot variables.

Definition 8-10. Jacobian matrix of an r-axes manipulator. Let

$$d\mathbf{D} = (da\, db\, dc\, d\alpha\, d\phi\, d\theta)^{\mathrm{T}} \quad \text{and} \quad d\boldsymbol{\xi} = (d\xi_1 \ldots d\xi_r)^T.$$

Then the Jacobian matrix

$$\mathbf{J}(\boldsymbol{\xi}) = \frac{d\mathbf{D}}{d\boldsymbol{\xi}}(\boldsymbol{\xi})$$

such that

$$d\mathbf{D} = \mathbf{J}(\boldsymbol{\xi})\, d\boldsymbol{\xi}$$

is the Jacobian matrix of the manipulator.

Remark 8-3. Note, carefully, that the Jacobian matrix itself cannot be used to calculate the actual physical differential displacement of the end effector; that is given by

$$d\mathbf{r}_0 = \begin{bmatrix} d\boldsymbol{\kappa} & \vdots & d\mathbf{c} - d\boldsymbol{\kappa}\mathbf{c} \\ \cdots & \cdots & \cdots \\ \mathbf{0} & \vdots & 1 \end{bmatrix} \mathbf{r}_0$$

Of course, we may use the entries in $\mathbf{J}(\boldsymbol{\xi})$ to determine the relevant terms in this expression.

The remainder of this section deals with the calculation of the Jacobian matrix for some particular manipulators. There are a number of approaches to achieve this goal. We shall present only the most direct approach, involving the derivatives of terms in the DH matrix of the manipulator.

The method is deceptively simple. We begin with (8-24) and determine the differential entries of the hand matrix. The translational components immediately yield the desired differential relationships. To determine those for the differential rotations, we multiplu the differential rotation matrix from the differential hand matrix by the transpose of the original rotation matrix as contained in the DH matrix. The resultant skew-symmetric matrix provides the rotational differential relationships. This latter process is the same as that for the derivation of the angular velocity given in Chap. 2.

The first example is yet another exploitation of the simple two-link manipulator. However, a careful study of this example will considerably ease the digestion of the subsequent derivation of the Jacobian matrix for the AdeptOne robot.

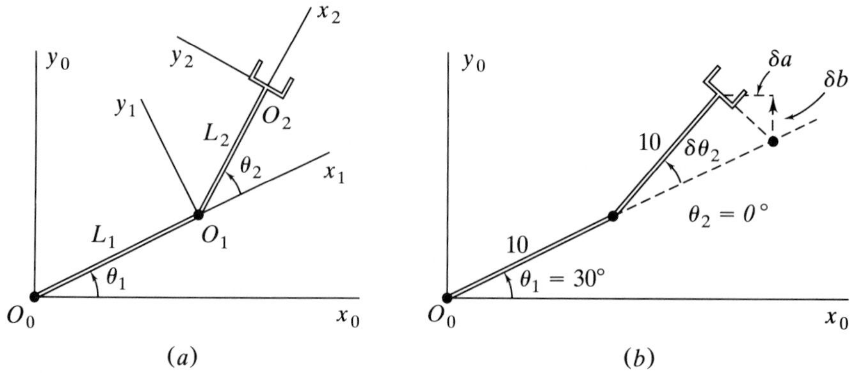

FIGURE 8-18
The planar two-link manipulator.

Example 8-12 The planar two-link manipulator. The two-link manipulator in Fig. 8-18 has a gripper that remains aligned with the x_2-axis. The links are free to move in the $x_0 y_0$-plane.

(*a*) Determine the Jacobian matrix for the manipulator.
(*b*) Discuss the relationship between the number of axes of this manipulator and its degrees of freedom.
(*c*) Consider a differential displacement $(da, d\theta)$ and calculate the required values of $(d\theta_1, d\theta_2)$ when $da = -0.1$, $d\theta = 0.02$, $\theta_1 = 30°$, $\theta_2 = 0$, $L_1 = L_2 = 10$; sketch the result.

Solution

(*a*) The DH matrix for this manipulator is

$$\mathbf{H}_2 = \begin{bmatrix} C\psi & -S\psi & 0 & L_2C\psi + L_1C\theta_1 \\ S\psi & C\psi & 0 & L_2S\psi + L_1S\theta_1 \\ 0 & 0 & 1 & 0 \\ 0 & 0 & 0 & 1 \end{bmatrix}$$

where $\psi = \theta_1 + \theta_2$. By design, this is equal to the hand matrix which here is given by

$$\mathbf{H} = \begin{bmatrix} a_x & o_x & n_x & p_x \\ a_y & o_y & n_y & p_y \\ a_z & o_z & n_z & p_z \\ 0 & 0 & 0 & 1 \end{bmatrix}$$

For this two-axes robot with variables θ_1 and θ_2, the differentials of the hand matrix are thus given by (8-24):

$$dh_{11} = da_x = -S\psi\, d\psi \qquad dh_{12} = do_x = -C\psi\, d\psi \qquad dh_{13} = dn_x = 0$$

$$dh_{21} = da_y = C\psi\, d\psi \qquad dh_{22} = do_y = -S\psi\, d\psi \qquad dh_{23} = dn_y = 0$$

$$dh_{31} = da_z = 0 \qquad dh_{32} = do_z = 0 \qquad dh_{33} = dn_z = 0$$

$$dh_{14} = dp_x = da = (-L_2S\psi - L_1S\theta_1)\, d\theta_1 - L_2S\psi\, d\theta_2$$

$$dh_{24} = dp_y = db = (L_2C\psi + L_1C\theta_1)\, d\theta_1 + L_2C\psi\, d\theta_2$$

$$dh_{34} = dp_z = dc = 0$$

It remains to determine $d\alpha$, $d\phi$, and $d\theta$ from the now known general differential rotation matrix. We postmultiply this matrix by the transpose of the rotational partition of the matrix $\mathbf{H}_2$. The result is

$$\begin{bmatrix} 0 & -d\theta & d\phi \\ d\theta & 0 & -d\alpha \\ -d\phi & d\alpha & 0 \end{bmatrix} = d\psi \begin{bmatrix} -S\psi & -C\psi & 0 \\ C\psi & -S\psi & 0 \\ 0 & 0 & 0 \end{bmatrix} \begin{bmatrix} C\psi & S\psi & 0 \\ -S\psi & C\psi & 0 \\ 0 & 0 & 1 \end{bmatrix}$$

$$= d\psi \begin{bmatrix} 0 & -1 & 0 \\ 1 & 0 & 0 \\ 0 & 0 & 0 \end{bmatrix}$$

As expected, we are forced to conclude that there is only a differential rotation about the z-axis given by

$$d\theta = d\psi = d\theta_1 + d\theta_2$$

The collection of the two nonzero displacement relationships, da and db, together with $d\theta$ then yields the Jacobian matrix implicit in the transformation

$$\begin{pmatrix} da \\ db \\ d\theta \end{pmatrix} = \begin{bmatrix} -L_1 S\psi - L_1 S\theta_1 & -L_2 S\psi \\ L_2 C\psi + L_1 C\theta_1 & L_2 C\psi \\ 1 & 1 \end{bmatrix} \begin{pmatrix} d\theta_1 \\ d\theta_2 \end{pmatrix}$$

(*b*) We first recall that the unconstrained motion of a rigid body in two dimensions has three degrees of freedom. This requires at least a three-axes robot to provide corresponding independent motions. (Note that this is a necessary but not sufficient condition; additional axes do not necessarily provide the additional degrees of freedom.) Since there are only two robot variables here, we can only hope to control two degrees of freedom. To obtain a unique relationship between differential displacements and the corresponding robot variables, it becomes necessary to drop one of the components with the idea that we shall simply take whatever we can get for the value of this component. This is one approach to obtaining a square Jacobian matrix whose inverse we can calculate.

(*c*) For this manipulator we have the following motion pairs: $(da, d\theta)$, $(db, d\theta)$, and (da, db). Consider then the first of these possibilities; the result is

$$\begin{pmatrix} da \\ d\theta \end{pmatrix} = \begin{bmatrix} -L_2 S\psi - L_1 S\theta_1 & -L_2 S\psi \\ 1 & 1 \end{bmatrix} \begin{pmatrix} d\theta_1 \\ d\theta_2 \end{pmatrix}$$

The Jacobian of this transformation is

$$\begin{vmatrix} -L_2 S\psi - L_1 S\theta_1 & -L_2 S\psi \\ 1 & 1 \end{vmatrix} = -L_1 S\theta_1 = J(\theta_1, \theta_2)$$

so that this transformation becomes singular only for $\theta_1 = 0$. The inverse transformation is given by

$$\begin{pmatrix} d\theta_1 \\ d\theta_2 \end{pmatrix} = \frac{1}{L_1 S\theta_1} \begin{bmatrix} -1 & -L_2 S\psi \\ -1 & L_2 S\psi + L_1 S\theta_1 \end{bmatrix} \begin{pmatrix} da \\ d\theta \end{pmatrix}$$

with Jacobian

$$j(a, \theta) = \frac{1}{-L_1 S\theta_1}$$

which has no singular points. For the given numerical values, the approximations for $\delta\theta_1$ and $\delta\theta_2$ are given by

$$\begin{pmatrix} \delta\theta_1 \\ \delta\theta_2 \end{pmatrix} = \begin{bmatrix} -0.2 & -1 \\ 0.2 & 2 \end{bmatrix} \begin{pmatrix} -0.1 \\ 0.02 \end{pmatrix} = \begin{pmatrix} 0 \\ 0.02 \end{pmatrix}$$

a result depicted in Fig. 8-18*b*. Having chosen the displacement δa and the differential rotation $\delta\theta$, the required $\delta\theta_1$ and $\delta\theta_2$ yield a value for δb given by

$$\delta b = (L_2 C\psi + L_1 C\theta_1)\,\delta\theta_1 + L_2 C\psi\,\delta\theta_2$$

$$= \left(10 \cdot \frac{\sqrt{3}}{2}\right)(0.02) = 0.173$$

We are stuck with this value. The other possible combinations may be treated in a similar fashion.

Our final example in this segment concerns the Jacobian matrix for the AdeptOne robot.

Example 8-13 The AdeptOne robot. Calculate the Jacobian matrix for the AdeptOne robot.

Solution. Again, we cannot hope to achieve the six degrees of freedom of motion implied by unconstrained motion in three dimensions, since the robot has only five axes. Consequently, we expect the Jacobian matrix to be a 6×5 matrix. Its derivation is carried out in exactly the same manner as that for the simple manipulator in the preceding example.

The equality of the hand matrix and the DH matrix of the manipulator,

$$\mathbf{H} = \mathbf{H}_5$$

yields the following identities:

$$a_x = C\theta_5 C\psi \qquad o_x = -S\theta_5 C\psi \qquad n_x = S\psi$$

$$a_y = C\theta_5 S\psi \qquad o_y = -S\theta_5 S\psi \qquad n_y = -C\psi$$

$$a_z = S\theta_5 \qquad o_z = C\theta_5 \qquad n_z = 0$$

$$p_x = hC\theta_5 C\psi + L_2 C\beta + L_1 C\theta_1$$

$$p_y = hC\theta_5 S\psi + L_2 S\beta + L_1 S\theta_1$$

$$p_z = hS\theta_5 - d_3 + d_1$$

where $\psi = \theta_1 + \theta_2 - \theta_4$, $\beta = \theta_1 + \theta_2$. As before, the equalities for the displacement components immediately yield the corresponding differential relationships, based on $\boldsymbol{\xi} = (\theta_1\,\theta_2\,d_3\,\theta_4\,\theta_5)^{\mathrm{T}}$,

$$da = (-hC\theta_5 S\psi - L_2 S\beta - L_1 S\theta_1)\,d\theta_1 + (-hC\theta_5 S\psi - L_2 S\beta)\,d\theta_2 + hC\theta_5 S\psi\,d\theta_4 - hS\theta_5 C\psi\,d\theta_5$$

$$db = (hC\theta_5 C\psi + L_2 C\beta + L_1 C\theta_1)\,d\theta_1 + (hC\theta_5 C\psi + L_2 C\beta)\,d\theta_2 - hC\theta_5 C\psi\,d\theta_4 - hS\theta_5 S\psi\,d\theta_5$$

$$dc = -dd_3 + hC\theta_5\,d\theta_5$$

The differentials of the rotational part of the hand matrix are

$$da_x = -C\theta_5 S\psi\,d\psi - S\theta_5 C\psi\,d\theta_5 \qquad do_x = S\theta_5 S\psi\,d\psi - C\theta_5 C\psi\,d\theta_5$$

$$da_y = C\theta_5 C\psi\,d\psi - S\theta_5 S\psi\,d\theta_5 \qquad do_y = -S\theta_5 C\psi\,d\psi - C\theta_5 S\psi\,d\theta_5$$

$$da_z = C\theta_5\,d\theta_5 \qquad do_z = -S\theta_5\,d\theta_5$$

$$dn_x = C\psi\,d\psi$$

$$dn_y = S\psi\,d\psi$$

$$dn_z = 0$$

The multiplication of the resultant differential matrix by the transpose of the rotational partition of the matrix $\mathbf{H}_5$ yields the product

$$\begin{bmatrix} da_x & do_x & dn_x \\ da_y & do_y & dn_y \\ da_z & do_z & dn_z \end{bmatrix} \begin{bmatrix} C\theta_5 C\psi & C\theta_5 S\psi & S\theta_5 \\ -S\theta_5 C\psi & -S\theta_5 S\psi & C\theta_5 \\ S\psi & -C\psi & 0 \end{bmatrix}$$

$$= \begin{bmatrix} 0 & -d\psi & -C\psi\, d\theta_5 \\ d\psi & 0 & -S\psi\, d\theta_5 \\ C\psi\, d\theta_5 & S\psi\, d\theta_5 & 0 \end{bmatrix} = \begin{bmatrix} 0 & -d\theta & d\phi \\ d\theta & 0 & -d\alpha \\ -d\phi & d\alpha & 0 \end{bmatrix}$$

from which we conclude

$$\begin{pmatrix} d\alpha \\ d\phi \\ d\theta \end{pmatrix} = \begin{pmatrix} S\psi\, d\theta_5 \\ -C\psi\, d\theta_5 \\ d\theta_1 + d\theta_2 - d\theta_4 \end{pmatrix}$$

We thus deduce the following Jacobian matrix for this manipulator

$$\mathbf{J}(\xi) = \begin{bmatrix} -hC\theta_5 S\psi - L_2 S\beta - L_1 S\theta_1 & -hC\theta_5 S\psi - L_2 S\beta & 0 & hC\theta_5 S\psi & -hS\theta_5 C\psi \\ hC\theta_5 C\psi + L_2 C\beta + L_1 C\theta_1 & hC\theta_5 C\psi + L_2 C\beta & 0 & -hC\theta_5 C\psi & -hS\theta_5 S\psi \\ 0 & 0 & -1 & 0 & hC\theta_5 \\ 0 & 0 & 0 & 0 & S\psi \\ 0 & 0 & 0 & 0 & -C\psi \\ 1 & 1 & 0 & -1 & 0 \end{bmatrix} \tag{8.25}$$

Remark 8-4. There are a number of different methods for the calculation of the Jacobian matrix of a manipulator. The approach used and illustrated here is equivalent to that of Whitney.[4] In a sense we have given the matrix equivalent of his vectorial approach. It thus goes hand in hand with our previous emphasis on the simultaneous development of vector and matrix methods. Another common expression used for the Jacobian matrix of a manipulator is that of Paul.[5] He calculates the differential change in the hand configuration due to a differential displacement of rotation of each link and then sums these changes to obtain the total differential change in the hand matrix.

Remark 8-5. We comment briefly on some differences in notation. In particular, we shall provide some comparison with the notation in Paul.[5] Paul's matrix $\mathbf{A}_j = \boldsymbol{H}_{j-1,j}$, ${}^i\mathbf{T}_j = \mathbf{H}_{ij}$, $i < j$, and his $\mathbf{T}_i = \mathbf{H}_i$. He also uses numerous additional superscripts and subscripts to denote partial transformations and to identify specific reference frames.

We close our discussion of kinematics with some comments on the selection of DH parameters and reference frames. First, such assignments are not unique. The parameters α_i and a_i are generally fixed parameters for a given link, the parameters θ_i and d_i serve as robot variables or control parameters, and links are assigned in such a way that only one of them is adjustable for a given link—something that sometimes requires links of zero length. Parameter values are generally based on a fixed reference position or home position for a robot. The DH assignation of reference frames and parameters, while useful from a kinematic point of view, is quite inconvenient in a kinetics context, where reference frames embedded in the links with origins at the centers of mass of the links are far more convenient. Indeed, we shall make use of this latter approach in our next section dealing with robot equations of motion.

8-2 MANIPULATOR EQUATIONS OF MOTION

Although equations of motion appear in various guises and under a variety of names (such as Euler-Lagrange and Newton-Euler), the end result is the expression of Euler's laws of motion as stated in Sec. 3-4. While D'Alembert did have axioms equivalent to Euler's first and second laws, mainly for particles, Euler was the first to be able to routinely formulate and solve problems in the theory of rigid and deformable body motion. To a large extent, the acceptance of later formulations rested on their proven equivalence to Euler's laws. The various attached names thus refer to differences in formulation and derivation, rather than to differences in the end results.

Different formulations may have individual advantages in certain situations. Some lend themselves more easily to routine computer generation, and others are more suited to dealing with large-scale multibody problems. Still others are preferred simply because the users need not deal directly with forces and accelerations. We shall use Euler's approach here for a number of reasons, the most obvious being the student's background—the same reason for the choice of the development in Chap. 3. Furthermore, for manipulators with up to, say, six links, the derivations, while onerous, are still manageable and clearly expose the use of actuator forces and moments, so essential for robot control.

One of the major uses of these equations is the modeling and simulation of controlled robot motion. However, more often than not, algorithms that work well on paper tend to be fickle when implemented on actual machinery. This is due, in part, to the relative simplicity of the models, which often omit such effects as elasticity, friction, slack, and other deviations from perfection that characterize real machinery.

We begin the discussion with the simple physical pendulum, since this scalar equation of motion may be viewed as a prototype for the more general formulations to follow. Interspersed with the examples, we shall cite various standard forms of these equations, interpret them in light of the examples, and illustrate their substance, though not their complexity.

Example 8-14 The one-armed manipulator with Coulomb friction. We consider another variation of Example 3-6 involving a physical pendulum of mass m and length L. Suppose an actuator moment M^a exists at the base of the pendulum, together with a resisting Coulomb friction couple proportional to the radial force. Obtain the equation of motion of this manipulator.

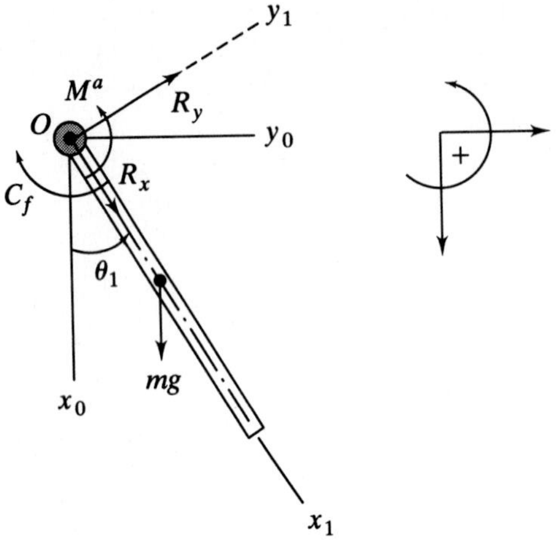

FIGURE 8-19
The one-armed manipulator with friction.

Solution. The force and moment free body is shown in Fig. 8-19. We shall assume that the Coulomb friction couple C_f has magnitude

$$C_f = \mu\epsilon|R_x|$$

where R_x is the radial reaction component at the support O, μ is the coefficient of friction between the hub and the sleeve, and ϵ is the hub radius. Of course, the couple acts opposite to the direction of motion.

For simplicity, we shall consider only the ranges θ_1, $\dot{\theta}_1$, and $\ddot{\theta}_1$ positive, with $0 \leq \theta_1 \leq \pi/2$. Since R_x is involved in the problem formulation, we first make use of Euler's law of linear momentum. The acceleration of the center of mass is

$$\boldsymbol{a}_G = -\frac{L}{2}\dot{\theta}_1^2\hat{\imath}_1 + \frac{L}{2}\ddot{\theta}_1\hat{\jmath}_1$$

and

$$(R_x + mg\cos\theta_1)\hat{\imath}_1 + (R_y - mg\sin\theta_1)\hat{\jmath}_1 = m\left(-\frac{L}{2}\dot{\theta}_1^2\hat{\imath}_1 + \frac{L}{2}\ddot{\theta}_1\hat{\jmath}_1\right)$$

with

$$R_x = -mg\cos\theta_1 - m\frac{L}{2}\dot{\theta}_1^2$$

as a consequence.

The use of Euler's law of moment of momentum yields

$$M^a - C_f - mg\frac{L}{2}\sin\theta_1 = I_0\ddot{\theta}_1$$

and when the expression for C_f is included, this becomes

$$\frac{1}{3}mL^2\ddot{\theta}_1 + \mu\epsilon m\frac{L}{2}\dot{\theta}_1^2 + \left(mg\frac{L}{2}\sin\theta_1 + \mu\epsilon mg\cos\theta_1\right) = M^a \qquad (8\text{-}26)$$

As mentioned, we shall provide several standard forms of the equations of motion for manipulators. The first generalization follows from the previous scalar example to the matrix equation

$$\mathbf{M}(\boldsymbol{\xi}, t)\ddot{\boldsymbol{\xi}} + \mathbf{b}(\boldsymbol{\xi}, \dot{\boldsymbol{\xi}}, t) + \mathbf{c}(\boldsymbol{\xi}, t) = \mathbf{q}(\boldsymbol{\xi}, \dot{\boldsymbol{\xi}}, t) \tag{8-27}$$

where $\mathbf{M}$ is a matrix of mass and inertial terms, $\boldsymbol{\xi}$, as always, denotes the axes variables of the manipulator, $\mathbf{b}$ is a column matrix of Coriolis terms involving products of velocities and position variables, $\mathbf{c}$ is usually a column matrix of gravitational terms, and $\mathbf{q}$ provides the applied forces and moments.

Consciously or unconsciously, the laws of motion provide the crucial connection between the geometry of motion and the applied forces and moments; from a computational point of view, they provide conditions to be counted toward the solution for the unknown quantities that have been introduced.

If the motion $\theta_1(t)$ is known, the applied moment required to produce it may easily be computed from (8-26). Conversely, the application of different moments $M^a(t)$ and a subsequent integration of the equation allows us to compute the corresponding motion $\theta_1(t)$. The latter problem is generally the more difficult to solve, by far. This is not reflected in the following literal definition, since reference to an inverse problem generally implies the greater difficulty in execution.

Definition 8-11 Forward and inverse problems of dynamics. Specification of the forces and moments and the subsequent determination of the robot displacements and velocities is termed the *forward dynamics problem*. Specification of the robot displacements and the subsequent determination of the forces and moments is termed the *inverse dynamics problem*.

Thus the calculation of $M^a(t)$ in (8-26) from a specified $\theta_1(t)$ would be an inverse dynamics problem.

Example 8-15 The polar manipulator. In Example 3-7 we calculated the actuator force and moment required for the controlled motion of the polar manipulator. Write these equations in matrix form.

Solution. In Example 3-7 we obtained the following expressions for the required actuator moment and force:

$$M^a(t) = m_1 g c_1 \cos\theta_1 + m_2 g c_2 \cos\theta_1$$
$$+ \left[c_1^2 m_1 + c_2^2 m_2 + I_{G_1} + I_{G_2}\right]\ddot{\theta}_1 + 2 m_2 c_2 \dot{c}_2 \dot{\theta}_1$$

$$F^a(t) = -m_2 g \sin\theta_1 - m_2 \ddot{c}_2 + m_2 c_2 \dot{\theta}_1^2$$

where $\theta_1(t)$ and $c_2(t)$ were the robot variables. The matrix form of these equations is

$$\begin{bmatrix} M_{11} & M_{12} \\ M_{21} & M_{22} \end{bmatrix} \begin{pmatrix} \ddot{\theta}_1 \\ \ddot{c}_1 \end{pmatrix} + \begin{bmatrix} N_{111}\dot{\theta}_1^2 + N_{112}\dot{\theta}_1\dot{c}_1 + N_{121}\dot{c}_1\dot{\theta}_1 + N_{122}\dot{c}_2^2 \\ N_{211}\dot{\theta}_1^2 + N_{212}\dot{\theta}_1\dot{c}_1 + N_{221}\dot{c}_1\dot{\theta}_1 + N_{222}\dot{c}_2^2 \end{bmatrix} + \begin{pmatrix} G_1 \\ G_2 \end{pmatrix}$$

$$= \begin{pmatrix} M^a(t) \\ F^a(t) \end{pmatrix}$$

where

$$M_{11} = I_{G_1} + I_{G_2} + m_1c_1^2 + m_2c_2^2 \qquad M_{22} = -m_2$$

$$M_{12} = M_{21} = 0$$

$$N_{112} = 2m_2c_2 \qquad N_{211} = m_2c_2$$

$$N_{111} = N_{121} = N_{122} = N_{212} = N_{221} = N_{222} = 0$$

$$G_1 = (m_1c_1 + m_2c_2)gC\theta_1$$

$$G_2 = -m_2gS\theta_1$$

Clearly, this equation has the form indicated by (8-27). We have included the coefficients N_{ijk} since we always have the indicated possible velocity products. The reason for the use of N_{i12} and N_{i21} will become more apparent later.

With the previous equation in mind, we may write the n equations of an n-axes robot in the form

$$\sum_{j=1}^{n} M_{ij}\ddot{\xi}_j + \sum_{j=1}^{n}\sum_{k=1}^{n} N_{ijk}\dot{\xi}_j\dot{\xi}_k + G_i = Q_i \qquad i = 1,\ldots,n \tag{8-28}$$

where it must be kept in mind that M_{ij}, N_{ijk}, and G_i are all generally functions of ξ.

The next example brings us more in line with what might be termed common manipulator equations, and it will lead us up to two final standard forms of these equations. We shall work the problem in some detail to help the student in absorbing the coalescence of the various dynamic concepts.

Example 8-16 The simple planar two-link manipulator. The manipulator in Fig. 8-20 is operating in the vertical plane and thus is subject to a gravitational acceleration g. The links are slender homogeneous rods of lengths L_1 and L_2 and masses m_1 and m_2, respectively. Derive the equations of motion of this manipulator and put them into the standard form exhibited by (8-28).

Solution. We shall approach this problem in the ingrained fashion. We first determine all of the needed kinematic information and then make use of the equations of motion in the form

$$\boldsymbol{M}_{G_i} = \frac{d\boldsymbol{H}_{G_i}}{dt} \qquad \text{and} \qquad \boldsymbol{F}_i = m_i\boldsymbol{a}_{G_i}$$

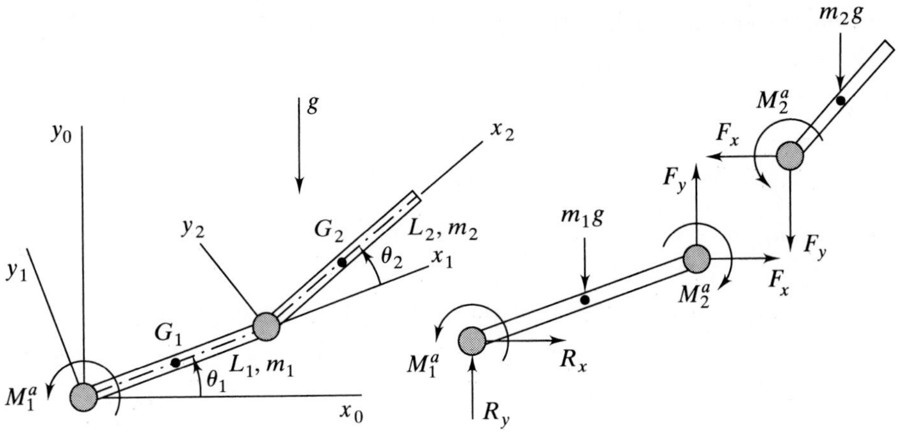

FIGURE 8-20
The planar two-link manipulator.

for each link. For a planar problem there are then three governing equations for each link.

We first obtain the accelerations of the mass centers. The motions of the mass centers are

$$\boldsymbol{r}_{G_1} = \frac{1}{2}L_1\hat{\boldsymbol{\imath}}_1 \qquad \text{and} \qquad \boldsymbol{r}_{G_2} = L_1\hat{\boldsymbol{\imath}}_1 + \frac{1}{2}L_2\hat{\boldsymbol{\imath}}_2$$

and the absolute angular velocities of the frames $(0xyz)_1$ and $(0xyz)_2$ are

$$\boldsymbol{\omega}_1 = \dot{\theta}_1\hat{\boldsymbol{k}}_1 \qquad \text{and} \qquad \boldsymbol{\omega}_2 = \dot{\psi}\hat{\boldsymbol{k}}_2 \qquad \dot{\psi} = \dot{\theta}_1 + \dot{\theta}_2$$

The velocities are obtained from the motions as

$$\boldsymbol{v}_G = \frac{1}{2}L_1\boldsymbol{\omega}_1 \times \hat{\boldsymbol{\imath}}_1 = \frac{1}{2}L_1\dot{\theta}_1\hat{\boldsymbol{\jmath}}_1$$

and

$$\boldsymbol{v}_{G_2} = L_1\boldsymbol{\omega}_1 \times \hat{\boldsymbol{\imath}}_1 + \frac{1}{2}L_2\boldsymbol{\omega}_2 \times \hat{\boldsymbol{\imath}}_2 = L_1\dot{\theta}_1\hat{\boldsymbol{\jmath}}_1 + \frac{1}{2}L_2\dot{\psi}\hat{\boldsymbol{\jmath}}_2.$$

Another differentiation yields the accelerations as

$$\boldsymbol{a}_{G_1} = \frac{1}{2}L_1\left(-\dot{\theta}_1^2\hat{\boldsymbol{\imath}}_1 + \ddot{\theta}_1\hat{\boldsymbol{\jmath}}_1\right)$$

$$\boldsymbol{a}_{G_2} = L_1\left(-\dot{\theta}_1^2\hat{\boldsymbol{\imath}}_1 + \ddot{\theta}_1\hat{\boldsymbol{\jmath}}_1\right) + \frac{1}{2}L_2\left(-\dot{\psi}^2\hat{\boldsymbol{\imath}}_2 + \ddot{\psi}\hat{\boldsymbol{\jmath}}_2\right)$$

Since we ultimately want an equation written in world coordinates, we now convert these equations to the world basis $\hat{\imath}_0$, $\hat{\jmath}_0$, and $\hat{k}_0$ with

$$\hat{\imath}_1 = \cos\theta_1\,\hat{\imath}_0 + \sin\theta_1\,\hat{\jmath}_0 \qquad \hat{\imath}_2 = \cos\psi\,\hat{\imath}_0 + \sin\psi\,\hat{\jmath}_0$$

$$\hat{\jmath}_1 = -\sin\theta_1\,\hat{\imath}_0 + \cos\theta_1\,\hat{\jmath}_0 \qquad \hat{\jmath}_2 = -\sin\psi\,\hat{\imath}_0 + \cos\psi\,\hat{\jmath}_0$$

The final expressions for the accelerations are then given by

$$\boldsymbol{a}_{G_1} = \frac{L_1}{2}\left(-\dot{\theta}_1^2\cos\theta_1 - \ddot{\theta}_1\sin\theta_1\right)\hat{\imath}_0 + \frac{L_1}{2}\left(-\dot{\theta}_1^2\sin\theta_1 + \ddot{\theta}_1\cos\theta_1\right)\hat{\jmath}_0$$

$$\boldsymbol{a}_{G_2} = \left[L_1\left(-\dot{\theta}_1^2\cos\theta_1 - \ddot{\theta}_1\sin\theta_1\right) + \frac{1}{2}L_2\left(-\dot{\psi}^2\cos\psi - \ddot{\psi}\sin\psi\right)\right]\hat{\imath}_0$$
$$+\left[L_1\left(-\dot{\theta}_1^2\sin\theta_1 + \ddot{\theta}_1\cos\theta_1\right) + \frac{1}{2}L_2\left(-\dot{\psi}^2\sin\psi + \ddot{\psi}\cos\psi\right)\right]\hat{\jmath}_0$$

The equations of motion for link 1 are

$$(R_x + F_x)\hat{\imath}_0 + (R_y + F_y - m_1 g)\hat{\jmath}_0 = m_1\boldsymbol{a}_{G_1}$$

$$M_1^a - M_2^a + \frac{1}{2}L_1R_x\sin\theta_1 - \frac{1}{2}L_1R_y\cos\theta_1$$
$$-\frac{1}{2}L_1F_x\sin\theta_1 + \frac{1}{2}L_1F_y\cos\theta_1 = I_{G_1}\ddot{\theta}_1$$

and those for link 2 are given by

$$-F_x\hat{\imath}_0 + (-F_y - m_2 g)\hat{\jmath}_0 = m_2\boldsymbol{a}_{G_2}$$

$$M_2^a - \frac{1}{2}L_2F_x\sin\psi + \frac{1}{2}L_2F_y\cos\psi = I_{G_2}\ddot{\psi}$$

These yield the following judiciously written six equations:

$$R_x = -F_x - m_1\frac{L_1}{2}\left(\dot{\theta}_1^2\cos\theta_1 + \ddot{\theta}_1\sin\theta_1\right) \tag{8-29a}$$

$$R_y = -F_y + m_1 g + m_1\frac{1}{2}L_1\left(-\dot{\theta}_1^2\sin\theta_1 + \ddot{\theta}_1\cos\theta_1\right) \tag{8-29b}$$

$$M_1^a = I_{G_1}\ddot{\theta}_1 + M_2^a - \frac{1}{2}L_1(R_x - F_x)\sin\theta_1 + \frac{1}{2}L_1(R_y - F_y)\cos\theta_1 \tag{8-29c}$$

$$F_x = m_2\left[L_1\left(\dot{\theta}_1^2\cos\theta_1 + \ddot{\theta}_1\sin\theta_1\right) + \frac{1}{2}L_2\left(\dot{\psi}^2\cos\psi + \ddot{\psi}\sin\psi\right)\right] \tag{8-29d}$$

$$F_y = m_2\left[-g + L_1\left(\dot{\theta}_1^2\sin\theta_1 - \ddot{\theta}_1\cos\theta_1\right) + \frac{1}{2}L_2\left(\dot{\psi}^2\sin\psi - \ddot{\psi}\cos\psi\right)\right] \tag{8-29e}$$

$$M_2^a = \frac{1}{2}L_2(F_x\sin\psi - F_y\cos\psi) + I_{G_2}\ddot{\psi} \tag{8-29f}$$

The remaining objective is to obtain the actuator moments M_1^a and M_2^a purely in terms of θ_1 and θ_2 and their derivatives. This is accomplished for M_2^a by substituting the preceding expressions for F_x and F_y [Eqs. (8-29d) and (8-29e)]

into (8-29f), with the result

$$M_2^a = \ddot{\theta}_1\left[\frac{1}{2}L_1L_2m_2\cos\theta_2 + \frac{1}{4}L_2^2m_2 + I_{G_2}\right] + \ddot{\theta}_2\left[\frac{1}{4}L_2^2m_2 + I_{G_2}\right] + \dot{\theta}_1^2\left(\frac{1}{2}L_1L_2m_2\sin\theta_2\right) + \frac{1}{2}L_2m_2g\cos\psi \quad (8\text{-}30)$$

For the calculation of M_1^a we first eliminate R_x and R_y from (8-29c) by using (8-29a) and (8-29b). The subsequent use of (8-29d) and (8-29e), together with (8-30), then yields the desired expression for M_1^a, given by

$$\begin{aligned} M_1^a = {} & \ddot{\theta}_1\left[I_{G_1} + I_{G_2} + \frac{1}{4}m_1L_1^2 + m_2\left(L_1^2 + \frac{1}{4}L_2^2 + L_1L_2\cos\theta_2\right)\right] \\ & + \ddot{\theta}_2\left[I_{G_2} + \frac{1}{4}m_2L_2^2 + \frac{1}{2}L_1L_2m_2\cos\theta_2\right] \\ & + \dot{\theta}_1\dot{\theta}_2[-L_1L_2m_2\sin\theta_2] + \dot{\theta}_2^2\left[-\frac{1}{2}L_1L_2m_2\sin\theta_2\right] \\ & + \frac{1}{2}L_1m_1g\cos\theta_1 + m_2g\left(\frac{1}{2}L_2\cos\psi + L_1\cos\theta_1\right) \end{aligned} \quad (8\text{-}31)$$

To write these equations for M_1^a and M_2^a in standard form, we again introduce

$$M_{11} = I_{G_1} + I_{G_2} + \frac{1}{4}m_1L_1^2 + m_2\left(L_1^2 + \frac{1}{4}L_2^2 + L_1L_2C\theta_2\right)$$

$$M_{12} = M_{21} = I_{G_2} + \frac{1}{4}m_2L_2^2 + \frac{1}{2}L_1L_2m_2C\theta_2$$

$$M_{22} = I_{G_2} + \frac{1}{4}m_2L_2^2$$

along with

$$N_{111} = 0 \qquad N_{112} = N_{121} = -\frac{1}{2}L_1L_2m_2S\theta_2 \qquad N_{122} = -\frac{1}{2}L_1L_2m_2S\theta_2$$

$$N_{211} = \frac{1}{2}L_1L_2m_2S\theta_2 \qquad N_{212} = N_{221} = N_{222} = 0$$

$$G_1 = \frac{1}{2}L_1m_1gC\theta_1 + m_2g\left(\frac{1}{2}L_2C\psi + L_1C\theta_1\right) \qquad G_2 = \frac{1}{2}L_2m_2gC\psi$$

with the general form

$$\sum_{j=1}^{2} M_{ij}\ddot{\theta}_j + \sum_{j=1}^{2}\sum_{k=1}^{2} N_{ijk}\dot{\theta}_j\dot{\theta}_k + G_i = Q_i \qquad i = 1,2$$

Remark 8-6. It is sometimes noted that the distinction between internal and external forces and moments with the present context is not as relevant as the distinction between actuator or actively controlled forces and passive reactions. Rather, both distinctions are important and must be kept in mind. The applicable laws, such as Newton's laws and Euler's laws of motion, clearly require a distinction between external and internal forces or moments, active or not. Conversely, in adding up the work of a system, we can no longer make the broad assertion that the work done by the internal forces is 0.

For example, in the preceding problem we took moments about the centers of mass of the individual links in order to make the derivation routine. The external moment M_1^a may also be calculated by writing Euler's second law with respect to O_0. Note carefully that the internal actuator moment M_2^a does not appear in this equation.

We now introduce a further refinement of the standard equations of motion. It can be shown (see Hamel[6]) that for multibody systems with normal connections (in essence, hinges producing only forces and moments), some additional assertions may be made. That is, we still have the equations

$$\sum_{j=1}^{n} M_{ij}\ddot{\xi}_j + \sum_{j=1}^{n}\sum_{k=1}^{n} C_{ijk}\dot{\xi}_j\dot{\xi}_k + G_i = Q_i \tag{8-32}$$

where we may now assert that M_{ij} forms a symmetric matrix and that the C_{ijk} are the Christoffel symbols given by

$$C_{ijk} = \frac{1}{2}\left(\frac{\partial M_{ik}}{\partial \xi_j} + \frac{\partial M_{ij}}{\partial \xi_k} - \frac{\partial M_{jk}}{\partial \xi_i}\right)$$

We remind the reader that all of the coefficients should be viewed as functions of $\boldsymbol{\xi}$.

As a final manipulation of the equations of motion, we introduce the path variable s. Toward this purpose, we assume that some kind of trajectory planning in the world coordinates has resulted in a trajectory whose parametric equations are available to us as

$$\mathbf{w}(s) = \begin{pmatrix} x_0(s) \\ y_0(s) \\ z_0(s) \end{pmatrix}$$

The manner of traversal of this trajectory—that is, s as a function of time—is still taken to be unknown. Next, we assume that a closed form solution for the inverse kinematics problem is available, so that we have

$$\boldsymbol{\xi} = \boldsymbol{\xi}(\mathbf{w}(s)) = \boldsymbol{\xi}^*(s)$$

Clearly, $\boldsymbol{\xi}^*(s)$ is a different function from $\boldsymbol{\xi}(\mathbf{w})$; however, we shall suppress this distinction, since it is clear that all of the functions are to be considered functions of s for the remainder, with the exception of $Q_i(t)$. With $s = s(t)$, we obtain

$$\dot{\boldsymbol{\xi}} = \frac{d\boldsymbol{\xi}}{ds}\dot{s}$$

and
$$\ddot{\boldsymbol{\xi}} = \frac{d\boldsymbol{\xi}}{ds}\ddot{s} + \frac{d^2\boldsymbol{\xi}}{ds^2}\dot{s}^2$$

Substitution of these expressions into (8-32) yields

$$E_i(s)\ddot{s} + F_i(s)\dot{s}^2 + G_i(s) = Q_i(t) \qquad i = 1, 2, \ldots, n \tag{8-33}$$

where

$$E_i(s) = \sum_{j=1}^{n} M_{ij}(s)\frac{d\xi_j}{ds}(s)$$

$$F_i(s) = \sum_{j=1}^{n}\sum_{k=1}^{n} C_{ijk}(s)\frac{d\xi_j}{ds}(s)\frac{d\xi_k}{ds}(s) + \sum_{j=1}^{n} M_{ij}(s)\frac{d^2\xi_j}{ds^2}(s)$$

Here, $G_i(s) = G_i(\boldsymbol{\xi}(s))$ and $Q_i(t)$ is the same as before. In essence, (8-33) serve as constraints on the possible choices of $s(t)$ in control problems.

We have only touched on the rudiments of the generation of equations of motion. Their transformation to a numerically pliable form for large-scale systems is an extensively cultivated art in practice. Quite often, a particular form is only useful for a particular robot type.

8-3 MANIPULATOR CONTROL

Control is getting there in any way we can. Anything beyond that is concerned with optimal control or, more appropriately, "better control," since sufficient conditions for optimality are rarely applied, nor do existing conditions lend themselves to applications in complex problems. Thus optimal control is better termed extremal control, indicating that a particular control is based on only necessary conditions for optimality.

Control theory and methods enter robot motion in two ways: controlled motion of the individual joints, which is usually a feedback control based on linear automatic control methods; and the controlled motion of the end effector, where methods of optimal control may come into play. Optimization in the former case generally involves PID controllers; in the latter case we shall base our results on Pontryagin's maximum principle.

Trajectory planning may or may not precede the application of optimal control methods. That is, a trajectory or curve passing through a specified set of points may have been selected with only the manner of traversal of this curve still to be optimized. Trajectories in joint control generally refer to angular displacements, velocities, and accelerations as functions of time, while the term may refer to actual curves in three dimensions, when the motion of the end effector is being described. We shall provide a number of examples dealing with these distinctions. Many of the examples are necessarily simplified or academic, to make them amenable to analysis and to provide a clarity of method which might otherwise be obscured with algebraic manipulation.

There are some useful preliminaries. Quite often one deals with linearized system equations, and we shall thus present a routine approach to the linearization of a nonlinear system around some operating point. Furthermore, two-dimensional trajectory planning makes use of cubic splines, and we shall thus provide a relatively detailed treatment of these, continuing our discussion from Chap. 1.

8-3-1 Linear and Nonlinear Control Problems

We shall introduce some standard equation forms for both linear and nonlinear systems. These standard forms serve as the fundamental system equations for control problems. In addition, we shall present a linearization of nonlinear systems about some operating point and show that the two standard forms may be related in this fashion.

THE NONLINEAR PROBLEM. For the nonlinear problem formulation, we consider n first-order differential equations in the form

$$\dot{\mathbf{x}} = \mathbf{f}(\mathbf{x}, \mathbf{u}) \qquad t \in [0, t_1] \tag{8-34}$$

with $\mathbf{x} \in \mathbb{R}^n$ as the system state, $\mathbf{u} \in \mathbb{R}^r$ as the control, and with $\mathbf{x}(0) = \mathbf{x}^0 \in \theta^0$ some set of permissible initial values and $\mathbf{x}(t_1) = \mathbf{x}^1 \in \theta^1$ a set of permissible terminal values. A function $\mathbf{s}(t) = \mathbf{s}(\mathbf{x}^0, \mathbf{x}^1; t)$ is a solution of (8-34), provided $\mathbf{s}(\mathbf{x}^0, \mathbf{x}^1; 0) = \mathbf{x}^0$, $\mathbf{s}(\mathbf{x}^0, \mathbf{x}^1; t_1) = \mathbf{x}^1$, and

$$\dot{\mathbf{s}}(t) = \mathbf{f}(\mathbf{s}(t), \mathbf{u}(t))$$

for $t \in [0, t_1]$. Any such solution will also be termed an *admissible trajectory* since the components of $\mathbf{s}$ may be viewed as the parametric equations of a curve in $\mathbb{R}^n$. Generally, each choice of $\mathbf{u}(t)$ will yield a different trajectory. Finding controls that generate admissible trajectories is the *nonlinear control problem* for a manipulator. Usually, there is an infinite number of such trajectories and controls that produce them, and one then attempts to select one in accordance with some preference—the essence of the nonlinear optimal control problem.

THE LINEAR PROBLEM. The standard first-order form of the equations for the linear control problem is

$$\begin{aligned} \dot{\mathbf{x}} &= \mathbf{A}\mathbf{x} + \mathbf{B}\mathbf{u} \qquad t \in [0, t_1] \\ \mathbf{y} &= \mathbf{C}\mathbf{x} \end{aligned} \tag{8-35}$$

where $\mathbf{x} \in \mathbb{R}^n$ is the system state, $\mathbf{A}$ is the $n \times n$ state matrix, $\mathbf{B}$ is the $n \times r$ input matrix, and $\mathbf{u} \in \mathbb{R}^r$ is the input or control vector for the system. The matrix $\mathbf{C}$ is a $k \times n$, $k \leq n$, output matrix expressing the fact that the states we can actually measure or observe are usually less than the defining states for the system. Again, one stipulates $\mathbf{x}(0) \in \theta^0$ and $\mathbf{x}(t_1) \in \theta^1$. A solution is defined exactly as for the nonlinear problem, and different choices of $\mathbf{u}(t)$ yield different solutions or trajectories. The selection of controls that yield a solution is termed the *linear control problem*. Again, there is generally an infinite number of such controls and corresponding solutions. The optimal control problem deals with a selection in accordance with some quantifiable preference.

LINEARIZATION OF THE NONLINEAR SYSTEM. More often than not, the nonlinear control problem becomes intractable, and one thus resorts to a linearization of the problem in the hope that the linearized version will provide insight and perhaps even suffice in controlling the nonlinear system. One such standard problem deals with the controlled small deviation from a nonlinear trajectory. The linearization of the nonlinear system (8-34) relies on the existence of the Taylor series expansion for vector functions of several variables (Fleming[1]). Let $(\mathbf{x}_0, \mathbf{u}_0)$ be a specified "point." Note that "point" here really refers to two functions $(\mathbf{x}_0(t), \mathbf{u}_0(t))$ whose values at an instant t are $(\mathbf{x}_0, \mathbf{u}_0)$. We are thus considering a Taylor series at each instant. For $(\mathbf{x}, \mathbf{u})$ in a neighborhood of $(\mathbf{x}_0, \mathbf{u}_0)$, the Taylor series expansion of $\mathbf{f}(\mathbf{x}, \mathbf{u})$ about $(\mathbf{x}_0, \mathbf{u}_0)$ yields

$$\mathbf{f}(\mathbf{x}, \mathbf{u}) = \mathbf{f}(\mathbf{x}_0, \mathbf{u}_0) + \begin{bmatrix} \dfrac{\partial f_1}{\partial x_1}(\mathbf{x}_0, \mathbf{u}_0) & \cdots & \dfrac{\partial f_1}{\partial x_n}(\mathbf{x}_0, \mathbf{u}_0) \\ \vdots & & \vdots \\ \dfrac{\partial f_n}{\partial x_1}(\mathbf{x}_0, \mathbf{u}_0) & \cdots & \dfrac{\partial f_n}{\partial x_n}(\mathbf{x}_0, \mathbf{u}_0) \end{bmatrix} (\mathbf{x} - \mathbf{x}_0)$$

$$+ \begin{bmatrix} \dfrac{\partial f_1}{\partial u_1}(\mathbf{x}_0, \mathbf{u}_0) & \cdots & \dfrac{\partial f_1}{\partial u_r}(\mathbf{x}_0, \mathbf{u}_0) \\ \vdots & & \vdots \\ \dfrac{\partial f_n}{\partial u_1}(\mathbf{x}_0, \mathbf{u}_0) & \cdots & \dfrac{\partial f_n}{\partial u_r}(\mathbf{x}_0, \mathbf{u}_0) \end{bmatrix} (\mathbf{u} - \mathbf{u}_0)$$

$$+ \text{ higher-order terms}$$

To firm up this idea, suppose we consider the previously mentioned common use of such an expansion.

Suppose a trajectory $\mathbf{x}_0(t)$ has been specified for a nonlinear system. Due to inaccuracies and disturbances in the system, the actual trajectory traversed by the manipulator may be $\mathbf{x}(t)$, where we assume that $\mathbf{x}(t)$ does not differ too much from $\mathbf{x}_0(t)$. Let

$$\mathbf{y}(t) = \mathbf{x}(t) - \mathbf{x}_0(t)$$

be the instantaneous error between these two trajectories. Similarly, we may view $\mathbf{u}_0(t)$ as the control that provides the specified trajectory and $\mathbf{u}(t)$ as the control that ultimately yields $\mathbf{x}(t)$. Then we take

$$\mathbf{v}(t) = \mathbf{u}(t) - \mathbf{u}_0(t)$$

to be the cause of the deviation, or, conversely, we may consider it as an aid in reducing the deviation. Note that $\mathbf{y}(t)$ generally is not a solution of the original nonlinear problem; however, for small $\mathbf{y}(t)$, we have

$$\begin{aligned}\dot{\mathbf{y}}(t) &= \dot{\mathbf{x}}(t) - \dot{\mathbf{x}}_0(t)\\ &= \mathbf{f}(\mathbf{x}(t), \mathbf{u}(t)) - \mathbf{f}(\mathbf{x}_0(t), \mathbf{u}_0(t))\\ &= \mathbf{A}(t)(\mathbf{x}(t) - \mathbf{x}_0(t)) + \mathbf{B}(t)(\mathbf{u}(t) - \mathbf{u}_0(t))\\ &= \mathbf{A}(t)\mathbf{y}(t) + \mathbf{B}(t)\mathbf{v}(t)\end{aligned}$$

Since $\mathbf{A}$ and $\mathbf{B}$ depend on the time, this is now a *nonautonomous* linear control problem in $\mathbf{y}(t)$ with control input $\mathbf{v}(t)$. A common choice for the control $\mathbf{v}(t)$ is one that will minimize the square of the error,

$$J(\mathbf{v}(\cdot)) = \int_0^{t_1} \mathbf{y}^T(t)\mathbf{y}(t)\, dt$$

If we assume that the error is 0 initially and finally, then we would addend the conditions $\mathbf{y}(0) = \mathbf{y}(t_1) = \mathbf{0}$.

As an example we shall consider a linearization of the equations of motion of a manipulator.

Example 8-17. We first note that the equation of motion of a manipulator [Eq. (8-27)] may also be written (with no explicit dependence of the coefficients on t) in the form

$$\mathbf{M}(\boldsymbol{\xi})\ddot{\boldsymbol{\xi}} + \mathbf{g}(\boldsymbol{\xi}, \dot{\boldsymbol{\xi}}) = \mathbf{q}(t)$$

To be more specific, suppose $\boldsymbol{\xi} = \boldsymbol{\theta} = (\theta_1\, \theta_2)^{\mathrm{T}}$ so that $\boldsymbol{\theta} \in \mathbb{R}^2$. The equation has the specific form

$$\begin{bmatrix} M_{11}(\boldsymbol{\theta}) & M_{12}(\boldsymbol{\theta}) \\ M_{21}(\boldsymbol{\theta}) & M_{22}(\boldsymbol{\theta}) \end{bmatrix}\begin{pmatrix} \ddot{\theta}_1 \\ \ddot{\theta}_2 \end{pmatrix} + \begin{pmatrix} g_1(\boldsymbol{\theta}, \dot{\boldsymbol{\theta}}) \\ g_2(\boldsymbol{\theta}, \dot{\boldsymbol{\theta}}) \end{pmatrix} = \begin{pmatrix} q_1(t) \\ q_2(t) \end{pmatrix}$$

(*a*) Write this equation in standard first-order form for the nonlinear control problem.

(*b*) Linearize the equations derived in part (*a*) about the operating values $\boldsymbol{\theta} = \dot{\boldsymbol{\theta}} = \mathbf{0}$ and $q_1 = q_2 = 0$.

Solution

(*a*) We first multiply the equation by $\mathbf{M}^{-1}$ to obtain

$$\begin{pmatrix} \ddot{\theta}_1 \\ \ddot{\theta}_2 \end{pmatrix} = \mathbf{M}^{-1}(\boldsymbol{\theta})\left[-\mathbf{g}(\boldsymbol{\theta}, \dot{\boldsymbol{\theta}}) + \mathbf{q}(t)\right]$$

where we take

$$\mathbf{M}^{-1}(\boldsymbol{\theta}) = \begin{bmatrix} M_{11}^{-1}(\boldsymbol{\theta}) & M_{12}^{-1}(\boldsymbol{\theta}) \\ M_{21}^{-1}(\boldsymbol{\theta}) & M_{22}^{-1}(\boldsymbol{\theta}) \end{bmatrix}$$

an inverse which always exists for practical problems because of several nice properties enjoyed by **M**. Next, we augment the state space by defining

$$\theta_1 = x_1 \qquad \dot{\theta}_1 = x_2 \qquad \theta_2 = x_3 \qquad \dot{\theta}_2 = x_4 \qquad \text{and} \qquad q_1 = u_1 \qquad q_2 = u_2$$

In terms of $\mathbf{x} = (x_1\ x_2\ x_3\ x_4)^T$, we then have the equations

$$\dot{x}_1 = x_2$$

$$\dot{x}_2 = M_{11}^{-1}(x_1, x_3)[-g_1(\mathbf{x}) + u_1] + M_{12}^{-1}(x_1, x_3)[-g_2(\mathbf{x}) + u_2]$$

$$\dot{x}_3 = x_4$$

$$\dot{x}_4 = M_{21}^{-1}(x_1, x_3)[-g_1(\mathbf{x}) + u_1] + M_{22}^{-1}(x_1, x_3)[-g_2(\mathbf{x}) + u_2]$$

which clearly have the desired form

$$\dot{\mathbf{x}} = \mathbf{f}(\mathbf{x}, \mathbf{u}) = \begin{pmatrix} f_1(\mathbf{x}, \mathbf{u}) \\ f_2(\mathbf{x}, \mathbf{u}) \\ f_3(\mathbf{x}, \mathbf{u}) \\ f_4(\mathbf{x}, \mathbf{u}) \end{pmatrix}$$

(*b*) For the linearization of these equations, we shall evaluate enough of the derivatives to indicate the trend. For $f_1(\mathbf{x}, \mathbf{u}) = x_2$ and $(\mathbf{x}, \mathbf{u}) = (\mathbf{0})$ we have

$$\frac{\partial f_1}{\partial x_1}(\mathbf{0}) = O = \frac{\partial f_1}{\partial x_3}(\mathbf{0}) = \frac{\partial f_1}{\partial x_4}(\mathbf{0}) \qquad \text{and} \qquad \frac{\partial f_1}{\partial x_2}(\mathbf{0}) = 1$$

For $f_2(\mathbf{x}, \mathbf{u})$ we obtain the following expressions:

$$\frac{\partial f_2}{\partial x_1}(\mathbf{0}) = M_{11}^{-1}(\mathbf{0})\left[-\frac{\partial g_1}{\partial x_1}(\mathbf{0})\right] + \frac{\partial M_{11}^{-1}}{\partial x_1}(\mathbf{0})[-g_1(\mathbf{0})]$$
$$+ M_{12}^{-1}(\mathbf{0})\left[-\frac{\partial g_2}{\partial x_1}(\mathbf{0})\right] + \frac{\partial M_{12}^{-1}}{\partial x_1}(\mathbf{0})[-g_2(\mathbf{0})]$$

$$\frac{\partial f_2}{\partial x_2}(\mathbf{0}) = M_{11}^{-1}(\mathbf{0})\left[-\frac{\partial g_1}{\partial x_2}(\mathbf{0})\right] + M_{12}^{-1}(\mathbf{0})\left[-\frac{\partial g_2}{\partial x_2}(\mathbf{0})\right]$$

$$\frac{\partial f_2}{\partial x_3}(\mathbf{0}) = M_{11}^{-1}(\mathbf{0})\left[-\frac{\partial g_1}{\partial x_3}(\mathbf{0})\right] + \frac{\partial M_{11}^{-1}}{\partial x_3}(\mathbf{0})[-g_1(\mathbf{0})]$$
$$+ M_{12}^{-1}(\mathbf{0})\left[-\frac{\partial g_2}{\partial x_3}(\mathbf{0})\right] + \frac{\partial M_{12}^{-1}}{\partial x_3}(\mathbf{0})[-g_2(\mathbf{0})]$$

$$\frac{\partial f_2}{\partial x_4}(\mathbf{0}) = M_{11}^{-1}(\mathbf{0})\left[-\frac{\partial g_1}{\partial x_4}(\mathbf{0})\right] + M_{12}^{-1}(\mathbf{0})\left[-\frac{\partial g_2}{\partial x_4}(\mathbf{0})\right]$$

the remaining derivatives being similarly computed. For the control input matrix, we have

$$\frac{\partial f_1}{\partial u_1}(\mathbf{0}) = \frac{\partial f_1}{\partial u_2}(\mathbf{0}) = 0$$

$$\frac{\partial f_2}{\partial u_1}(\mathbf{0}) = M_{11}^{-1}(\mathbf{0}) \qquad \text{and} \qquad \frac{\partial f_2}{\partial u_2}(\mathbf{0}) = M_{12}^{-1}(\mathbf{0})$$

with similar results for the remaining derivatives. The linearized equations then have the form

$$\begin{pmatrix} \dot{x}_1 \\ \dot{x}_2 \\ \dot{x}_3 \\ \dot{x}_4 \end{pmatrix} = \begin{bmatrix} 0 & 1 & 0 & 0 \\ \dfrac{\partial f_2}{\partial x_1}(\mathbf{0}) & \dfrac{\partial f_2}{\partial x_2}(\mathbf{0}) & \dfrac{\partial f_2}{\partial x_3}(\mathbf{0}) & \dfrac{\partial f_2}{\partial x_4}(\mathbf{0}) \\ & \cdots & & \end{bmatrix} \begin{pmatrix} x_1 \\ x_2 \\ x_3 \\ x_4 \end{pmatrix}$$

$$+ \begin{bmatrix} 0 & 0 \\ \dfrac{\partial f_2}{\partial u_1}(\mathbf{0}) & \dfrac{\partial f_2}{\partial u_2}(\mathbf{0}) \\ \cdots & \end{bmatrix} \begin{pmatrix} u_1 \\ u_2 \end{pmatrix}$$

since $\mathbf{y} = \mathbf{x} - \mathbf{0}$ and $\mathbf{v} = \mathbf{u} - \mathbf{0}$.

8-3-2 Cubic Splines

Example 1-5 gave a brief introduction to this topic. We shall now generalize this treatment and provide the usual background.

The term *spline* derives from a draftsperson's device used extensively in nautical and aeronautical engineering. It is a flexible ruler that can be held in place by weight and hence made to pass through each of a set of points, the connecting curve essentially being that of a bent beam. Indeed, if $y(x)$ denotes the deflection of the elastic line of a beam with constant cross section, then the load-deflection equation for the beam in terms of a distributed load $w(x)$ is given by

$$EI\frac{d^4y}{dx^4}(x) = w(x)$$

where E is Young's modulus and I is the cross-sectional area moment of inertia with respect to the section's neutral line. If the transverse loading on the beam is 0 (e.g., the beam is loaded only by couples at the ends), then

$$\frac{d^4y}{dx^4} = 0$$

is the governing equation. The most important implication of this equation is the continuity of the curvature. That is, we avoid the jumps so undesirable from the point of view of an object accelerating along such a curve. For shipbuilders,

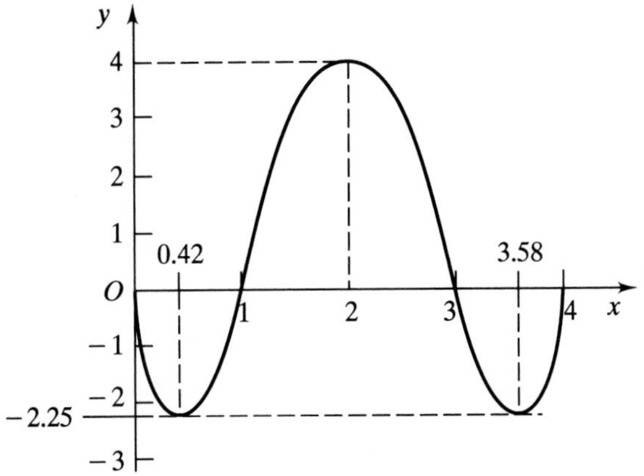

FIGURE 8-21
A quartic through five points.

it provided a curve into which the stringers in a boat hull could be "naturally" deformed. We note that the solution of the equation is a cubic,

$$y(x) = ax^3 + bx^2 + cx + d$$

Our more specific purpose here is to pass a smooth curve† through n points (x_i, y_i) in the plane. At first sight, a simple polynomial of large enough degree would seem to be a natural choice, since it is easy to show the existence and uniqueness of a suitable polynomial of degree $r \leq n - 1$. In addition, there are a variety of algorithms for the determination of such polynomials. As an example suppose we were to pass a *single* polynomial through the points $(x_1, y_1) = (0, 0)$, $(x_2, y_2) = (1, 0)$, $(x_3, y_3) = (2, 4)$, $(x_4, y_4) = (3, 0)$, and $(x_5, y_5) = (4, 0)$. The result, after solving the obvious simultaneous equations, is the fourth-degree polynomial

$$P(x) = x^4 - 8x^3 + 19x^2 - 12x$$

depicted in Fig. 8-21. As previously mentioned, a problem with using simple polynomials for this purpose is the possible wide excursion of the path before again passing through a required point (e.g., swinging to a position $y = -2.25$ before returning to 0). In part, the use of several polynomials in sequence is meant to overcome this difficulty.

According to Böhmer,[7] which we shall use as one of our desk references, the term *spline function* was first coined by Schoenberg[8] in one of the first papers on this topic, in 1946. We provide the following formal definition of such a function.

Definition 8-12 Cubic spline. Suppose n points (x_i, y_i) with $a = x_1 < \cdots < x_n = b$ have been specified. Let $\Pi_n(x_i, x_{i+1})$ be the set of polynomials of degree

†Actually, we require more from a mathematical point of view.

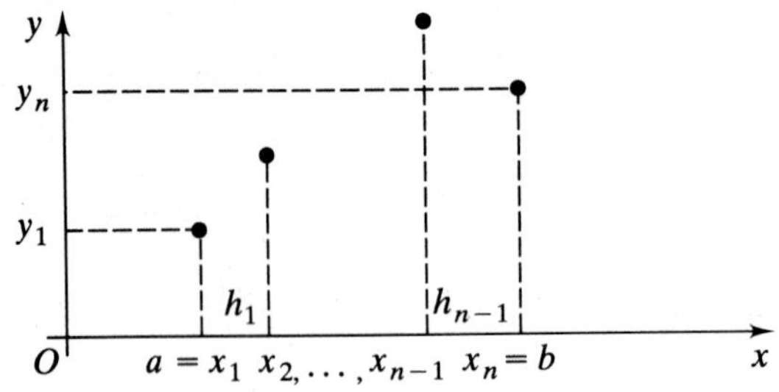

FIGURE 8-22
Points to be splined.

$r \leq n$ restricted to the interval (x_i, x_{i+1}). A *cubic spline* is a function $y(\cdot)$: $\mathbb{R} \to \mathbb{R}$ such that

(a) its restriction to (x_i, x_{i+1}) belongs to $\Pi_3(x_i, x_{i+1})$;
(b) $y(\cdot) \in C^2[a, b]$, the class of functions with continuous second derivative.

If, in addition, we have

(c) $$\frac{d^2y}{dx^2}(a) = \frac{d^2y}{dx^2}(b) = 0$$

then $y(\cdot)$ is termed a *natural spline function.*

We now derive a set of defining equations for a collection of cubic splines through a set of points (x_i, y_i), $i = 1, \ldots, n$, as shown in Fig. 8-22. The following derivation and notation are based on our second desk reference, Gerald and Wheatley.[9] Let

$$y(x) = a_i(x - x_i)^3 + b_i(x - x_i)^2 + c_i(x - x_i) + d_i \tag{8-36}$$

be the cubic polynomial splining the points (x_i, y_i) and (x_{i+1}, y_{i+1}). We then have the identities

$$y(x_i) = y_i \qquad \text{and} \qquad y(x_{i+1}) = y_{i+1} \tag{8-37}$$

We shall also make use of the derivatives

$$\begin{aligned} y'(x) &= 3a_i(x - x_i)^2 + 2b_i(x - x_i) + c_i \\ y''(x) &= 6a_i(x - x_i) + 2b_i \end{aligned} \tag{8-38}$$

In line with Gerald and Wheatley,[9] we let S_i be the second derivative at (x_i, y_i), and S_{i+1} the second derivative at (x_{i+1}, y_{i+1}); that is,

$$S_i = y''(x_i) \qquad \text{and} \qquad S_{i+1} = y''(x_{i+1}) \tag{8-39}$$

The ith interval will be denoted by $h_i = x_{i+1} - x_i$. The objective is to solve for a_i, b_i, c_i, and d_i in terms of the given coordinates (x_i, y_i).

The use of (8-37) to (8-39) yields

$$a_i = \frac{S_{i+1} - S_i}{6h_1} \qquad b_i = \frac{S_i}{2} \qquad \text{and} \qquad d_i = y_i \tag{8-40}$$

The evaluation of (8-36) at x_{i+1} yields

$$y_{i+1} = a_i h_i^3 + b_i h_i^2 + c_i h_i + d_i$$

and

$$c_i = \frac{1}{h_i}(y_{i+1} - y_i) - \left(a_i h_i^2 + b_i h_i\right) \tag{8-41}$$

Equating the slopes of adjoining polynomials at (x_i, y_i) results in

$$c_i = 3a_{i-1}(x_i - x_{i-1})^2 + 2b_{i-1}(x_i - x_{i-1}) + c_{i-1}$$

After some manipulation this yields the recursion relationship

$$\frac{6}{h_i}(y_{i+1} - y_i) - \frac{6}{h_{i-1}}(y_i - y_{i-1}) = S_{i-1}h_{i-1} + S_i(2h_i + 2h_{i-1}) + S_{i+1}h_i \tag{8-42}$$

Example 8-18. Rework Example 1-5 by making use of the recursion relationship (8-42).

Solution. Note that only the y-coordinates are involved in (8-42) and that the $h_i = 1$ for every i. We have

$$y_1 = 2 \qquad y_2 = 2 \qquad y_3 = 3 \qquad \text{and} \qquad y_4 = 4$$

Substitution of these values into (8-42) yields

$$i = 2 \qquad 6(3 - 2) - 6(2 - 2) = S_1 + 4S_2 + S_3$$

$$i = 3 \qquad 6(4 - 3) - 6(3 - 2) = S_2 + 4S_3 + S_4$$

or the simultaneous equations

$$4S_2 + S_3 = 6 - S_1$$

$$S_2 + 4S_3 = -S_4$$

two equations in four unknowns. To be able to solve, we thus need to specify two of the unknowns. This is usually done by specifying the first and the last value of the second derivative, a requirement that we have already incorporated in the way we have written the equations. When we use the values of the earlier example, namely:

$$S_1 = 0 \qquad \text{and} \qquad S_4 = -24$$

then the final results for S_2 and S_3 are $S_2 = 0$ and $S_3 = 6$. The coefficients of the polynomials are given by

$$i=1 \qquad 1 \le x < 2$$

$$a_1 = \frac{S_2 - S_1}{6h_1} = 0$$

$$b_1 = \frac{S_1}{2} = 0$$

$$c_1 = \frac{1}{h_1}(y_2 - y_1) - \left(a_1 h_1^2 + b_1 h_1\right) = (2-2) - (0+0) = 0$$

$$d_1 = y_1 = 2$$

The corresponding cubic is thus reduced to $y(x) = 2$:

$$i=2 \qquad 2 \le x < 3$$

$$a_2 = 1 \qquad b_2 = 0 \qquad c_2 = 0 \qquad d_2 = 2$$

$$y(x) = (x-2)^3 + 2$$

$$i=3 \qquad 3 \le x \le 4$$

$$a_3 = -5 \qquad b_3 = 3 \qquad c_3 = 3 \qquad d_3 = 3$$

$$y(x) = -5(x-3)^3 + 3(x-3)^2 + 3(x-3) + 3$$

In the example the substitution of the y_i yielded a set of simultaneous equations for the S_i. Quite generally, we have the following set of simultaneous equations, obtained from (8-42) with $i = 2, \ldots, n-1$,

$$\begin{bmatrix} h_1 & 2h_2 + 2h_1 & h_2 & 0 & 0 & 0 \\ 0 & h_2 & 2h_3 + 2h_2 & h_3 & 0 & \cdot \\ 0 & 0 & h_3 & 2h_4 + 2h_3 & h_4 & \cdot \\ & & \cdots & \cdots & & \cdot \\ 0 & 0 & 0 \quad \cdots & h_{n-2} & 2h_{n-1} + 2h_{n-2} & h_{n-1} \end{bmatrix} \begin{pmatrix} S_1 \\ S_2 \\ \vdots \\ S_{n-1} \\ S_n \end{pmatrix}$$

$$= 6 \begin{pmatrix} \frac{1}{h_2}(y_3 - y_2) - \frac{1}{h_1}(y_2 - y_1) \\ \frac{1}{h_3}(y_4 - y_3) - \frac{1}{h_2}(y_3 - y_2) \\ \cdots \\ \frac{1}{h_{n-1}}(y_n - y_{n-1}) - \frac{1}{h_{n-2}}(y_{n-1} - y_{n-2}) \end{pmatrix} \tag{8-43}$$

Example 8-19. Consider again the example we gave at the beginning of this section, involving a quartic made to pass through five given points. The points through which the curve was made to pass are shown in the following table. Determine the cubic spline functions through these points, based on the assumption $S_1 = S_5 = 0$.

i	x_i	y_i
1	0	0
2	1	0
3	2	4
4	3	0
5	4	0

Solution. First, note that $h_i = 1$ for all i. The system of equations for the derivatives S_i is obtained directly as

$$\begin{bmatrix} 1 & 4 & 1 & 0 & 0 \\ 0 & 1 & 4 & 1 & 0 \\ 0 & 0 & 1 & 4 & 1 \end{bmatrix} \begin{pmatrix} S_1 \\ S_2 \\ S_3 \\ S_4 \\ S_5 \end{pmatrix} = \begin{pmatrix} 24 \\ -48 \\ 24 \end{pmatrix}$$

With $S_1 = S_5 = 0$ these equations reduce to

$$4S_2 + S_3 = 24$$
$$S_2 + 4S_3 + S_4 = -48$$
$$S_3 + 4S_4 = 24$$

Their simultaneous solution yields the curvatures

$$S_1 = S_5 = 0 \qquad S_2 = 10.29 \qquad S_3 = -17.16 \qquad S_4 = 10.29$$

The corresponding cubics for the various intervals are given by

$$[0,1) \qquad y(x) = 1.72(x^3 - x)$$
$$[1,2) \qquad y(x) = -4.58(x-1)^3 + 5.15(x-1)^2 + 3.43(x-1)$$
$$[2,3) \qquad y(x) = 4.58(x-2)^3 - 8.58(x-2)^2 + 4$$
$$[3,4] \qquad y(x) = -1.72(x-3)^3 + 5.15(x-3)^2 - 3.43(x-3)$$

The resultant spline through all of these points is sketched in Fig. 8-23.

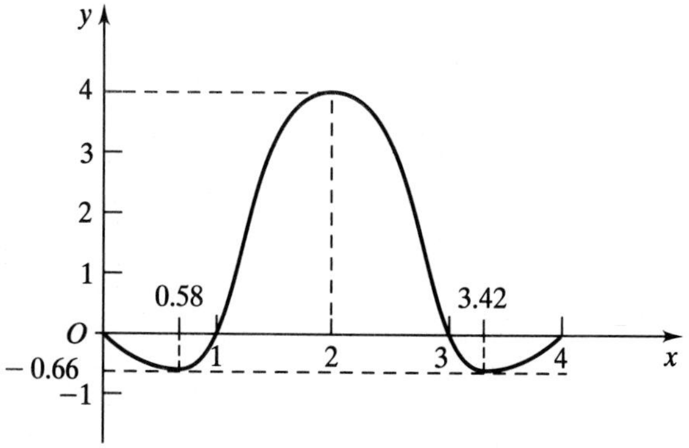

FIGURE 8-23
The quartic replaced by the spline.

We close this section with some comments on the optimality properties of cubic splines. According to Böhmer[7], in 1957 Holladay[10] was the first to note that a beam composed of spline functions had a minimum strain energy. More specifically, if $\bar{y}(\cdot)$ is any possible elastic curve of a beam with constant bending stiffness EI and

$$V(\bar{y}(\cdot)) = \frac{1}{2}\int_a^b \frac{M^2(x)}{EI}\,dx = c\int_a^b \left(\frac{d^2\bar{y}}{dx^2}(x)\right)^2 dx$$

is the strain energy of the beam viewed as a functional (function of functions) of $\bar{y}(\cdot)$, then the cubic spline $y(\cdot)$ through points between a and b satisfies

$$V(y(\cdot)) = \min_{\bar{y}(\cdot)} V(\bar{y}(\cdot))$$

In addition, it can be shown that the *natural cubic spline* is the *unique* minimizing spline passing through a specified set of points.

We remind the reader once more that these splines are interpolation functions between points in two dimensions. Thus their use is restricted to the two-dimensional motion of the tool point, for example, or to the calculation of individual robot variables as functions of time. In both situations the calculations must take into account velocity and acceleration restrictions which are always present in robot motion.

8-3-3 Optimal Paths of the End Effector

The final objective is the controlled motion of the end effector, its position, velocity, and orientation. The achievement of this objective is based on the controlled motion of the individual joints or robot axes. Thus control methods ultimately differ only in the manner in which this joint motion is produced and prescribed. The following example illustrates this connection.

Example 8-20 The two-link manipulator. Suppose the tool point is to move along the curve C as shown in Fig. 8-24a. Discuss the manner in which the motion from point A to point B may be achieved.

Solution. We assume that the curve C, the tool point trajectory, has been planned so as to avoid all obstacles as well as undesirable motion characteristics, such as jumps in the curvature. The remaining prescription follows our examples in Chap. 2, where we simply look for a parametrization of the curve C such that $\boldsymbol{r}_0(0) = \boldsymbol{r}_A$ and $\boldsymbol{r}_0(t_1) = \boldsymbol{r}_B$ with $\boldsymbol{v}_0(0) = \boldsymbol{v}_0(t_1) = \boldsymbol{0}$.

Corresponding to these initial and terminal conditions in world space, we have equivalent conditions in joint space. That is, in terms of A and B we require:

$$\begin{aligned}
A:&\quad \theta_1(0) = \theta_{1A} &\quad \dot{\theta}_1(0) = 0\\
&\quad \theta_2(0) = \theta_{2A} &\quad \dot{\theta}_2(0) = 0\\
B:&\quad \theta_1(t_1) = \theta_{1B} &\quad \dot{\theta}_1(t_1) = 0\\
&\quad \theta_2(t_1) = \theta_{2B} &\quad \dot{\theta}_2(t_1) = 0
\end{aligned}$$

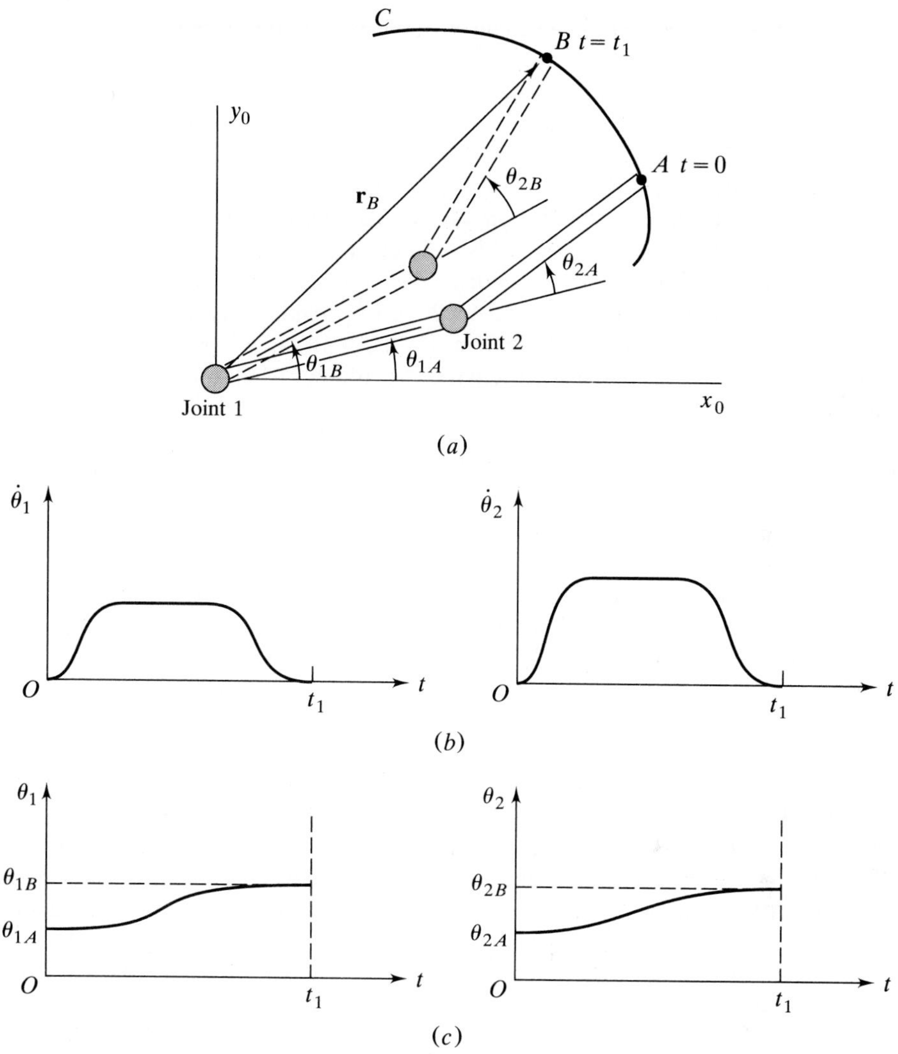

FIGURE 8-24
Joint and end-effector motion.

All of the intermediate points for the joint motion lie on position and velocity curves such as those shown in Figs. 8-24*b* and *c*.

As is the case with all design problems, the final design or control will always include some effort at achieving better control. We emphasize the adjective "better" rather than optimal, since truly optimal control can rarely be guaranteed. Once we accept that some kind of optimally controlled motion is the goal, then the whole robot should be designed with this goal in mind.

For example, if motion in as little time as possible is the most desirable aspect, then this objective should govern the design of the whole robot. Instead, robots are often designed with great rigidity (meaning hefty) to maintain greater accuracy, and the achievement of high speeds may then set inordinate power requirements. The power consumption itself may often impose additional limitations. In short, the desired versatility of the robot as a machine generally requires some compromise between various desiderata. The manner in which such a compromise can be reached is the subject of what is commonly termed *multicriteria optimization*, or *multicriteria optimal control*, a subject dealt with extensively in Stadler.[11] Our aim here will be to provide some basic background in optimal control as generated by the use of Pontryagin's maximum principle and PID controllers as used in automatic control. We shall emphasize problem formulation rather than complexity.

THE OPTIMAL CONTROL PROBLEM. We have previously provided a discussion of the general control problem; we now add a preference to characterize optimal control. For completeness, we shall repeat some of this previous discussion.

We begin with the term *trajectory*. It is common to refer to curves in $\mathbb{R}^n$ as trajectories, whether they characterize the physical motion of a point P or not. Thus the motion of the tool point in $\mathbb{R}^3$ is a trajectory or curve in the traditional sense; the state trajectory $\mathbf{x}(t)$ in $\mathbb{R}^n$ is one in the broader sense. We return to the nonlinear control problem with

$$\dot{\mathbf{x}} = \mathbf{f}(\mathbf{x}, \mathbf{u}) \qquad t \in [0, t_1] \tag{8-44}$$

$\mathbf{x} \in \mathbb{R}^n$, $\mathbf{u} \in \mathbb{R}^r$ as the state equation, and we require that $\mathbf{x}(0) = \mathbf{x}^0 \in \theta^0$ and $\mathbf{x}(t_1) = \mathbf{x}^1 \in \theta^1$. With no further requirements, a control $\mathbf{u}(\cdot)$ is an *admissible* control if it produces a solution of (8-44), satisfying the initial and final conditions. It is useful to view a solution $\mathbf{x}(t)$ with different controls, producing different trajectories, as shown in Fig. 8-25.

More often than not, there is an infinite number of admissible controls that accomplish the specified task, and it obviously becomes desirable to make a good or optimal selection from among them. That is, we should like to compare

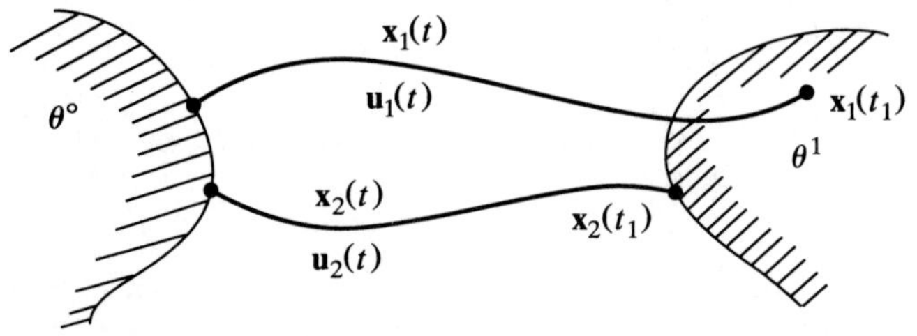

FIGURE 8-25
Different controls... different trajectories.

controls in some fashion. The most direct way is to introduce a criterion functional

$$g(\mathbf{u}(\cdot)) = \int_0^{t_1} f_0(\mathbf{x}(t), \mathbf{u}(t))\, dt \tag{8-45}$$

with an adage such as "smaller is better." [Note that the integrated $f_0(\cdot)$ is not in any way related to the $\mathbf{f}(\cdot)$ in the equation for $\dot{\mathbf{x}}$.] The implication is an ordering of the controls in accordance with

$$\mathbf{u}_1(\cdot) \preceq \mathbf{u}_2(\cdot) \quad \Leftrightarrow \quad g(\mathbf{u}_1(\cdot)) \le g(\mathbf{u}_2(\cdot))$$

where $\preceq$ is read as "is preferred or equivalent to." Given any two controls, we are now able to decide which one is better. A natural next step is the definition of a best control. A control $\mathbf{u}^*(\cdot)$ is termed an optimal (minimizing) control iff

$$\mathbf{u}^*(\cdot) \preceq \mathbf{u}(\cdot) \quad \Leftrightarrow \quad g(\mathbf{u}^*(\cdot)) \le g(\mathbf{u}(\cdot))$$

for all $\mathbf{u}(\cdot)$. All $\mathbf{u}(\cdot)$ turns out to be somewhat too broad from a mathematical as well as a practical point of view, and one thus includes some restrictions on the controls $\mathbf{u}(\cdot)$ such as bounds, $a_i \le u_i(t) \le b_i$, or the insistence that $\mathbf{u}(\cdot)$ belong to some function class $\mathscr{F}$. Collectively, it is thus assumed that $\mathbf{u}(\cdot)$ belongs to some control constraint set $\mathscr{U}$. We now have the ingredients for the basic optimal control problem statement:

Obtain control(s) $\mathbf{u}^*(\cdot) \in \mathscr{U}$, such that

$$g(\mathbf{u}^*(\cdot)) \le g(\mathbf{u}(\cdot))$$

for all $\mathbf{u}(\cdot) \in \mathscr{U}$, subject to

$$\dot{\mathbf{x}} = \mathbf{f}(\mathbf{x}, \mathbf{u}) \qquad t \in [0, t_1]$$

with $\mathbf{x}(0) = \mathbf{x}^0$ and $\mathbf{x}(t_1) = \mathbf{x}^1$, where we have restricted ourselves to given initial and final states for simplicity.

There are many guises to this problem; we have chosen a variant that suffices for our purposes.

The next step, of course, concerns the manner in which we may derive such an optimal control. Such derivations are generally based on the use of necessary conditions for optimal control—in our case, conditions embodied in Pontryagin's maximum principle. We shall make little attempt at mathematical rigor, but simply cite the conditions with the same abandon with which they are usually used. And, if the approach leads to a practical better control, it becomes irrelevant whether any mathematical conditions were satisfied or not in constructing it.

THE MAXIMUM PRINCIPLE. The conditions stated here are as simple in their statement as they are complex in their actual application. We shall subsequently illustrate their use.

The Hamiltonian for the problem is

$$H(\boldsymbol{\lambda}, \mathbf{x}, \mathbf{u}) = \lambda_0 f_0(\mathbf{x}, \mathbf{u}) + \boldsymbol{\lambda}^{\mathrm{T}} \mathbf{f}(\mathbf{x}, \mathbf{u})$$

Subject to a number of mathematical conditions, the following statements embody the essentials of the maximum principle:

Let $\mathbf{u}^*(\cdot) \in \mathscr{U}$ be an optimal control. Then there exists a *nonzero* vector function $(\lambda_0^* \, \boldsymbol{\lambda}^*(t))^{\mathrm{T}}$ whose components are solutions of the adjoint equations

$$\dot{\lambda}_i^*(t) = -\frac{\partial H}{\partial x_i}(\boldsymbol{\lambda}^*(t), \mathbf{x}^*(t), \mathbf{u}^*(t))$$

such that

1. For all $t \in [0, t_1]$,

$$\sup_{u \in U} H(\boldsymbol{\lambda}^*(t), \mathbf{x}^*(t), \mathbf{u}) = H(\boldsymbol{\lambda}^*(t), \mathbf{x}^*(t), \mathbf{u}^*(t)) = \text{const.} \geq 0$$

2. $\lambda_0^* = \text{const.} \leq 0$
3. $\boldsymbol{\lambda}^*(t)$ is normal to the tangent spaces of the terminal manifolds at $t = 0$ and $t = t_1$; that is, $\boldsymbol{\lambda}^*(0) \perp T_{\theta^0}$ and $\boldsymbol{\lambda}^*(t_1) \perp T_{\theta^1}$. Thus, if $\mathbf{x}(0)$ is specified, for example, then $\boldsymbol{\lambda}^*(0)$ is arbitrary; if $\mathbf{x}(0)$ is not specified, then the implication is $\boldsymbol{\lambda}^*(0) = \mathbf{0}$. These normality conditions are called *transversality conditions*.

For convenience, the asterisk will be omitted in calculations with the exception of its use for emphasis in isolated instances.

All of these conditions are of little use if the optimal control for a given problem does not exist. From a theoretical as well as a practical point of view, establishing the existence of optimal control is essential before embarking on conditions for its calculation. The engineer is usually undaunted by such considerations and simply uses the necessary conditions.

A solution based only on the use of necessary conditions is called an *extremal* control. The concept of extremal control is analogous to the calculation of critical points in a simple calculus minimization problem. Thus such an extremal may actually correspond to either a maximum or a minimum. If, however, we have a working control available, as is often the case, then a comparison of criterion values can still help us make a decision about the character of the extremal control. At any rate, optimal controls can be shown to exist under rather general conditions (see Lee and Markus,[12] for example).

Our first example simply serves to illustrate the use of necessary conditions. It provides a transition of sorts from the student's experience in calculus to the control theoretic approach. Suppose we wish to obtain the shortest distance from a point in the plane to a line in the same plane. For definiteness, say the point is $(1, 3)$ and we wish to find the distance to the line $y = 2x - 2$, a situation we have depicted in Fig. 8-26a. With (x, y) as an arbitrary point on the line, we need only minimize

$$\begin{aligned} L(x) &= \sqrt{(x-1)^2 + (y(x) - 3)^2} \\ &= \sqrt{5x^2 - 22x + 26} \end{aligned}$$

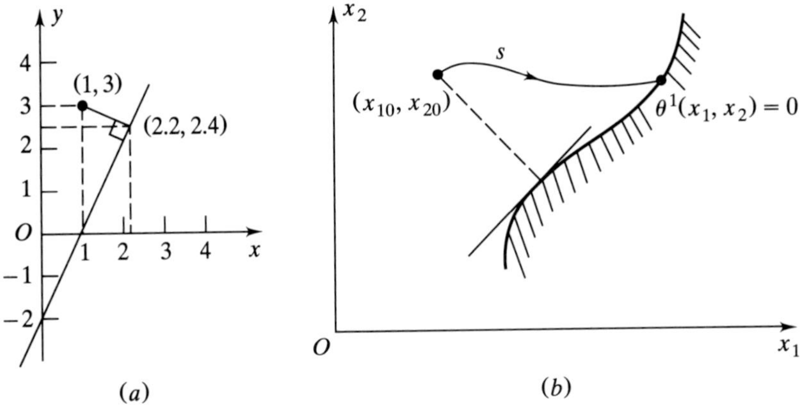

FIGURE 8-26
Minimum distance from a point to a line.

The usual necessary condition yields

$$\frac{dL}{dx} = \frac{5x - 11}{\sqrt{5x^2 - 22x + 26}} = 0$$

or $x = 2.2$ and $y = 2.4$. Viewed in terms of the arc length s, we would attempt to minimize

$$s_1 = \int_0^{s_1} ds$$

where s is measured along any possible trajectory from the point (x_0, y_0) to the terminal set $\theta(x, y)$. To obtain a control theoretic formulation, suppose we now parametrize s, x, and y in terms of t so that

$$s_1 = \int_0^{t_1} |v(t)|\, dt$$

and $v(t) = \sqrt{\dot{x}^2 + \dot{y}^2}$. For a constant v we may then formulate the following optimal control problem.

Example 8-21 Minimum time to travel from a point to a curve. We propose the following minimum time problem: Minimize

$$g_1(\mathbf{u}(\cdot)) = \int_0^{t_1} dt$$

subject to

$$\dot{x}_1 = u_1 \qquad x_1(0) = x_{10} = 1$$

$$\dot{x}_2 = u_2 \qquad x_2(0) = x_{20} = 3$$

and the termination requirement $\theta^1(x_1, x_2) = x_2 - 2x_1 + 2$. Control is restricted to the control constraint set $\mathscr{U} = \{(u_1, u_2) \in \mathbb{R}^2 \colon u_1^2 + u_2^2 = 1\}$, with the terminal time t_1 left unspecified.

Solution. The Hamiltonian for the problem is

$$H(\boldsymbol{\lambda}, \mathbf{x}, \mathbf{u}) = \lambda_0 + \lambda_1 u_1 + \lambda_2 u_2$$

with adjoint equations

$$\dot{\lambda}_1 = -\frac{\partial H}{\partial x_1} = 0 \quad \Rightarrow \quad \lambda_1(t) = \lambda_1 = \text{const.}$$

$$\dot{\lambda}_2 = -\frac{\partial H}{\partial x_2} = 0 \quad \Rightarrow \quad \lambda_2(t) = \lambda_2 = \text{const.}$$

To calculate the supremum of H with respect to $\mathbf{u} \in \mathscr{U}$, we write

$$H = \lambda_0 + \lambda_1 u_1 + \lambda_2 \sqrt{1 - u_1^2}$$

A necessary condition for H to be a maximum with respect to u_1 is

$$\frac{dH}{du_1} = \lambda_1 - \frac{\lambda_2 u_1}{\sqrt{1 - u_1^2}} = 0 \quad \Rightarrow \quad \frac{u_1}{u_2} = \frac{\lambda_1}{\lambda_2}$$

The initial transversality conditions are trivially satisfied since $\mathbf{x}_0$ is given. The terminal transversality conditions require that the adjoint vector $\boldsymbol{\lambda}(t_1) = (\lambda_1(t_1)\, \lambda_2(t_1))^T$ be normal to the tangent plane to the terminal surface at the terminal point. Thus, if $\boldsymbol{\eta} = \eta_1 \hat{\imath}_1 + \eta_2 \hat{\imath}_2$ is a vector in the tangent plane T_{θ^1} to the surface $\theta^1(x_1, x_2) = x_2 - 2x_1 + 2$, then we have

$$\nabla \theta^1(x_1, x_2) \cdot \boldsymbol{\eta} = 0$$

since $\nabla \theta^1(x_1, x_2)$ is normal to T_{θ^1}, and

$$\boldsymbol{\lambda} \cdot \boldsymbol{\eta} = 0$$

as required by the transversality conditions, resulting in

$$-2\eta_1 + \eta_2 = 0 \quad \Rightarrow \quad \eta_2 = 2\eta_1$$

$$\lambda_1 \eta_1 + \lambda_2 \eta_2 = 0 \quad \Rightarrow \quad \lambda_1 = -2\lambda_2$$

The implication for extremal control is

$$u_1 = -2u_2$$

which, in view of the control constraint, leads to extremal (actually, optimal) control

$$\mathbf{u}^*(t) = \left(\frac{2}{\sqrt{5}} \; \frac{-1}{\sqrt{5}} \right)^T$$

The integration of the state equations yields

$$x_1(t) = 1 + \frac{2}{\sqrt{5}}t$$

$$x_2(t) = 3 - \frac{1}{\sqrt{5}}t$$

For termination on the terminal manifold θ^1, we must have

$$3 - \frac{1}{\sqrt{5}}t_1 = 2 + \frac{4}{\sqrt{5}}t_1 - 2 \quad \Rightarrow \quad t_1 = \frac{3}{5}\sqrt{5}$$

and the transfer trajectory terminates at

$$x_1(t_1) = 1 + \frac{2}{\sqrt{5}}3\frac{\sqrt{5}}{5} = 2.2$$

$$x_2(t_1) = 2.4$$

as expected. Thus optimal control reaches the terminal set in minimum time $t_1 = \frac{3}{5}\sqrt{5}$.

Finally, we need to investigate the possibility of abnormal control with $\lambda_0 = 0$. The Hamiltonian becomes

$$H(\boldsymbol{\lambda}, \mathbf{x}, \mathbf{u}) = \lambda_1 u_1 + \lambda_2 u_2 = 5\lambda_2 u_2 = 0$$

which requires $\lambda_2 = \lambda_1 = 0$, a violation of the necessary condition that there exist a nonzero adjoint vector. We conclude that abnormal control is not possible and take $\lambda_0 = -1$. We may then use the null condition for the Hamiltonian to solve for the adjoint variables themselves as

$$-1 + 5\lambda_2 u_2 = 0 \quad \Rightarrow \quad \lambda_1 = \frac{2}{5}\sqrt{5} \text{ and } \lambda_2 = -\frac{1}{5}\sqrt{5}$$

This completes the solution of the problem.

The following two additional examples are classical problems in optimal control. However, this does not diminish their usefulness from a practical point of view. The first example deals with the minimum time control of the one-armed manipulator. The second example provides the derivation of optimal control for a standard linear quadratic problem, the so-called tracking problem, whose relevance to robotics is well established. As usual, we shall make use of some desk references on optimal control. For a geometric treatment of the subject, the classical text by Leitmann[13] is unsurpassed. Mathematical background is provided by Lee and Markus[12]; and Athans and Falb[14] serves as a compendium of control problem variants and the required adjustments in necessary conditions.

Example 8-22 Minimum time control for the one-armed manipulator. We take the governing equation to be the linearized equation [Eq. (8-26)] without the Coulomb friction. The resultant governing equation is

$$\ddot{\theta}_1 + \omega^2\theta_1 = k\frac{M^a(t)}{M_0} \qquad \omega^2 = \frac{3g}{2L} \qquad k = \frac{3M_0}{mL^2}$$

where the applied torque is limited to the range $|M^a(t)| \leq M_0$. This system is to be transferred from an initial state $\theta_1(0) = \delta_1$, $\dot{\theta}_1(0) = \dot{\delta}_1$ to a final state $\theta_1(t_1) = \dot{\theta}_1(t_1) = 0$ in minimum time.

(*a*) State the optimal control problem in standard normalized and null-controlled form.

(*b*) Derive a general expression for the extremal control.

(*c*) Synthesize an optimal control and sketch the switching surfaces in phase space.

(*d*) Sketch the optimal phase space trajectory if $k = 2$, $\omega = 2$ and the initial state is given as $\theta_1(0) = 1$, $\dot{\theta}_1(0) = 2$.

Solution

(*a*) We formulate the problem in standard first-order form. The introduction of the new variables

$$x_1 = \frac{\omega}{k}\theta_1 \qquad x_2 = \frac{1}{k}\dot{\theta}_1 \qquad \text{and} \qquad u = \frac{M^a}{M_0}$$

yields

$$\dot{x}_1 = \omega x_2$$

$$\dot{x}_2 = u - \omega x_1$$

with

$$x_1(0) = \frac{\omega}{k}\theta_1(0) = \frac{\omega}{k}\delta_1 = x_{10} \qquad x_2(0) = \frac{1}{k}\dot{\delta}_1 = x_{20}$$

and with terminal values $x_1(t_1) = x_2(t_1) = 0$ based on $|u(t)| \leq 1$. The time t_1 is not specified. Formally, we have the following optimal control problem: Minimize

$$g_1(u(\cdot)) = \int_0^{t_1} dt$$

subject to $|u(t)| \leq 1$ and

$$\begin{pmatrix} \dot{x}_1 \\ \dot{x}_2 \end{pmatrix} = \begin{bmatrix} 0 & \omega \\ -\omega & 0 \end{bmatrix} \begin{pmatrix} x_1 \\ x_2 \end{pmatrix} + \begin{pmatrix} 0 \\ u(t) \end{pmatrix} \tag{8-46}$$

with $x_1(0) = x_{10}$, $x_2(0) = x_{20}$, and $x_1(t_1) = x_2(t_1) = 0$.

Note that it is always possible to normalize a given interval constraint on the control as shown. Furthermore, it is common to formulate control problems as problems in null controllability, where the final values of the state are to be driven to 0. Thus, if we wish to drive a system state (y_1, y_2) from $(0, 0)$ to a final state (y_1^1, y_2^1), then a change of variable

$$x_1 = y_1^1 - y_1$$

$$x_2 = y_2^1 - y_2$$

will yield the corresponding null-control problem.

(*b*) We make use of the maximum principle to deduce extremal control. The Hamiltonian for this system is given by

$$H(\boldsymbol{\lambda}, \mathbf{x}, u) = -1 + \lambda_1 \omega x_2 + \lambda_2(-\omega x_1 + u)$$

where a discussion of $\lambda_0 = 0$ has been omitted. The corresponding adjoint equations are

$$\begin{aligned} \dot{\lambda}_1 &= -\frac{\partial H}{\partial x_1} = +\omega\lambda_2 \\ \dot{\lambda}_2 &= -\frac{\partial H}{\partial x_2} = -\omega\lambda_1 \end{aligned} \tag{8-47}$$

The simultaneous solution of the adjoint equations yields

$$\lambda_1(t) = -A\cos(\omega t + \phi) \qquad \text{and} \qquad \lambda_2(t) = A\sin(\omega t + \phi) \tag{8-48}$$

We now enforce some specific requirements implied by the maximum principle. The statement of necessary conditions requires that u be selected to maximize H. (Note that in this context H needs to be thought of simply as a function of $\boldsymbol{\lambda}$, $\mathbf{x}$, and $\mathbf{u}$ without reference to their ultimate time dependence.) It then follows that the extremal control

$$u^* = +1 \qquad \text{for} \quad \lambda_2(t) \geq 0$$

$$u^* = -1 \qquad \text{for} \quad \lambda_2(t) < 0$$

Since u bangs back and forth between its maximum and its minimum value, this type of control is also termed *bang-bang* control, and since the switching intervals are determined by the sign of $\lambda_2(t)$, it is called the *switching function*. The extremal control may thus be written in the general form

$$u^*(t) = \operatorname{sgn} \lambda_2(t)$$

where the *signum function* is defined by

$$\operatorname{sgn} K = \begin{cases} 1 & K \geq 0 \\ -1 & K < 0 \end{cases}$$

(c) The previous conditions are those used to deduce open loop control, control as a function of time. More often than not, it is desirable to construct optimal feedback control since it tends to be self-correcting. The construction of a feedback control law from an open loop control law is called *control synthesis*. Within the context of piecewise constant control, the usual result is a separation of the state space into distinct regions separated by switching surfaces. We now outline the construction of such a feedback control (as well as the open loop control) for this problem. Greater details may be found in Athans and Falb.[14]

For u = const., the solution of the state equations (8-46) is given by

$$x_1(t) = A_1 \sin(\omega t + \psi) + \frac{u}{\omega}$$
$$x_2(t) = A_1 \cos(\omega t + \psi) \tag{8-49}$$

with A_1 and ψ to be determined by initial and continuity conditions. The substitution of these solutions and those of the adjoint equations into the Hamiltonian yield

$$H(\boldsymbol{\lambda}^*, \mathbf{x}^*, u^*) = -1 - AA_1\omega \cos(\phi - \psi) = 0$$

One way the switching function $\lambda_2(t)$ cannot affect the choice of control is for $\lambda_2(t)$ to be 0 over some time interval. We ask if this is a possibility. Suppose so. Then $\lambda_1(t)$ is 0 also and the final implication is $H = -1$ rather than 0—a contradiction of necessary conditions. Allowing $\lambda_0 = 0$ would violate the existence of $\boldsymbol{\lambda}(t) \neq 0$.

With $\lambda_2(t) = A \sin(\omega t + \phi)$, the relationship between $\lambda_2^*(t)$ and $u^*(t)$ then has the form shown in Fig. 8-27. Based on this sketch, we draw the following conclusions:

1. Optimal control can remain constant for no more than π/ω seconds.

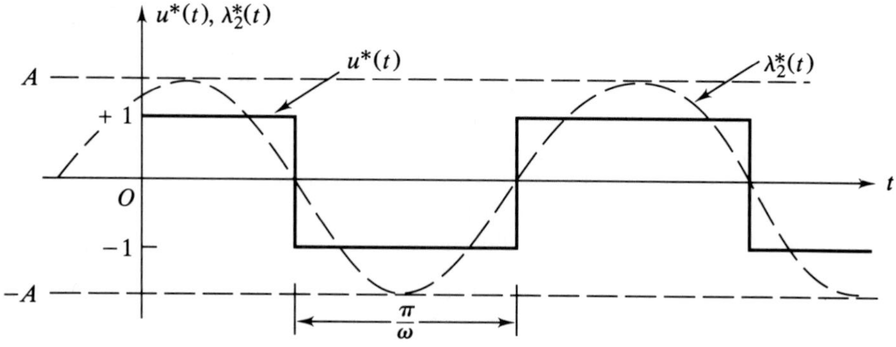

FIGURE 8-27
Switching of control with $\lambda_2^*(t)$.

2. Switching may occur an arbitrary number of times. This is in contrast with other linear time optimal control problems, where a maximum number of possible switches may be deduced.

We now turn to a phase space representation of the optimal trajectories. The plot of position versus velocity—in our case, the plot of x_2 versus x_1 in x_1x_2-space—is termed the phase space plot of the motion. The parametric equations of this plot are given by

$$x_1(t) = A_1 \sin(\omega t + \psi) + \frac{u}{\omega}$$

$$x_2(t) = A_1 \cos(\omega t + \psi)$$

Elimination of the parameter t yields

$$\sin^2(\omega t + \psi) + \cos^2(\omega t + \psi) = \frac{1}{A_1^2}\left[\left(x_1 - \frac{u}{\omega}\right)^2 + x_2^2\right] = 1$$

$$\Rightarrow \quad \left(x_1 - \frac{u}{\omega}\right)^2 + x_2^2 = A_1^2 \tag{8-50}$$

Since $u = \pm 1$ these are two families of circles with centers at $-1/\omega$ and $+1/\omega$, as shown in Fig. 8-28. Based on increasing t in the parametric equations for x_1 and x_2, points traverse the phase trajectories in the indicated directions. In view of the switching of $\lambda_2(t)$, the longest we can stay on a given circle is for half of it; that is, for $t_s = \pi/\omega$.

Of these families of circles, only the heavy-lined segments corresponding to circles with $A_1 = 1/\omega$ yield the desired result of driving the system state to the null state. Hence the final segment of any optimal phase trajectory must always be a segment of one of these semicircles. Furthermore, initial states

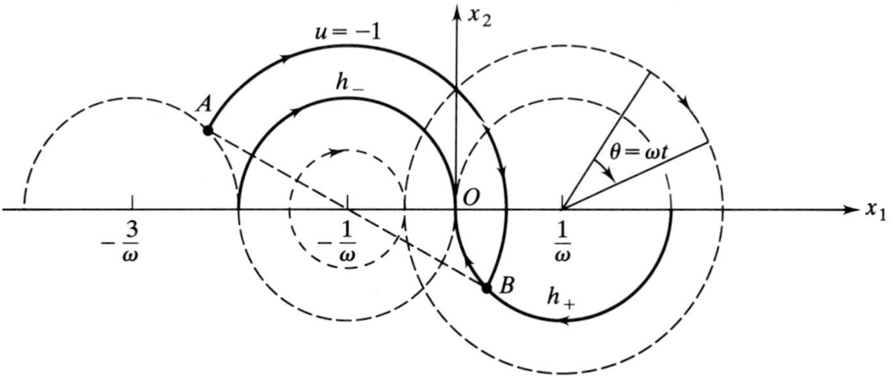

FIGURE 8-28
Phase plane trajectories.

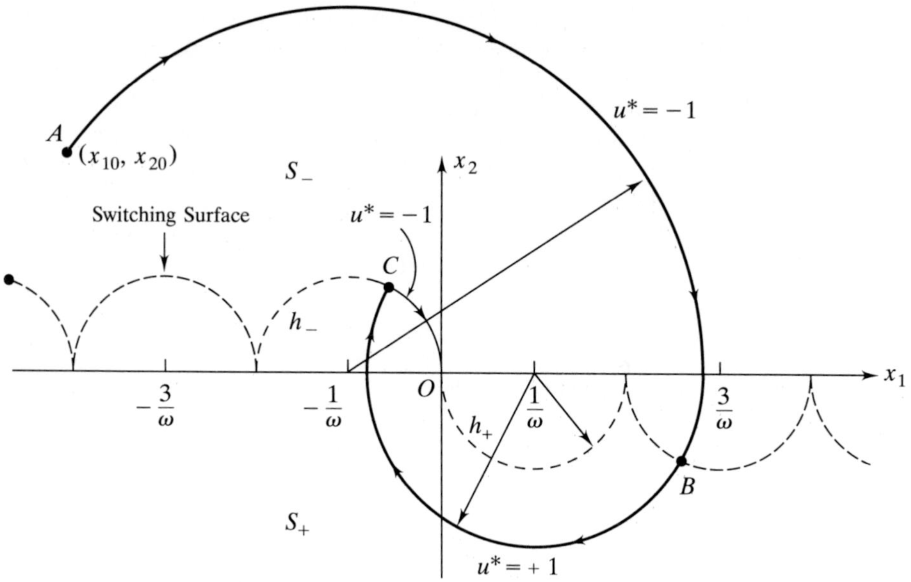

FIGURE 8-29
A typical switching sequence.

which lie on these segments can be forced to null by the appropriate choice of u, in less than t_s seconds.

With the exception of the initial segment and the final segment of an optimal phase trajectory, all switches must occur in $t_s = \pi/\omega$ seconds. Thus all intermediate pieces are semicircles. Since we must reach the home segments h_- and h_+, we ask ourselves from which points in x_1x_2-space we can reach a home segment in less than t_s seconds. A farthest such point is A on a copy of h_- and the connected semicircle terminating at B on h_+. For the initial point A the optimal control sequence thus is

$$u = -1 \quad \text{for } AB \quad t = t_s \text{ seconds}$$

$$u = +1 \quad \text{for } BO \quad t = t_{BO} \text{ seconds}$$

A repeated classification of such points eventually leads to a control law dividing x_1x_2-space into two half-spaces separated by the switching surface, consisting of copies of the semicircles h_- and h_+ repeated at odd multiples of $1/\omega$, as shown in Fig. 8-29. Depending on the half-space in which an initial point is located, the initial control then is ± 1; the whole sequence is generated by considering each intermediate switching state as a new initial state. More specifically, the upper half-space is labeled S_- and the lower half-space S_+ as shown. Extremal control is thus synthesized with

$$u^* = u^*(x_1, x_2) = \begin{cases} +1 & \text{for all } (x_1, x_2) \in S_+ \cup h_+ \\ -1 & \text{for all } (x_1, x_2) \in S_- \cup h_- \end{cases}$$

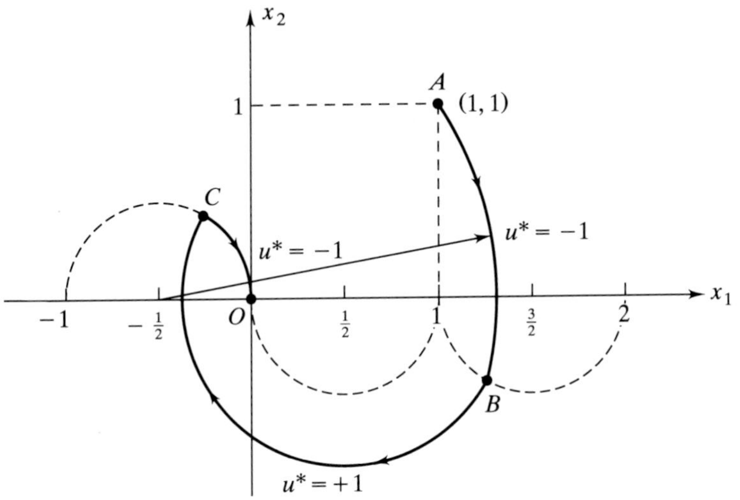

FIGURE 8-30
A numerical example.

A typical trajectory is depicted in Fig. 8-29. Beginning at the initial state A, we use $u^* = -1$ to move on a semicircle about $-1/\omega$ until we reach B; there we switch to $u^* = +1$ and move on a semicircle about $+1/\omega$ to C, where a switch to $u^* = -1$ then takes us to the null state.

(*d*) As a final look at this problem, we work out the phase plane trajectory for the numerical values $\omega = 2$, $k = 2$ and $\theta_1 = 1$, $\dot{\theta}_1 = 2$. In practice, we should need to supply the appropriate parametrization in terms of t, and we shall thus include the computation of the state $(x_1(t), x_2(t))$ on each control interval.

The motion begins at the initial state

$$x_{10} = \frac{2}{2} \cdot 1 = 1.0 \qquad \text{and} \qquad x_{20} = \frac{1}{2} \cdot 2 = 1.0$$

Since the initial state lies above the switching surface, the motion begins with $u^* = -1$, then switches to $u^* = +1$ and again to $u^* = -1$ to complete the motion. The corresponding phase plane trajectory is depicted in Fig. 8-30. We shall treat each segment separately.

Segment 1 (AB in Fig. 8-30). For $u^* = -1$ and $t \geq 0$, the initial conditions $(1, 1)$ at $t = 0$ yield

$$x_1(t) = 1.803 \sin(2t + 0.983) - 0.5$$
$$x_2(t) = 1.803 \cos(2t + 0.983)$$

To obtain the switching point, we solve the simultaneous equations

$$(x_1 + 0.5)^2 + x_2^2 = 3.25$$
$$(x_1 - 1.5)^2 + x_2^2 = 0.25$$

and obtain the intersection of the two circles at (1.25, −0.436). The use of

$$1.803\cos(2t_1 + 0.983) = -0.436$$

for example, then yields $t_1 = 0.416$ s (as long as we have chosen seconds as our basic time unit).

Segment 2 (BC in Fig. 8-30). For $u^* = +1$ and $t \geq 0.416$, the initial conditions now are continuity conditions at $t = 0.416$ s, with

$$1.25 = A_1 \sin(2 \cdot 0.416 + \psi) + 0.5$$

$$-0.436 = A_1 \cos(2 \cdot 0.416 + \psi)$$

The resultant state is given by

$$x_1(t) = -0.867\sin(2t - 1.876) + 0.5$$

$$x_2(t) = -0.867\cos(2t - 1.876)$$

The termination part for this segment is easy to obtain. It lies diagonally across through (0.5, 0) on h_-. It is $(-0.25, 0.436)$. The time of arrival is $\pi/2$ seconds later at $t_2 = 1.987$.

Final Segment (CO in Fig. 8-30). On the final segment, control is $u^* = -1$ with $t \geq 1.987$. Similarly enforced continuity conditions yield

$$x_1(t) = 0.50\sin(2t - 3.453) - 0.5$$

$$x_2(t) = 0.50\cos(2t - 3.453)$$

both of which are 0 when $t_f = 2.51$ s.

Remark 8-7. It can be shown that the previously derived extremal control $u^*(\cdot)$ is indeed optimal. Thus the corresponding transfer time is a minimum.

It is useful to return to the physical example of the one-armed manipulator and visualize the states at which switching occurs. From a strict point of

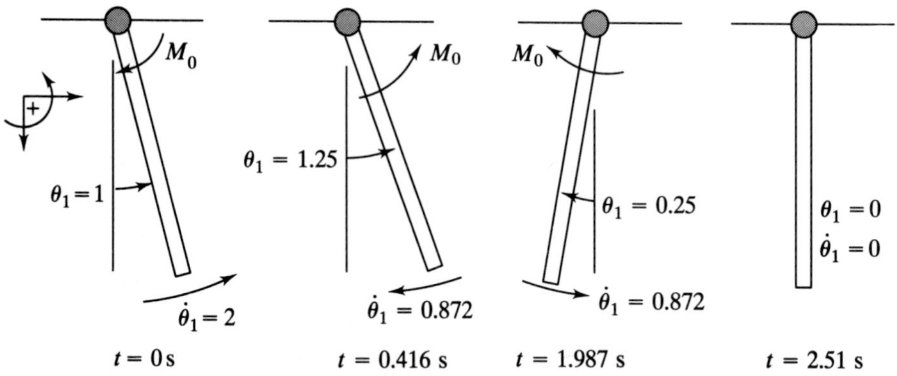

FIGURE 8-31
Time optimal control of the one-armed manipulator.

view, the chosen initial conditions (a terminal state) are out of the "small" motion range. The larger state was chosen to increase the number of switches required. The pendulum states are depicted in Fig. 8-31.

Remark 8-8. The standard problem formulation here creates the impression that the outcome is independent of the magnitude of M_0. It is not. The dependence is buried in the constant $k = (3M_0)/mL^2$.

We shall consider one more example in some detail: the linear-quadratic problem with linear state equations and a criterion integrand that is quadratic in **u** and **x**. In particular, we shall develop the expression for optimal control for the tracking problem previously introduced, when we linearized the nonlinear control problem.

We have already encountered one criterion that fits this category—namely, the use of the square of the error as an integrand. The selection of the square of the control variable is related to the energy required in carrying out the control process.

For example, suppose we wish to calculate the work done against a resistance R by the applied voltage $u(t)$ for the circuit shown in Fig. 8-32a. With current $i(t)$ the work done over a time interval $[0, t_1]$ is

$$W = \int_0^{t_1} u(t) i(t)\, dt = \frac{1}{R} \int_0^{t_1} u^2(t)\, dt$$

The mechanical analog is the energy dissipated in a viscous damper as shown in Fig. 8-32b. If $v(t)$ is the motion of the right end point of the damper and $u(t)$ is the force exerted by the system on the damper, then the work done in a time interval $[0, t_1]$ is

$$W = \int_0^{t_1} u(t) \cdot v(t)\, dt = \frac{1}{b} \int_0^{t_1} u^2(t)\, dt$$

Thus the corresponding optimization problem reflects the natural desire to minimize the amount of work or energy required for a particular task.

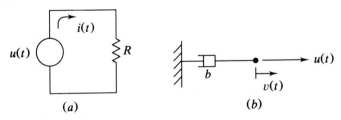

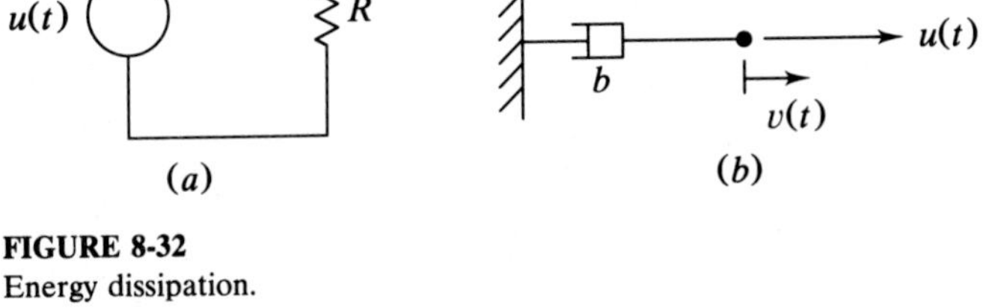

FIGURE 8-32
Energy dissipation.

It is common to combine the energy and the error integrands in a single criterion with

$$g_2(\mathbf{v}(\cdot)) = \tfrac{1}{2}\int_0^{t_1}\left[\mathbf{y}^{\mathrm{T}}(t)\mathbf{Q}(t)\mathbf{y}(t) + \mathbf{v}^{\mathrm{T}}(t)\mathbf{R}(t)\mathbf{v}(t)\right] dt$$

Generally, the simultaneous minimization of the error and of the energy involves conflicting demands imposed upon the system, so that a compromise is required. The emphasis placed on a particular criterion is reflected in the choice of the weighting matrices $\mathbf{Q}$ and $\mathbf{R}$. The following example illustrates the outcome of this compromise.

Example 8-23 The tracking problem (or the state regulator problem). Suppose we take the governing equation for the error $\mathbf{y}(t) = \mathbf{x}(t) - \mathbf{x}_0(t)$ to be given by

$$\dot{\mathbf{y}} = \mathbf{A}\mathbf{y} + \mathbf{B}\mathbf{v}$$

with nonzero initial error, so that $\mathbf{y}(0) = \mathbf{y}_0$. The admissible control $\mathbf{v}(\cdot)$ is taken to be bounded with $|\mathbf{v}(t)| < \infty$ but is unconstrained otherwise. The terminal time t_1 is presumed given. The objective is to keep $\mathbf{y}(t)$ near $\mathbf{0}$ [or $\mathbf{x}(t)$ near $\mathbf{x}_0(t)$] while using as little energy as possible.

(*a*) Provide a formal optimal control problem statement.

(*b*) Derive extremal control $\mathbf{v}^*(t)$ and discuss the system response.

Solution

(*a*) A formal optimal control problem statement is given by: Obtain control(s) $\mathbf{v}^*(t) \in \mathscr{V}$ which minimize

$$g_2(\mathbf{v}(\cdot)) = \tfrac{1}{2}\int_0^{t_1}\left[\mathbf{y}^{\mathrm{T}}(t)\mathbf{Q}(t)\mathbf{y}(t) + \mathbf{v}^{\mathrm{T}}(t)\mathbf{R}(t)\mathbf{v}(t)\right] dt$$

subject to $\mathbf{v}(t) \in \mathscr{V} = \{\mathbf{v}(t): |\mathbf{v}(t)| < \infty\}$,

$$\dot{\mathbf{y}} = \mathbf{A}\mathbf{y} + \mathbf{B}\mathbf{v} \qquad \mathbf{y}(0) = \mathbf{y}_0 \qquad t \in [0, t_1]$$

with t_1 specified. In addition, it is usually assumed that the matrix $\mathbf{Q}$ is *positive semidefinite* and $\mathbf{R}$ is *positive definite*. We remind the reader that these terms require the symmetry of $\mathbf{Q}$ and $\mathbf{R}$ and that we thus must have $\mathbf{a}^{\mathrm{T}}\mathbf{Q}\mathbf{a} \geq 0$ and $\mathbf{b}^{\mathrm{T}}\mathbf{R}\mathbf{b} > 0$ for all nonzero conformable $\mathbf{a}$ and $\mathbf{b}$.

(*b*) The deduction of extremal control is again based on the use of the maximum principle. The Hamiltonian is given by

$$H(\boldsymbol{\lambda}, \mathbf{x}, \mathbf{v}) = -\tfrac{1}{2}\left[\mathbf{y}^{\mathrm{T}}\mathbf{Q}\mathbf{y} + \mathbf{v}^{\mathrm{T}}\mathbf{R}\mathbf{v}\right] + \boldsymbol{\lambda}^{\mathrm{T}}[\mathbf{A}\mathbf{y} + \mathbf{B}\mathbf{v}] \tag{8-51}$$

with corresponding adjoint equations given by

$$\dot{\boldsymbol{\lambda}} = -\frac{\partial H}{\partial \mathbf{y}} = +\mathbf{Q}\mathbf{y} - \mathbf{A}^{\mathrm{T}}\boldsymbol{\lambda} \tag{8-52}$$

Again, we seek $\mathbf{v}$ so as to maximize H; for unconstrained control

$$\frac{\partial H}{\partial \mathbf{v}} = \mathbf{0}$$

is a necessary condition for a maximum. This results in

$$\frac{\partial H}{\partial \mathbf{v}} = -\mathbf{R}\mathbf{v} + \boldsymbol{\lambda}^{\mathrm{T}}\mathbf{B} = \mathbf{0}$$

or

$$\mathbf{v} = \mathbf{R}^{-1}\mathbf{B}^{\mathrm{T}}\boldsymbol{\lambda} \tag{8-53}$$

where the existence of $\mathbf{R}^{-1}$ is guaranteed by the positive definiteness of $\mathbf{R}$. Furthermore, since

$$\frac{\partial^2 H}{\partial \mathbf{v}^2} = -\mathbf{R}$$

it follows that this Hessian matrix is negative definite, and we are thus assured that this choice of $\mathbf{v}$ actually maximizes H. (Note the similarity of these conditions with the first and second derivative tests for an optimum in calculus problems.)

Rather than continuing the solution process in the usual fashion, we now ask ourselves the question: Subject to what requirements on the matrix $\mathbf{K}(t)$ does there exist an overall solution for which

$$\boldsymbol{\lambda}(t) = \mathbf{K}(t)\mathbf{y}(t)\ ? \tag{8-54}$$

We first take a look at the requirements arising from transversality conditions. The initial transversality conditions are trivially satisfied since $\mathbf{y}(0) = \mathbf{y}_0$ is specified, allowing $\boldsymbol{\lambda}(0)$ to be arbitrary. The terminal transversality conditions imply

$$\boldsymbol{\lambda}(t_1) = \mathbf{0} \quad \Rightarrow \quad \mathbf{K}(t_1)\mathbf{y}(t_1) = 0$$

and we conclude $\mathbf{K}(t_1) = \mathbf{0}$, since $\mathbf{y}(t_1)$ is not specified.

Substitution of (8-54) into the expression for extremal control yields the feedback controller

$$\mathbf{v} = \mathbf{R}^{-1}\mathbf{B}^{\mathrm{T}}\mathbf{K}\mathbf{y} \tag{8-55}$$

which may then be substituted into the state equations to yield

$$\begin{aligned}\dot{\mathbf{y}} &= \mathbf{A}\mathbf{y} + \mathbf{B}\mathbf{R}^{-1}\mathbf{B}^{\mathrm{T}}\mathbf{K}\mathbf{y} \\ &= [\mathbf{A} + \mathbf{B}\mathbf{R}^{-1}\mathbf{B}^{\mathrm{T}}\mathbf{K}]\mathbf{y}\end{aligned} \tag{8-56}$$

Finally, the assumption must also satisfy the adjoint equation (8-52) so that

$$\dot{\boldsymbol{\lambda}} = \mathbf{K}\dot{\mathbf{y}} + \dot{\mathbf{K}}\mathbf{y} = \mathbf{Q}\mathbf{y} - \mathbf{A}^{\mathrm{T}}\boldsymbol{\lambda}$$

or

$$\mathbf{K}[\mathbf{A} + \mathbf{B}\mathbf{R}^{-1}\mathbf{B}^{\mathrm{T}}\mathbf{K}]\mathbf{y} + \dot{\mathbf{K}}\mathbf{y} = \mathbf{Q}\mathbf{y} - \mathbf{A}^{\mathrm{T}}\mathbf{K}\mathbf{y}$$

which leads to the following matrix differential equation to be satisfied by $\mathbf{K}(t)$ —namely,

$$\dot{\mathbf{K}} = \mathbf{Q} - \mathbf{A}^{\mathrm{T}}\mathbf{K} - \mathbf{K}\mathbf{A} - \mathbf{K}\mathbf{B}\mathbf{R}^{-1}\mathbf{B}^{\mathrm{T}}\mathbf{K} \tag{8-57}$$

[We term (8-57) the Riccati equation for this problem; its solution $\mathbf{K}(t)$ is called the *gain matrix*.]

The equation is a nonlinear equation in $\mathbf{K}(t)$, and numerical means are generally required to solve it. However, since all of the coefficient matrices in the equation are known, $\mathbf{K}(t)$ may be computed in advance of the implementation of the feedback controller. The matrix $\mathbf{K}(t)$ always exists, is unique, and remains bounded. The corresponding control $\mathbf{v}^*(\cdot)$ is the unique optimal control for this problem, so that the criterion takes on its minimum possible value.

We summarize the solution of the tracking problem:

1. We determine the solution of the matrix Riccati equation
$$\dot{\mathbf{K}} = \mathbf{Q} - \mathbf{A}^T\mathbf{K} - \mathbf{K}\mathbf{A} - \mathbf{K}\mathbf{B}\mathbf{R}^{-1}\mathbf{B}^T\mathbf{K}$$
subject to $\mathbf{K}(t_1) = \mathbf{0}$.
2. The optimal control is then given by
$$\mathbf{v}^*(t) = \mathbf{R}^{-1}\mathbf{B}^T\mathbf{K}\mathbf{y}$$
3. The corresponding state equation has the form
$$\dot{\mathbf{y}} = [\mathbf{A} + \mathbf{B}\mathbf{R}^{-1}\mathbf{B}^T\mathbf{K}]\mathbf{y} \tag{8-58}$$
Its solution is
$$\mathbf{y}^*(t) = \mathbf{\Phi}(t)\mathbf{y}_0$$
where $\mathbf{\Phi}(t)$ is the fundamental matrix for the system (8-58).
4. The local minimum of the criterion function is given by
$$g(\mathbf{v}^*(\cdot)) = \tfrac{1}{2}\int_0^{t_1}\mathbf{y}^{*T}(t)\big[\mathbf{Q}(t) + \mathbf{K}(t)\mathbf{B}(t)\mathbf{R}^{-1}(t)\mathbf{B}(t)\mathbf{K}(t)\big]\mathbf{y}^*(t)\,dt$$

Note that in writing the criterion in this form, we have used the symmetry of $\mathbf{K}(t)$ and the fact that if $\mathbf{R}$ is a positive-definite matrix, then so is $\mathbf{R}^{-1}$. As a desk reference for the considerable amount of linear algebra involved here, the text by Strang[15] is highly recommended.

One of the obvious uses of tracking control is to provide system adjustments when intentional or unintentional disturbances are present. For example, the specified trajectory might be the recorded trajectory of the robot without a load; tracking may then be used to assure adherence to this path in the presence of a load. Similarly, it can compensate for other disturbances due to a variety of causes, such as friction, elasticity of the robot, slipping of transmission belts, and so on.

As the first example illustrated, optimal control theory can provide both the optimal path and its optimal traversal. As mentioned, however, much of the optimal control in robotics is concerned only with the optimal traversal of an otherwise specified path, planned by other means, often in some ad hoc fashion. One frequent such approach is to plan the space trajectory only at a sequence of points, to record the corresponding individual joint positions, and then to use some interpolation scheme to provide smooth connectedness of the joint locations and hence (with some caveats) for the space trajectory.

Optimal control is a rich and evolving discipline. Here, we have provided only a glimpse of its diversity. In the next section we turn to joint control, an application of control theory dominated by automatic control methods.

8-3-4 Joint Control

We now turn from joined to joint control. As practiced today, it is mainly a linear automatic control problem, with much of the manipulation carried out in s-space. In contrast to the previous section, where we discussed optimal control with respect to specific criteria, much of the effort here is directed toward obtaining a better, or an improved, control without explicit reference to criteria. Rather, the system improvements deal with the assurance of system stability and the reduction of overshoot and rise time for the system's response to a step input. This latter task is one of the main uses of PID controllers, a superposition of proportional, integral, and derivative control segments.

Once the trajectory of the end effector has been determined, the actual execution of the trajectory becomes a matter of joint control. The joint trajectories are deduced by using the inverse kinematics of the manipulator. For reasons of speed and practicality, the space trajectory itself is often specified only as a sequence of points and velocities, with corresponding sequences derived and specified for the individual joints. These sequences of values to be taken on by the joint variables are then connected by trajectories planned for each particular joint. As mentioned previously, cubic splining is one of the methods used to accomplish this latter task. The following example will illustrate this approach as well as a number of additional aspects of trajectory planning.

We shall use the polar manipulator of Chap. 2 as the vehicle for the illustration. We first plan a plane trajectory for the end effector and then specify the robot variables, as in Example 2-17. We then suppose that only a discrete number of points on the trajectory and corresponding joint locations are available. We plan the joint motion by connecting the given joint locations with cubic splines; and, finally, we compare the splined path with the actual path as required by the exact inverse kinematics. Collectively, the example provides a clear illustration of the steps required in planning the prescribed joint motions.

Example 8-24 The polar manipulator. The end effector or tool point E is to move along the straight-line path AB shown in Fig. 8-33a, from the point $(6, 0)$ to the point $(0, 8)$, in such a way that the initial and final velocities are 0. The length of the sleeve for the prismatic joint is taken to be $a = 4$ in, the length of the arm itself is taken to be $L_2 = 8$ in. Furthermore, we take the velocity and acceleration to be bounded by $|\boldsymbol{v}_0(t)| \leq 10$, $|\boldsymbol{a}_0(t)| \leq 20$, along with $|d\boldsymbol{a}_0/dt(t)| \leq 40$.

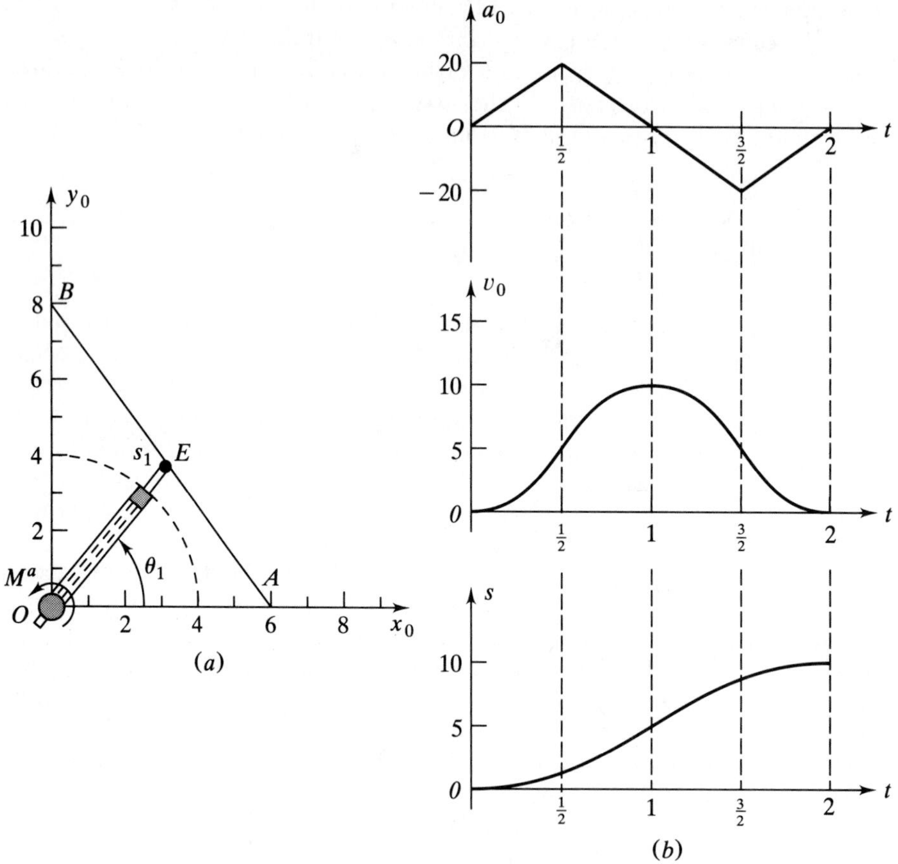

FIGURE 8-33
(*a*) The polar manipulator; (*b*) motion profile along the path *AB*.

(*a*) Determine a suitable motion for the end effector.

(*b*) Determine the corresponding (x_0, y_0) parametrization of the motion.

(*c*) Determine the corresponding parametrization in terms of the joint variables (s_1, θ_1).

(*d*) Determine the actuator couple M^a required to execute the first segment of the required motion.

(*e*) Rather than taking the whole end-effector motion as given, suppose that only some discrete points are available for the determination of joint motion. Suppose that pairs (t_i, s_i) are specified in such a way and provide a suitable joint trajectory by using cubic splining. Compare the splined trajectory to the exact trajectory as obtained from the world path parametrization.

Solution

(*a*) We begin with the construction of the acceleration profile for the specified world path AB. We shall insist on the continuity of the acceleration as well as beginning and ending the motion with zero acceleration. The simplest such profile incorporating the specified bounds is given by the one shown in Fig. 8-33*b*. Its integration yields the corresponding velocity and motion profile for the end effector, as shown in the remainder of Fig. 8-33*b*. In view of the symmetry of the motion, we provide analytical expressions for only the first part of the motion, until $t = 1$ s:

$$a_0 = \begin{cases} 40t & 0 \le t < \dfrac{1}{2} \\ 40(1 - t) & \dfrac{1}{2} \le t < 1 \end{cases}$$

$$v_0 = \begin{cases} 20t^2 & 0 \le t < \dfrac{1}{2} \\ -20(1 - t)^2 + 10 & \dfrac{1}{2} \le t < 1 \end{cases}$$

$$s = \begin{cases} \dfrac{20}{3}t^3 & 0 \le t < \dfrac{1}{2} \\ \dfrac{20}{3}(1 - t)^3 + 10t - 5 & \dfrac{1}{2} \le t < 1 \end{cases}$$

(*b*) The parametrization of the world trajectory is given by

$$\boldsymbol{r}_0(t) = s(t)\left(-\frac{3}{5}\hat{\boldsymbol{\imath}}_0 + \frac{4}{5}\hat{\boldsymbol{\jmath}}_0\right) + 6\hat{\boldsymbol{\imath}}_0$$

or

$$x_0(t) = -\frac{3}{5}s(t) + 6$$

$$y_0(t) = \frac{4}{5}s(t)$$

(*c*) As in Chap. 2, the corresponding parametrization in the joint variables is

$$s_1(t) = \sqrt{s^2(t) - 7.2s(t) + 36} - 4$$

$$\theta_1(t) = \text{Arctan}\left(\frac{4s(t)}{30 - 3s(t)}\right)$$

where $s(t)$ is, of course, the previously derived motion along the world path AB.

(*d*) The previous questions address issues of kinematic motion control. Suppose we digress for a moment and consider the possibility of force and torque control for the motion. Specifically, suppose we wish to prescribe the required actuator moment for the interval $[0, \frac{1}{2})$. The requisite equation of motion is

TABLE 8-3
Locations of the end effector

t	**0**	**0.5**	**1.0**	**1.5**	**2.0**
(x_0, y_0)	(6, 0)	(5.5, 0.67)	(3, 4)	(0.5, 7.33)	(0, 8)
$s(t)$	0	0.833	5	9.167	10

obtained from Example 3-7 as

$$\left[c_1^2 m_1 + c_2^2(t) m_2 + I_{G_1} + I_{G_2}\right]\ddot{\theta}_1(t) + 2m_2 c_2(t)\dot{c}_2(t)\dot{\theta}_1(t)$$
$$+\left(m_1 c_1 + m_2 c_2(t)\right) g \cos\theta_1(t) = M^a(t)$$

where $c_2(t)$, the location of the center of mass of the prismatic link, is given by $c_2(t) = s_1(t) + 4 - \frac{L}{2}$, where L is the total length of the sliding bar.

(*e*) We now suppose that the trajectory has not been completely parametrized, but that only some discrete times and locations of the end effector are available. To be specific, suppose only the locations and times given in Table 8-3 have been recorded. We shall consider points generated by the inverse kinematics of the manipulator only for the prismatic joint. The corresponding points in (t, s_1)-space are listed in Table 8-4.

As mentioned, it is common to plan trajectories in joint space by using cubic splines to connect the sequence of points obtained by using inverse kinematics. We shall use minimum curvature splines, with the initial and the final values of the second derivative set equal to 0. The resultant spline is represented by the following cubics in the respective intervals:

$$i=1 \qquad 0 \le t < 0.5 \qquad s_1(t) = -2.07t^3 - 0.40t + 2.00$$

$$i=2 \qquad 0.5 \le t < 1.0 \qquad s_1(t) = 9.69(t-0.5)^3 - 3.10(t-0.5)^2 - 1.95(t-0.5) + 1.54$$

$$i=3 \qquad 1.0 \le t < 1.5 \qquad s_1(t) = -12.93(t-1)^3 + 11.43(t-1)^2 + 2.22(t-1) + 1.00$$

$$i=4 \qquad 1.5 \le t \le 2.0 \qquad s_1(t) = 5.31(t-1.5)^3 - 7.96(t-1.5)^2 + 3.95(t-1.5) + 3.35$$

A comparison of the exact joint trajectory and the splined trajectory is shown in Fig. 8-34. It would seem that a continuous linear acceleration profile is well approximated by cubic splines.

TABLE 8-4
Discrete points for the prismatic joint

t	**0**	**0.5**	**1.0**	**1.5**	**2.0**
$s_1(t)$	2.00	1.54	1.00	3.35	4.00

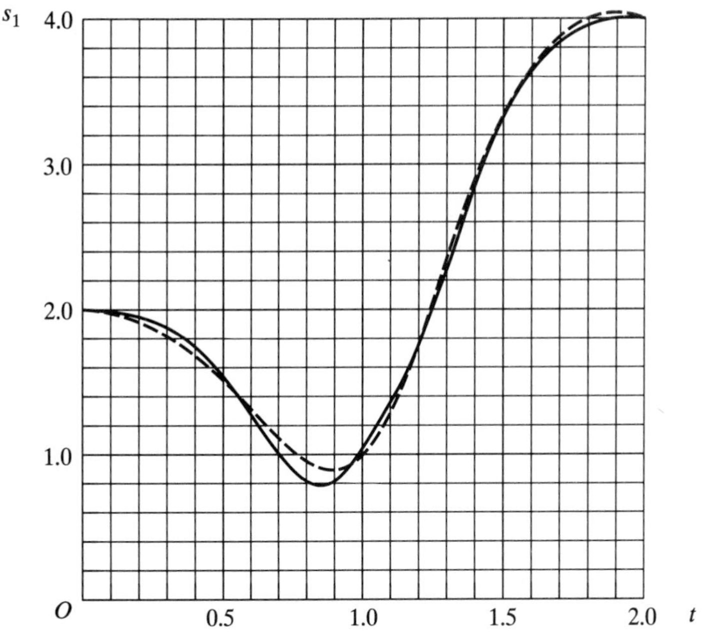

FIGURE 8-34
A comparison of splined and exact joint trajectory: (—) exact; (----) splined.

The preceding example illustrates how a suitable joint trajectory may be derived once the world trajectory has been supplied, either completely or as a sequence of desired locations and times. For the remainder of this section, we shall assume that the joint trajectories or states have been specified for each joint, either in the previous manner or in some equivalent fashion.

We now turn to the manner in which such joint trajectories can be maintained and assured. Virtually all joint control systems in use are feedback systems, where some or all of the current system state is measured, compared to the required state, and system adjustments are then made to reduce the error between the two—the desired output and the actual output.

Suppose the joint trajectory is specified as $\theta^d(t)$, the superscript indicating that it is the desired trajectory as provided by some mathematical system model or as taught to the system in some manner. Ultimately, this trajectory is fed to the system as an equivalent current or voltage signal. The eventual system output is the actual state $\theta(t)$, which is measured and compared to $\theta^d(t)$. Some type of system error is then used as the stimulant to produce system change; usually, the error is some amplification of the difference between input and output state, or $e(t) = k(\theta^d(t) - \theta(t))$. Presumably, $e(t) = 0$ is the desired stimulant at steady-state operation. Since the representation of feedback systems gives the impression that this error is actually used to drive the system, the student may well wonder what it is that continues to drive the system once the

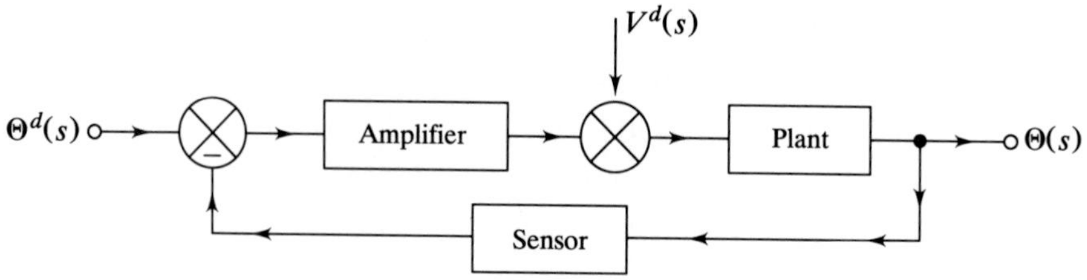

FIGURE 8-35
A typical joint feedback loop.

goal of zero error has been achieved. There must be some agent that continues to move the system at the now desired output $\theta^d(t)$. This is the purpose of the bias voltage $V^d(s)$, which we have indicated at the second summer just before the plant in Fig. 8-35, which depicts a typical joint feedback loop. Thus what actually continuously drives the plant is $V^d(s) + E(s)$, the bias voltage together with the error, with $V^d(s)$ remaining when the error is 0. We shall term such a continuously applied voltage the *set point*, or *set trajectory*, for the control system.

There are two prevalent types of set trajectory implementations. The first possibility is depicted in Fig. 8-36*a*, where the system motion occurs in the neighborhood of some mean trajectory. We take this mean trajectory to be the set trajectory, provided as a bias $V^d(s)$, and we take the system input to be the deviation therefrom, as depicted in Fig. 8-36*b*. For example, the set trajectory might be the robot motion without a load, and the deviation $\theta^d(t)$ might be the theoretically determined correction when a load is to be included. For a second possibility, $V^d(s)$ and $\theta^d(s)$ both may be representative of the set trajectory, as is the case in some DC motor drives.

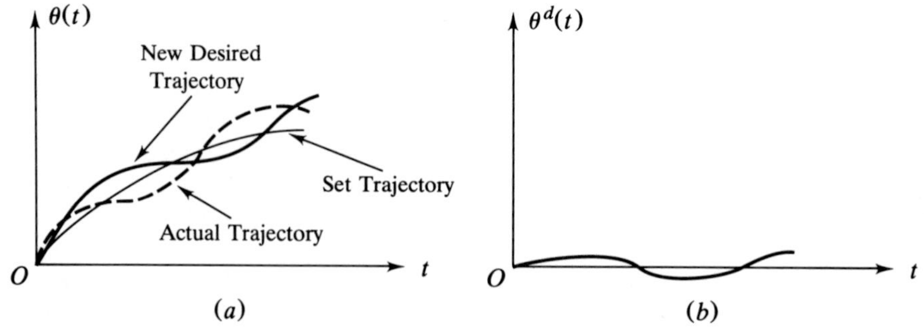

FIGURE 8-36
(*a*) Set trajectory and fluctuation; (*b*) desired addition to the set trajectory.

COMPENSATORS AND CONTROLLERS. Earlier we emphasized that feedback changes a system, whereas open loop control left the system unchanged. This change of the system may be detrimental; obviously, we strive to make it beneficial. When the simple linear feedback of the system state is inadequate to achieve the desired system behavior, we compensate by adding additional system components for the sole purpose of achieving a desired system behavior. These components are compensators or controllers, any distinction between them being murky at best.

There are some common approaches to the inclusion of such components in feedback systems. To illustrate, let $G_p(s)$ and $H_p(s)$ represent the system components of the simple plant or process depicted in Fig. 8-37*a*. Let $G_c(s)$ be the system function of a controller or compensator. The four standard compensator configurations—cascade compensator, feedback compensator, input compensator, and output compensator—are presented in Figs. 8-37*b*–*e*. There are, of course, other combinations for more complex systems, and more than one compensator may be used to achieve desired performance.

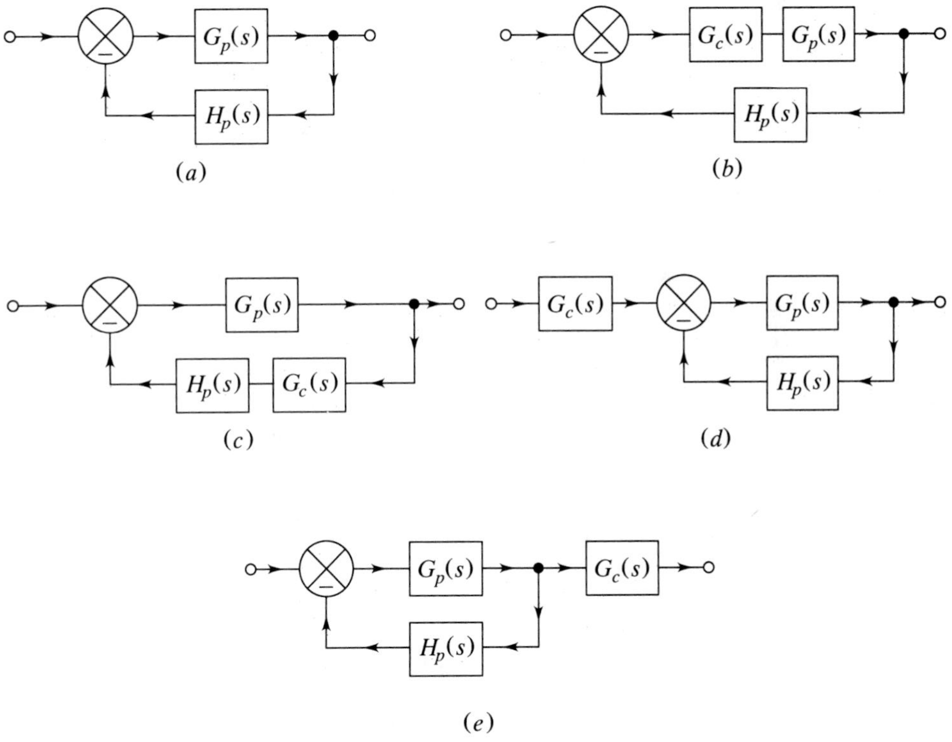

FIGURE 8-37
(*a*) Simple feedback system; (*b*) cascade compensator; (*c*) feedback compensator; (*d*) input compensator; (*e*) output compensator.

Quite generally, a compensator is a system of the form

$$G_c(s) = K_c \frac{\prod_{i=1}^{m}(s - z_i)}{\prod_{i=1}^{n}(s - p_i)} \tag{8-59}$$

with K_c and the poles p_i and zeros z_i serving as the design variables for the compensator. They are to be selected to achieve design objectives for the combined system of plant and compensator. There are two frequent uses of compensators: One is the assurance of system stability, to be achieved by the proper placement of the system poles; the other consists of the selection of the design parameters, to fulfill specific design requirements imposed on the system overshoot and settling time when subjected to a step input. The former is a desired effect in the frequency domain; the latter, in the time domain. We illustrate the method with a simple example where an underdamped oscillatory system is to be transformed to an overdamped system by the proper selection of a compensator.

Example 8-25 Compensation. Suppose our plant consists of the feedback system shown in Fig. 8-38*a*. The resultant open loop system function is that of a damped harmonic oscillator with damping factor $\zeta < 1$. An oscillatory response is deemed undesirable, however, and it is therefore suggested that a compensator be used to change the system response to that of an overdamped system. Design a suitable compensator to achieve this task and indicate the range of its applicability.

Solution. The open loop system function for the system in Fig. 8-38*a* is given by

$$G(s) = \frac{\frac{1}{s}}{1 + \frac{1}{s}\frac{1}{s+1}} = \frac{s+1}{s^2 + s + 1}$$

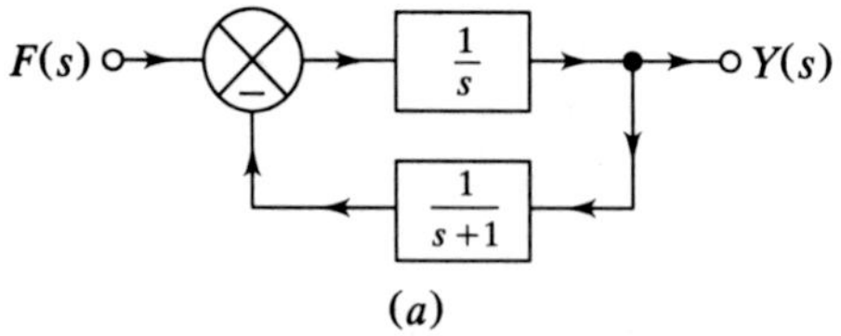

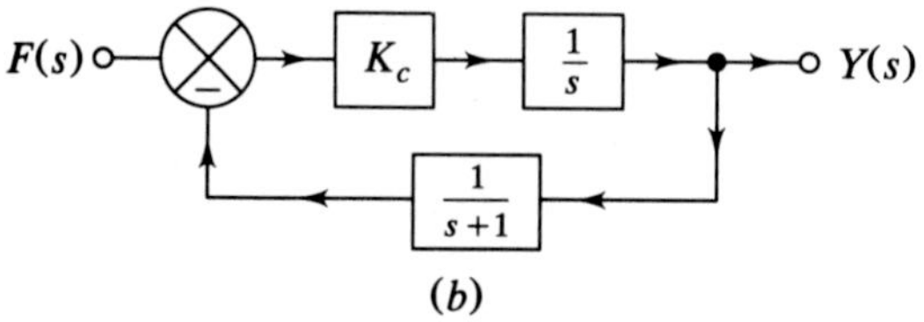

FIGURE 8-38
(*a*) Underdamped system; (*b*) compensated overdamped system.

The denominator for the standard harmonic oscillator has the form

$$s^2 + 2\zeta\omega s + \omega^2.$$

For the present system we thus have $\omega = 1$, $2\zeta\omega = 1$ with $\zeta = \frac{1}{2}$ as a consequence—an underdamped oscillatory system.

Suppose we now introduce a cascading compensator of the form $G_c(s) = K_c$ so that the compensated system has the form shown in Fig. 8-38*b*. The resultant open loop system function is

$$G(s) = \frac{K_c(s+1)}{s^2 + s + K_c}$$

A comparison with the standard system yields

$$\omega = \sqrt{K_c} \qquad \zeta = \frac{1}{2\sqrt{K_c}} \qquad \Rightarrow \qquad K_c < \frac{1}{4}$$

to assure an overdamped system with $\zeta > 1$.

Controllers differ from compensators in purpose rather than substance. By the very meaning of the word, a compensator is meant to compensate for original system inadequacies; the intent of a controller is to steer the system to a desired performance. Optimality concepts enter the realm of automatic controls mostly in terms of controllers, which improve rather than optimize system performance. The most prominent among such "improvement" controllers is the PID controller.

THE PID CONTROLLER. The PID controller is an outgrowth of the traditional proportional controller. Its premise is straightforward—namely, to use a linear combination of proportional, differential, and integral controller in the form

$$G_c(s) = k_p + k_d s + \frac{k_i}{s} \tag{8-60}$$

If $e(t)$ is the system input and $v(t)$ is the output, then the time domain expression for this controller is given by

$$v(t) = k_p e(t) + k_d \frac{de}{dt}(t) + k_i \int_0^t e(\tau)\, d\tau$$

The coefficients serve as design variables which are to be selected to optimize system performance. The latter is usually characterized in terms of the steady-state error, the overshoot, the rise time, and the settling time for the system response to a unit step input. Clearly, all of the possible combinations of P, I, and D are only special cases of compensators. The PID controller itself, for example, is a special case of the second-degree compensator

$$G_c(s) = K_c \frac{(s - z_1)(s - z_2)}{(s - p_1)(s - p_2)}$$

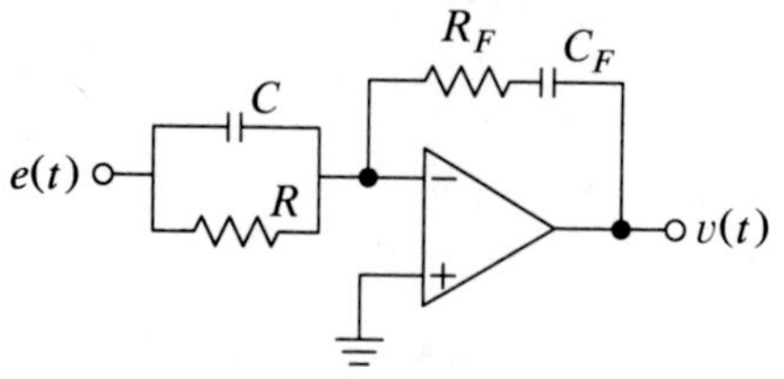

FIGURE 8-39
A simple PID controller.

Thus the compensators incorporate the PID controllers and provide the desired performance for time-invariant lumped linear systems. They are relatively easy to implement electronically; exceptions are hydraulic and pneumatic systems, where PID controllers can be constructed but more complex compensators may not be implementable. A simple PID controller, consisting of suitable elements in sequence, is shown in Fig. 8-39.

One final comment before we turn to some examples. The low power at which electronic compensators operate is insufficient to drive the motors, and power amplifiers generally intercede between controller and motor.

Example 8-26. Consider the simplified joint control system with a cascaded PD controller as shown in Fig. 8-40. The unity feedback is used to produce an error signal $e(t) = \theta^d(t) - \theta(t)$, where $\theta^d(t)$ is the desired angular position and $\theta(t)$ is the actual one.

(a) Determine the system function with $\theta^d(t)$ as input and $\theta(t)$ as output.

(b) Consider a unit step input $u(t)$ and discuss the system response. Use the initial and final value theorems for Laplace transforms to determine the initial values of $\theta(t)$ and $\dot{\theta}(t)$ and the steady state for the system.

(c) Obtain the relationship between k_p and k_d if the system is to be critically damped.

(d) Adjust k_p and k_d to obtain a low overshoot and a low rise time.

Solution

(a) The system function has the form

$$G(s) = \frac{\Theta(s)}{\Theta^d(s)} = \frac{k_p + k_d s}{J_m s^2 + k_d s + k_p}$$

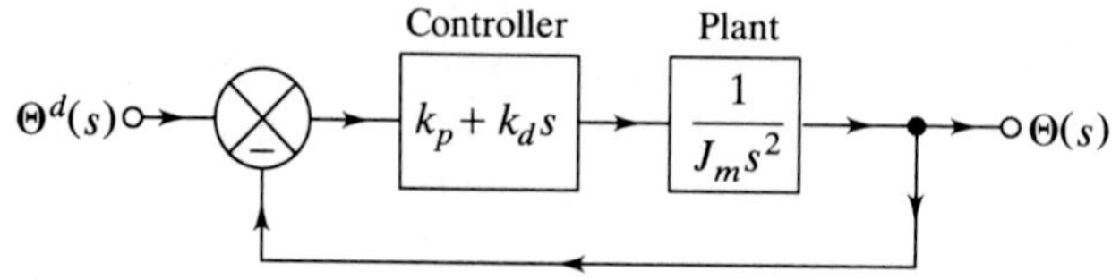

FIGURE 8-40
A simplified joint control system.

The introduction of

$$2\zeta\omega = \frac{k_d}{J_m} \qquad \text{and} \qquad \omega^2 = \frac{k_p}{J_m} \tag{8-61}$$

and the division of the numerator and the denominator of $G(s)$ by J_m yields

$$G(s) = \frac{\omega^2 + 2\zeta\omega s}{s^2 + 2\zeta\omega s + \omega^2}$$

so that we may simply use ω and ζ as design parameters.

(*b*) The Laplace transform of $u(t)$ is $\Theta^d(s) = U(s) = 1/s$. With this input

$$\Theta(s) = \frac{\omega^2 + 2\zeta\omega s}{s^2 + 2\zeta\omega s + \omega^2}\frac{1}{s} \tag{8-62}$$

We use the initial value theorem

$$\lim_{t\to 0} f(t) = \lim_{s\to\infty} sF(s)$$

to obtain

$$\theta(0) = \lim_{s\to\infty} s\Theta(s) = 0$$

and

$$\dot{\theta}(0) = \lim_{s\to\infty} s(s\Theta(s)) = 2\zeta\omega$$

The use of the terminal value theorem

$$\lim_{t\to\infty} f(t) = \lim_{s\to 0} sF(s)$$

yields the steady-state values

$$\theta(\infty) = \lim_{s\to 0} s\Theta(s) = 1$$

$$\dot{\theta}(\infty) = \lim_{s\to 0} s(s\Theta(s)) = 0$$

In the time domain the governing differential equation is given by

$$\begin{aligned}\frac{d^2\theta}{dt^2} + 2\zeta\omega\frac{d\theta}{dt} + \omega^2\theta &= \omega^2\theta^d(t) + 2\zeta\omega\frac{d\theta^d}{dt}\\ &= \omega^2 u(t) + 2\zeta\omega\delta(t)\end{aligned}$$

since the derivative of the unit step function is the δ-function. The solution of this differential equation is

$$\theta(t) = 1 + e^{-\zeta\omega t}\left[\frac{\zeta}{\sqrt{1-\zeta^2}}\sin\omega_d t - \cos\omega_d t\right] \tag{8-63}$$

with

$$\dot{\theta}(t) = e^{-\zeta\omega t}\omega\left[2\zeta\cos\omega_d t + \frac{1-2\zeta^2}{\sqrt{1-\zeta^2}}\sin\omega_d t\right] \tag{8-64}$$

where $\omega_d = \omega\sqrt{1-\zeta^2}$ is the damped frequency. The initial values are $\theta(0) = 0$ and $\dot{\theta}(0) = 2\zeta\omega$, as predicted by the initial value theorem.

The inquisitive student should be a little disturbed by this result, based on the fact that the system functions are obtained with all initial conditions set equal to 0. Then why is $\dot{\theta}(0) \neq 0$? The nonzero initial value for $\dot{\theta}(t)$ is due to the input $\delta(t)$. Simply put, initial values are generally limits as t approaches 0 from the right [e.g., $f(0^+)$], whereas the inclusion of the δ-function requires that we look at limits as t approaches 0 from the left [e.g., $f(0^-)$.] Thus the inclusion of δ-function inputs either requires a special treatment of such cases or a self-consistent approach, as used by Chen[16] who simply defines the Laplace transform with lower limit 0^- and derives all properties with this view from the left. When $f(\cdot)$ is continuous at $t = 0$, there is no difference, and otherwise the approach routinely includes the use of δ-function inputs.

(*c*) In many situations overshoot is to be avoided at all costs, and one then insists on a critically damped system. Based on the relationships given by (8-61) with $\zeta = 1$, we have

$$k_d = 2\sqrt{J_m k_p}$$

(*d*) We first express the maximum overshoot in terms of the damping factor ζ. The condition $\dot{\theta}(t_0) = 0$ yields

$$\tan \omega_d t_0 = \frac{2\zeta\sqrt{1-\zeta^2}}{2\zeta^2 - 1} = u(\zeta)$$

with corresponding expressions

$$\sin \omega_d t_0 = 2\zeta\sqrt{1-\zeta^2}$$

$$\cos \omega_d t_0 = 2\zeta^2 - 1$$

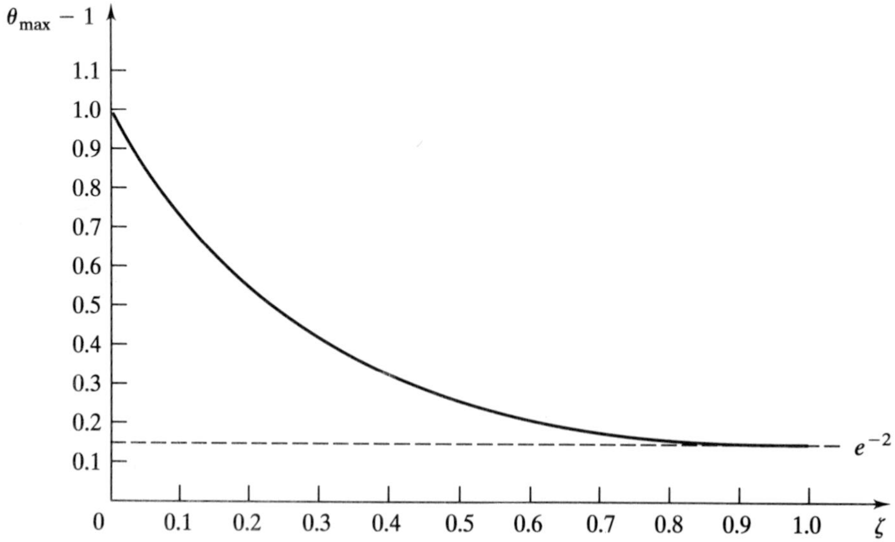

FIGURE 8-41
Maximum overshoot versus ζ.

The resultant maximum displacement is given by

$$\theta_{max} = \theta(t_0) = 1 + \exp\left[-\frac{\zeta}{\sqrt{1-\zeta^2}}\text{ Arctan } u(\zeta)\right] \tag{8-65}$$

A plot of the maximum overshoot versus ζ is shown in Fig. 8-41. Since $\dot{\theta}(0) = 2\zeta\omega$ we may actually achieve both a quicker rise time and a smaller overshoot by choosing ζ as large as possible. The problem of minimizing the overshoot on $\zeta \in (0, 1)$ actually has no solution, since

$$\lim_{\zeta \to 1} \exp\left[-\frac{\zeta}{\sqrt{1-\zeta^2}}\text{ Arctan } u(\zeta)\right] = e^{-2} \tag{8-66}$$

and $\zeta = 1$ is not included in the design interval. However, a choice of $\zeta = 0.99$ with an overshoot of 0.14 is a minimum for all practical purposes. With this choice for ζ, we have

$$\omega t_0 = 1.98$$

If we now suppose that k_d is bounded with $k_d \leq k_0$, as it usually would be, then we may take $k_d = k_0$ and

$$\omega = 0.505\frac{k_0}{J_m}$$

from which the peak time t_0 and the proportional gain k_p then follow as

$$t_0 = 3.92\frac{J_m}{k_0} \quad \text{and} \quad k_p = 0.255\frac{k_0^2}{J_m}$$

The previous example served to illustrate the overall effect and purpose of the inclusion of controllers. The remaining examples will be more realistic—hence more complex—and thus will lend themselves less to the exact analysis just illustrated.

The next example deals with a direct drive system. Rather than dealing with specific design criterion for a single-system configuration, we shall evolve several system refinements.

Example 8-27 Direct drive control for a single joint. We shall restrict our discussion to the use of an armature-controlled DC motor since they are in most prevalent use. We assume that the joint angle $\theta^d(t)$ has been specified as a twice differentiable function of t in one of the previously discussed manners. The overall objective is the construction of an automatic feedback control system that tracks this prescribed time behavior. The governing equations for the motor are taken to be (7-62) and (7-63):

$$J_m\frac{d\omega_m}{dt} + b_m\omega_m = k_T i_a - T_L \tag{8-67}$$

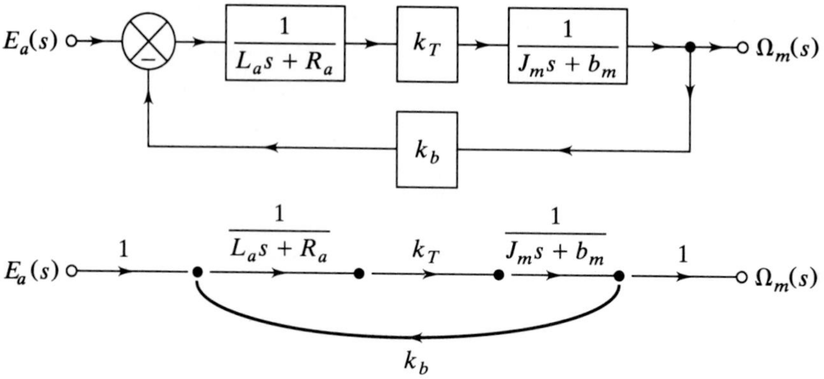

FIGURE 8-42
Block diagram and signal flow graph for armature-controlled direct drive.

for the motion of the armature, and

$$L_a \frac{di_a}{dt} + R_a i_a = e_a - k_b \omega_m \tag{8-68}$$

for the armature circuit. With $T_L = 0$ for the moment, with $e_a(t)$ as input, and with $\omega_m(t)$ as output, the system function is given by (7-65):

$$G_\theta(s) = \frac{\Omega_m(s)}{E_a(s)} = \frac{k_T}{(L_a s + R_a)(J_m s + b_m) + k_T k_b} \tag{8-69}$$

The corresponding block diagram and signal flow graph are shown in Fig. 8-42. The feedback loop is an essentially internal one, representing the back emf of the motor. For the remainder, we shall take the armature voltage $e_a(t)$ as our primary cause in providing the desired angular position $\theta^d(t)$; that is, $e_a(t) \propto \dot{\theta}^d(t)$.

Denote the desired angular velocity by $\omega_m^d(t)$. Then the armature voltage $e_a^d(t)$, which will result in this angular velocity, may be calculated from (8-69). The result is

$$L_a J_m \frac{d^2\omega_m}{dt^2} + (L_a b_m + R_a J_m)\frac{d\omega_m}{dt} + (R_a b_m + k_b k_T)\omega_m = K_T e_a^d(t) \tag{8-70}$$

For example, the angular velocity for the polar manipulator was given by

$$\dot{\theta}_1(t) = \frac{120}{(30 - 3s(t))^2 + (4s(t))^2} \frac{ds}{dt}(t)$$

$$= \frac{8t^2}{3 - 4t^3 + 3.70t^6}$$

when the interval $0 \le t < \frac{1}{2}$, with $s(t) = \frac{20}{3}t^3$, is considered. The substitution of this expression into (8-70) yields the required armature voltage $e_a^d(t)$. Conversely, in a mathematically perfect system, the use of $e_a^d(t)$ in (8-68) would provide the $i_a(t)$ which, when substituted in (8-67), would yield that $\omega_a^d(t)$ which, when used in (8-68), would leave the current $i_a^d(t)$ unchanged. Once again, for a fixed $e_a^d(t)$,

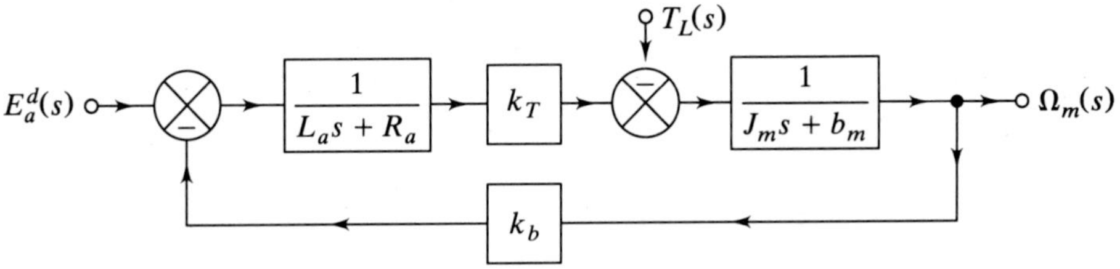

FIGURE 8-43
A disturbance enters the picture.

nothing in the system would change, and only a change in $e_a^d(t)$ would produce a change in the remaining parameters.

Suppose now that there is an external disturbance to the system, characterized by the inclusion of the torque T_L. The inclusion of the disturbance leads to the altered block diagram shown in Fig. 8-43 and to an angular velocity $\omega_m(t)$, which is not the desired one, $\omega_m^d(t)$. We now note that the feedback loop actually tracks the desired angular velocity.

Suppose $\omega_m(t) < \omega_m^d(t)$. Then the voltage input into the armature circuit increases, increasing the torque and hence the angular velocity. A similar adjustment attains when $\omega_m(t) > \omega_m^d(t)$.

As in the previous example, we may improve system performance by including a controller. We shall use a position feedback, together with the PD controller, as shown in Fig. 8-44—again, a cascade controller. Note the inclusion of the bias voltage $E_a^d(s)$, provided to maintain the desired motion. The corresponding closed loop system function relating the output position to the desired position (with zero bias and zero disturbance) is given by

$$\begin{aligned} G_\theta(s) &= \frac{\Theta_m(s)}{\Theta_m^d(s)} \\ &= \frac{k_p k_T + k_d k_T s}{L_a J_m s^3 + (L_a b_m + R_a J_m)s^2 + (R_a b_m + k_T k_b + k_d k_T)s + k_p k_T} \end{aligned} \tag{8-71}$$

Usually, the electric time constant, $L_a/R_a \ll J_m/b_m$, the mechanical time constant, and we thus neglect the former in comparison to the latter. With this simplification the system function [Eq. (8-71)] takes on the familiar form

$$G_\theta(s) = \frac{k_p k_T + k_d k_T s}{R_a J_m s^2 + (R_a b_m + k_T k_b + k_d k_T)s + k_p k_T}$$

The introduction of the standard parameters

$$2\zeta\omega = \frac{1}{R_a J_m}(R_a b_m + k_T k_b + k_d k_T)$$

$$\omega^2 = \frac{k_p k_T}{R_a J_m}$$

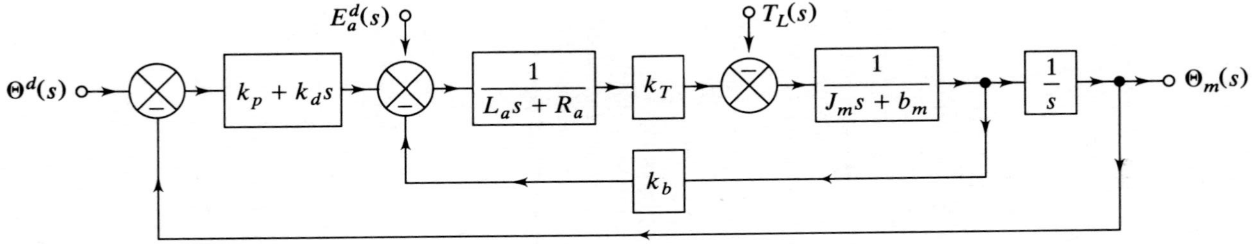

FIGURE 8-44
The system with PD controller.

yields the standardized system function in the form

$$G_\theta(s) = \frac{\omega^2 + (2\zeta\omega - K)s}{s^2 + 2\zeta\omega s + \omega^2} \qquad K = \frac{1}{R_a J_m}(R_a b_m + k_T k_b)$$

To conclude this discussion, we turn briefly to the unit step response of this system, given by

$$\Theta_m(s) = \frac{\omega^2 + (2\zeta\omega - K)s}{s^2 + 2\zeta\omega s + \omega^2} \cdot \frac{1}{s}$$

This time, the initial values are

$$\lim_{t\to 0} \theta_m(t) = \lim_{s\to\infty} s\Theta_m(s) = 0$$

$$\lim_{t\to 0} \dot{\theta}_m(t) = \lim_{s\to\infty} s^2\Theta_m(s) = 2\zeta\omega - K$$

so that high choices of ω and ζ will again tend to improve the system rise time. The steady-state system performance is similarly obtained as

$$\lim_{t\to\infty} \theta_m(t) = \lim_{s\to 0} s\Theta_m(s) = 1$$

$$\lim_{t\to\infty} \dot{\theta}_m(t) = \lim_{s\to 0} s^2\Theta_m(s) = 0$$

If we again insist on critical damping, then we have, with $\zeta = 1$,

$$k_d = 2\sqrt{k_p}\sqrt{\frac{R_a J_m}{k_T}} - \left(\frac{R_a b_m}{k_T} + k_b\right)$$

relating the choice of k_d and k_p. We omit a discussion of overshoot and rise time since it may be carried out in pretty much the same manner as was done in the preceding example.

As our final example in this section, we shall continue the discussion on hydraulic actuators given in Chap. 7. We shall proceed in much the same manner as we did for the DC drive. We first write the system equations in standard first-order form and draw the system block diagram and signal flow graph. Finally, we establish the overall system function and indicate some possibly desirable adjustments of the controller parameters.

Our problem formulation here will be slightly more complex than that given in Chap. 7, in that we shall consider an arbitrary set point for the system instead of the rather specialized $(\bar{x}_1, \bar{p}) = (0, 0)$ used in the previous discussion.

We emphasize once more that actual fluid flow dynamics are quite nonlinear and that all of the following defined quantities are deviations from some steady-state system behavior.

Example 8-28 Automatic control for the hydraulic actuator. Based on the mathematical model of a hydraulic system in Sec. 7-1-3, carry out the following steps directed toward the modeling of a hydraulic control system:

(*a*) Derive the governing equation(s) for an arbitrary set point $(\bar{x}_1, \bar{p})$ and express these equations in the standard first-order form

$$\dot{\mathbf{y}} = \mathbf{Ay} + \mathbf{Bv}$$

(*b*) Construct the corresponding block diagram and signal flow graph, including a proportional controller of the form $v(t) = -k_{1p}x_2(t) + k_{2p}u(t)$.

(*c*) Determine the system function when the input is the open loop component of the controller and the output is the displacement of the mass.

Solution

(*a*) Suppose we take our general set point to be $(\bar{x}_1, \bar{p})$. This results in a valve flow

$$\bar{q} = f(\bar{x}_1, \bar{p})$$

In a neighborhood of the set point, we then have

$$q - \bar{q} = k_1(x_1 - \bar{x}_1) - k_2(p - \bar{p})$$

which we shall write as

$$r = k_1 z_1 - k_2 w$$

where r, z_1, and w are the incremental flow, valve displacement, and pressure, respectively, and k_1 and k_2 are termed the volumetric flow and pressure flow coefficients. In this context $k_2 \geq 0$, generally. The set point is generally a function of time. That is, at specified intervals, it maybe necessary to linearize the system about different set points as dictated by the overall motion requirements. Of course, this also requires a recalculation of k_1 and k_2. The frequency of changing set points depends on the time required for the system to reach a state approximating steady-state behavior in order to maintain control. The system state is to be maintained as close as possible to each successive set point. The valve opening is taken to be the cause of all causes, and we thus maintain a bias $\bar{x}_1$; we emphasize this bias only in the system block diagram (see Fig. 8-45), where we have indicated it at the first summer. Thus, when $x_1 - \bar{x}_1$ becomes small, the valve opening is maintained at $\bar{x}_1$.

As before, we accept the following contributions to the flow rate,

$$r = A\frac{dx_2}{dt} + \frac{V}{B}\frac{dw}{dt} + k_L w$$

where $x_2(t)$ is now the incremental piston displacement measured from the position of the piston at set point. Equating the two expressions for the flow rate leads to the first of the governing equations:

$$k_1 z_1 - k_2 w = A\frac{dx_2}{dt} + \frac{V}{B}\frac{dw}{dt} + k_L w \tag{8-72}$$

The second of the governing equations is the dynamic equation for piston and load

$$m\frac{d^2x_2}{dt^2} = Aw - b\frac{dx_2}{dt} - kx_2 \tag{8-73}$$

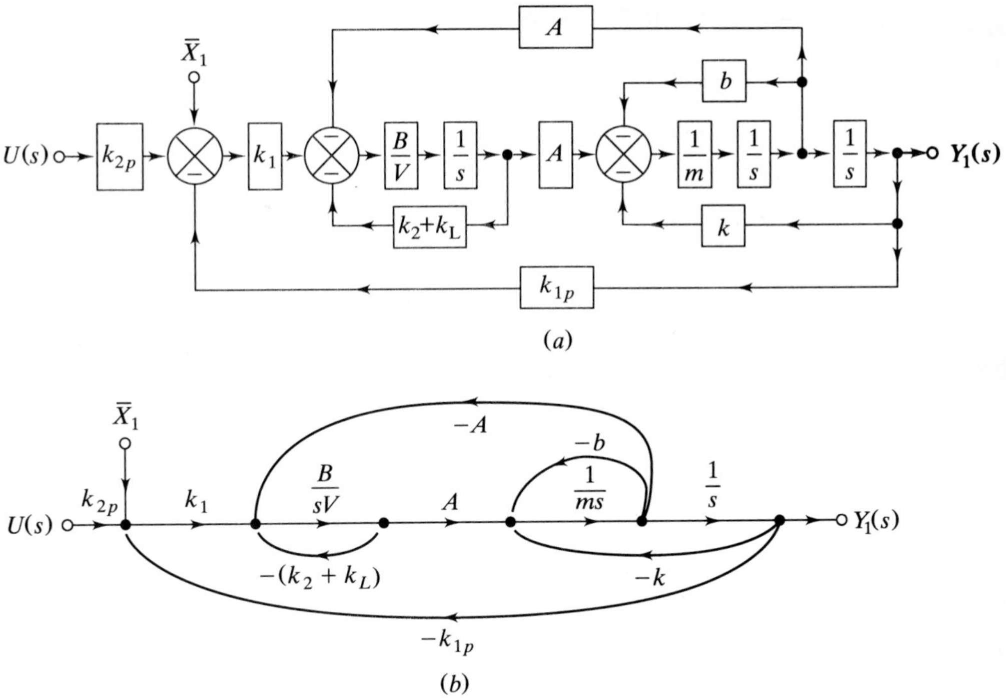

FIGURE 8-45
Hydraulic control system. (*a*) Block diagram; (*b*) signal flow graph.

These equations are now written in standard first-order form by introducing the usual auxiliary variables and control notation. Let

$$y_1 = x_2 \qquad y_2 = \dot{x}_2 \qquad y_3 = w \qquad \text{and} \qquad z_1 = v$$

The state space equations then are

$$\begin{pmatrix} \dot{y}_1 \\ \dot{y}_2 \\ \dot{y}_3 \end{pmatrix} = \begin{bmatrix} 0 & 1 & 0 \\ -\dfrac{k}{m} & -\dfrac{b}{m} & \dfrac{A}{m} \\ 0 & -\dfrac{AB}{V} & -(k_2 + k_L)\dfrac{B}{V} \end{bmatrix} \begin{pmatrix} y_1 \\ y_2 \\ y_3 \end{pmatrix} + \begin{pmatrix} 0 \\ 0 \\ \dfrac{Bk_1}{V} \end{pmatrix} v$$

(*b*) A common controller used in such control systems is one that has both open and closed loop components. Suppose we introduce the controller

$$v(t) = -k_{1p}y_1(t) + k_{2p}u(t)$$

With this controller the system equations take on the final form

$$\begin{pmatrix} \dot{y}_1 \\ \dot{y}_2 \\ \dot{y}_3 \end{pmatrix} = \begin{bmatrix} 0 & 1 & 0 \\ -\dfrac{k}{m} & -\dfrac{b}{m} & \dfrac{A}{m} \\ -\dfrac{B}{V}k_1k_{1p} & -\dfrac{AB}{V} & -(k_2+k_L)\dfrac{B}{V} \end{bmatrix} \begin{pmatrix} y_1 \\ y_2 \\ y_3 \end{pmatrix} + \begin{pmatrix} 0 \\ 0 \\ \dfrac{B}{V}k_1k_{2p} \end{pmatrix} u \tag{8-74}$$

To draw the corresponding block diagram, we first take the Laplace transform of (8-74) and introduce a summer for each of the variables. The transformed equations are

$$sY_1(s) = Y_2(s)$$

$$sY_2(s) = -\frac{k}{m}Y_1(s) - \frac{b}{m}Y_2(s) + \frac{A}{m}Y_3(s)$$

$$sY_3(s) = -\frac{B}{V}k_1k_{1p}Y_1(s) - \frac{AB}{V}Y_2(s) - \frac{B}{V}(k_2+k_L)Y_3(s)$$

$$+\frac{B}{V}k_1k_{2p}U(s)$$

In drawing any block diagram, we have various choices for the amount of detail that we may wish to include for a given subsystem. Here, we choose to present every detail by including all of the essentially internal feedback loops as well as the integrators as separate system components. The resultant block diagram and signal flow graph are shown in Fig. 8-45.

(*c*) With $\overline{X}_1 = 0$ the system function may be derived in a straightforward manner from the Laplace-transformed system equations given previously, or we may use Mason's rule to deduce it from the signal flow graph. In either case we obtain

$$G(s) = \frac{Y_1(s)}{U(s)}$$

$$= \frac{k_{2p}/k_{1p}}{\dfrac{V}{ABk_1k_{1p}}[ms^2+bs+k]\left[s+\dfrac{B}{V}(k_2+k_L)\right] + \dfrac{As}{k_1k_{1p}} + 1} \tag{8-75}$$

With the exception of having to deal with a cubic polynomial in the denominator, the system analysis and design now proceed in much the same manner as before. We may again look at the step function response and attempt an optimal selection of the controller parameters k_{1p} and k_{2p}. The proportional controller may be produced mechanically by using appropriate levers, or it may be produced electrically by using position sensors and a servo to move the valve. We shall not pursue any of these concepts here.

Quite generally, controller or compensator parameters change the root structure of the denominator and the numerator of the system function. The primary limitations on these parameters are thus stability requirements, such as an insistence that all poles reside in the left half plane. The meandering of the poles as a function of the changes in the system parameters is the subject of root locus analysis. The perusal of these and related topics is the subject of automatic control theory. Here, we have only gotten the proverbial foot in the door.

Our final section deals with the performance evaluation of the robot itself as a sophisticated machine, and many of the measures consequently are the same as those employed in the categorization of other machines.

8-4 THE MEASURE OF THE ROBOT

This section is the appropriate closing section. After all is said and done, the following terminology and definitions serve to evaluate the performance of the final product—the robot. Fortunately, the various claims of accuracy and repeatability of robots are somewhat more consistent now than they were five years ago; some uniform standards were proposed in 1988 by the American National Standards Institute. In Doeblin[17], about 170 pages are devoted to the discussion of the static and dynamic characteristics of instruments. Here, the instrument is the robot, and we shall restrict our discussion to only three concepts that are used in the evaluation of robot performance: resolution, accuracy, and repeatability. The former is deterministic; the latter two concepts are statistical in nature.

Suppose we consider the instrument as some transducer where the quantity to be measured is termed the input, and the corresponding measurement the output. For example, if an absolute encoder has an angular resolution of

$$r_\theta = \frac{2\pi}{2^4} = 0.3927 \sim 22.5°$$

then any change in angle of less than 22.5° cannot be detected.

In the same fashion we may view the robot as an instrument with a certain resolution, when all or some of the joints are made to move in discrete steps. Only a discrete set of points then is accessible to the end effector. As might be expected, a concept of resolution in this case is not quite as straightforward as in the resolution of a single joint, for example, since a variety of translational and rotational resolutions are interacting with one another. We propose a definition of resolution that is based on what is known as a multicriteria optimization process. We begin with the definition of an accessible point.

Definition 8-13 Accessible point. Let $\boldsymbol{\xi} = (\xi_1 \ldots \xi_n)^T$ represent a controlled setting of the robot coordinates and let $\mathbf{w} = (x\,y\,z)^T$ be a world point. Let $\mathbf{f}(\cdot)$: $\mathbb{R}^n \to \mathbb{R}^3$ be the mapping that maps a robot point $\boldsymbol{\xi}$ into a world point $\mathbf{w}$; that is,

$$\mathbf{f}(\boldsymbol{\xi}) = \mathbf{w}$$

A point $\mathbf{w}$ in the robot work space is accessible if and only if there exists a controlled setting $\boldsymbol{\xi}$ such that $\mathbf{f}^{-1}(\mathbf{w}) = \boldsymbol{\xi}$.

We shall also have need of the following partial order on $\mathbb{R}^2$. Let $\mathbf{z}_0, \mathbf{z}_1$ be two points in $\mathbb{R}^2$ with $\mathbf{z}_0 = (x_0\ y_0)^T$ and $\mathbf{z}_1 = (x_1\ y_1)^T$. Then the natural order on $\mathbb{R}^2$ is given by

$$\mathbf{z}_0 \leq \mathbf{z}_1 \quad \text{iff} \quad x_0 \leq x_1 \quad y_0 \leq y_1$$

and

$$\mathbf{z}_0 < \mathbf{z}_1 \quad \text{iff} \quad x_0 \leq x_1 \quad y_0 \leq y_1 \quad \mathbf{z}_0 \neq \mathbf{z}_1$$

Furthermore, let Z (finite) $\subset \mathbb{R}^2$. Then $\mathbf{z}^* \in Z$ is called a minimal point of Z if and only if there is no $\mathbf{z} \in Z$ for which $\mathbf{z} < \mathbf{z}^*$.

With this background we now construct the resolution for a robot. We shall phrase it in terms of the presumed motion of the robot end effector along a straight-line segment. In view of the discrete accessibility of the work space, it is clear that relatively few points would lie exactly on the line, and we thus introduce an allowable deviation from the line; that is, the points may lie in some tube surrounding the line. Let AB be a suitable straight-line segment of length L (e.g., connecting two accessible boundary points A and B of the robot work space). Let $\epsilon > 0$ be the radius of a circular tube with AB as its center line, in which all acceptable deviations from the straight-line path AB must lie. Let $\mathbf{w}_i$, $i \in I = \{0, \ldots, n\}$, be all the accessible points belonging to the interior of this tube. Let $\mathbf{d}_i$ be the normal projection of the $\mathbf{w}_i$ on the line AB as shown in Fig. 8-46. Let n_i be the normal distance of the point $\mathbf{w}_i$ from the line AB and order the n_i according to magnitude with $n_1 = \min_{i \in I} |n_i - \epsilon|$; let N be the set of all n_i. Corresponding to each n_k, let I_k be the index set for the points $\mathbf{w}_i$ which remain in the tube (or its boundary) for radius $\epsilon_k = n_k$ and calculate

$$\delta_k = \max_{i \in I_k} |\mathbf{d}_i - \mathbf{d}_{i-1}|$$

The set $\mathscr{R} = \{(n_k, \delta_k): n_k \in N\}$ will be termed the *resolution set* for the robot. Let $\mathscr{R}$ be ordered with the natural order on $\mathbb{R}^2$.

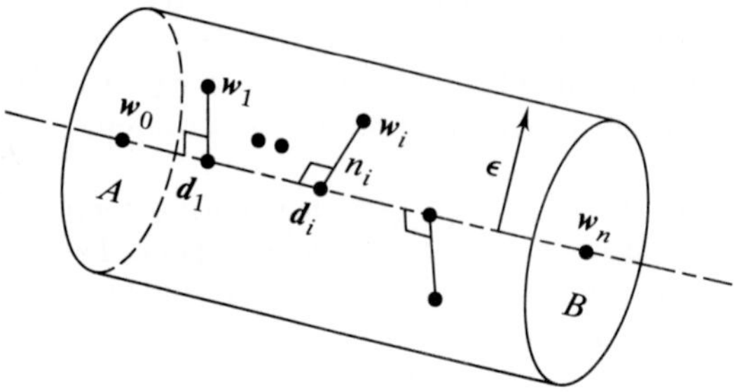

FIGURE 8-46
Resolution in a tube.

Definition 8-14 Resolution of a robot. A pair $(n^*, \delta^*) \in \mathscr{R}$ is a resolution of the robot if and only if it is a minimal point of $\mathscr{R}$ with respect to the natural order on $\mathscr{R}$.

It is clear that the resolution changes with the tube size. The choice of the pair in the definition is such that decreasing the maximum interval results in an increase of the radius and, conversely, decreasing the radius results in an increase of the maximum interval. Omitted are all pairs from which it is still possible to improve both entries simultaneously or for which one may still be improved without changing the others. Once again, we shall use the polar manipulator to illustrate this concept.

Example 8-29 The resolution of the polar manipulator. We suppose that the radial resolution is 1 cm and that the angular resolution is 10°. The result is the polar grid indicated in Fig. 8-47. The work space of the robot is taken to be the indicated semicircular band. The line AB is at a distance of 4.5 cm from the y_0-axis; it is a secant line of the semicircular work space, with A and B in the boundary of the work space. As our primary band we take $\epsilon = 1$, a "tube" of 1 cm radius about the center line AB. Since the situation is symmetric, we shall restrict our discussion to the left quadrant. Calculate the resolution of this robot with respect to the specified line.

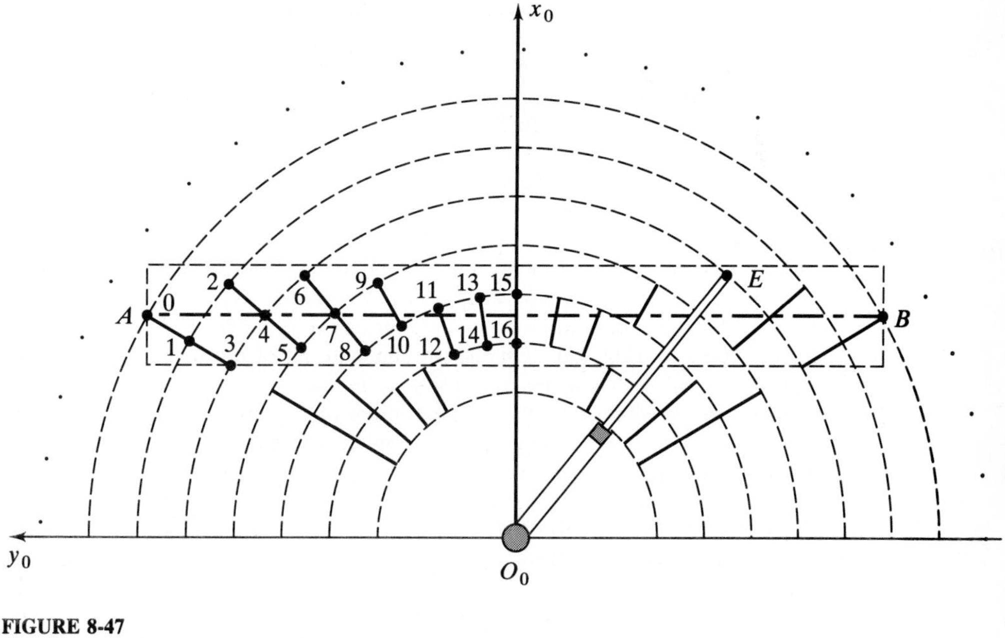

FIGURE 8-47
Resolution for the polar manipulator.

TABLE 8-5

w_i	x_0	y_0	d_i		n	n_k
w_0	4.500	7.794	0.866		0	$n_1 = 1.000$
w_1	4.000	6.928	0.800		0.500	$n_2 = 0.862$
w_2	5.142	6.128	0.066		0.642	$n_3 = 0.741$
w_3	3.500	6.062	0.700	0.766	1.000	$n_4 = 0.696$
w_4	4.500	5.362	0.766		0	$n_5 = 0.670$
w_5	3.857	4.596	0.096		0.643	$n_6 = 0.643$
w_6	5.362	4.500	0.643		0.862	$n_7 = 0.642$
w_7	4.596	3.857	0.643		0.096	$n_8 = 0.561$
w_8	3.830	3.214	0.214		0.670	$n_9 = 0.500$
w_9	5.196	3.000	0.500		0.696	$n_{10} = 0.424$
w_{10}	4.330	2.500	0.790		0.170	$n_{11} = 0.198$
w_{11}	4.698	1.710	0.342		0.198	$n_{12} = 0.170$
w_{12}	3.759	1.368	0.500		0.741	$n_{13} = 0.096$
w_{13}	4.924	0.868	0.173		0.424	
w_{14}	3.939	0.695	0.695		0.561	
w_{15}	5.000	0	0		0.500	
w_{16}	4.000	0			0.500	

Solution. In Table 8-5 we list the points in order in accordance with their y_0-components. We then list all of the normal distances and then the selection of the n_i in their proper order. In Table 8-6 we list all of the points (n_k, δ_k) as well as the final selections that actually serve as the resolutions. To illustrate the elimination procedure, we begin with $n_1 = 1.000$; the corresponding maximum interval occurs between $\mathbf{w}_0$ and $\mathbf{w}_1$ with $\delta_1 = 0.866$. We then eliminate n_1 as a bound and consider the next smaller tube radius $n_2 = 0.862$. Since the normal distance n_1 corresponded to $\mathbf{w}_3$, we now eliminate $\mathbf{w}_3$ from our listing. When $\mathbf{w}_3$ is eliminated, the new difference will be between $\mathbf{w}_2$ and $\mathbf{w}_4$. We have shown this step in Table 8-5. The continuation of this process eventually yields all of the pairs (n_k, δ_k) listed in Table 8-6. Finally, we eliminate all of the pairs where we may improve n_k without changing δ_k. This selection process eventually results in the minimal pairs or what we term the ϵ-resolutions of the robot. For these latter pairs a decrease in the tube radius clearly implies an increase in the size of the maximum interval.

Some additional insight may be gained by taking a brief look at the dilemmas of a revolute manipulator. The simple manipulator shown in Fig. 8-48 is to move the point E along the line $y_0 = 4$ from right to left, beginning at the extreme position indicated. The inner link has a length of 5 cm, and the outer one a length of 4 cm. The angular resolution of each arm is 10°. If we take the positions in sequence, as they can be reached by the robot along the line, the

TABLE 8-6

n_k	δ_k	n_k^*	δ_k^*
$n_1 = 1.000$	0.866	$n_5 = 0.670$	0.866
$n_2 = 0.862$	0.866	$n_6 = 0.643$	1.357
$n_3 = 0.741$	0.866	$n_7 = 0.642$	1.505
$n_4 = 0.696$	0.866	$n_9 = 0.500$	1.566
$n_5 = 0.670$	0.866	$n_{10} = 0.424$	2.432
$n_6 = 0.643$	1.357	$n_{11} = 0.198$	3.420
$n_7 = 0.642$	1.505	$n_{12} = 0.170$	5.000
$n_8 = 0.561$	1.566	$n_{13} = 0.096$	7.714
$n_9 = 0.500$	1.566	$n_{14} = 0$	10.724
$n_{10} = 0.424$	2.432		
$n_{11} = 0.198$	3.420		
$n_{12} = 0.170$	5.000		
$n_{13} = 0.096$	7.714		
$n_{14} = 0$	10.724		

motion would appear awkward at best. The first step is below-shoulder level; the next step requires a 40° counterclockwise rotation for the inner link and an 80° clockwise rotation for the outer link; and the end effector would have to deviate considerably and then return to its final position. The next position is more or less a toss-up between two possible positions for the second link; the next step is relatively normal. However, the following position is one that would bring the inner arm all the way down to the horizontal position and require a 160° rotation for the outer link, and so on. These extreme excursions of the motion are to be avoided, the one way to remove them is to insist on either below-shoulder or above-shoulder motion. In this context the shortest distance between two points may be a curve rather than a straight line.

All of this discussion has dealt only with purely geometric considerations, with all components assumed to be perfectly rigid. Influences such as friction and elasticity, as well as dynamic effects, have not been included.

We close our comments on resolution with some suggested broader problems:

1. The following inverse problem, as suggested by Jon Moore: Determine the required joint resolutions to achieve a specified resolution for the robot.

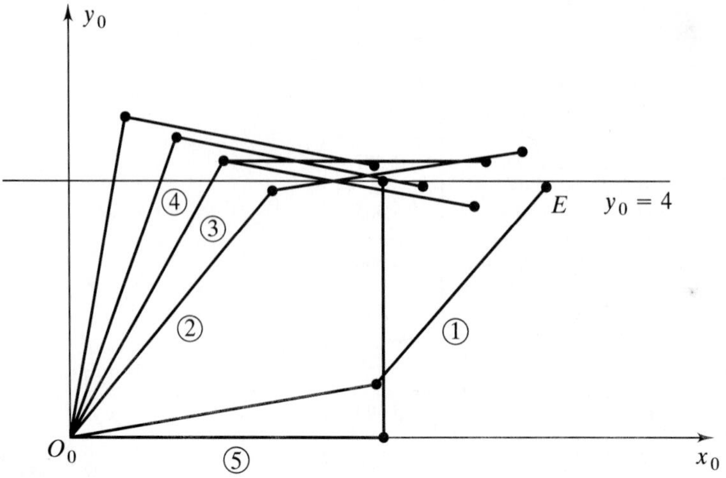

FIGURE 8-48
Dilemmas of the revolute manipulator.

2. It may be advisable to divide the robot work space into resolution sectors, much in the way a computer hard disk is subdivided into information retrieval and storage sectors.
3. With ever-increasing storage capacity, it may become advisable to record all or a judicious selection of positions within a given sector and to use this information to generate motion.

Both subsequent measures of the robot, accuracy and repeatability, are based on probability and statistics, and it therefore behooves us to review enough of these concepts for the following to make sense.

A *sample space* Z is a collection of possible outcomes of a given experiment. Any function defined on Z—that is, any function whose domain is Z—is called a *random variable* on Z. If the range of the function is a subset of $\mathbb{R}$, the real numbers, then the random variable is *continuous*; if the range is a countable collection of real numbers, then we speak of a *discrete* random variable. For example, within the present context, we may choose some target point $\overline{\mathbf{w}} = (\bar{x}, \bar{y}, \bar{z})$ and we may approach this target point 50 times by a variety of approach paths. Each approach will generally yield a point $\mathbf{w}$ which is not the target point itself. The collection of approaches constitutes our sample space Z. Any function $X(\cdot)$: $Z \to \mathbb{R}$ is a continuous random variable on Z. For example, $X(\cdot)$ may be the distance function $D(\overline{\mathbf{w}}, \cdot\,)$, whose values are given by

$$D(\overline{\mathbf{w}}, \mathbf{w}) = \sqrt{(x - \bar{x})^2 + (y - \bar{y})^2 + (z - \bar{z})^2}$$

providing the deviation from the target point.

The probability that the deviation or outcome D of an approach will lie in some particular interval $[a, b]$ is given by the integral

$$\mathscr{P}(a < D < b) = \int_a^b f(x)\,dx$$

We term $f(\cdot)$: $\mathbb{R} \to \mathbb{R}$ the *probability density function*, describing the likely outcomes of the specified collection of experiments. An immediate consequence is that the probability of the isolated event $\{x\}$, $\mathscr{P}(\{x\}) = 0$. Quite generally, a probability density function is required to satisfy

1. $f(x) \geq 0$ for all $x \in \mathbb{R}$.
2. $\int_{-\infty}^{\infty} f(x)\,dx = 1$.
3. $\mathscr{P}(a < x < b) = \int_a^b f(x)\,dx$

Experience over literally centuries has shown that a variety of experiments exhibit very specific probabilistic behavior. One such probability density or distribution is the Gaussian curve

$$f(x) = \frac{1}{\sqrt{2\pi}\,\sigma} e^{-(x-\mu)^2/2\sigma^2}$$

whose general appearance is depicted in Fig. 8-49. We also term this curve a Gaussian or normal distribution, and x a normal random variable.

The particular shape of the curve is characterized by the parameters μ and σ, the *mean* and the *standard deviation* of the curve, respectively. Theoretically, the mean or expected value of the random variable $X(\cdot)$ is given by

$$\mu = E[X(\cdot)] = \int_{-\infty}^{\infty} x f(x)\,dx$$

and the variance of $X(\cdot)$ is given by

$$\sigma^2 = E\left[(X - \mu)^2\right] = \int_{-\infty}^{\infty} (x - \mu)^2 f(x)\,dx$$

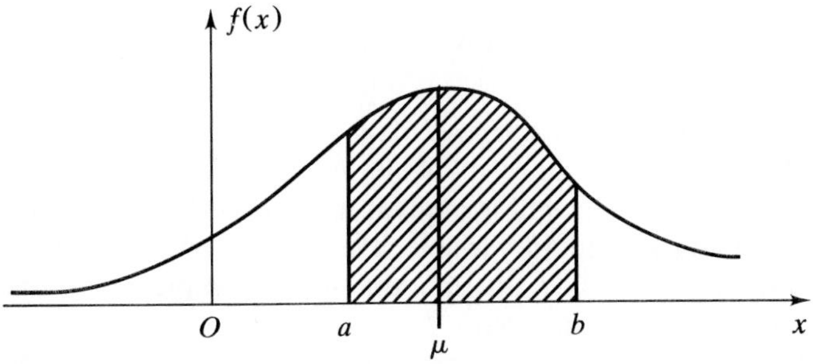

FIGURE 8-49
The Gaussian distribution.

Remark 8-9. At this point the reader is likely to be somewhat confused with all of the different X's floating around. The continuous random variable $X(\cdot)$ is a *function* from Z into the reals; a specific value of this function, denoting the outcome of an experiment ζ in Z, is given by $X = X(\zeta)$; finally, x simply denotes any real number in $\mathbb{R}$ or x is the "generic outcome."

Remark 8-10. Some intervals centered on μ and the probabilities (expressed as percentages) that the outcomes will lie in these intervals are of special interest:

$[-\sigma, \sigma]$	contains 68% of the outcomes;
$[-2\sigma, 2\sigma]$	contains 95% of the outcomes;
$[-3\sigma, 3\sigma]$	contains 99.7% of the outcomes.

Thus a statement such as "three-sigma accuracy" refers to the fact that 99.7% of the outcomes of the experiment will lie within the interval $[-3\sigma, 3\sigma]$, centered on μ.

The previous concept of a probability distribution was based on an infinite number of outcomes, either imagined to be infinite or so large in number that it could be considered to be infinite. From a practical point of view, however, we can never conduct an infinite number of experiments; we can never attain more than a *sampling* of our infinite set of possible outcomes. We term the original set—the totality of all observations—a *population* and any subset of it a *sample*. The use of such a sample to infer some property of the population is called *statistical inference*; it is what we do when we run a finite number of tests and deduce therefrom the characteristics of the overall performance.

A collection of n independent random variables $X_1(\cdot), \ldots, X_n(\cdot)$ (functions from Z to $\mathbb{R}$), each with the same probability distribution [taken to be $f(x)$ here], is termed a *random sample* of size n of the population. That is, we take the probability of $X_i = X_i(\zeta)$ to be $f(x_i)$. The corresponding *sample mean* and *sample standard deviation* are defined by

$$\bar{X} = \frac{1}{n} \sum_{i=1}^{n} X_i$$

and

$$S = \sqrt{\frac{1}{n-1} \sum_{i=1}^{n} \left(X_i - \bar{X}\right)^2}$$

respectively. Without going into detail, the use of $n - 1$ rather than n makes this expression an estimation of S rather than the actual standard deviation. Such a function of the observed values of a random variable is itself a random variable called a *statistic*. As a random variable it enjoys its own probability distribution. The particular probability distribution of the sample mean and sample deviation are the subject of the *central limit theorem*.

The real beauty of the central limit theorem lies in the fact that the distribution of the sample means is a normal distribution regardless of the distribution of the population from which the samples are taken. If the samples are taken from a population with a normal distribution with mean μ and standard deviation σ, then the sample means have a normal distribution with mean μ and standard deviation $\sigma/\sqrt{n}$, provided the sample size n is large enough, a rule of thumb being $n \geq 30$. For an expanded discussion on probability and statistics for engineers, the reader is referred to the text by Walpole and Myers.[18]

We will use these statistical concepts to define the accuracy and repeatability of a robot. The precise definitions are based on the following general framework and assumptions:

Some point (or points) $\overline{\mathbf{w}} = (\bar{x}, \bar{y}, \bar{z})$ is specified within the robot's work space. The set of experiments, Z, consists of all of the attempts to reach the target point $\overline{\mathbf{w}}$; the outcome of each such attempt is the point actually reached, denoted by $\mathbf{w}$. This suggests the definition of the continuous random variable $D(\overline{\mathbf{w}}; \cdot): Z \rightarrow \mathbb{R}$, the distance from $\overline{\mathbf{w}}$. The outcome of each experiment is a distance $d = D(\overline{\mathbf{w}}; \mathbf{w})$, and we assume that $D(\overline{\mathbf{w}}; \cdot)$ has a normal distribution $f(d)$ over Z, with mean μ and standard deviation σ. A random sample of size n might consist of n paths p_i and termination points $\mathbf{w}_i$ with corresponding random variable $D_i(\overline{\mathbf{w}}; \cdot)$. If the conditions for each approach are "pretty much the same," we may assume that each of the random variables $D_i(\overline{\mathbf{w}}; \cdot)$ also has normal distribution $f(d)$. Subject to these assumptions, the random sample is normally distributed and the sample mean and sample deviation tend to μ and $\sigma/\sqrt{n}$ and hence may be considered to be good approximations thereof for large enough n. The concepts of accuracy and repeatability are based on a random sampling of Z and the corresponding sample mean and deviation. We now make accuracy more precise.

Remark 8-11. There is some problem in defining the distance as a random variable, since $d \geq 0$ always and we are thus ignoring the whole interval $(-\infty, 0)$. Some statements may thus lose some of their statistical meaning; the approach will, however, serve its purpose as a method for comparing robots as long as all participants adhere to the guidelines.

Accuracy deals with the robot's ability to reach arbitrary points in the work space, points that it has not been taught—indeed points that presumably have never been occupied by the robot's end effector. The first definition deals with accuracy based on a variety of routes to the same specified point.

Suppose a point $\mathbf{w}$ has been specified. Consider then m randomly selected points within the robot's work space and use software to program m routes from these points to the specified point. From among these m routes, n are then selected randomly and executed. These n routes constitute the random sample.

Definition 8-15 Single-point accuracy. Let $\overline{\mathbf{w}}$ be the specified point and let $\mathbf{w}_i$ be the point attained by the ith trial. Let

$$D_i = \sqrt{(\bar{x} - x_i)^2 + (\bar{y} - y_i)^2 + (\bar{z} - z_i)^2}$$

denote the error in this ith approach. Furthermore, let

$$\bar{D} = \frac{1}{n} \sum_{i=1}^{n} D_i$$

be the sample mean and let

$$S = \sqrt{\frac{1}{n-1} \sum_{i=1}^{n} (D_i - \bar{D})^2}$$

be the sample standard deviation. Let

$$r = \bar{D} + 3S$$

Then we define r as the *3S-accuracy* (three sigma accuracy) of the robot.

Remark 8-12. With $3S$ (three-sigma) accuracy of the robot, we simply attempt to guarantee that 99.7% of the outcomes will lie in this neighborhood of the target point.

We illustrate the computational routine with an example.

Example 8-30. Suppose a robot is being tested for accuracy by randomly selected approaches to the point (2, 1, 3) in its work space. A random sample of 10 approaches (sufficient for the illustration) has yielded the near misses $\mathbf{w}_i$ listed in Table 8-7. Assume that the random sample is normally distributed and compute the mean, the standard deviation, and the three-sigma accuracy of the robot.

TABLE 8-7

$\mathbf{w}_i$	x_i	y_i	z_i	D_i	$(D_i - \bar{D})^2$
$\mathbf{w}_1$	2.012	1.020	2.970	0.038	0.001600
$\mathbf{w}_2$	1.981	0.970	3.152	0.157	0.006241
$\mathbf{w}_3$	1.975	1.022	3.021	0.039	0.001521
$\mathbf{w}_4$	2.111	1.015	3.002	0.112	0.001156
$\mathbf{w}_5$	1.995	1.005	3.017	0.018	0.003600
$\mathbf{w}_6$	2.112	0.985	3.003	0.113	0.001225
$\mathbf{w}_7$	2.003	1.040	2.992	0.041	0.001369
$\mathbf{w}_8$	1.908	1.080	3.115	0.168	0.008100
$\mathbf{w}_9$	2.001	1.032	2.937	0.071	0.000049
$\mathbf{w}_{10}$	1.999	0.981	2.996	0.019	0.003481

Solution. The calculations are straightforward. The distances D_i are calculated from

$$D_i = \sqrt{(x_i - \bar{x})^2 + (y_i - \bar{y})^2 + (z_i - \bar{z})^2}$$

with

$$D_1 = \sqrt{(2.012 - 2)^2 + (1.020 - 1)^2 + (2.97 - 3)^2} = 0.038$$

for example. The mean is obtained as

$$\bar{D} = \frac{1}{n} \sum_{i=1}^{n} D_i = \frac{1}{10} \sum_{i=1}^{10} D_i = 0.078$$

and the standard deviation is

$$S = \sqrt{\frac{1}{n-1} \sum_{i=1}^{n} (D_i - \bar{D})^2} = \sqrt{\frac{0.028342}{9}} = 0.056$$

The three-sigma accuracy for the robot is given by

$$r = 0.078 + 0.168 = 0.246$$

We continue our discussion with the multipoint accuracy as defined by the American National Standards Institute.[19] Since the intent is to set a standard for a comparison of robot systems, the attendant test instructions are considerably more detailed.

Let C_w be the geometric center of the robot work space and introduce a base reference frame whose x_0-axis passes through the projection of the centroid, as shown in Fig. 8-50a. Next, the test plane is a plane parallel to the plane defined by the points $(1, 0, 0)$, $(0, 1, 0)$, and $(0, 0, -1)$ and passing through the work space centroid C_w. The standard test path must lie within the test plane.

The line segment E_1E_2, parallel to the x_0y_0-plane, passing through C_w and initiating and terminating on the work space boundary, is the reference center line for the standard test path. Ultimately, this standard test path is to be located within the rectangle formed by U_1L_1 and $U_{K+1}L_{K+1}$, as depicted in Fig. 8-50b. The test path will consist of K segments with equal length S_L, where S_L is either 200, 500, or 1000 mm and where S_L is chosen as large as possible with $K \geq 3$. The segment sides will have length $D_L = \frac{1}{2}S_L$; the final overall length of the test path rectangle will be an integral multiple of $K \geq 3$ with $E_1F_1 = E_2F_2$ and with the segments labeled as shown. In addition, a certain orientation of the payload must be maintained. Let $(0xyz)_m$ be the axis system of the end effector, with z_m as its roll axis; then the z_m-axis must remain normal to the test plane (or nearly so) throughout the test sequence. Instead of the many deviations from a single point, multiple-point accuracy deals with the individual deviations at many points in a pattern.

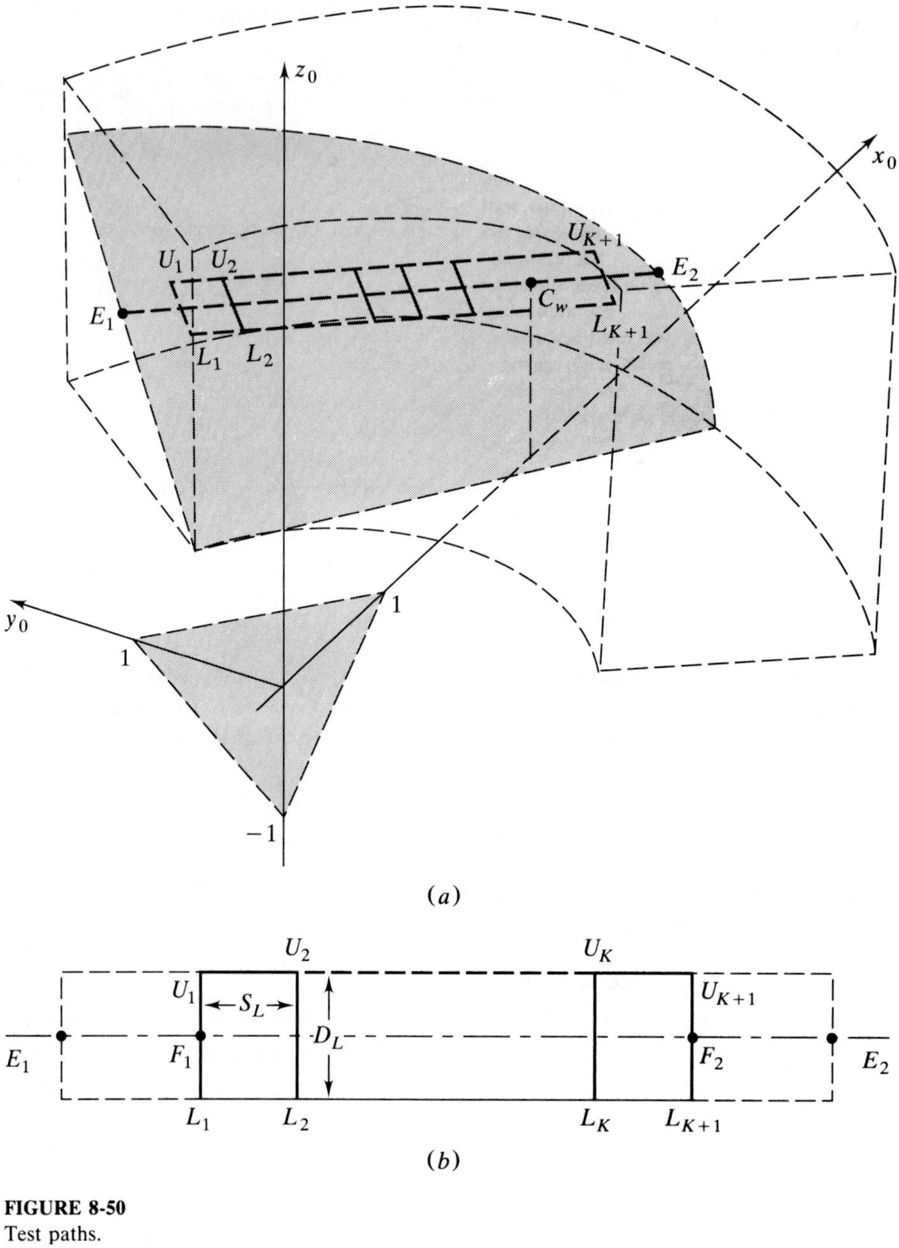

FIGURE 8-50
Test paths.

Definition 8-16 Multiple-point accuracy. The standard test path shall consist of $N \geq 50$ vertices. The order in which these vertices are visited shall be random. Let $\mathbf{D}_i$ be the deviation vector from the specified vector to the position actually attained. The magnitude of $\mathbf{D}_i$ is given by

$$D_i = \sqrt{(x_i - \bar{x}_i)^2 + (y_i - \bar{y}_i)^2 + (z_i - \bar{z}_i)^2}$$

where (x_i, y_i, z_i) is the point actually attained near the ith vertex and $(\bar{x}_i, \bar{y}_i, \bar{z}_i)$ are the coordinates of the ith vertex. The deviation mean is

$$\bar{D} = \frac{1}{N} \sum_{i=1}^{N} D_i$$

and the standard deviation is

$$S = \sqrt{\frac{1}{N-1} \sum_{i=1}^{N} (D_i - \bar{D})^2}$$

where $N \geq 50$ is the total number of vertices visited. Let $r = \bar{D}$ be the radius of a sphere centered at any one of the command points $(\bar{x}_i, \bar{y}_i, \bar{z}_i)$. We shall term r the multiple-point accuracy of the robot.

Accuracy is an elusive concept in practice. While we are able to mathematically define our position to as many decimals as we wish, the point the robot can actually attain depends on the robot's resolution and on that of our position-measuring instruments.

Another term dealing with robot accuracy is repeatability, which we shall define next. Again, we shall base our definition on the standard provided by ANSI.[19] Repeatability, as the word implies, concerns the revisiting of a target point that has been previously occupied by the robot. The point may have been taught or programmed. Here, our statistical evaluation will be based on the measurements along a route which follows three specific vertices selected from the previously established pattern–namely, L_1, $L_{K/2}$ or $L_{(K+1)/2}$, and L_{K+1}.

Definition 8-17 Repeatability. The robot is programmed to perform a cycle which includes the three vertices along the test path. One test sequence shall consist of $n \geq 500$ continuous cycles. During each cycle the deviation of the actual position from the programmed one shall be measured at each of the vertices which we shall identify by a, b, and c. During the ith cycle let $(x, y, z)_{ai}$ denote the attained point and let $(\bar{x}, \bar{y}, \bar{z})_a$ denote the specified point for vertex a. Then the deviation at a is given by

$$D_{ai} = \sqrt{(x_{ai} - \bar{x}_a)^2 + (y_{ai} - \bar{y}_a)^2 + (z_{ai} - \bar{z}_a)^2}$$

the deviations D_{bi} and D_{ci} are similarly obtained. The mean of the deviations is

$$\bar{D} = \frac{1}{3n} \sum_{i=1}^{n} (D_{ai} + D_{bi} + D_{ci})$$

The corresponding standard deviation is

$$S = \sqrt{\frac{1}{3n-1} \sum_{i=1}^{n} \left[(D_{ai} - \bar{D})^2 + (D_{bi} - \bar{D})^2 + (D_{ci} - \bar{D})^2 \right]}$$

Let $r = \bar{D} + 3S$ be the radius of a sphere centered at any target point of the robot. Then 99.7% of the repeat approaches lie within this sphere, and we term r the three-sigma repeatability of the robot.

The definitions that we have given contain only the essentials of the tests to be conducted. In particular, we have made no mention of the test load (usually a steel cube) and the orientation it is to maintain during the motion—the point on the robot at which all of these measurements are to take place has not been specified, nor have we indicated warm-up time or that the position measurements have to be carried out with noncontact sensors. As is the case with all standardized tests, there is a litany of detail that must be followed and adhered to in order to make these tests at once uniform and random. To some extent, the statistical validity of the tests is irrelevant. Provided that all of the participants use the same tests and compute the same parameters, they will provide a basis for the comparison of robots. We refer the reader to Mathews and Hill[20] for additional detail on standardized tests; the material in Albertson[21] should also be of interest.

The previous concepts of accuracy and repeatability are all static concepts, in that the robot's position is measured when at rest. Still needed is what might be termed a concept of dynamic accuracy. The main thing to be avoided in approaching a target point is overshoot. It is generally desirable to control the system in such a way that there is no overshoot—in essence, to creep up to the target whenever feasible. We close this section with a brief discussion of ideas relevant to such a concept of dynamic accuracy.

Suppose the position, the velocity, and the acceleration of a point are 0 at some given instant. Does this imply that the point will remain at rest? Of course not. For a point in rectilinear motion, with

$$x(t) = (t-1)^3$$

we have $x(1) = \dot{x}(1) = \ddot{x}(1) = 0$. However, the point will clearly continue to move for $t > 1$. What allowed the point to continue to move was the fact that $\dddot{x} = 6$, the jerk, was nonzero. In essence, energy may be contained in any and all derivatives of a motion. Only when all derivatives of a motion are 0 at a given time $\bar{t}$ would it become theoretically impossible for the system to begin moving again. That is, cutting off power to the system at $t = \bar{t}$ would assure that it remained at rest at $t = \bar{t}$. From a physical point of view, there would always be enough friction in a system to hinder the motion at some point. We thus simply assert that in creeping up to a target, it is desirable to bring as many derivatives of the motion as possible to 0.

EXERCISES

8-1. Suppose we are given a circle of radius 2 with center at the origin. Let $s(t)$ be the arc length along the circle with $s = 0$ at the point $(2, 0)$ and $s = 4\pi$ after one traversal of the circumference. Suppose we wish to travel on the circle in such a way that $s(0) = 0$, $s(2) = 4\pi$, $v(0) = 0$, and $v(2) = 0$. Assume that the existing parametrization of the circle is

$$x(\theta) = 2\cos\theta$$

$$y(\theta) = 2\sin\theta$$

(*a*) Use a cubic polynomial to construct $s(t)$ to satisfy the stated requirements. Sketch s versus t and indicate the range over which the representation is valid.

(*b*) Obtain the corresponding parametrization of the circle by using Eq. (8-2) to solve for $\theta(t)$.

(*c*) Determine the time t for which the point P is at the location $(-2, 0)$. Does $t = \frac{1}{2}$ correspond to the location $(0, 2)$? If not, determine the time at which P is at $(0, 2)$.

8-2. Suppose the parametrization of a curve C is given by

$$x(\theta) = \theta$$

$$y(\theta) = \frac{2}{3}\theta^{3/2}$$

(*a*) Sketch and name the curve.

(*b*) Derive a parametrization of the curve for which the arc length $s(t)$ satisfies

$$s(0) = 0 \qquad s(2) = 6 \qquad v(0) = 0 \qquad v(2) = 0$$

(*c*) Determine the coordinates of the point at which P comes to rest at $t = 2$.

8-3. Suppose a transformation $f(\cdot)\colon \mathbb{R}^2 \to \mathbb{R}^2$ is given by

$$f(x, y) = 2xy\hat{\imath} + (x^2 - y^2)\hat{\jmath} = u_1(x, y)\hat{\imath} + u_2(x, y)\hat{\jmath}$$

(*a*) Calculate the Jacobian and the Jacobian matrix for this transformation.

(*b*) Determine the singular points of the transformation.

(*c*) Introduce the new transformation $g(\cdot)\colon \mathbb{R}^2 \to \mathbb{R}^2$ defined by

$$g(r, \theta) = x(r, \theta)\hat{\imath} + y(r, \theta)\hat{\jmath} = r\cos\theta\,\hat{\imath} + r\sin\theta\,\hat{\jmath}$$

and obtain the composite transformation

$$\mathbf{h}(r, \theta) = \mathbf{f}[\mathbf{g}(r, \theta)]$$

(*d*) Use your result from part (*c*) to calculate $\mathbf{f}^{-1}(\cdot)$ and check your result by showing that

$$\mathbf{f}\left[\mathbf{f}^{-1}(u_1, u_2)\right] = \begin{pmatrix} u_1 \\ u_2 \end{pmatrix}$$

8-4. Given the transformation

$$u = e^x \cos y$$
$$v = e^x \sin y$$

(*a*) Is this transformation globally one to one? Explain.
(*b*) Determine the inverse transformation for

$$-\frac{\pi}{2} \le y \le \frac{\pi}{2}$$

(*c*) Calculate the Jacobian of the transformation.
(*d*) Calculate the Jacobian of the inverse transformation and show that it is the reciprocal of that of the transformation.
(*e*) Obtain a linear approximation of the transformation in a neighborhood of the origin and write the corresponding linear equation in terms of the increments of (u, v) and (x, y). Calculate the exact change in (u, v) and the approximate change in (u, v) as (x, y) changes from $(0, 0)$ to $(0.1, -0.15)$.

8-5. The parametric equations of two lines are given by

$$\text{line 1} \quad \begin{aligned} x &= 3t + 1 \\ y &= -4t + 1 \\ z &= -2t + 1 \end{aligned} \qquad \text{line 2} \quad \begin{aligned} x &= -4t + 3 \\ y &= 2t - 1 \\ z &= 3t + 2 \end{aligned}$$

(*a*) Determine the shortest distance between the two lines and the points of intersection of this shortest line segment with the two lines.
(*b*) Show that this shortest segment is perpendicular to both lines.
(*c*) Sketch your result.

8-6. Example 8-10 provided the forward kinematics of the AdeptOne manipulator.
(*a*) Determine the individual DH matrices $\mathbf{H}_{ij}$ connecting the joint reference frames. That is, determine $\mathbf{H}_{i-1,i}$ for $i = 1, 2, \ldots, 5$.
(*b*) Use the matrices obtained in (*a*) to calculate $\mathbf{H}_{i5}$, $i = 1, \ldots, 4$, and ultimately $\mathbf{H}_5$.

8-7. Sketch the position of the AdeptOne robot (see Fig. 8-13) for the robot variable values $\theta_1 = 90°$, $\theta_2 = 0$, $\theta_4 = -90°$, $\theta_5 = 0$, with d_3 unspecified. Include all of the reference frames with their proper orientation in your sketch. Calculate the corresponding matrix $\mathbf{H}_5$ and show that $\hat{\imath}_5$, $\hat{\jmath}_5$, and $\hat{k}_5$ have the correct directions.

8-8. Derive the expression for the inverse of the DH matrix [Eq. (8-9)].
(*a*) Use a mainly theoretical approach involving the product of the homogeneous rotation matrix with the homogeneous translation matrix.
(*b*) Calculate the inverse by a brute-force approach using the definition

$$\mathbf{A}^{-1} = \frac{1}{\det \mathbf{A}} \operatorname{Adj} \mathbf{A}$$

where Adj **A** is the adjoint matrix of **A**.

8-9. Show that (8-14) and (8-15) are equal. For the derivation you may take the Atan 2 function to be equal to the Arctan function.

8-10. Show that (8-14) can be written in the form

$$\theta_1 = \operatorname{Atan2}(\bar{y} - \bar{x}A, \bar{x} + \bar{y}A)$$

where $$A = \frac{\sqrt{(L_1 + L_2)^2 - (\bar{x}^2 + \bar{y}^2)}}{\bar{x}^2 + \bar{y}^2 + L_1^2 - L_2^2}$$

8-11. Carry out the details of the derivation in going from (8-11) to (8-13).

8-12. Show that $\hat{\boldsymbol{o}} \times \hat{\boldsymbol{a}} = \hat{\boldsymbol{n}}$ for $\hat{\boldsymbol{o}}$, $\hat{\boldsymbol{a}}$, and $\hat{\boldsymbol{n}}$ as defined in the equation $\mathbf{H} = \mathbf{H}_5$ for the AdeptOne robot.

8-13. Provide the details of the derivation of (8-21) beginning with (8-20) and show that (8-21) is equivalent to (8-13).

8-14. Begin with (8-19) and derive Eq. (8-22). Then show that (8-16) and (8-22) are equivalent. For the purpose of this derivation, consider only the regular arctangent function rather than the modified Atan 2 function.

8-15. Recall that the degree of freedom of a rigid body depends on the subspace in which it is operating. In Example 8-12 it was shown that a manipulator may have too few axes to attain the degrees of freedom of the manipulator. One way to deal with this difficulty was to simply consider subcombinations of the differential displacements and to take whatever arose for the remainder. For the two-link manipulator in Example 8-12:

(*a*) Obtain the Jacobian matrix and the Jacobian for the combinations $(db, d\theta)$ and (da, db).

(*b*) Determine the singular points of these transformations and calculate their inverse Jacobian matrices.

(*c*) Calculate the numerical values for $(d\theta_1, d\theta_2)$ when $(db, d\theta) = (-0.2, 0.02)$ and $(da, db) = (-0.1, -0.2)$.

Furthermore, calculate the value of the remaining differential and sketch the corresponding manipulator configurations before and after the displacement. In all of the numerical work, use $L_1 = L_2 = 10$, $\theta_1 = 30°$, and $\theta_2 = 90°$ as the basis for the calculations.

8-16. Whitney's method for the calculation of the manipulator Jacobian matrix is discussed as the vector cross-product method in Klafter, Chmielewski, and Negin.[22] We follow the description given there, since it is more accessible to the student. Let

$$\boldsymbol{p} = p_x \hat{\boldsymbol{\imath}}_0 + p_y \hat{\boldsymbol{\jmath}}_0 + p_z \hat{\boldsymbol{k}}_0$$

$$\boldsymbol{v} = v_x \hat{\boldsymbol{\imath}}_0 + v_y \hat{\boldsymbol{\jmath}}_0 + v_z \hat{\boldsymbol{k}}_0$$

$$\boldsymbol{\omega} = \omega_x \hat{\boldsymbol{\imath}}_0 + \omega_y \hat{\boldsymbol{\jmath}}_0 + \omega_z \hat{\boldsymbol{k}}_0$$

be the position, the velocity, and the angular velocity of the hand frame with respect to the world frame. Take the combined column vector $(\mathbf{v}\ \boldsymbol{\omega})^{\mathrm{T}}$ to be given by

$$\begin{pmatrix} \mathbf{v} \\ \boldsymbol{\omega} \end{pmatrix} = \mathbf{J}(\boldsymbol{\xi})\dot{\boldsymbol{\xi}}$$

where the ith column of $\mathbf{J}(\boldsymbol{\xi})$ is given by

$$\mathbf{J}_i(\boldsymbol{\xi}) = \begin{cases} \begin{pmatrix} \hat{\boldsymbol{n}}_{i-1} \times \boldsymbol{p}_{i-1,6} \\ \hat{\boldsymbol{n}}_{i-1} \end{pmatrix} & \text{for a revolute joint} \\[2ex] \begin{pmatrix} \hat{\boldsymbol{n}}_{i-1} \\ \mathbf{0} \end{pmatrix} & \text{for a prismatic joint} \end{cases}$$

Here, $\boldsymbol{p}_{i-1,6}$ is the position vector of the origin of the hand frame with respect to the $(i-1)$th frame, the components being taken with respect to the base or world frame, and $\hat{\boldsymbol{n}}_{i-1}$ is a unit vector along the axis of rotation for joint i, also expressed in terms of world components. For a six-link manipulator with only revolute joints, the Jacobian matrix of the manipulator is given by

$$\mathbf{J}(\boldsymbol{\xi}) = \begin{bmatrix} \hat{\boldsymbol{n}}_0 \times \boldsymbol{p}_{06} & \hat{\boldsymbol{n}}_1 \times \boldsymbol{p}_{16} & \cdots & \hat{\boldsymbol{n}}_5 \times \boldsymbol{p}_{56} \\ \hat{\boldsymbol{n}}_0 & \hat{\boldsymbol{n}}_1 & & \hat{\boldsymbol{n}}_5 \end{bmatrix}$$

Use this approach to calculate the Jacobian matrix for the AdeptOne robot.

8-17. Consider again the two-link manipulator treated in Example 8-16. In the example we used Euler's equations with respect to the link mass centers for each link. Calculate the required actuator moment M_1^a by using Euler's second law for the two-link system with respect to the fixed origin O_0 of the world coordinate system $(0xyz)_0$.

8-18. The PUMA 560 robot, made by Unimation, is a frequently treated textbook example, mainly because it has been around for some time and because information concerning the robot is readily available. Figure E8-18 shows a 560 robot which is just a shadow of itself in order to properly display the relevant coordinate systems and the DH parameters. A dashed line connecting origins implies their coincidence. The sketch is drawn with the robot variables θ_i at the values: $\theta_1 = 90°$, $\theta_2 = 0$, $\theta_3 = 90°$, and $\theta_4 = \theta_5 = \theta_6 = 0°$.
(*a*) Tabulate the DH parameters for this manipulator.
(*b*) Determine the homogeneous DH matrices $\mathbf{H}_{ij}$.
(*c*) Determine the absolute transformation matrix $\mathbf{H}_2$ for this manipulator.

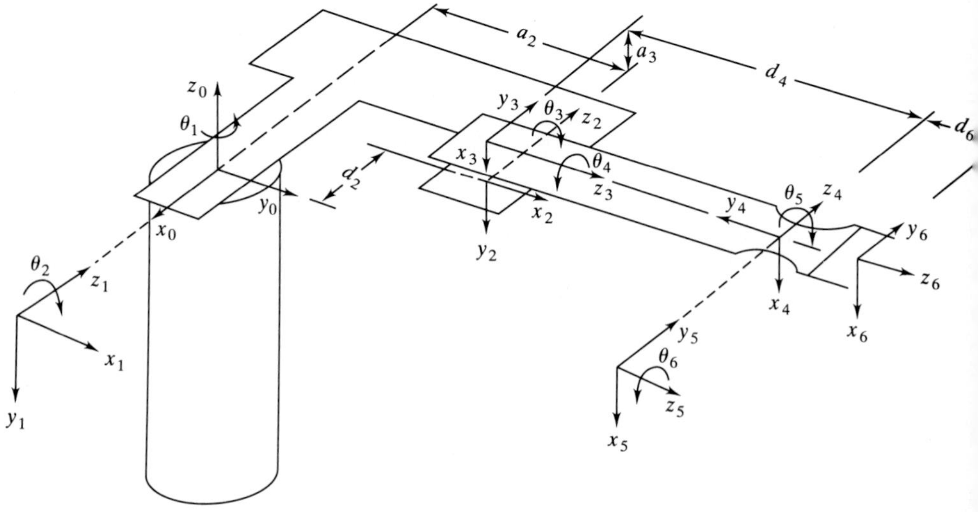

FIGURE E8-18

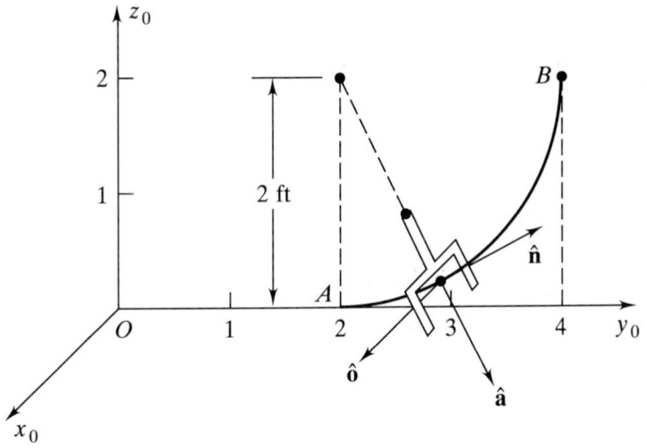

FIGURE E8-19

8-19. Consider again the specification of position and orientation of the nth reference frame as embodied in the hand matrix **H**. Suppose that the tool point E is to trace the quarter circle located in the y_0z_0-plane, from A to B, as shown in Fig. E8-19. The point is to move along the circle with the constant speed $v = 2\omega$ while the nth reference frame maintains an orientation with $\hat{n}$ normal to the curve, as shown. Orient the reference frame with $\hat{o} = \hat{j}_n$, $\hat{a} = \hat{k}_n$, and $\hat{n} = \hat{\imath}_n$. Calculate the hand matrix that follows this prescription. Proceed as follows:

(*a*) Calculate the position components p_x, p_y, and p_z.

(*b*) Determine $\hat{\imath}_n$, $\hat{j}_n$, and $\hat{k}_n$ in terms of $\hat{\imath}_0$, $\hat{j}_0$, and $\hat{k}_0$ and use the definition of the rotation matrix to complete the calculation of **H**.

(*c*) Check your results by calculating $\boldsymbol{r}_0$ when $\boldsymbol{r}_n = \hat{j}_n$ and the tool point is at A and at B.

8-20. In spite of the extensive use of linearized equations in control theory, linear approximations may be quite poor and may prove useful only in the immediate neighborhood of the operating point. Consider the function $f(x, y) = x^3y^2$.

(*a*) Determine the linear approximation of this function around the operating point $(\bar{x}, \bar{y}) = (2, 2)$.

(*b*) Fix x at $\bar{x} = 2$ and determine the range of y for which the error introduced by using the linear approximation is less than 5%. That is, if $g(x, y)$ denotes the expression for the linear approximation, determine the range of y for which

$$\frac{f(\bar{x}, y) - g(\bar{x}, y)}{f(\bar{x}, y)} \leq .05$$

8-21. Consider the arbitrary motion of the double pendulum in Fig. E8-21. The links have equal length L and each of the particles has mass m. The pendulum moves in a gravitational field.

(*a*) Obtain the vector equations of motion for each particle by an application of Newton's second law. Combine the four component equations in a matrix

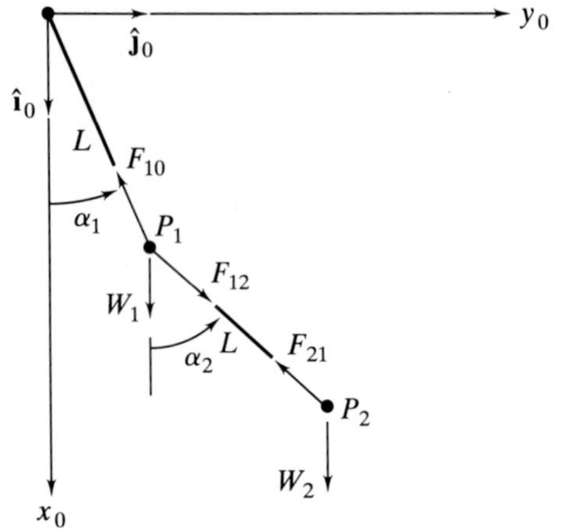

FIGURE E8-21

equation of the form

$$\mathbf{M}(\alpha_1, \alpha_2)\begin{pmatrix} \ddot{\alpha}_1 \\ \ddot{\alpha}_2 \end{pmatrix} + \mathbf{g}(\alpha_1, \alpha_2, \dot{\alpha}_1^2, \dot{\alpha}_2^2) = (mg) + \mathbf{q}(\alpha_1, \alpha_2, t)$$

where $\mathbf{q}$ is a matrix involving the internal forces.

(*b*) Premultiply both sides of this equation by the transpose of the system Jacobian matrix

$$\frac{1}{L}\mathbf{J}^T(\alpha_1, \alpha_2) = \begin{bmatrix} -\sin\alpha_1 & \cos\alpha_1 & -\sin\alpha_1 & \cos\alpha_1 \\ 0 & 0 & -\sin\alpha_2 & \cos\alpha_2 \end{bmatrix}$$

to obtain the system equation in the form

$$\begin{bmatrix} 2 & \cos(\alpha_1 - \alpha_2) \\ \cos(\alpha_1 - \alpha_2) & 1 \end{bmatrix}\begin{pmatrix} \ddot{\alpha}_1 \\ \ddot{\alpha}_2 \end{pmatrix}$$

$$+ \begin{pmatrix} \sin(\alpha_1 - \alpha_2)\dot{\alpha}_2^2 \\ -\sin(\alpha_1 - \alpha_2)\dot{\alpha}_1^2 \end{pmatrix} = -\frac{g}{L}\begin{pmatrix} 2\sin\alpha_1 \\ \sin\alpha_2 \end{pmatrix}$$

(*c*) Obtain the linearized equations corresponding to the assumption of "small" α_1 and α_2.

8-22. Complete the linearization of the equation of motion used in the illustration of Example 8-17. That is, compute the remaining partials of $f_3(\mathbf{x}, \mathbf{u})$ and $f_4(\mathbf{x}, \mathbf{u})$ evaluated at $(\mathbf{x}, \mathbf{u}) = (\boldsymbol{0}, \boldsymbol{0})$.

8-23. Derive the necessary conditions implied by the maximum principle for the following specific optimal control problem: Minimize

$$g(u(\cdot)) = \int_0^{t_1}\left[x_1^2(t)u(t) + x_2^2(t)u^2(t)\right] dt$$

subject to

$$\dot{x}_1 = x_1^2 - x_2^2$$

$$\dot{x}_2 = x_1^2 x_2$$

with arbitrary initial values (x_1^0, x_2^0) for x_1 and x_2 and with terminal values that are required to lie on the circle $x_1^2 + x_2^2 = 4$; that is, with (x_1^1, x_2^1) required to belong to the terminal manifold specified by $\theta^1(x_1, x_2) = x_1^2 + x_2^2 - 4 = 0$. The terminal time t_1 is unspecified and you may take $\lambda_0 = -1$ in the following. Proceed as follows:

(*a*) Write the Hamiltonian for the system and derive an expression for the extremal control $u^*(t)$ in terms of x_1 and x_2. Show that your extremal provides a maximum of the Hamiltonian as a function of u. What is the value of $H(\boldsymbol{\lambda}^*(t), \mathbf{x}^*(t), \mathbf{u}^*(t))$?

(*b*) Derive the corresponding adjoint equations and state the implications of the initial and terminal transversality conditions as they apply to the adjoint variables.

8-24. Determine the minimum distance from the point $(-2, -1)$ to the parabola $y = \frac{1}{2}x^2$.

(*a*) Use the traditional calculus approach.

(*b*) Formulate an appropriate minimum time optimal control problem as was done in Example 8-21.

(*c*) Solve the optimal control problem. Be sure to evaluate all parameters corresponding to optimal control, including the values of the adjoint variables and the optimal time.

8-25. A robot arm attached to a motor is to be modeled as a slender rod with a homogeneous cylinder at its end, as shown in Fig. E8-25. The slender rod has a length of $L = 0.4$ m with a mass density of 2 kg/m, and the cylinder at its end has a radius of 5 cm and a total mass of 2 kg. The motor at the base O is capable of supplying a maximum torque of 10 N · m.

(*a*) Determine the equation of motion for this system.

(*b*) Suppose the system is to be driven from the initial conditions $\theta_1(0) = 0.15$ rad and $\dot{\theta}_1(0) = 2$ rad/s to the null state in minimum time. Formulate an appropriate minimum time null control problem in its standard form, as represented by (8-46).

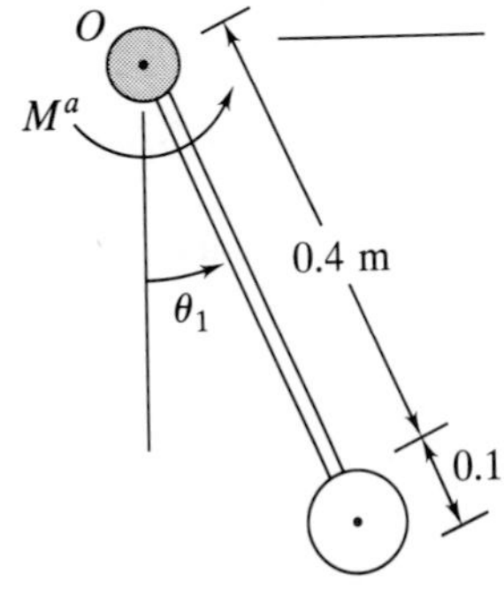

FIGURE E8-25

(*c*) Sketch the switching surfaces in the phase plane and the optimal phase trajectory for this problem. Calculate θ_1 and $\dot{\theta}_1$ at the first switch.

(*d*) Use your sketch to calculate the switching times, the total time required, and list the optimal switching sequence $u^*(t)$ that drives the system to 0 in minimum time.

8-26. The general tracking problem was treated in Example 8-23. Consider a scalar version of this problem. Minimize

$$g_2(v(\cdot)) = \frac{1}{2}\int_0^{t_1}\left[c_1 y^2(t) + c_2 v^2(t)\right] dt \qquad c_1 > 0 \qquad c_2 > 0$$

subject to

$$\dot{y} = ay + bv \qquad y(0) = y_0 \qquad t \in [0, t_1]$$

with t_1 specified.

(*a*) Formulate the Hamiltonian, the corresponding adjoint equations, and the remaining necessary conditions for optimal control. Determine the extremal control and the differential equation to be satisfied by $k(t)$ in $\lambda(t) = k(t)y(t)$.

(*b*) Consider the particular case with equal weighting constants $c_1 = c_2 = 1$, $a = \frac{1}{8}$, $b = 1/\sqrt{8}$, and $t_1 = 1$. Solve for $k(t)$ on the interval $-4 \leq k(t) \leq 2$ and show that your solution $k(t)$ satisfies the differential equation for $k(t)$. [In this context you may find it useful to note $\int(dt/t) = \ln|t| + C$.]

(*c*) For the same parameter values and $k(t)$ as obtained in part (*b*), calculate the response $y(t)$ with $y(0) = y_0$.

8-27. In part (*d*) of Example 8-24, the equation describing the inverse dynamics of the manipulator was given in the form

$$A_1(t)\ddot{\theta}_1(t) + A_2(t)\dot{\theta}_1(t) + A_3(t)\cos\theta_1(t) = M^a(t)$$

The equation may be used to calculate the torque required to produce some specified motion. Use the equation to calculate the moment $M^a(t)$ required to produce the motion specified in the example. That is, calculate all of the quantities on the left side of this equation. You may express your answer in terms of s and $\dot{s}$ rather than in terms of t.

8-28. In part (e) of Example 8-24, a sequence of trajectory points of $s_1(t)$ was connected by cubic splines. Carry out the details of the calculations that will yield these splines corresponding to $i = 1$, 2, 3, and 4.

8-29. In part (*e*) of Example 8-24, the discrete values of the joint variable $s_1(t)$ were provided in Table 8-4. These points were then smoothly connected with cubic splines. Carry out the same calculations for the joint variable $\theta_1(t)$.

(*a*) Tabulate the values of $\theta_1(t)$ corresponding to the given discrete trajectory points.

(*b*) Calculate the requisite cubics representing the natural cubic splines through these points.

(*c*) Present your results in a figure similar to Fig. 8-34.

8-30. Suppose you are given the simple feedback system in Fig. E8-30. You are to introduce a proportional controller with gain $0.2 \leq k_p \leq 2.0$ to achieve the lowest possible output $|Y(s)|$.

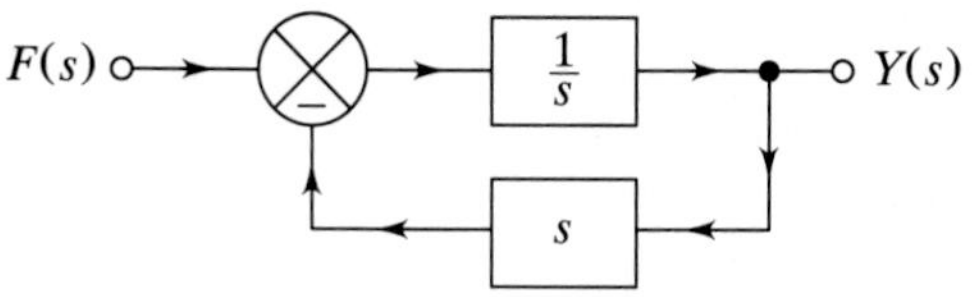

FIGURE E8-30

(*a*) Determine the system function $G(s)$ and the response $Y(s)$ for each of the four standard configurations in Fig. 8-37. Sketch the block diagram for each configuration.

(*b*) Determine that configuration that will minimize $|Y(s)|$ and specify the corresponding choice of k_p.

8-31. Derive the expression for θ_{max} as given in (8-65). Begin with (8-63), derive (8-64), determine the critical times t_0 for which $\dot{\theta}(t_0) = 0$, and finally θ_{max}.

8-32. Note that (8-65) is a function of ζ only. Show that $\phi(\zeta) = \theta_{max} - 1$ is a monotonically decreasing function of ζ. That is, show that $d\theta_{max}/d\zeta < 0$ for $0 \le \zeta < 1$.

8-33. Provide the details of the limit given by (8-66). Be sure to justify each step in the limiting process.

8-34. Derive the system function, Eq. (8-75). Begin with (8-74), take the Laplace transform, obtain a single equation involving only $Y_1(s)$ and $U(s)$, and hence the system function $G(s) = Y_1(s)/U(s)$.

8-35. Begin with the signal flow graph, Fig. 8-45*b*, and use Mason's rule to deduce the system function, Eq. (8-75). Be sure to provide all of the details of the derivation.

8-36. The natural order on $\mathbb{R}^2$ may be depicted in terms of a quarter space (cone) with origin (vertex) at the point to which other points are to be compared with "$\le$." Points in the cone or on its boundary are comparable to the point at which the cone is located. Fig. E8-36 depicts a number of points $\mathbf{z}_i$ in the positive orthant of $\mathbb{R}^2$. Right angle cones are drawn at $\mathbf{z}_3$ and $\mathbf{z}_5$.

(*a*) Determine the manner in which the points $\mathbf{z}_3$ and $\mathbf{z}_5$ are related to the remaining points. If they cannot be related with respect to "$\le$," so state.

(*b*) Which of the points are minimal points with respect to "$\le$"?

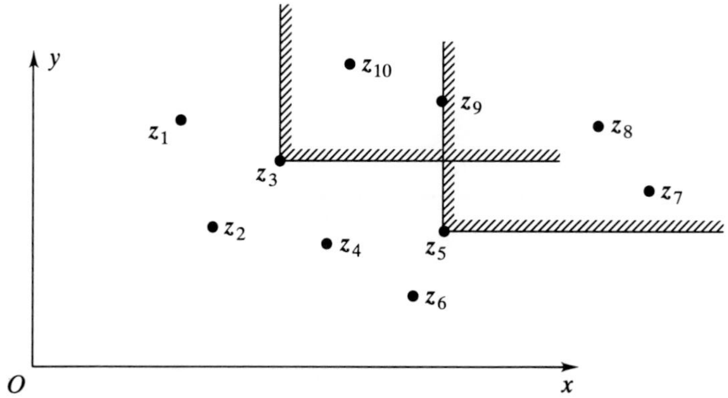

FIGURE E8-36

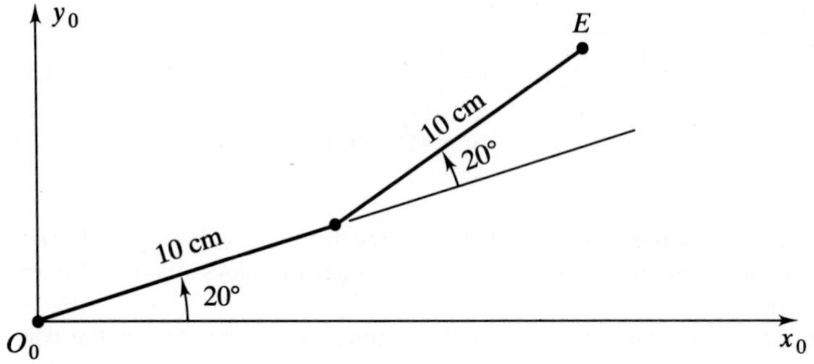

FIGURE E8-37

8-37. The accuracy of a robot really cannot be better than its resolution, no matter how it is defined. Another approach to the resolution of a robot might be this: For a given accessible point, determine the closest new accessible point. When this is done for a whole region in the robot's work space, one may then take the maximum of all of the minimum distances to be the resolution of the robot with respect to that region. Suppose a simple two-arm SCARA robot (see Fig. E8-37) with arms of length 10 cm is at the accessible point specified by $\theta_1 = \theta_2 = 20°$. Suppose each arm individually has an angular resolution of 0.1°. Calculate the closest accessible point based on angular displacements of $\Delta\theta_i = \pm 0.1°$.

(*a*) Determine and organize all of the possible accessible positions.

(*b*) Determine the position that is closest to the original point and specify the rotations required to attain it. Which rotations correspond to the farthest distance from the original point?

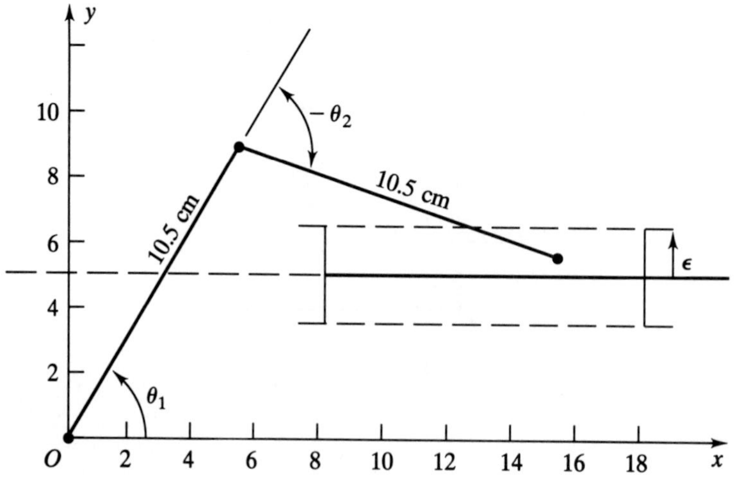

FIGURE E8-38

8-38. Consider again the simple two-arm SCARA manipulator. Suppose the individual arms have a resolution of 10°. Calculate the resolution set for the line segment [8, 18] on the line $y = 5$ cm as shown in Fig. E8-38. To simplify matters, allow only the above-shoulder configuration indicated. Take each arm to have a length of 10.5 cm (a length derived from the available protractor with a scale of 60 intervals to the inch). Take a boundary tube with radius $\epsilon = 1.5$ cm. The reference or home position is specified by $\theta_1 = \theta_2 = 0$. (Calculation to two decimals suffices.)

It may happen (as it does here) that none of the accessible points are on the desired curve, including the end points. We take the points whose x-components are closest to the desired segment (containing the segment between them) to be the end points of the interval. We take the (approximate) traversal of the specified curve to be of primary importance, and we thus stop the selection of the resolution set with the selection that would eliminate one or both of the end points.

8-39. Let $f(x)$ be a Gaussian distribution with mean μ and standard deviation σ and show that

$$\int_{-\infty}^{\infty} f(s)\,dx = 1 \qquad \text{and} \qquad \mu = \int_{-\infty}^{\infty} xf(x)\,dx$$

(*Hint:* You may find it useful to note that the integral of any odd function from $-\infty$ to ∞ is 0.)

8-40. Suppose you are testing the single-point accuracy of a robot based on random approaches to a specified point P. Recall that $3S$ accuracy was taken to assure that 99.7% of the outcomes would be within the sphere of radius $r = \overline{D} + 3S$. Determine the constant k that would provide assurance that 50% of the outcomes would lie within the region $r = \overline{D} + kS$. That is, determine k such that

$$\mathscr{P}(\mu - k\sigma < x < \mu + k\sigma) = \tfrac{1}{2}$$

assuming that the outcomes of the experiment are normally distributed with mean μ and standard deviation σ.

To work this problem, you will need to make use of the error function

$$\operatorname{erf} x = \frac{1}{\sqrt{2\pi}} \int_0^x e^{-y^2/2}\,dy$$

along with the partial table of values

x	erf x
0.55	0.20884
0.60	0.22575
0.65	0.24215
0.70	0.25804
0.75	0.27337

8-41. A robot is being tested to determine its repeatability. For simplicity, suppose it is one of our simple planar robots. Consider the test path shown in Fig. E8-41. During each random cycle, the robot's end effector is made to pass through the checkpoints $(\bar{x}, \bar{y})_a = (1, 4)$, $(\bar{x}, \bar{y})_b = (2, 3)$, and $(\bar{x}, \bar{y})_c = (3, 2)$. In five such cycles, the robot achieves the proximities of the checkpoints as listed in the table of Fig. E8-41. Calculate the three-sigma repeatability of the robot.

x_{ai}	y_{ai}	x_{bi}	y_{bi}	x_{ci}	y_{ci}
1.002	3.998	2.012	3.007	2.988	1.990
1.013	3.987	1.998	3.014	2.991	1.988
0.989	4.018	1.993	2.985	3.017	1.995
0.918	4.012	2.005	2.982	3.010	2.005
1.010	3.991	2.015	2.992	3.008	2.014

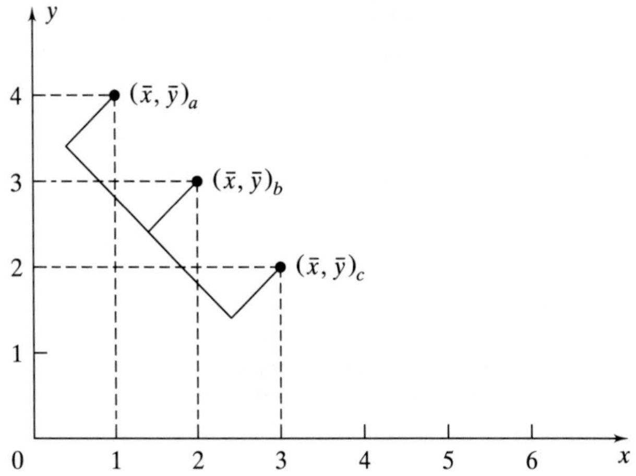

FIGURE E8-41

REFERENCES

1. Fleming, W. H.: *Functions of Several Variables*, Addison-Wesley, Reading, Mass., 1965.
2. Taylor, A. E.: *Advanced Calculus*, Ginn and Company, Boston, Mass, 1955.
3. Goel, P. K.: "The Inverse Kinematics Solution, Closed-form Dynamics and Simulation of AdeptOne Industrial Robot," *IEEE International Conference on Robotics and Automation*, Philadelphia, April 24–29, pp. 1688–1693, 1988.
4. Whitney, D. E.: "The Mathematics of Coordinated Control of Prosthetic Arms and Manipulators," *Transactions of the ASME*, *Journal of Dynamic Systems*, *Measurement and Control*, vol. 122, pp. 303–309, 1972.
5. Paul, R. P.: *Robot Manipulators, Mathematics, Programming and Control*, MIT press, Cambridge, Mass., 1981.
6. Hamel, G.: *Theoretische Mechanik*, Springer, Berlin, 1967.
7. Böhmer, K.: *Spline-Funktionen*, B. G. Teubner, Stuttgart, Germany, 1974.
8. Schoenberg, I. J.: "Contributions to the Problem of Approximation of Equidistant Data by Analytic Functions," *Quarterly of Applied Mathematics*, vol. 4, pp. 45–99 and 112–141, 1946.
9. Gerald, C. F., and P. O. Wheatley: *Applied Numerical Analysis*, (3rd ed., Addison-Wesley, Reading, Mass., 1984.
10. Holladay, J. C.: "Smoothest Curve Approximation," *Mathematical Tables Aids Computation*, vol. 11, pp. 233–243, 1957.

11. Stadler, W. (Ed.): *Multicriteria Optimization in Engineering and in the Sciences*, Plenum, New York, 1988.
12. Lee, E. B., and L. Markus: *Foundations of Optimal Control Theory*, Wiley, New York, 1967.
13. Leitmann, G.: *An Introduction to Optimal Control*, McGraw-Hill, New York, 1966.
14. Athans, M., and P. L. Falb: *Optimal Control*, McGraw-Hill, New York, 1966.
15. Strang, G.: *Linear Algebra and Its Applications*, Academic, New York, 1980.
16. Chen, C.-T.: *Control System Design*, Saunders College Publishing, New York, 1993.
17. Doeblin, E. O.: *Measurement Systems (Applications and Design)*, 4th ed., McGraw-Hill, New York, 1990.
18. Walpole, R. E., and R. H. Myers: *Probability and Statistics for Engineers and Scientists*, 3rd ed., Macmillan, New York, 1985.
19. American National Standards Institute (ANSI): "Point-to-Point and Static Performance Characteristics—Evaluation," Report for Industrial Robots and Robot Systems, ANSI/RIA 15.05-1-1990, July 1990.
20. Mathews, S. H., and J. W. Hill: "Repeatability Test System for Industrial Robots," SME Technical Paper MS84-1045, 1984.
21. Albertson, P.: "Automated Evaluation Eases Robot-Performance Specification," *EDN*, pp. 159–169, October 1984.
22. Klafter, R. D., T. A. Chmielewski, and M. Negin: *Robotic Engineering: An Integrated Approach*, Prentice-Hall, Englewood Cliffs, N.J., 1989.

AUTHOR INDEX

SUBJECT INDEX

The arrangement of the subject index allows for three interpretations:

1. The indented word may be viewed as preceding the key word.
2. The indented word may be viewed as following the key word.
3. Indented words may refer to subject matter which is simply related to the key word.

The intended interpretation will be evident.

Q

R

S